HANDBUCH DER ETHNOTHERAPIEN
HANDBOOK OF ETHNOTHERAPIES

DIE DEUTSCHE BIBLIOTHEK – CIP-EINHEITSAUFNAHME
Handbuch der Ethnotherapien. Handbook of Ethnotherapies - 2002
HANDBUCH DER ETHNOTHERAPIEN. HANDBOOK OF ETHNOTHERAPIES /
hrsg. von Christine E. Gottschalk-Batschkus & Joy C. Green
im Auftrag von ETHNOMED – Institut für Ethnomedizin e.V. - München
Hamburg : BoD, 2002
ISBN 3-8311-4184-3

VERLAG UND VERTRIEB:
BoD Print on Demand
Hamburg

COPYRIGHT:
© ETHNOMED – Institut für Ethnomedizin e.V., Melusinenstr. 2, D-81671 München, Germany

HANDBUCH DER ETHNOTHERAPIEN

HANDBOOK OF ETHNOTHERAPIES

HERAUSGEGEBEN VON
EDITED BY

CHRISTINE E. GOTTSCHALK-BATSCHKUS
& JOY C. GREEN

IM AUFTRAG VON / ON BEHALF OF

ETHNOMED – INSTITUT FÜR
ETHNOMEDIZIN E.V.
ETHNOMED - INSTITUTE FOR
ETHNOMEDICINE
MELUSINENSTR. 2 · D-81671 MÜNCHEN ·
GERMANY

PHOTO DESIGN:
MARC M. BATSCHKUS

DRUCKDATENAUFBEREITUNG
PRINT DATA MANAGEMENT
HERBERT VON BRANDENSTEIN

MIT EINER EINLEITUNG VON
WITH AN INTRODUCTION BY
CLAUDIA MÜLLER-EBELING

BOD 2002

Herausgeber / Editors:

Christine E. Gottschalk-Batschkus & Joy C. Green
ETHNOMED - Institut für Ethnomedizin e.V.
Melusinenstr. 2
D – 81671 München
Germany
Tel/Fax: ++49-89-40 90 81 29
E-Mail: ethnomedizin@web.de
Website: www.institut-ethnomed.de

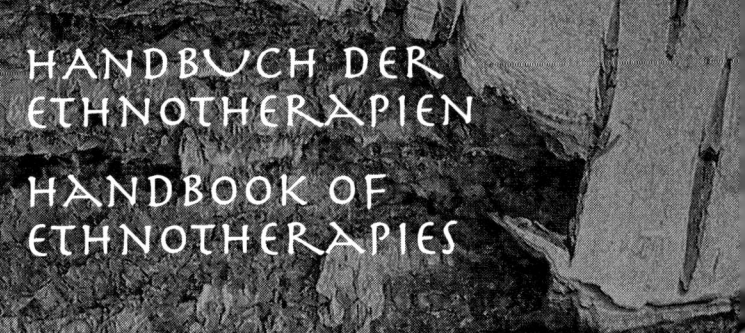

HANDBUCH DER ETHNOTHERAPIEN
HANDBOOK OF ETHNOTHERAPIES

INHALT / CONTENTS

Danksagung / Acknowledgements — 10

EINLEITUNG UND ÜBERBLICK
INTRODUCTION AND OVERVIEW

NICHT ALLE HEILER SIND SCHAMANEN – EIN ÜBERBLICK ÜBER DIE VIELFALT DER HEILMETHODEN
Not all Healers are Shamans – A Survey about the Variety of Healing Methods
Claudia Müller-Ebeling — 13 / 17

EIN SCHAMANISCHES MANIFEST: DIE PRINZIPIEN INDIGENEN WISSENS
A Shamanic Manifesto: The Principles of Indigenous Knowledge
Stanley Krippner — 21 / 29

VOM SCHAMANENTUM ZUR MODERNEN NATURTHERAPIE
From Shamanism to Nature Therapy
Holger Kalweit — 37 / 45

GEBET UND SPIRITUELLE HEILUNG IM MEDIZINISCHEN UMFELD
Prayer and Spiritual Healing in Medical Settings
David Aldridge — 53 / 65

ALTE WELT / OLD WORLD

Europa und westliche Kulturen
Europe and western cultures

MAGISCH-RELIGIÖSE HEILRITUALE IN DER ZENTRALSCHWEIZ
Magic-Religious Healing Rituals in Central Switzerland
Kurt Lussi — 77 / 87

MAGISCHE HEILUNG - VOLKSMEDIZINISCHE PRAKTIKEN DES VULTURGEBIETES SÜDITALIENS
Traditional Healing in the Vulture Area of Southern Italy
Andrea Pieroni & Cassandra Leah Quave — 97 / 109

Afrika / Africa

DIE PRAXIS EINER PEPO HEILERIN IN TANSANIA
The Practice of a PEPO Healer in Tanzania
Jessica Erdtsieck — 119 / 133

IGBO HEILER UND WEGE ZUR HEILUNG VON GEISTESKRANKHEITEN IN SÜDOST NIGERIA
Igbo Medicine: Practitioners and Ways of Healing Insanity in Southeast Nigeria
Patrick Iroegbu — 145 / 157

DIE MAFA IN NORDKAMERUN
The Mafa in Northern Cameroon
Godula Kosack — 169 / 183

SÜDAFRIKANISCHE MEDIZINPFLANZEN IN DER ZULU-VOLKSMEDIZIN
Medicinal Plants Used in Zulu Folk Medicine
John A. O. Ojewole — 197 / 209

NAHER OSTEN / NEAR EAST

Israel

VOLKSMEDIZIN BEI ORIENTALISCHEN JUDEN IN ISRAEL
Folks Medicine Among Oriental Jews in Israel
Ofra Greenberg — 221 / 229

Türkei / Turkey

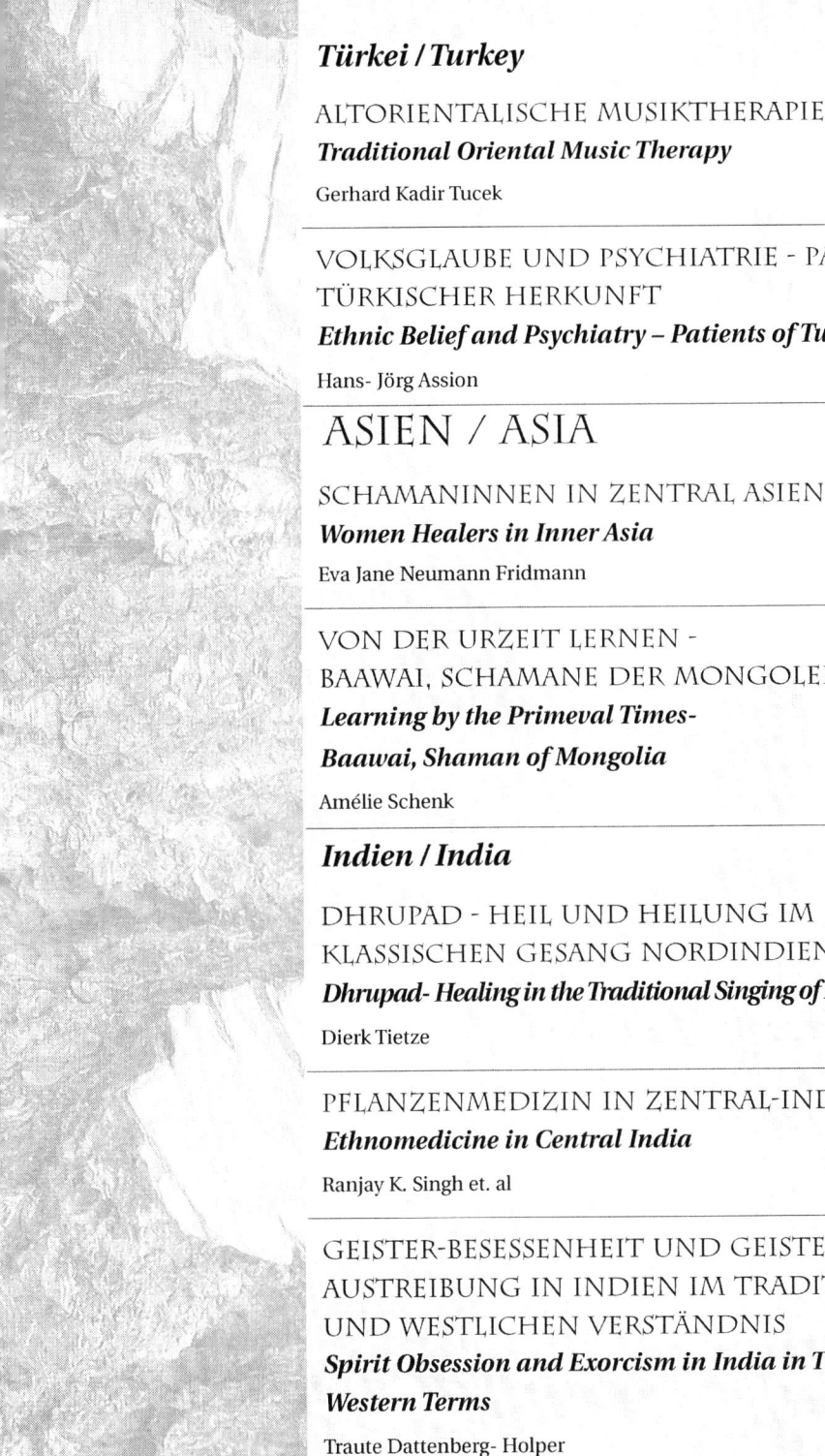

ALTORIENTALISCHE MUSIKTHERAPIE
Traditional Oriental Music Therapy

Gerhard Kadir Tucek   237 / 253

VOLKSGLAUBE UND PSYCHIATRIE - PATIENTEN TÜRKISCHER HERKUNFT
Ethnic Belief and Psychiatry – Patients of Turkish Origin

Hans- Jörg Assion   269 / 281

ASIEN / ASIA

SCHAMANINNEN IN ZENTRAL ASIEN
Women Healers in Inner Asia

Eva Jane Neumann Fridmann   291 / 301

VON DER URZEIT LERNEN - BAAWAI, SCHAMANE DER MONGOLEI
Learning by the Primeval Times- Baawai, Shaman of Mongolia

Amélie Schenk   311 / 317

Indien / India

DHRUPAD - HEIL UND HEILUNG IM KLASSISCHEN GESANG NORDINDIENS
Dhrupad- Healing in the Traditional Singing of Northern India

Dierk Tietze   323 / 331

PFLANZENMEDIZIN IN ZENTRAL-INDIEN
Ethnomedicine in Central India

Ranjay K. Singh et. al   337 / 341

GEISTER-BESESSENHEIT UND GEISTER-AUSTREIBUNG IN INDIEN IM TRADITIONELLEN UND WESTLICHEN VERSTÄNDNIS
Spirit Obsession and Exorcism in India in Traditional and Western Terms

Traute Dattenberg- Holper   347 / 355

VOLKSMEDIZIN BEI DEN ZEME NAGAS IN INDIEN
Folk Medicine Among the Zeme Nagas of India
Babul Roy   361 / 367

Bangladesh
CHAKMA TALIKA CIKITSA – DAS THERAPEUTISCHE SYSTEM DER CHAKMA VON BANGLADESH
The Therapeutic System of the Chakma of Bangladesh
Mahmoud Tareq Hassan Khan   373 / 381

Nepal
JHARPHUK - EINE SCHAMANISCHE HEILBEHANDLUNG IN NEPAL
Jharphuk - A Shamanistic Healing Ritual in Nepal
Andreas Reimers   387 / 397

NEUE WELT / NEW WORLD

Nordamerika / North America

TRADITIONELLE HEILVERFAHREN IN DER KULTUR DER ALTEN ORDNUNG DER AMISH
The Approach of Traditional Healing in the Old Order Amish Culture
Sharyn Buccalo   407 / 413

DIE THERAPEUTISCHE SEITE DER HAITIANISCHEN RELIGION VODOU IN NEW YORK CITY
Therapeutic Aspects of Vodou in New York City
Bettina E. Schmidt   419 / 425

Mittel- & Südamerika
Central America & South America

Einheimische Systeme / Indigenous Systems

KALLAWAYA MEDICINE: AN ANDEAN SYSTEM OF CURING AND HEALING
Kallawaya Medicine: An Andean System of Curing and Healing
Stanley Krippner   431 / 437

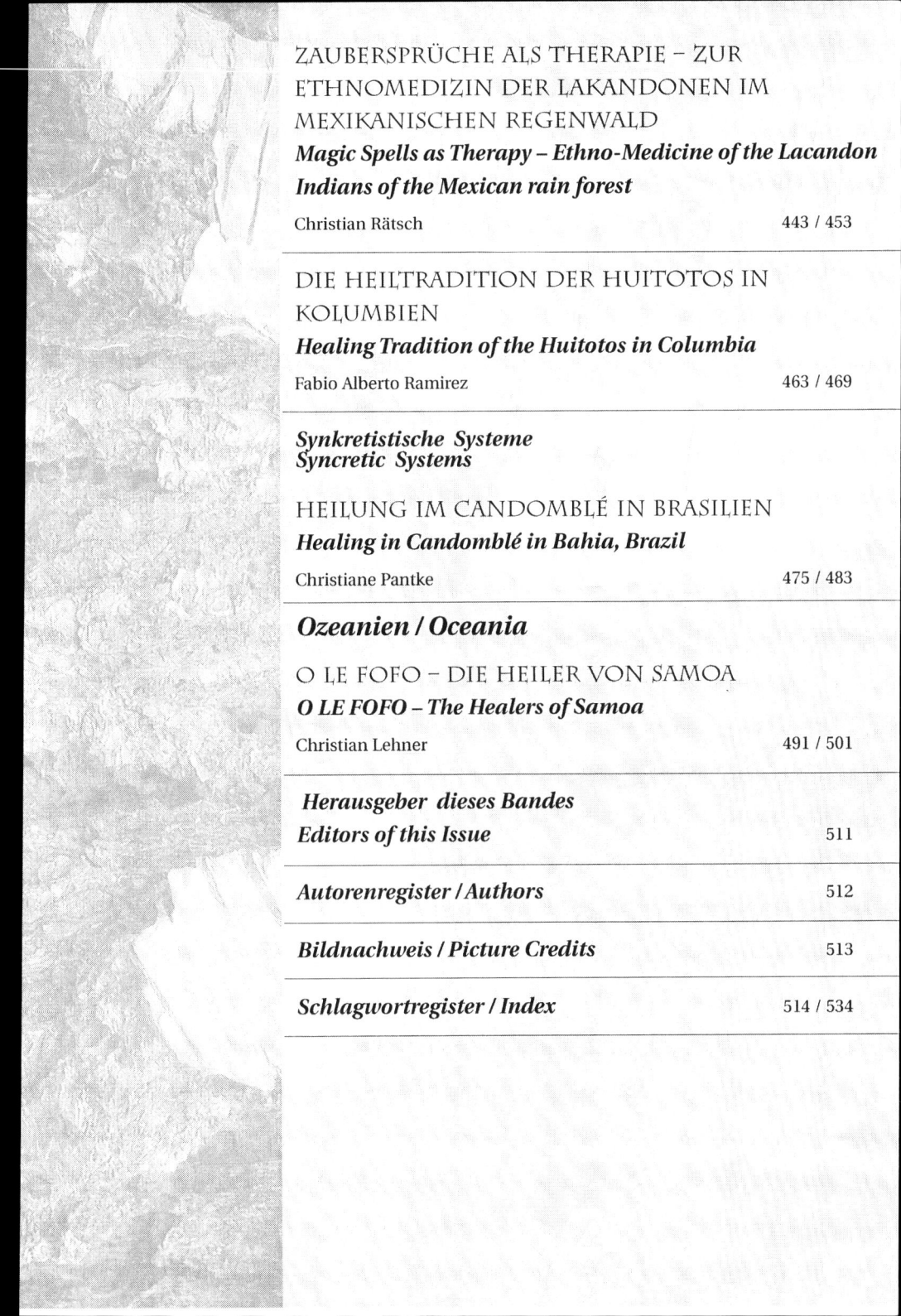

ZAUBERSPRÜCHE ALS THERAPIE – ZUR ETHNOMEDIZIN DER LAKANDONEN IM MEXIKANISCHEN REGENWALD
Magic Spells as Therapy – Ethno-Medicine of the Lacandon Indians of the Mexican rain forest
Christian Rätsch   443 / 453

DIE HEILTRADITION DER HUITOTOS IN KOLUMBIEN
Healing Tradition of the Huitotos in Columbia
Fabio Alberto Ramirez   463 / 469

Synkretistische Systeme
Syncretic Systems

HEILUNG IM CANDOMBLÉ IN BRASILIEN
Healing in Candomblé in Bahia, Brazil
Christiane Pantke   475 / 483

Ozeanien / Oceania

O LE FOFO – DIE HEILER VON SAMOA
O LE FOFO – The Healers of Samoa
Christian Lehner   491 / 501

Herausgeber dieses Bandes
Editors of this Issue   511

Autorenregister / Authors   512

Bildnachweis / Picture Credits   513

Schlagwortregister / Index   514 / 534

VORWORT UND DANKSAGUNG

PREFACE AND ACKNOWLEDGEMENT

Christine E. Gottschalk-Batschkus
&
Joy C. Green

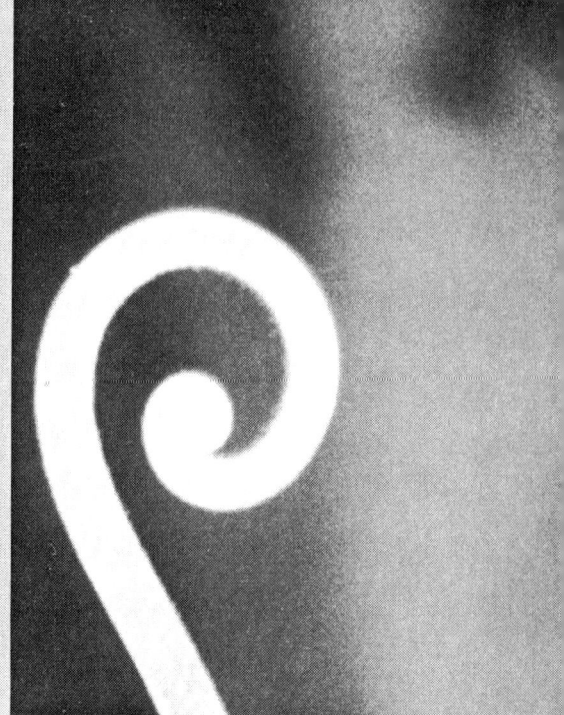

Traditionelle und moderne Medizin
Die meisten Heiler und traditionellen Medizinsysteme, so geheim und mysteriös ihre Techniken auch erscheinen, versuchen ihre Patienten wieder zu Harmonie und Balance mit sich, ihrer Umgebung und dem Kosmos zu führen.
Diese allem übergeordneten Grundwahrheiten von Gesundheit und Heilung in traditionellen Medizin-Systemen, seit Anbeginn der Menschheit bewährt und behütet, treten in diesem Buch so offensichtlich zutage, dass wir uns fragen, ob die moderne Schulmedizin durch deren Außerachtlassung hier nicht einen ganz entscheidenden Fehler macht und somit die Ergebnisse ihrer Anstrengungen immer begrenzt bleiben müssen.

Wichtige Hinweise!
Desweiteren wollen und müssen wir darauf hinweisen, dass der Schreibstil der Autoren weitgehend original belassen wurde und die Meinung der des jeweiligen Autoren entspricht und nicht die Meinung der Herausgeber wiedergibt. Für Therapieempfehlungen, Rezepturen und Anweisungen sei an die eigene Urteilsfähigkeit des Lesers appelliert; die Handlungsweisen verschiedener Völker und die traditionellen Anwendungen sind als ethnografische Daten und nicht als Behandlungs- oder Therapieempfehlung zu werten. Die Herausgeber übernehmen keine Verantwortung für eigene Versuche der Leser..

Transfer und unermüdlicher Einsatz
Wir wollen an dieser Stelle für das unermüdliche, ehrenamtliche Engagement der ETHNOMED- Mitarbeiter danken, ohne die dieses enorme Werk niemals hätte entstehen können. Außer den üblichen Arbeiten bei der Herausgabe waren noch sehr spezielle zeitraubende und aufwendige Aufgaben zu bewältigen:
Mancher Autor verfasste seine Arbeit in Englisch, der dieser Sprache kaum mächtig ist und das über Themen, die hochkomplex sind und menschliche Weisheiten wiedergeben, für die der interviewte Heiler oftmals Jahrzehnte seines Lebens studiert hat. Um das Wesentliche der Inhalte aus der Menge der Angaben herauszuarbeiten bedurfte es der Hilfe zahlreicher erfahrener Experten: Ethnologen zu ethnologischen Angaben, Ärzten zu medizinischen Sachverhalten, Musikern zu musikalischen Fachtexten, Ethnopharmakologen zur korrekten Wiedergabe der Pflanzenangaben. Und dies alles unter der Prämisse den Stil und die Aussagen der Autoren möglichst unverändert zu lassen.

Traditional and modern medicine
Most healers and medicine systems, no matter how secret and mysterious they may seem, try to lead their patients back into harmony and balance within themselves and with their surrounding.
This dominating truth about health and healing in traditional medicine systems is relied upon and protected since the earliest beginning of mankind.We ask ourselves if modern western medicine is not mistaken to ignore that important wisdom of old healing systems, and therefore will always limit its success in entirly healing a patient.

Important Notes!
Furthermore we would like and have to mention that the writing styles of our authors as well as their personal opinions are left in their original form and that their opinions are not representing the editors opinion. Therapy recommandations, precriptions and orders need to be judged by the readers; the actions and traditional rituals carried out by the different folks need to be seen as ethnographical facts and not to be understood as recommandations for treatments or therapies. The editors do not take over responsibility for experimental try-outs of the readers.

Transfer and neverending effort
At this point we want to thank the ETHNOMED- team for their untiring and honorary effort. This book would not exist without them. Beside the regular work of publication very special, time- consuming jobs had to be taken care of: some authors wrote their pamphlets in english, not really being familiar with the language, about very complex and deep subjects containing their life wisdom and their work from decades. To sensitively filter out the essentiel context of the pamphlets, the help of many experienced experts was necessary: ethnologists for ethnological facts, doctors for medical concerns, musicians for musical facts, ethno-pharmacologists for correct reproduction quality of botanical facts. Whereas the main concern has always been to leave the style and message of the author as pure and unchanged as possible.

Danksagung / Acknowledgement

Gedankt sei für alles hier ganz herzlich:
We would like to give our warmest thanks to:

Christian Abele,
Ingo Armbruster,
Kerstin Bauer,
Sieglinde Batschkus,
Paul Baumann,
Judith Beyer,
Judith Blab,
Stephanie Borm,
Oliver Bosch,
Herbert von Brandenstein,
Dorothea Daus,
Eveline Ernst,
Cordula Exner,
Arne Frercks,
Cordula Gehlert Wohlfahrt,
Christine Granados Hughes,
Andrea Grasse,
Karl Heinz Heiss,
Thorsten Holzschneider,
Daniel Kirchhoff,
Stephanie Kuhn,
Sven Kulenkampff,
Hermann Lechleitner,
Björn Lehmann,
Sandra Lüttich,
Eva Makkos,
Johanna-Kathrin Malsch,
Dominique Marquis,
Karin Murad Merwanji,
Kat Morgenstern,
Karin Moser,
Martina Moser,
Birgit Neumann,
Kristina Nilsson,
Jolanta Nowak,
Adelheid Ohlig,
Marie von Otting,
Sylvia Peipe,
Bojanka Pajtler,
Udo Richter,
Barbara Roberts,
Florian Rubner,
Matthias Schmidt,
Katharina Scholz,
Dominik Schweizer,
Simone Siahdohoni,
Guido Terlinden,
Artur Tesche,
Silke Kerstin Tönsjost,
Gerd Venghaus,
Jan Wacker,
Wiebke Wollenweber

und ganz besonders unseren Männern, and especially our husbands, *Marc M. Batschkus* und *Dennis Meyerding* und unseren Kindern, and our children, *Garance, Jenny, Louise, Joanne, Tamiko, Phyllis* und *Victor*, die uns in unermüdlicher Weise bei der Arbeit unterstützt, erduldet, ermuntert, entlastet, ermutigt und inspiriert haben, who supported, tolerated, motivated, relieved, and inspired us in their wonderful loving way.

München im Juni 2002
Christine E. Gottschalk-Batschkus & Joy C. Green

NICHT ALLE HEILER SIND SCHAMANEN – EIN ÜBERBLICK ÜBER DIE VIELFALT DER HEILMETHODEN

von Claudia Müller-Ebeling

In diesem *Handbuch der Ethnotherapien* geht es um vielfältige Heilmethoden.
Heiler und Schamanen aus fernen Ländern führen uns zeitlich zurück in unsere eigene europäische Vergangenheit und entführen uns auch geographisch in andere, außereuropäische Kulturen.
Dabei entdecken wir, dass die Vergangenheit in alternativen Heilverfahren lebendig ist, die sich bei uns in den letzten Jahrzehnten entwickelten. Und wir erkennen, dass andere Kulturen gänzlich andere Konzepte von Diagnose und Heilung haben – und Krankheit und Gesundheit unter Umständen anders definieren als wir!

In den Kapiteln des Handbuchs zeigen sich Gemeinsamkeiten wie auch Unterschiede. So vertraut oder exotisch fremd uns diese vielfältigen Ansätze auch erscheinen mögen – sie alle teilen dasselbe Ziel: Das Erkennen von Krankheiten und die Heilung der Patienten. Was sie kulturübergreifend miteinander verbindet - und gleichzeitig von der westlichen Schulmedizin unterscheidet - ist das Konzept der Einheit von Körper, Geist und Seele.

Die westliche Schulmedizin widmet sich vornehmlich dem Körper. Den Geist lässt sie meistens, die Seele immer außer Betracht. Sie analysiert den Patienten als isolierte Einheit und meist unabhängig von seiner Umgebung. Bei uns geschehen

ärztliche Untersuchungen hinter verschlossenen Türen und gehen nur Arzt und Patient etwas an.
Außereuropäische Heilsysteme beschäftigen sich mit der Einheit von Körper, Geist und Seele. Darin unterscheiden sie sich vom naturwissenschaftlichen Ansatz. Sie betrachten Patienten im Kontext von Familie, Gesellschaft, Natur und Kosmos. Diagnose und Therapie sind eine öffentliche Angelegenheit und keine Privatsache. Ähnlich verhielt es sich mit Heiltraditionen, die in unserer Kultur in der Vergangenheit lebendig waren und heute in alternativen Heilverfahren zunehmend mehr Beachtung finden.

Schamanismus

Schamanismus ist keine Religion, sondern eine Technik, durch die mit Hilfe von veränderten Bewusstseinszuständen Einblick in Vergangenheit, Gegenwart und Zukunft gewonnen und geheilt werden kann. Diese Technik ist etwa 60.000 Jahre alt und war früher weltweit verbreitet. In manchen Kulturen blieb er bis heute lebendig, vor allem in Asien und Südamerika. Je nach Kultur bildete sich Schamanismus unterschiedlich aus.

Mancherorts sind beide Geschlechter aktiv tätig (Nepal, Sibirien), anderswo ist Schamanismus fast ausschließlich Sache von Frauen (Korea) oder aber Männersache (Amazonas).

In Nepal, Ladakh und (eingeschränkt) auch in der Mongolei, arbeiten Heiler bei der Heilung von Patienten zusammen. Sie unterstützen sich gegenseitig bei aufwendigen Heilzeremonien und wechseln einander ab. Auch wenn es fähige, kraftvolle wie auch weniger mächtige, schwächere Schamanen gibt, existiert nicht wirklich eine Hierarchie untereinander. Man respektiert die Fähigkeiten gegenseitig und ergänzt sich.

In Korea und im Amazonasgebiet ist diese archaische Heiltechnik hingegen kämpferisch und wettbewerbsorientiert. Dort kämpfen Heiler um Macht und Einfluss - und zwar sowohl in der sichtbar materiellen Welt der Menschen, als auch in der unsichtbaren Welt von Hilfsgeistern und Dämonen. Heiler attackieren sich in Trance ggf. gegenseitig und jagen sich mächtige Schutz- und Hilfsgeister ab.

Die eine Variante ist nicht besser oder schlechter als die andere, auch wenn uns die friedliche Form "besser gefallen" mag. Das schamanische Universum ist zyklisch - im Gegensatz zu unserem linearen Weltbild. Nichts ist gut oder schlecht, richtig oder falsch *per se*, sondern nur in Bezug auf etwas anderes. Dazu ein simples Beispiel: Die Sonne ist willkommen und wohltätig, wo es lange Zeit im Jahr kalt und dunkel ist. In trockenen, heißen Wüstenregionen jedoch sehnt man sich eher nach Wolken und Regen.

Es ist für uns westlich geprägte Menschen, die wir geradezu süchtig sind, nach Werteinteilungen, Hierarchien und Bewertungen, von dramatischer Wichtigkeit, dies wirklich zu begreifen in aller Konsequenz und Tiefe!
Doch nicht jeder Heiler und jede Heilerin außerhalb Europas ist Schamane oder Schamanin. Der Begriff *Schamane* kommt aus dem *Tungusischen* (eine *Altai*sprache in Sibirien) und meint: "schütteln", "außer sich sein", "in

Verzückung/ Trance geraten". Die Trance ist also ein wesentlich bestimmender Aspekt. Schamane ist nur, auf wen die (im Idealfall) fünf Faktoren zutreffen:

1. Die Berufung zu dieser Aufgabe durch die unsichtbare Welt (durch Krankheiten, Visionen, soziale Ausgrenzung, Träume etc.).

2. Die Fähigkeit, in Trance zu fallen, sie willentlich steuern und wieder verlassen zu können.

3. Jahrelange Lehrzeit bei anderen Schamanen, um die Strukturen der unsichtbaren Welt zu verstehen und Techniken von Diagnose und Therapie zu erlernen.

4. Öffentliche Prüfung, um die erworbenen Fähigkeiten zu beweisen.

5. Schwur, diese Fähigkeit ausschließlich zum Wohle anderer einzusetzen und nicht für persönliche egoistische Zwecke, in den Dienst der Allgemeinheit zu stellen, Tag und Nacht, ohne geregelte Arbeitszeiten.

Heil-Experten

Daher sind nicht alle Heiler und Heilerinnen automatisch auch Schamanen und Schamaninnen. Jede Kultur fand andere Bezeichnungen für spezifische Heiltätigkeiten. Hier drei ausgewählte Beispiele.

Nordamerikanische Indianer

sind Medizinmänner oder -frauen. Sie verfügen über Kenntnisse von Mensch, Natur und Kosmos, die sie in Rituale umsetzen, um Einzelne und Gruppen mit allen Komponenten ins Gleichgewicht zu bringen. Dazu fallen sie nicht notwendigerweise in Trance.

Afrikaner

sind *Fetisch*zauberer, Orakelpriester, *Inyanga* oder *Izangomas*. Die Kenntnisse werden geheim gehalten und geheim vermittelt. Dabei spielt Magie eine wesentliche Rolle, wie auch Hierarchie. Die Magie kann sowohl für heilende als auch tödliche Zwecke eingesetzt werden. Darin unterscheiden sich afrikanische Heilrichtungen vom Amazonasschamanismus, wo der Kampf auf der Ebene der Schamanen ausgetragen wird, nicht aber zum Wehe der Patienten.

Balinesen, Brasilianer oder Bewohner von Haiti (Karibik)

sind Tempeltänzer oder Medien, *Voodoo/ Candomblé*-Priester, bzw. Anhänger. Sie werden spontan von einem Gott/ Geist/ einer Macht besessen, ohne Trance willentlich herbeiführen, lenken oder verlassen zu können. Sie erinnern sich nicht an das Trancegeschehen, werden nicht ausgebildet und setzen ihre natürliche Veranlagung, in Trance fallen zu können nicht für Heilzwecke ein - auch wenn der Zustand für sie selbst und die Umgebung einen sozialstabilisierenden Wert hat.

Die drei knappen Beispiele können in dieser Kürze lediglich eigene Überlegungen anregen, um ein differenziertes Verständnis der kulturellen Hintergründe zu stimulieren, denen sich das *Handbuch der Ethnotherapien* widmet. Sie können nur eine Ahnung vermitteln, wie vielfältig und geographisch unterschiedlich Konzepte, Motivationen und Methoden von Experten sind, die sich der Einheit von Körper, Geist und Seele widmen und den Menschen in mannigfaltige Bezüge zu Gesellschaft, Natur und Kosmos stellen - und zwar sowohl auf materieller, wie auch immaterieller Ebene.

Diese Unterschiede sind wesentlich begründet durch ökologische Lebensräume und historische Prozesse, über die man sich in weiterführender Literatur eingehend informieren kann, was lohnenswert und spannend ist.
Ebenso anregend und informativ empfinden wir auch das vorliegende Werk, das *Handbuch der Ethnotherapien*.

Autorin
DR. PHIL. CLAUDIA MÜLLER-EBELING
Ethnologin und Kunsthistorikerin. Zu ihren wissenschaftlichen Spezialgebieten gehört vor allem die visionäre Kunst, Dämonisierung der Natur in der Kunstgeschichte, *Thanka*malerei und Schamanismus. Ihre Arbeit hat in zahlreichen Publikationen wie z.B. "Schamanische Wissenschaften", "Hexenmedizin", "Schamanismus und Tantra in Nepal". Niederschlag gefunden.
Kontakt: E-Mail: ethnomedizin@web.de

NOT ALL HEALERS ARE SHAMANS – A SURVEY ABOUT THE VARIETY OF HEALING METHODS

by Claudia Müller-Ebeling

In the *Handbook of Ethnotherapies* we find various healing methods. Healers and shamans from distant countries lead us back into our own European past and carry us off geographically into other, non-European countries.
We discover that natural, alternative healing methods, that developed through the past decades, are alive. And we also discover that other cultures have entirely different diagnoses and healing methods and different definitions of disease and health, than we do.

The book shows mutual and varying aspects in the chapters. No matter how familiar or exotic these manifold concepts might appeal to us, they all serve the same goal: the perception of a disease and the healing of the patient.
The cross-over relation through all cultures – and the main difference to Western school medicine- is the concept of the unity of body, spirit and soul.

The Western school medicine is dedicated to the body; the spirit is partially disregarded while the soul is disregarded all the time. The patient is analysed as an isolated unit, irrespective of his environment. In our society medical examinations take place behind shut doors and concern only the doctor and the patient.
Non-European healing systems deal with the unity of body, spirit and soul. In this

---

* Translated by Joy C. Green and Kat Morgenstern.

they differ from the Western scientific methods. The patient is seen in the context of family, society, nature, and cosmos. Diagnosis and therapy are public affairs and not kept in privacy.
Similar healing traditions were practiced in our past culture and are now being used more and more in the today´s alternative healing methods.

Let us take a survey of Shamanic cultures and various kinds of healers and shamans to begin with.

Shamanism

Shamanism is not a religion but a technique, which utilizes the aid of altered states of consciousness to gain insights into the past, present or future and thus facilitates a healing process. This technique is about 60.000 years old and in the past was widespread. In some cultures it has remained a living tradition to this day – particularly in Asia and South America. Shamanism has developed in accordance with its specific cultural context.

In some areas both genders are actively involved (Nepal, Siberia), elsewhere it may be exclusively either a female (Korea) or male (Amazon) person.

In Nepal, Ladakh and, to some extend, Mongolia, healers and patients are both actively involved in the healing process. They support each other during elaborate healing ceremonies and alternate their roles. Although some shamans may be more capable and powerful than others, there is no hierarchical structure among them. The varying abilities are mutually respected and complement each other.

In Korea and in the Amazon on the other hand, this archaic healing technique takes a more fierce and competitive form. Healers fight for their power and influence (status) – both in the visible, material world as well as in the invisible world of spirit allies and daemons. Healers may even attack each other during a trance and pursue each other's power allies and protective spirits.

Neither variation is better or worse than the other, although we might 'prefer' the more peaceful variant. In contrast to our own linear worldview, the Shamanic universe in its essence is cyclic. Nothing is good or evil, right or wrong *per se*, but only in relation to something else. A simple example illustrates the point: In regions where it is cold and dark for long periods of time the sun is welcome and benevolent. In dry and scorching hot desert regions on the other hand people are usually rather longing for clouds and rain. For us, with our westernised programming, being almost addicted to categorization, hierarchies and value judgements, it is of crucial importance to truly comprehend this point in all its consequence and significance.

But not each and every healer outside of Europe is a shaman. The term '*shaman*' derives from a *Tungus* term (an *Altaic* language of Siberia) and means 'to shake', 'to be besides one self' 'to fall into trance or ecstasy'.
Trance, therefore is an essential and defining aspect. Ideally a shaman is defined as someone who fulfills the following five characteristics:

1. To have been summoned by the forces of the invisible world and called to perform the Shamanic work (e.g. by means of diseases, visions, social exclusion, dreams etc.)

2. The ability to enter, control or exit the state of trance by the power of one's own will.

3. Many years of apprenticeship with other shamans in order to understand the structures of the invisible world and learn diagnostic an therapeutic techniques

4. A public trial to prove and demonstrate the assimilated skills

5. Pledging an oath to use these abilities exclusively for the benefit of others and refrain from using them for personal, egoistical purposes; to serve the public, day and night without a regulated work schedule.

Healing Experts

Thus not all healers are automatically also shamans. Every culture has adopted different expressions for various healing occupations. Here is a selection of three examples:

Native North American Indians are *'medicine men'* or '- *medicine women'*, since they have assimilated knowledge concerning human beings, nature and the cosmos, which they incorporate into rituals in order to re-establish a balance between an individual or a group and the other components. A trance is not necessary for this process.

Africans are *fetish sorcerers, oracle priests, Inyanga* or *Izangomas.*
Knowledge is kept secret and is secretly transmitted. Magic plays a crucial part, so does hierarchy. Magic can be utilized for either curative or lethal intents. In this respect African healing traditions vary from Amazonian shamanism, where the battle is carried out on the level of the shamans, but never to harm the patients.

Balinese, Brazilians and Haitians (Caribbean) are *temple dancers* or *mediums, Voodoo/ Candomblé priests* or their followers.
Spirit possession occurs spontaneously. The God, spirit or power enters a person, though the possessed individual is unable to willingly bring about, control or exit a trance state. They do not remember what happened during a trance, have not undergone any training and do not utilize their natural ability to fall into trance for any healing purposes, though their (trance) state has a socially stabilizing effect, both for themselves and for their environment.

Due to brevity these three short examples can merely stimulate personal thinking

processes to encourage a more differentiated understanding of the cultural backgrounds addressed in this *Handbook of Ethnotherapies*. They can only convey a faint idea of how diverse and geographically varied concepts, motivations and approaches of these specialists are, who are dedicating themselves to the unity of body, spirit and soul.
They place the human being within the context of their manifold relations to society, nature and cosmos – both in the material and well as the immaterial world.

The differences are essentially based on the ecology of environments and historical processes. They can – and should be – experienced by the reader in the manifold of the available literature, most informing and exciting, and informative – so we think – as the *Handbook for Ethnotherapies*.

Author
DR. PHIL. CLAUDIA MÜLLER-EBELING
Ethnologist and Art historian.
Her scientific fields are the visionary art, demonization of nature in historian arts as well as *Tanka*-paintings and shamanism. Her work is published in numerous books like "Schamanische Wissenschaften", "Hexenmedizin", and "Schamanismus und Tantra in Nepal".
Contact: E-Mail: ethnomedizin@web.de

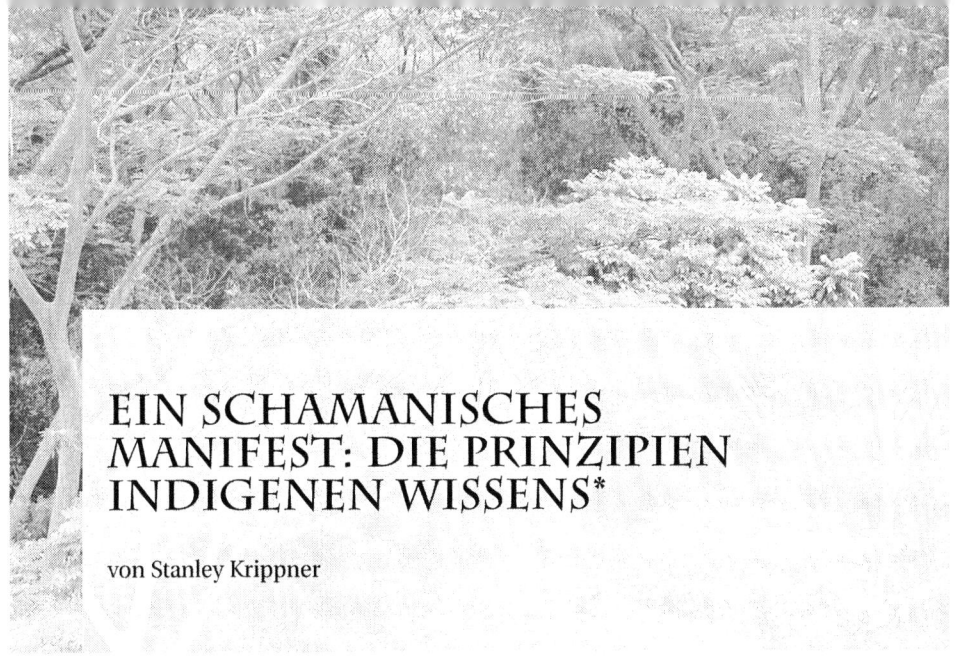

EIN SCHAMANISCHES MANIFEST: DIE PRINZIPIEN INDIGENEN WISSENS*

von Stanley Krippner

Im April 1998 hielt ich in Brasilien an der Internationalen Ganzheitlichen Universität in Brasilia, in der Stadt des Friedens, ein Seminar.
In der gleichen Woche fand die nationale Zusammenkunft der *pajes* in der Stadt des Friedens statt. *Pajes* oder Schamanen aus etwa 40 Stammesgebieten waren zusammengekommen, um gegen die "Ökopiraterie", den Diebstahl ihrer Ressourcen und des Wissens ihres Stammes durch die biotechnologische Industrie zu kämpfen.
Dieses Treffen wurde von der "O Fundacao National de India", der Nationalen Stiftung für Indianer, gefördert. Während dieser Zeit konnte ich mich mit einigen der *pajes* austauschen, da wir alle im selben Restaurant in der Stadt des Friedens speisten.
Mir wurde auch erlaubt, das Camp der *pajes*, welches sich in der Nähe eines wunderschönen Wasserfalls befand, zu besuchen. Einige der *pajes* waren gleichzeitig Häuptlinge, da in kleineren Stämmen diese Funktionen manchmal von einer Person ausgeübt werden.
Der *paje*, mit dem ich mich am regelmässigsten traf, hieß Itambe` Pataxo, ein Vertreter des *Pataxo*-Volkes und bekannter Aktivist, der gegen die Unaufmerksamkeit gegenüber den indigenen Kulturen im Rahmen der Feierlichkeiten zum Jahrestag der portugiesischen Ankunft in Brasilien im Jahr 1500 protestierte (Hasse 1999).
Mit ihm läutete ich die Friedensglocke, die der Stadt des Friedens von einer privaten japanischen Stiftung zur Würdigung der Arbeit der Universität im Bereich der Konfliktbewältigung überreicht wurde. Ein paar Jahre zuvor repräsentierte ich

---

* Dankbare Anerkennung sei Joaquim Pose für die Unterstützung beim Übersetzen aus dem Spanischen ausgedrückt. Übersetzung aus dem Englischen: Matthias Schmidt, Udo Richter und Björn Lehmann

die Vereinigten Staaten, als die Glocke, begleitet von japanischen Tänzern und Musikern, überreicht wurde. Itambe` erzählte mir, dass 1996 eine amerikanische Firma, Coriel Cell Repositories, und ein brasilianischer Arzt zusammenarbeiteten, um kommerzielle Arbeit in einem vom Karitiana-Stamm bewohnten Dorf im Nordwesten Brasiliens durchzuführen.

Von der Nationalen Stiftung für Indianer wurde ihnen die Erlaubnis erteilt, ein regionales Tier zu erforschen. Aber statt dessen nahmen sie Blutproben von Angehörigen des *Karitiana*-Volkes, die den Fremden in ihrer Naivität vertrauten . Ähnlich war der Ablauf bei Stammesangehörigen der Sururi, um von ihnen Blutproben zu bekommen.

Beide Stämme sind in der Nähe von Porto Velho, der Landeshauptstadt des Staates Rondonia, beheimatet. 1998 berichtete der brasilianische Journalist VELOSO, dass Coriel Cell Repositories über ihre Webseite sowohl die Decodierung der Indianer-DNA als auch Blutproben verkaufte.

VELOSO beschrieb das *Karitiana*-Dorf als kleine Enklave, in der etwa 200 Indianer ein armes, aber friedvolles Leben als Subsistenz-Bauern führten und Reis, Bohnen und Mais auf ihren 800 Morgen Land anbauten. Als das betrügerische Vorgehen aufgedeckt wurde, verurteilte eine Kommission des Abgeordnetenhauses die Aktion; Maßnahmen wurden jedoch nicht ergriffen.

Der empörendste Fakt war nach Aussage des Schamanenhäuptlings Cizino Karitiana, dass die Forscher von einem Vertreter der Nationalen Stiftung für Indianer begleitet wurden, der nichts unternahm, um den Missbrauch zu unterbinden. An jenem verhängnisvollen Tag wurde der Häuptling von acht "Forschern" eingeladen, ihr Führer auf dem Weg zu einer Höhle zu sein. In der Zwischenzeit nahmen zwei im Dorf zurückgebliebene "Forscher" von allen Stammesangehörigen, inklusive Babys und Alten, Blutproben.

Die "Forscher" erzählten den Indianern, dass sie krank seien und ihr Blut untersucht werden müsse, damit sie geheilt werden könnten. Als Cizino von der Höhle zurückkehrte, sollte auch er eine Blutprobe abgeben, oder er würde das ganze Dorf anstecken. Durch dieses Eindringen beabsichtigen "Forscher" in verschiedenen Gebieten der Erde, herauszufinden, warum Indianer gegen tropische Krankheiten immun zu sein scheinen, und wie sie unter extremen Wetterbedingungen leben können.

Mit Hilfe dieser Informationen produzieren diese "Forscher" Medikamente, die die Abwehrkräfte von Soldaten bei Einsätzen in ähnlichen Teilen der Erde oder unter vergleichbaren Wetterbedingungen erhöhen.

Als Zilene Kaingangue, eine Vertreterin der Nationalen Stiftung für Indianer, von Veloso interviewt wurde, merkte sie an: "*Strikte Gesetze sind nicht genug. Die große Verpflichtung, unsere eigene Medizin nicht preiszugeben, obliegt uns, den Indianern.*" Sie berichtete, dass ihr Vater, Domingos Kaingangue, ein im Staat Parana sehr bekannter paje, der auch bei der Zusammenkunft war, im Jahre 1995 von einigen "Forschern" aufgesucht wurde.

Er gab ihnen eine Reihe von Rezepturen gegen verschiedene Erkrankungen von Krebs bis zur gewöhnlichen Erkältung. Kurze Zeit später wurden diese Rezepturen ohne Erlaubnis des Dorfes und ohne jegliche finanzielle Entschädigung in einem Buch veröffentlicht. Zilene beklagte, dass die biotechnologische Industrie "Millionen Dollar Gewinn aus unseren Kenntnissen" macht. Am Ende der wochenlangen Zusammenkunft erstellten die *pajes* eine Charta über die Prinzipien des indigenen Wissens, welche landesweit veröffentlicht wurde.

Ich erhielt eine Kopie der Charta und versprach Citambe Pataxo sie, zu verteilen, sobald ich in die Vereinigten Staaten zurückgekehrt sein würde. Was folgt, ist eine Übersetzung dieses Dokuments aus dem portugiesischen Original:

Vor vielen Jahren, am Anbeginn der Zeit, waren wir brasilianischen Indianer bereits hier und es gab Millionen von uns. In diesen Zeiten lehrten unsere Vorfahren schon, dass alles, was existiert, mit dem grossen Zyklus des Lebens in Verbindung steht. In der Natur ist jedes Detail wichtig. Das Wasser der Flüsse und der Zuläufe, die Wälder, kleine und grosse Tiere, alles hat seinen eigenen Zweck.
Sie wurden hier plaziert, um den Zyklus des Lebens aufrechtzuerhalten und ihr Wissen mit den Menschen zu teilen. In Tausenden von Jahren haben wir respektvoll am Zyklus des Lebens, jeden Tag von der Natur lernend, teilgenommen. Die Erde war für unser Volk die grosse Mutter und sie ist es immer noch. Die Natur gibt uns Nahrung für unsere Kinder.
Die Natur lehrt uns den Gebrauch von Pflanzen, um die Krankheiten unserer Leute zu heilen. Die Eindringlinge erschienen vor 500 Jahren und alles änderte sich an diesem Platz, an dem wir gelebt haben. Viele unserer Stämme wurden durch Krankheit und Krieg dezimiert.
Am Anfang waren wir sechs Millionen an der Zahl. Heute sind wir bloß noch Dreihunderttausend. Die Eindringlinge haben die kostbaren Bodenschätze, das Holz und sogar das Land genommen. Unsere grosse Mutter weint traurig und wir weinen mit ihr. Wenn wir zum Fluss gehen, ist er verschmutzt. Viele von uns können nicht mehr im Wald jagen, da er nicht mehr existiert. Wenn wir zu den Geistern sprechen wollen, antworten sie nicht, da Traktoren ihre Häuser zerstört haben.
Wir sind sicher, dass die Lebensweise, die uns auferlegt wurde, eine "Zivilisation" war, die nicht einmal für die Eindringlinge funktionierte. Als Indianer widerstehen wir immer noch dieser "Zivilisation". Wir führen unsere Traditionen und unseren Respekt für die große Mutter Erde fort. Aber diese Aktivitäten bewirken, dass wir von den Eindringlingen als "faule Wilde" abgestempelt werden. Wir verstehen ihre Lehren nicht. Wir verstehen Lehren nicht, die den Wald zerstören, die Flüsse verschmutzen und die Fische töten.
Wir begreifen keine Lehren, die die Alten aufgeben, ihre Kinder missachten und ihre Frauen missbrauchen. Wir verstehen das Verlangen der Eindringlinge nicht, nicht nur die Natur und die Kräfte des Universums, sondern auch andere Menschen beherrschen zu wollen.
All ihre Macht und all ihre Waffen haben sie nicht glücklich gemacht. Wir kennen die Arzneien, die viele ihrer Erkrankungen, Schmerzen und Krankheiten, für die ihre Gelehrten keine Heilmittel haben, heilen würden. Unser Wissen könnte ihnen sogar helfen, mit den unterschiedlichen Plagen, die ihre Felder befallen, umzugehen. Während dieser nationalen Zusammenkunft der *pajes* waren wir zum erstenmal in der Lage, mit unseren Verwandten aus ganz Brasilien über unser traditionelles Wissen zu sprechen. Wir fanden heraus, dass die Eindringlinge einmal mehr wie Tiere der Nacht erschienen, um unseren kostbarsten Besitz zu stehlen.
Dieser kostbare Besitz ist das Wissen, welches im Kopf eines jeden *pajes* und in unseren Stammestraditionen bewahrt wird. Sie stehlen dieses Wissen im Namen des Friedens, im Namen der Menschlichkeit und im Namen der Wissenschaft. Nachdem sie dieses Wissen geplündert haben, verkaufen sie es an den, der am meisten dafür bietet. Bei der nationalen Zusammenkunft der *pajes* haben wir viel Zeit damit verbracht, über diese Vorkommnisse zu sprechen und wir beschlossen,

unsere Herzen zu schliessen und unser Wissen zu schützen.
Wie erließen eine Forderung: Hört auf, von uns zu stehlen. Hört auf, uns wie Forschungsobjekte zu behandeln.
Stoppt die Zerstörung der Wälder, Flüsse und Tiere. Wir fordern Respekt für unsere Vergangenheit und für unsere Kultur. Wir fordern nicht nur von der brasilianischen Regierung, sondern auch von anderen Weltautoritäten eine Reaktion auf folgende Vorschläge:

1. Ein Haufen Gesetze wurden von der brasilianischen Regierung und von vielen anderen Regierungen der ganzen Welt erlassen. Es gibt Gesetze, die unsere Leute und unser traditionelles Wissen beschützen, Gesetze, die die Wälder, die Flüsse und die Luft beschützen. Aber in Brasilien und auf der ganzen Welt gibt es zu viele Gesetze und zu wenig Taten. Für uns haben diese Gesetze keinen Wert, da die Regierungen die Gesetze, die sie erlassen, nicht beachten. Wir fordern, dass Regierungen ihre eigenen Gesetze, die geschaffen wurden, um einheimische Menschen zu schützen, durchsetzen.

2. Es gibt Patentrechte, die im Namen von Außenstehenden das erfassen, was in Wahrheit uns gehört. Diese Gesetze sind weder gut noch gerecht für indigene Menschen. Diese Gesetze erlauben den Diebstahl unseres Wissens. Wir fordern ein neues Gesetz, eines, das den *pajes* als Repräsentanten von Einheimischen eine Stimme gibt, eines, das uns die Rechte für Dinge die uns gehören, garantiert. Wir möchten gehört werden und wir wollen, dass unsere Wünsche respektiert werden, wann auch immer Gesetze hinsichtlich dieses Anliegens beschlossen werden.

3. Das Blut von einigen unserer Stammesverwandten, der *Karitiana* und der *Surui*, wurde von ihren Körpern und aus Brasilien genommen und wird nun als genetische Handelsware verkauft. Wir fordern, dass die brasilianische Regierung mit den anderen Regierungen der Welt spricht, um diese Praxis zu beenden.

4. Das Blut der *Karitiana* und der *Surui* wurde weit weg gebracht und ist nun Geld wert. Diese Stämme wurden zurückgelassen mit dem Versprechen, Hilfe zu erhalten von denen, die ihr Blut nahmen. Wir fordern, dass an die *Karitiana* und *Surui* eine gerechte Abfindung für den Schaden gezahlt wird, den dieser Diebstahl bei ihnen verursachte.

5. Viele Fremde kommen in unser Land, werden willkommen geheißen, führen Nachforschungen durch, sprechen mit uns, tragen viele lebende Dinge aus unseren Wäldern und Flüssen weg und kehren dann nicht

zurück. Statt dessen gehen sie in die Städte, schreiben Bücher, produzieren Filme, drucken Postkarten. Dann verkaufen sie all diese Güter mit Gewinn, während unsere Leute weiterhin arm, ohne Fürsorge und ohne Unterstützung bleiben. Die Nationale Stiftung für Indianer verkündet, dass sie diese Eintrittswege kontrolliert, allerdings haben wir bisher nicht gesehen, dass mit dieser Kontrolle richtig verfahren wurde. Wir fordern, dass die brasilianische Regierung anfängt, mit der Nationalen Stiftung für Indianer zusammen zu arbeiten, um das Betreten von Fremden in indigene Gebiete zu kontrollieren.

6. Die Nationale Stiftung für Indianer existiert seit langer Zeit und durch ihre Dienste haben viele Fremde unser Land besucht. Was wurde mit den Ergebnissen dieser Besuche gemacht? Wie hat diese Arbeit unseren Leuten geholfen? Wann wird diese Unterstützung eintreffen? Die Nationale Stiftung für Indianer muss antworten. Die Nationale Stiftung für Indianer soll einen Bericht über diese Angelegenheit verfassen und ihn den *pajes* präsentieren.

7. Wir wissen, dass verschiedene Pflanzen, Tiere, Insekten und sogar Proben unseres eigenen Blutes von Brasilien in andere Länder exportiert werden. Unser Land ist wie ein offener Markt, den jeder betreten kann und mitnehmen darf, was immer er möchte. Wir fordern, dass die brasilianische Regierung ihre eigenen Eintrittswege besser überwacht, um einen besseren Schutz ihres eigenen Herrschaftsgebietes zu erlangen.

8. Wir wissen, dass es viele Universitäten in den grossen Städten und viele brasilianische Forscher gibt. Warum müssen sie Gegenstände wegnehmen, um sie zu studieren? Warum müssen wir teure Medikamente kaufen, von denen viele von der Anwendung unseres eigenen Wissens herrühren? Das Volk der *Macuxi* zum Beispiel hat über Jahre eine pflanzliche Medizin benutzt, die nun an einer Universität untersucht und wahrscheinlich in Zukunft an uns zurück verkauft wird. Die brasilianische Regierung muss die von indigenen Menschen bereits unternommenen Forschungen anerkennen und unterstützen.

9. Die Zukunft unseres traditionellen Wissens, eines seltenen und kostbaren Schatzes für die gesamte Menschheit, könnte gefährdet sein. Unsere *pajes* und unsere Ältesten sterben an Krankheiten, die es in den alten Tagen nicht gab. Viele unserer Kinder und jungen Leute sterben an Krankheiten und Hunger. Deshalb fordern wir, dass die Autoritäten uns bei der Erhaltung unserer Gesundheit unterstützen und das Überleben unserer Leute garantieren.

10. Die Erde ist unsere große Mutter, und die Natur die größte Apotheke, die auf der Welt existiert. Ohne die Natur wird unser traditionelles Wissen weder für unsere Leute noch für den Rest der Menschheit nützlich sein. Die Gier der Eindringlinge hat zur Verwandlung unserer natürlichen Schätze zu Geld geführt. Diese Gier hat unseren Leuten Krankheit, Hunger und Tod gebracht. Während der Feuer im nördlichen Staat Roraima wurden viele Tiere, Kräuter und Ranken, die wir in unserer Heilkunst benutzten, vernichtet und existieren nicht mehr. Unsere grosse Mutter ist tödlich verwundet und wenn sie stirbt, werden auch wir sterben. Wenn sie stirbt, werden die Eindringlinge keine Zukunft haben. Deshalb fordern wir Schutz für unsere Gebiete. Wir fordern durch Festlegung von Grenzen die Garantie für den Raum, der für unser physisches und kulturelles Überleben notwendig ist.

11. Wir wissen, dass die brasilianische Regierung nicht die einzige Regierung ist, die für das Leben und den Lebensraum der indigenen Bevölkerung verantwortlich ist. Alles, was aus unseren Gebieten exportiert wird, wie Holz, Mineralien, Tiere, unser Blut, geht in ferne Länder. Deshalb sind diese Länder genauso für unser Leiden, wie für das Leiden unserer Verwandten in der ganzen Welt verantwortlich. Es gibt eine Internationale Charta indigener Menschen. Wir fordern, dass die Vereinten Nationen und das Europäische Parlament eine feste Position einnehmen, um diese Charta zu garantieren und zu verlangen, dass die Regierungen der Welt Umweltangelegenheiten und indigene Völker mit dem Respekt und dem Ernst behandeln, den sie verdienen. Unsere abschließenden Worte bezeugen unsere unglücklichen Gefühle.

Wir beendeten diese Zusammenkunft sehr bekümmert über das, was wir sahen und von unseren Verwandten hörten. Außerdem ist da eine große Traurigkeit in unseren Herzen, nachdem wir die gewalttätige "zivilisierte" Welt in Aktion beobachtet haben. Jetzt werden wir unsere Herzen verschliessen und das Wissen unserer Vorfahren in unseren Herzen tragen.
Dies geschieht nicht, weil wir egoistisch sind. Wir handeln so, weil wir unser indigenes Wissen schützen müssen, um eine bessere Zukunft nicht nur für uns, sondern für die ganze Menschheit zu garantieren. Wir werden diese Punkte mit unseren Verwandten, die nicht an dieser Konferenz teilnahmen, diskutieren. Wir werden ihnen die Geschichten, die wir bei diesem Treffen hörten, erzählen. Wir werden jeden, der uns zuhört, warnen.
Wir würden gerne dieses Dokument, in dem unsere Sorgen festgehalten wurden, in die ganze Welt versenden, weil wir immer noch hoffen, dass wir die Eindringlinge lehren können, dass wir alle am grossen Zyklus des Lebens teilnehmen.
Wir sind Kinder der grossen Mutter Erde und wir sind hier, um in Frieden zu leben. Frieden ist die Tochter des Respekts. Solange es keinen Respekt für unsere Leute

gibt, wird es keinen wirklichen Frieden unter uns geben. Wir haben 500 Jahre neben den Eindringlingen gelebt. Diese 500 Jahre sind voll Trauer und Konflikt. Trotzdem leben wir immer noch. Unsere Frauen tragen jeden Tag Früchte ("Our women bear fruit ..." Anm. d. Übers.), wie es auch die Erde tut. Wir kommen von der Erde und werden hier bleiben. Wir können der ganzen Menschheit helfen und wir wollen ihr helfen. Aber auch wir brauchen Hilfe. Zur gleichen Zeit können wir nicht über Diebstahl und Verwüstung hinwegsehen.
Es ist an der Zeit, dass es aufhört. Dies ist unser Wort.
Von Francisco Apurina, von der Apuria-Nation, Waixa Javae von der Javae-Nation, Domingos Kaingangue von der Kaingang-Nation, Maluare Karaja von der Karaja-Nation, Cizino Karatiana von der Karatiana-Nation, Maria Diva Maxacali von der Maxacali-Nation, Citambe Pataxo von der Pataxo-Nation, Joaozinho Xavante von der Xavante-Nation, Joao Xerente von der Xerente-Nation, Vertreter der Kraho-Nation, der Terena-Nation und 30 anderen indigenen Stammesnationen. Stadt des Friedens, Brasilia, 17. April 1998

Oktober 1998 wurde eine ähnliche Konferenz in den Vereinigten Staaten abgehalten. Die verbündeten Stämme der Salish und der Kootenai und die Montana/Wyoming Gesundheitsvereinigung waren Gastgeber einer Konferenz über nordamerikanische Genforschung und einheimische Völker in Polson, Montana.
Diese Konferenz brachte Stammesoberhäupte, Wissenschaftler, Bioethiker, Stammesanwälte und Erzieher zusammen, um über Streitfragen human-genetischer Forschung in Verbindung mit indigenen Menschen zu diskutieren. Auffallend war die Abwesenheit von Vertretern des nordamerikanischen Komitees für das menschliche Genomvielfaltsprojekt, trotz wiederholter Einladungen durch die Organisatoren.
Ein bei der Konferenz anwesender Stammesanwalt kritisierte das Protokoll des Projekts: "Es fordert nichts außer einer Einverständniserklärung. Wer wird beurteilen, ob das Einverständnis sachkundig ist?" Ein anderer Anwalt beobachtete: "Es sollten keine Forschungen (an Menschen) betrieben werden, solange dabei kein Vorteil für die untersuchte Bevölkerung entsteht. ...
Ich vermute, dass, wenn es keine Patente geben würde, die meisten dieser Streitfragen gar nicht erst aufkommen würden." (HARRY 1999). Um es anders auszudrücken, auf beiden Konferenzen wurden viele ähnliche Belange zum Ausdruck gebracht.
Letztendlich wurde die "ethische" Herangehensweise zum Studium menschlicher Diversität ernsthaft in Frage gestellt (z.B. WINANT 1994).
Im Gegensatz dazu bringt die "emische" Behandlung des Themas den Gebrauch von Selbst- und Fremdkategorisierungen von Menschen mit sich, um Rassen-identitäten und Bedeutungen zu schaffen. Dieser Annäherungsversuch sieht Rasse nicht als "natürliches" Attribut, sondern als eins, das sozial erschaffen und spezifisch für eine bestehende Gesellschaft ist.
In Brasilien z.B. überwiegt die Auffassung von Hautfarbe, Haarstruktur und Gesichtsmerkmalen gegenüber der Abstammung, um eine Rassenidentität zu schaffen (HARRIS, CONSORTE, LANG & BYRNE 1993).
Wenn indigene Menschen dagegen protestieren, Blutproben für genetische Tests zu geben, erheben sie einen berechtigten Einwand gegen die Verdinglichung der Rassenstereotypen, die ein Vermächtnis von Nichtbefähigung und Diskriminierung hinterlassen haben.

Autor
STANLEY KRIPPNER, PH.D.
Professor für Psychologie am Saybrook Graduate School and Research Center, San Francisco, Kalifornien. Er hat Schamanen in Nord- und Südamerika, Europa, Asien und Afrika beobachtet und mit ihnen zusammengearbeitet und präsentiert seine Erkenntnisse in Dutzenden von Artikeln und in seinem Buch "Spiritual Dimensions of Healing: From Tribal Shamanism to Contemporary Health Care."
Kontakt: E-Mail: skrippner@saybrook.edu

Literatur
HARRIS, M., CONSORTE, J., LANG, J. & BYRNE, B. 1993. Who are the whites? Imposed census categories and the racial demography of Brazil. *Social Forces*, 72, 451-462.
HARRY, D. 1999, February. Tribes meet to discuss genetic colonization. *Anthropology newsletter*, p.15.
HASSE, G. 1999, April 19. Paje' nao quer festa para Cabral (Shaman does not want a festival for Cabral). *Epoca*, pp. 46-47.
VELOSO, B. 1998, April 21. Pajes se unem contra biopirataria (Shamans unite against biopiratism). *Correio Braziliense*, p. 16.
WINANT, H. 1994. *Racial conditions: Politics, theory, comparisons*. Minneapolis: University of Minnesota Press.

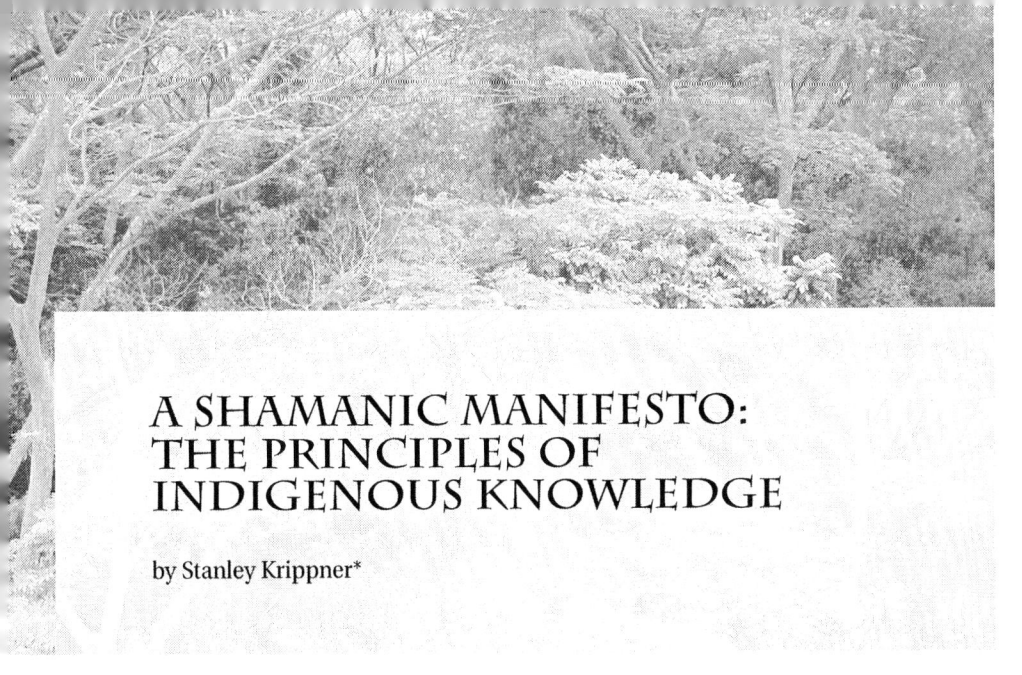

A SHAMANIC MANIFESTO: THE PRINCIPLES OF INDIGENOUS KNOWLEDGE

by Stanley Krippner*

In April, 1998, I gave a seminar at the International Holistic University, located at the City of Peace, Brasilia, Brazil. During that same week, the National Encounter of *Pajes* was being held at the City of Peace.

Pajes, or shamans, from some 40 tribal nations in Brazil, had assembled to combat "ecopiratism," the theft by the biotechnology industry of their resources and tribal knowledge. This encounter was sponsored by O Fundacao Nacional de India, the National Foundation for the Indians. I was able to interact with many of the pajes during meal times, as we all ate at the same restaurant at the City of Peace. I also was allowed to visit the encampment of the *pajes* which was located near a beautiful waterfall. Some of the *pajes* were also chiefs, as these functions are sometimes combined in small tribes. The *paje* with whom I had the most frequent contact was Itambe' Pataxo, representative of the Pataxo Nation, a well-known activist who has protested the inattention given to indigenous cultures in the anniversary plans surrounding Portugal's arrival in Brazil in 1500 (HASSE 1999). With him, I rang the Peace Bell, a gift to the City of Peace from a private Japanese Foundation in honor of the university's work in the area of conflict resolution.

A few years earlier, I had represented the United States when the Peace Bell was dedicated, to the accompaniment of Japanese dancers and musicians. Itambe' told me that in 1996, an American company, Coriel Cell Repositories, and a Brazilian physician had teamed up for a clandestine commercial operation in a village inhabited by the Karitiana tribe in northwestern Brazil.

They had obtained permission from the National Foundation for the Indians to study a regional animal, but instead drew blood samples from members of the Karitiana Nation who naively trusted the outsiders. A similar procedure was

---

* Grateful acknowledgement is expressed to Joaquim Pose for his assistance in translating this document.

followed to obtain blood samples from the Surui tribe. Both tribes are located in the state of Rondonia near Porto Velho, the state capital. VELOSO (1998), a Brazilian journalist, reported that through its website, Coriel Cell Repositories has been selling the decodification of the Indians' DNA as well as their blood samples. VELOSO described the Karitiana village as a small enclave of some 200 Indians who live a poor but peaceful life as subsistence farmers, growing rice, beans, and corn on their 800 acres. When the scam was uncovered, a special commission from Brazil's House of Deputies denounced the scheme, but no action was taken. According to the shaman-chief Cizino Karitiana, the most outrageous aspect of the incident was that the researchers were accompanied by a representative of the National Foundation for the Indians who did nothing to stop the abuse. On the fateful day, the shaman-chief was invited to be the guide for eight "researchers" as they travelled to a cave. In the meantime, two "researchers" stayed in the Karitiana village and drew blood from everyone, including elders and babies. The "researchers" told the Indians that they were sick and that their blood needed to be examined in order for them to be healed.

When Cizino returned from the cave, he was also told to donate blood, or he would contaminate the entire village. The information gleaned from these incursions is in demand from "researchers" in various parts of the world who ask why these Indians appear to be immune to tropical illnesses, and how they can function in extreme weather conditions. With this information, these "researchers" produce medicines that increase soldiers' resistance during combat in parts of the world with similar illnesses or weather conditions.

A representative for the National Foundation for the Indians, Zilene Kaingangue, was interviewed by Veloso and commented, "It is not enough to have rigorous laws. The important commitment is among ourselves, the Indians, not to give away our own medicines." She told Veloso that her father, Domingos Kaingangue, a well-known *paje* in the state of Parana who was present at the encounter, received some "researchers" in 1995. He gave them a number of prescriptions for various illnesses ranging from cancer to the common cold.

A short time later, these prescriptions were published in a book without the village's authorization or any kind of financial compensation. Zilene claimed that the biotechnology industry "makes millions of dollars in profits from our knowledge." At the end of the week-long encounter, the *pajes* produced a Charter of the Principles of Indigenous Knowledge which was publicized throughout the country. I was given a copy of this Charter and promised Citambe Pataxo that I would distribute it once I returned to the United States.

What follows is a translation of this document from the original Portuguese: Many years ago, at the beginning of time, we Brazilian Indians were already here, and there were millions of us. In those times, our ancestors were already teaching that all that exists is linked to the great cycle of life. In nature, each detail is important. The waters of the rivers and the tributaries, the forests, both large and small animals, all have their own purpose. They were placed here in order to maintain the cycle of life and to share their knowledge with human beings. Through thousands of years, we have participated respectfully in this cycle of life, learning from nature every day.

The Earth was the Great Mother to our people, and still is. Nature gives us nourishment for our children. Nature teaches us how to use plants to heal the illnesses of our people. The invaders arrived five hundred years ago, and everything changed in this place where we used to live. Many of our tribes were decimated by illness and by war. In the beginning, we were six million in number. Today we are a mere three hundred thousand. The invaders have taken the precious minerals, the wood, and even the land. Our Great Mother cries sadly, and we cry with her. When we go to the river, it is polluted. Many of us can not hunt in the forest because it no longer exists. When we want to talk to the spirits, they do not answer us because tractors have trampled their homes.

We are certain that the way of life that was imposed upon us was a "civilization" that did not even work out for the invaders. As Indians, we still resist this "civilization." We maintain our traditions and our respect for Great Mother Earth. But these activities cause us to be labelled "lazy savages" by the invaders. We do not comprehend their teachings. We do not understand teachings that destroy the forest, that pollute the rivers, and that kill the fish.

We do not comprehend teachings that abandons the elderly, mistreats their children, and abuses their women. We do not comprehend the invaders' anxiety to dominate not only nature and the forces of the universe, but other people as well. All of their power and all of their weapons have not made them happy. We know the medicines that would cure many of their illnesses and pains, sicknesses for which their wise men have no remedies.

Our knowledge could even help them deal with the various plagues that are affecting their farms. At this National Encounter of *Pajes*, we were able to talk about our traditional knowledge with our relatives from all over Brazil for the first time. We found that once more the invaders, like animals of the night, have been coming to our land to steal our most precious possession.

This precious possession is the knowledge that is stored inside the head of each paje and in our tribal traditions. They steal this knowledge in the name of peace, in the name of humanity, and in the name of science. After they plunder this knowledge, they sell it to the one who offers the best price for it. At the National Encounter of *Pajes*, we spent a great deal of time talking about these issues, and we decided to close our hearts and protect our knowledge. We issued a command: Stop stealing from us. Stop treating us as objects of research. Stop the destruction of the forests, rivers, and animals. We demand respect for our past and for our culture. We also demand that not only the Brazilian government, but other world authorities as well, respond to the following proposals:

> 1. A pile of laws has been established by Brazil and many other governments throughout the world. There are laws that protect our people and our traditional knowledge, and that protect the forests, rivers, and air. But in Brazil and all over the world there are too many laws and not enough action. For us, these laws have no value because governments do not follow the laws they make. We demand that governments enforce their own laws that were made to protect indigenous people.

> 2. There are patent laws that register under the names of outsiders what, in truth, belongs to us. These laws are neither good nor just for indigenous people. These laws permit the theft of our knowledge. We demand a new law, one that gives voice to the pajes as representatives of indigenous people, one that guarantees that we have the rights to what is ours. We want

to be heard and we want our wishes to be respected whenever laws are made concerning this matter.

3. The blood of some of our tribal relatives, the *Karitiana* and the *Surui*, was taken away from their bodies and away from Brazil, and is now being sold as genetic merchandise. We demand that the Brazilian government speak with the other governments of the world in order to stop this practice.

4. The blood of the *Karitiana* and the *Surui* was taken far away and is now worth money. These tribes were left with the promise that they would receive some help from those who took their blood away. We demand a just indemnity be paid to the Karitiana and the *Surui* people for the damage this theft caused them.

5. Many outsiders go to our land, are welcomed, conduct research, talk to us, and carry away many living things from the forests and rivers, then do not return. Instead, they go to the cities, write books, make movies, print postcards, then sell all of these items for profit while our people remain poor, without care, and without support. The National Foundation for the Indians proclaims that it controls these entryways yet we never saw this control handled in the right way. We demand that the Brazilian government begin working with the National Foundation for the Indians to control the entry of outsiders in indigenous lands.

6. The National Foundation for the Indians has existed for a long time, and through its services, many outsiders have visited our land. What has been done with the results of these visits? How has this work helped our people? When will this assistance arrive? The National Foundation for the Indians must answer. The National Foundation for the Indians should produce a report about this matter and present it to the *pajes*.

7. We know that various plants, animals, insects, and even our own blood samples are exported from Brazil to other countries. Our land is like an open market, where anyone can enter and carry away whatever they like. We demand that the Brazilian government monitor its own gateways in order to establish a better protection of its own patrimony.

8. We know that there are many universities in the big cities, and that there are many Brazilian researchers. Why do they have to remove items in order to study them? Why do we have to buy expensive medicines, many of which

resulted from applications of our own knowledge? For example, the *Macuxi* tribe has used an herbal medicine for years that is now being studied at a university, and will probably be sold back to us in the future. The Brazilian government needs to acknowledge and support the research already done by indigenous people.

9. The future of our traditional knowledge, a rare and precious resource for all humankind, might not be secure. Our *pajes* and our elders are dying with illnesses that did not exist in the old days. Many of our children and our young people are dying of illness and starvation. Therefore, we demand that the authorities assist us in maintaining our health and guaranteeing the survival of our people.

10. The Earth is our Great Mother. Nature is the largest pharmacy that exists in the world. Without nature, our traditional knowledge will not be useful to our people or to the rest of humanity. The invaders' greed has resulted in the transformation of our natural resources into money. This greed has brought sickness, starvation, and death to our people. During the fires in the northern state of Roraima, many animals, herbs, and vines that we used in our medicines perished, and no longer exist. Our Great Mother Earth is mortally wounded, and if she dies, we will die as well. If she dies, the invaders will have no future. Therefore, we demand protection of our lands. We demand the guarantee, through demarcation, of the space that is necessary for our physical and cultural survival.

11. We know that the Brazilian government is not the only government responsible for the indigenous people's lives and environment. Everything that is exported from our lands, such as wood, minerals, animals, and our blood, go to distant countries. Therefore, these countries are also responsible for our suffering, and the suffering of our relatives throughout the world. There is an International Charter of Indigenous Peoples. We demand that a firm position be taken by the United Nations and by the European Parliament in order to guarantee this Charter and to require that the governments of the world treat environmental issues and the indigenous people with the respect and seriousness they deserve.

Our final words are not those of happiness. We ended this encounter very distressed with what we saw and what we heard about our relatives. In addition, there is a great sadness in our hearts after observing the violent "civilized" world in action. Now we are going to close our hearts, and keep in our heads the knowledge of our ancestors. This is not because we are selfish. We are doing this because we must protect our indigenous knowledge to guarantee a better future not only for our people, but for the entire world.

We will discuss these issues with our relatives who did not attend this encounter. We will tell them the stories we heard at this meeting. We will warn everybody who will listen to us. We would like to have this document, in which our concerns are recorded, sent all over the world, because we still hope to teach the invaders that we all participate in the great cycle of life. We are children of the Great Mother Earth, and we are here to live in peace, which is the daughter of respect. As long as there is no respect for our people, there will be no real peace among us.

We have been coexisting with the invaders for 500 years. These 500 years are full of sadness and conflict. Nevertheless, we are still alive. Our women bear fruit every day, as does the Earth. We are from the Earth and we will stay here. We can help all humanity, and we want to help them. But we need help as well. At the same time, we can not condone the theft and the devastation. It is time for this to stop. This is our word.

Francisco Apurina, from the Apurian Nation, Waixa Javae, from the Javae Nation Domingos Kaingangue, from the Kaingang Nation Maluare Karaja, from the Karaja Nation Cizino Karatiana, from the Karatiana Nation Maria Diva Maxacali, from the Maxacali Nation Citambe Pataxo, from the Pataxo Nation Joaozinho Xavante, from the Xavante Nation Joao Xerente, from the Xerente Nation Representatives from the Kraho Nation, the Terena Nation, and 30 other indigenous tribal nations.

City of Peace, Brasilia, 17 April 1998.

In October, 1998 a similar conference was held in the United States. The Confederated Salish and Kootenai Tribes and the Montana/Wyoming Health Board hosted a conference on North American Genetic Research and Native People in Polson, Montana.

This conference brought together tribal leaders, scientists, bioethicists, tribal attorneys, and educators to discuss issues relating to human genetic research and indigenous peoples. Notably absent from the conference were representatives from the North American Committee of the Human Genome Diversity Project, despite repeated invitations by conference organizers. A tribal attorney at the conference criticized the Project's protocol, noting that "It doesn't demand anything but informed consent. Who will judge if the consent is informed?" Another lawyer observed, "No research [on humans] should be done unless there's a benefit to the population to be studied....If there were no patents, my guess is that most of these issues would be gone" (HARRY 1999). In other words, many similar concerns were voiced at the two conferences.

Finally, the "etic" approach to the study of human diversity has been seriously questioned (e.g., WINANT 1994). In contrast, the "emic" approach entails the use of people's self-categorizations and others to establish racial identities and meanings. This approach sees race not as a "natural" attribute, but one that is socially constructed and specific to a given society. In Brazil, for example, the perception of skin color, hair texture, and facial features outweigh heritage to establish a racial identity (HARRIS, CONSORTE, LANG, & BYRNE 1993). When indigenous people protest against giving blood samples for genetic testing, they are also making a legitimate objection to the reification of racial stereotypes that have left a legacy of disempowerment and discrimination in their wake.

Author
STANLEY KRIPPNER, PH.D.
Professor of Psychology at Saybrook Graduate School and Research Center, San Francisco, California. He has observed and worked with shamans in North and South America, Europe, Asia, and Africa, presenting his findings in dozens of articles and in the book *Spiritual Dimensions of Healing: From Tribal Shamanism to Contemporary Health Care*. Contact: E-Mail: skrippner@saybrook.edu

References

HARRIS, M., CONSORTE, J., LANG, J., & BYRNE, B. 1993. *Who are the whites? Imposed census categories and the racial demography of Brazil*. SOCIAL FORCES, 72, 451-462.

HASSE, G. 1999, April 19. *Paje' nao quer festa para Cabral* [Shaman does not want a festival for Cabral]. Epoca, pp. 46-47.

HARRY, D. 1999, February. *Tribes meet to discuss genetic colonization*. Anthropology Newsletter, p. 15.

VELOSO, B. 1998, April 21. *Pajes se unem contra biopirataria* [Shamans unite against biopiratism]. Correio Braziliense, p. 16.

WINANT, H. 1994. *Racial conditions: Politics, theory, comparisons*. Minneapolis: University of Minnesota Press.

VOM SCHAMANENTUM ZUR MODERNEN NATURTHERAPIE

von Holger Kalweit

Der unmittelbare Kontakt zur Natur
Schamanentum, wie es in Stammeskulturen ausgeübt wird, besitzt heute für Europäer eine zunehmende Ausstrahlung. Klassisches Schamanentum von Stammeskulturen ist jedoch nicht übertragbar auf moderne Gesellschaften. Alle diesbezüglichen Versuche verkommen zu bloßer Nachahmung. Ich habe daher eine neue Therapie entworfen, die Naturtherapie. In der Naturtherapie ist die Natur selbst der Heiler und Schamane. Der Beruf des Therapeuten ist damit aufgehoben, an dessen Stelle tritt die Einweihung in die Natur, bzw. der Kontakt zu den vielen Lebewesen, aus denen sie sich zusammensetzt.
Das ist das innere Wesen des Schamanentums, und das kann von modernen Menschen ausgeübt werden. Das heißt jedoch: Der Abendländer muss seine eigene Form des Herangehens an die Natur entwickeln, er kann sich billigerweise nicht an indianische, tibetische oder afrikanische Traditionen anlehnen.
Woraus schöpft der Mensch seine Lebenskraft, wenn nicht aus der gläsernen Reinheit der Bergsees und dem milchigen Morgennebel, aus dem Vogelflug und dem Wolkendunst? Naturtherapie ist eine Reise in die Wildnis der Seele und die Seele der Wildnis. Natur ist der größte Heiler.
Natur lässt sich nur ganz allein erfahren. Daher beginnt Naturtherapie mit langen

Aufenthalten unter Bäumen, am Bachquell, im Steinkreis. Je länger ich allein bin in der Natur, Tag und Nacht, bei Regen, bei glühender Sonne, desto mehr enthüllen sich die Gesetze der Natur und zugleich dazu tritt unsere Seelennatur hervor, als Ebenbild der äußeren Natur, befreit von Ballast unserer Kultur. Die große Einsamkeit in der Höhle oder am Kratersee schleift wie der Bergbach den Fels alles künstliche Kulturgehabe und die vielen Ichaufblähungen ab.

Entwicklung der Naturtherapie

Die Naturtherapie wurde von mir in den 80-er Jahren aus dem Schamanentum und der Mythologie der Stammeskulturen entwickelt. Ich erforschte das Schamanentum, den Tod, die Mythen der Völker, unter anderem der Germanen und Kelten sowie die Psychophysik unseres Plasmakörpers; daraus entstanden zwei neue Therapien: die Dunkeltherapie und die Naturtherapie. Unzufrieden mit der modernen Psychologie, die keine Wurzeln im alten Wissen der Völker hat und weder ihren Ursprung noch ihr Ziel kennt, suchte ich nach einer für den Abendländer angemessenen Übertragung des Schamanentums und der archaischen Naturkenntnisse: Naturtherapie ist das Ergebnis.

Brückenschlag zu anderen Lebensformen

Naturtherapie findet nicht im sterilen Therapeutenzimmer statt, sondern draußen in der Waldakademie, wo wir im Verein mit Bäumen und Gräsern ein Ereignis feiern. Nicht als isolierte Menschen, sondern im Verein mit Pflanzen und Tieren versuchen wir uns als Lebensform unter anderen zu erfahren. Das wilde Zwiegespräch mit dem Berg findet tatsächlich statt, sofern wir Berg und Gipfel als Partner erfahren. Der Umgang mit anderen Lebensformen, Tieren, Pflanzen und Steinen steht also im Mittelpunkt der Naturtherapie.

Seinsöffnung

In der Naturtherapie geht es um Seinsöffnung, Öffnung für das ungeschminkte, "asoziale", "unmenschliche" Sein wie es ist, ohne unsere Benennungen und Ansichten. Der Baum hat keinen Namen, kein Biologe hat ihn je erfasst. Ich erfahre den Baum, den Stein, die Wolke, verwandle mich in sie. Ich bin die Haselnuss, die Schleiereule, der Schieferfels. Beim langen Sitzen an der scharfen Klippe, beim stillen Betrachten der smaragdgrünen Steinader verwandle mich in diese. Voraussetzung aber ist die innere Leere, das Gereinigtsein von allen Gedanken und jedem Kulturballast. Mit der Verwandlung offenbart sich uns eine Ebene uns umgebender, uns durchdringender übermenschlicher Seinsgröße. Seinsöffnung ist erreicht. Die Psyche ist der Kultur entrissen und wieder Natur geworden.

Entsagung, Preisgabe, Opfer

An erster Stelle stehen Übungen zur inneren Reinigung. Reinigung wird bewirkt durch Entsagung, durch Preisgabe und Öffnung unserer menschlichen Verfassung, durch das Opfern dessen, was man liebt und nicht entbehren zu können meint. Dem schließen sich an: lange Naturaufenthalte in der Einsamkeit, mehrtägige Visionssuchen, Pilgerfahrten zu Naturheiligtümern oder Kultstätten, Dunkeltherapie in unterirdischen Grotten und Tunneln, Meditation auf heiligen Bergen und in antiken und urzeitlichen Tempelarealen.

Visionssuche

In der Einsamkeit - der Zweisamkeit mit der Natur - erkennen wir die Symbolsprache des Lebendigen. Vögel und Wolken gleiten wie Freunde an uns vorbei, der Farn wedelt bedeutungsvoll, das Energiewesen hinter den Naturformen spricht zu uns als tiefes Mitgefühl, als Ahnung und Vision. Alle Naturformen sind Zeichen energetischer Felder. Diese wirken auf uns ein nicht über den Verstand, sondern umittelbar auf die Seele. Alle Naturformen und -wesen scheinen schon gespeichert in uns als Urformen, die es nur wiederzuerkennen gilt. In der Naturschau kommen dann äußere und innere Natur zusammen, wir werden, was wir wahrhaftig sind. Diese Ursprache von Natur und Seele wiederzuentdecken ist der Zweck des Zwiegesprächs in der Wildnis. Visionssuche und Naturschau finden nur im Sommer und allein statt.

Dunkeltherapie

Zum klassischen Prozess der Wesensschau gehört die Dunkeltherapie; der Aufenthalt in Höhlen oder abgedunkelten Räumen. Ich führe Dunkeltherapie bis zu sieben Wochen durch.

Naturverehrung, Naturfeste

Wie kann man Quellen und Sträuchern gegenübertreten?: Durch den Ritus der Verehrung! Der Ritus setzt einen Rahmen, innerhalb dessen wir uns Libellen und Lurchen nähern können. Dem aber geht stets die lange Einsamkeit in der Natur voraus, die uns öffnet, reinigt und in den Stand der Schau versetzt. In der Naturzeremonie bekleiden wir uns nur mit Naturmaterialien und gestalten eine Verehrungszeremonie für die Naturkraft hinter den Sumpfgräsern oder dem Eichenhain; auf diese Weise durchdringt Natur unser Denken und Fühlen und die Erfahrung unserer Gleichheit mit allen Naturwesen vertieft sich.

Naturritual und Mysterienfeier

Die in der Naturschau und Einsamkeit gewonnen Erfahrungen sollen verkörpert werden, und zwar durch Naturzeremonien, in denen die gemachten Einsichten als Dramen, zeremonielle Handlungen und Choreographien nachgespielt werden. Die Teilnehmer verwandeln sich dabei in die darzustellenden Archetypen. Bei jedem Treffen wird kontemplativ ein Archetyp der Natur ergründet und dann inszeniert; diese Feste können Namen haben wie: Am Totenfluss, Geistertanz, Feueropfer, Anrufung der vier Himmel, Insel des Jetzt, Geisterkanu, Herrin der Waldtiere, Phallus und Vulva oder Die nackte Göttin.

Reisen zu Urkulturen

Naturtherapie heißt Rückwendung zum Wissen der alten Kulturen, insbesondere zu dem von Stammeskulturen, denn wir können von deren Lebensform lernen. Die Geschichte der Menschheit gipfelt nicht in der Moderne, diese hat die Natur vergessen; sie gipfelt in der Schau, durch die alte Völker das ganze Wesen des Seins durchdrungen und eine umfassende Naturwissenschaft entwickelt haben.

Reisen zu den großen Naturschauspielen, zu Stämmen und Kultstätten
Wir bieten Naturaufenthalte in verschiedenen Ländern und Reisen in abgelegene Gebiete von Stammeskulturen an. Die großen Wüsten, Hochgebirge, Urwälder und Meere sollen im Verein mit dem alten Wissen der Naturvölker erfahren werden. Das Reisen und die Pilgerfahrten sind integraler Bestandteil der Naturtherapie, weil sie erweitern, erneuern, erheben.

Autor
DIPL. PSYCH. HOLGER KALWEIT
Psychologe, Psychotherapeut, Ethnologe. Schamanismusforscher mit Schwerpunkt Hawaii, Tibet und Mexiko. Seine besondere Aufmerksamkeit gilt den Urüberlieferungen der Völker über Weltentstehung, Geburt der Menschheit, Weltkatastrophen und Kulturentwicklung. Er entwickelte auf der Grundlage des Schamanentums eine neue Therapie, die Naturtherapie, und aus dem tibetischen Dunkelretreat die Dunkeltherapie.
Kontakt: Holger Kalweit, Grünwalder Str. 30, D-79853 Lenzkirch-Kappel, Tel/Fax: +49-7653-9458

Literatur

KALWEIT, H. 1981. Transpersonal Anthropology and the Comparison of Cultures, In: Phoenix: *Journal of Transpersonal Anthropology*, 1981, V, 2: 97-105.
- (Hrsg.). 1983. *Frank Hamilton Cushing. Ein weisser Indianer. Mein Leben mit den Zuni.* Walter Verlag, Olten.
- 1984. *Traumzeit und innerer Raum. Die Welt der Schamanen.* Scherz Verlag, München.
- 1984. Formen transpersonaler Psychotherapie bei nichtwestlichen Kulturen. In: *Integrative Therapie* 10 (3): 253-262.
- & SCHENK, AMELIE (Hrsg.). 1984. *Heilung des Wissens. Forscher erzählen von ihrer Begegnung mit dem Schamanen - Der innere und der äußere Weg des Wissens.* Goldmann Verlag, München.
- 1987. *Urheiler, Medizinleute und Schamanen. Lehren aus der archaischen Lebenstherapie.* Kösel Verlag, München.
- 1987. Himalaya Orakel. In: KALWEIT/SCHENK: *Heilung des Wissens.* Goldmann Verlag, München S. 260-287.
- 1989. When Insanity is a Blessing: The Message of Shamanism. In: GROF, STANISLAV & CHRISTINA (Hgg.): *Spiritual Emergency. When Personal Transformation Becomes a Crisis.* Los Angeles, S. 77-97.
- 1994. Lightening Shamans. *Jahrbuch für Ethnomedizin und Bewußtseinsforschung*, 3: 161-169.
- 1994. Schamanische Trance und die Theorie des Bewußtseinskontinuums. In: *Jahrbuch für Transkulturelle Medizin und Psychotherapie.* Hgg. R. VAN QUEKELBERGHE & D. EIGNER, 1994: 17-41.
- 1995. Der Sitz der Seele in traditionellen Kosmologien. *Ethnopsychologische Mitteilungen*, 1995, 4, 1: 37-71.
- 1995. Urschamanen und das Goldene Zeitalter . *Curare. Zeitschrift für Ethnomedizin*, (1995) 18, 1: 153-160.
- & A. Schenk. 1995. Der Doppelkörper als Grundlage der Trance in der tibetischen Psychologie. *Curare. Zeitschrift für Ethnomedizin* 18 (1995) 2: 467-496.
- 1997. Übertragung der Lebensenergie bei tibetischen Schamanen. *Ethnopsychologische Schriften*, Hrsg. R. V. QUEKELBERGHE, Landau 1997, S. 25-52.
- 1987. Yin, Yang und die Drachenenergie. In: *Ethnopsychologische Mitteilungen*, 1987 (2), S. 109-145.
- 1998. Schamanische Energie-Ökologie: Das Bündnis von Seelen- und Naturfeld. In: GOTTWALD/RÄTSCH, *Schamanische Wissenschaften.* Diederichs Verlag, München S. 96-120.
- Dunkeltherapie - Eine traditionelle Selbstbefreiungsmethode und ihre Verwendung in der modernen Praxis. In: *Curare Sonderband: Ethnotherapien.* Verlag für Wissenschaft und Bildung. Hrsg. C. E. GOTTSCHALK-BATSCHKUS & CH. RÄTSCH S. 223-227.
- & Amélie Schenk. 1998 Schamanische Heilung durch Reisen ins Totenreich. In: *Jahrbuch für Transkulturelle Medizin und Psychotherapie* 1998/99, Verlag für Wissenschaft und Bildung, Berlin. Hrsg. von STANLEY KRIPPNER & HOLGER KALWEIT, S. 103-124.
- 2001. *Das Totenbuch der Germanen. Die Edda - die Wurzeln eines wilden Volkes.* AT-Verlag, Aarau.
- 2002. *Das Totenbuch der Kelten. Das Bündnis zwischen Anderswelt und Erde.* AT-Verlag, Aarau.
- *Naturtherapie. Wilde Zwiegespräche mit Himmel und Erde.* In Vorbereitung.

SCHENK, A.. 1994. Schamanen auf dem Dach der Welt. ADEVA Graz.
- 2000. *Herr des Schwarzen Himmels. Zeren Baawai - Schamane der Mongolei.* O. W. Barth Verlag, München.

FROM SHAMANISM TO NATURE THERAPY*

by Holger Kalweit

Contact to Nature

Shamanism, as practised in tribal cultures, has an increasing attraction for Europeans today. However, the classical shamanism of tribal cultures can not simply be transferred to modern societies - attempts to do so result in mere imitations.

Therefore I have developed a new kind of therapy, Nature Therapy. Within Nature Therapy, nature itself is both, healer and shaman and the profession of the therapist is abolished. Instead there is an initiation into nature and the many lifeforms that make up nature. That is the inner essence of shamanism, as it can be practised by modern people. This means, however, that Western people should develop their own ways of dealing with nature. They cannot just rely on patterns from Indian, Tibetan or African traditions.

Where does a human obtain their lifeforce from, if not from the glassy pureness of a mountain lake and the milky morning fog, from flying birds and misty clouds? Nature Therapy is a trip into the wilderness of the soul and into the soul of the wilderness. Nature is the greatest healer. Nature can only be experienced in itself. Therefore Nature Therapy begins with long stays under trees, at springs and within stone-circles. The longer one stays in nature by oneself, night and day - in the rain,

---

* Translated by Andrea Grasse

in the hot sun - the better the laws of nature are revealed. At the same time our soul-nature appears as an image of outer nature, liberated from the ballast of our culture. In a cave or at a crater-lake, the great loneliness grinds away all artificial cultural affectations and the swollen ego, like the mountain-brook grinds away rocks.

Development of Nature Therapy

In the eighties I developed Nature Therapy from shamanism and the mythology of tribal cultures. I researched shamanism, death and myths of peoples among them Teutonic and Celtic myths, as well as on the psychophysics of our plasmabody. Two new therapies emerged from this: darkness therapy and Nature Therapy. Dissatisfied with modern psychology, which is not rooted in ancient wisdom and does not know its origin or goal, I looked for a suitable way of making shamanism and the archaic nature-knowledge useful to Western man: Nature Therapy is the result.

Bridging to other life forms
Nature Therapy does not take place in a sterile therapeutic room, but in the outside wood academy, where we celebrate an event together with trees and grass. We try to experience ourselves as one lifeform among others - not as isolated men, but together with plants and animals.

The wild dialogue with the mountain actually takes place, if we experience the mountain and the peak as partners. Hence, the central focus of Nature Therapy is in relations to other forms of life like animals, plants and stones.

Opening up for existence
Nature Therapy deals with opening up for existence, opening up for the unpainted, "anti-social, "inhuman existence as it is, without our cultural codes and points of views.

The tree has no name, no biologist has ever comprehended it. I experience the tree, the stone, the cloud and transform myself into them. I am the hazelnut, the barn-owl, the slate. While sitting next to a sharp cliff, while silently contemplating the emerald-green stone-vein, I become it. Inner emptiness - being purified from thoughts and cultural ballast - is the basic requirement for the transformation.

A level of surrounding, penetrating superhuman existence is revealed by transforming. Opening up, the existence is reached. Psyche is separated from culture and becomes nature again.

Renunciation, abandonment, sacrifice

First there are exercises for inner purification. Purification is caused by renunciation, through abandonment and opening our human frame of mind, by sacrificing what we love and what we think we cannot live without. Afterwards long and lonely stays in nature, several days of vision quest, pilgrimages to nature sanctuaries or places of worship, Darkness Therapy in subterranean grottos or tunnels, meditations on holy mountains and in antique and prehistoric temple areas follow.

Vision Quest

In loneliness together with nature we recognise the symbolic language of living. Birds and clouds pass by like friends, ferns wave meaningfully, the energy behind natural forms speaks to us as deep empathy, as notion and vision. All forms of nature are signs of energetic fields. These have an immediate effect on our souls rather than on our intellects. All forms of nature and natural beings seem to be stored within us as archetypical original forms, which only need to be recognised.

Then outer and inner nature reunite in nature vision. We become what we truly are. The re-discovery of this original language of nature and soul is the purpose of the dialogue in the wilderness. Vision quest and nature vision only take place in summer and individually.

Darkness Therapy
Darkness Therapy, the stay in caves or darkened rooms, belongs to the classical process of essence vision. I guide Darkness Therapy sessions of up to seven weeks duration.

Nature reverence, nature celebrations
How can one face springs and shrubs? Through the rite of reverence! This rite gives a frame, within which we are able to approach dragon-flies and amphibians. But before that there is always a long stay in nature loneliness, which opens us, purifies us and puts us into the state of vision. In the nature ceremony we are dressed with

natural materials only and we conduct a reverence ceremony for the nature force behind swamp grasses or the oak grove. In this way nature penetrates our thoughts and feelings, and the experience of our equality with all nature beings deepens.

Nature ritual and mystery celebration
The experiences won within nature vision and loneliness should be embodied through nature ceremonies in which the insights are played out as dramas, ceremonial acts and choreographies.

Through these, participants transform themselves into archetypes. At each meeting an archetype of nature is contemplatively explored and enacted afterwards. These ceremonies could have names like:

At the River of Death, Ghost Dance, Sacrifice of Fire, Invocation of the Four Heavens, Island of Now, Ghost Canoe, Mistress of Forest Animals, Phallus and Vulva or The Naked Goddess.

Journeys to original cultures

Nature Therapy means turning back to the knowledge of old cultures, especially tribal cultures, because we can learn from these forms of life. The history of mankind does not culminate in modernity, which has forgotten nature. It culminates in the contemplation through which ancient people penetrated the whole essence of being and developed a comprehensive nature science.

Journeys to great nature spectacles, to tribes and places of worship

We offer stays in nature in different countries and journeys to remote areas of tribal cultures. Big deserts, high mountain regions, jungles and seas should be experienced together with the old knowledge of nature peoples. Travelling and pilgrimage are integral parts of Nature Therapy, because they extend, renew and transcend our existence.

Author

DIPL.-PSYCH. HOLGER KALWEIT

Psychologist, psychotherapist, ethnologist, shamanism researcher. Areas - Hawaii, Tibet and Mexico. His focus is on ancient deliveries about origins of the world, birth of mankind, world catastrophes and culture development. He developed a new therapy based on Shamanism, Nature Therapy. He also developed Darkness Therapy from the Tibetan darkness retreat.

Contact: Holger Kalweit, Grünwalder Str. 30, D-79853 Lenzkirch-Kappel, Tel/Fax: +49-7653-9458

References

KALWEIT, H. 1981. Transpersonal Anthropology and the Comparison of Cultures, In: Phoenix: *Journal of Transpersonal Anthropology,* 1981, V, 2: 97-105.
- (Hrsg.). 1983. *Frank Hamilton Cushing. Ein weisser Indianer. Mein Leben mit den Zuni.* Walter Verlag, Olten.
- 1984. *Traumzeit und innerer Raum. Die Welt der Schamanen.* Scherz Verlag, München.
- 1984. Formen transpersonaler Psychotherapie bei nichtwestlichen Kulturen. In: *Integrative Therapie* 10 (3): 253-262.
- & SCHENK, AMELIE (Hrsg.). 1984. *Heilung des Wissens. Forscher erzählen von ihrer Begegnung mit dem Schamanen - Der innere und der äußere Weg des Wissens.* Goldmann Verlag, München.
- 1987. *Urheiler, Medizinleute und Schamanen. Lehren aus der archaischen Lebenstherapie.* Kösel Verlag, München.
- 1987. Himalaya Orakel. In: KALWEIT/SCHENK: *Heilung des Wissens.* Goldmann Verlag, München S. 260-287.
- 1989. When Insanity is a Blessing: The Message of Shamanism. In: GROF, STANISLAV & CHRISTIANA (Hgg.): *Spiritual Emergency. When Personal Transformation Becomes a Crisis.* Los Angeles, S. 77-97.
- 1994. Lightening Shamans. *Jahrbuch für Ethnomedizin und Bewußtseinsforschung,* 3: 161-169.
- 1994. Schamanische Trance und die Theorie des Bewußtseinskontinuums. In: *Jahrbuch für Transkulturelle Medizin und Psychotherapie.* Hgg. R. VAN QUEKELBERGHE & D. EIGNER, 1994: 17-41.
- 1995. Der Sitz der Seele in traditionellen Kosmologien. *Ethnopsychologische Mitteilunge*n, 1995, 4, 1: 37-71.
- 1995. Urschamanen und das Goldene Zeitalter . *Curare. Zeitschrift für Ethnomedizin,* (1995) 18, 1: 153-160.
- & A. Schenk. 1995. Der Doppelkörper als Grundlage der Trance in der tibetischen Psychologie. *Curare. Zeitschrift für Ethnomedizin* 18 (1995) 2: 467-496.
- 1997. Übertragung der Lebensenergie bei tibetischen Schamanen. *Ethnopsychologische Schriften,* Hrsg. R. V. QUEKELBERGHE, Landau 1997, S. 25-52.
- 1987. Yin, Yang und die Drachenenergie. In: *Ethnopsychologische Mitteilungen,* 1987 (2), S. 109-145.
- 1998. Schamanische Energie-Ökologie: Das Bündnis von Seelen- und Naturfeld. In: GOTTWALD/RÄTSCH, *Schamanische Wissenschaften.* Diederichs Verlag, München S. 96-120.
- Dunkeltherapie - Eine traditionelle Selbstbefreiungsmethode und ihre Verwendung in der modernen Praxis. In: *Curare Sonderband: Ethnotherapien.* Verlag für Wissenschaft und Bildung. Hrsg. C. E. GOTTSCHALK-BATSCHKUS & CH. RÄTSCH S. 223-227.
- & Amélie Schenk. 1998 Schamanische Heilung durch Reisen ins Totenreich. In: *Jahrbuch für Transkulturelle Medizin und Psychotherapie* 1998/99, Verlag für Wissenschaft und Bildung, Berlin. Hrsg. von STANLEY KRIPPNER & HOLGER KALWEIT, S. 103-124.
- 2001. *Das Totenbuch der Germanen. Die Edda - die Wurzeln eines wilden Volkes.* AT-Verlag, Aarau.
- 2002. *Das Totenbuch der Kelten. Das Bündnis zwischen Anderswelt und Erde.* AT-Verlag, Aarau.
- *Nature Therapy. Wilde Zwiegespräche mit Himmel und Erde.* In Vorbereitung.
SCHENK, A.. 1994. Schamanen auf dem Dach der Welt. ADEVA Graz.
- 2000. *Herr des Schwarzen Himmels. Zeren Baawai - Schamane der Mongolei.* O. W. Barth Verlag, München.

GEBET UND SPIRITUELLE HEILUNG IM MEDIZINISCHEN UMFELD *

von David Aldridge

"If you can't handle your feelings, how can you avoid harming your spirit? If you can't control your emotions, but nevertheless try to stop yourself following them, you will harm yourself twice over. Those who do this double injury to themselves are not counted amongst those with long life"

CHANG TZU IN PALMER [1]

"Thus far you have harmonized with your body, having the usual nine apertures, and you have not been struck midway through life with blindness or deafness, lameness nor any deformity, so in comparison to many you are fortunate. So why do you wander around grumbling about Heaven? Be gone, Sir!"

CHANG TZU IN PALMER [1]

Gebet in der Medizin

Gebet findet zunehmend Verwendung in verschiedenen Heilungsmethoden. Der Einsatz von Gebet wird mit spezifischen Behandlungsergebnissen [2,3] in Verbindung gebracht und gilt in der medizinischen Praxis als akzeptabel [4]. VANDECREEK et al. [5] stellten fest, dass ambulant behandelte Brustkrebspatienten für Gebet als komplementäre Therapie Interesse zeigen und Beten auch aktiv praktizieren. Obwohl erste klinische Untersuchungen der positiven Wirkungen von Gebeten keine schlüssigen Ergebnisse brachten [6-8], ergaben neuere Studien aus einer breiter

---

* Übersetzung aus dem Englischen: Christina Wagner

angelegten medizinischen Perspektive und mit mehr Patientengut durchaus positive Wirkungen von fürsprechendem Beten. Mehrere Autoren vertreten die Auffassung, dass religiöse Zugehörigkeit und Religionsausübung ebenfalls relevant sind, selbst wenn sie sich nicht direkt positiv auswirken, und dass Ärzte diese Aspekte berücksichtigen sollten [4,9-12].

SAUDIA et al. [13] untersuchten die hilfreiche Wirkung von Gebet als direkte Bewältigungsstrategie bei Patienten vor herzchirurgischen Eingriffen. 96 Versuchspersonen gaben an, Gebete als Mittel zur Bewältigung der mit einer Herzoperation verbundenen Belastung einzusetzen, und 70 davon stuften die Nützlichkeit von Beten ganz oben auf einer entsprechenden Skala ein. Beten wurde als hilfreicher, direkter Bewältigungsmechanismus wahrgenommen, unabhängig davon, ob die Befragten glaubten, ihr Leben sei durch sie selbst bestimmt oder durch eine höhere Macht. Diese Studie ist insofern bedeutsam, als sie unterstreicht, dass Gebet als direkte Bewältigungsstrategie eingesetzt wird. Patienten mit Nierenleiden setzten sowohl Beten als auch eine objektive Auseinandersetzung mit dem Leiden am häufigsten zur Stressbewältigung ein [14]. Ein interessanter Aspekt ist die Tatsache, dass auf der pragmatischen Ebene der Patient das Beten und die objektive Auseinandersetzung mit dem Leiden nicht ausschließlich, sondern komplementär im Rahmen eines Wertesystems einsetzt. Mit Beten als Bewältigungstrategie wird Belastung gemildert.

Bei der Behandlung von Alkoholismus gibt es seit langer Zeit Einflüsse spiritueller Erwägungen auf die Behandlungsstrategien [15-18], von der Temperenzlerbewegung einmal abgesehen. Behandlungen von Patienten mit Alkoholmissbrauch waren häufig Kombinationen aus körperlichen Entspannungsmethoden, psychologischen Methoden der Suggestion und Auto-Suggestion, sozialen Methoden der Gruppentherapie und Dienst an der Gemeinschaft sowie spirituellen Gebetstechniken. Diese Verfahren finden noch heute Anwendung und sind auf Drogen- und Medikamentenabhängigkeit und -missbrauch ausgeweitet worden [19-24]. Bei Abhängigen sind geringe religiöse Bindungen festzustellen, und spirituelle Bindungen scheinen mit Erholung korreliert zu sein [22], während Religiosität als vorteilhafter Bewältigungfaktor angesehen werden könnte [25].

Mehrere Autoren beschreiben das Gebet als wertvollen Faktor bei der Betreuung älterer Patienten in verschiedenen kulturellen Traditionen [26-34].

Bemühungen um medizinische Hilfe und Gebet schließen sich nicht gegenseitig aus [35], denn Beten gilt als aktive Reaktion angesichts belastender medizinischer Probleme. Eine Studie mit 160 Ärzten ergab, dass Ärzte daran glauben, Religion hätte eine positive Wirkung auf die körperliche Gesundheit, religiöse Fragen sollten angesprochen werden und ältere Patienten bitten durchaus einmal ihren Arzt, mit ihnen zu beten [29]. Ein wichtiger Faktor bei dieser Befragung ist das Wertesystem des Arztes selbst, was sich wiederum auf die Bereitschaft des Patienten auswirken kann, über solche Themen zu sprechen.

Byrds Studie
Die Studie von RANDOLPH BYRD [36] am San Francisco General Hospital gilt als Meilenstein in der Forschung zum Thema Heilen. Er stellte die Frage, ob fürsprechendes Beten zu einem jüdisch-christlichen Gott Auswirkungen auf die

Erholung und medizinische Verfassung des Patienten im Krankenhaus hat, und falls Wirkungen festzustellen sind, worin diese bestehen. Die Hypothese lautet, dass fürsprechendes Gebet eine vermittelnde Funktion im Heilungsprozess hat.

Fürsprechende Gebete wurden als Behandlungsmethode für 192 randomisiert eingeteilte Patienten angesetzt, während weitere 201 Patienten eine Kontrollgruppe bildeten. Alle 393 Patienten erhielten die vorgesehene medizinische Standardversorgung. Die fürsprechenden Personen waren "wiedergeborene" Christen, die ein aktiv christliches Leben führten, mit täglichen Gebeten und Engagement in den örtlichen Kirchengemeinden. Jeder Patient wurde randomisiert drei bis sieben Fürsprechenden zuordnet, denen der Vorname des Patienten, seine Diagnose und sein allgemeiner Zustand mitgeteilt wurden. Die Gebete erfolgten außerhalb des Krankenhauses in einiger Entfernung. Jeder Fürsprecher wurde aufgefordert, täglich um eine schnelle Erholung und um das Ausbleiben von Komplikationen und Todesfällen zu beten. Die Ärzte wurden über den Versuch informiert, wussten aber nicht, zu welcher Gruppe die Patienten gehörten.

Alle Patienten erhielten während des Versuchs durchgängig die medizinische Standardversorgung. Somit war das Beten keine Alternative, sondern ein Zusatz zur Standardversorgung.
Auf den ersten Blick sind die statistischen Ergebnisse der Studie von BYRD beeindruckend, da den Gebeten generell eine positive Wirkung zugeschrieben wird. In der Tat zeigt die Studie einen rührenden Glauben der Mediziner an statistische Ergebnisse, teilweise deshalb, weil die Ergebnisse medizinisch Sinn machen. Es gibt eine Abnahme an Stauungsinsuffizienz, Herz-Lungen-Stillstand und Lungenentzündung, es sind weniger Antibiotika notwendig, weniger harntreibende Mittel, und Beatmungsgeräte müssen seltener eingesetzt werden.

Mein Einwand bei solchen Studien besteht darin, dass sie zwar Kausaleffekte von Gebet aufzeigen, aber einen wichtigen Aspekt des Betens auslassen, der nicht instrumental, sondern spirituell ist. Während sich eine solche spirituelle Veränderung vollzieht und sichtbar wird, kann sich der Zeitrahmen für dieses Sichtbarwerden durchaus über den zeitlichen Rahmen des Versuchs selbst ausdehnen. Viele möglicherweise mit der Heilung in Verbindung stehende Veränderungen können durchaus zunächst verborgen bleiben.

Erforschung der spirituellen Heilung im medizinischen Umfeld
Gebet ist nur eine der als spirituell geltenden Formen des Heilens. Es gibt unterschiedliche andere Formen des spirituellen Heilens, welche umfassend von DOSSEY [9], BENOR [37,38], BRAUD und SCHLITZ (1989) und SOLFVIN [39] beschrieben worden sind. Die NATIONAL FEDERATION OF SPIRITUAL HEALERS IN ENGLAND [40] definiert spirituelles Heilen als die Wiederherstellung des Gleichgewichts von Körper, Geist und Seele des Empfängers in der Absicht, die Selbstheilung zu fördern und dem Empfänger ein Gefühl des Wohlbefindens und Friedens zu geben (S. 2). In einer weiteren Beschreibung geht es darum, einen inneren friedlichen Mittelpunkt zu finden und Verbindung zu einer universellen Quelle des Friedens und der Liebe herzustellen, welche zum Wohle anderer weitergeleitet wird. Diese Verbindung mit einer universellen Kraft steht auch im Zentrum der "therapeutischen Berührung"

und belegt den Zusammenhang mit alten Heiltraditionen[41].
Der für die Heilung erforderliche Bewusstseinszustand entzieht sich zwar der Erforschung, es gab aber recht umfangreiche Studien über physische Folgeerscheinungen spiritueller Heilungsphänomene; dazu gehörten auch kontrollierte Versuche [42]. Es sind Enzyme und Körperchemikalien in vitro untersucht worden, ebenso die Auswirkungen des Heilens auf Zellen und niedere Organismen (einschließlich Bakterien, Pilze und Hefen), auf menschliches Zellgewebe in vitro, auf die Motilität einfacher Organismen und Pflanzen, auf Tiere und auf menschliche Probleme. Spirituelles Heilen wird oft als reine Plazebo-Reaktion abgetan, jedoch weisen Untersuchungen an niederen Organismen und Zellen auf einen direkten Einfluss hin. Selbst wenn wir berücksichtigen, dass erwartete Wirkungen Einfluss auf experimentell gewonnene Daten haben, ergeben sich dennoch zahlreiche Erkenntnisse, die einer Erklärung bedürfen [39,43].

Allgemeine Praxis
Einige Allgemeinmediziner erklärten sich bereit, sich in ihrer alltäglichen Praxis mit dem Konzept der spirituellen Heilung zu befassen und es in ihre Tätigkeit aufzunehmen, spirituelle Erklärungen bei einigen Patientengesprächen einfließen zu lassen oder bei den Überweisungen anzugeben [9,44-47]. COHEN [46] betont den Wert von Berührung, Zeit und Mitempfinden, die der Heiler anbieten kann, und die positiven Effekte von Überweisungen. In dieser Vorgehensweise zeigen sich die Vorteile der Zusammenarbeit in einem überweisenden Verbund von behandelnden Ärzten.

KING et al. [48] untersuchten insbesondere Patienten, die an religiöse Überzeugung gebundene Heiler und Ärzte wegen ihrer Gesundheitsprobleme konsultieren, um herauszufinden, wie oft Ärzte Patienten sehen, die sich mit Glaubensheilung befassen, und mehr über die Einstellung zu und Erfahrung mit Glaubensheilung bei Ärzten zu erfahren. Ungefähr die Hälfte (52%) der 594 teilnehmenden Mediziner wussten von mindestens einem ihrer Patienten, der eine Erfahrung mit Glaubensheilung hatte. Die meisten Ärzte trafen nicht häufiger als einmal pro Jahr auf einen solchen Patienten. 55% bejahten und 20% verneinten die Aussage, dass das Vertrauen auf Glaubensheiler häufig zu schwerwiegenden medizinischen Problemen führt. 44% waren jedoch der Meinung, dass Ärzte und Glaubensheiler bei der Heilung einiger Patienten zusammenarbeiten können, und 23% meinten, Glaubensheiler könnten mit ihrer Kraft manche Menschen heilen, denen Ärzte nicht helfen können. Hausärzte waren geteilter Meinung über das Glaubensheilen; eine Mehrheit äußerte sich eher skeptisch, eine recht große Minderheit zeigte sich positiv eingestellt.

Chronische Beschwerden und erfolglose Behandlung
In der Studie von BROWN (1995) über chronische Beschwerden in einer englischen Allgemeinarztpraxis mit sechs beteiligten Medizinern wurden erwachsene Patienten mit chronischen Beschwerden von ihrem Allgemeinarzt an eine Heilklinik überwiesen. Bei der Auswahl der Patienten suchte der Allgemeinmediziner auch solche aus, die über sechs Monate hinweg Beschwerden hatten und nicht gut auf übliche Behandlungsmethoden angesprochen hatten, andere mit Zweitüberweisungen oder zur Beratung. Die Behandlungssitzungen dauerten je 20 Minuten einmal pro Woche über insgesamt acht Wochen. Bei der spirituellen Heilung wurde ein "Handauflegen" eingesetzt zur "Lenkung heilender Energien";

eine Evaluation erfolgte mit einem Fragebogen zur Lebensqualität mit festgelegten Populationsgrößen zum Vergleich (SF-36). Nach acht Wochen traten signifikante Veränderungen bei einer Patientengruppe mit schlechtem Gesundheitszustand auf in bezug auf Rollenbeschränkungen, soziale Funktion, Schmerz, allgemeinen Gesundheitszustand und Vitalität. Diese Veränderungen blieben nicht bestehen bis zu einer Evaluation nach 26 Wochen vom Beginn der Studie an gerechnet. Wie der Autor schreibt, können wir keine spezifischen Schlüsse bezüglich der Heilmethode ziehen, da es keine Kontrollgruppe gab. Es war jedoch bei einer Gruppe chronisch kranker Patienten, die auf vorherige Behandlung nicht angesprochen hatte, eine Verbesserung feststellbar.

Chronische Symptome in der Allgemeinarztpraxis sind auch Gegenstand der Studie von DIXON [49]. Ebenso wie in der oben genannten Studie mit mehreren Allgemeinmedizinern in einer Gemeinschaftspraxis wurden Patienten mit seit sechs Monaten anhaltenden Beschwerden, die auf Behandlung nicht ansprachen, an einen Heiler überwiesen. Die Patienten erhielten die Information, sie würden einen Heiler aufsuchen – es war nicht von einem Glaubensheiler oder spirituellen Heiler die Rede, und der Betreffende werde mit seinen Händen nahe am Körper des Patienten den Durchgang des Lichts durch den Patienten veranschaulichen, das Ganze begleitet von entspannender Musik. Wir erfahren nichts über die Kontrollbedingungen, und der Einsatz entspannender Musik beeinträchtigt die Untersuchung der Behandlung, da Musiktherapie bekanntermaßen angstlösend wirkt[50]. Im Vergleich zu den Kontrollgrößen war jedoch nach drei Monaten eine Verbesserung bezüglich Angst und Depression feststellbar, die nach sechs Monaten bei der behandelten Gruppe noch anhielt. Funktionale Verbesserungen nach dem Nottingham Health Profile nach drei Monaten bestanden nach Ablauf von sechs Monaten nicht mehr in signifikantem Maß. Diese Patienten hatten vorher nicht auf Behandlung angesprochen, und die Verbesserung der allgemeinen Befindlichkeit weist auf ein generelles Erholungspotential hin, das für die klinische Praxis von Wert ist.

Eine breitergefasste Ökologie der Betreuung
Die Forderung nach ganzheitlicher Behandlung haben einige Gruppierungen im Bereich der Pflege nachhaltig übernommen, die uns daran erinnern, dass in der Betreuung der Patienten auch spirituelle Bedürfnisse berücksichtigt und geäußert werden müssen [4,51-62]. Innerhalb dieser verschiedenen Ansätze gibt es einen Grundkonsens, demzufolge Leiden und Schmerz als Teil einer umfassenderen Lebenserfahrung zu akzeptieren sind und für Patienten und Pflegende von tieferer Bedeutung sein können [44,63]. Der Schwerpunkt liegt dabei auf der persönlichen Gottesvorstellung, auf den Quellen für Kraft und Hoffnung, auf der Bedeutung von religiösen Praktiken und Ritualen für die Patienten und ihre Wertvorstellungen [55].

Wenn das Behandlungsziel palliativ ist, bei Krebspatienten im Endstadium mit einer Lebenserwartung von sechs Monaten und weniger, dann besteht das wichtigste Ziel in der Verbesserung der Lebensqualität für den Patienten [64]. Bei Interviews von 120 Krebspatienten im Endstadium ergab sich, dass die für sie wichtigsten Themen existentieller, spiritueller, physischer und emotionaler Art waren oder familienbezogen, und dass während des gesamten Krankheitsverlaufs diese Dinge in der Behandlung selten angesprochen wurden. Ein weiterer Anlass zur Sorge ist die Tatsache, dass Ärzte in 15% der Fälle den Schweregrad von

Symptomen unterschätzen[65], und dies hat wichtige Auswirkungen auf palliative Interventionen und darauf, inwieweit die Sichtweise des Patienten ernstgenommen wird.

Ärzte, Pflegepersonal und Geistliche arbeiten häufig in der Betreuung Sterbender zusammen [31,64,66-68], und eine gemeinschaftliche Betreuung durch ein Team, die auch die Familienangehörigen und Freunde des Patienten miteinschließt, scheint von Nutzen zu sein [69-72]. Bei dem prinzipiellen Nutzen für den Sterbenden geht es um eine Verringerung der zustandsbedingten Angst, um allgemeines Wohlbefinden und ein erhöhtes spirituelles Bewusstsein, unabhängig von Geschlecht, Familienstand, Alter oder Diagnose[73]. Das heißt nicht, dass jeder Mediziner sich mit all diesen Komponenten befassen muss, sondern vielmehr, dass die Beteiligten die Bedürfnisse des Patienten erkennen und auf entsprechende Ressourcen zurückgreifen können. Die auf Schmerzbewältigung spezialisierte Krankenschwester und der Priester, der sich mit Leiden auskennt, arbeiten gemeinsam mit dem Patienten, der Schmerzen erleidet. Aber der Patient leistet einen aktiven Beitrag. Unterstützung durch technisches Gerät ist lebenswichtig, aber optimale Betreuung bedeutet auch emotionalen Rückhalt, und dazu können Techniken der Entspannung, Visualisierung und Meditation gehören [74].

Betreuende brauchen Betreuung
Immer mehr Krebspatienten werden daheim in häuslicher Pflege betreut [75]. In der Untersuchung von HILEMAN et al. ging es in erster Linie darum, die Bedeutung von Bedürfnissen zu identifizieren, kategorisieren und evaluieren, die 492 mit häuslicher Pflege befasste Personen äußerten, und festzustellen, inwieweit diesen Bedürfnissen entsprochen wurde. Betreuende, also Personen, die unbezahlt bei der körperlichen Versorgung Kranker oder der Bewältigung der Krankheit halfen, wurden aus den Unterlagen zweier gemeinnütziger Krebsorganisationen auf Gemeindeebene und zweier ambulanter Onkologiestationen ausgewählt. Es wurden sechs Kategorien an Bedürfnissen definiert: psychologische, informative, pflegerische, persönliche, spirituelle und haushaltsbezogene Bedürfnisse. Diese Bedürfnisse änderten sich im Verlauf der Zeit und machten häufige Anpassungen erforderlich; jedoch wurden sowohl bei den Patienten als auch bei den sie Versorgenden Bedürfnisse festgestellt. Wenn wir unsere Outcome-Messungen immer nur auf den einzelnen Patienten ausrichten, machen wir den schweren Fehler, sein soziales Umfeld außer acht zu lassen.

In einer Dreimonatsstudie über die wahrgenommenen Bedürfnisse und Ängste von 166 erwachsenen Familienangehörigen von Patienten auf der Intensivstation *62* wurden Bedürfnisse und situationsbedingte Ängste seitens der Familien in ihren Zusammenhängen untersucht. Befürchtungen, persönliche Ängste, alters- und familienbedingte Bedürfnisse machten 38% der Variationsbreite der Situationsängste aus. Weitere 33% betrafen spirituelle Bedürfnisse und situationsbedingte Sorgen. In bedrohlichen Situation brauchen Familien Bewältigungsstrategien. ZIGMOND [76] schreibt: "Untereinander, in den privatesten Gruppen entwickeln wir eher persönliche und idiosynkratische Überzeugungen, Rituale und Protokolle, um die potentiellen Stürme oder Einöden der Ungewissheit abzuwehren" (S. 69). Die spirituelle Dimension wehrt zwar vielleicht nicht die Ungewissheit ab, bietet aber eine hilfreiche Strategie zum Verständnis oder zur Bewältigung der Ungewissheit.

Spirituelle Faktoren sind auch für die Pflegenden von Bedeutung. In 77 Fällen wird der Zusammenhang von religiös/spiritueller Bewältigung und speziellen auch psychologischen Belastungszuständen untersucht, die bei privaten Betreuern auftreten, welche zuhause wohnende behinderte ältere Menschen versorgen. Spirituelle Bewältigungsstrategien haben einen indirekten Einfluss auf die Belastung der Pflegenden aufgrund der Qualität der Beziehung zwischen Betreuenden und Patienten. Bei Betreuenden mit religiösen oder spirituellen Überzeugungen wurde eine bessere Beziehung zu den Betreuten festgestellt, was sich in geringerer Depression und gesteigerter Hingabe an die Rolle des Pflegenden niederschlug.

Spiritualität im Umgang mit AIDS-Patienten
In umfassenden Behandlungsprogrammen für AIDS-Patienten wird empfohlen, auch das spirituelle Wohlergehen der Patienten und seinen Einfluss auf ihr allgemeines Wohlbefinden zu berücksichtigen [78-86]. Wer sich spirituell wohlfühlte und auf diese Weise Sinn und Zweck im Leben finden konnte, erwies sich auch als widerstandsfähiger [87]. COOKE [88] erinnert uns daran, dass die Betreuung von HIV-Infizierten nicht nur anstrengend ist, sondern auch hohe emotionale Anforderungen stellt. Andere Autoren betonen ebenfalls die Bedeutung des Spirituellen und machen auch auf die verwirrenden Probleme aufmerksam, die sich aus der Verurteilung verschiedener Aspekte der Sexualität durch einige Religionen ergeben, und auf die Auswirkungen auf HIV- oder AIDS-Patienten [89].

Der Begriff spirituelles Heilen wird hier im Kontext orthodoxer medizinischer Praxis als komplementärer oder begleitender Ansatz verwendet; der Begriff "Spirit" oder Geist wird aber auch anders gebraucht. Da es kein Mittel gegen AIDS gibt, können sich HIV-Infizierte auch um alternative Therapien und traditionelle Heilmethoden bemühen. In einer Klinik für HIV/AIDS-Patienten in einem Innenstadtbezirk in New Jersey haben HIV-infizierte Hispano-Amerikaner die Überzeugung geäußert, dass es gute und böse Geister gibt und dass diese Geister eine kausale Rolle bei ihrer Infektion spielten, entweder allein oder in Verbindung mit dem AIDS-Virus [90]. Sie suchten nach spirituellen traditionellen Heilmethoden zur körperlichen und spirituellen Linderung und zum Schutz vor Bösem. Eine Minderheit hoffte darauf, geheilt zu werden. Wir müssen uns bewusst machen, dass es solche Heiltraditionen und alternative Heilpraktiken gibt; wir können nicht davon ausgehen, dass spirituelles Heilen sich mit konventionellen Auffassungen moderner westlicher Methoden deckt.

Outcomes nicht eindeutig
RICHARDS und FOLKMAN [91] stellten fest, dass von 125 HIV-positiven und –negativen Personen, deren Partner kürzlich an AIDS gestorben waren, 68 im Gespräch spontan von spirituellen Phänomenen berichteten. Spirituelle Vorstellungen halfen bei der Verarbeitung des Todes und wurden als Trostquelle angesehen. Diejenigen, die spirituelle Phänomene ansprachen, wiesen auch stärker ausgeprägte Depressionen und Ängste auf und weniger positive Stimmungslagen, verwendeten mehr adaptive Bewältigungsstrategien und meldeten mehr körperliche Symptome als diejenigen, die spirituelle Phänomene nicht erwähnten. Diese Ergebnisse stammen von Partnern von Patienten; sie bestätigen auch, was KING [10] feststellte, dass nämlich ausgeprägtere spirituelle Überzeugungen einen unabhängigen Prädiktor für negative Outcomes nach neun Monaten darstellen

bei Patienten, die in die Notaufnahme eines Londoner Krankenhauses eingeliefert wurden. Patienten mit chronischen Beschwerden, die häufiger Gebete zur Schmerzbewältigung einsetzen, meldeten auch ein höheres Maß an Beeinträchtigung [92].

Bestimmte Überzeugungen zu fördern und sie als spirituell zu bezeichnen birgt auch eine Gefahr in sich: sie können uns abbringen von dem, was als pragmatisches Verständnis für das Alltagsleben erforderlich ist. Ein entscheidendes Element spirituellen Verständnisses ist, dass man die vernünftige und angemessene Anwendbarkeit erkennen kann, nicht dass man sich in der Wiederholung ritueller Übungen und in Wunschdenken ergeht. Die treibende Kraft hinter der Entwicklung moderner Schmerzmittel kann ebenso höheren Ursprungs sein wie die Ausübung meditativer Techniken. Wichtig ist nur zu wissen, wann und wie sie einzusetzen sind [44].

Urteilsfähigkeit
Spirituelles Heilen birgt noch andere Gefahren. Es gibt spirituelle Heiler, die ihren Patienten fantastische Heilerfolge in Aussicht stellen. Andere Patienten hören, dass sie sich nicht erholen, weil sie es entweder selbst nicht wollen oder andere nicht genügend lieben oder sich innerlich dem Heiler widersetzen. Es gab Fälle, in denen Heiler Patienten von konventioneller medizinischer Behandlung abgeraten haben. Solche Ansätze sind schlicht falsch. Urteilsfähigkeit ist hier der Schlüssel. Wer Wunder sucht oder irgendeine magische Intervention durch heilende Kräfte, den wird die Mahnung zur Vorsicht und Vernunft vielleicht enttäuschen. Urteilsfähigkeit hat nichts zu tun mit Verkleidung mit besonderen Gewändern, dramatischen Handbewegungen oder magischen Beschwörungen. Das Einhüllen in Gewänder, die für unsere Zeit oder kulturelle Umgebung unangemessen sind, ist ein warnender Hinweis auf spirituellen Bankrott, nicht etwa auf erweiterte Kräfte[93]; dasselbe gilt für Sprachen aus anderen Kulturkreisen. Wer Subtiles und Verborgenes sucht, wird diesen Ansatz zwar weniger dramatisch, aber nicht weniger effektiv finden. Eine von erweiterter Urteilskraft geprägte Einstellung lässt sich auf alle Modalitäten des Heilens anwenden, einschließlich der konventionellen Medizin. Urteilsfähigkeit kann das Spirituelle zurückführen auf die subtile Ebene, auf der es existiert. Damit sich Geist materiell manifestiert, ist die Urteilsfähigkeit der Ärzte erforderlich und derer, die von ihnen betreut werden.

Eine integrative Perspektive
Wenn wir das Beten einer Untersuchung unterziehen, sollten wir zumindest sicherstellen, dass bei unseren Beobachtungen auch die für die Beurteilung des Heilerfolges relevanten Kriterien berücksichtigt werden. Das Gebet bringt nicht nur Erleichterung mit sich, sondern es wird ein neues Verständnis erwartet, buchstäblich eine Bewusstseinsveränderung.

Wenn Spiritualität als Suche nach dem Göttlichen und Erlangung der Einheit definiert wird, stellt Beten das Vehikel für diese Erlangung dar (ALDRIDGE 2000). Auch mit einem gebrochenen Bein kann man beten, aber laufen kann man nicht. Diesen Unterschied zu kennen, bedeutet eine elementare Erkenntnis. Die Absicht des Betens besteht darin, mit dem Göttlichen verbunden zu sein; dann fallen alle anderen Sorgen von uns ab. Für Kranke erhält Krankheit einen anderen Stellenwert; sie kann sogar verschwinden. Sucht man nach einem direkten

Zusammenhang von Ursache und Wirkung beim Beten, dann lässt man die im Lauf von Jahrhunderten gewonnenen spirituellen Lehren außer acht, dann verkennt man den Sinn von Krankheit und auch den Sinn des Betens selbst.

Dass der Geist den Heilungsprozess beeinflusst, wird immer deutlicher. Dies ist eine Erkenntnis aus der Welt der Gesetze von Ursache und Wirkung, auch Naturwissenschaft genannt. Es gibt auch Erkenntnisse, die manche als Spiritualität bezeichnen. Beide sind wichtig. Beide sind nicht zu vernachlässigen. Heilung entsteht aus dem Erlernen der Beziehung zwischen beiden Formen der Erkenntnis. In beiden Perspektiven der Erkenntnis oder des Wissens, nämlich Naturwissenschaft und Spiritualität, erfolgt Lernen durch Lehre und Anleitung. Ist uns die Welt in all ihrer Fülle von einer höheren Macht gegeben, dann haben gewiss die Segnungen medizinischen Wissens, die Hingabe vieler in der Medizin Tätiger und die Lehren von Krankheit und Heilung denselben Ursprung.

Autor
PROF. DR. PHIL. DAVID ALDRIDGE

Lehrstuhl für Qualitative Forschung in der Medizin an der Universität Witten/Herdecke. Senior Research Fellow at St Mary´s Hospital, London. Qualitative Forschung. Familiensystemische Aspekte des Suizid. Habilitation im Bereich Musiktherapie. Wissenschaftliche Schwerpunkte: Entwicklung der wissenschaftlichen Fundierung der Musiktherapie, Forschungsmethodik in komplementären medizinischen Ansätzen; Verbindung von Kunst und Wissenschaft. Kontakt: E-Mail: davida@uni-wh.de

Literatur
1. Palmer M. The book of Chang Tzu. London: Arkana, Penguin, 1996.
2. Duckro P, Magaletta P. The effect of prayer on physical health: Experimental evidence. Journal of Religion and Health 1994; 33:211-219.
3. McCullough M. Prayer and health: Conceptual issues, research view, and research agenda. Journal of Psychology and Theology 1995; 25:15-29.
4. Magaletta P, Duckro P. Prayer in the medical encounter. Journal of Religion and Health 1996; 35:203-209.
5. VandeCreek L, Rogers E, Lester J. Use of alternative therapies among breast cancer out patients compared with the general population. Alternative Therapies 1999; 5:71-76.
6. Joyce C, Welldon R. The efficacy of prayer: a double-blind clinical trial. Journal of Chronic Diseases 1965; 18:367-377.
7. Rosner F. The efficacy of prayer: scientific v. religious evidence. Journal of Religion and Health 1975; 14:294-298.
8. Collipp P. The efficacy of prayer: a triple blind study. Medical Times 1969; 97:201-204.
9. Dossey L. Healing words: The power of prayer and the practice of medicine. New York: Harper Collins, 1993.
10. King M, Speck P, Thomas A. The effect of spiritual outcome from illness. Social Science and Medicine 1999; 48:1291-1299.
11. King M, Dein S. The spiritual variable in psychiatric research. Psychological Medicine 1998; 28:1259-1262.
12. King MB. Psychiatry and religion, context, consensus and controversies, by D. Bhugra. Br J Psychiatry 1997; 170:93-94.
13. Saudia T, Kinney M, Brown K, Young W. Health locus of control and helpfulness of prayer. Heart Lung 1991; 20:60-5.

14. Sutton T, Murphy S. Stressors and patterns of coping in renal transplant patients. Nursing Research 1989; 38:46-9.
15. Bergmark K. The Links and Alcoholics Anonymous: Two "A.A" movements in Sweden. In: Eisenbach-Stagl I, Rosenqvist P, eds. Diversity in unity. Studies of Alcoholics Anonymous in eight societies. Helsinki: Nordic Council for Alcohol and Drug Research, 1998:75-89.
16. Carroll S. Spirituality and purpose in life in alcoholism recovery. Journal of Studies on Alcohol 1993; 54:297-301.
17. McCarthy K. Early alcoholism treatment: the Emmanuel Movement and Richard Peabody. Journal for the Study of Alcohol 1984; 45(1):59-74.
18. Eisenbach-Stagl I. How to live a sober life in a wet society: Alcoholics Anonymous in Austria. In: Eisenbach-Stagl I, Rosenqvist P, eds. Diversity in unity. Studies of Alcoholics Anonymous in eight societies. Helsinki: Nordic Council for Alcohol and Drug Research, 1998:131-147.
19. Buxton M, Smith D, Seymour R. Spirituality and other points of resistance to the 12-step recovery process. Journal of Psychoactive Drugs 1987; 19:275-86.
20. Green L, Fullilove M, Fullilove R. Stories of spiritual awakening - The nature of spirituality in recovery. Journal of Substance Abuse Treatment 1998; 15:325-331.
21. Mathew R, Georgi J, Wilson W, Mathew V. A retrospective study of the concept of spirituality as understood by recovering individuals. Journal of Substance Abuse Treatment 1996; 13:67-73.
22. Miller W. Researching the spiritual dimensions of alcohol and other drug problems. Addiction 1998; 93:979-990.
23. Navarro J, Wilson S, Berger L, Taylor T. Substance abuse and spirituality: A program for native American students. American Journal of Health Behavior 1997; 21:3-11.
24. Peteet J. A closer look at the role of a spiritual approach in addictions treatment. Journal of Substance Abuse Treatment 1993; 10:263-267.
25. Kendler KS, Gardner CO, Prescott CA. Religion, psychopathology, and substance use and abuse: A multimeasure, genetic-epidemiologic study. Am J Psychiatry 1997; 154:322-329.
26. Koenig H, Hays J, George L, Blazer D, Larson D, Landerman L. Modeling the cross-sectional relationships between religion, physical health, social support, and depressive symptoms. American Journal of Geriatric Psychiatry 1997; 5:131-144.
27. Gorham M. Spirituality and problem solving with seniors. Perspectives. 1989; 13:13-6.
28. Chatters L, Taylor R. Age differences in religious participation among black adults. Journal of Gerontology 1989; 44(5):S183-9.
29. Koenig H, Bearon L, Dayringer R. Physician perspectives on the role of religion in the physician,older patient relationship. Journal of Family Practice 1989; 28:441-8.
30. Markides K. Aging, religiosity, and adjustment: a longitudinal analysis. Journal of Gerontology 1983; 38:621-5.
31. Reed P. Spirituality and well-being in terminally ill hospitalized adults. Research in Nursing and Health 1987; 10:335-44.
32. Taylor R, Chatters L. Nonorganizational religious participation among elderly black adults. Journal of Gerontology 1991; 46.
33. Garrett G. A natural way to go? Death and bereavement in old age. Professional Nurse 1991; 6:744-6.
34. Foley L, Wagner J, Waskel S. Spirituality in the lives of older women. Journal of Women & Aging 1998; 10:85-91.
35. Bearon L, Koenig H. Religious cognitions and use of prayer in health and illness. Gerontologist. 1990; 30(2):249-53.
36. Byrd R. Positive therapeutic effects of intercessory prayer in a coronary care unit population. Southern Medical Journal 1988; 81:826-9.
37. Benor D. Healing Resarch: Volume 1, Professional Supplement. Southfield, MI: Visdion Publications, 2001.
38. Benor D. Healing Research: Volume 1, Spiritual Healing: Scientific Validation of a Healing Revolution. Southfield, MI: Vision Publications, 2001.
39. Solfin J. Mental healing. In: Krippner S, ed. Advances in Parapsychological Research. Jefferson,N.C: McFarland and Co., 1984:31-63.

40. NFSH. National Federation of Spiritual Healers Code of Conduct. The Director, NFSH: Sunbury on Thames, Middlesex TW16 6RG, England, 1999.
41. Fischer S, Johnson P. Therapeutic Touch: A viable link in midwifery. Journal of Nurse-Midwifery 1999; 44:300-309.
42. Benor D. Survey of spiritual healing. Complementary Medical Research 1990; 4:9-33.
43. Wirth D. The significance of belief and expectancy within the spiritual healing encounter. Social Science and Medicine 1995; 41:249-260.
44. Aldridge D. Spirituality, healing and medicine. Return to the silence. London: Jessica Kingsley Publishers, 2000.
45. Brown C. Spiritual healing in general practice. Complementary Therapies in Medicine 1995; 3:230-233.
46. Cohen J. Spiritual healing in a medical context. Practitioner 1989; 233 (1473):1056-7.
47. Pietroni PC. Spiritual interventions in a general practice setting. Holistic Medicine 1986; 1:253-262.
48. King D, Sobal J, Haggerty J, Dent M, Patton D. Experiences and attitudes about faith healing among family physicians. Journal of Family Practice 1992; 35:158-62.
49. Dixon M. Does 'healing' benefit patients with chronic symptoms? A quasi-randomized trial in general practice. Journal of the Royal Society of Medicine 1998; 91:183-188.
50. Aldridge D. Music therapy research and practice in medicine. From out of the silence. London: Jessica Kingsley, 1996.
51. Dossey B. Barbara Dossey on holistic nursing, Florence Nightingale, and healing rituals. Alternative Therapies 1999; 5:79-86.
52. Boutell K, Bozett F. Nurses' assessment of patients' spirituality: continuing education implications. Journal of Continuing Education in Nursing 1990; 21:172-6.
53. Clark J, Dawson L. Personal religiousness and ethical judgements: An empirical analysis. Journal of Business Ethics 1996; 15:359-372.
54. Burkhardt M. Spirituality: an analysis of the concept. Holistic Nursing Practitioner 1989; 3:69-77.
55. Soeken K, Carson V. Responding to the spiritual needs of the chronically ill. Nursing Clinics of North America 1987; 22(3): 603-11.
56. Labun E. Spiritual care: an element in nursing care planning. Journal of Advanced Nursing 1988; 13:314-20.
57. Grasser C, Craft B. The patient's approach to wellness. Nursing Clinics of North America 1984; 19:207-18.
58. Potts R. Spirituality and the experience of cancer in an African - American community: Implications for psychosocial oncology. Journal of Psychosocial Oncology 1996; 14:1-19.
59. Ferrell B, Grant M, Funk B, OtisGreen S, Garcia N. Quality of life in breast cancer Part II: Psychological and spiritual well-being. Cancer Nursing 1998; 21:1-9.
60. Rustoen T, Hanestad B. Nursing intervention to increase hope in cancer patients. Journal of Clinical Nursing 1998; 7:19-27.
61. Harrington V, Lackey N, Gates M. Needs of caregivers of clinic and hospice cancer patients. Cancer Nursing 1996; 19:118-125.
62. Rukholm E, Bailey P, Coutu-Wakulczyk G, Bailey W. Needs and anxiety levels in relatives of intensive care unit patients. Journal of Advanced Nursing 1991; 16:920-8.
63. Nagai Jacobson M, Burkhardt M. Spirituality: cornerstone of holistic nursing practice. Holistic Nursing Practitioner 1989; 3:18-26.
64. Greisinger A, Lorimor R, Aday L, Winn R, Baile W. Terminally ill cancer patients - Their most important concerns. Cancer Practice 1997; 5:147-154.
65. Stephens RJ, Hopwood P, Girling DJ, Machin D. Randomized trials with quality of life endpoints: Are doctors' ratings of patients' physical symptoms interchangeable with patients' self-ratings? Qual Life Res 1997; 6:225-236.
66. Roche J. Spirituality and the ALS patient. Rehabilitation Nurse 1989; 14:139-41.
67. Conrad N. Spiritual support for the dying. Nursing Clinics of North America 1985; 20: 415 - 26.
68. McMillan S, Weitzner M. Quality of life in cancer patients - Use of a revised hospice index. Cancer Practice 1998; 6:282-288.

69. Aldridge D. A team approach to terminal care: personal implications for patients and practitioners. Journal of the Royal College of General Practitioners 1987; 37:364.
70. Aldridge D. A community approach to cancer in families. Journal of Maternal and Child Health 1987; 12:182-185.
71. Aldridge D. Families, cancer and dying. Family Practice 1987; 4:212-218.
72. Aldridge D. One body: a guide to healing in the Church. London: S.P.C.K., 1987.
73. Kaczorowski J. Spiritual well-being and anxiety in adults diagnosed with cancer. Hospital Journal 1989; 5:105-16.
74. Peteet J, Stomper P, Ross D, Cotton V, Truesdell P, Moczynski W. Emotional support for patients with cancer who are undergoing CT: semistructured interviews of patients at a cancer institute. Radiology 1992; 182:99-102.
75. Hileman J, Lackey N, Hassanein R. Identifying the needs of home caregivers of patients with cancer. Oncol Nurs Forum 1992; 19:771-7.
76. Zigmond D. Three types of encounter in the healing arts: Dialogue, dialectic, and didacticism. Holistic Medicine 1987; 2:69-81.
77. Chang B, Noonan A, Tennstedt S. The role of religion/spirituality in coping with caregiving for disabled elders. Gerontologist 1998; 38:463-470.
78. Belcher A, Dettmore D, Holzemer S. Spirituality and sense of well-being in persons with AIDS. Holistic Nursing Pract.ice 1989; 3:16-25.
79. Flaskerud J, Rush C. AIDS and traditional health beliefs and practices of black women. Nursing Research 1989; 38:210-5.
80. Gutterman L. A day treatment program for persons with AIDS. American Journal of Occupational Therapy 1990; 44:234-7.
81. Ribble D. Psychosocial support groups for people with HIV infection and AIDS. Holistic Nursing Practice 1989; 3:52-62.
82. Kaplan M, Marks G, Mertens S. Distress and coping among women with HIV infection: Preliminary findings from a multiethnic sample. American Journal of Orthopsychiatry 1997; 67:80-91.
83. Hall B. Patterns of spirituality in persons with advanced HIV disease. Research in Nursing and Health 1998; 21:143-153.
84. Holt J, Houg B, Romano J. Spiritual wellness for clients with HIV/AIDS: Review of counselling issues. Journal of Counselling and Development 1999; 77:160-170.
85. Warner-Robbins C, Christiana N. The spiritual needs of persons with AIDS. Family and Community Health 1989; 12:43-51.
86. Sowell R, Misener T. Decisions to have a baby by HIV-infected women. Western Journal of Nursing Research 1997; 19:56-70.
87. Carson V, Green H. Spiritual well-being: a predictor of hardiness in patients with acquired immunodeficiency syndrome. Journal of Professional Nursing 1992; 8:209-20.
88. Cooke M. Supporting health care workers in the treatment of HIV-infected patients. Prim Care 1992; 19:245-56.
89. Jenkins RA. Religion and HIV: Implications for research and intervention. J Soc Issues 1995; 51:131-144.
90. Suarez M, Raffaelli M, OLeary A. Use of folk healing practices by HIV-infected Hispanics living in the United States. AIDS Care 1996; 8:683-690.
91. Richards T, Folkman S. Spiritual aspects of loss at the time of a partner's death from AIDS. Death Studies 1997; 21:527-552.
92. Ashby J, Lenhart R. Prayer as a coping strategy for chronic pain patients. Rehabilitation Psychology 1994; 39:205-208.
93. Marsham R. Sufi orders. In: Shah I, ed. Sufi thought and action.London: Octagon Press, 1990:112-122.

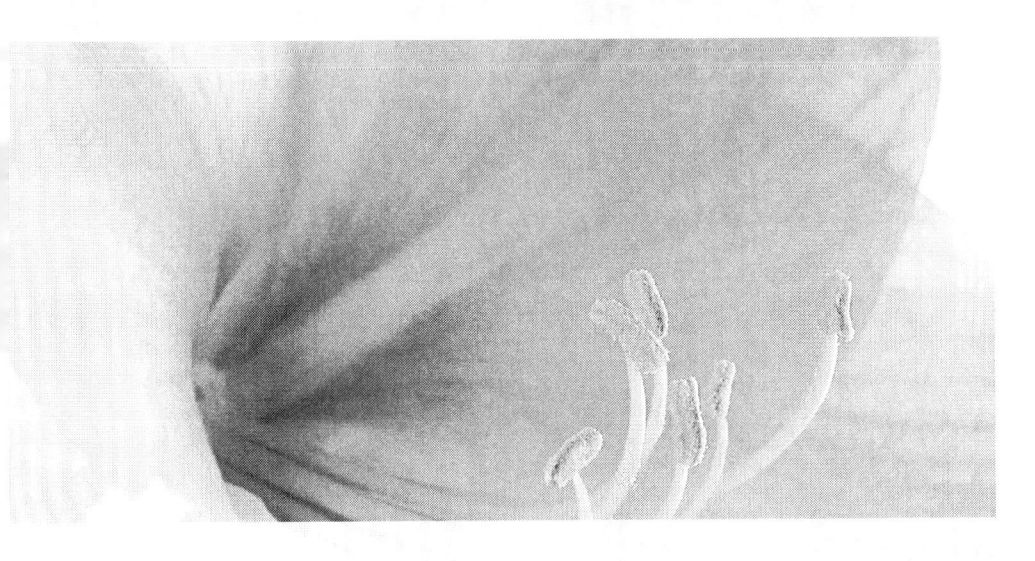

PRAYER AND SPIRITUAL HEALING IN MEDICAL SETTINGS

by David Aldridge

"If you can't handle your feelings, how can you avoid harming your spirit? If you can't control your emotions, nevertheless try to stop yourself following them, you will harm yourself twice over. Those who do this double injury to themselves are not counted amongst those with long life"
CHANG TZU IN PALMER [1]

"Thus far you have harmonized with your body, having the usual nine apertures, and you have not been struck midway through life with blindness or deafness, lameness nor any deformity, so in comparison to many you are fortunate. So why do you wander around grumbling about Heaven? Be gone, Sir!"
CHANG TZU IN PALMER [1]

Prayer in medicine

Prayer is increasingly used in approaches to healing. The use of prayer is related to specific health outcomes [2,3] and is acceptable within medical practice [4]. VANDECREEK et al. [5] found that there is both an interest in, and a practice of, prayer as a complementary therapy for breast cancer outpatients.

Although initial clinical research into the benefits of prayer was inconclusive [6-8] more recent studies, from a broader medical perspective and with larger study populations, have shown that intercessory prayer is beneficial. Several authors argue that religious affiliation and practice are also relevant, even if not beneficial, and that physicians should choose to attend to them [4, 9-12].

SAUDIA, et al [13] investigated the helpfulness of prayer as a direct coping mechanism used by patients prior to having cardiac surgery. Ninety-six subjects indicated that prayer was used as a coping mechanism in dealing with the stress of cardiac surgery, and 70 of these subjects gave it the highest possible rating on the Helpfulness of Prayer Scale. Prayer was perceived as a helpful, direct-action coping mechanism and was independent of whether individuals believed that their lives were controlled by themselves or a powerful other. The importance of this study is that it emphasises prayer as direct action that the individual uses as a coping strategy.

For renal patients, prayer and looking at the problem objectively were used most in coping with stress [14]. It is interesting to see that at the pragmatic level of the patient, prayer and looking at the problem objectively are not exclusive but complementary activities in a system of beliefs. This is stress relief using prayer as a coping strategy.

In the treatment of alcoholism there has been an historical influence of spiritual considerations included in treatment plans [15-18] apart from the temperance movement. Such treatments for alcohol abuse were often composite packages using physical methods of relaxation, psychological methods of suggestion and auto-suggestion, social methods of group support and service to the community, and spiritual techniques of prayer. These procedures are still in use today and have been extended into the realm of chemical dependency and substance abuse [19-24]. Individuals suffering from substance problems are found to have a low level of religious involvement, and spiritual engagement appears to be correlated with recovery [22] while religiosity may be an advantageous coping factor [25].

Prayer is described by several authors as valuable in care for the elderly across several cultures [26-34].

Medical help seeking and prayer are not mutually exclusive [35], as prayer is considered to be an active coping response in the face of stressful medical problems. A study of 160 physicians found that physicians believe that religion has a positive effect on physical health, that religious issues should be addressed and that the older patient may ask the physician to pray with them [29]. An influential factor in this questioning is the belief system of the practitioner, which may influence in turn the willingness of the patient to talk about such matters.

Byrd's study

RANDOLPH BYRD's study [36] at the San Francisco General Hospital has achieved landmark status in the topography of healing research. He asked whether intercessory prayer to a Judeo-Christian God has an effect on the patient's recovery and medical condition while in hospital, and if there is an effect, what are its characteristics. The hypothesis is that intercessory prayer mediates the process of healing.

Intercessory prayer was taken as the treatment method for the 192 randomly allocated patients, another 201 patients formed a control group. All 393 patient had standard medical care as expected. The intercessors were "born-again" Christians with an active Christian life of daily devotional prayer who partook of fellowship in their local churches. Each patient was randomised to between three to seven intercessors who were given the patient's first name, diagnosis and general condition. The prayer was done from outside the hospital from a distance.

Each intercessor was asked to pray daily for a rapid recovery and for the prevention of complications and death. Physicians were informed of the trial but did not know to which group the patients belonged. Standard medical treatment was given throughout to all patients. Thus prayer was an adjunct to standard medical care not an alternative. At first glance the statistical results of Byrd's study are impressive, with an overall improvement being attributed to prayer. It does indeed show a touching faith on the behalf of medical scientists in statistical results, partly because the results make medical sense. There is less congestive heart failure, cardio-pulmonary arrest, pneumonia, fever antibiotics are needed, less diuretic medication and less ventilator support.

My concern with these studies is that while they do demonstrate causal effects of prayer, they miss an important aspect of prayer which is not instrumental, and is spiritual. As this spiritual change unfolds and becomes explicit, the time frame for that explication may extend beyond the time scale of the trial itself. Indeed, many of the changes that can be related to the healing may at first be hidden.

Spiritual healing research in medical settings

Prayer is only one form of healing that is regarded as spiritual. There are a variety of other forms of spiritual healing and these are comprehensively described by DOSSEY [9] BENOR [37, 38], BRAUD and SCHLITZ (1989), and SOLFVIN [39]. The National Federation of Spiritual Healers in England [40] define spiritual healing as restoring the balance of body, mind and spirit in the recipient with the intention of promoting self-healing, to bring a sense of well-being and peace to the recipient. A further description concerns itself with finding an inner peaceful core, connecting with a universal source of peace and love that is channelled for the benefit of another. This connection with a universal force is also at the centre of "therapeutic touch" and belies its connections with ancient systems of healing [41].

While the state of mind necessary for healing has been elusive to research there has been quite extensive research into the physical sequelae of spiritual healing phenomena which has included investigations using controlled trials [42]. Enzymes and body chemicals in vitro have been studied, as have the effects of healing on cells and lower organisms (including bacteria, fungus and yeasts), human tissue cells in vitro, the motility of simple organisms and plants, on animals and on human problems. While spiritual healing is often dismissed as purely a placebo response, the evidence from studies of lower organisms and cells would indicate that there is direct influence. Even if we introduce the idea of expectancy effects as an influence on experimental data, we are still left with a body of knowledge which begs understanding [39, 43].

General practice

At the level of daily practice some general practitioners have been willing to entertain the idea of spiritual healing and incorporate it into their practice, to use spiritual explanations for some of their patient contact, or as part of their referral network [9, 44-47]. COHEN [46] emphasises the value of touch, time and compassion which the healer can offer, and the benefits of referral. Such practice points out the value of working together as a referral network of practitioners.

KING et al. [48] focused on patients who use faith healers and physicians to care for their medical problems to learn about how often physicians see patients who are involved in faith healing, and to learn more about physicians' attitudes about, and experiences with, faith healing. Approximately one half (52%) of the 594 participating physicians were aware of at least one patient in their practice who had had a faith-healing experience. Most physicians came in contact with such patients no more frequently than once a year. Fifty-five percent agreed and 20% disagreed that reliance on faith healers often leads to serious medical problems. However, 44% thought that physicians and faith healers can work together to cure some patients, and 23% believed that faith healers divinely heal some people whom physicians cannot help. Family physicians were divided in their views about faith healing, with a majority expressing scepticism about faith healing and a sizeable minority favourable toward it.

Chronic complaints and recalcitrance

In BROWN's study (1995) of chronic problems in an English general practice of six doctors, adult patients with chronic complaints were referred by their general practitioner to a healing clinic. In choosing the patients, the general practitioner included those who had had a problem of six months duration and had not responded well to usual interventions, other secondary referrals or counselling. Treatment sessions lasted 20 minutes once a week for an eight week period. The spiritual healing used a "laying on of hands approach" to "channel healing energies" and was assessed using a validated quality of life questionnaire that has established population norms for comparison (SF-36). There were significant changes after eight weeks in what was a group of patients with poor health status in role limitations, social function, pain, general health and vitality. These improvements were not extended to an assessment after 26 weeks from the beginning of the study. As the author says, we cannot make any specific conclusions regarding the healing approach as there were no treatment controls. However, for a group of chronic patients, recalcitrant to previous intervention, there was improvement.

Chronic symptoms in general practice are also the focus of DIXON's study [49]. Like the above study with several general practitioners working together, patients with a condition that had lasted for six months, which was unresponsive to treatment, were referred to a healer. The patients were told that they were going to see a healer rather than a faith or spiritual healer, who would then pass her hands close to the patient visualising the passage of light through the patient accompanied by relaxing music. We are not told of the control condition, and the use of relaxing music confounds the treatment given that the use of music as music therapy is a known anxiolytic [50]. However, compared to the control scores, there was an improvement in anxiety and depression scores after three months that was maintained at six months for the treatment group. Functional improvements on the Nottingham Health Profile at three months were not maintained at a significant level after six months. These patients were previously unresponsive to treatment and the improvement in general mood state scores indicates a general setting for recovery that is of worth for clinical practice.

A broader ecology of care

The demand for whole person treatment has been strenuously adopted by some nursing groups who remind us that in caring for the patient there is a need to include spiritual needs and to allow the expression of those needs [1, 51-62]. Within these approaches there is a core of opinion which accepts that suffering and pain are part of a larger life experience, and that they can have meaning for the patient, and for the caregivers [44, 63]. The emphasis is placed upon the person's concept of God, sources of strength and hope, the significance of religious practices and rituals for the patient and their belief system [55].

When the goal of treatment is palliative, in terminally ill cancer patients with a prognosis of 6 months or less, the most important outcome is improving patient quality of life [64]. Interviews with 120 terminally ill cancer patients show that their most important concerns encompass existential, spiritual, familial, physical, and emotional issues and that throughout their illness these concerns were rarely a focus of their care. What is of further concern is that doctors underestimate symptom severity 15% of the time [65], and this has important implications for palliative interventions and the way in which patient understandings are taken seriously.

Doctors, nurses and clergy have worked together to care for the dying [31, 64, 66-68], and a community team approach which includes the family of the patient and his or her friends appears to be beneficial [69-72]. These principle benefits are concerned with a lessening of state-trait anxiety, general feelings of well being and an increasing spiritual awareness for the dying person regardless of gender, marital status, age, or diagnosis [73]. This does not imply that each practitioners has to address all of these components, rather that those involved identify that which is necessary for the patient and can call upon the appropriate resources. The nurse specialising in pain management works with the priest understanding suffering and together with the patient that is in pain. But the patient plays an active contributory role. Technical support is vital but optimal care involves emotional support and these may include techniques of relaxation, visualisation and meditation [74].

Caregivers need care
Increasing numbers of patients with cancer are being cared for by home caregivers[75]. The primary purpose of the study of HILEMAN et al. was to identify, categorize, and assess the importance of needs expressed by 492 home caregivers and to determine how well these needs were satisfied. Caregivers, unpaid people who helped with physical care or coping with the disease process, were selected from the records of two non-profit community cancer agencies and two hospital outpatient oncology clinics. Six need categories were identified: psychological, informational, patient care, personal, spiritual, and household. Those needs changed over time and required frequent reassessment but it was the caregivers as well as the patients who were seen as in need. If we continually refine our outcome measures to assess the individual patient then we are committing a big mistake by ignoring his ecological milieu.

In a three month study of the perceived needs and anxiety levels of 166 adult family members of intensive care unit (ICU) patients [62] family needs and situational anxiety were significantly related. Worries, trait anxiety, age and family needs explained 38% of the variation of situational anxiety. In addition, spiritual needs and situational anxiety explained 33% of the variation of family needs. In threatening situations families need strategies to cope. As ZIGMOND [76] writes "On our own, or in our most intimate groups, we devise more personal and idiosyncratic beliefs, rituals and protocols to ward off the potential storms or deserts of uncertainty" (p69). The spiritual dimension, while perhaps not warding off uncertainty, offers a satisfactory strategy by which uncertainty may be understood and coped with.

Spiritual factors are also important for the caregivers. [77] CHANG et.al. examines how religious/spiritual coping is related to specific conditions of caregiving and psychological distress among informal caregivers to community-residing disabled elders. Spiritual coping strategies influence caregiver distress indirectly through the quality of the relationship between caregiver and care recipient. Caregivers who used religious or spiritual beliefs to cope with caregiving had a better relationship with those who were being cared for, which is associated with lower levels of depression and an increased dedication to the role of caring.

Spirituality in the treatment of persons living with AIDS
Comprehensive treatment programs for people living with AIDS recommend that the spiritual welfare of the patient, and its influence on their well-being, should be included [78-86]. Individuals who were spiritually well and able to find meaning and purpose in their lives were also found to be hardier[87]., COOKE [88] reminds us that the care of HIV-infected patients is demanding as well as the emotional demands of caring for HIV-infected people. Other authors, while supporting an emphasis on the spiritual, also direct our attention to the confounding problem of religions that condemn various aspects of sexuality and the ramifications this has for the person living with HIV or AIDS [89].

While the term spiritual healing is used here within the context of orthodox medical practices as a complementary or adjuvant approach, the term spirit has other applications. In the absence of a medical cure for AIDS, HIV-infected individuals may seek alternative therapies and folk healing practices. In inner-city New Jersey, HIV-infected Hispanics receiving care at an HIV/AIDS clinic believed in good and evil spirits and that such spirits had a causal role in their infection, either alone or in conjunction with the AIDS virus [90]. They sought spiritual folk healing for physical relief, spiritual relief, and protection from evil. A minority hoped for cure. We must be aware of the prevalence of folk beliefs and alternative healing practices and cannot assume that when we talk of spiritual healing that it will fit into the conventional views of Western approaches.

Ambiguity in outcomes

RICHARDS & FOLKMAN [91] found spiritual phenomena were spontaneously reported in interviews of 68 of 125 recently bereaved HIV-positive and HIV-negative partners of men who died from AIDS. Spiritual understandings helped assimilate the deaths and were seen as sources of solace. Those reporting spiritual phenomena also showed higher levels of depression and anxiety and lower levels of positive states of mind, used more adaptive coping strategies, and reported more physical health symptoms than those who did not report spiritual phenomena. While these findings are with partners of patients, it reflects the work of KING [10] who found that stronger spiritual belief is an independent predictor of poor outcome at nine months for patients admitted to the acute services of a London hospital. Chronic pain patients who endorse a greater use of prayer to cope with their pain also reported a greater degree of disability [92]..

A distinct danger of promoting understandings, and calling them spiritual, is that they may deflect from pragmatic understandings that are necessary for daily life. An essential element of spiritual understanding is discernment of reasonable and proper applicability not the repetition of ritual exercises and wishful thinking. The guiding impulse behind the development of modern analgesics may be as divine as the exercise of meditative techniques. Knowing when and how to use them is the important factor [44].

Discernment
There are other dangers in spiritual healing.Some patients are promised fantastic healings by spiritual healers. Others are told that they are not recovering either because they do not want to, or that they do not love others enough, or that they are secretly resisting the healer. Some healers have been known to advise patients to refrain from conventional medical treatments. Such approaches are simply wrong.. Discernment is the key. For those seeking miracles or some sort of magical intervention through healing powers, this cautious reasoned approach may be disappointing. Discernment involves no dressing up in special clothes, nor any fancy hand-passes or magical incantations. Dressing up in clothes inappropriate to the period or the local culture is a warning of spiritual bankruptcy not enhanced powers [93] as is the use of languages strange to the culture. For those seeking the subtle and the hidden, this approach remains less dramatic but no less effective. The attitude of enhancing discernment is one that can be adapted for all healing modalities, including conventional medicine. Discernment can return the spiritual to the subtle level at which it exists. For spirit to be manifested in material effects requires the discernment of practitioners and of those whom they serve.

An integrative perspective
If we are to submit prayer to a test, then we should at least be certain that the observations we will make incorporate the relevant criteria for assessing recovery. Prayer not only brings relief but the expectation is of a new understanding, literally a change in consciousness.
If spirituality is defined as the search for the divine and the achievement of unity, then prayer is the vehicle for this achievement (ALDRIDGE 2000). You can still pray with a broken leg. You cannot run with a broken leg. Knowing the difference between the two is an elementary awareness. The intention of prayer is to be with the divine; then all other cares will fall away. For the sick, illness takes on a different meaning. It too may disappear. To look for a direct cause and effect with prayer is to defy the spiritual teachings throughout the centuries, failing to see the purposes of both sickness and prayer itself.
That the mind influences healing is becoming apparent. This is a knowledge of the world of laws of cause and effect, called science. There is also a knowledge that some call spirituality. Both are important. Neither is to be neglected. Healing comes from learning the relationship between both forms of knowledge. In both perspectives of knowledge, science and spirituality, learning is achieved through teaching and guidance. If the world is given to us by the divine in all its richness, then surely the blessings of medical knowledge, the dedication of various practitioners, and the lessons of illness and healing are provided by the same source.

Author

PROF. DR. PHIL. DAVID ALDRIDGE

Qualitative research in medicine, Witten/Herdecke University. Senior Research Fellow at St Mary's Hospital, London. Qualitative research. Family systemic aspects of suicide. Lecturing qualification in music therapy. Research interests: development of scientific basis of music therapy, research methodology in complementary medicine; combination of arts and science.
Contact: E-Mail: davida@uni-wh.de

References

1. Palmer M. The book of Chang Tzu. London: Arkana, Penguin, 1996.
2. Duckro P, Magaletta P. The effect of prayer on physical health: Experimental evidence. Journal of Religion and Health 1994; 33:211-219.
3. McCullough M. Prayer and health: Conceptual issues, research view, and research agenda. Journal of Psychology and Theology 1995; 25:15-29.
4. Magaletta P, Duckro P. Prayer in the medical encounter. Journal of Religion and Health 1996; 35:203-209.
5. VandeCreek L, Rogers E, Lester J. Use of alternative therapies among breast cancer out patients compared with the general population. Alternative Therapies 1999; 5:71-76.
6. Joyce C, Welldon R. The efficacy of prayer: a double-blind clinical trial. Journal of Chronic Diseases 1965; 18:367-377.
7. Rosner F. The efficacy of prayer: scientific v. religious evidence. Journal of Religion and Health 1975; 14:294-298.
8. Collipp P. The efficacy of prayer: a triple blind study. Medical Times 1969; 97:201-204.
9. Dossey L. Healing words: The power of prayer and the practice of medicine. New York: Harper Collins, 1993.
10. King M, Speck P, Thomas A. The effect of spiritual outcome from illness. Social Science and Medicine 1999; 48:1291-1299.
11. King M, Dein S. The spiritual variable in psychiatric research. Psychological Medicine 1998; 28:1259-1262.
12. King MB. Psychiatry and religion, context, consensus and controversies, by D. Bhugra. Br J Psychiatry 1997; 170:93-94.
13. Saudia T, Kinney M, Brown K, Young W. Health locus of control and helpfulness of prayer. Heart Lung 1991; 20:60-5.
14. Sutton T, Murphy S. Stressors and patterns of coping in renal transplant patients. Nursing Research 1989; 38:46-9.
15. Bergmark K. The Links and Alcoholics Anonymous: Two "A.A" movements in Sweden. In: Eisenbach-Stagl I, Rosenqvist P, eds. Diversity in unity. Studies of Alcoholics Anonymous in eight societies. Helsinki: Nordic Council for Alcohol and Drug Research, 1998:75-89.
16. Carroll S. Spirituality and purpose in life in alcoholism recovery. Journal of Studies on Alcohol 1993; 54:297-301.
17. McCarthy K. Early alcoholism treatment: the Emmanuel Movement and Richard Peabody. Journal for the Study of Alcohol 1984; 45(1):59-74.
18. Eisenbach-Stagl I. How to live a sober life in a wet society: Alcoholics Anonymous in Austria. In: Eisenbach-Stagl I, Rosenqvist P, eds. Diversity in unity. Studies of Alcoholics Anonymous in eight societies. Helsinki: Nordic Council for Alcohol and Drug Research, 1998:131-147.
19. Buxton M, Smith D, Seymour R. Spirituality and other points of resistance to the 12-step

recovery process. Journal of Psychoactive Drugs 1987; 19:275-86.
20. Green L, Fullilove M, Fullilove R. Stories of spiritual awakening - The nature of spirituality in recovery. Journal of Substance Abuse Treatment 1998; 15:325-331.
21. Mathew R, Georgi J, Wilson W, Mathew V. A retrospective study of the concept of spirituality as understood by recovering individuals. Journal of Substance Abuse Treatment 1996; 13:67-73.
22. Miller W. Researching the spiritual dimensions of alcohol and other drug problems. Addiction 1998; 93:979-990.
23. Navarro J, Wilson S, Berger L, Taylor T. Substance abuse and spirituality: A program for native American students. American Journal of Health Behavior 1997; 21:3-11.
24. Peteet J. A closer look at the role of a spiritual approach in addictions treatment. Journal of Substance Abuse Treatment 1993; 10:263-267.
25. Kendler KS, Gardner CO, Prescott CA. Religion, psychopathology, and substance use and abuse: A multimeasure, genetic-epidemiologic study. Am J Psychiatry 1997; 154:322-329.
26. Koenig H, Hays J, George L, Blazer D, Larson D, Landerman L. Modeling the cross-sectional relationships between religion, physical health, social support, and depressive symptoms. American Journal of Geriatric Psychiatry 1997; 5:131-144.
27. Gorham M. Spirituality and problem solving with seniors. Perspectives. 1989; 13:13-6.
28. Chatters L, Taylor R. Age differences in religious participation among black adults. Journal of Gerontology 1989; 44(5):S183-9.
29. Koenig H, Bearon L, Dayringer R. Physician perspectives on the role of religion in the physician,older patient relationship. Journal of Family Practice 1989; 28:441-8.
30. Markides K. Aging, religiosity, and adjustment: a longitudinal analysis. Journal of Gerontology 1983; 38:621-5.
31. Reed P. Spirituality and well-being in terminally ill hospitalized adults. Research in Nursing and Health 1987; 10:335-44.
32. Taylor R, Chatters L. Nonorganizational religious participation among elderly black adults. Journal of Gerontology 1991; 46.
33. Garrett G. A natural way to go? Death and bereavement in old age. Professional Nurse 1991; 6:744-6.
34. Foley L, Wagner J, Waskel S. Spirituality in the lives of older women. Journal of Women & Aging 1998; 10:85-91.
35. Bearon L, Koenig H. Religious cognitions and use of prayer in health and illness. Gerontologist. 1990; 30(2):249-53.
36. Byrd R. Positive therapeutic effects of intercessory prayer in a coronary care unit population. Southern Medical Journal 1988; 81:826-9.
37. Benor D. Healing Resarch: Volume 1, Professional Supplement. Southfield, MI: Visdion Publications, 2001.
38. Benor D. Healing Research: Volume 1, Spiritual Healing: Scientific Validation of a Healing Revolution. Southfield, MI: Vision Publications, 2001.
39. Solfin J. Mental healing. In: Krippner S, ed. Advances in Parapsychological Research. Jefferson,N.C: McFarland and Co., 1984:31-63.
40. NFSH. National Federation of Spiritual Healers Code of Conduct. The Director, NFSH: Sunbury on Thames, Middlesex TW16 6RG, England, 1999.
41. Fischer S, Johnson P. Therapeutic Touch: A viable link in midwifery. Journal of Nurse-Midwifery 1999; 44:300-309.
42. Benor D. Survey of spiritual healing. Complementary Medical Research 1990; 4:9-33.
43. Wirth D. The significance of belief and expectancy within the spiritual healing encounter. Social Science and Medicine 1995; 41:249-260.
44. Aldridge D. Spirituality, healing and medicine. Return to the silence. London: Jessica Kingsley Publishers, 2000.
45. Brown C. Spiritual healing in general practice. Complementary Therapies in Medicine 1995; 3:230-233.
46. Cohen J. Spiritual healing in a medical context. Practitioner 1989; 233 (1473):1056-7.
47. Pietroni PC. Spiritual interventions in a general practice setting. Holistic Medicine 1986; 1:253-262.

48. King D, Sobal J, Haggerty J, Dent M, Patton D. Experiences and attitudes about faith healing among family physicians. Journal of Family Practice 1992; 35:158-62.
49. Dixon M. Does 'healing' benefit patients with chronic symptoms? A quasi-randomized trial in general practice. Journal of the Royal Society of Medicine 1998; 91:183-188.
50. Aldridge D. Music therapy research and practice in medicine. From out of the silence. London: Jessica Kingsley, 1996.
51. Dossey B. Barbara Dossey on holistic nursing, Florence Nightingale, and healing rituals. Alternative Therapies 1999; 5:79-86.
52. Boutell K, Bozett F. Nurses' assessment of patients' spirituality: continuing education implications. Journal of Continuing Education in Nursing 1990; 21:172-6.
53. Clark J, Dawson L. Personal religiousness and ethical judgements: An empirical analysis. Journal of Business Ethics 1996; 15:359-372.
54. Burkhardt M. Spirituality: an analysis of the concept. Holistic Nursing Practitioner 1989; 3:69-77.
55. Soeken K, Carson V. Responding to the spiritual needs of the chronically ill. Nursing Clinics of North America 1987; 22(3): 603-11.
56. Labun E. Spiritual care: an element in nursing care planning. Journal of Advanced Nursing 1988; 13:314-20.
57. Grasser C, Craft B. The patient's approach to wellness. Nursing Clinics of North America 1984; 19:207-18.
58. Potts R. Spirituality and the experience of cancer in an African-American community: Implications for psychosocial oncology. Journal of Psychosocial Oncology 1996; 14:1-19.
59. Ferrell B, Grant M, Funk B, OtisGreen S, Garcia N. Quality of life in breast cancer Part II: Psychological and spiritual well-being. Cancer Nursing 1998; 21:1-9.
60. Rustoen T, Hanestad B. Nursing intervention to increase hope in cancer patients. Journal of Clinical Nursing 1998; 7:19-27.
61. Harrington V, Lackey N, Gates M. Needs of caregivers of clinic and hospice cancer patients. Cancer Nursing 1996; 19:118-125.
62. Rukholm E, Bailey P, Coutu-Wakulczyk G, Bailey W. Needs and anxiety levels in relatives of intensive care unit patients. Journal of Advanced Nursing 1991; 16:920-8.
63. Nagai Jacobson M, Burkhardt M. Spirituality: cornerstone of holistic nursing practice. Holistic Nursing Practitioner 1989; 3:18-26.
64. Greisinger A, Lorimor R, Aday L, Winn R, Baile W. Terminally ill cancer patients - Their most important concerns. Cancer Practice 1997; 5:147-154.
65. Stephens RJ, Hopwood P, Girling DJ, Machin D. Randomized trials with quality of life endpoints: Are doctors' ratings of patients' physical symptoms interchangeable with patients' self-ratings? Qual Life Res 1997; 6:225-236.
66. Roche J. Spirituality and the ALS patient. Rehabilitation Nurse 1989; 14:139-41.
67. Conrad N. Spiritual support for the dying. Nursing Clinics of North America 1985; 20:415-26.
68. McMillan S, Weitzner M. Quality of life in cancer patients - Use of a revised hospice index. Cancer Practice 1998; 6:282-288.
69. Aldridge D. A team approach to terminal care: personal implications for patients and practitioners. Journal of the Royal College of General Practitioners 1987; 37:364.
70. Aldridge D. A community approach to cancer in families. Journal of Maternal and Child Health 1987; 12:182-185.
71. Aldridge D. Families, cancer and dying. Family Practice 1987; 4:212-218.
72. Aldridge D. One body: a guide to healing in the Church. London: S.P.C.K., 1987.
73. Kaczorowski J. Spiritual well-being and anxiety in adults diagnosed with cancer. Hospital Journal 1989; 5:105-16.
74. Peteet J, Stomper P, Ross D, Cotton V, Truesdell P, Moczynski W. Emotional support for patients with cancer who are undergoing CT: semistructured interviews of patients at a cancer institute. Radiology 1992; 182:99-102.
75. Hileman J, Lackey N, Hassanein R. Identifying the needs of home caregivers of patients with cancer. Oncol Nurs Forum 1992; 19:771-7.
76. Zigmond D. Three types of encounter in the healing arts: Dialogue, dialectic, and

didacticism. Holistic Medicine 1987; 2:69-81.
77. Chang B, Noonan A, Tennstedt S. The role of religion/spirituality in coping with caregiving for disabled elders. Gerontologist 1998; 38:463-470.
78. Belcher A, Dettmore D, Holzemer S. Spirituality and sense of well-being in persons with AIDS. Holistic Nursing Pract.ice 1989; 3:16-25.
79. Flaskerud J, Rush C. AIDS and traditional health beliefs and practices of black women. Nursing Research 1989; 38:210-5.
80. Gutterman L. A day treatment program for persons with AIDS. American Journal of Occupational Therapy 1990; 44:234-7.
81. Ribble D. Psychosocial support groups for people with HIV infection and AIDS. Holistic Nursing Practice 1989; 3:52-62.
82. Kaplan M, Marks G, Mertens S. Distress and coping among women with HIV infection: Preliminary findings from a multiethnic sample. American Journal of Orthopsychiatry 1997; 67:80-91.
83. Hall B. Patterns of spirituality in persons with advanced HIV disease. Research in Nursing and Health 1998; 21:143-153.
84. Holt J, Houg B, Romano J. Spiritual wellness for clients with HIV/AIDS: Review of counselling issues. Journal of Counselling and Development 1999; 77:160-170.
85. Warner-Robbins C, Christiana N. The spiritual needs of persons with AIDS. Family and Community Health 1989; 12:43-51.
86. Sowell R, Misener T. Decisions to have a baby by HIV-infected women. Western Journal of Nursing Research 1997; 19:56-70.
87. Carson V, Green H. Spiritual well-being: a predictor of hardiness in patients with acquired immunodeficiency syndrome. Journal of Professional Nursing 1992; 8:209-20.
88. Cooke M. Supporting health care workers in the treatment of HIV-infected patients. Prim Care 1992; 19:245-56.
89. Jenkins RA. Religion and HIV: Implications for research and intervention. J Soc Issues 1995; 51:131-144.
90. Suarez M, Raffaelli M, OLeary A. Use of folk healing practices by HIV-infected Hispanics living in the United States. AIDS Care 1996; 8:683-690.
91. Richards T, Folkman S. Spiritual aspects of loss at the time of a partner's death from AIDS. Death Studies 1997; 21:527-552.
92. Ashby J, Lenhart R. Prayer as a coping strategy for chronic pain patients. Rehabilitation Psychology 1994; 39:205-208.
93. Marsham R. Sufi orders. In: Shah I, ed. Sufi thought and action. London: Octagon Press, 1990:112-122.

MAGISCH RELIGIÖSE HEILRITUALE IN DER ZENTRALSCHWEIZ

von Kurt Lussi

Verborgene Welt am Fuß des Pilatus*

Nach außen deutet fast nichts darauf hin, dass die Gegend am Fuße des Pilatus durchsetzt ist von magisch-religiösen Bezugspunkten, an denen die Geister der Vergangenheit seit Menschengedenken ihren Aufenthalt haben. Von dieser geheimnisvollen Anderswelt, die das Land nördlich der Stadt Luzern wie ein unsichtbares Netz überzieht, gibt es eigentlich nichts zu sehen außer einigen merkwürdigen Steinen, seltsamen Kreuzen und gottverlassenen Kapellen.

Gewiss, in der Schweiz gibt es bekanntere und für den Fremden besser erschlossene Gegenden als das Voralpengebiet. Und das Land besitzt auch sagenumwobenere Sehenswürdigkeiten, als den erratischen Block von Roggliswil, den außerhalb des Kantons Luzern kaum jemand kennt.

Abb. 1: Doppelbalkiges Kreuz bei Sigigen, Kanton Luzern. Es schützt vor dem Heer der Toten, das in stürmischen Nächten hier vorbeizieht. Im Hintergrund der Pilatus, das Reich der Geister, Kobolde und Drachen. *Berg bei Luzern

Handbuch der Ethnotherapien – ETHNOMED 2002

Über die Grenzen hinaus bekannt ist der Teufelsstein von Göschenen, der beim Bau des Gotthardtunnels nur mit Glück der Sprengung entgangen ist. Auf Druck der Bevölkerung hatte man ihn seinerzeit versetzt. Jetzt steht er etwas verloren zwischen Autobahn und wild schäumender Reuss. Beflaggt und zur Schau gestellt ist er bloß noch ein totes Relikt und ein Zeichen für den Tribut, den ein immer mehr überhand nehmender Verkehr fordert. Täglich fahren jetzt Personenautos und schwere Lastwagen über seinen ursprünglichen Standort, als ob sie einen Jahrhunderte alten Mythos an der Wiederkehr hindern müssten.

Der Vergleich zwischen dem erratischen Block von Roggliswil und dem Teufelsstein von Göschenen ist bezeichnend für die Gegensätze, die das Leben am Fuß der Alpen bestimmen. Nach außen gibt sich die Zentralschweiz zwar modern und aufgeschlossen. Kaum wahrnehmbar für Außenstehende existiert im Verborgenen jedoch eine Anderswelt, die zu wesentlichen Teilen von magisch-religiösen Vorstellungen geprägt ist.

Nach der Einführung des Christentums ist der Glaube an eine von Göttern und Ahnen beseelte Natur keineswegs verdrängt worden. Die neu eingeführte Religion hat sich stattdessen schon früh mit den bestehenden Auffassungen vermischt, indem heidnische Riten christlich umgedeutet worden sind. Umgekehrt hat das Volk viele christliche Glaubensgrundsätze auf seine Weise interpretiert und in das Bestehende eingefügt. Aus der Vermischung zwischen christlicher Religion und überlieferter Tradition ergab sich im Laufe der Zeit ein Weltbild, das weder ein rein christliches, noch ein heidnisches ist. Die zahlreichen Kapellen, Kreuze und Bildstöcke, die den Lebensraum der Innerschweiz bis heute prägen, sind deshalb nicht nur heilige Orte im christlichen Sinne. Viele sind gleichzeitig auch Schauplätze unheimlicher Erzählungen, an denen trotz der Heiligkeit dieser Orte kopflose Geister, schwarze Hunde und der *Türstzug*, das Heer der ins Jenseits ziehenden Seelen, auftreten.

Diese Auffassungen haben sich in den Vorstellungen vom Entstehen der Krankheiten und ihrer Heilung niedergeschlagen. Die Krankheit wird durch scheinbar negativ wirkende heidnische Mächte verursacht. Die Heilung erfolgt durch christliche oder dem Christentum angeglichene und als positiv begriffene Rituale.

In dieser Welt ist der moderne Mensch hin und her gerissen. Er vertraut zwar der modernen Medizin, bleibt aber gleichzeitig der Tradition verhaftet.

Die traditionellen Vorstellungen von Krankheit und Heilung

Entstehung von Krankheiten
Wie bei allen Völkern ist auch in der Zentralschweiz der alte Glaube zu finden, dass Krankheiten von bösartigen und meist unsichtbaren Dämonen oder dem Teufel selbst verursacht werden. Nach dieser Auffassung ist die Krankheit ein selbständig auftretendes Wesen, das vom Menschen Besitz ergreift, ihn quält und plagt bis er stirbt oder vom Dämon befreit wird. Dieser Glaube hat sich in der Umgangssprache erhalten. Der Mensch wird nicht einfach krank, sondern die Krankheit packt ihn und wirft ihn ins Bett.

Besonders anschaulich zeigt sich dies beim Albtraum. Der vom Alb befallene Mensch hat das Gefühl, ein Dämon schleiche sich an und krieche von den Füßen her langsam zur Gurgel, wodurch ein Gefühl des Gepacktwerdens entsteht. Auch der nachfolgende Erfahrungsbericht zeigt, dass die Krankheit als "Ding" oder "Wesen" begriffen wird:

"Vielleicht zwei Monate später erwachte ich erneut und fühlte im Halbschlaf etwas auf meinem Körper liegen. Es drückte mich nieder und ich hatte große Mühe, die Herrschaft über meinen Körper zu bekommen. Sobald ich diese wieder hatte, verschwand der Druck. Zuvor war ich außerstande, auch nur mit der Wimper zu zucken.

Das wiederholte sich nun öfters. Es gab Zeiten, da wurde ich durch das Zittern meines Körpers geweckt, der die Anwesenheit der Wesenheit wahrnahm, bevor sie mir zu Bewusstsein kam. Das Zittern hörte nach dem Erwachen erst allmählich auf und ich konnte eine gute Stunde nicht mehr weiterschlafen. Bei den folgenden ‚Besuchen' wurde der Druck immer heftiger; ich wurde regelrecht auf das Bett

Abb. 2
Der hl. Antonius von Padua. Der nach ihm benannte Segen "Ecce crucem" schützt gegen Besessenheit. Durch die beigeheftete Berührungsreliquie wird das Bildchen zu einem Schutzamulett.

hinunter gedrückt. Mein Körper war völlig gelähmt und nur mit größter Willenskraft, manchmal bis zu zehn Minuten kämpfend, "bekam" ich meinen Körper wieder zurück. Immer wenn ich den Druck abgeschüttelt hatte, meinte ich das ‚Ding' in Richtung Badezimmer verschwinden zu spüren."

Nebst Dämonen und Geistern kommen auch bösartig gesinnte Menschen in Frage, die durch Zauberei Krankheiten verursachen. Und schließlich kann auch Gott selbst den Menschen für seine Verfehlungen mit Krankheiten strafen. Krank wird demnach, wer sein Leben nicht im Einklang mit den Gesetzen Gottes führt. Daher werden bei Krankheiten Bußwallfahrten unternommen und die Heiligen um Schutz und Hilfe angerufen.

Heilung

Kaum überblickbar sind die magischen Mittel, mit denen Krankheiten vertrieben werden. Sie können unterteilt werden in Gebete (Segensgebete, Wortzauber), magische Handlungen, Gegenstände (Heilkräuter und Tiere mit magischer Wirkung), lebende Menschen (Blut, Harn, Speichel, Schweiß), Leichenteile (Totenzähne) und die Elemente Erde, Wasser und Feuer.

Weitaus am häufigsten und bis heute in Gebrauch sind die kirchlichen beziehungsweise magisch-religiösen Heilmittel und Rituale. Dazu gehören der Reliquienkult, die Krankheitsheiligen, Wallfahrten, kirchliche Gebete (wie zum Beispiel Exorzismen), Krankensegen und geweihte oder an heiligen Dingen anberührte Gegenstände. Die Gebete, Handlungen und Gegenstände haben den Zweck, auf einer anderen Bewusstseinsebene den Mächten des Bösen entgegenzutreten.

Die nachfolgenden drei Beispiele beziehen sich auf die Anrufung von Krankenheiligen, Heilung mit geweihten Gegenständen (Loretokind) und den Krankenexorzismus. Die fürbittende Anrufung eines Krankenheiligen ist das einfachste und zugleich häufigste magisch-religiöse Ritual, der Exorzismus das stärkste. Dazwischen liegt der Gebrauch geweihter und an einem Gnadenbild berührter Gegenstände (Loretokind).

1. Heilige als Helfer bei Krankheiten – St. Burkard von Beinwil

Heilige sind Menschen, die im irdischen Leben dem Licht Gottes begegnet und nach ihrem Tod mit ihm verschmolzen sind. Sie werden mit einer Lichtscheibe, dem Nimbus, dargestellt. Diese Form der Darstellung ist keine willkürliche, sondern sie beruht auf realen Erfahrungen, die von besonders begnadeten Menschen im Zustand tiefster mystischer Versenkung gemacht werden.
Nach der Lehre der katholischen Kirche bewirken die Heiligen keine Wunder, sondern sie sind Bindeglieder zwischen Gott und den Menschen. In den von der Kirche approbierten Bittgebeten werden sie deshalb nicht direkt, sondern immer nur fürbittweise angesprochen.

Besondere Ereignisse im Leben und Sterben des Heiligen machen ihn zum Patron bestimmter Krankheiten. Aufschluss über die Zuständigkeit eines Heiligen geben die zahlreichen Heiligenlegenden und Gebetbücher. Die vierzehn wichtigsten katholischen Heiligen werden zu einer Gruppe, den vierzehn Nothelfern, zusammengefasst. Je nach Gegend und Umständen werden einige weggelassen und durch andere ersetzt.

Die wichtigsten und im ganzen Alpenraum verbreiteten Helfer bei Krankheiten sind:

St. Blasius	Halsleiden
St. Erasmus	Leibschmerzen (Unterleib, Magen)
St. Veit	Epilepsie
St. Dyonisios	Kopfschmerzen
St. Margaretha	Patronin der Gebärenden
St. Katharina	schwere Sprache
St. Sebastian	Pest und pestartige Seuchen
St. Apollonia	Zahnschmerzen

Ein nur in der Zentralschweiz (Kantone Aargau, Luzern und Zug) angerufener Heiliger bei Krankheiten allgemeiner Art ist St. Burkard von Beinwil. Es handelt sich dabei nicht um den ersten Bischof von Würzburg, sondern um den gleichnamigen Leutpriester von Beinwil im Freiamt (Schweiz).

St. Burkard von Beinwil wurde im 12. Jahrhundert in Langenmatt, einem Bauerngut oberhalb des Klosters Muri geboren. Er verstarb am 18. Mai 1192 im Ruf der Heiligkeit. Schon 1228 wird er in Urkunden des Klosters Muri "St. Burkard" genannt. Das Wasser des bei der Kirche fließenden Brunnen gilt als heilkräftig.

Die Heilung geschieht durch die Zentrierung des Geistes mit Hilfe von Gebet und Meditation. Zur Unterstützung dieses Vorgangs trinkt der Kranke vom heiligen Brunnen, indem er sich dorthin begibt oder sich das Wasser bringen lässt. Im Zustand der mystischen Versenkung geschieht die Zwiesprache des Kranken mit Gott und dem Heiligen.

Erst jetzt erfolgt die Anrufung, indem sich der Kranke mit dem nachfolgenden Bittruf an Gott wendet, ihn durch die Fürsprache des Heiligen von der Krankheit zu befreien.

"Allmächtiger Gott, du hast deinen treuen Diener Burkard mit wunderbaren Gnadengaben ausgezeichnet. Ich bitte, o Herr, befreie durch die kräftige Fürsprache dieses deines Priesters Burkard auch mich und meine Schutzbefohlenen von allen Krankheiten und Übeln des Leibes und der Seele; gib mir Geduld im Leiden, Starkmut in allen Prüfungen, die du mir auferlegst. Schenke mir die Kraft, nach seinem Vorbild dir zu dienen, dich allzeit zu loben und zu preisen und deinen mächtigen Namen zu verkünden. Durch Jesus Christus, unseren Herrn. Amen."

2. Krankensegnungen mit dem Loretokind von Salzburg

Im Christentum gebühren Anbetung und Verehrung einzig und allein Gott. Sofern die Heiligen nicht fürbittweise angerufen werden, widerspricht die Heiligenverehrung der Lehre der römisch-katholischen Kirche. Da der Volksglaube die Verehrung eines einzigen Gottes jedoch nur schwer erträgt, hat die Kirche im Laufe der Zeit dennoch eine Reihe von Zugeständnissen machen müssen.

Zu diesen gehört die Verehrung von Gnadenbildern. Nach der christlichen Lehre

Abb. 3: Das Loretokindlein von Salzburg. Am Original im Kloster der Kapuzinerinnen berührte Kopie des Gnadenbildes.

bewirken Bilder keine Wunder. Und wenn dabei dennoch Wunderzeichen geschehen, heißt es in der katholischen Handpostille, so bewirkt sie Gott allein, bewogen durch die Fürsprache Christi, Marias oder der Heiligen, die sie darstellen.

Im Volksglauben existiert dagegen die auf vorchristliche Zeit zurückgehende Vorstellung, wonach die Gnadenbilder mit besonderer Kraft erfüllt sind. Das gleiche gilt auch für Gegenstände oder Abbilder, die gesegnet und am Original anberührt werden.

Heilritual mit dem Loretokind

Ein Beispiel dafür ist das "Loretokind" im Kloster der Kapuzinerinnen in Salzburg. Das winzige, knapp 10 cm hohe Elfenbeinfigürchen stellt das Jesuskind dar. Es wird in einem Holzkästchen aufbewahrt, das "Stammenhaus" oder "Stammhäusel" genannt wird.

Für den Privatgebrauch werden auch außerhalb des Einzugsgebiets des Klosters originalgetreue Nachbildungen des Gnadenbildes oder Andachtsbildchen zur Heilung von Krankheiten verwendet. Sie werden auf Anfrage hin abgegeben oder verschickt. Vor dem Versand werden sowohl die Figürchen als auch die Bildchen gesegnet und am Original berührt.

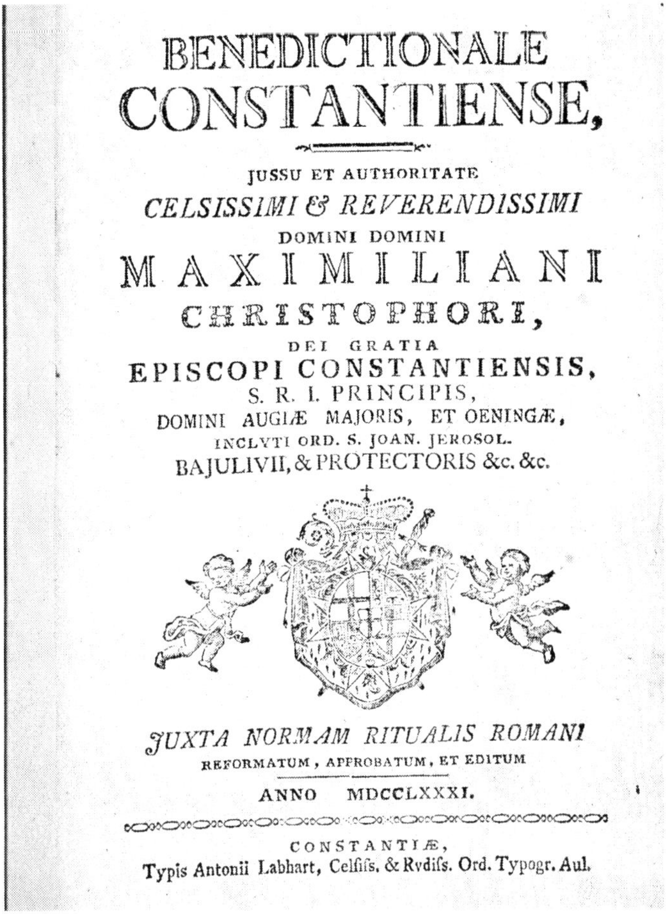

BENEDICTIONALE
CONSTANTIENSE,
JUSSU ET AUTHORITATE
CELSISSIMI & REVERENDISSIMI
DOMINI DOMINI
MAXIMILIANI
CHRISTOPHORI,
DEI GRATIA
EPISCOPI CONSTANTIENSIS,
S. R. I. PRINCIPIS,
DOMINI AUGIÆ MAJORIS, ET OENINGÆ,
INCLVTI ORD. S. JOAN. JEROSOL.
BAJULIVII, & PROTECTORIS &c. &c.

JUXTA NORMAM RITUALIS ROMANI
REFORMATUM, APPROBATUM, ET EDITUM
ANNO MDCCLXXXI.

CONSTANTIÆ,
Typis Antonii Labhart, Celſiſs. & Rvdiſs. Ord. Typogr. Aul.

Abb. 4
Benedictionale Constantiense von 1781. Im Anhang finden sich Exorzismen gegen verschiedene Formen der Besessenheit.

Zur Heilung wird das Bild auf den Kopf oder die leidende Stelle aufgelegt. Beim Auflegen, dem sogenannten "Aufsetzen", muss das nachfolgende Gebet gesprochen werden, wobei an den im Gebet mit einem Kreuz bezeichneten Stellen mit dem Figürchen oder dem Andachtsbild ein Segenskreuz gemacht werden muss. (Das Gebet ist auf der Rückseite der Bildchen aufgedruckt.)

Segensgebet
"Es segne Dich Gott † der Vater, der dich erschaffen, † der Sohn, der Dich erlöst, † der Heilige Geist, der dich geheiligt hat. Der Segen der heiligsten Dreifaltigkeit sei mit Dir auf allen Deinen Wegen und bewahre Deinen Leib und Deine Seele vor allem Unheil. Amen.

Mit Deinem göttlichen Kindlein segne uns, o Du allerreinste Jungfrau-Mutter Maria! O allmächtiges Jesulein, in dem die ganze Fülle der Gottheit wohnt, das Du ganz Liebe und Güte bist, reich für alle, die dich anrufen. Du Quelle des Lebens und der

Heiligkeit, des vollkommenen Trostes, Du unser Friede, unsere Versöhnung, Du Rettung aller, die auf Dich hoffen, Deinem Herzen vertraue ich an (diese Seele, dieses Anliegen, dieses Leid ...). Blicke darauf und dann tue, was Deine Liebe Dir eingibt! – O liebreichstes Jesulein, das Du schon durch unzählige Gnadenerweise Dein Wohlgefallen an der Verehrung Deiner heiligsten Kindheit in diesem Bilde geoffenbart hast, erbarme Dich unser! – Verherrliche Deinen heiligsten süßesten Namen auch an uns! Sei uns Jesus! Sei uns Heiland! Amen."

3. Privatexorzismus

Unerklärliche oder langwierige Krankheiten werden oft auf die Besessenheit durch Teufel oder Dämonen zurückgeführt. Die Art der Krankheit, heißt es in einem 1729 in Konstanz gedruckten Exorzistenbüchlein, spielt dabei eine untergeordnete Rolle, weil "der Teüffel alle erdenckliche Krancheiten nacharten kann, also das ein natürliche Krancheit von solcher böser sehr hart und schwär zu erkennen ist".

Um festzustellen, ob die Krankheit eine natürliche oder übernatürliche Ursache hat, macht nach dem erwähnten Exorzistenbüchlein eine fromme Person über dem Kranken das Kreuzzeichen. Dann befiehlt sie dem Dämon, sofern das Leiden von ihm herrühre, augenblicklich innezuhalten. Wird der Kranke für kurze Zeit von den Schmerzen befreit, hat das Leiden eine übernatürliche Ursache, die mit den Mitteln der Kirche bekämpft werden kann.

Exorzismus für Kranke

Der Kranke wird geheilt, indem ein besonders bevollmächtigter Priester den im Körper steckenden Dämon im Namen Gottes anruft und ihm befiehlt, den Kranken zu verlassen.
Dabei ist es wichtig, dass der Priester die kirchlichen Vorschriften genauestens befolgt. Es müssen nicht nur die richtigen Texte gewählt werden. Auch die Reihenfolge ist entscheidend. Anleitungen und Texte finden sich im Anhang der kirchlich approbierten Benedictionale.

Eine einfachere Form ist der Privatexorzismus, den jedermann unter Anwendung des Kreuzzeichens und des Weihwassers sprechen darf. Auch beim Privatexorzismus ruft der Exorzist Gott und die Heiligen um Beistand an. Dann befiehlt er dem Dämon, seinen Aufenthaltsort zu verlassen und nicht mehr zurückzukehren.

Privatexorzismus

Vor dem Beten des Exorzismus werden ein Kruzifix und Weihwasser bereitgestellt. Nach einigen vorbereitenden Gebeten (Psalmen, Allerheiligen-Litanei) spricht man am Bett des Kranken:

"Im Namen Jesu und Mariä befehle ich euch, ihr höllischen Geister, weichet von uns (ihnen) und von diesem (jenem) Orte und waget nicht wiederzukehren und uns (sie) zu versuchen und uns (ihnen) zu schaden.
Jesus! Maria! (3mal)
Heiliger Michael, streite für uns! Heilige Schutzengel, bewahret uns vor allen Fallstricken des bösen Feindes!"

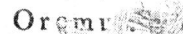

Abb. 5
Exorzismus
gegen Dämonen
und Kruzifix.

> 262 SECTIO VIII. *Ordo triplex*
>
> Oremus
>
> Deus, & Pater D[omini nostr]i JEsu Christi, invoco Nomen sanc[tum] tuum, & clementiam tuam supplex [exoro], ut adversus hunc, & omnem im[mundum] spiritum, qui vexat hoc plasma tuu[m, au]xilium præstare digne[ris. Per e]undem Dominum nostrum JEs[um ...]
>
> *His finitis [Exorcista loco ali]ali sedens ceu judex a Deo [constitutus, vo]ut non tamen clamorosa Exo[rcismu]m pronuntiet, ut sequitur:*
>
> EZORCISMUS [AD] DÆMONEM
> AB ENERGUM[ENO E]XPELLENDUM.
>
> Contra te male[dicte] dæmon (*vel* si plures estis) contra vos, [spirit]us immundi, & apostatici, qui Domi[num] Deum vestrum dereliquistis, & oblit[i estis] Dei Creatoris vestri, constitutus sum a[...], ego N. Minister Christi, & Ecclesiæ; id [ea auc]toritate, quam accepi a Deo, & ab E[cclesia] in ordine Exorcistatus, in Nomine sanc[tissimæ] Trinitatis, & in virtute Domini nostri J[Esu Ch]risti, præcipio vobis omnibus, & sing[ulis, e]t in omnibus, quæ nunc vobis præcepe[ro, sin]e ulla mora ad amussim mihi obediatis.
>
> Præcipio ergo vobis eadem auctoritate, ut in exitu vestro non audeatis vos, nec quicun-

Hier ist das Spritzen von Weihwasser angezeigt. Dann wird der nachfolgende Segen gesprochen und an den mit einem Kreuz bezeichneten Stellen mit dem Kruzifix ein Kreuzzeichen gemacht:

"Der Segen † des Vaters, die † Liebe des Sohnes und die Kraft † des Heiligen Geistes; der mütterliche Schutz der Himmelskönigin, der Beistand der hl. Engel und die Fürbitte der Heiligen – sei mit uns (dir, ihnen) und begleite uns (dich, sie) überall und allezeit! Amen."

Autor

KURT LUSSI
geb. 1956 in Luzern, Wissenschaftlicher Mitarbeiter am Historischen Museum Luzern und Konservator der Schenkung Dr. Josef Zihlmann. Tätigkeit als Referent, Autor und Ausstellungsmacher. Forschungsschwerpunkte sind die Praxis des Volksglaubens und der Volksmedizin im Alpenraum. Herausgeber der Reihe "Volksfrömmigkeit und Brauchtum" sowie freier Mitarbeiter verschiedener Jahrbücher und Fachzeitschriften.
Kontakt: E-Mail: k-lussi@bluewin.ch

Literatur

LUSSI, K. 2002: *Im Reich der Geister und tanzenden Hexen. Jenseitsvorstellungen, Dämonen und Zauberglaube*. Aarau.
NIEDERBERGER, F. 1910: *Religiöse Sitten und Sagen aus Unterwalden*, 2. Teil. Sarnen.
SCHEUBER, J. K 1960: *Bauern-Gebetbuch*. Einsiedeln.
SCHMID, J. 1972: *Collectanea Chronica und denkwürdige Sachen pro Chronica Lucernensi et Helvetiae* (Quellen und Forschungen zur Kulturgeschichte von Luzern und der Innerschweiz), Bd. 4, 3. Teil. Luzern.
WUTTKE, A. 1925: *Der deutsche Volksaberglaube der Gegenwart*. Leipzig.
ZENETTI, L. 1987: *Das Jesuskind. Verehrung und Darstellung*. München.
ZIHLMANN, J. 1989: *Volkserzählungen und Bräuche. Handbuch luzernischer Volkskunde*. Hitzkirch.

MAGIC-RELIGIOUS HEALING RITUALS IN CENTRAL SWITZERLAND*

by Kurt Lussi

The secret world at the foot of the Pilatus**

It is not really visible from afar that the area at the foot of the Pilatus is covered with magic-religious significant points where the spirits of the past live since the beginning of mankind. Except for the strange stones, the peculiar crosses and the godforsaken chapels, nothing can really be seen of this mysterious otherworld which covers the county north of the city of Luzern like an invisible net.

Certainly there are better known and for the foreigner more accessible regions than the Low Alps. The country does have more legendary sights than the erratic block of Roggliswil which is hardly known outside the Canton Luzern.
The Devil Stone ("Teufelsstein") of Göschenen is well known across the borders. Only by chance it was spared from the blasting during the construction of the Gotthard-Tunnel. Pressed by the local population, the constructors moved the

---

Fig. 1: Double cross at Sigigen, Kanton Luzern, Switzerland. It protects against the host of the death passing by in stormy nights. In the background is Pilatus, the realm of spirits, dwarfs, and dragons. * Translated by Björn Lehmann. ** Mountain close to Luzern.

rock at that time. Now it stands a little lost between the freeway and the wild, roaring Reuss. Flagged and displayed it is merely a dead relict and a sign for the toll taken from the steadily increasing traffic. Every day passenger vehicles and heavy trucks drive across its pristine location, as if they had to prevent the return of a centuries-old myth.

The comparison between the erratic block of Roggliswil and the Devil Stone of Göschenen is a good sign of the contrasts which define life at the the foot of the Alps. Outwardly, Switzerland acts modern and open-minded. However for the outsider, hardly noticeable, there exists another world in secret which is largely marked by magic-religious views.

The belief in nature animated by gods and ancestors did not vanish after the adoption of Christianity. Instead, the newly introduced religion mixed with the preexisting beliefs by reinterpreting pagan rites into christian ones. On the other hand, people have interpreted many christian beliefs in their own way and adapted them to the existing. Out of the mixture of christian religion and the traditions arose a world view, in the course of time, which is neither purely christian nor pagan. Numerous chapels, crosses and Bildstöcke (posts on ways or roads made of stone or wood with a crucifix or an image of a saint) which define the living space of Central Switzerland until today, are not only holy places in christian terms. Many of them are at the same time scenes of eerie tales where - in spite of the sacredness of these places - spirits without heads, black dogs and the Türstzug, the army of souls on their way to eternity, appear.

These conceptions had a very strong influence on the beliefs of the origin of illnesses and healing. The illness is caused by pagan powers with an obviously negative effect. The healing results from christian rituals or from rituals which are adapted to Christianity and are regarded as positive.

In this modern world the human being is pulled to and fro. It trusts modern medicine but stays attached to traditon at the same time.

Traditional beliefs on illness and healing

Like all people in the world, people in Central Switzerland as well believe that sickness is caused by evil spirits or by the devil himself. According to this concept, illness is an independent entity which can take possession of a person, grab him or her, tortures and annoys until he or she dies, unless the person is freed from the demon. This belief has been maintained in common language. People do not just get sick, but the illness grabs and throws them into bed.

This can be vividly seen in nightmares ("Albtraum"). People who are infested with an "Alb" (mythical creature) feel as if demons are creeping up to them and crawling slowly from the feet up to the throat. A feeling like being seized arises. The following experience shows that illness is regarded as a "thing" or an "entity":

"Maybe two months later I woke up again and half-asleep, I felt like there was something lying on my body. It pressed down on me and it took a lot of effort to regain control over my body. As soon as I had regained control the pressure vanished. Before that I couldn't even blink. This kept constantly repeating. There were times when I woke up by the trembling of my body which perceived the presence of the

entity before it reached my consciousness. The trembling only faded slowly after my awakening and I couldn't go back to sleep for another hour. During the following "visits" the pressure became stronger; I was literally pressed into the bed. My body was totally paralysed and only with strongest willpower, sometimes fighting as long as ten minutes, I "got my body back." Always, when I had shaken off the pressure, I felt like I noticed the thing disappear in the bathroom."

Along with demons and spirits, evil people can also cause illness by using magic. And, finally, God can punish people for offences with sickness. This means that someone who does not live in harmony with God's amendments will get sick. For this reason, penance pilgrimages are undertaken and people call upon the saints for protection and help.

Fig. 2:
The holy Antonius of Padua. The blessing "Ecce crucem.", named after him protects against obsession. With the attached relic the picture becomes a guarding amulett.

Healing

The magic remedies which can be used to expel illnesses are almost too numerous to overview.
They can be subdivided into prayers (blessing prayers, magic spells), magic rites, objects, (healing herbs and animals with magic effects), living humans (blood, urine, saliva, sweat), bodyparts (teeth of the dead) and the elements earth, water and fire.
Widespread and still in practice today are the ecclesiastical or magic-religious remedies and rituals. Part of these are the relic cults, the illness saints, pilgrimages, religious prayers (e.g. exorcism), patient blessings and objects that came into contact with sacred or holy artefacts. The anticipated goal of these prayers, rites and objects is to encounter the powers of evil in another state of consciousness.

The following three examples refer to the calling of illness saints, healing with sacred objects (Loretokind) and sickness exorcism. The interceding calling of an illness saint is the easiest and most practiced magic-religious ritual, exorcism the strongest. In between lies the use of objects which are sacred and have come into contact with a mercy image (Loretokind).

1. Saints as helpers during illnesses – St. Burkard von Beinwil

Saints are people who saw the light of God in their lifetime and became one with it after their death.
They are represented with a light-disc, the Nimbus (halo). This form of presentation is not arbitrary but is based on real experiences made by divinely gifted people in states of mystic depth. According to the teachings of the Catholic church, saints do not work wonders but they are the connecting link between God and human beings. Therefore in the Church prayers they are not addressed directly but always with the use of intercessions.

Special events in the life and death of a saint make him the patron of specific illnesses. The numerous saint legends and prayer books provide information about the competence of a saint. The fourteen most important Catholic saints are combined as a group, the fourteen helpers in times of trouble. Depending on the area and circumstances some are omitted and replaced by others.
The most important and common helpers (throughout the area of the Alps) in case of sickness are:

St. Blasiu	problems with the throat
St. Erasmus	bodily pain (lower body, stomach)
St. Veit	epilepsy
St. Dyonisios	headaches
St. Margaretha	patron of the pregnant
St. Katharina	hard language
St. Sebastian	plague and plague-like diseases
St. Apollonia	toothaches

St. Burkard von Beinwil is a saint who is only called upon in Central Switzerland (Cantons Aargau, Luzern and Zug) for general sicknesses. It is not the first bishop of Würzburg but the affable priest of the same name of Beinwil in Freiamt

(Switzerland). St. Burkard von Beinwil was born in Langenmatt, on a farm above the monastery Muri in the twelfth century.
He died on the18th of May, 1192 with the reputation of holiness. 1228 he was already called "St. Burkard" in documents of the monastery Muri. The water from the well close to the church is known to have healing powers.

The healing process works with the concentration of the mind with the help of prayers and meditation. To reinforce this procedure the patient drinks from the holy fountain by going there himself or having water brought to him. In the state of mystical depth the patient's dialogue with God and the saint takes place.
Now the invocation starts: the sick person turns to God with the following petition to heal him from his illness by intercession of the saint.

"Almighty God, you have honoured your faithful servant Burkard with wonderful gifts. I ask you, oh Lord, by the the powerful intercession of your priest Burkard, liberate me and my people from all sicknesses and evil of the body and the soul; give me patience in my suffering, courage in all tests which you impose on me. Give me the power to serve you like he did, to praise you ever and ever and announce your mighty name.
With Jesus Christ, our Lord. Amen."

2. Blessings of the sick with the Loretokind of Salzburg

In Christianity worship and reverence are reserved for God only. As long as the saints are not called upon in terms of intercession saint-reverence contradicts the teaching of the Roman-Catholic church.
But since people's belief can hardly endure the admiration of only one god the church had to make some concessions over the course of time.

One of which is the worship of mercy images. According to christian teachings images do not work wonders. Nonetheless there are signs of miracles showing, the catholic Handpostille (small reference booklet) says that they are signs of God being persuaded by the intercession of Christ, Maria or the saints which they represent.

However, within people's beliefs there is a vision which dates back to pre-christian times according to which mercy images are filled with special powers.
The same is true for objects or pictures which have been praised and have come into contact with the original.

Healing ritual with the Loretokind

A good example is the "Loretokind" in the Capuchin convent in Salzburg. A small ivory-figure (almost 10cm in height) represents the child Jesus. It is kept in a wooden box which is called "Stammenhaus" or "Stammhäusel".

Outside of the convent's trading area replicas of the mercy image or small devotion pictures are privately used to heal illnesses. They are distributed at the convent or sent by mail upon request. Before the shipment the figures and the pictures are brought into contact with the original.

Fig. 3: The child of Loreto in Salzburg. Copy of the miraculous image, that had touched the original in the convent of the Capuchines.

During the actual healing the picture is put on the head or the aching spot. While putting it there (the so-called "putting-on" (Aufsetzen)) the following prayer must be recited.
Every time when a cross appears in the text a blessing cross must be made with the small figure or the devotion picture. (The prayer is printed on the back of the pictures.)

Blessing prayer

"May you be blessed by God †, the Father who created you, † the Son who unbans you, † the Holy Ghost who has sanctified you. May the blessing of the most holy Trinity be with you on all your paths and prevent your body and your soul from all evil. Amen.

Bless us with your divine child, oh you immaculate Virgin Mother Maria! Oh, almighty child Jesus full of God's abundance so that you are wholly love and kindness, opulent for all who call upon you.
You, wellspring of life and holiness, of complete solace, you, our peace, our conciliation, you salvation of all who believe in you, your heart I entrust (this soul, this concern, this suffering, ...). Look upon it and then follow what your love tells you. [...] Be our Jesus! Be our saviour! Amen."

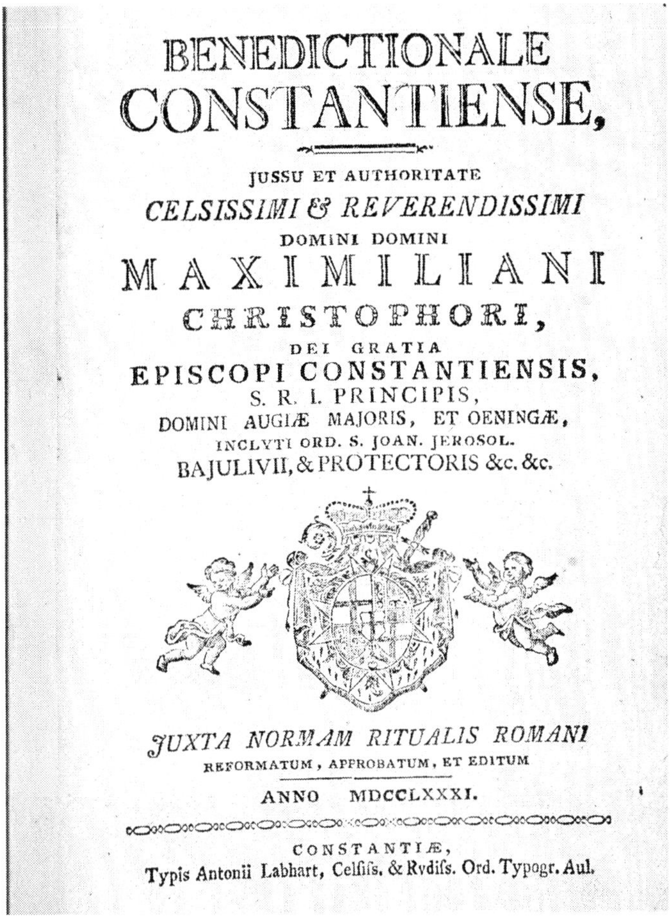

Fig. 4:
Benedictionale Constantiense of 1781. Find attached in the appendix exorcisms against different forms of obsession.

3. Private exorcism

Unexplainable or long-lasting illnesses are often attributed to posession by a devil or demon. The kind of illness only plays a small role according to an exorcism booklet printed in Konstanz in 1729: "the devil can imitate all thinkable illnesses which means that a natural illness can hardly be differentiated from an evil one." In order to find out wether the sickness has a natural or a supernatural cause a religious person makes a cross above the patient according to the mentioned exorcist booklet. Then he or she commands the demon - if it is responsible for the suffering - to stop immediately. If the patient is freed from his pains for a short period of time the suffering is caused by supernatural powers which can be fought with means of the church.

Exorcism for the sick

The patient is healed by a specially authorized priest who calls upon the demon in the body in the name of God and commands it to leave the sick person. It is

> 262　SECTIO VIII.　*Ordo triplex*
>
> Oremus
>
> Deus, & Pater Domini nostri JEfu Chrifti, invoco Nomen fanctum tuum, & clementiam tuam fupplex ore, ut adverfus hunc, & omnem immundum fpiritum, qui vexat hoc plafma tuum, auxilium præftare digneris. Per eundem Dominum noftrum JEfum.
>
> *His finitis Exorcifta veluti fedens ceu judex a Deo conftitutus, gravi non tamen clamorofa Exorcifmum pronuntiet, ut fequitur:*
>
> EZORCISMUS AD DÆMONEM
> AB ENERGUMENO EXPELLENDUM.
>
> Contra te maledicte dæmon (*vel* fi plures eftis) contra vos, fpiritus immundi, & apoftatici, qui Dominum Deum veftrum dereliquiftis, & obliti eftis Dei Creatoris veftri, conftitutus fum a Deo ego N. Minifter Chrifti, & Ecclefiæ; ideo auctoritate, quam accepi a Deo, & ab Ecclefia in ordine Exorciftatus, in Nomine fanctæ Trinitatis, & in virtute Domini noftri JEfu Chrifti, præcipio vobis omnibus, & fingulis ut in omnibus, quæ nunc vobis præcepero fine ulla mora ad amuffim mihi obediatis.
>
> Præcipio ergo vobis eadem auctoritate, ut in exitu veftro non audeatis vos, nec quicun-

Fig. 5: Exorcism against demon and crucifix

important that the priest strictly complies with church regulations. He must not only choose the right texts but must follow the correct order as well. Instructions and texts are found in the appendix of the official church benediction.
A simpler form is a private exorcism which may be spoken by everyone with the use of the cross sign and the holy water. In private exorcism the exorcist calls upon God and the saints as well. Then he commands the demon to leave his whereabouts and not to come back anymore.

Private exorcism

Before the exorcism prayer starts, a crucifix and holy water are provided. After a few preparing prayers (psalms and All-Hallows-litanies) the exorcist speaks at the bed of the patient:
"In the name of Jesus and Maria I command you, you infernal spirits move away from us (them) and from this (that) place and do not dare coming back and to try us (them) and to harm us (them). Jesus! Maria! (three times) Holy Michael, fight for us! Holy guardian angels, save us from all the pitfalls of the evil enemy!"

Now holy water is being sprayed. Then the following blessing is spoken and a cross sign is made with the crucifix at the marked spots:

"The blessing † of the father, the † love of the son and the power † of the holy ghost; the motherly protection of the heavenly queen, the assistance of the holy angels and the intercession of the saints – may you be with us (you, them) and accompany us (you, them) everywhere and forever! Amen."

Author
KURT LUSSI
born 1956 in Luzern, scientific associate of the Historic Museum of Luzern and official responsible for the conservation of the donation Dr. Josef Zihlmann. Function as abstractor, author and manager of exhibitions. Main points of research are the practice of people's beliefs and people's medicine in the Alps. Editor of the magazine "People's devoutness and tradition" and freelancer of different yearbooks and professional journals.
Contact: E-Mail: k-lussi@bluewin.ch

References
LUSSI, K. 2002: *Im Reich der Geister und tanzenden Hexen. Jenseitsvorstellungen, Dämonen und Zauberglaube.* Aarau.
NIEDERBERGER, F. 1910: *Religiöse Sitten und Sagen aus Unterwalden, 2. Teil.* Sarnen.
SCHEUBER, J. K 1960: *Bauern-Gebetbuch.* Einsiedeln.
SCHMID, J. 1972: *Collectanea Chronica und denkwürdige Sachen pro Chronica Lucernensi et Helvetiae* (Quellen und Forschungen zur Kulturgeschichte von Luzern und der Innerschweiz), Bd. 4, 3. Teil. Luzern.
WUTTKE, A. 1925: *Der deutsche Volksaberglaube der Gegenwart.* Leipzig.
ZENETTI, L. 1987: *Das Jesuskind. Verehrung und Darstellung.* München.
ZIHLMANN, J. 1989: *Volkserzählungen und Bräuche. Handbuch luzernischer Volkskunde.* Hitzkirch.

MAGISCHE HEILUNG - VOLKSMEDIZINISCHE PRAKTIKEN DES VULTURGEBIETES SÜDITALIENS*

von Cassandra Quave & Andrea Pieroni

Einführung

In der medizinischen, anthropologischen und ethnopharmakologischen Forschung ist die Evaluation von Feldforschungsdaten ist von zentraler Bedeutung. Diese werden mit sozialwissenschaftlichen als auch naturwissenschaftlichen Methoden erhoben um die interdisziplinären Aspekte der traditionellen Heilrituale und der Volksheilmittel zu studieren.

Als Teil einer ethnobiologischen und anthroprologischen -medizinischen Feldstudie aus den nördlichen Lucania- oder der Basilicata-Region in Süditalien, haben wir Daten über die dort auftretenden Krankheiten und volksmedizinischen Praktiken erhoben, die bis heute in drei kleinen arbëreschen Gemeinden angewendet werden, nämlich:

Barile (*Barilli*), Ginestra (*xhinestra*) & Maschito (*mashquiti*) und zwei benachbarte italienische Gemeinden: Ripacandida und Venosa. Obwohl über 50 botanische Arten und über 20 tierische und industrielle Produkte dokumentiert wurden, die in den Ethnopharmakologien dieser Region speziell angewendet werden (PIERONI et al. in press), werden hier nur die Quellen diskutiert, die in Zusammenhang mit magischen oder spirituellen Heilungsriten stehen.

Vulturgebiet Lucania

Das vulkanische Vulturgebiet der nördlichen Basilikata (Lucania) besteht aus 7 Dörfern und kleinen Städten, die hauptsächlich von Landwirtschaft und Fabrikarbeit leben. Die sanften Hügel des Landes sind übersät mit Weingärten (*vitis vinifera var, Aglia nico*), Olivenhainen (*olea europaea* und *Durum*) und

---

Abb. 1: "Zia Elèna" (E.M., geb. 1908),eine 93-jährige Heilerin von Maschito
* Übersetzung aus dem Englischen: Judith Blab und Sandra Lüttich

Weizenfeldern (*triticum durum*). Die vorherrschende Religion ist der Katholizismus und der ältere Anteil der Bevölkerung besteht vorwiegend aus frommen Christen - das trifft vor allem auf Frauen zu, die mehrheitlich mindestens einmal täglich zur Kirche gehen.

Das Vulturgebiet ist insofern einzigartig, da es dietraditionelle süditalienische Kultur erhält, als auch auf der schnell verfallenden arbëresch - albanischen Kultur fußt. Diese ist in den drei Dörfern Ginestra, Barile und Maschito noch zu finden. Die Konzentration der arbëresch-albanischen Kultur in diesem Gebiet ist recht auffällig, vor allem wenn man bedenkt, dass nur fünf solche Gemeinschaften in ganz Lucania existieren. Diese drei Dörfer sind auch abgetrennt vom Großteil der anderen arbëreschen Gemeinden, die sich in Calabrien, Sizilien, Campanien und Apulien konzentrieren.

Die Arbëreschë

Die *Arbëreschë* sind Nachkommen von Südalbanern, die sich während des 15. Jahrhunderts in diversen Inlandsgebieten der süditalienischen Regionen ansiedelten. Heutzutage leben schätzungsweise 80.000 arbëresch-albanisch sprechende Menschen (allesamt zweisprachig mit italienisch) in isolierten italienischen Dörfern.

Diese Zahl mag hoch angesetzt sein, da sie auf der gesamten Bevölkerungsanzahl der "Arbëresch-Gemeinden" basiert und nicht auf der Anzahl von Menschen innerhalb jeder einzelnen Gemeinde, die wirklich die Sprache sprechen können. Dieser Anteil kann in vielen Orten nicht größer als 10% sein.

Die arbëresch-albanische Sprache gehört zu der toskisch-albanischen Untergruppe der albanischen Sprachen, welche die einzig überlebenden Sprachen der alten Paleo-Balkan-Gruppe (Illyrien, Messapic und Thrakien) der indoeuropäischen Familie darstellen (AAVV 2000). Arbëresch -albanisch wird von "UNESCO Rotbuch der gefährdeten Sprachen" als eine "gefährdete Sprache" klassifiziert (SALMINEN 1999). Die kulturellen Überreste des Arbëreschen in der beobachteten Region sind nur bei einigen Vertretern der älteren Generation (55 und mehr Jahre alt) noch vorhanden. Sie erinnern sich zwar noch an die Sprache und die Volksbräuche, aber sie spielen im täglichen Leben keine aktive Rolle mehr.

Ethnomedizin

Traditionelle Volksheilmittel hatten immer einen wichtigen Platz in den traditionellen Heilsystemen rund um die Welt. Über die Zeit hinweg entwickelten die Menschen verschiedene Methoden zur Heilung von Krankheit mittels Gebrauch von einheimischen Pflanzen und Anwendungen ihres sozio-religiösen Glaubenssystems. Indigenes, volkstümliches und traditionelles Heilen bezieht sich auf "unorthodoxe therapeutische Praktiken, die auf indigenen kulturellen Traditionen basieren und die außerhalb des offiziellen Gesundheitssystems operieren" (JILEK 1994).

Diese Heiltraditionen sind notwendigerweise kulturell spezifisch und werden oft nur in dem entsprechenden sozio-kulturellen Rahmen mit Erfolg angewandt. Genesung von Krankheit innerhalb eines traditionellen volksmedizinischen Systems hängt auch von einer starken Verknüpfung mit spirituellen Glaubensmodellen ab und ist ein Ausdruck des Plazeboeffektes. Unkonventionelle, medizinische Praktiken werden oft dargestellt als Manifestationen von

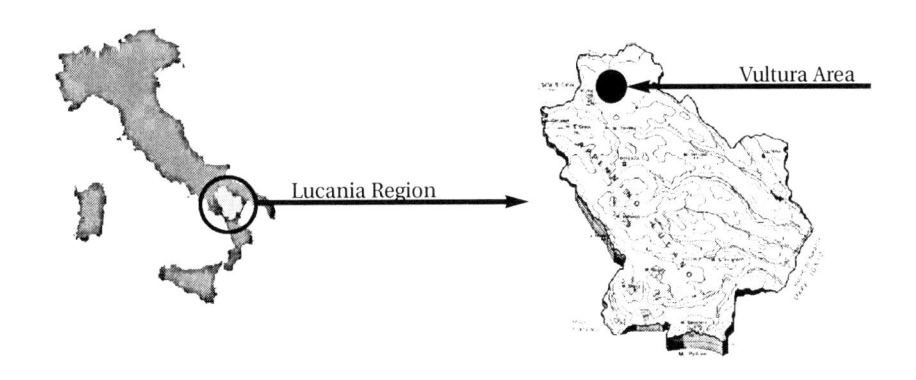

Abb. 2: Geografische Lokalisation des Vulture Gebietes.

magischen Dingen und sind angesiedelt im Bereich von Aberglaube und Religion. WAYLAND HAND definierte in seiner Analyse über die magische Komponente der Volksheilung die Wichtigkeit des Glaubens an den therapeutischen Erfolg, indem er feststellt:
"Diese magischen Handlungen, die als begleitende Umstände zu mehr Routine führen und oft gewöhnliche Arten der medizinischen Behandlung sind, mögen entweder auf einer übernatürlichen oder sakralen Kraft basieren. .–...Sie bringen ein zusätzliches Maß an Kraft und Heilungseffekt bei einem hingebungsvollen Glaubenden – und sie allein - sichern den Erfolg der Therapie " (HAND 1980).
In diesem Bereich der Medizin wird der Heilungsprozess durch das Zusammenwirken von symbolischen Objekten, Nummern, gesprochenen Formeln und Handlungen verstärkt.
Gemäß den Standards der Biomedizin ist dieser Erfolg nur durch den Plazeboeffekts erklärbar. Im Vulturgebiet sind Heiler und Patienten der gleichen Überzeugung: "*chi no crede no puo essere aiutato*" oder "der/ die nicht glaubt, dem kann nicht geholfen werden". Diese Aussage ist ein Beispiel einer allgemeinen Erkenntnis, dass therapeutischer Erfolg, in dieser speziellen volksmedizinischen Rahmenarbeit, abhängig ist vom Willen des Patienten, an die Behandlung zu glauben.
Folglich nimmt der Heiler die Rolle eines Führers denn eines Arztes ein. Seine Arbeit ist es, den Patienten auf einem Weg der Selbsterkenntnis zur Heilung zu führen. Dazu stehen Verfahren der Autosuggestion und psychotherapeutische Methoden zur Verfügung.

Krankheit wird nicht nur durch magische Verfahren geheilt, sondern hat auch magische Ursachen. Im Falle von gewissen Krankheiten wie *mal d´arco* ("Krankheit des Regenbogens") und einigen Fällen von *malocchio* ("Böser Blick") ist eine wechselseitige Beziehung zwischen der Erkrankung und ihrer Heilung klar zu erkennen.
Der Glaube an "magische Ansteckung" und ihre Rolle in der Übertragung von Krankheit zwischen lebenden (und nicht lebenden) Dingen bestimmt den Umgang mit Leiden und beeinflusst den Heilungsprozess an sich.

Das ethnomedizinische Konstrukt
In der traditionellen Heilkunde existieren spezifische ethnomedizinische Kategorien in der Vulturgegend (QUAVE & PIERONI 2001). Es konnten sieben Unterteilungen von Krankheiten identifiziert werden, die durch die Anwendung von folgenden Arten magisch-religiöser Ritualen geheilt werden können:

- Gesprochene Formeln (oft begleitet von einer leichten Massage)
- Gesprochene Formeln und biologische Stoffe, als Medizin angewandt
- Gesprochene Formeln und biologische Stoffe, als rituelle Objekte benutzt
- Gesprochene Formeln und nicht biologische Stoffe, für rituelle Objekte
- Gesprochene Formeln und westliche Arzneimittelkunde als Medizin

und solche Krankheiten, die durch nicht-magische Behandlung geheilt werden: **Biologische** (pflanzliche oder tierische Heilmittel), sowie **industrielle** Produkte und Arzneimittel, sowie andere medizinische Verfahren, die in der westlichen schulmedizinischen Behandlung unter der Anweisungen eines Arztes angewandt werden.
Obwohl jede Unterteilung dieses Aufbaus eine wichtige Rolle in der medizinischen Versorgung der Region spielt, werden wir uns nur auf solche Krankheiten konzentrieren, die den Gebrauch von gesprochene Formeln in einem magisch-religiösen Zusammenhang stellen.
Volksmedizinische Krankheiten wurden identifiziert und werden benutzt, um solche Erscheinungen wie Kopfschmerzen, Nasenbluten, Brustentzündung, penile Entzündungen, Migräne, Bauchschmerzen, Unterleibsschmerzen, Hautentzündungen, Hepatitis, Mumps und Zahnschmerzen zu beschreiben. Der Aufbau dieser volkstümlichen Klassifizierungen von Krankheiten und Leiden ist komplex. Er beschreibt Krankheitsursachen, die entweder magisch- spirituell oder biologisch strukturiert sind, abhängig vom Krankheitsbild. In diesem Zusammenhang ist interessant zu bemerken, dass alle Kranheiten magisch-spirituellen Ursprungs mit Gebeten geheilt werden können, nicht jedoch alle Krankheiten biologischer Genese. Es existiert eine strikte Trennung zwischen diesen Krankheiten, die man mit Gebeten heilen kann und solchen, die eine phytotherapeutische oder pharmazeutische Behandlung benötigen.

Quelli che possono aiutare (die, die helfen können)
Wer sind die Heiler? In der Vulturregion werden sie eigentlich nicht mit dem Wort "Heiler" (*aiutare*) beschrieben, sondern mit "Helfer" (*aiutare*) assoziiert. Diese "Helfer" sind in der Region weit verbreitet, aber scheinen verstärkt in den kleinen Arbëreschdörfern bei Barille und Ginestra aufzutreten. Dort ist die traditionelle Kultur noch nicht komplett von der dominanten italienischen Kultur verdrängt worden. Die Arberësh-Heiler werden in diesem Gebiet aufgrund des sozio-kulturellen Wandels immer weniger.
Ripacandida z.B ist der nächste Nachbar von Ginestra. Dort gibt es heute nur noch einen nicht mehr praktizierender Heiler. Viele Ältere dieser Gemeinschaft konnten sich noch an verschiedene andere "Helfer" erinnern.
Das Schwinden von traditionellen Heilern in dieser beschriebenen Gemeinschaft hat auch zum Verschwinden von kulturgebundenen Krankheiten wie den "bösen

Blick", *malocchio*, in der Bevölkerung geführt. Dieses offensichtliche Mangel an Vertretern der magisch- religiösen Heikunst in Ripacandida war überraschend, besonders im Vergleich zu dem nahe wohnenden Ginestravolk, in dem es mindestens sechs Frauen und einen Mann gibt, die bei spezifischen Leiden helfen können.
Ein chakteristisches Merkmal der traditionellen Heiler ist ihr fortgeschrittenes Alter.

Der Älteste ist 93 Jahre alt, der Jüngste ist 51, durchschnittlich herrscht das Alter von 60 oder 70 vor. Die Heiler beherrschen die Formeln und Rituale sowie die häufigsten Volkskrankheiten (*malocchio cigli alla testa*) wie Migräne, Wurmbefall (helminthiasis) und *mal di gola* (Halsschmerzen). Die lesekundigen Heilern (meist unter 75 Jahre) führen zudem kleine Büchlein, in denen sie seltener werdende magische Krankheiten und deren Behandlung dokumentieren *mal viento* ("Windkrankheit"), *fuoco morto* ("tote Feuerkrankheit"), *fuoco di sant antonio* ("Sankt Antonius Feuerkrankheit"), und *mal d´arco* ("Regenbogenkrankheit") erwähnt wurden).
Diese Notizbücher wurden manchmal innerhalb der Familien von einem Heiler an seinen Nachfolger weitergereicht. Alle der untersuchten Notizbücher waren in dem gebräuchlichen, süditalienischen Dialekt geschrieben. In den Abëreschgemeinschaften gibt es heute nur zwei anerkannte "Helfer" "- eine 93 Jahre alte Frau aus Maschito und eine 80 Jahre alte Frau aus Barile, die fähig waren, den Heilungsformeln in der traditionellen abëreschen Sprache auszusprechen. Heute benutzen sie jedoch selten diese Sprache in ihren Heilzeremonien und bevorzugen stattdessen den lokalen, süditalienischen Dialekt, der von allen ihren Patienten verstanden wird.
Es wurde nie klar festgestellt, warum oder wann der Gebrauch der arbëreschen Sprache im Heilungsprozess verloren gegangen ist, doch es wird vermutet, dass vielleicht die besser "zu verstehende" Sprache schrittweise dominant wurde, genauso wie die Vermischung von traditioneller arbërescher Kultur mit der norditalienischen Kultur. Es ist wahrscheinlich, dass die Worterkennung oder zumindest die Vertrautheit mit dem Klang der formelhaften Reime eine wichtige Rolle spielt und zum Erfolg des Plazeboeffekts beiträgt. Ebenso wichtig ist zu bemerken, dass nicht alle Heiler fähig sind, alle Leiden in diesem magisch-religiösen Schema zu behandeln.
Manche werden als Spezialisten angesehen wie z.B. Knochenheiler, die nur kleinere orthopädische Verletzungen und Muskelleiden behandeln, sowie andere, die nur einen bestimmten Typ von Leiden heilen (z.B. *malocchio*). Es gibt auch "Meisterhelfer", die Kenntnisse über eine Reihe von Leiden besitzen, und die sowohl verehrt als auch aufgesucht werden von ihren eigenen und umgebenden Gemeinschaften wegen ihrer besonderen Heilungsfähigkeiten.
Als letztes ist eine spezifische Klasse von Heilern zu erwähnen, die nicht als "Helfer" in diesem System betrachtet werden, sondern die Fähigkeit besitzen, eine spezielle Krankheit zu heilen, die *nervi accavallati* ("gekreuzte Nerven"). Dies ist eine eigene Krankheit, in der ein unverheiratetes Geschwisterpaar (nicht geschlechtsabhängig), die noch zuhause wohnen und deren Vater gestorben ist, durch eine spezielle Zeremonie, die eine Beschwörungsformel und rituelle Gegenstände einschließt, helfen können. Diese Geschwister sind jedoch nicht fähig, eine andere Krankheit als diese zu heilen.

Der Heilungsprozess

Ein generelles Muster, das der Komplexität dieses medizinischen Systems zugrunde liegt, ist in der Sequenz des rituellen Heilungsprozesses zu erkennen. Der erste Schritt, wie auch in jedem anderen Volks- oder biomedizinischen System, ist die Präsentation der Krankheit vor einem anerkannten Heiler und der Beginn der Diagnosestellung. Wenn ein Patient an einer Krankheit leidet, die sich physisch äußert, zum Beispiel durch einen Hautausschlag, wird meist zuerst der Rat einer älteren, weiblichen Verwandten oder einer Nachbarin eingeholt, die als primäre Ratgeber dienen.

Nachdem die Symptome des Leidens mit dem Patienten besprochen worden sind, lenken diese Ratgeber die Patienten in Richtung einer der sieben Bereiche der Behandlung dieses ethnomedizinischen Konstrukts. Ist die Ratgeberin der Meinung, die Krankheit sei das Resultat einer magisch-rituellen Übertragung oder Vergiftung, wird der Patient angewiesen, den "Helfer" der Gemeinde aufzusuchen, der als Spezialist für dieses spezielle Leiden angesehen wird. Falls ein solcher Spezialist nicht in der eigenen Gemeinschaft existiert, der Patient aber überzeugt ist, dass das Leiden aus einer Form von magischer Übertragung oder Vergiftung resultiert, so wird die Unterstützung eines "Helfers" einer benachbarten Gemeinde ersucht. Ganz nach Brauch der süditalienischen Kultur, werden Besucher warmherzig herein gebeten. Man sitzt zusammen bei einer warmen Tasse Espresso, und so beginnt auch oft der Heilungsprozess.

Nach allgemeiner Unterhaltung beginnt der Patient, dem "Helfer" die Symptome seines Leidens zu schildern und höflich um Hilfe zu bitten. Die unterschiedlichen Mittel zur Diagnose sind jeweils abhängig von Heiler und den speziell dargebotenen Symptomen. Bei dem Beispiel des Hautausschlags, welcher den drei Krankheitskategorien (*mal viento*, *fuoco morto* und *fuoco di Sant´Antonio*) zugeordnet wird, untersucht der "Helfer" die physische Präsentation des Ausschlages gründlich. Er wird dann einen Beurteilungsprozess einleiten, indem er den Patienten dazu befragt, wo dieser sich in den letzten Tagen aufgehalten hat und ob ihm irgend etwas aufgefallen sei, wie z.B. ungewöhnliche Winde (kalt oder stark).

Diese Befragung nach dem Aufenthaltsort ist wichtig für die Diagnose bestimmter Hautausschläge, da die Ätiologie als magisch-spirituelle Kraft erkannt wird, die man in Gegenden antrifft, wo in der Vergangenheit ein Mord stattgefunden hat. Daraufhin kann das Leiden abhängig von der Darstellung der Krankheit und den magisch-spirituellen Indikatoren diagnostiziert werden.

Nur durch die Erkenntnis der Ursachen kann der nächste Schritt der Behandlung begonnen werden.

Obwohl die Behandlung bei jeder Krankheit anders verläuft und abhängig von der Darstellung und der zugeordneten Ursache des Leidens ist, existieren doch einige generelle Trends in der Kunst des magisch-spirituellen Heilens. Die Heilungszeremonie beginnt damit, dass sich sowohl "Helfer" als auch Patient - gemäß des katholischen Brauches - selbst bekreuzigen (*nome della croce*). Jede Prozedur wird begleitet von einer gesprochenen Formel oder einem Gebet, das speziell an die zu behandelnde Krankheit gerichtet ist. Diese Formel wird gewöhnlich drei Mal wiederholt, gefolgt von drei *Padre Nostro* (Vater Unser), drei *Ave Maria* und drei *Gloria al Padre*. Abhängig jeweils von den Vorlieben des Heilers wird mitunter auch auf ein oder zwei dieser katholischen Gebete verzichtet. Kreuze werden in jeder Behandlung gemacht, entweder direkt über der Körperregion ohne körperlichen Kontakt (bei Hautausschlägen üblich), oder

durch körperlichen Kontakt im betroffenen Bereich (üblich in Fällen, in denen auch Massage angewendet wird).
Abhängig von der Krankheit wird diese Bewegung mit einem rituellen Gegenstand oder einfach mit der Hand des Heilers ausgeführt. In Fällen, in denen ein rituelles Objekt verwendet wird (außer bei *pelo alla menna* = Brusthaarkrankheit), kann dieses als eine Art beschützende Barriere zwischen Patient und Heiler dienen, welche die Passage biologisch ansteckender (in diesem System bisher nur als "magisch ansteckend" verstanden) Krankheiten verhindert. Alle Krankheiten, die den Gebrauch eines rituelles Objekt erfordern (außer *mal di pancia* = Bauchschmerzen), müssen bei Nacht behandelt werden und stehen oft in Verbindung mit speziellen spirituellen Einschränkungen (kein Kirchenbesuch, bis entweder die Symptome nachlassen oder die Behandlung abgeschlossen ist). Innerhalb jeder Zeremonie gibt es bestimmte Indikatoren, welche die richtige Diagnose und die erfolgreiche therapeutische Sitzung bestätigen. Gähnen oder Husten zum Beispiel sind wichtige symbolische Ausdrücke einer erfolgreich verlaufenen Therapie.
Gähnt der Patient im Falle des *malocchio* während der Behandlung, so bestätigt dies die Diagnose und wird als Zeichen für die Anwesenheit eines entweder spirituellen oder magischen "bösen" Wesens angesehen. Das Gähnen oder Husten des Heilers ist genauso ein Zeichen dafür, dass der Geist der zu behandelnden Krankheit anwesend ist, und aus dem Patienten in die umgebende Luft heraustritt, oder dem symbolischen Raum des zeremoniellen Ortes (oft Küche oder Esszimmer des Heilers) entweicht.
In diesem Moment (laut einiger Heiler) kann der *malocchio* in den Körper des Heilers oder der Heilerin eindringen, dadurch den Körper des Patienten verlassen und somit die Kopfschmerzen kurieren. Unter diesen Umständen wird der "Helfer" nach abgeschlossener Behandlung des Patienten den selben Heilungsprozess noch einmal am eigenen Körper durchführen, ähnlich einem Post-Heilungs- und Reinigungsprozess (entspricht etwa dem Händewaschen westlicher Ärzte), diesmal mit dem Ziel der Selbstheilung des *malocchio*. Am Ende jedes Heilungsprozesses wird die Krankheit einem höheren heiligen Wesen präsentiert, wie z.B. einem speziellen Heiligen, Jesus Christus, dem Vater, dem Sohn oder dem heiligen Geist.
Manchmal schließt die Präsentation auch heilige Pflanzen mit ein, so wie im Falle San *Savuco´s. Savuco* ist der süditalienische Name des gemeinen Holunderbeeren-Baums (*Sambucus nigra*). Das Anrufen eines heiligen Wesens ist krankheitsbezogen und meist beeinflusst durch die physische Präsentation der zu behandelnden Krankheit. Zum Beispiel bei der Behandlung von *mal di gola* (Halsschmerzen) wird San Biagio gerufen, der als Beschützer des Halses in katholischer Tradition angesehen wird. Für "stärkere" Krankheiten, wie z.B. *malocchio und mal di testa* wird ein mächtigeres Wesen, wie z.B. die Dreieinigkeit bestehend aus Vater, Sohn und heiligem Geist, zur Hilfe gerufen. Die Wichtigkeit dieser Dreieinigkeit wird deutlich in jeder Heilungsprozedur, denn der Zahl "drei" wird eine besondere Bedeutung zugemessen. Wie auch bei anderen "magischen" Handlungen, spielt die Wiederholung eine wesentliche Rolle in diesen volksmedizinischen Heilungen. Ein Gebet wird jeweils drei Mal wiederholt (ausgenommen ist die zeremonielle Heilung von *mal di denti* (Zahnschmerzen), welche entweder 27 oder 33 Mal wiederholt wird) und die Behandlungsphase "starker" Krankheiten muss an drei aufeinanderfolgenden Tagen ausgeführt werden, um zur Heilung zu führen.

Wenn ein Patient auch nach dreitägiger Behandlung noch immer Symptome aufweist, dann wird die Behandlung um weitere drei Tage verlängert, woraufhin noch einmal drei Behandlungstage folgen (insgesamt neun Tage), gilt die Krankheit als nicht geheilt. Falls die Krankheit auch nach neuntägiger Behandlung noch immer vorhanden ist, gibt es unterschiedliche Vorgehensweisen. In manchen Fällen wurde von Patienten berichtet, dass sie nach der ersten erfolglosen Behandlung die Hilfe anderer "Helfer" aufgesucht hätten, die dann letztlich durch eine andere Diagnose und Behandlung die Krankheit heilen konnten.
Es ist ebenso dokumentiert, dass im Falle erfolgloser Therapien auch auf eine andere Form der Medizin (meist Biomedizin) zurückgegriffen wird.
Die Magie der Zahl drei ist auch in anderen Formen magischer Medizin in vielen anderen Kulturen bekannt und wird auch in Verbindung mit "treatments of crossroads, boundaries, directions, sunwise and withershins" =Behandlungen von Kreuzungen und Grenzen, Richtungen angewendet (HAND 1980).
Dieser Symbolismus der Kreuzungen, der in beinahe allen Volkskrankheiten dieses magisch-religiösen Systems angesprochen wird, repräsentiert - abhängig vom Informanten - entweder einen Ort der Sicherheit oder der Verletzlichkeit in Bezug auf magische Vergiftung oder Übertragung unterschiedlicher Leiden. Diese örtlichen Gegebenheiten werden mitunter in die Heilungsprozedur bestimmter Leiden integriert, indem etwas für eine andere Person dort zurückgelassen wird. Dieser Vorgang des Zurücklassens, besonders in der üblichen Verbindung mit dem "nicht zurückblicken", ist ein Tabu, das genauso alt ist, wie der ausdrückliche Befehl an Lot (zu Zeiten Soddom und Gomorrahs), sich nicht umzuwenden. Ein exzellentes Beispiel ist der Brauch, rituell vorbereitetes Salz auf einer Kreuzung hinter sich zu werfen und davon zu gehen, ohne noch mal zurück zu blicken, um so einen *malocchio* zurückzulassen. Entsprechend dieser Behandlung wird dann die nächste Person, die zu dieser Kreuzung kommt, den *malocchio*, den die erste Person zurückgelassen hat, aufnehmen.
Ein weiteres Beispiel für solch magische Übertragungen wird am besten verdeutlicht durch die Krankheit *mal d`arco* (Krankheit des Regenbogens), für deren Behandlung zeremoniell gesammelter Urin des Nachts auf einer Kreuzung vergossen wird. Die nächste Person, die vorbeikommt, wird auch hier die Krankheit in sich aufnehmen - und der frühere Patient geheilt sein. Bei der Hinterfragung dieses feindseligen Aktes der Übertragung der eigenen Krankheit auf eine andere, unbetroffene Person, erklärten alle befragten Personen einstimmig, das es sich dabei nicht um eine "böse Tat" oder gar einen "Fluch" handle, sondern der Vorgang vielmehr als Mittel der Heilung verstanden wird.
Vielleicht kann dieser Akt besser erklärt werden durch die Erkenntnis, dass die Person, die den Urin als symbolisches Mittel der Übertragung zurücklässt, nicht weiß, wer als nächster die Kreuzung passieren und somit die Krankheit aufnehmen wird.
Das bedeutet, dass diese magische Krankheits-Übertragung nicht vorsätzlich stattfindet, wie es z. B. der Fall wäre, würde der Urin etwa auf den Stufen des Nachbarn vergossen werden - und somit auch nicht als üble Tat angesehen wird. Die Methode des Verfluchens ist jedoch auch in dieser Region bekannt. In jeder Kultur, in der magische oder abergläubische Dinge als "gutes Tun" gewertet werden, existieren ebenso solche Elemente, die als "schlecht" angesehen werden. Wir konnten lediglich einen Mann ausfindig machen, der in dieser Region für solchen Schadenszauber bekannt ist.

Doch seine Verweigerung eines Interviews verhindert eine genauere Beschreibung der Ausführung solcher Handlungen. Was wir jedoch wissen ist, dass zwischen beiden Spektren dieses magisch-religiösen Systems (jene, die "helfen" oder "verfluchen") einige entscheidenden Unterschiede bestehen.

Jemand, der Rituale durchführt um zu verfluchen, wird sowohl gefürchtet als auch gemieden in der Gemeinschaft. Es wird angenommen, dass diese entgeldlich für ihre Dienste entlohnt werden. Diejenigen allerdings, die helfen, werden per se nicht bezahlt, sondern erhalten vielmehr kleine Geschenke bestehend aus Nahrung oder hausgemachten Dingen.

Während sowohl diejenigen, die "helfen" als auch diejenigen, die "verfluchen" dazu neigen, betreffend ihrer speziellen Fähigkeiten ein Element der Geheimhaltung zu hegen - besonders verbreitet unter "Meisterheilern", die auch über die Grenzen ihrer Gemeinde hinaus bekannt sind - ist es offensichtlich, dass jene, denen die Fähigkeit des Verfluchens nachgesagt wird, das größere Geheimnis daraus machen.

"Helfer", die hinsichtlich ihrer Fähigkeit befragt wurden, Leiden zu heilen, denen ein Fluch zugrunde liegt, antworten alle, dass dies nicht möglich sei - nur ein erfahrener Priester könne versuchen, so eine Notlage zu beheben.

Als eine über achtzigjährige "Helferin" befragt wurde, ob sie die Fähigkeit besitzen würde, Verfluchungen auszusprechen- um Gutes zu tun- antwortete sie komischerweise, *"Hör zu meine Tochter. Wenn ich in der Lage wäre solche Dinge zu tun, dann wäre ich nicht hier mit dem ..."* dabei zeigte sie auf ihren Mann, der sich mit einem Freund auf der Straße unterhielt, *"...sondern mit einem Prinzen!"*.

Sie fuhr fort zu erklären, "Ich kann nur tun, was Gott und die Jungfrau Maria wünschen, dass ich es tun soll - und das auch nur, um denen zu helfen, denen ich helfen kann." Es ist nicht zu leugnen, dass alle, die sich als "Helfer" in ihrer Gemeinschaft verdient machen, gläubige Katholiken sind. Jedoch stellt diese Tatsache immer noch ein kleines Mysterium dar in unserer Beurteilung (Evaluation), da viele dieser Heilungsriten nicht in vollem Umfang religiös sind und keiner strikten katholischen Doktrin folgen - sondern vielmehr heidnische Elemente des magischen Symbolismus und sogar die Heilung von Objekten wie z.B. Pflanzen in ihre gesprochenen Formeln und Zeremonien mit einbeziehen.

Magische Elemente, die den Zeitpunkt bestimmter Behandlungen betreffen, stellen ein interessantes Paradoxon dar in der Beurteilung dieser Mischung von heidnischer und katholischer Zeremonie. Bei jenen Krankheiten, die als Manifestation magischer oder spiritueller Ursachen auftreten, muss die Behandlung - abhängig von der jeweiligen Krankheit - entweder vor Sonnenaufgang oder nach Sonnenuntergang durchgeführt werden.

Dies ist keine ungewöhnliche Vorgehensweise und wurde schon in früheren Arbeiten zur europäischen Volksmedizin dokumentiert, denn "... der gesamte Zeitraum von Sonnenuntergang bis Sonnenaufgang ist - unter bestimmten Umständen - besonders wirksam für die Heilung, da es eine günstige Zeit ist, um magische Aufgaben durchzuführen" (HAND 1980).

Diese Besonderheit des speziellen Zeitraumes sowie die Geheimhaltung magischer Handlungen kann auch in Verbindung zu der Tatsache betrachtet werden, dass der frühe Morgen ebenso die bevorzugte Zeit ist (in Bezug auf phytotherapeutisch Aktivität) für das Sammeln von Heilkräutern.

Diskussion

Die ethnomedizinischen Praktiken solcher europäischer Regionen wie Süditalien, die durch ihren kulturellen Reichtum geradezu überquellen, stellen eine höchst interessante Quelle für zukünftige folkloristische und anthropologische Studien dar.

Das traditionelle Heilungssystem, das meistens Phyto- und Psychotherapie vereint, hat in der Vergangenheit dieser Kultur dazu gedient, einen wirksamen holistischen Ansatz für Gesundheit und Heilung hervorzubringen. Unglücklicherweise hatte das Einfließen "moderner" Biomedizin, der meistens der holistische Ansatz fehlt, einen Einfluss sowohl auf die arbëresche als auch die italienische Kultur in der Vulture-Region.

Interviews mit Informanten im Alter von bis zu 55 Jahren in Ginestra zeigten, dass die meisten Personen nicht in die Heilungsmethoden der "Helfer" vertrauen. Moderne Biomedizin, präsentiert durch örtliche Ärzte, Apotheken und nahegelegene Krankenhäuser wie z.B. in Rionero und Venose, werden immer stärker als erster Anlaufpunkt bei Krankheit bevorzugt. Das Gegenteil ist der Fall bei der älteren Generation (ab 55 Jahre). Bei Problemen wie Kopfschmerzen, Hautausschlag, Übelkeit und Bauchschmerzen wird zuerst die Hilfe eines Heilers aufgesucht, oder ein Heilkraut verwendet.

Nur wenn das Problem durch die traditionelle Behandlung nicht korrigiert werden konnte, wird von Angehörigen dieser Altersgruppen auch ein westlich geschulter Mediziner aufgesucht. Der Generationsunterschied in der Region ist groß, und es kann davon ausgegangen werden, dass diese Heilungsmethode den fortlaufenden Übergang zur Moderne nicht überleben wird. Das bestätigt sich auch in dem absoluten Mangel an Lehrlingen dieser Heilkunst. Mit jedem Tod eines "Helfers" gehen nicht nur die Worte ihrer Zeremonien verloren, sondern auch ein großer Teil dieser reichen Kultur, zu der auch das gesamte Gesundheits-Glaubens-System zählt, verschwindet.

Anmerkungen

Gelder für diese Studie wurden durch eine Kombination verschiedener Stipendien zur Verfügung gestellt: Mars Nutritional Research Council, Urbana, IL, USA; National Kappa Alpha Theta Foundation, USA; und der Foundation for Science and Disability, USA.

Zusammenfassung

Drei *Arbërschë* Gemeinden im nördlichen Teil der Region Basilicata (Süditalien) wurde eine ethnomedizinische Studie ausgeführt. Rituelle Heilungspraktiken, die den Gebrauch gesprochener Formeln, biologischer Objekte und ritueller Objekte miteinbeziehen, werden am Beispiel verschiedener Volkskrankheiten untersucht. Diskutiert werden Ätiologie, Vorsorge, Diagnose und Behandlungen sowie Einschränkungen, Zeit und heilige Wesen, die während der Behandlung gerufen werden. Schlagwörter Ethnomedizin; Süditalien; albanisches *Arbërschë*; rituelles Heilen; folkloristische Studien; Ethnobotanik

Autoren

CASSANDRA QUAVE
Unabhängige Forscherin in Atlanta, Georgia (USA). Ihr Forschungsfeld bezieht sich auf ethnomedizinische Praktiken, Ethnobiologie und Folklore des mediterranen Raumes und NW Amazoniens.
Kontakt: University of London, School of Pharmacy, Centre for Pharmacognosy and Phytotherapy, 29/39 Brunswick Square, London WC1N 1AX, U.K.,
E-Mail: cassandraquave@hotmail.com

DR. RER. NAT., DOTT. ANDREA PIERONI
Ethnobiologe und Ethnopharmakologe, ist Forschungsassistent im Center for Pharmacognosy and Phytotherapy der School of Pharmacy, Universität London (UK) Sein Forschungsschwerpunkt bezieht sich auf "medizinische Nahrung" im ethnischen Kontext im Mittelmeerraum.
Kontakt: Center for Pharmacognosy and Phytotherapy, The School of Pharmacy, University of London, 29-39 Brunswick Square, London WC1N 1AX, UK. E-Mail: a.pieroni@etnobotanica.de, andrea.pieroni@ulsop.ac.uk, uzs51a@IBM.RHRZ.uni-bonn.de

Literatur

AAVV. 2000. *The Indo-European Database.* http://indoeuro.bizland.com.
Boggi, R. 1977. *Magia, Religione e Classi Subalterne,* Firenze, Italy: Guaraldi Editore.
Coltro, D. 1983. *Dalla Magia alla Medicina Contadina e Popolare,* Firenze, Italy: Sansoni Editore.
Di Nola, A.M. 1976. *L`Arco di Rovo. Impotenza ed Aggressività in due Rituali del Sud,* Torino, Italy: Boringhieri.
Di Stasi, L. 1981. *Mal occhio: The Underside of Vision.* San Francisco: North Point Press.
Dundes, A. (Ed.) 1981. *The Evil Eye, a Folklore Casebook,* New York/London:Garland Publishing.
Elworthy, F. 1958. *The Evil Eye: The Origins and Practices of Superstition,* New York: The Julian Press, Inc.
Gallini, C. 1973. *Dono e Malocchio,* Palermo, Italy: Flaccovio Editore.
Gatto-Trocchi, C. 1982. *Magia e Medicina Popolare in Italia,* Rome, Italy: Newton Compton.
Hand, W. 1980. *Magical Medicine: The Folkloric Component of Medicine in the Folk Belief, Custom, and Ritual of the Peoples of Europe and America,* Berkeley, CA: University of California Press.
Jilek, W.G. 1994. *Transcultural Psychiatric Research Review,* 31 (3), 219-258.
Hauschild, T. 1994. *Studien zum religiösen Diskurs in Süditalien: eine lukanischeHagiographie,* Tübingen, Germany.
Maloney, C. 1976. *The Evil Eye.* New York: Columbia University Press.
Migliore, S. 1997. *Mal'uocchiu: Ambiguity, Evil-Eye, and the Language of Distress,* Canada:University of Toronto Press.
Pieroni, A., Quave, C., Nebel. S., Heinrich, M. 2001. *Fitoterapia,* in press.
Quave, C.L., Pieroni, A. 2001. *Paper presented at the 3rd International Congress of Ethnobotany,* Naples, Italy, 22-30 September 2001, 94-OC-S7.
Salminen, T. 1999. UNESCO *Red Book Report on Endangered Languages: Europe.* http://www.helsinki.fi/~tasalmin/europe_report.html.
Stephenson, P.H. 1979. *Culture, Medicine and Psychiatry,* 3, 247-265.
Pazzini, A. 1980. *Storia tradizioni e leggende nella medicina popolare,* Milano, Italy: Recordati editore.

MAGICAL HEALING – TRADITIONAL FOLK-MEDICAL PRACTICES OF THE VULTURE AREA OF SOUTHERN ITALY

by Cassandra Quave & Andrea Pieroni

Introduction

In medical anthropological and ethnopharmacological research, the evaluation of field data using both social and natural scientific methods is central in order to study interdisciplinary aspects of both ritual healing procedures and biological remedies used in the local popular pharmacopoeias. In Italy, in the last decades, ethnomedical findings related to popular medical practices have been very rarely interdisciplinary studied.

As part of an ethnobiological and anthropo-medical field study carried out in the north Lucania or Basilicata region, Southern Italy (Fig. 2), we recorded data dealing with the representation of illness and folk-medical practices still in use in three small Arbëresh communities: Barile (*Barilli*), Ginestra (*Xhinestra*), and Maschito (*Mashqiti*) and two neighbouring Italian communities: Ripacandida and Venosa. While over 50 botanical species and over 20 animal or industrial products were identified with specific uses in the ethno-pharmacopoeias of this region (PIERONI et al., in press), only those remedies associated with magical or spiritual healing rites will be discussed here.

Vulture area, Lucania

The Vulture volcanic area of northern Basilicata (Lucania) is composed of seven villages and small cities sustained primarily by agriculture and factory labor. The rolling hills of the countryside are dotted with vineyards (*Vitis vinifera* var. Aglianico), olive groves (*Olea europaea*), and durum wheat fields (*Triticum durum*). The predominant religion is Catholicism and the elderly portion of the population are generally devout Catholics – this is especially true for women, the

Fig. 1: "Zia Elèna" (E.M., born 1908), a ninety-three year old healer of Maschito majority of which attend church at least once a day.

The Vulture area is unique in the fact that as well as maintaining the "traditional" South Italian culture, it also sustains some of the rapidly decaying Arbëresh Albanian culture in three villages: Ginestra, Barile, and Maschito. The concentration of the Arbëresh Albanian culture in this area is quite significant considering that only five such communities exist in all of Lucania. These three villages are also isolated from the bulk of other Arbëresh communities which are concentrated in Calabria, Sicily, Campania, and Apulia.

The Arbëreshë

The Arbëreshë are descendants of south Albanians who immigrated during the 15th Century to diverse inland areas of the South-Italian regions. At present, an estimated 80,000 Arbëresh Albanian speakers (all bilingual in Italian) remain in isolated villages in Italy. This figure, however, may be exaggerated as it is based on the whole populations of "Arbëresh municipalities" and not on the exact number of people within each municipality that can actually speak the language, which may be as low as 10% in many places.

The Arbëresh Albanian language belongs to the Tosk Albanian subgroup of the Albanian languages, which represent the only surviving languages from the ancient Paleo-Balkan group (Illyrian, Messapic, and Thracian) of the Indo-European family (AAVV 2000). Arbëresh Albanian has been classified as an "endangered language" by the "UNESCO Redbook of the Endangered Languages" (SALMINEN 1999). The cultural remnants of the Arbëreshë in the studied area are evident only in some of the older generation (55+ years old), in which the language and folk-customs can still be remembered, but not normally used on a daily basis.

Ethnomedicine

Traditional popular remedies have always had an important place in healing systems throughout the world. Over time, people have developed various means of curing the ill through the use of native plants and icons of their socio-religious belief system. Indigenous, folk, or traditional healing refers to "*non-orthodox therapeutic practices based on indigenous cultural traditions and operating outside official health care systems*" (JILEK 1994). These healing traditions are necessarily culturally specific and are often met with success only when applied within such a socio-specific cultural framework. Recovery from illness within a traditional folk-medical system is also dependent upon a strong interconnection with spiritual belief models and expression of the placebo effect.

Non-conventional medical practices are often referred to as manifestations of things magical and in the realm of superstition and religious beliefs. Wayland Hand, in his analysis on the magical component of folk curing, gave definition to this concept of magical healing and the importance of belief on therapeutic success in stating:

These magical acts, which serve as attendant circumstances to more routine, and often common kinds of doctoring, may rest either on a supernatural or sacral power... they bring an added measure of power and healing efficacy... In the hands of a devout believer, these magical procedures – and they alone – insure the success of the therapy (HAND 1980).

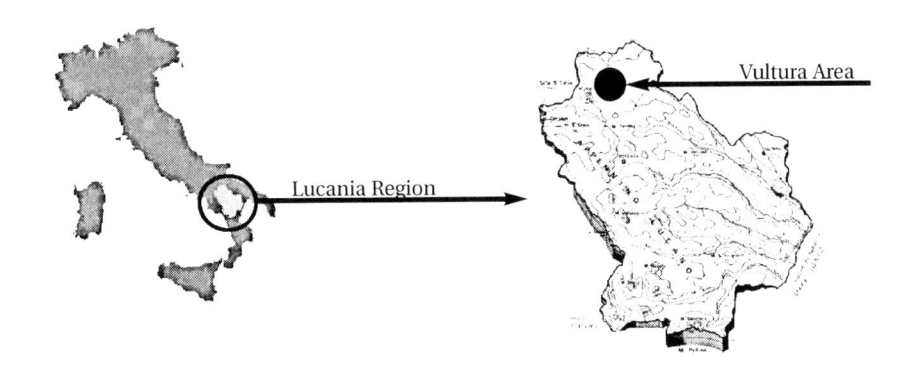

Fig. 2: Geographical location of the Vulture area.

Under this realm of medicine, the healing process is strengthened by the incorporation of symbolic objects, numbers, oral formulas, and actions – yet does not always incorporate pharmacotherapeutic agents – and thus success, under the standards of biomedicine, is subsequently explicable only through a heavy reliance on the power of the placebo effect. In Vulture, it is common knowledge both amongst healers and patients alike that "*chi non crede non può essere aiutato*", or "*he/she who does not believe cannot be helped*". This statement is one example of a general recognition that therapeutic success in this specific folk-medical framework is dependent upon the patient`s willingness to believe in the treatment itself. Thus, the healer serves more the role of guide than physician, whose job is to walk the patient through a path of self, trance-based, or psychotherapeutic healing.

Illness is not only healed through magical means, but is also often acquired via similar routes. In the case of certain illnesses, such as *mal d`arco* ("illness of the rainbow") and some cases of *malocchio* ("evil-eye"), a circular relationship between the acquisition and expulsion of disease is clearly demonstrated. This theme of "magical contagion" – and its role in the transfer of illness between living (and sometimes nonliving) things – shapes the local theory of symbolic transmission of ailments, and thus impacts the healing process itself.

The ethnomedical construct

Specific ethnomedical distinctions exist within the framework of healing in the Vulture area (QUAVE & PIERONI 2001). We have identified seven divisions of illness – those that are healed through the use of magico-religious rituals and incorporate:
> oral formulas (often accompanied by light massage),
> oral formulas and biological materials applied as medicinals,
> oral formulas and biological materials used as ritual objects,
> oral formulas and non-biological materials used as ritual objects,
> oral formulas and Western pharmaceuticals applied as medicinals

and those illnesses which are healed through the non-ritualistic application of: biological (wild or cultivated botanicals or animal products) or industrial materials and pharmaceuticals or other medical procedures applied within a Western "biomedical" framework under the instruction of a physician.

Although each division of this construct plays an important role in medical care in the region, we will focus only on those illnesses that incorporate the use of oral formulas in a magico-religious context.

Twenty-two folk-medical illnesses were identified and are employed to describe such conditions as headaches, nose bleeds, mastitis, penile inflammation, migraines, stomachaches, abdominal pain, dermatitis, hepatitis, mumps, and toothache. The construction of this folk-classification of illness and disease is complex and includes aetiologies structured as either magico-spiritual or biological, depending upon the form of expression of the illness.

It is interesting to note that while all folk-illnesses with a spiritual aetiology can be treated through the use of prayers (oral-formulas) – not all illnesses of biological aetiology can be healed in this manner. There is a strict division between those illnesses that one can heal with prayers and those that also necessitate a biological intervention in the form of medicinal plants or pharmaceuticals.

Quelli che possono aiutare (those who can help)

Who are the healers? In the region Vulture, they are not actually described with the term for "healer" (*guaritore*), but instead with the verb for "help" (*aiutare*). These "helpers" are spread throughout the region, but seem to be most concentrated in the smaller Arbëresh villages of Barile and Ginestra where the traditional culture has not yet been completely overrun by the dominant Italian culture. This unequal distribution is most likely due to differences in the speed of socio-cultural transition between communities and not, instead, to the previous lack of such healers in these surrounding Italian communities.

Ripacandida, for example, is the closest neighbor of Ginestra, and today there remains only one (non-practicing) healer in the community. Many elderly of the community were able, however, to recall several different "helpers", including one man, who had all either died or have moved to other areas of Italy for medical or family reasons.

This deficit of traditional medical leaders in this particular community has also contributed to a decreased prevalence of such "culture-bound" ailments as *malocchio* in the population. This apparent lack of representatives to the magico-religious healing art in Ripacandida was most surprising especially when compared to the nearby Ginestra which houses at least six women and one man who can "help" specific ailments.

All of the healers shared one major characteristic in common: that of old age. While the oldest is 93 years old, most averaged in their sixties to seventies, with the youngest being 51. It was not unusual to find that of the healers who were literate (mostly those younger than seventy-five), in addition to knowing the oral-formulas and rituals for today's more common ailments (*malocchio*, *cigli alla testa* [migraine], *vermi* [helminthiasis], *mal di gola* [sore throat]) they also maintained small notebooks in which were recorded the oral-formulas and ritual procedures for the treatment of those illnesses which are less common today than they had been in the past (*mal viento* ["wind-illness"], *fuoco morto* ["dead fire illness"], *fuoco di Sant´ Antonio* ["St. Antonio´s fire illness"], and *mal d´arco* ["rainbow illness"].

These notebooks were sometimes passed down from deceased family members or elders who had taught them the healing art. All of the notebooks viewed were written in the common south Italian dialect.

Of the Arbëresh communities, only two identified "helpers" – one ninety-three year-old woman from Maschito and one eighty year-old woman from Barile – were able to perform the healing process in the traditional Arbëresh language. Today, however, they seldom use this language in their healing ceremonies, opting instead for the local south-Italian dialect that is recognized by all of their patients. It was never clearly determined why or when the use of the Arbëresh language was lost in the healing process, but it can be suggested that perhaps the more "recognizable" of the two languages became gradually dominant over time as the transition from traditional Arbëresh culture blended with that of the modern Italian culture in these small communities. It is probable that word recognition, or at least familiarity with the formation of sounds used in the formulaic rhymes, plays an important role in the success of placeboic effect and the patient`s perception of healing.

It is important to note that not all "helpers" are able to treat all eligible ailments in this magico-religious schema. Some are considered specialists in the healing of only one class of ailments (such as bone-healers who treat only minor orthopedic and muscular ailments) whereas others treat only one type of ailment (such as one who can treat only *malocchio*). There are also those "master helpers" who are knowledgeable of a diverse range of ailments and who are subsequently both well revered and sought out in their own and other surrounding communities for their particular healing abilities. Lastly, there exists one specific class of healers who are not considered "helpers" in this system, yet are recognized to have the ability to heal one particular illness – that of *nervi accavallati* ("crossed nerves"). This is a particular illness in which only an unmarried pair of siblings (not gender-dependent) who still live at home, and whose father has died may "help" following a specific ceremony involving an oral formula and ritual objects. These siblings, however, are not able to heal any illness other than this one.

The healing process

Underlying the complexity of this medical system, a general pattern can be identified in the sequence of the ritualistic healing process. The first step, as in any other folk or biomedical system, is the presentation of illness to a designated healer and initiation of the diagnostic process.

When a patient develops an illness with a physical presentation such as a skin rash, they often first seek the advice of an older female relative or neighbor who serves as the primary advisor. This advisor, after discussing the symptoms of the ailment with the affected person, will guide them in the direction described in one of the seven divisions of treatment for this ethnomedical construct.

If the advisor feels that the illness is a result of some magico-religious transfer or contagion, the person is advised to see the "helper" in that community who is deemed the specialist for this particular ailment. If a specialist for such an ailment does not exist in their own community, and the patient is convinced that the ailment is in fact the result of some form of magical contagion or transfer, aide from a known "helper" in a nearby community is sought.

As is common in this south Italian culture, visitors are graciously admitted into homes with an offer to sit and chat over a cup of warm espresso – and so often initiates this healing process. After general conversation, the visiting patient will describe the symptoms of the ailment to the "helper" and politely ask for aide. Depending upon the healer and the particular symptoms being represented, diverse means of diagnosis may take place. For the example of a skin rash – which is consequently broken down into three categories of illness (*mal viento, fuoco morto,* and *fuoco di Sant´Antonio*) – the "helper" will thoroughly examine the physical presentation of the rash and then initiate a process of evaluation by questioning the patient as to where they have walked in the past few days and had they noticed anything strange – for example any strange winds (cold or strong). This question of location of physical passage is important in the diagnosis of certain skin rashes as the aetiology is recognized as a magico-spiritual force that is encountered by walking nearby the area in which a person was reportedly murdered in the past. Then, depending upon these factors – the presentation of illness and magico-spiritual indicators recognized by the healer – the ailment may be diagnosed. It is only through this clear recognition of causation that the next step of treatment may be taken.

While treatments vary from illness to illness and are dependent upon the manifestation and perceived origin of the condition – there do exist some general trends in this magico-religious healing art. The healing ceremony begins with both the "helper" and patient making a *nome della croce* (Catholic cross) on their own bodies. Each procedure entails the use of an oral formula, or prayer, specific to the illness being treated. This prayer is normally said three times and is followed by three *Padre Nostro,* three *Ave Maria,* and three *Gloria al Padre*. Depending upon the preference of the particular healer, one or more of these common Catholic prayers may not be utilized.
Motions of a cross are made in every procedure either directly above the region without bodily contact (most common in cases of dermatitis), or are made through bodily contact on the affected area (most common in cases where massage is also incorporated). Depending upon the illness, a ritual object or just the healer`s hand will be used to make this crossing motion.

In cases in which a ritual object is utilized (excluding *pelo alla menna* ["breast-hair illness"]), the object may serve as a sort of protective barrier between the patient and healer, preventing the passage of biologically contagious (yet only recognized as "magically contagious" in this system) disease between patient and healer. All illnesses that require the use of such a ritual object (excluding *mal di pancia* [stomachache]) must be treated at night and are often accompanied by special spiritual restrictions (not entering the church until either the symptoms are relieved or the period of treatment is complete).
There are certain indicators within the ceremony that attest to a correct diagnosis and successful therapeutic session. Yawning and coughing, for example, are important as symbolic expressions of the successful progression of some therapies. In the case of *malocchio*, if the patient yawns during a treatment, this verifies the diagnosis and confirms that the "evil" entity, either spiritual or magical, is present. The yawning or coughing of the healer, likewise is a sign that the spirit of the illness being treated is present and is coming out of the patient into the surrounding air or symbolic space of the ceremonial location (which is often the helper`s kitchen or dining area). It is at this point (only amongst some helpers) that the *malocchio* can actually enter his or her body, leaving the patient and thus curing the headache. Under these circumstances, the "helper", once finished with the treatment of the patient, will undergo the healing process once more on his or herself as a sort of post-healing sanitation process (much like that of a physician

who washes his or her hands after a conducting biomedical procedure), this time with the aim of self-healing for *malocchio*.

At the end of each healing procedure, the illness is presented to a higher holy entity such as a specific Saint (sometimes including even "sanctified" plants, as in *San Savuco* – where *savuco* is the South-Italian name of the common elderberry tree [*Sambucus nigra*]), Jesus Christ, or to the Father, Son, and Holy Spirit. The calling of a holy entity is illness-specific and is usually related in some way to the physical presentation of the illness being treated. For example, in the treatment of *mal di gola* (sore throat), San Biagio, who is the protector of the throat in Catholic tradition, is called. For "strong" illnesses such as *malocchio, mal di testa*, and *mal viento*, a more "powerful" entity such as the trinity of *Padre, Figlio, e Spirito Santo* (Father, Son, and Holy Spirit) is called forth for help.

The importance of this trinity is also evident in every healing procedure as a distinct emphasis is placed on the number "three". As in other kinds of "magical" acts – repetition plays an integral role in these folk-medical cures. A prayer is always repeated three times (excluding the ceremonial healing of *mal di denti* [toothache] which is repeated a total of 27 times or 3^3) and the treatment period for "strong" illnesses must be carried out in subsets of three consecutive days until healed. For example, if a patient is still symptomatic after three days of treatment, then three more days of treatment will ensue, and three more days after this (totaling nine days of treatment) will be sought if the illness is not yet cured. It is not always clear what happens after nine days of treatment have been completed and the illness is still present, but in some cases it has been reported by patients that they have sought out treatment from other "helpers" after the first method was unsuccessful and were subsequently healed due to a different diagnosis and treatment. It has also been documented for some other instances of unsuccessful therapy that another form of medicine (generally biomedicine) is then usually sought.

The magic of threes is apparent throughout other forms of magical medicine in many diverse cultures and is also invoked in various connections with "*treatments of crossroads and boundaries, directions, sunwise, and withershins*" (HAND 1980). This symbolism of the crossroads is addressed in nearly all of the folk-illnesses of this magico-religious system and, depending upon the informant, represents either a place of safety or of vulnerability in regards to the magical contagion and transfer of diverse ailments. Such locations are even integrated into the healing procedure for certain ailments in which something is left behind there for another person to acquire. This action of leaving something behind, and especially the common adjunction of "not looking back" is a taboo as old as the injunction to Lot in the days of Soddom and Gomorrah. One excellent example is the practice of tossing ritually prepared salt over one`s shoulder into a crossroad and continuing to walk away without looking back in order to leave behind a case of *malocchio*. According to this treatment, the next person to come to that crossroads will then acquire the *malocchio* that the first person left behind. Another example of such a magical transfer of illness is best illustrated in the case of *mal d`arco* ("illness of the rainbow"), in which ceremonially collected urine is poured into a crossroads at night. The next person to pass by will acquire the illness that you left behind and you are hence cured. When questioned as to the malevolence of this act of passing one`s illness onto another unsuspecting person, people unanimously explained that it wasn`t an "evil" act – and especially is not considered a "curse" that you are placing on someone – but simply a means of healing.

Perhaps this can be better explained by the recognition that the person leaving the urine behind as a symbolic means of transfer does not actually know who will walk by next and acquire the illness. Thus, this magical transfer of illness is not deemed intentional – such as it would be if perhaps the urine was poured instead on a neighbor`s doorstep – and is therefore not perceived as an "evil" act.

This conception of "evil" acts by placement of a *fattura* (curse) does, however, also exist in the region. In any culture in which things magical or superstitious are called upon to do "good"– there are also those that call upon these elements to do "bad". We were able to locate only one man in the region who is known for doing such acts and are not able to speak with much authority as to the process of completing these acts due to his refusal to take part in an interview.

What we do know, however, is that between these two spectrums of this magico-religious health system is that there exist some key differences between those that "help" and those that "curse". Ones who perform rituals for "curses" are both feared and avoided in the community. It is perceived that they are paid monetarily for their services whereas those that "help" are not paid per se, but instead presented with small gifts of food or other small, often homemade, items. While both those who "help" and who "curse" tended to harbor some element of secrecy pertaining to their special knowledge – particularly amongst those "master healers" who are well sought out for their services from the surrounding in addition to their own communities – it was evident that those who where even rumored to have the knowledge for making "curses" were the most secretive.

"Helpers", when asked about their ability to heal ailments caused by curses, all replied that this was not possible – that only an experienced priest can attempt to help such plights. When one helper in her mid-eighties was questioned as to whether she had the ability to make curses – even for doing good – she comically replied, "*Listen to me my daughter. If I were able to do these things, I wouldn`t be here with that –*" as she pointed to her oblivious husband who was talking to a friend in the street, "*but with a prince!*".

She continued in explaining that, "*I can only do as God and the Virgin Mary wishes me to do – and that is to help those that I can.*" It is undeniable that all of those who serve as "helpers" to their communities are devout Catholics. Yet, this fact still presents a bit of mystery for our evaluation as many of these healing rites are not wholy religious in that they do not follow a strict Catholic doctrine – but instead incorporate many paganic elements of magical symbolism and even the sanctification of objects such as plants in their oral formulas and ceremonies.

Magical elements concerning the timing of certain treatments also represent an interesting paradox in the evaluation of this mixture of pagan and Catholic ceremony. For example, amongst those illnesses perceived as manifestations of things spiritual or magical – treatments must be carried out either before sunrise or after sunset, depending upon the illness. This, as documented in earlier works on European folk-medicine, is not an uncommon practice, "*…the whole period from sundown until sunrise, under certain circumstances, is efficacious for curing, just as it is a propitious time for the carrying out of magical offices*" (HAND 1980). This peculiarity of timing, in addition to providing a blanket of secrecy to magical acts, could also be linked to the fact that early morning also happens to be a favorable time (in terms of phytotherapeutic activity) for the collection of medicinal herbs.

Discussion

The ethnomedical practices of such European regions as Southern Italy, which are overflowing with cultural richness, represent a most interesting source for future folkloristic and anthropological studies. The traditional system of healing, which often incorporates phytotherapy with psychotherapy, has served to effectively provide a holistic approach to health and healing within this culture in the past. Unfortunately, the influx of "modern" biomedicine, which is often lacking in such a holistic mode, has had its impact on both the Arbëresh and Italian cultures of the Vulture region. For example, interviews with people aged 55 and younger in Ginestra confirmed that most, in fact, do not believe that the "helpers" way of healing actually works. Western medicine, available in the form of a local physician, pharmacy, and nearby hospitals in Rionero and Venosa, are increasingly preferred as a first response to an illness episode. The opposite, however, is still true for the elder generation (55 + years old). For problems such as headaches, dermatitis, nausea, and stomachache, the help of a healer or herb is sought first and the aid of a Western medicinal is solicited only if the problem is not corrected after a period of traditional treatment.

This generation gap in the region is wide and it can be easily postulated that this mode of healing will not survive the current transition to modernity. This is confirmed by the absolute lack of apprentices to this art of healing. With the death of each "helper", more than just the words to their ceremonies are lost, a large part of this rich culture, including an entire health-belief model is lost as well.

Acknowledgements

Funding for this study was provided by a combination of several grants: Mars Nutritional Research Council, Urbana, IL, USA; National Kappa Alpha Theta Foundation, U.S.A. and the Foundation for Science and Disability, U.S.A.

Abstract

An ethnomedical study of three Arbërshë communities in the northern part of the Region Basilicata, Southern Italy, was carried out. Ritual healing practices, including the use of oral formulas, biological materials and ritual objects, are examined for several folk-illnesses. Aetiology, prevention, diagnosis, and treatments, including restrictions, time, and holy entities who are "called" during treatment are discussed.

Keywords

Ethnomedicine; Southern Italy; Albanian Arbërshë; Ritual Healing; Folkloric Studies; Ethnobotany

Authors

CASSANDRA QUAVE, an independent researcher, is based in Atlanta, Georgia (USA). Her research focus is centered on the ethnomedical practices, ethnobiology, and folklore of the Mediterranean and NW Amazonia. Contact: University of London, School of Pharmacy, Centre for Pharmacognosy and Phytotherapy, 29/39 Brunswick Square, London WC1N 1AX, U.K., E-Mail: cassandraquave@hotmail.com.

DR. RER. NAT.. DOTT. ANDREA PIERONI, ethnobiologist and ethnopharmacologist, is Research Assistant at the Centre for Pharmacognosy and Phytotherapy of the School of Pharmacy, University of London (UK). His research focus is represented by "medicinal foods" in ethnic contexts in the Mediterranean. Contact: Centre for Pharmacognosy and Phytotherapy, The School of Pharmacy, University of London, 29-39 Brunswick Square, London WC1N 1AX, UK, E-Mail: a.pieroni@etnobotanica.de.

References

AAVV. 2000. *The Indo-European Database.* http://indoeuro.bizland.com.
BOGGI, R. 1977. *Magia, Religione e Classi Subalterne,* Firenze, Italy: Guaraldi Editore.
COLTRO, D. 1983. *Dalla Magia alla Medicina Contadina e Popolare,* Firenze, Italy: Sansoni Editore.
DI NOLA, A.M. 1976. *L`Arco di Rovo. Impotenza ed Aggressività in due Rituali del Sud,* Torino, Italy: Boringhieri.
DI STASI, L. 1981. *Mal occhio: The Underside of Vision.* San Francisco: North Point Press.
DUNDES, A. (Ed.) 1981. *The Evil Eye, a Folklore Casebook,* New York/London:Garland Publishing.
ELWORTHY, F. 1958. *The Evil Eye: The Origins and Practices of Superstition,* New York: The Julian Press, Inc.
GALLINI, C. 1973. *Dono e Malocchio,* Palermo, Italy: Flaccovio Editore.
GATTO-TROCCHI, C. 1982. *Magia e Medicina Popolare in Italia,* Rome, Italy: Newton Compton.
HAND, W. 1980. *Magical Medicine: The Folkloric Component of Medicine in the Folk Belief, Custom, and Ritual of the Peoples of Europe and America,* Berkeley, CA: University of California Press.
JILEK, W.G. 1994. *Transcultural Psychiatric Research Review,* 31 (3), 219-258.
HAUSCHILD, T. 1994. *Studien zum religiösen Diskurs in Süditalien: eine lukanischeHagiographie,* Tübingen, Germany.
MALONEY, C. 1976. *The Evil Eye.* New York: Columbia University Press.
MIGLIORE, S. 1997. *Mal'uocchiu: Ambiguity, Evil-Eye, and the Language of Distress,* Canada:University of Toronto Press.
PIERONI, A., QUAVE, C., NEBEL. S., HEINRICH, M. 2001. *Fitoterapia,* in press.
QUAVE, C.L., PIERONI, A. 2001. Paper presented at the 3rd International Congress of Ethnobotany, Naples, Italy, 22-30 September 2001, 94-OC-S7.
SALMINEN, T. 1999. UNESCO *Red Book Report on Endangered Languages: Europe.* http://www.helsinki.fi/~tasalmin/europe_report.html.
STEPHENSON, P.H. 1979. *Culture, Medicine and Psychiatry,* 3, 247-265.
PAZZINI, A. 1980. *Storia tradizioni e leggende nella medicina popolare,* Milano, Italy: Recordati editore.

DIE PRAXIS EINER PEPO HEILERIN IN TANSANIA*

von Jessica Erdtsieck

Vermittler zwischen Geistern und Menschen spielen eine zentrale Rolle im afrikanischen religiösen Leben. Sie verhindern nicht den Weg zwischen Mensch und Gott, sondern stellen eher eine Verbindung zwischen ihnen dar. Manche dieser Vermittler können als das afrikanische Äquivalent zu den Schamanen gesehen werden. Unser heutiges Verständnis des Schamanen ist viel der einflussreichen Arbeit von Lévi Strauss (1963) zu verdanken. Er zeigte auf, dass der Schamane den Kranken in seiner Gesellschaft eine Sprache verleiht, mit der unausgedrückte und anderweitig nicht ausdrückbare psychische Zustände unmittelbar zum Ausdruck gebracht werden können.

In der afrikanischen Gesellschaft drückt die Sprache der Kranken den Sinn der Krankheit und die Offenbarung aus. Dieser Artikel beschäftigt sich mit der Praxis einer anerkannten, traditionellen Heilerin in Tansania, deren heilendes Eingreifen visionäres Sehen in den betroffenen Patienten auslöst. Während dieses zuerst einmal den Patienten die Möglichkeit gibt, ihr eigenes Wohlbefinden zu verbessern, könnte dies auch ein Mittel werden, um Krankheit und Übel in der Gesellschaft zu bekämpfen.

Einleitung

Seit Beginn meines anthropologischen Studiums (seit 1990) über die Rolle von spirituellen Kräften und die Anwendung und Wirksamkeit therapeutischer Techniken traditioneller Heiler in Tansania, habe ich einige schamanische Wahrsager getroffen. Ich begann mich zu wundern, warum so wenig über sie und ihre Arbeit bekannt war, besonders weil die Gemeinschaft sie für die

---

Abb. 1: Nambela, die Heilerin, mit ihrem Enkel
* Übersetzung aus dem Englischen: Eva Makkos

kompetentesten aller Heiler halten. Obwohl viele Wissenschaftler über die spirituelle Welt afrikanischer Völker geschrieben haben, ist die ethnographische Literatur über die indigenen Kenntnisse und die Heilerrolle der Schamanen bzw der Geistheiler in Afrika sehr gering; Schamanismus wird daher oft als nichtexistent auf diesem Kontinent angesehen
Es gibt auch große Unklarheiten in Definition und Funktion der einheimischen Heiler in Afrika. Bezeichnungen wie Zauberärzte, Medizinmänner, Wahrsager und Kräuterkundige werden abwechselnd benutzt um eine große Vielfalt von Praktizierenden zu beschreiben.
In Ostafrika, wo die Nationalsprache *Kiswahili* gesprochen wird, heißen Geistheiler oder Schamanen allgemein *Waganga* (Einzahl: *Mganga*) von dem Verb *kuganga*, welches heilen, kurieren bedeutet. Die Heiler, die verschiedene Fertigkeiten kombinieren sind normalerweise schamanische Wahrsager und werden *Waganga wa pepo* genannt, wörtlich Heiler, die vom Geist oder von unsichtbaren Kräften inspiriert werden. Das Wort *pepo* stammt vom Verb "*kupepea*", d.h. "in der Luft herumfuchteln", wohingegen "*upepo*" "Wind" heißt. Die *Waganga wa pepo* haben Wissen über Rituale und Medizinpflanzen teilweise durch eine Ausbildung erhalten, meist jedoch werden sie durch die Anweisungen der Geister gelenkt. Sie wissen, wie man Schutzmittel gegen das Eindringen von Geistern oder Hexen in Form von Amuletten, Talismanen oder Medizin anwendet. Im Gegensatz zum Zauberer (*Mchawi*), der Riten und Zaubersprüche für illegale Zwecke verwendet, tut es der *Waganga wa pepo* für legale Zwecke und zum Wohle der Gemeinschaft. Als Spezialist für unsichtbare Kräfte, hat er/sie oft mit durch Geister hervorgerufenen Symptomen zu tun, bekannt als *ugonjwa wa pepo* oder *pepo*-Krankheit.

Dieses bezeichnet eine große Bandbreite von psychosomatischen und mentalen Beschwerden, die ohne richtige Behandlung für jemanden, der von Geistern besessen ist (*kupagawa na pepo*) chronisch werden könnten. Aufgrund der Vielfalt der geistigen Kräfte (Mächte) hat jeder *mganga wa pepo* verschiedene Begabungen und Fähigkeiten, um bestimmte Arten von Geist- Besessenheiten zu behandeln.
Die Menschen betrachten diese Spezialisten als diejenigen, die für die sozialen Beziehungen, das körperliche und emotionale Wohlbefinden zuständig sind und jeder Praxis von schwarzer Magie (*uchawi*) entgegenwirken. In Tansania erklären die *Pepo* Heiler von leitenden Kräften in Träumen oder von Visionen inspiriert zu werden, die es ihnen möglich machen, den Grund einer Krankheit oder eines Unglücks zu erkennen und einen Ratschlag bezüglich einer Heilung oder einer Lösung zu geben. *Pepo* Heiler durchleben oft eine Krankheit und Krise bevor sie den Weg als Heiler beginnen, ähnlich wie die Schamanen. Die erste spirituelle Erfahrung erfolgt unvorhergesehen und kann in einem beliebigen Alter oder Lebensabschnitt der Person auftreten. Es geschieht Menschen, die gar keinen Wunsch haben Heiler zu werden oder/und die keine Tradition von Heilern in der Familie haben. Berichte erzählen, dass ein Wandlungsprozess begonnen hat aufgrund von Ablehnung oder Ignoranz der ausgesuchten Person, die Anwesenheit von geistigen Kräften zu akzeptieren.
Diese Kräfte möchten sich deutlich manifestieren und ein Hauptanliegen für diese Person und seine nächsten Angehörigen werden. Widersteht die ausgesuchte Person der geistigen Kraft oder lehnt sie sie ab, so wird sich ihr Gesundheitszustand stetig verschlechtern.
Sobald die Person und die nächsten Angehörigen zuhören und bestimmte

Abb. 2: Ausdruck eines Patienten, der in einem Trance-Zustand Visionen hat

Aufgaben ausführen, wird das Leben wieder ‚normal'. Diese neu gewonnene spirituelle Erfahrung erlaubt es der Person nach und nach, die Probleme anderer auf körperlicher, sozialer und oft geistiger Ebene zu behandeln. Kurz gesagt, wo dieser Prozess zuerst dazu dient Ausgeglichenheit in das persönliche und familiäre Leben zurückzubringen, wird diese Erfahrung konsequenterweise auch anderen dienen (siehe WALSH 1990). Die Frage bleibt, wie es einem Patienten, der geistige Leiden durchlebt, möglich ist, spirituelle Fähigkeiten zu entwickeln und wie diese zum Heilungsmechanismus in Bezug stehen. In diesem Aufsatz erläutere ich es an dem Beispiel der Vorgehensweise einer Heilerin in Südwest Tansania, mit der ich ca 1 Jahr gearbeitet habe (1990/1991). Sie heißt Nambela und leitet eine große traditionelle Gesundheitspraxis in der ländlichen, abgelegenen Mbeya Region. Anschließend folgt eine kurze Beschreibung der Umgebung, in der Nambela, eine *Nyiha*, als *Pepo* Heilerin praktiziert.

Lage und Setting von Nambela's Heilpraxis

Nambela gehört zu der *Bantu* sprechenden ethischen Gruppe *Nyiha*, die Teil einer Anhäufung von eng verwandten Völkern ist, die eine sehr ähnliche Sprache sprechen. Ihre Stammesnachbarn sind die *Nyamwanga*, die *Fipa*, die *Wanda*, die

Iwa und die *Mambwe* (WILLIS 1996). Sie sind kulturell und historisch verknüpft mit vielen Völker der *Tangayika Nyasa* Korridor Gegend, deren Beziehungen weit über diese unmittelbare Region hinausgeht. Zu ihnen gehören die *Nyakyusa*, die zusammen mit den eng verwandten *Sumkuma* die größte und einflussreichste ethnische Gruppe in Tansania (über 2 Millionen) bilden. So hat sich die traditionelle *Nyiha* Kultur nicht in Isolation entwickelt, sondern wurde von anderen Völkern und Ideen beeinflusst. In den letzten Jahrzehnten fanden Veränderungen schneller statt, da die *Nyiha* mit vollkommen fremden Kulturen und Ideen konfrontiert waren, deren Gesamteinfluss sich vielleicht als größer herausstellen wird, als alle anderen vorherigen Einflüsse. Im 20. Jahrhundert haben viele *Niyha* begonnen, das Christentum zu akzeptieren, aber dies bedeutet nicht, dass traditionelle religiöse Gebräuche aufgegeben wurden.

Vor der Unabhängigkeit (1962) hielten einige *Nyiha* Häuptlinge oder *Muwene* (*sing.Mwene*), die christlich eingestellt waren, Bußtage ab, um das Wohlwollen der Ahnen zu erhalten und eine gute Ernte zu sichern. Ein guter Häuptling hatte bei dieser Gelegenheit alle Ahnen bei ihrem Namen zu nennen, egal ob Frauen oder Männer. Nach dem Gebet wurde ein Feuer gemacht, bei dem sich alle trafen und mit großer Freude sangen. Bei dieser Gelegenheit konnten sich alle Anwesenden aussprechen und Unstimmigkeiten untereinander bereinigen. Die *Nyiha* glaubten, dass die Ahnen nichts für sie tun konnten, solange sie sich nicht gegenseitig vergeben hatten.
Im Falle von Krankheit oder Unglück wurde ein Wahrsager konsultiert, um offen zu legen, ob ein gebrochenes Tabu oder Hexerei im Spiel war. Falls die "*muzimu*" verantwortlich gemacht wurden, fanden die Wahrsager heraus, welcher Verstoß gemacht wurde und was benötigt wurde um es wieder gut zumachen. Oft hatte der Verstoß mit dem Versagen zu tun, verschiedene verwandtschaftliche Verpflichtungen zu erfüllen. In diesem Fall hatte das Familienoberhaupt ein Opfer in Form von selbstgebrautem Bier, einem Schaf oder einer Kuh zu bringen. Falls viele Leute der Linie oder des Unter-Clans betroffen waren, trafen sie sich an der heiligen Beerdigungsstätte ihrer Vorfahren (genannt: "*ivitimbango*") um zu beten.
Der Glaube an die Kraft der Ahnen war stark, aber ebenso stark war der Glaube an "*Mulungu*" oder Gott.
Die Ahnen einer jeden Familie wurden mit einer bestimmten Baumgruppe dargestellt, immer in der Nähe ihrer lebenden Nachkommen. In dem Schatten dieser Bäume wurden ihre Seelen geglaubt.
Ein Mann (niemals eine Frau) segnete ein Geflügel, eine Ziege oder ein Schaf für den Geist des Vorvaters. Schreine, die winzigen Hütten ähnlich sahen wurden benutzt und Gaben (meistens aus Bier oder Mehl) wurden hineingegeben. Allgemein wurden Opfergaben ("*matambiko*") an die väterlichen Ahnen gemacht, dies wurde "*mababu*" genannt. Die *Nyiha* waren immer ein sehr religiöses Volk, was sich heute noch in der Praxis der Heilerin Nambela zeigt, die zur Zeit meines Aufenthaltes (1990-1991) einer der angesehendsten Heilerinnen in der *Mbeya* Region war.
Nambela begann ihre Arbeit als ein *Mganga wa pepo* 1965 als sie ca 37 Jahre alt war. Dies geschah nach einem Leben voller Krisen, in dem sie unter einem kranken *pepo* (Swahili) oder *impepo* (Kinhiha) litt. Dieses äußerte sich hauptsächlich in stechenden Schmerzen und Zeiten mentaler Probleme, wie Verwirrung. Nach langen Jahren der Ablehnung gegen ihren spirituellen Ruf fand Nambela endlich einen Heiler, der ihr das Vertrauen gab, dass sie durch Entwickeln ihrer visionären

Abb. 3: Befreiung von *pepo;* die Patienten rennen

Fähigkeiten eine Heilung ihrer Beschwerden erfahren würde. Dies wurde gefolgt von einer plötzlichen Initiation, während derer sie für zwei Tage das Bewusstsein verlor, während sie Anweisungen von göttlichen, heilenden Geistern empfing.

Kontext der Wahrsager-Sitzungen

Wenn die Personen in dem Lager ankommen, werden sie sofort von einem der Patienten empfangen (im Allgemeinen jemand, der als Assistent von Nambela benannt wurde). Oft müssen die Klienten für einen oder mehr Tage reisen, und diejenigen, die für eine Behandlung bleiben, bringen außerdem wichtige Haushaltsutensilien und Essen mit. Täglich kommen zwischen fünf und zehn Patienten an, die oft von einem oder mehreren Familienmitgliedern oder Freunden begleitet werden.

Denjenigen, die von weither kommen, wird eine Hütte zugewiesen, in der sie sich ausruhen oder kochen können, während sie auf die erste Sitzung mit Nambela warten. Gewöhnlich geschieht dies am Vormittag zwischen 8 und 11 Uhr. Falls es notwendig sein sollte, ist Nambela aber auch am späten Nachmittag oder am Abend verfügbar, abhängig von der Anzahl der anwesenden Patienten und dem Zeitdruck aufgrund anstehender Gartenarbeiten und persönlicher familiärer Verpflichtungen. Im allgemeinen finden Nambela's Wahrsagersitzungen jedoch täglich statt. Sobald Nambela für eine Diagnosesitzung bereit ist, informiert sie ihre Assistenten, die selbst Patienten in einem fortgeschrittenen *pepo*- Stadium sind. Sie sind vertraut mit den täglichen Abläufen von Nambelas Arbeit.

Sie versammeln die neu angekommenen Klienten und lassen sie einer nach dem anderen für die Konsultation niedersitzen. Dieses geschieht in der Mitte des Lagers zwischen Nambelas Haus und der Hütte des Patienten. Nambela setzt sich an einem ganz bestimmten Platz in der Nähe ihres Hauses am Boden nieder, oft mit gekreuzten Beinen. Der Klient sitzt ein paar Meter vor ihr mit nach vorn zeigenden, ausgestreckten Beinen. Die Assistenten erzählten mir, dass dies die beste Art für Nambela sei, "Informationen" über die Person zu erhalten. Da die Diagnose-Sitzung eine öffentliche Sache ist, können andere Klienten, Patienten oder Besucher zusehen. Ein oder mehrere Assistenten helfen den Neuankömmlingen und falls notwendig, übersetzen sie *Kinyiha*, die Mundart von Nambela, in Kiswahili, die Landessprache Tansanias. Nambela wahrsagt in einem Halb-Trance-Zustand, normalerweise beginnend bei Beziehungsproblemen zu körperlichen Beschwerden übergehend. Bevor Nambela in Trance geht mit dem üblichen *pepo* Zittern, fragt Namblea den Klienten woher er/sie kommt und zu welchem Stamm er/sie gehört. Dann konzentriert sie sich auf den Klienten (und seine/ihre Familie), um die verschiedenen beteiligten Aspekte des Problems herauszufinden. Was immer sie erfährt (fühlt, hört, sieht) oder weiß, wird sofort mitgeteilt, gleich ob dies direkt oder indirekt in Zusammenhang mit dem jetzigen Zustand oder der Situation des Klienten steht. Wenn sie bemerkt, dass der Klient sich mancher Dinge nicht bewusst ist oder nicht gewillt ist, sie zuzugeben, wiederholt Nambela ihre Worte emotionaler oder stellt diesbezügliche Fragen.

Solange der Klient sich weigert, diesen Punkt einzusehen, fühlt sich Nambela gehindert fortzufahren. Anschließend berichtet sie über die körperlichen Beschwerden oder Schmerzen des (der) Klienten. Obwohl dies nicht immer der Grund gewesen sein mag, weshalb dieser zu ihr gekommen ist, gibt es oft etwas zu berichten. Wenn sich mehr Details oder negative Aspekte im Zusammenhang mit dem Klienten entfalten, z.B. Tod aufgrund eines Familienstreits, Mord oder Zauberei, reagiert Nambela sehr stark auf den Schmerz oder das Problem des Klienten. Diese Art von starken Vibrationen, die Nambela wahrnimmt, rufen die Reaktion hervor. Zum Glück war mein Team- Kollege Patterson an Nambelas *pepo* Sprache gewöhnt. Außerdem hatte er schon seine eigenen Erfahrungen mit *pepo*, auf die er sich verlassen konnte. Ohne seine Hilfe wäre es unmöglich gewesen, eine vernünftige Übersetzung einer diagnostischen Sitzung zu machen, die ich zu diesen Zweck aufgenommen habe.
Unabhängig davon, ob die Klienten aktiv mit Nambela sprachen oder nicht, wurde mir klar, dass das Geschehen der Wahrsagerei von grenzwertigen Entscheidungs-prozessen geprägt wird (TURNER 1980:17).Die visionären Leistungsfähigkeiten sind ständig im Austausch mit Überlegungen, um Ursache und Zusammenhang der Probleme zu offenbaren.
Dies erfordert Entscheidungen, die der Klient schwerlich alleine treffen kann. So dient die verbale Therapie des Wahrsagens einem psychotherapeutischen Zweck. Ist es aber nicht sehr verunsichernd, von jemandem analysiert zu werden, der zur gleichen Zeit auch Richter ist ?

Im Gegensatz zum westlichen medizinischem Vorgehen, bei dem der Klient den Arzt über seine Beschwerden informiert, erklärt hier der Wahrsager dem Klienten, was nicht in Ordnung ist. Falls der Wahrsager nicht in der Lage ist, die emotionalen und sozialen Auswirkungen seiner Worte einzuschätzen, kann beachtlicher Schaden entstehen. Die Rolle des schamanischen Heilers entspricht somit sehr dem eines Psychotherapeuten. Beide, der Schamane und der Psychotherapeut, stellen eine direkte Beziehung mit dem Bewusstsein des Patienten und eine indirekte Beziehung mit seinem Unterbewusstsein her – der Psychotherapeut durch zuhören, der Schamane durch Redekunst.

Pepo Ätiologie: Eine Beratung mit Nambela.
Das folgende Beispiel betrifft eine Frau, die mit einem kleinen Kind kam. Nankala, eine Heiler-Novizin, hatte sie mitgebracht, um die Meinung ihrer Lehrerin Nambela zu erfahren.

Nambela: ‚In Deiner Verwandtschaft gibt es jemanden der mit pepo zu tun hat (kuchima). In deiner Heimat hat ein Unfalltod stattgefunden(kifo cha ghafula).'

Frau: ‚Ja, mein Vater hat sich erhängt.'

Nambela:‚Du wirst auch durch einen Unfall sterben, wenn du nicht den Geist deines Vaters gehen läßt. Ich sehe zwei Frauen und einen Mann sterben! Kind (sie spricht die Frau an), nimm deinen Platz am Boden ein (um pepo aufzuwecken). Du musst ein pepo Erwachen mindestens dreimal verspüren, um den Zorn des Blutes zu mindern, der deine Gedanken umgibt seit dem Tod Deines Vaters. Gott wird Dir helfen! Hast du seinen Geist gehen lassen?'

Frau: ‚Nein, haben wir nicht.'

Nankala:‚Bei mir reagierte diese Frau mit einem sehr starken pepo, so wie Leute, die stark unter mentalen Krankheiten leiden (ugonjwa ya kichaa).'

Nambela: ‚Gut, so wird es ihr hier auch ergehen; denn falls sie pepo nicht erfährt, besteht die Gefahr, dass sie in den Wald wandert und verloren geht. Wenn Du den Geist Deines Vaters gehen lässt, tust du dies auch für alle Alten und alle Kinder. Falls sie pepo erfährt, wird das für sie von Vorteil sein, denn sie wird ihre Kraft anschließend wieder erlangen!'

Nambela beschreibt die Symptome der Frau nicht noch einmal, da sie schon vorher von der Novizin Nankala diagnostiziert wurden. Sie weiß nun natürlich schon, was in der Familie der Klientin vorgefallen ist. Wichtig ist dabei die Tatsache, dass die Frau einen *Pepo* Status hat, aufgrund des Selbstmordes ihres Vaters. Ein Selbstmord oder Mord wird, wie auch Unfälle, als ein plötzlicher Tod bezeichnet. Dies widerspricht einem natürlichen Tod, der aufgrund von Krankheit oder hohem Alter eintritt.
Ein plötzlicher Tod muss abgeschlossen werden (*kufunga kiparazi*) indem ein Opfer (eine Kuh, ein Schaf, ein Huhn, abhängig von den Bindungen und den Bedürfnissen des Verstorbenen) und /oder spezielle Kräuter, in und um das Haus oder auf das Grab platziert werden. Der Verstorbene wird als Schatten oder "*mzimu*" bezeichnet, der losgelassen werden muss, damit er in die Welt der Toten übertreten kann. Dies verhindert, dass der Schatten einen lebenden Verwandten so schädigen könnte, dass er selbst, als Ergebnis davon, durch dieselben Leiden gehen müsste und dasselbe Schicksal erleiden, wie der Verstorbene. Außerdem muss man sagen, dass laut Nambela die Kraft des Geistes oder *pepo* mit dem Tod zu Ende geht, wohingegen der Schatten bleibt. Zusätzlich ist Nambela der Ansicht, dass alle Menschen mit *pepo* geboren sind und je nach Geschehnissen, kann es der Grund für Krankheiten sein ebenso wie ein Mittel zum Heilen. Kurz, die Balance

des *pepo* ist essentiell für das Wohlbefinden einer Person.
Die charakteristischen Symptome einer *pepo* Erkrankung sind Sodbrennen, Herzklopfen, Ruhelosigkeit, Schwäche und Gewichtsverlust. Dieses kann mit mentalen Problemen verknüpft sein, wie z.B. Depression, Verwirrung, Aggression und geistige Abwesenheit ("*ugonjwa*" oder mentale Krankheit). Probleme im Zusammenhang mit der *pepo* Krankheit umfassen auch:

1) Krämpfe,

2) Paralyse,

3) plötzlicher Tod,

4) Pech,

5) Schwarze Magie.

Nambela konnte bisher 3 verschiedene Arten der *pepo* Krankheit identifizieren. Als erstes nannte sie "*pepo wa mtu*", die beinhaltet, dass der innere Geist einer Person nicht im Gleichgewicht ist. Zweitens erwähnt sie "*pepo wa jin*i", eine ‚fremde' Geisteskraft ist in Disharmonie und sucht sich ein Opfer aus. Solch ein 'fremder' Geist kann ein Naturgeist sein oder ein verstorbener Geist mit Ursprung außerhalb des *Nyiha* Territoriums. Drittes verweist sie auf "*pepo ya mzimu*", die Geisteskraft eines verstorbenen Ahnens, der durch Beleidigung oder Verletzung eines Tabus innerhalb der Familie erzürnt wurde. Eine Disharmonie in einem dieser Stadien kann eine *pepo* Krankheit oder "*ugonjwa ya pepo*" hervorrufen.
Während der Weissagung identifiziert Nambela, welche(s) der Stadien den Klienten betreffen.
Mit anderen Worten, wenn *pepo* in einem Zustand von Disharmonie war, konnte es durch Geister von Lebenden oder Toten oder nicht-menschlichen Kräften beeinflusst werden. Laut Nambela ist jedoch ein guter, gesunder *pepo* immer unter dem Einfluss einer schützenden oder heiligen Geisteskraft, auch "*pepo nzuri*" genannt. In diesem Fall nannte es Nambela auch *pepo wa Mungu (Mulungu* in *Kinyiha*). Wenn schwarze Magie praktiziert wurde oder bestimmte Geister gesandt wurden, um jemanden zu schaden, konnte dies nur in der Abwesenheit solcher heiligen Kräfte Erfolg haben.

Religiöse und musikalische Heilsitzungen

Nachdem Nambela festgestellt hatte, worauf das Problem ihres Patienten beruhte, konnte die psychotherapeutische Behandlung beginnen. Die Gruppentherapie bestand hauptsächlich aus der Teilnahme an rhythmischen Gesang-Sessions, die täglich von Patientengruppen abgehalten wurden. Manchmal wurde diese mit einem Ritual kombiniert, um Geister oder andere unsichtbare Kräfte zu besänftigen, die einen Einfluss auf den eigenen inneren Geist oder den *pepo* haben. Nambela selbst nahm an dieser Aktivität nicht teil, obwohl sie manchmal aus der Ferne mitsang, entweder durch mitsummen der Lieder oder durch Beobachten der Reaktionen der Patienten.

In der zeit meines Aufenthaltes unterbrach sie manchmal kurz das Geschehen, um eine Anweisung zu geben. Dies geschah z.B. um in einem Patienten *pepo* zu erwecken oder um eine lange Session zu beenden, da die Beteiligten eine Ruhepause brauchten. Im Allgemeinen lag diese tägliche Gruppenaktivität in der Verantwortung der Patienten selbst, angeregt und geleitet wurden sie von einem oder mehreren erfahrenen Patienten (Assistenten). Mehrmals täglich hörte ich den Ruf "*Wimbo, Wimbo*" (was "Lieder, Lieder" bedeutet) zu solch einem Treffen. Dieser laute Ruf erreichte auch mich, was sehr praktisch war. Ich wohnte damals nicht weit weg vom Lager, nur eine kleine Kaffeeplantage lag dazwischen.

Während der ersten Monate zogen mich diese Treffen sehr an und ich konnte herausfinden, unter welchen Umständen sie stattfanden. Das Singen wurde einberufen, wenn ein neu angekommener Patient dringend 'Behandlung' brauchte, oder wenn einer der anderen Patienten oder Nambela selbst plötzlich von *pepo* ergriffen worden waren. Nambela deutete einige ihrer Träume als eine Warnung für soziale und persönliche Belange anderer. Wenn Einheimische oder Patienten betroffen waren, rief dies beinahe immer eine Reaktion bei einem oder mehreren der Anwesenden hervor. Manchmal beschuldigte sie jemanden, faul oder ignorant zu sein oder Krankheit und Unglück hervorzurufen. Wenn eine Frau keine gute Mutter und Partnerin war, konnte Nambela wütend reagieren. Auch wurden Patienten, die unmoralisches Verhalten im Lager zeigten, wie z.B. Verheiratete, die anderweitig sexuelle Affairen hatten, nicht von dieser Zur-Schau-Stellung ausgeschlossen. Diskussionen kamen auf, wenn die Betroffenen sich zu verteidigen versuchten und andere Patienten bestätigten, was vorgefallen war. Bei anderen Gelegenheiten hatte Nambela dieselben Träume wie einer ihrer Patienten, der dann begierig wissen wollte welche Botschaft dieser Traum vermitteln sollte. Wenn alle diese Dinge geklärt waren, begann Nambela die Gebete.

Die Gebete waren an Jesus Christus und an Gott gerichtet und stellten deren Beitrag an der Heilung für alle dar. Gott "der einzige Heiler" wurde gebeten, Nambela und den Patienten ein starkes *pepo* zu geben, um ihren Heilungsprozess zu unterstützen. Danach rannte sie im Lager in *Pepo* herum und machte Prophezeiungen über lokale und nationale Ereignisse. Oft murmelte sie dieselbe Information für Wochen und Monate, dabei fügte sie neue Entwicklungen hinzu. Wenn sie dann in ihre normale Bewusstseinslage zurückgelangt war, hatte sie diese Nachrichten teilweise völig vergessen Während sie rannte und prophezeite kam der Punkt, an dem sie Medizin einsammelte.

Sie nahm ihr Beil und ihren Korb und rannte in die Wälder. Wenn Nambela auf Wurzelsuche gegangen war, zogen alle auf die andere Seite des Lagers und begannen zu singen. In manchen Fällen fand sofortige Aktion in ihrer Mitte statt, indem einer oder mehreren Personen, die Schmerzen hatten, zugesungen wurde. Nambela kam nach ein oder zwei Stunden zurück, schwer atmend und den Korb voll mit Wurzeln. Manchmal begann sie wieder zu rennen, als Reaktion auf die ‚aufgeladene' Atmosphäre, die sich in der Zwischenzeit entwickelt hatte. Manchmal ruhte sie sich zu Hause aus, wechselte die Kleidung (wie es am Sonntag üblich war) und beobachtete die Aktivitäten im Lager, während sie Freunde oder Familienmitglieder traf.

Diese Sonntagstreffen gingen bis tief in die Nacht, abgesehen von einer kurzen Pause gegen 17 Uhr. Die Atmosphäre, in dem diese Treffen stattfanden, waren für manche Patienten ein Auslöser, der dazu führte, dass sie rannten, tanzen, sich rollten, bewegungslos im Schlamm oder in der heißen Sonne lagen, oder zu jemandem unsichtbaren sprachen. Andere wahrsagten oder behandelten andere Patienten (mit der Hand oder mit der Hilfe von Pflanzen), sammelten Medizin (*dawa*) oder fanden verborgene Zaubergeräte (*vipembe*). Diese verschiedenen Zustände waren bezeichnend für den *pepo* Zustand, d.h. jede Person hat eine spezifische Verhaltensweise, sei es mehr introvertiert oder extrovertiert.

Nachfolgend ist eine Beschreibung der Rolle von *pepo* in den allgemeinen Gesang-Sessions, als ein Ausdrucksmittel von emotionaler und therapeutischer Bedeutung.

Die Begegnung mit pepo Erwachung

Um die Gesänge zu erlernen, sollten die Personen sich an einem bestimmten Platz am Boden hinsetzen, der in der Mitte des Lagers war. Dabei waren die Beine gerade ausgestreckt und die Hände lagen locker auf den Oberschenkeln. Normalerweise war es notwendig, eine Weile im Lager zu verbringen, um seinem *pepo* Zeit zu geben 'zu erwachen' und von seinem losgelösten *pepo* profitieren zu können.

Der Zeitraum, den es benötigte um sein *Pepo* loszulösen hing von persönlichen Faktoren ab. Wenn Nambela sich sehr Sorgen um einen Patienten machte, berief sie ein sofortiges Treffen ein und während des Singens konzentrierte sich jeder auf diesen einen Patienten. Grundsätzlich jedoch saßen die Patienten am Boden, während eine Gruppe anderer Patienten um sie herum sangen. Familienmitglieder, die neue Patienten begleiteten, hatten sich in weiterer Ferne aufzuhalten, da sie den Prozess des erwachenden *pepo* stören konnten. Geld musste auch zurückgelassen werden, da dies ebenfalls einen negativen Einfluss haben konnte. Neue Patienten wurden eingeladen auszusprechen, was sie dachten. Falls sie dazu nicht sofort bereit waren, wurden sie nach einigen Songs wiederum gebeten und falls dann immer noch Stille herrschte, wurde ein neuer Versuch bei einer anderen Gelegenheit unternommen. Für manche Patienten war dieser Reinigungsprozess essentiell. Erst nachdem sie den Mut gefunden hatten zu sprechen, wurde das Befreien ihres *pepo* erreicht. Die meisten Personen brauchten jedoch mehrere Tage oder sogar Wochen, um sich den Liedern zu öffnen.

Ihr *pepo* wurde als 'noch schlafend' betrachtet. Immer mehr wurde ihr *pepo* auf die Gesänge sensibilisiert, einfach nur ihre Anwesenheit oder durch mitsingen. Gelegentlich gelang es schon bei der ersten Session das *Pepo* von Personen zu finden (erwecken und loslösen). Es wurde gesagt, dass jemand der schnell reagierte ein starkes *pepo* hatte und deshalb sensibler war und wahrscheinlicher die Fähigkeit hatte ‚Dinge zu sehen'. Nambela sagte dies einem Patienten entweder während der ersten diagnostischen Sitzung oder im Laufe seines Aufenthaltes. Manchmal ermutigte sie jemanden, seine Fähigkeiten zu entwickeln wie sie es getan hatte und dieses Geschenk zu nutzen. Sie tat dies bei den Leuten, die sich sonst Sorgen gemacht hätten aufgrund ihres starken und sensitiven *pepo*s. Dies konnten Frauen oder Männer sein.

Zu Beginn des Treffens nahmen nur wenige teil. Aber schon nach wenigen Songs kamen immer mehr dazu. Neue Patienten wurden ausdrücklich zu den Sessions eingeladen und bald war jeder mit den Liedern vertraut. Je mehr Leute teilnahmen, desto intensiver wurde die Atmosphäre, während die Hingabe und Aufmerksamkeit um die am Boden sitzende Gruppe sich erhöhte. Es gab Augenblicke, in der die richtige Atmosphäre nicht entstand, obwohl viele Leute teilnahmen. Ich fühlte, dass alles stark von der Hingabe des Solosängers abhing. Sie waren auch Patienten und nicht immer fühlten sie sich stark oder gut genug, um die Führung zu übernehmen. Wenn der Solosänger in diesem Fall nicht ersetzt wurde, endete die Sessions an diesem Punkt.

Als generelles Merkmal, das zu spüren war, sobald *pepo* sich befreite, war ein Zittern oder Schütteln des Körpers. Dann legte die Person sich langsam hin, immer noch zitternd oder sich schüttelnd. Die Gruppe herum machte sofort den Weg frei, richtete dabei immer noch die Aufmerksamkeit auf die betreffende Person bis diese über den Boden rollte. Dann wurde der Kreis geöffnet. Der Zweck der Lieder, *pepo* zu erwecken war erfüllt worden und der Kreis wurde wieder geschlossen. Wieder richtete sich die Aufmerksamkeit auf andere Patienten, die in der Mitte saßen.

Die Auslösung von *pepo* steht eigentlich für den Trance-Zustand, in dem eine Person den Punkt erreicht, an dem ihre/seine Willenskraft von einer anderen Kraft übernommen wird. Diese Situation wird durch ein Muster allgemeiner Erregungen, die durchlaufen werden, erreicht. Während meiner Versuche mit *pepo* (meiner eigenen und der anderer) fand ich heraus, dass ein starkes Gefühl im Bauch entstand, wenn *pepo* auf die Lieder zu reagieren begann. Es gab jedoch auch Personen, die dieses Empfinden zuerst in ihren Füßen oder Beinen hatten. Diese Leute litten unter Druck in den Beinen und so musste sich die Spannung auch zuerst dort lösen. Dies wurde als die schwierigste Situation angesehen, *pepo* zu befreien, da es zuerst in den Bauch wandern und durch die Brust den Weg zum Kopf finden musste.

Da ich begierig war dies alles zu erfahren, nahm ich oft während der Sessions am Boden Platz. Nambela sagte mir, dass mein *pepo* im Bauch konzentriert war. Wenn ich von dort ‚erwachen' würde, wäre es auch für mich möglich mein *pepo* freizulassen. Ich wusste nur zu gut, dass ich seit meiner Kindheit unter Magenbeschwerden und Verstopfung litt.

Diese Beschwerden wurden durch Yoga besser und ich bemerkte, dass besonders eine Entspannung des Nervensystems die Verbesserung verursachte. So war es für mich keine Überraschung, dass ich als Reaktion auf die Songs (die Erwachung *pepo*s) eine starke Reaktion im Hauptnervenzentrum spürte, das um den Bauchnabel herum sitzt. Aber ich bemerkte diese Empfindung nur bis zum Hals und nicht weiter. Wenn aber die Empfindungen nicht zur Kopfkrone gelangen, kann die Erweckung des *Pepo* nicht vollendet werden. Mit anderen Worten konnte der Geist nicht vom Kopf gelöst werden *(pepo anapasua rasi)* und blieb somit im Körper des *Pepo* Patienten.

Diskussion über das *Pepo*-Heilen.

Nambelas Wissen über den Körper scheinte auf dem zu basieren, was sie während des Wahrsagens sieht. Auf diese Art erhält sie auch Informationen über die Symptome und die Lösung, z.B. welche Art von Heilkräutern einzusetzen waren. Nambela schreibt die Wirkung der Heilkräuter, oder *dawa ya miti shamb*a (wörtlich: Pflanzenmedizin vom Feld) der Kraft der Natur und Gottes zu. Sie sagte dieses oft am Ende einer Weissagung und wiederholte es oft während den wöchentlichen religiösen Gebeten. Nambela sagte jedesmal:"Gott wird dir helfen, *(Mungu atasaidia)* da Gott der einzige Heiler ist".

 So wie sie sich als ein Mittler zwischen Gott und den Leuten empfand, war dies auch die Pflanze. Nambela hob den Zusammenhang oft hervor, dass die Pflanzen nur dann wirken konnten, wenn die Menschen ihre Probleme oder Fehler geklärt hatten. Eine Einstellung, die in der Vergangenheit bei den *Nyiha* üblich war. Sobald alle Probleme von Grund auf, im Herzen, geklärt waren *(kutoa mawazo za moyo)*, wurden die *pepo* Patienten ermutigt, *pepo* Kräfte mittels der Musiksessions zu erfahren. Die Lieder, die während der Gruppensessions gesungen wurden, vermittelten viele Informationen über den emotionalen, sozialen und religiösen

Aspekt von *pepo*. Aber wichtiger war, dass ein völliges Sich-öffnen zu den Liedern erreicht wurde.
Zu diesem Zweck versammelten sich die Sänger um das Ohr des Patienten. Alle Patienten nahmen an diesem Prozess teil, und da ich oft selbst auch teilgenommen hatte, wusste ich, wie einfach es war, aufzuhören zu denken, da mich die starken Schwingungen völlig vereinnahmten. Es war einfach zu verstehen, wie dies einen hypnotisierenden Effekt auf jeden haben konnte. Die Befreiung von *pepo* resultierte aus einem Trance-Zustand, indem die Willenskraft der Person von einer anderen Kraft übernommen wurde. Wenn dies sehr energetisch geschah, veranlasste Nambela den Patienten herauszufinden, ob er eine Bestimmung hatte, *pepo* Heiler zu werden. Aber auch ohne diese Berufung hatten viele Patienten visionäre Fähigkeiten, nachdem sie die Befreiung von *pepo* eine zeitlang erfahren hatten.

In diesem Artikel wurde gezeigt, wie durch die Verwendung von Liedern, die Musik der Wegbereiter zu veränderten Bewusstseinzuständen sein kann. Die Patienten konnten Erfahrungen haben, die über die körperliche, emotionale und spirituelle Veränderungen hinausgingen. Sie stiegen von einer persönlichen zu einer überpersönlichen Ebene auf.
Diese Erfahrungen hatten ein vorteilhaftes Ergebnis, da sie die Patienten mit ihren unterdrückten Gefühlen konfrontierten, die an der Basis ihrer spirituellen Auseinandersetzung standen. Durch die Reinigung von Körper und Geist konnten die Patienten ihr Gleichgewicht wieder herstellen, ihre Selbstheilungskräfte anregen und erlebten spirituelles Wachstum. Mit anderen Worten veränderte die spirituelle Auseinandersetzung, sowohl das Individuum als auch die gesamte Gruppe in positivem Sinne. Dieser Prozess läuft stark parallel zu den Erfahrungen mit dem Kundalini Yoga (AVALON 1974).

Zusammenfassung
1. Solange *pepo* schlief, fühlte es sich an wie ein Bündel von Hitze oder Kraft in bestimmten, unteren Körperteilen. Während Patienten dies erfuhren, zitterten sie innerhalb der Wirbelsäule, wo sie ein inneres Feuer erfuhren. Daher schrien die Sänger oft : "*chema, chema, amka pepo*" ("bring es zum Kochen und lass *pepo* aufwachen").

2. Wenn das Gefühl des inneres Feuers vom Abdomen höherstieg und eventuell durch die Hilfe des Singens den Kopf an dessen Krone verließ, erwachte und befreite sich somit *pepo*. An diesem Punkt verloren die Personen die Kontrolle, und eine andere Kraft ergriff von ihrem Geist und Körper Besitz.

3. Die Patienten mit stärkeren spirituellen Kräften profitierten früher von den Heilsitzungen. Ihr Bewusstsein öffnete sich weiter in dem Moment persönlichen Wohlbefindens. Visionen begleiteten sie und der Impuls, anderen durch das Finden von Heilpflanzen zu helfen, sowie Böses aufzuzeigen.

4. Diejenigen mit einem starken *pepo* (*pepo joto*, wörtl. einem heißem *pepo*) wurden ermutigt, Kontrolle über ihre spirituellen Kräfte zu erhalten und ebenfalls Heiler zu werden. In diesem Fall hatten sie sich an *pepo* Vorschriften zu halten (*sheria wa pepo*). Die Hauptregeln bestanden aus Essenseinschränkungen,

entsprechend der Hinweise der Geister und kein Missbrauch mit ihren neu erhaltenen spirituellen Kräfte zu betreiben. Die neuen Heiler wurden ernsthaft darauf hingewiesen, dass ihr Schutz und persönliches Wohlergehen nun in den Händen der Geister lag.

Daher hatten sie auch keinen Grund, Bezahlung für Behandlungen zu verlangen. Um Störungen im Kommunikationsaustausch zwischen Geistern und Heilern gering zu halten, sollten die neuen Heiler keinen Alkohol trinken und keine sexuellen Beziehungen, außer mit ihrem eigenen Partner unterhalten. Diejenigen Heiler, die diese Vorschriften nicht einhielten, litten nicht nur wieder unter Krankheit, sondern sie sahen auch ihre Fähigkeiten und Kräfte dahinschwinden oder enden.

Diese Parallele mit dem Kundalini mag darauf hinweisen, dass bestimmte historische Beziehungen zwischen Yoga, okkulten Praktiken und Schamanismus bestehen (ELIADE 1983).

Wichtiger ist jedoch, dass spirituelle Kräfte oder die Fähigkeit zum Hellsehen sehr kulturell geformt sind und das die Erfahrung subjektiv und damit sehr individuell bleibt. Geister, Teufel, Götter oder Engel mögen keine Kraft oder Realität für diejenigen haben, die nicht an deren Existenz glauben. Für diejenigen, die ihnen durch ihren Glauben Energie geben, sind sie sehr real. In afrikanischen Kulturen, in denen sich die Menschen eingeschränkt fühlen ihre Emotionen zu zeigen, sind traditionelle Heilmethoden ein wichtiger Ort der Befreiung. Gleichzeitig eröffnet sich hier die Möglichkeit der Übertragung und Weitergabe eines kulturellen Heilererbes.

Autor

DR. JESSICA ERDTSIECK

Master in Anthropologie, studierte Anthropologie an der Universität Amsterdam und ist nun in der Endphase ihrer Dr. Phil. Promotionsthese. Diese beinhaltet eine vergleichende Studie von *pepo* Heilern in Tansania mit den verschiedenen Arten von geistigen Kräften, die Heiler benutzen und der Bezug zu der geographischen, historischen und kulturellen Dynamik. Da sich fast alle Berichte von traditionellen Heilern auf männliche Spezialisten konzentrieren, richtet sie ihr Hauptaugenmerk auf die Rolle der weiblichen Heilerinnen.

Kontakt: E-Mail: J.Erdtsieck@frw.uva.nl

References

AVALON, A. 1974. *The serpent power.* New York.

ELIADE, M. 1983. *Le chamanisme et les techniques archaiques de l'extase.* Paris.

ERDTSIECK, J. 1993. *Spiritual forces in illness and healing. The role of pepo in the life and healing practice of a female healer in the Southwestern highlands of Tanzania.* Nijmegen, Third World Centre (Occ. paper nr. 32).

ERDTSIECK, J. 1997. *Pepo as an inner healing force. Practices of a female spiritual healer in Tanzania.* Amsterdam (Bulletin 343).

ERDTSIECK, J. 2001. *Nambela mganga wa pepo; Mambo afanyayo mganga wa tiba ya asili kwa uwezo wa pepo nchini Tanzania.* Dar es Salaam University Press.

FULLER-TORREY, E. 1972. Witchdoctors and psychiatrists. The common roots of psychotherapy and its future. New York.
GROF, S. & Ch. 1989. *Spiritual emergency. When personal transformation becomes a crisis.* Los Angeles.
HARNER, M. 1982. *The way of the shaman.* New York.
JANZEN, J., NGOMA. 1982. *Discourses of healing in Central and Southern Africa.* Berkeley.
KAKAR, S. 1982. *Shamans, mystics and doctors.* Boston.
KATZ, R. 1982. *Boiling energy.* Cambridge (Mass.).
KELLO-AYOT, H.O. 1976. *Topics in East-African history.* Nairobi.
KESBY, J.D. 1977. *The cultural regions of East Africa.* London.
KIEV, A.. 1974. *Magic, faith and healing.* New York.
LÉVI-STRAUSS, C. 1967. *Structural anthropology.* New York.
LEWIS, I. (ed.). 1971. *Ecstatic religion. An anthropological study of spirit possession and shamanism.* New York.
MBITI, J.S. 1969. *African religions and philosophy.* East African Educational Publishers.
PEEK, P. (ed.) 1968. *African divination systems. Ways of knowing.* Bloomington.
PRINCE, R. (ed.). 1968. *Trance and possession states.* Montreal.
SHORTER, A. 1974. *East-African societies.* London.
WALSH, R.N. 1990. *The spirit of shamanism.* Los Angeles.

THE PRACTICE OF A PEPO HEALER IN TANZANIA

by Jessica Erdtsieck

Intermediaries between spirits and men are central in African religious life. They do not block the way between man and God, but rather they form bridges. Certain intermediaries can be seen as the African equivalent of shamans. Our contemporary understanding of the shaman owes much to the influential work of CLAUDE LÉVI-STRAUSS *(1963) who pointed out that the shaman provides a sick member of his society with a language by means of which unexpressed and otherwise inexpressible psychic states can be immediately expressed. In African society the language of sick people is imbedded in spirit illness and spirit manifestation.*

This article deals with the practice of a reputed traditional healer in Tanzania whose main healing intervention can spur visionary sights in afflicted patients. Where this firstly enables patients to improve their individual well being it may also become a means to combat illness and evil in society.

Introduction

Ever since my anthropological study (from 1990 onwards) about the role of spiritual forces and the application and effectiveness of therapeutic techniques of traditional healers in Tanzania, I have met a number of shaman diviners.

It made me wonder why so little is known about them and their work, especially because the community considers them to be the most competent of all healers.

Although many scholars have written about the spiritual world of African peoples, ethnographic literature about the indigenous knowledge and healing roles of shaman or spirit healers in Africa is limited; to such an extent that shamanism is often regarded as not to exist at all on this continent. There is also much confusion

Fig 1: Nambela, the healer, and grandchild

about the definition and functions of indigenous healers in Africa. Terms such as witch doctors, medicine men, diviners and herbalists are used interchangeably to denote a wide variety of practitioners. In East Africa, where the national language is Kiswahili, indigenous healers are generally called *waganga* (singular *mganga*) from the verb *kuganga* which means to heal, to cure.

Those healers who combine various skills are usually shaman diviners, also called *waganga wa pepo* (literally meaning healers who are inspired by spiritual or unseen forces). The word *pepo* originates from the verb *kupepea* meaning "to wave about in the air", whereas *upepo* means "wind". The *waganga wa pepo* have gained knowledge on rituals and medicinal plants in part by training but foremost upon instruction of the spirits. They know how to apply protective means against the intrusion of spirits or witches in the form of amulets, charms or medicine.

In contrast to the sorcerer *(mchawi)* who uses rites and spells for illegal purposes, the *mganga wa pepo* will do so for legal ends and for the benefit of the community. As a specialist of unseen forces, he/she deals often with symptoms caused by spirits, known as *ugonjwa wa pepo or pepo*-illness. This term denotes a broad range of psychosomatic and mental complaints that may become chronic without proper treatment for a person possessed by spirits (*kupagawa na pepo*). Due to a great variety of spiritual forces, each *mganga wa pepo* will have different qualities and skills so as to handle particular types of spirit intrusion. People look at these specialists as the ones to take care of social relations, physical and emotional wellbeing and to act against any practice of black magic *(uchawi)*.

In Tanzania, *pepo* healers claim to be inspired by guiding forces in dreams or by means of visionary sights, enabling them to reveal the cause of illness or misfortune and to advise about a cure or solution. *Pepo* healers go often through illness and crisis before entering a career as a healer, much like shamans do. The initial spiritual intrusion happens involuntary and may occur at any given age or life period of an individual. It happens to people who have no desire whatsoever to become a healer or who have no tradition of healers in the family. Accounts explain that a transformation process is anticipated by denial or ignorance from the chosen individual to accept the presence of spiritual forces.

These forces wish to manifest themselves as to communicate a matter of major concern to the individual and next close of kin. Resisting or ignoring their presence will gradually make the individual suffer. Once the individual and next of kin listen and perform certain tasks, life will return back to 'normal'. The newly gained spiritual competence gradually allows the person to deal with other people's problems of a physical, social and often spiritual nature. This serves first to bring balance back in personal and family life, consequently it is to serve others (see also WALSH 1990).

The question remains how a patient, suffering from a spiritual affliction, is able to develop spiritual skills and how this relates to healing mechanisms. In this paper I will discuss this in the light of principle interventions as practiced by a female healer in Southwest Tanzania with whom I stayed for nearly one year (1990/1991). She is called Nambela and she manages a large traditional health care practice in a vast rural area situated in Mbeya region. Below I give an outline of the setting in which Nambela, as a *Nyiha*, practices as a *pepo* healer.

Fig 2: Expression of patient having visionary sights while in a trance state

The setting of Nambela's healing practice

Nambela belongs to the *Bantu* speaking *Nyiha* ethnic group which forms part of a cluster of closely related peoples sharing similar languages. Their tribal neighbours are the *Nyamwanga*, the *Fipa*, the *Wanda*, the *Iwa* and the *Mambwe* (WILLIS 1966). They are historically and culturally interrelated with many of the peoples of the *Tanganyika Nyasa* Corridor area, whose relationships extend beyond this immediate region. Among them are the *Nyakyusa*, who together with the closely related *Sukuma* form the largest and most influential ethnic group of Tanzania (over 2 million). Hence traditional *Nyiha* culture has not evolved in isolation but affected, and in turn was affected, by other peoples and ideas. In recent decades change accelerated as the *Nyiha* have been exposed to completely foreign cultures and ideas whose overall impact may prove to be greater than all their previous experiences. In the twentieth century many *Nyiha* have come to accept Christianity, but this does not mean that traditional religious customs have been abandoned.

Before independence (1962) some *Nyiha* chiefs or *Muwene* (sing. *Mwene*) who were Christian held repentance days to get the sympathy of the ancestral spirits to assure a good crop. A good chief was to address all his ancestors by name, be it men or women at such occasions. After the prayer, a fire was made while everybody gathered and sang with excitement. At that occasion all present would 'clear their throats' and 'spit out' what they had against each other. The *Nyiha* believed that the ancestors could not do anything for them as long as they had not forgiven each other. When illness or disaster struck, a diviner was consulted to reveal if a broken taboo or witchcraft was involved. If the *muzimu* were held responsible, the diviners would find out what offence had been made and what was needed to make up for it. Often the offence had to do with the failure to carry out certain kinship obligations. In that case the head of the family was to make a sacrifice of home brewed beer, a sheep or a cow. If many people of the lineage or sub-clan were affected, they would gather at the sacred burial place of their predecessors, called the *ivitimbano*, for prayers. Belief in the ancestors' power was strong but so was the belief in *Mulungu* or God. The spirits of each family were associated with a particular grove of trees in the vicinity of the home of their living descendants, where they were thought to live in the shade of these trees. A man (never a woman) would consecrate a fowl, a goat or a sheep to the spirit of a forefather. Shrines that resembled miniature huts were in use and offerings (usually of millet beer or flour) were placed inside them. In general sacrificial offerings *(matambiko)* were made to the patrilineal ancestors, also called the *mababu*.

As such, the *Nyiha* always were very religious people and till today this is reflected in the practice of the healer Nambela, who at the time of my stay from 1990-1991, was one of the most prominent healers in *Mbeya* region. Nambela started her practice as *mganga wa pepo* in 1965 when she was about 37 years old. This happened after a life of crisis in which she suffered from an ill *pepo* (Swahili) or *impepo* (Kinyiha), resulting foremost in stabbing pains and periods of mental problems, like confusion. After many years of resistance to her spiritual calling, Nambela eventually found a healer who gave her confidence about the fact that by developing her visionary capacities she would finally find a cure of her complaints. This was followed by a sudden initiation during which she lost consciousness for two days while receiving instructions from divine healing spirits.

Context of the divination sessions

When people arrive at the compound, they are immediately welcomed by one of the patients Usually someone who has been appointed as an assistant of Nambela. Often clients have to travel for one or more days, and those who come to stay for treatment also bring along essential household items and food. About five to ten clients arrive daily who are often accompanied by one or more relatives or friends. Those who have come from far are allocated a hut to rest in or to cook a meal, while awaiting the first occasion to meet Nambela. Usually this happens in the morning, between 08.00 a.m. and 11.00 a.m. But if necessary, Nambela also makes herself available late in the afternoon or in the evening, depending on the number of clients present, and the time pressure due to seasonal cultivating activities and personal family duties. In general, however, Nambela's divination sessions are held daily.

As soon as Nambela is ready for a diagnostic session, she informs her assistants, who themselves are patients in an advanced state of *pepo* transformation. Being familiar with the daily concerns of Nambela's work, they gather the clients who have recently arrived and make them sit down one at a time for consultation. This

Fig 3: Liberation of *pepo;* patients running

is done in the middle of the compound in between Nambela's house and the patient's huts. Nambela takes her seat at a fixed spot on the ground near her house, often with legs crossed. The client is seated a few yards in front of her and has to face Nambela with the legs pointing straight forward. The assistants told me that this was the best way for Nambela to receive 'information' about the person. Since the diagnostic session is a public affair, other clients, patients or visitors, may be watching. One or more assistants help the newcomers and if necessary they translate *Kinyiha*, the vernacular of Nambela, into *Kiswahili*, the national language of Tanzania. Nambela divines in a semi-trance state, usually proceeding from relational problems to physical complaints.

Since the divination session is a public affair, other clients or visitors may be watching as the person for whom Nambela divines is seated on the ground a few yards away from her in the open. Before entering a trance by the typical shivering of *pepo*, Nambela will ask a client where he/she is coming from and from which tribe he/she is. Then she concentrates on the client (and his/her family) to discover the various aspects of the problem involved. Whatever she experiences (feels, hears, sees) or knows may be expressed instantly, whether or not these are direct or indirect matters connected to the client's present situation or state.

If she notices that the client is not aware of certain facts or not willing to admit them, Nambela may repeat what she said more emotionally or ask related questions. As long as the client refuses to see the point, Nambela may feel obstructed to continue. Next she reports the physical complaints or pain of the client(s). Though this may not always be the reason for a client to see her, there is often something to be reported. As more details or negative features in the context of the client gradually unfold, for instance a death due to a family feud, a murder or witchcraft, Nambela will react very dramatically to the pain or problems of clients. The kind of strong vibrations Nambela perceives induces this reaction. Fortunately my field assistant Patterson was well used to Nambela's speech with *pepo*. Besides, he had his own *pepo* experiences to rely on. Without his help, it would have been quite impossible to come to a fair transcription and translation of diagnostic sessions, which I have recorded for this purpose.

Whether or not clients were actively communicating with Nambela, it became clear to me that the divinatory drama is marked by a moment of liminal reflexivity (Turner 1980: 17). Here the visionary capacities are constantly in exchange with reflections to reveal the cause and context of the problem(s) that subsequently calls for a decision that cannot easily be taken by the client alone. Therefore the verbal therapy in divination serves a psychotherapeutic aim. For is it not most convincing to be mirrored by someone who is at the same time considered to be a judge? In contrast to the Western medical approach, where the client informs the doctor about his or her complaints, here the diviner explains to the client what is wrong. If the diviner is not able to assess the emotional and social implications of what (s)he is saying, considerable damage could be caused. The role of the shaman healer is therefore much like that of the psychoanalyst. Both the shaman and the analyst establish a direct relationship with the patients' conscious and an indirect relationship with his unconscious - the analyst through listening, the shaman through oratory.

Pepo etiology: a consult with Nambela

The following example concerns a woman who has come with a small child. Nankala, a novice healer, has brought her along for a second opinion by her tutor Nambela.

Nambela: *'Among your relatives, there is someone who has been running with pepo (kuchima). At your homeground there is a case of accidental death (kifo cha ghafula).'*
Woman: *'Yes, my father hanged himself.'*
Nambela: *'You will also die by accident, if you don't "close" the spirit of your father. I see two women and a man will die! Child (adressing the woman), take your place on the ground (to wake up pepo). You will need to experience pepo awakening at least three times, in order to reduce the trouble of the blood that surrounds your mind ever since the death of your father. God will help you! Did you close his spirit?'*
Woman: *'No, we did not.'*
Nankala: *'This woman reacted with a very strong pepo at my place, in the way that people do who suffer severely from mental illness (ugonjwa ya kichaa).'*
Nambela: *'Alright, here too it will work for her, for if she does not run with pepo, she may wander off in the woods and get lost. When you close your father's spirit, you will close it for all the elders and all children. If she runs off with pepo it is fortunate for her as it will help her to get strength again!'*

Nambela gives no description of the symptoms of the woman who had already been diagnosed by the novice healer Nankala before. She already knows, however, what has happened in the client's family. Important is the fact that the woman has an 'ill' state of *pepo* because her father committed suicide. A suicide or murder is referred to as a sudden death, just as accidents are. This is opposed to natural deaths, which occur of illness or old age. A sudden death must be closed (*kufunga kiparazi*) by means of a sacrifice (a cow, a sheep or a chicken depending on the ties with and the demands of the deceased) and/or special herbs, which are placed in and around the house or on the grave. The deceased is referred to as a shadow or *mzimu*, which must be closed as to fulfill the passage to the world of the dead. This prevents the shadow from becoming harmful to a living relative who may as a result go through the same hardships and meet the same destiny as the deceased. In addition, it needs to be said that to Nambela spirit force or *pepo* stops to exist upon death whereas the shadow remains.

Furthermore, Nambela holds the opinion that all humans are born with *pepo* and as it fluctuates, it may be the cause of illness as well as it can mean a cure. In short, the state of balance with respect to *pepo* is essential to personal wellbeing. The characteristic symptoms of *pepo* illness are heartburn, heart-palpitation, restlessness, weakness and weight loss. This could be intertwined with mental problems like depression, confusion, aggression and withdrawal (*ugonjwa kichaa* or mental illness). Problems related to *pepo* illness comprised also:

1) convulsions,

2) paralysis,

3) sudden deaths,

4) bad luck and

5) black magic.

Yet Nambela could identify three different forms of *pepo* illness. Firstly she could refer to *pepo wa mtu* or the inner spirit of a person being out of balance. Secondly she could mention *pepo wa jini*, an 'alien' spirit force being in disharmony and intruding a victim. Such an 'alien' spirit could be a nature spirit or a deceased spirit originating outside *Nyiha* territory. Thirdly she could refer to *pepo ya mzimu*, a spiritual force of a deceased ancestor who was angered by an offence or a violation of a taboo in the extended family. A disharmony in either level could bring about *pepo* illness or *ugonjwa ya pepo*. During divination Nambela would identify which one(s) was affecting the client. In other words, when *pepo* was in a state of disharmony it could be influenced by spirits of living, dead or non-human forces. According to Nambela, however, a 'good' or 'healthy' *pepo* was always under the influence of a protective or divine spirit force, also a *pepo nzuri*. In that case Nambela called it also *pepo wa Mungu (Mulungu in Kinyiha)*. When bad magic was practised or certain spirits had been sent to harm a person this could only succeed in the absence of such divine forces.

Religious and musical healing sessions

After Nambela had established what was wrong with a patient by using divination, psychotherapeutic treatment of the patient could begin. The main group therapy consisted of participation in rhythmic singing sessions that were kept daily by groups of patients. Sometimes this was combined with rituals to appease spirits or other unseen powers that have an influence on one's inner spirit or *pepo*. Nambela herself was not involved in this activity, although sometimes she joined the singing from a distance, either by humming along with the songs or by watching the reactions of the patients. During my stay she would occasionally halt the proceedings to give an instruction. This happened for instance to let another patient take his or her turn in awakening *pepo* or, to stop a long session because the participants needed a rest. Basically however, this daily group activity was a responsibility of the patients themselves, instigated and conducted by one or more experienced patients (assistants).

A few times a day I would hear the calling for such a gathering as someone shouted: '*Wimbo, Wimbo*' (meaning songs, songs). The loud calling warned me as well, which was very handy. I lived only a few yards away from the compound, with just a small coffee plantation in between. During the first months I was always attracted to the gatherings and by and large I could find out under which conditions they were taking place. The singing took place when a newly arrived patient needed urgent 'treatment', or one of the regular patients or Nambela herself were suddenly seized by *pepo*.

Nambela interpreted some of her dreams as warnings about the social or personal affairs of others. Whenever local people or patients were involved this nearly always provoked a reaction by one or more persons present at the gathering. Sometimes she accused a person of being lazy or ignorant, causing illness and bad luck. When a woman failed to be a good mother and partner, Nambela could react furiously. Also patients who showed immoral behaviour on the compound, like married people maintaining sexual affairs with each other, were not excluded from exposure. Discussions could arise, as the accused tried to defend themselves and other patients confirmed what went on. On other occasions Nambela had the same dream as one of the patients, who would then be eager to find out what message it contained.

Once all this was cleared Nambela started the prayers. The prayers were directed to Jesus Christ and God, stating their contribution in achieving a cure for all. God 'the only healer' was asked to give Nambela and the patients a strong *pepo* to help them in their healing process. She would repeatedly run around the compound with *pepo* after the prayers and make prophecies about local and national events. Often she uttered the same information for weeks or months, adding recent developments. Once back in her 'normal' consciousness these messages were sometimes totally forgotten. While she was running and prophesying, she would finally come to the stage where she would fetch medicine. At that moment she took her hatchet and basket and ran off into the woods.

When Nambela left in search of the roots, everybody moved away to the other side of the compound and started singing. In certain cases immediate action was taken in the middle to direct the singing to one or more people who were in pain. Nambela returned after one or two hours breathing heavily and carrying the basket filled with roots. Sometimes she would start running again, in a reaction to the 'charged' atmosphere that had evolved in the meantime. Eventually she would rest at home, change her clothes (as everybody did on Sunday) and watch the activities on the compound, while meeting friends or members of the family.

These Sunday gatherings continued until late at night, apart from a short interval around 5 p.m. The atmosphere in which these gatherings took place would sooner or later trigger several participants, resulting in a spectacle in which people were staggering, running, swinging, rolling, lying motionless down in the mud or the hot sun, or talking to something invisible. Others were divining or treating other patients (manually or with the help of plants), fetching medicine *(dawa)* or locating hidden witchcraft items *(vipembe)*. These different expressions were intrinsic to the state of *pepo,* meaning that each person had a specific pattern(s) of behavior, be it more introvert or extrovert. Below follows a description of the role of *pepo* in regular singing sessions, being a means of expression with emotional and therapeutic significance.

The encounter with *pepo* awakening

To experience the songs, people had to take their place on a particular spot on the ground in the middle of the compound with their legs straight ahead of them, their hands relaxed on their thigh. Usually it was necessary to stay for a while on the compound in order to give *pepo* time to 'wake up' and to benefit from the outcome of a released *pepo*. A fast or slow reaction to awaken and to release *pepo* was due to personal factors. If Nambela was very worried about a patient, she would call for an immediate gathering and while singing everybody paid attention to this one patient. As a rule, however, patients sat down on the ground while a group of people (other patients) were singing around them. Family members who accompanied new patients had to stay at a distance since they could disturb the process of 'awakening' *pepo*. Money had to be left behind because this too had a negative impact. New patients were invited to speak what was on their mind. If they were not willing to do so at once, this was repeated after a few songs and if silence still prevailed, a new attempt was given on another occasion. To certain patients this clearing process turned out to be essential. Only after they had found the courage to speak out was the release of *pepo* achieved. Most of the people needed several days or even weeks to open up to the songs. They were considered to have a *pepo* that was still 'asleep'. Little by little their *pepo* would become more sensitive to the songs, even by just being present or singing along. Occasionally it could happen that the first session made a person trigger (awake and release) *pepo*. It was said that somebody who reacted fast was having a 'strong' *pepo* and therefore was more sensitive or liable to have the abilities of 'seeing things'. Nambela would tell a patient about this either during the first diagnostic session or in the course of the stay. Sometimes she would encourage a person to develop these abilities like she did and use this gift for the same purpose. She did so to those people who otherwise would often be troubled by their strong and sensitive *pepo*. These could be either men or women.

At the start of a gathering only a few people were participating. It was only after a few songs that more and more people joined in. New patients were explicitly invited to join the sessions and soon everybody would get acquainted with the songs. The more people joined, the more intense the atmosphere could become, as the dedication and attention increased around the group sitting on the ground. There were occasions when the right atmosphere could not be created, no matter how many people were around.

I felt that all this depended very much on the devotion of the solo singers. They too were patients and they did not always feel strong or well enough to take the lead. If the solo singer was not replaced then the singing session would just end.

As a general feature, as soon as *pepo* was felt to 'free' itself this was accompanied by a shivering and/or shaking of the body. At the next stage the person would slowly start to lie down, still shivering or shaking. The surrounding group immediately cleared the way, still directing all their attention to the person concerned until he or she started to roll over the ground.

The circle of people would then open. The purpose of the songs to liberate *pepo* was achieved and the circle would close again. And again the attention was directed to other patients, who sat down in the middle. The liberation of *pepo* actually stands for the state of trance in which a person achieves a situation where his or her willpower is taken over by another power. This situation is reached through a pattern of general sensations that are seen as essential preceding stages. In the course of my trials with *pepo* (both my own and that of others) I discovered, that an intensified feeling is sensed in the belly as pepo starts to react to the songs. However, there were also people who felt this sensation first of all in their feet or legs. These people suffered from pressure in their legs and so the tension had first to free itself there. This was considered the most difficult situation in which to achieve the liberation of *pepo* as it had to climb first to the belly and the chest to make its way to the head.

As I was eager to experience all this myself, I often took my place on the ground during the sessions. Nambela told me that my *pepo* was concentrated in my belly. If it were to 'wake up' from there, it would be possible for me also to liberate pepo. I was only too well aware of the fact that ever since my childhood, I have suffered from complaints of belly oppression and obstruction. These complaints gradually lessened due to my yoga activities and I noticed that in particular a relaxation of the nervous system caused this improvement. So it did not come as a surprise to me that in a reaction to the songs, or the 'awakening' of *pepo*, I felt an intense reaction in the main nervous centre, seated around the navel. But I only got as far as to notice the sensation in my neck but never any further. Whenever these sensations failed to reach the crown of the head the awakening could not be completed. In other words, the spirit could not be split from the head (*pepo anapasua rasi*) and thus remained in the body of the *pepo* patient.

Discussion about *pepo* healing

Nambela's knowledge of the human body seems based on what she perceives clairvoyantly during the divination. In this way too she receives information about the symptoms and the solution e.g. the type of herbal remedies that were to be applied. Nambela would attribute the efficacy of herbal medicine, or *dawa ya miti shamba* (lit. plant medicines from the field), to the power of nature and God. This she often stated at the end of a divination session but was repeated during the weekly religious prayers in which Nambela always said 'God will help you (*Mungu atasaidia*), for God is the only healer'. Just as she considered herself to be an intermediary between God and the people, so was the plant. Nambela regularly stressed in this context that medicine would only be effective if people had cleared their problems or faults, an approach that had been common among the *Nyiha* in the past.

As soon as all problems are cleared from the heart (*kutoa mawazo za moyo*) *pepo* patients would be encouraged to experience and manifest *pepo* forces by means of musical sessions. The songs that were sung during group singing sessions contained a lot of information about the emotional, social and religious aspects of *pepo*. But more important was that a total opening to the songs was achieved. For this purpose the singers gathered around the patients ear. All patients participated in this process and since I often took part too I noticed how easy it was to stop thinking, for the strong vibrations of the voices would completely occupy me. It was easy to understand that this has a hypnotizing effect on everyone.

The liberation of *pepo* resulted in a state of trance In which a person's willpower was taken over by another power. When this happened vigorously Nambela divined the patient to find out if he had a calling to be a *pepo* healer. Yet also without having a calling, most patients had visionary sights after having experienced the liberation of *pepo* for a length of time.

It was demonstrated in this article how, by the use of songs, music opened a gateway to altered states of consciousness. Patients could encounter experiences that went beyond the physical involving emotional, mental and spiritual changes which stretched out from the personal to the transpersonal level (experiences that go beyond the personal). These experiences could have a beneficial outcome as they confronted patients with their suppressed feelings which were at the bases of their spiritual afflictions. By clearing both mind and body people should restore their balance, spur their self-healing principle, and encounter spiritual growth. In other words, the individual affliction gradually transformed into a positive experience, both for the individual as well as the social group. This process is strongly parallel with *Kundalini yoga* experiences (AVALON 1974).

Let me summarize:

1. When *pepo* was asleep this was felt like a bundle of heat or power in a certain part of the lower body. As patients experienced this sensation they shivered from within the spine where an internal fire was experienced. Therefore the singers often shouted: *chema, chema, amka pepo* or "come to a boil and let *pepo* wake up".

2. As the sensation of an internal fire would rise up from the abdomen with the help of the singing it would eventually leave the head via the crown, thereby awakening and liberating pepo. At this stage, people lost control while another power took over their mind and body.

3. Those patients with stronger spirit forces sooner benefited from the healing sessions. In other words, their consciousness opened further as personal wellbeing was achieved which was accompanied by visionary sights and the impulse to help others by finding medicinal plants and exposing evil.

4. Those with strong *pepo* (*pepo joto*, literally a hot *pepo*) were encouraged to gain control over their spiritual powers and become novice healers. In this case they had to abide by *pepo* regulations (*sheria wa pepo*). The major disciplines were food restrictions, to be followed upon indication of the spirits, and not to misuse their newly gained spirit powers. The novice healers were profoundly made aware that protection and personal wellbeing were now in the hands of the spirits. Subsequently they had no need to ask a fee for treatment. To diminish the disturbances in communication between the spirits and the healer, the novice healers were not to take alcoholic drinks, and not to maintain sexual affairs with others than one's own partner. Those healers who violated these regulations not only suffered from illness again, they also saw their skills and powers diminish or end.

This parallel with my personal *Kundalini yoga* practices may indicate that certain historical relationships exist between yoga, occult practices and shamanism (ELIADE 1983). More important is, however, that spiritual forces or clairvoyant

abilities are largely culturally shaped and that the experience remains subjective and thus highly individual. Spirits, devils, gods or angels may have no power or reality to those who do not believe in their existence.
To others who do give them energy through their beliefs, they are very real. In African cultures, where people may feel restricted to show their emotions, traditional healing practices are an important arena for expression. Simultaneously this arena also allows for the transmission and diffusion of a cultural healing heritage.

Author
DR. JESSICA ERDTSIECK
Masters in Anthropology, studied anthropology at the University of Amsterdam and is now in the final stage of writing a PhD thesis which concerns a comparative study of *pepo* healers in Tanzania. This thesis deals with the various types of spirit forces that healers use and how these forces relate to geographical, historical and cultural dynamics. So far most accounts of traditional healers have been focused around male specialists therefore in her thesis she directs the main attention to the roles of female healers.
Contact: E-Mail: J.Erdtsieck@frw.uva.nl

References
AVALON, A. 1974. *The serpent power.* New York.
ELIADE, M. 1983. *Le chamanisme et les techniques archaiques de l'extase.* Paris.
ERDTSIECK, J. 1993. *Spiritual forces in illness and healing. The role of pepo in the life and healing practice of a female healer in the Southwestern highlands of Tanzania.* Nijmegen, Third World Centre (Occ. paper nr. 32).
ERDTSIECK, J. 1997. *Pepo as an inner healing force. Practices of a female spiritual healer in Tanzania.* Amsterdam (Bulletin 343).
ERDTSIECK, J. 2001. *Nambela mganga wa pepo; Mambo afanyayo mganga wa tiba ya asili kwa uwezo wa pepo nchini Tanzania.* Dar es Salaam University Press.
FULLER-TORREY, E. 1972. Witchdoctors and psychiatrists. The common roots of psychotherapy and its future. New York.
GROF, S. & Ch. 1989. *Spiritual emergency. When personal transformation becomes a crisis.* Los Angeles.
HARNER, M. 1982. *The way of the shaman.* New York.
JANZEN, J., NGOMA. 1982. *Discourses of healing in Central and Southern Africa.* Berkeley.
KAKAR, S. 1982. *Shamans, mystics and doctors.* Boston.
KATZ, R. 1982. *Boiling energy.* Cambridge (Mass.).
KELLO-AYOT, H.O. 1976. *Topics in East-African history.* Nairobi.
KESBY, J.D. 1977. *The cultural regions of East Africa.* London.
KIEV, A.. 1974. *Magic, faith and healing.* New York.
LÉVI-STRAUSS, C. 1967. *Structural anthropology.* New York.
LEWIS, I. (ed.). 1971. *Ecstatic religion. An anthropological study of spirit possession and shamanism.* New York.
MBITI, J.S. 1969. *African religions and philosophy.* East African Educational Publishers.
PEEK, P. (ed.) 1968. *African divination systems. Ways of knowing.* Bloomington.
PRINCE, R. (ed.). 1968. *Trance and possession states.* Montreal.
SHORTER, A. 1974. *East-African societies.* London.
WALSH, R.N. 1990. *The spirit of shamanism.* Los Angeles.

IGBO HEILER UND WEGE ZUR HEILUNG VON GEISTESKRANKHEITEN IN SÜDOST NIGERIA*

von Patrick Iroegbu

Einführung

Nur sehr wenig Aufmerksamkeit wurde den kulturspezifischen Wegen zur Heilung von Geisteskrankheiten gewidmet bis KLEINMANN (1980) das "erklärende Modell", welches sich mit kulturellen und biomedizinischen Fragen der Ethnopsychiatrie beschäftigt, erforschte.

Dieser Text soll nun die *Igbo*-Heiler in Südost Nigeria vorstellen. Ihre Methoden zur Heilung der Geisteskrankheiten aus größerem symbolischen Blickwinkel sollen aufgezeigt werden. Es soll dargestellt werden wie Semantik und traditionelle Praktiken zu beachtenswerten Heilerfolgen führen können. Ich behaupte, dass Menschen, konfrontiert mit den verschiedensten alltäglichen Krankheiten, dazu neigen, sich auf der Suche nach Heilung zwischen den verschiedenen Heilungsangeboten im Kreis drehen. Diese Suche nach dem Sinn der Krankheit und der Heilung findet abseits der wissenschaftlichen Schulmedizin statt, der es oft nicht gelingt, effektive Ergebnisse zu erzielen. Weiter wird dargestellt, wie *Igbo*-Mediziner ihren Patienten helfen, das eigene Krankheitsgeschehen in Bezug auf die Weltordnung zu verstehen, wobei sie das kulturelle System verantwortlich für den jetzigen Zustand des Patienten machen.

Der Versuch der (Krankheits-) Analyse bezieht Symbolik und Semantik mit ein. Er betrachtet die Erlösung von den Ursachen des mentalen Leidens bei gleichzeitiger Anwendung tierischer und pflanzlicher Heilmittel. Es wird versucht, einen Einblick in ethnomedizinische Blickwinkel und Praktiken der *Igbo* zu gewähren, die ihnen helfen, ihr Gesundheitssystem, ihre Gesellschaft und ihre Welt zu ordnen. Die Beobachtung der Heilungsformen des Wahnsinns soll verständlich

---

* Übersetzung aus dem Englischen: Udo Richter, Wiebke Wollenweber, Johanna-Kathrin Malsch, Jan Wacker, Matthias Schmidt und Oliver Bosch, überarbeitet von Joy C. Green.

machen, wie Therapie angewandt wird im Kontext mit sozialen und symbolischen Erfordernissen. Desweiteren enthüllt diese Schrift einige verborgene, magische Mysterien in den komplexen Symbolsystemen und der Pflanzen- und Tierwelt des therapeutischen Bereiches.

Hervorzuheben sind die Praktiken des "Bindens" (*Tying ritual*) und deren Auswirkungen auf die Ursachen des Leidens. Es wird dargestellt, welche Geister und hexerische Energien dabei verwandt werden.

Heilungsverständnis

Im Gegensatz zu biomedizinischen Psychiatern sehen Heiler Geisteskrankheiten nicht als unheilbar an. Heilung zielt vielmehr darauf ab, Verwirrungen der Gefühle und der sozialen Ordnung wiederherzustellen, als die Symptome zu behandeln. Eine komplexe Ätiologie der Geisteskrankheiten stellt einen Rahmen für die Erklärungen der Krankheiten, des Todes und des Unglücks dar. Erklärungen, welche angeführt werden, reichen von angesammelter menschlicher Gewalt bis zum Zorn der Ahnen. Aus der kollektiv-sozialen und kulturellen Vorstellung heraus betrachtet, sind Depressionen, Angst, Demenz, Epilepsie, manische Syndrome und biopsychosoziale Formen der geistigen Erkrankung weit verbreitet.

Igbo-Heiler

Igbo-Heiler werden *Dibia* genannt, und stehen mit der Medizin-Gottheit *Agwu* in Verbindung. Ihre Entwicklung zur vollen Kunst des Heilens ist sehr kompliziert und beinhaltet die Berufung, Initiationsriten und ein langes Studium über die Gottheit *Agwu*. Der weitverbreitete Ausdruck *Dibia* bedeutet Heiler, Medizinmann, Priester, Medizinhändler. Heiler beschäftigen sich mit aller Art medizinischer und therapeutischer Aktivität, um die Heilung der körperlichen Krankheit, der sozialen und kosmologischen Ordnung und der Gesellschaft sicherzustellen. Sie befassen sich mit aktiven und inneren Prozessen, sowie Prophezeiung, Erinnerungen an vergangene Handlungen, Glauben und dem Umgang mit Leidenschaft, um den Raum der Normalität von allen negativen Mustern zu befreien. Durch das Wiederherstellen der emotionalen und geistigen Gesundheit einer geistesgestörten Person mit einen gut ausgeklügelten rituellen Akt wird eine Energieverbindung gepflegt. Geisteskrankheit – im Sinne der *Igbo* – ist ätiologisch eng mit dem Verhalten des Kollektivs gegenüber dem Schicksal, im sozialen Gefüge und im Haushalt verknüpft. Es zeigt an, dass die Gesellschaft es verpasst hat, Probleme zu lösen, wodurch eine Lücke für das Eindringen anderer unreifer Kräfte entsteht, welche eine fragwürdige Pathologie und lächerliche Verhaltensweisen über die erkrankten Personen und über die Gesellschaft bringen. Dadurch wird der Zerfall geltender Formen der Ehre und Identität vorangetrieben, welcher sich nun als Lebensschwierigkeiten in dem Körper des Geistesgestörten manifestieren. Mit anderen Worten: wenn in irgendeiner Gesellschaft Widersprüche sehr häufig auftreten, ist es sehr wahrscheinlich, dass Verhaltensstörungen und geistige Verwirrungen gehäuft auftreten. Um weniger geisteskranke Leute hervorzubringen, müsste eine Gesellschaft ihre Probleme lösen, um so die geistig Klaren und Dynamischen zu unterstützen.

Heilung, wie sie hier diskutiert wird, beinhaltet eine spezielle Organisation von Kräften. Zuerst will der Heiler den Erkrankten neu mit Kraft versorgen um ihn aus seiner Unfähigkeit zu lösen und die Schwäche, die ihn besetzt hält, durch Stärke zu ersetzen.

Der wichtigste Gesichtspunkt hierbei ist, dass der Heiler eng mit der erkrankten Person und seiner Familie zusammenarbeitet, um das zu entwickeln, was der Kranke braucht, um von seiner Geisteskrankheit erlöst zu werden. Aus ethnographischen Erhebungen heraus wird deutlich, dass zwei erklärende Heilungsmodelle sehr häufig auftauchen in der Behandlung der Geisteskrankheit. Namentlich die symbolische Behandlung und die Wurzel-Pflanzentherapie.

Heilen durch symbolische Erlösung
Die *Igbo* verstehen Heilung der Geisteskrankheit als Resultat aus einem Rahmen symbolischer Erlösung. Hierbei geht es darum, die Geisteskrankheit zu heilen durch die Befreiung der eingedrungenen Kräfte. Es ist bedeutend, für meine Aussage die Frage zu stellen, was symbolische Erlösung ist, und warum der Begriff sehr gut passt für das Verständnis, das Heiler von der Heilung der Geisteskrankheit haben.

Definition
Der Gebrauch von Wurzeln und Pflanzen für die Heilung der Geisteskrankheit funktioniert alleine nicht. Es fängt an mit wichtigen therapeutischen Zeremonien, um den Zustand des kranken Patienten zu lindern. Diese Zeremonie wird "Symbolische Erlösung" genannt. Sie bereitet den Weg für die Wurzel- und Pflanzengebräue, die effektiv im Körper wirken. Die Vorstellung von symbolischer Erlösung bezieht sich auf beides: die therapeutische Aktion und der rituelle Gebrauch der Pflanzen im Umgang mit der Krankheit. Das therapeutische Handeln bezeiht sich auf Beides: auf die Ursachen und auf die Symptome.
Ohne das symbolische Erlösungsmuster der Ethnotherapie würde der Gebrauch von Drogen (Pflanzen, Kräuter) die Krankheit nur bis zu einem bestimmten Punkt lindern. Nur wenn symbolische Erlösung stattfindet, werden Bedrohungen eliminiert, um den Genesungsprozess zu erleichtern und das Netz der verwandtschaftlichen Verhältnisse neu zu strukturieren. Dann hat der Patient eine gute Chance, geheilt zu werden. Volksheiler, denen es gelingt, zerstörte Beziehungen wieder herzustellen, fahren fort, Therapien zu formulieren, die die ökologischen Begebenheiten und den physischen und sozialen Zustand des Patienten behandeln, um eine endgültige Heilung zu erreichen.
Psychiater haben selten diesen Erfolg . Es werden Psychopharmaka verabreicht und damit nur der körperliche Aspekt der Krankheit behandelt. Der gesamte Rahmen der symbolischen Erlösung ist jedoch für eine Gesamtheilung des Patienten notwendig. Ein Prozess auf der Suche nach den Ursachen hängt immer damit zusammen, warum bestimmte Dinge auf bestimmte Weise geschehen. In diesem Punkt geht es darum, klarzustellen, warum einige Leute sogar nach dem Grund fragen, der hinter bestimmten Dingen steht, von denen ihnen erzählt worden ist, dass sie sie getan hätten.
Das System des Auflösens einer Quelle der Störung funktioniert wie eine Art Verschleierung, welche manipuliert ist, um andere Realitäten fernzuhalten. Sie sind also da, um andere Realitäten zu verbergen.
Therapie in diesem Zusammenhang bedeutet, Raum- und Rahmenbedingungen zu schaffen, um die Quelle der Aggression und Bedrängnis zu bekämpfen. Sie beschäftigt sich nicht zuerst mit dem Patienten und seinen Symptomen.
Der grundlegende Unterschied zwischen solchen indigenen Therapien und biomedizinischen psychiatrischen Behandlungen ist, dass Volksheiler Beziehun-

gen heilen, wobei Psychiater lediglich Körper heilen. Diese Maßnahme unterstützt nicht den Einklang im Körper, bzw. den Konsens zwischen der sozialen Gruppe und der Lebenswelt des Betroffenen. Menschliche Gefühle haben eine physikalische Auswirkung auf unseren Körper und interagieren mit unseren Zellen und unserem Gewebe. Ihre Therapie kann Erfahrungen des Leidens in komplexe biologische Prozesse, welche in der Folge eine heilende Wirkung haben, umwandeln, indem Erlebnisse aufgearbeitet werden.

Ein weiterer wichtiger Punkt ist der Umgang mit Rückfällen aus Phasen der Zustandsbesserung eines Patienten. Während Psychiater dies als einen Rückfall in die Krankheit betrachten, deuten Heiler es als erneuten Besuch aus der Geisterwelt. Es wird als übermenschlich ausgedrückte kulturelle Kraft verstanden. Nun ist es wichtig, den Patienten nicht als erkrankte Person zu behandeln, sondern ihn als Botschafter der Quelle dieser Störung (Gottheit, Geisterwelt) zu verstehen. Therapien sind so aufgebaut, daß sie den Patienten eine neue Vision des Lebens vermitteln und ihn nicht entmutigen oder isolieren.

Also beinhaltet die Heilung der Geisteskrankheit die Beziehung zwischen Geist und Körper genauso wie das soziale Umfeld und die Lebenswelt.

Im esoterischen Bereich gibt es viele Informationen *sui generis*, zusammen mit Phänomenen, die wir nicht verstehen, welche auf ihre Entdeckung warten. Es ist das grundlegende Ziel der Heilung der Geisteskrankheit den Willen der zerstörenden Kraft zu brechen. Es wird deutlich, dass der therapeutische Wille, obwohl schwer zu quantifizieren, eine entscheidende Rolle spielt, was den Erfolg der Therapie betrifft. Dort, wo der therapeutische Wille schwach ist, kann die Effektivität des "symbolischen Erlösens", welchem der Gebrauch von Wurzeln und Kräutern folgt, neutralisiert werden. Es scheint, als ob große therapeutische Willenskraft die Potenz der Wurzeln und Kräuter schärft, und so maßgebend ist, um den störenden Kräften, der Quelle des Leidens standzuhalten und diese einzudämmen.

Die *Igbo* glauben außerdem, dass bestimmte Bäume Unterhaltungen mithören und aufnehmen können. Bäume können Geräusche absorbieren und wahrnehmen, dies führt zu dem anthropomorphen Glauben, dass Bäume hören können. Bäume interagieren in extensiven Ritualen, die Geburt, Wachstum, Heirat, Krankheit und Tod beinhalten. *Igbo* betrachten Bäume als vitalste Symbole des Lebens und der Ewigkeit, im Gegensatz zu Gräbern als Symbole von Tod und Verblassen der Erinnerung.

Diese Dimension verbindet das Wissen ihrer Ahnen mit Herbalismus in symbolischer Erlösung für die Heilung das Wahns. Bäume drücken genealogische Kontinuität aus und helfen uns somit zu verstehen, wie andere untereinander kommunizieren und sich selbst organisieren.

Anwendungsformen

1.Fesselritual, ihe ekike oder amuma ekike
Dies ist eine Technik, die die Transformation von Kräften zur Wiederherstellung der Gesundheit (besonders bei Geisteskrankheit) darstellt. Der *Igbo* Begriff *igwo oria* ("um Krankheit zu heilen") ist nicht auf Gegenstände mit rein therapeutischen Anwendungen beschränkt. Er beinhaltet ebenfalls Formen der Beratung und bestimmte Arten der Gestik, deren effektive Anwendungen sich auf mehr als nur den einfachen Heilungsprozess erstrecken (cf.Iᴇ ᴡᴜ 1982; Eᴢᴇʟɪᴏʀᴀ 1994;85).

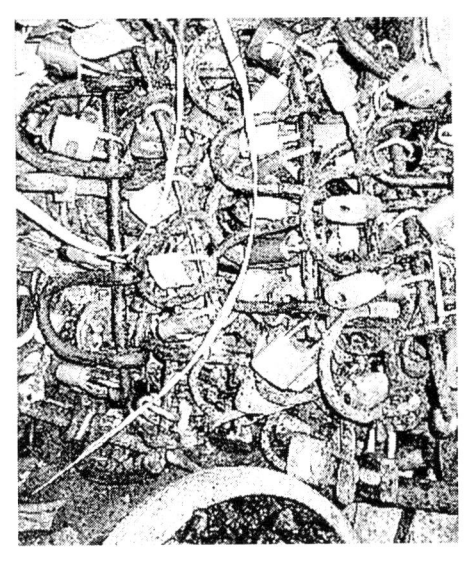

Abb. 1:
Schlösser, *igodo*

Abb. 1 zeigt rituelle Schlüssel, *igodo amuma*, die mit der Kraft belegt sind, Patienten von störenden Mustern zu befreien. Das rituelle Fesseln findet seine Anwendung mit dem Zweck, eine Person vor psychischen Stressfaktoren, Feinden und destruktiven Kräften zu beschützen.
Es sollen dadurch also jegliche Art von Attacken abgewehrt werden. Die Verwendung von Kraftobjekten spielt hierbei eine große Rolle. Am häufigsten werden Seile, Schnüre, Stricke oder Bindfäden verwendet (z.B. *uzoro*, wie die auf hohen Bäumen wachsende "Brotfrucht" (*treculia africana, ukwa*).
Des weiteren gibt es das *Trimphetta*-Seil (*akwara ngwo*), das aus *Raffia*-Schnur (*piassava: ngswo*) hergestellt wird und *tie* (*elaeis guineensis, ekwere nkwu*).Die Fähigkeit oder Kapazität der störenden Kraft, mit der umgegangen wird, soll eingeschnürt werden, wobei eine Deplazierung und Umlenkung der Störung angestrebt wird. Wenn das Fesseln beendet ist, wird die eingeschnürte Medizin (*ogwu*) normalerweise an einen beliebigen Platz des Hauses gehängt oder, je nach Fall, vergraben. In den meisten Fällen werden diese Amulette, die die Heilung von Geisteskrankheiten bewirken sollen, an Hauswände oder auf das Dach gehängt.
Ich fand heraus, dass das Fesseln Extraktion und Umlenkung der Krankheit zum Ziel hat. Es entfernt sie vom Körper, indem es diesem einen Eindruck von Normalität vermittelt. Lassen Sie mich, ohne tiefer auf die Erläuterung der Bedeutung von Symbolen einzugehen, beschreiben, was der Heiler Sunday Iroabuchi den von ihm für Behandlung von Geisteskrankheiten (*ara*) eingesetzten Objekten zuschreibt. Die von der Krankheit hervorgerufenen Störungen werden mit einem speziellen Behandlungsmuster, dass der Heiler durch Divination erkennt und dann in Gang setzt, konfrontiert. Als erstes wird der Patient durch einen rituellen Rahmen von seinen Schwächen befreit. Der erste Ritus versucht durch Ausdruck der Notwendigkeit von Opferung und Hingabe, die die Kranheit umgebenden Kräfte zu transformieren. Die Betonung und Untermauerung des Opfers zur Befreiung des Kranken wird weiter mit mit der Verstärkung des metaphysischen Begriffs von Macht verbunden.

Die Technik integriert die folgenden Dynamiken:
Schwäche ist eine Darstellung von Unfähigkeit und Untauglichkeit, und steht für einen schwachen Körper, Kraft für einen starken Körper, Fülle für Vermittlung um Kraft zu befreien und wieder herzustellen (bzw. Schwäche in Kraft zu transformieren), störende Elemente auszuschalten, zu trennen und zu vertreiben, und schließlich Genesung und Erhohlung zu erreichen.
Was bei dieser Art von Techniken besonders betont wird, ist die anfängliche Betrachtung des Patienten als schwaches Wesen in einem schwachen Körper. Die Identität des Körpers ist durch Verhaltenskrisen, besonders durch Anflüge von Wahn, angreifbar und verletzlich geworden. Die Dringlichkeit des Rituals führt den Patienten aus der Sackgasse der Schwäche heraus und bringt ihn auf eine, auf Kraft ausgerichtete Bahn. Er soll seinen gesunden Körper wiederfinden (*ahu isike*).
Auf diese Weise wird der Patient in eine Atmosphäre normaler Stärke gebracht, um mit alltäglichen Aufgaben umzugehen.

2. Loslassen durch Schlossöffnung, Aufschließen (igodo)
Eine andere Technik des Loslassens ist die des Aufschließens eines Raumes oder Weges (*ikpoghe uzo*). Die relevanten, hier verwendeten Symbole sind ein Schloss mit Schlüssel (*igodo*), die bezeichnend für ihr auf- und verschließen im Prozess des Loslassens sind. Eine belastend wirkende Kraft wird abgeschnitten und, wie beim Fesseln, vom Kontakt zur betreffenden Person abgeschirmt.
Der Schlüssel ist ein wichtiges symbolisches Werkzeug, das eine Vielzahl von Verwendungen findet. Während er für zur Herstellung von Glückstalismanen verwendet wird, findet man ihn in bestimmten Regionen ebenfalls als gegen andere Personen gerichtete Schadens- und Unglücksbringer.
Wie auch immer man ihn vorfindet, es wird immer das Auf- oder Verschließen bestimmter Absichten angestrebt. Die Verwendung von rituellen Schlüsseln (*igodo amuma*) ist deshalb effektiv, weil sie in Form von Abwehrmechanismen, die störende Kräfte vom geistig Erkrankten fernhalten und auch am Kranken festhaltenden Kräften einen Weg eröffnen, diesen zu verlassen. Um den Effekt der Behandlung zu steigern werden diese symbolischen Schlüssel mit großer Vorliebe eingesetzt. So wird geglaubt, dass wenn ein Schlüssel erstmal für den speziellen Zweck, den Weg einer Person oder einer Geisterkraft zu blockieren hergestellt wurde, damit auch ein solider Effekt erzielt wird. Ein Schlüssel mit der Kraft der Heilung von Geisteskrankheiten wird normalerweise in einem Behälter mit Eiern, Steinen und Muscheln, die ebenfalls transformatorische Kräfte besitzen sollen, aufbewahrt. Das Schloss wird vor dem Patienten hin- und herbewegt und schließlich hinter seinem Rücken geöffnet.

3. Verbinden des Menschen mit den Geistern und Gott, ekike mmuo na madu
Diese Methode zeigt eine unter Heilern weit verbreitete Technik, die das Fesseln/Verbinden vom Menschen, Geistern und Gott beinhaltet.
Diese Technik befreit und heilt den Kranken dadurch, dass sie ihn auf eine Ebene des "Kampfes gegen den Quell des Kummers *(ibuso nmuo okwu)*" trägt.
Um diese Konfrontation zu verstärken bindet der Heiler dem Patienten einen Umhang bzw. Mantel auf Brust und Hüfte, der mit Gegenständen bestückt ist, die den Menschen mit Gott und den Geistern verbinden sollen, wie es auf Bild 3 zu sehen ist. Brust (*obi*) und Hüfte (*ukwu*) gelten als besonders starke Zonen (*ifu ike*). Die weitere Behandlung mit Wurzeln und Kräutern gilt dabei den symptomatischen Manifestationen der Krankheit. Grundlegend müssen aber alle

Handlungen die Besserung bringen sollen, mit einer Neudefinition der Grenzen im Sinne der Rettung und Sicherung des Patienten, einhergehen.

4. Der Geisteskranke und Befreiung

Jeder Zustand von Geisteskrankheit erfordert eine Befreiung und einen Wechsel vom Patientenstatus hin zur Gesundheit. Unabhängig von der Personalität, die momentan aufrechterhalten wird, resultieren die körperlichen Beschwerden des Geisteskranken aus einer Störung der physischen, sozialen und moralischen Harmonie des normalen Lebens. Bei einem anderen wichtigen Ritual wird der Körper mit rituellem Pulver eingerieben. Dabei wird der Patient vorsichtig berührt und es wird ihm schwarzes Pulver in die Haut massiert.

Der Prozess als Ganzes erfordert das Eindringen der schwarzen Medizin in sieben Schnitte auf dem Kopf. Von diesen sieben Schnitten aus soll das fließende Blut im Sinne einer Reinigung die Medizin in das Gehirn und den Körper schwemmen.

Das Ziel ist praktisch das Gehirn von höhnischen Kräften zu isolieren, die einen Verlust von kosmologischer Energie hervorrufen.

5. Der Medizin-Topf

Der Medizin-Topf beinhaltet typische Materialien, wie unten gezeigt wird. Dazu gehören unter Anderem ein Affen- (*isi enwe*) und ein Hundekopf (*nkita*).

Alle Kraftobjekte werden in einem Topf (*ite*) aufbewahrt, der hier als Medizin-Topf vorgestellt wird. Dieser Topf wird in ein Becken (*efere*) gestellt, der bestimmte Wurzeln und symbolische Objekte wie Federn enthält.

Wenn die Situation es erfordert, werden die Gegenstände herausgenommen und zur Behandlung von Hirn und Körper verwendet. Unter Umständen werden der Affen- oder Hundeschädel als essenzielle Therapieelemente zur Transformation der störenden Kräfte benötigt.

Dabei gilt dem Affen die erste Wahl. Wenn keiner zur Verfügung steht, muss auf den Hundeschädel zurückgegriffen werden. Desweiteren ist *enwe* (Affe) gleichbedeutend mit Tauschpraktiken betreffenden Begriffen, wie etwa *onwo* (Tausch) und *weta bia were* (nehmen und geben), oder dem Ausdruck *weta isi bia were isi* (Kopf für Kopf bringen). Es wird betont, dass dem Gebrauch von rituellen Objekten dieser Art eine besondere Bedeutung beigemessen wird. Nachdem die Kraftobjekte zusammengeführt wurden, öffnet der Heiler den Affenkopf und gibt das Gehirn in einen Mörser. Der Schädelinhalt wird mit einer Wurzel vermischt, die der Behandlung von Epilepsie (*akwukwu*) dient.

Das zerstoßene Gemisch wird zu einem schwarzen Pulver verbrannt (*inu oke*) und unter gegebenen Umständen eingesammelt und soweit verstärkt, dass richtiges schwarzes Pulver entsteht. Dieses Produkt, das der Behandlung von Geisteskrankheit dient, wird *oke ononu* genannt.

Als nächster Schritt werden dem Kranken die Haare abgeschoren und es werden mit einer Rasierklinge (*mma akwa*) die sieben Einschnitte gemacht. In diese Schnitte, die die sieben Kräfte der Geistesstörung repräsentieren, wird dann *onunu* einmassiert, womit eine Verbindung zum inneren Teil des Körpers gewährleistet werden soll. Der Austauschprozess von dem hier die Rede ist, wird vervollständigt durch den Kontakt des Blutes mit den symbolischen Elementen. Dieser Zustand erklärt letztlich die kranke Person als von der Anwesenheit der störenden Kraft, und damit von ihren Erscheinungen und Blockaden befreit. Schließlich wird dem Patienten in der Folgezeit durch intensive Beratung und Wiederherstellung der Familienstrukturen zur Seite gestanden.

6. Die Aufstellung des Medizin-Topfes

Die Positionierung des Topfes (*ite ogwu*) ist, wie man der Abbildung 4 entnehmen kann, nicht wahllos. Bei näherer Betrachtung fällt auf, dass die Ausrichtung nicht nur nach dem Körper, sondern auch nach kosmologischen Zusammenhängen stattfindet. Der Topf befindet sich ständig im Blickfeld. Die Muster repräsentieren die obere Körperhälfte und die Welt darunter. Er besteht aus dem Mentalen und den vom Himmel kommenden Kräften. Das Becken (*efere*) oder die Schüssel (*oku*) ruhen auf der Erde, bzw. dem Land (*ala*).

Das Erdreich ist der Lebensraum der Geister und so wie der Topf mit dem Oberen, so verbindet er auch mit der Erde. Der Topf liefert ein Muster der kosmologischen Verknüpfungen bestehender Heilungssymbolik. In seiner Gesamtheit bildet das Ritual des Bindens und Loslösens einen Kanal, wie der Topf zeigt, um Emotionen auszudrücken und bietet der erkrankten Person ein Medium, in dem Enttäuschung und Frustration zum Ausdruck gebracht werden können. Damit soll auch der Weg aus der Gefangenschaft durch Gewalt und Verlust der sozialen Stellung beschritten werden.

7. Anbinden lebensspendender Kräfte

Der Bedarf Dinge zusammenzubinden kann nicht oft genug betont werden. Diese Technik nimmt bei den Heilern die zentralste Rolle bei der Behandlung psychiatrischer Störungen ein. Deshalb müssen im Vorfeld der Befreiung des Patienten seine Grenzen aufgelöst werden. Es ist weiterhin notwendig, die Bedeutung einiger Ritualobjekte zu erläutern, bzw. zu welchem Grad sich ihre Wirksamkeit auf den gesamten Ritualkomplex erstreckt.

Ein zentraler Inhalt ist die Gewinnung von Kraft. Kraft weckt das Bewusstsein von Stabilität, Normalität und Fortschritt, woraus die Erhaltung der Gesundheit resultiert.

8. Stimmungen und Farben

Wie aus dem vorhergehenden Text ersichtlich wird, erfordert die Behandlung geistiger Erkrankungen eine intensive Interaktion von Patient und Heiler, sowie eine Einheit der Erfahrungen im unmittelbaren und kosmologischen Umfeld. Die Interaktion variiert von Person zu Person. Um Verhaltensweisen zu ermitteln und darzustellen, bezieht sich der Heiler auf Farben, die bezeichnend für die Art des Konfliktes oder eine Übergangssituation sind. Des weiteren sind sie Zeichen für die Art und Weise, wie bestimmte Bilder von einer Gruppe kreiert oder widergespiegelt werden und wie sie mit der Geisterwelt, bzw. den von dort kommenden störenden Kräften in Verbindung stehen. Farben (*ucha ihe*) können dem Transfer bestimmter Sinninhalte (positive, sowie negative) von einem Kontext in den Anderen dienlich sein. Die *Igbo*heiler bevorzugen in ihrer Tradition die Farben Rot und Weiß für die symbolische Darstellung. Rot und Weiß werden von den Heilern am häufigsten zur Harmonisierung oder Überwindung der Gegensätze bestehender Werte verwendet. Es ist hier von besonderer Bedeutung, dass die Harmonie, welche der Heiler mit den beiden Farben herzustellen versucht, sich auf etwas schon bestehendes bezieht, etwas dass mit der Vereinigung von Bruchstücken im Sinne der Heilung von Geisteskrankheiten in Verbindung steht. Manchmal hält der Heiler es für angbrachter, je nach Umständen, auch die blaue Farbe zu benutzen. In der Entwicklung des Heilprozesses erkennen Heiler die Wirkung der Farben durch Handlesen und während der Herstellung von *onunu*, dem schwarzen Pulver (IROEGBU 2001). Farben wecken eine Stimmung, die es

Abb. 2:
ritueller Schlüssel,
igodo amuma

Abb. 3:
Fesseln eines
Mannes mit
Geistern und
Gott
ekike mmuo na madu

Abb. 4:
Medizin Topf

ermöglicht bestimmte Phänomene zu interpretieren. Der Patient muss sich innerhalb auf den Boden gezeichneter Linien (sich kreuzende Farblinien) aufhalten. So befindet er sich beispielsweise innerhalb eines weißen (*ocha*) oder gelben (*ode*) Kreises. Dies bedeutet, dem Patienten eine Welt zu erschaffen, in dem er der Axis mundi gleich im Zentrum des Kosmos steht, unterstützt und geschützt von Kerzen und Weihrauch oder bestimmten Pflanzen wie z.b. *ocimum viridis* (*nchanwu*), die eine sichere Atmoshäre für ihn erzeugen sollen. In diesem Moment wird der Heiler mit seinem Werk fortfahren, welches immer die systematische Erfassung der symbolischen Werte bestimmter Farben beinhaltet.

Weiterhin geschieht folgendes:
Die Wertung von Farben wie Rot, Weiß, Gelb, Blau und Schwarz, wird der Heiler sich systematisch vornehmen, z.B. Rot für bestimmte kritische Elemente in Bezug zum Gefahrenzustand des Patienten oder seinem Problem setzen.
Zugleich wird er diese Gefahr mit Weiß bekämpfen, mit dem Frieden, Harmonie und Geborgenheit zu invocieren. Im Alltag sowie im Ritual werden bestimmte Gegenstände aufgrund ihrer Farbe gewählt.
Die Bedeutung der Farben liegt im Symbolischen und erscheint in Heilritualen, gesellschaftlichen Initiationen, speziell der Titelverleihung, Macht- und Authoritätssymbolen von Führungskräften. In ihrer Studie über die Anatomie des Geistes (1996) hat CAROLINE MYSS sehr anschaulich die sieben Stufen von Macht und Heilung verknüpft. Die Farben werde in diverse Riten wie etwa Beschneidung, Initiation oder Namensgebung eingebracht. Die drei hauptsächlich mit Geistern assoziierten Farben sind Rot, Schwarz und Weiß.

Weiß steht, wie oben bereits eswähnt für Frieden und wird mit der Erscheinung von Geistern in Verbindung gebracht. Leichen werden deshalb ganz mit weißem Tuch zugedeckt, um sie in den Kontext von Geist, Frieden und Wiederkehr zu stellen.
Rot steht für Gefahr, Blut, Schädigung von Leben und die Zerstörung von Medizinkräften. Schwarz für sich genommen, tritt in Verbindung mit Exorzismus von Besessenheit auf. So tragen beispielsweise Männer oder Frauen, die zuvor exorziert wurden, schwarze Kleidung. Des weiteren spielt Schwarz eine Rolle bei Anrufungen im Sinne von Hexerei (KAPFERER 1997) und damit zusammenhängende Herstellung von Tränken u.a..
Bei der Behandlung von Geisteskrankheiten werden die drei Farben häufig vermischt. Beispielhaft werden hier bei Fesselritualen gefärbte Schnüre verwendet (siehe Bild 3).

Fazit

Ich habe hier verschiedene Arten von Fesselritualen und ihre, für die *Igbo*kultur signifikanten, Elemente zur Abwehr und Bekämpfung von durch Geister und Hexerei ausgelöste Geisteskrankheiten ausgewählt und beschrieben.
Wenn ein für den Patienten als zufriedenstellendes Niveau erreicht wurde, wird die Behandlung auf eine neue Ebene geführt. Es folgt eine medizinische Behandlung mit Kräutern, Wurzeln und anderen Stoffen, die ihre Wirksamkeit ebenfalls aus ihrer symbolischen Natur ziehen. Diese zweite Stufe der Behandlung erfordert genaueste Kenntnisse in Bezug auf Bäume, Wurzeln, Kräuter, Tiere und Mineralien, die durch eine Verbindung zu den Ahnen gewonnen wird. Die *Igbo* Medizin und ihre Praktiker beschäftigen sich mit einer Vielzahl von Fertigkeiten und Techniken, die in Bezug zur sozialen und kulturellen Bedeutung von

Abb. 5:
Heiler bringt Farben und Kraftfelder miteinander in Beziehung

Geisteskrakheit stehen. Die psychischen Heiler entfalten das subjektive Innenleben von Personen und helfen dem Patienten durch Gespräche, sich wieder in das soziale Gefüge und die damit zusammenhängenden Gesetze zu integrieren. Die Praktiker nähern sich normalerweise dem menschlichen Körper in systematischen Modi, die direkt mit ihrer Weltordnung, sozialen Beziehungen und der heilenden Natur mit planzlichen und tierischen Resourcen in Verbindung stehen.

Das Heilen des kranken Geistes und Körpers hat notwendigerweise eine Initiation in die therapeutische Praxis, die Aneignung der Ahnentradition und Auseinandersetzung mit derselben, sowie mit Symbolen und Ritualobjekten zur Folge. Der Heiler sucht nach der Ursache der Geisteskrankheit und versucht das sinnvolle Kategorisieren, Heilende Kräfte und das Moralbewusstsein des Patienten wiederzuerwecken.

Autor
PATRICK IROEGBU, PHD
Ph.D in Sozialwissenschaften im Bereich von Sozial- und Kulturanthropologie. Vertiefte Auseinandersetzung mit ethnomedizinischen und politischen Themen. Ausgebildet für analytische Untersuschungen und Ethnographie, sowie Wirtschaft Management und Entwicklung.
-Diplom 1983 in co-operative economics and management
-Bester des Jahrgangs
-Master Degree 1989 für development economics
-Master Degree 1994 für social & cultural anthropology
-Advanced Master Degree 1995 für social and cultural anthropology mit Spezialisierung in medical anthropology
-Doctorate Degree 2001 für medical anthropology.
Kontakt: #1, 11725-80 Street, Edmonton, Alberta T5B 2N4, Canada. Tel: 00780-982-6664, 0032-16/325760; 0032-16/583849; Gsm: 0496109004, Fax: 0032-16326000.
Email: piroegbu@hotmail.com

Literatur

AHYI, G.R. 1997. Traditional Models of Mental Health and Illness in Benin. In: HOUNTONDJI, P. (ed.), *Endogenous Knowledge: Research Trails.* Dakar: CODESRIA Book Series.
ASUNI, T. et al. 1994. *Mental health and disease in Africa.* Owerri: Spectrum Books Limited.
BIBEAU, G. 1997. Cultural psychiatry in a Creolising world: questions for a new research agenda. In: *Transcultural Psychiatry* Vol. 34(1): 9-41.
BALICK J. M. and COX P. A. 1997. *Plants, People and Culture: The Science of Ethnobotany.* New York: Scientific American Library. No. 60.
BLOCH, M. 1998. Why Trees, too, are good to think with: towards an anthropology of the meaning of life. In: RIVAL, L. (ed) *The Social Life of Trees. Anthropological Perspectives on Tree Symbolism.* Oxford: Oxford International Publishers Ltd.
---. 1989. *Ritual, History and Power.* Selected Papers in Anthropology. London: Anthlone Press.
DEVISCH, R. 1993. *Weaving the threads of life: The khita gyn-eco-logical healing cult among the Yaka.* Chicago: University of Chicago Press.
DE BOECK, F. 1994. Of Trees and Kings: Politics and Metaphors Among the Aluund of Southwestern Zaire. In: *American Ethnologist,* vol. 21, (3), 451-473.
DIRK, N. 1994. Ritual and Resistance: subversion as social fact. In: NICHOLAS DIRKS, GEOFF ELEY & SHERRY ORTNER (eds.), *Culture, Power, History.* Princeton, NJ: Princeton University Press.
EJIZU, C. I. 1986. *Ofo: Igbo Ritual Symbol.* Enugu: Fourth Dimensions Publishers. EZEABASILI, N. 1982. Traditional Ibo Ideas about Disease and Its Treatment. In: ERINOSHO, O.A. (ed.), *Nigerian Perspectives on Medical Sociology.* Virginia: College of William and Mary, Department of Anthropology. No. 19, pp. 17-28.
EZELIORA, B. 1994. *Traditional Medicine in Amesi.* Enugu: CECTA Nigeria Ltd.
IROEGBU, E. P. 2001. *Healing Insanity: An anthropological study of Igbo Medicine in southeastern Nigeria.* Ph. D Thesis, Catholic University of Leuven Belgium.
---. 1996. Traditional Psychiatry in Igbo Life and Culture (The Statesman, Owerri: Nigeria, March 29, pp.8-9; April 13, pp.8-9; April 15, p.11; April 19, p.11; May 1, p.11).
IWU, M.M. 1981. *Perspectives of Igbo Tribal Ethnomedicine. Ethnomedicine.* Enugu: SNAPP Press
---. 1982. *Traditional Igbo Medicine. Institute of Education.* University of Nigeria, Nsukka.
JORDAN, B. 1997. Authoritative Knowledge and Its Construction. In: DAVIS-FLOYD & SARGENT, C.F. (eds.) *Child Birth and Authoritative Knowledge.* Berkeley: University of California Press, pp.55-79.
KAPFERER, B. 1997. *The Feast of the Sorcerer: Practices of Consciousness and Power.* Chicago: University of Chicago Press.
KLEINMAN, A. 1980. *Patients and Healers in the Context of Culture: an Exploration of the Borderline between Anthropology, Medicine, and Psychiatry.* Berkley: California Press.
MYSS, C. 1996. *Anatomy of the spirit: the seven stages of power and healing.* New York: Three Rivers Press.
MALIDOMA, P.S. 1993. *Ritual: Power, Healing and Community.* Oregon: Swan raven & Company.
NWOGA, D. I. 1984. *Igbo Cosmology: Nka na Nzere.* Ahiajoku Lecture. Owerri: Culture Division.
NWOSU, L. 1980. *Symbols of Native Laws and Customs in Igboland.* Umuahia: Depe Press.
OJANUGA, D. 1979. *The Role of the Traditional Doctor in the Nigerian Health Services.* Thesis, University of Wisconsin.
PEEK, P. M. ed., 1991. *African Divination Systems.* Bloomington: Indiana University Press.
PRINCE, R. 1964. Indigenous Yoruba Psychiatry. In: *Magic, Faith and Healing.* ed. KIEV, A. 84-120. London: Collier-Macmillan, Ltd.
TAMBIA, J.S. 1985. "A Performative Approach to Ritual." In: id., *Culture, Thought and Social Action: An Anthropological Perspective,* pp. 123-66). London: Harvard University Press.
TIGANI EL MAHI. 1961. Techniques of Ethno-psychiatry in Relation to the Cultural Background of some Countries in Africa. In: LAMBO. T.A. (ed.), *First Pan-African Psychiatric Conference Report,* 118-120. Ibadan: Government Printers.
TURNER, V. 1967. *The Forest of Symbols: Aspects of Ndembu Ritual.* Ithaca, N.Y.: Cornel University Press.
UYANGA, J. 1979. The Characteristics of Patients of Spiritual Healing Homes and Traditional Doctors in Southeastern Nigeria. *Social Science and Medicine* 13A: 323-9.
UZOHO. V. 1984. *Igbo Traditional Medicine: Wealth in Our Culture to Tap and Utilise. Colloquium: Igbo Traditional Medicine.* Ahiajoku Lecture. Owerri: Culture Division.
ZELTER, A. 1998. Grassroots Campaigning for the World's Forests. In: RIVAL, L. (ed.), *The Social Life of Trees: Anthropological Perspectives on Tree Symbolism.* Oxford: Oxford International Publishers Ltd.

IGBO MEDICINE PRACTITIONERS AND WAYS OF HEALING INSANITY IN SOUTHEASTERN NIGERIA*

by Patrick Iroegbu

Introduction

Igbo medicine practitioners are called *dibia* and are associated with a medicine deity known as *agwu*. Their formation into the full art of healing is complicated and surrounds the intervention call, initiation rituals and long training around the *agwu* deity. The term *dibia* means healer, medicine man, priest, and native medicine dealer.

The designation refers to a multi-resourceful medical practitioner playing a multifaceted role in building and stabilising a healthy community. Thus, *di-bia* stands for a husband or life-giver such that a healer ties up, cools off, and blows away sources and crises that disturb normal life and society. Healers engage in all sorts of medical and therapeutic activity to ensure the cure of bodily illnesses, the social and cosmological order of the society. Operating in different therapeutic domains and expertise, they engage in active and internal processes that include divination (Peek 1991), memories of one's actions in life, beliefs and counselling with the desire to release all negative patterns.

This paper deals with *Igbo* medical practitioners regarding to heal insanity (or *ara*) in a larger symbolic perspective. It intends to show that when people are faced with diverse everyday illness realities, such as the one of insanity, they tend to circulate from one domain of healing to another in search of a satisfactory remedy. This search for meaning and satisfactory healing occurs irrespective of the presence of

* Revised by Joy C. Green

biomedical institutions, which largely fail to deliver efficacious results. As a consequence of the quest for a lasting cure of illness afflictions, the paper will, moreover, illustrate how *Igbo* medicine practitioners help their clients to make sense of their underlying illness episodes and world order, while they outline the cultural system leading the rebalancing and renewal of their society.

Conception of healing

Unlike biomedical psychiatrists, healers rarely perceive insanity as incurable. Insanity, in the *Igbo* context, apart from its ethiological argument, excitation in the household and social settings. It also signifies that society has failed to solve or reconcile its problems. In other words, when contradictions overweigh in any given society, the number of behavioural disorders and mental disturbances are likely to rise. Society would have to solve its problems in order to support the mentally well-adjusted and dynamic people and produce less insane people.

Healing involves particular organisation of forces. The intention of the healer is to first re-empower the vital elements to transform the insane from incapacity. This means to reinvent the body from hosting weakness to hosting strength. The main issue is that a healer works closely with each afflicted person and his care group. He develops a relevation to clear what the insane needs to be released of. Based on ethnographic data, two explanatory healing models appear very customary and useful in healing insanity, namely a symbolic treatment and a root-herbal (*mgborogwu*) therapy. For this publication, I concentrate on what healers do to manage the source of insanity. The second aspect focusing on herbalism, which refers to vegetal and animal resources, as well as Christian faith healing perspective will be examined in another article but can also be consulted in a dissertation I submitted to Catholic University of Leuven in June, 2001.

Curing Through Symbolic Release

The *Igbo* consider healing insanity to result from a frame of symbolic release. This is an important attribute to the control or cure of insanity.

Definition

The use of roots and herbs for the treatment of insanity does not apply by itself independently. It begins with important ceremonies, which are meant to be therapeutic to alleviate the condition of the insane patient. It is this ceremony that I call symbolic release. Psychiatrists cannot achieve the same interventions, in their cases, instances of success are rare (AHYI 1997:236). The entire framework of symbolic release amounts to explain that the socio-psycho-cultural work of healing is also one, which is transposed to intentions and processes, supposed to exist elsewhere. As to what happens in the various techniques of symbolic release, the (knotting) models deals with sources of disturbance. Disturbance in this case is located outside the patient's body or in-between the patient, his or her life-world and relevant others. This healing model is partly focused on the patient who has to be released and is based on the particular matter disturbing the patient. Therapy in this context means creating spaces and frameworks to combat the source of aggression and the affliction. It does not focus on the patient and his or her symptom first. It is to neutralise the force of the intentions or instigators in the disturbance. In summary, if the instigators are spirits, they must be cut off through a framework of pacification. And if they happen to be mischievous, evil spirits, genies of a particular distress factors, efforts will be made to placate them, shift them, or drive them out. They will be tied. The therapy is located in some other being, some other environment, within the social group, or in the spiritual world (AHYI 1997:227). The basic difference between such indigenous therapies and biomedical psychiatric treatment is that folk healers heal relationships by building or redynamising normality for the patient, whereas psychiatrists treat mainly the physical symptoms.

The symbolic release model proper to *Igbo* healing tradition can be said to embody the use of esoteric forces and the power of symbols. Therapies are made to give a patient a new vision in life without having to isolate or discourage him or her. The symbolic release is therefore a systematic practice that creates social bonds that all parties to the process of cure - the healer, patient and caregivers - obviously want to maintain. Healing insanity involves the mind-body relation as well as the social environment and the life-world.

In the esoteric domain, there is a lot of information sui generis waiting for discovery, tied in with phenomena we do not understand (AHYI 1997:246). It is basic that in the healing of insanity, the ultimate aim must be to affect or alter the 'will' of the intrusive force. The *Igbo* belief is that certain trees can overhear and record conversations. Connected with trees and sounds, the *Igbo* account the ability of trees to absorb sounds and other signals. This amounts to an anthropomorphic belief that a tree can hear conversations. It is the need to find the material manifestation within the natural environment. Some society believe that trees are symbolically important in the process of illness release and cure. Trees and humans interact in extensive rituals involving birth, growth, marriage, health, illness and death.

Examples of trees and woods linked to life crisis rituals and defences of boundaries

They see trees as most vital symbols of life and eternity as opposed to graves as symbols of death and fading of memory (cf. ZELTER 1998:221-231). This is the dimension linking up ancestral knowledge and herbalism in symbolic release for the healing of insanity.

In addition to that, let us recall that trees are commonly thought to be repositories of the souls of the death awaiting reincarnation. Trees are also made to hex the living with the earth and lineage. For example, the afterbirth (*alulo*, umbilical cord) of humans is very often tied to a tree or buried at its root. The *Igbo* call this a life insertion into the lineage world. Such a tree (usually a palm tree) is called *nkwu alo*, which becomes the child's alter ego. He or she sees him- or herself in the tree as well connected with the ancestral roots. In numerous symbolic representations, metaphors and stories, *nkwu alo* connotes life source and insertion containing bodily domains from afterbirth to the ashes of the dead. Trees seem to explain lived-in models based on sentient experience and practical knowledge to symbolise the reproductive couple, that is the genderless potential for self-regeneration. It is conceived as comprising both female and male principles. Some ethnographic information has been presented showing the occurrence of such symbolism in very different cultural contexts (e.g. BLOCH 1992A; DE BOECK 1994; RIVAL 1997). The association between tree and personality is important for healers who see the continuity of life-world and community stability standing within trees of life. Trees trigger their use to represent and heal broken boundaries. References to trees as symbols of kinship are common, and DE BOECK (1994) and DEVISCH (1993) have presented a solid example (see also RIVAL 1997). Trees express genealogical continuity and so help to make our understanding of how others address, rank and organise themselves. Taking into consideration the above dimensions and dynamics in the management of insanity, I will proceed to show some forms and techniques of symbolic release entailing how in reality it is being carried out to address cases of insanity.

Application Process
1. Tying ritual, ihe ekike or amuma ekike
This is the idiom reflecting the transformation of forces to restore health, in particular insanity. The *Igbo* expression *igwo oria* (to cure illness) is not limited to substances applied for a strictly therapeutic purpose. It includes also words, counseling, and gestures whose tested efficacy extends beyond the treatment of the ailment (cf. IWU 1982; EZELIORA 1994:85). Fig 1: *Locks, igodo*
Figure 1 shows a set of ritual keys, *igodo amuma* being in force as applied to release patients. Ritual tying is done to protect someone against psychiatric stress factors, enemies and malevolent forces. It wards off evil attacks. The use of enabling materials is important.
Mostly used are rope, twine, string, or a tying thread (e.g. *uzoro* growing from high trees like breadfruit - *treculia africana, ukwa*). Others are trimphetta cord *(akwara ngwo)* made from raffia string (*piassava: ngwo*) and tie tie (*elaeis* guineensis rope, *ekwere nkwu*). The capacity or ability of the intruding force concerned is meanwhile tied in. It is aimed at dislodging and redirecting the disturbance elsewhere. When tying is accomplished, the tied-in medicine (*ogwu*) is usually hung on any part of the building or buried.
In most cases, tied medicines connected with the cure of insanity are placed in hanging positions on the wall or roof of the house. I found that tying is done in order to take the illness away to somewhere else. It separates the body from it by entrusting the latter with a space of normality.
Without engaging further into the explanation of the relevance of symbols, let me state briefly what one healer Sunday Iroabuchi, attributed to the following objects he employs in healing insanity, *ara*.
The disturbing facts of the insanity as advised by divination will be faced with a specific treatment pattern a healer will set in motion.
First, a ritual framework is installed to release the patient from tethered weakness. The first rite sees to it that the forces surrounding the illness are transformed, bringing into active play the importance of offering and sacrifice in healing. The production and reinforcement of sacrifice to release the ill person combines also with the production and reification of metaphysical notion of power. The exercise involves the following dynamics.
Weakness depicts incapacity and disability, and stands for weak body, strength for strong body, wealth for mediation in order to liberate and restore strength (i.e., transfer weakness to strength), to knock out, separate and chase away disturbing elements, and finally treatment and recovery. What is underscored in the range of transforming techniques is how a patient is considered first as a weak being or body. It is one of which the body identity is made vulnerable for crisis of behaviour, namely episodic shores of insanity. The ritual exigency takes the patient out of the

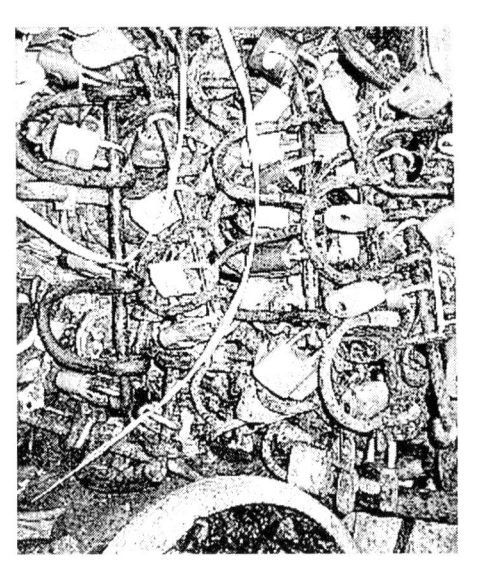

Fig. 1:
Locks, igodo

impasse of weakness to that of strength, that is, to recovering of a healthy body (*ahu isike*). In this way, the patient is immersed within a space of normal strength to cope with daily life tasks.

2. Release through opening of a key (igodo)
Another technique of release is to unlock the space or way (*ikpoghe uzo*). The important symbol used is a lock with key (*igodo*). This key is very significant in the release process through its locking and unlocking action. It depicts how a stressful intrusive force is cut off as it applies to tying technique aimed at shading something off from contact with someone *or* a thing.

The key represents an important tool for many ends. While it is significant in preparing medicines for good luck, it also occurs in areas such as harming and blocking the progress of another person. In whichever way it may be turned, it aims at locking up versus unlocking a particular intention. The use of ritual keys (*igodo amuma*) is effective because in the restrictive design to keep away forces that disturb the insane, they open the gate for any disturbance to quit from the condition of the patient. Practitioners use the key to make symbolic release to be effective.

It is believed that once a key is specially prepared for the purpose of blocking the way of someone or of the spirit force, it would have a solid effect.

With regard to healing insanity, basically, a ritual key, among the useful objects of transformation, is usually kept in a container with eggs, stone and cowrie shells. It is taken and moved from the front view of a patient to his or her behind, and then unlocked.

This method reveals a common practice among healers that consists in tying of man, God and spirits. It is a practice of rescuing and haling the insane involving astage known as "to fight the source of affliction" (*ibuso nmuo okwu*). To cement this encounter, a healer ties onto the patient's chest or waist the wrap or mantle of the human linkages with God and spirits. In particular, the two zones of the body, namely chest (*obi*) and waist (*ukwu*) denote zones of strength (*ifu ike*). Treatment with roots and herbs mixtures will also begin to address the illness regarding symptom manifestations. Any activities aimed to bring about release, involves the redrawing of boundries in view of the patinet's rescue and security.

4. The insane patient and release

Every situation of insanity requires a release and status change from patienthood to healthy person as a goal of treatment. Regardless of the type of personality, which an individual actually holds, the bodily dysfunction in insanity concerns a disturbance of the harmony between the physical, social and moral being within normal life. Another important rite called smearing the body with ritual powder. This goes with careful physical touching and rubbing of black powder to penetrate the body. And it comes after certain symbolic releases are considered satisfactory by the competent healer involved. The process as a whole entails the insertion of black medicinal concoction into seven cuts on the head.

It is from these seven incisions or marked openings that the flowing of blood is meant to lead this medicine inside the brain and body. The aim is to practically insulate the brain from further up-setting and loss of cosmological energy with the presence of taunting forces.

5. The medicine pot

The medicine pot contains significant materials, as shown below. These are a head of monkey (*isi enwe*), and dog (*nkita*) as well as other materials. All enabling materials are stored in one pot (*ite*), here referred to as medicine pot. This pot is placed inside a basin (*efere*) which contains several roots and symbolic objects such as feathers.

When the need arises, they are taken for use to treat the brain and body as the case may be. In the circumstance, the skull of monkey or dog is considered essential in the transformation of the forces that disturb the patient's brain. The monkey is considered as a first choice.

If unavailable, the skull of a dog may be used in its place. Moreover, *enwe* (monkey) is homonymous with terms denoting exchange practices, such as *enwe, onwo* (exchange) and *weta bia* were (give and take), as used for example, in the expression "bring head for a head" (*weta isi bia were isi*). The issue here is that ritual healing of insanity would be less sensible without its important ritual objects.

After gathering the enabling materials, the healer cuts open the skull of the monkey and empties the brain content into a grinding container. This brain content is mixed with a special root treating epileptic fits (*akwukwu*). The grounded mixture will be burned *(inu oke)* until it becomes charred or black powders. In this condition, it is collected and enhanced to the effect that all the burnt materials become real black powders. This mixture or state of the black elements is *oke onunu* for treating insanity.

When this is done, the hair of the ill person will be shaved off. A razor blade (*mma akwa*) will be used to cut seven incisions on the bare head. Into these seven incisions, representing the seven forces of spirit disturbance, the *onunu* will be smeared and pressed inside.

The significance of the ongoing head treatment through *onunu* smearing is to ensure a connection with the inner part of the body. The process of exchange spoken of here is completed through actual blood contact with the mixed symbolic elements involved. This stage finally declares the ill person liberated from sensory

Fig. 2:
Ritual key,
igodo amuma

Fig. 3:
Tying concerns
3. Tying
of man with
spirits and god,
ekike mmuo na madu

Fig. 4:
Medicine pot

visions and obstructions generated by the presence of the dislocating forces. Other treatments will follow, including counseling and the reformation of the patient's family ties.

6. The position of the medicine pot
The position of the medicine pot (*ite ogwu*), as shown in figure 4 following is not simply a matter of fancy. A closer examination reveals that the pot encompasses not only the body setting but also the interconnections in the life-world.
The pot is always kept open to gaze. It is patterned to represent the upper side of the body and the world above. So it consists of the head and things from above. The basin (*efere*) or bowel (*oku*) equally rests on the earth or land (*ala*).
The earth realm is the dwelling place of the spirits and as the pot connects the upper side so does it connect the earth.
The pot offers in no small measure a pattern of cosmological interweaving of healing symbols. Thus the whole ritual of release and retie in this context provides an outlet, as the pot shows, for expressing emotion, rebuttal, and avoidance. It also offers the oppressed ill person a medium to express his or her dissatisfaction and the coming out from this captivity associated with violence and loss of social importance.

7. Tying to life giving forces
The need to tie up things together cannot be overemphasised. Healers find the technique of tying as central as any meaningful thing which helps to break down the occluding effect of psychiatric disturbance. Healers therefore first engage in untying the bounds to liberate a patient. It is important therefore to further outline and stress the significance of some of the ritual objects and to what degree they stretch in healing insanity through a ritual action.
A central objective is to become strong. Strength evokes the idea of stability, normality and progress. This means staying healthy.

8. On moods and colours
From the above discussion it is clear that the healing of insanity demands an interaction between the patient and the healer as well as a unity of experience in the environmental and cosmological setting. This interaction differs from people to people. To determine or depict attitudes, the healer relies on colours, which can be indicative of how a conflict and transitional situation of a society reflect images and interact with the spirit forces and their ability to cause disturbance. Colours (*ucha ihe*) may be useful to transfer meaning (e.g., of well-being or of crisis) from one context to another.
The *Igbo* healers have a tradition of privileging the red and white colours in their symbolism. Red and white are mostly used by healers to overcome and harmonise the contradictions occurring in the pattern of values. It is of particular interest that the harmony which the healer needs to establish through the white and red refers to something, already stated, concerning the restoration of broken ties in the treatment or cure of insanity. At times the healer thinks best to use the blue colour depending on circumstances. As healing evolves, healers recognise the impact of colour in palm divination and the preparation of *onunu*, the black powder (IROEGBU 2001). Colours involve a potential mood for interpreting various phenomena.
As a rule, the patient is positioned inside marked lines and sometimes where marked colours intersect. Thus a white (*ocha*) or yellow (*ode*) circle that is drawn

Fi 5:
Healer relating colours and field of forces

on the ground will surround him or her. Doing this implies constituting a world where the patient belongs such as the axis mundi formed to serve as centre of the cosmos lighted with candles and burning incense or other plant resources, such as ocimum viridis (*nchanwu*), so as to obtain a secured ambience for him or her. At this moment, the healer will proceed with his cure, which always involves systematic exploitation of the symbolic value of the colour indication.

What will happen is also this: With value placed on colours, namely red, white, yellow, blue, and black, the healer will systematically relate, for example, the colour red to elements crucial to the patient's state of danger or his or her problem. Conversely, he will almost at the same time contradict this danger with the white colour advocating peace, harmony and settlement.

In everyday life and ritual, certain objects are chosen for their colour. Colours are used symbolically and appear in healing rituals, and in social initiations, notably title taking, power and authority symbols of leadership in society. In her study of the Anatomy of the Spirit (1996), CAROLINE MYSS creatively wove together the seven stages of power and healing.

Many rites such as circumcision, initiation, and naming involve different colours. The three principal colours associated with spirits are white, red and black. White signifies peace and the appearance of spirits are reported often in white colours. Corpses are equally covered with white colour in association with spirit colour, peace and recovery.

Red colour indicates danger, blood, harming life and destroying the potency of medicines (e.g., associated with menstrual blood). Black on its own falls into the practice of exorcism of possessive forces.

For example, if men or women are being exorcised, they wear black. Black plays a part in the rites in which the assistance of spirits is enlisted for purposes of sorcery or witchcraft (cf. KAPFERER 1997), and also in acquiring medicines for such purposes.

The three colours are often blended when used in healing insanity. This is exemplified in one of the tying rites to release the patient and is done with strips of coloured cloths.

Conclusion

I have elicited various strategies of tying ritual entailing the use of elements so significant in *Igbo* culture to block sources of spiritual and sorcerous attacks and bewitchment facing insanity. Once a level deemed suitable for a patient's release is attained, the treatment moves on to the next stage. What follows comes down to medical forms of treatment involving the use of roots and other substances, which are also made therapeutically effective through symbolic release. This second stage in the treatment involves real mastery of trees, roots, herbs, animal and mineral resources through the connection with ancestors.

In purpose and concern, *Igbo* medicine and its practitioners engage in a wide range of endogenous skills and practices regarding the social and cultural significance of healing insanity. The psychiatric healers unfold the inner subjective life of persons and their discourses that attempt to strengthen rather than limit the integration of social and cultural orders.

While eager to succeed, the practitioners mainly approach the human body in systematic modes that are relevant to the level of their world order, social relations, as well as the connection to the curative nature of plants and animal resources. Essentially, healing unsound mind and body entails necessary initiations into the medical practice, the reasoning and empowerment of the ancestral tradition, symbols and ritual objects. Practitioners, moreover, seek to address genuine causes of insanity and remobilise categories of meanings, healing forces, voices, moralities and ways of intersubjectivity.

Author

PATRICK IROEGBU, PhD

Ph.D in social sciences in the field of social and cultural anthropology. Majored in medical anthropology in ethno-medical issues and public policy. Grounded in analytic research and ethnography, as well as having previous education and training in co-operative economics, management, and developments.

High diploma 1983 in co-operative economics and management - best at graduation; Master Degree 1989 in development economics with great distinction; Master Degree 1994 in social & cultural anthropology with distinction; Advanced Master Degree 1995 in social and cultural anthropology with specialisation in medical anthropology passed with distinction; Doctorate Degree 2001, with great success, majored in medical anthropology.

Dissertation: Healing Insanity: An Anthropological study of Igbo Medicine in southeastern Nigeria.

Defence date: June 8th 2001, with great success. Publications: Several informed publications such as (1). Justice and the Bakassi Boys: An Emergent Liberation Gospel or What? In: The Oracle, international journal of culture, religion and

society, Vol. 1, No. 2. June 2001. (2). Mental illness in Igbo Life and Culture. In: The Statesman (Nig.) 1996. (3). Softening the stigma of mental illness. In: The Statesman (Nig.) 1996. (4). Marrying wealth, marrying money: repositioning Igbo men and women, 2001 (paper contribution to Gender Book, in press: Catholic University of Leuven Press, 2001); (5). Insanity and its aetiologies among the Igbo of Nigeria (paper at Satterthwaite Colloquium on Religion and Ritual, Manchester, 2000; (6). Igbo healers in the state context. Paper at the 9th General Assembly of CODESRIA on Globalisation and Social Sciences in Africa, 1998.
Contact: Africa Research Centre, Dept. Dept. Social & Cultural Anthropology, Catholic University of Leuven, Belgium, Tiensestraat 102, 3000 Leuven, Belgium   Tel: 0032-16325760; 0032-16583849; Gsm: 0032-496109004 Fax: 0032-16326000 E-mail: piroegbu@hotmail.com

References

AHYI, G.R. 1997. Traditional Models of Mental Health and Illness in Benin. In: HOUNTONDJI, P. (ed.), *Endogenous Knowledge: Research Trails.* Dakar: CODESRIA Book Series.
ASUNI, T. et al. 1994. *Mental health and disease in Africa.* Owerri: Spectrum Books Limited.
BIBEAU, G. 1997. Cultural psychiatry in a Creolising world: questions for a new research agenda. In: *Transcultural Psychiatry* Vol. 34(1): 9-41.
BALICK J. M. and COX P. A. 1997. *Plants, People and Culture: The Science of Ethnobotany.* New York: Scientific American Library. No. 60.
BLOCH, M. 1998. Why Trees, too, are good to think with: towards an anthropology of the meaning of life. In: RIVAL, L. (ed) *The Social Life of Trees. Anthropological Perspectives on Tree Symbolism.* Oxford: Oxford International Publishers Ltd.
---. 1989. *Ritual, History and Power.* Selected Papers in Anthropology. London: Anthlone Press.
DEVISCH, R. 1993. *Weaving the threads of life: The khita gyn-eco-logical healing cult among the Yaka.* Chicago: University of Chicago Press.
DE BOECK, F. 1994. Of Trees and Kings: Politics and Metaphors Among the Aluund of Southwestern Zaire. In: *American Ethnologist,* vol. 21, (3), 451-473.
DIRK, N. 1994. Ritual and Resistance: subversion as social fact. In: NICHOLAS DIRKS, GEOFF ELEY & SHERRY ORTNER (eds.), *Culture, Power, History.* Princeton, NJ: Princeton University Press.
EJIZU, C. I. 1986. *Ofo: Igbo Ritual Symbol.*   Enugu: Fourth Dimensions Publishers. EZEABASILI, N. 1982. Traditional Ibo Ideas about Disease and Its Treatment. In: ERINOSHO, O.A. (ed.), *Nigerian Perspectives on Medical Sociology.* Virginia: College of William and Mary, Department of Anthropology. No. 19, pp. 17-28.
EZELIORA, B. 1994. *Traditional Medicine in Amesi.* Enugu: CECTA Nigeria Ltd.
IROEGBU, E. P. 2001. *Healing Insanity: An anthropological study of Igbo Medicine in southeastern Nigeria.* Ph. D Thesis, Catholic University of Leuven Belgium.
---. 1996. *Traditional Psychiatry in Igbo Life and Culture* (The Statesman, Owerri: Nigeria, March 29, pp.8-9; April 13, pp.8-9; April 15, p.11; April 19,

p.11; May 1, p.11).
IWU, M.M. 1981. *Perspectives of Igbo Tribal Ethnomedicine. Ethnomedicine.* Enugu: SNAPP Press
---. 1982. *Traditional Igbo Medicine. Institute of Education.* University of Nigeria, Nsukka.
JORDAN, B. 1997. Authoritative Knowledge and Its Construction. In: DAVIS-FLOYD & SARGENT, C.F. (eds.) *Child Birth and Authoritative Knowledge.* Berkeley: University of California Press, pp.55-79.
KAPFERER, B. 1997. *The Feast of the Sorcerer: Practices of Consciousness and Power.* Chicago: University of Chicago Press.
KLEINMAN, A. 1980. *Patients and Healers in the Context of Culture: an Exploration of the Borderline between Anthropology, Medicine, and Psychiatry.* Berkley: California Press.
MYSS, C. 1996. *Anatomy of the spirit: the seven stages of power and healing.* New York: Three Rivers Press.
MALIDOMA, P.S. 1993. *Ritual: Power, Healing and Community.* Oregon:Swan raven & Company.
NWOGA, D. I. 1984. *Igbo Cosmology: Nka na Nzere. Ahiajoku Lecture.* Owerri: Culture Division.
NWOSU, L. 1980. *Symbols of Native Laws and Customs in Igboland.* Umuahia: Depe Press.
OJANUGA, D. 1979. *The Role of the Traditional Doctor in the Nigerian Health Services.* Thesis, University of Wisconsin.
PEEK, P. M. ed., 1991. *African Divination Systems.* Bloomington: Indiana University Press.
PRINCE, R. 1964. Indigenous Yoruba Psychiatry. In: *Magic, Faith and Healing.* ed. KIEV, A. 84-120. London: Collier-Macmillan, Ltd.
TAMBIA, J.S. 1985. "A Performative Approach to Ritual." In: id., *Culture, Thought and Social Action: An Anthropological Perspective,* pp. 123-66). London: Harvard University Press.
TIGANI EL MAHI. 1961. Techniques of Ethno-psychiatry in Relation to the Cultural Background of some Countries in Africa. In: LAMBO. T.A. (ed.), *First Pan-African Psychiatric Conference Report,* 118-120. Ibadan: Government Printers.
TURNER, V. 1967. *The Forest of Symbols: Aspects of Ndembu Ritual.* Ithaca, N.Y.: Cornel University Press.
UYANGA, J. 1979. The Characteristics of Patients of Spiritual Healing Homes and Traditional Doctors in Southeastern Nigeria. *Social Science and Medicine* 13A: 323-9.
UZOHO. V. 1984. *Igbo Traditional Medicine: Wealth in Our Culture to Tap and Utilise. Colloquium: Igbo Traditional Medicine. Ahiajoku Lecture.* Owerri: Culture Division.
ZELTER, A. 1998. Grassroots Campaigning for the World's Forests. In: RIVAL, L. (ed.), *The Social Life of Trees: Anthropological Perspectives on Tree Symbolism.* Oxford: Oxford International Publishers Ltd.

DIE MAFA IN NORDKAMERUN

von Godula Kosack

Das traditionelle Konzept von Gesundheit und Krankheit bei den *Mafa* in Nordkamerun
Gesundheit ist für die *Mafa* der Zustand des Einklangs mit dem Kosmos, das heißt mit den die transzendenten Welten bewohnenden Geistern und den Ahnen. Die den Himmel, die Erde, das Wasser, die Wege, die Felsen, die Bäume, die Häuser bewohnenden Geister sind den Menschen, für die sie zuständig sind, im allgemeinen wohl gesonnen und beschützen sie vor Angriffen von außen. Krankheit ist eine Unordnung, in dem die Menschen unmittelbar umgebenden Kosmos.
Selten erklärt sich eine Krankheit aus nur einer Ursache. Wenn eine Meningitis- oder Gelbfieberepidemie zahlreiche Kinder heimsucht, ist zwar bekannt, dass die Erkrankung auf Ansteckung zurückzuführen ist, aber dennoch wird mittels eines Orakels nach den tiefer liegenden Gründen geforscht.
Warum eine Familie im Unterschied zu einer anderen besonders von der Krankheit betroffen ist, mag daran liegen, dass Hexen/r die Kinder geschwächt haben oder dass die Ahnen oder Geister zürnen.
Wenn sich in einer Familie die Krankheits- oder Todesfälle häufen, wenn Wunden nicht heilen wollen oder periodisch wieder auftreten, wenn ein anderes Unglück passiert, ist es an der Zeit, einen Orakelsprecher (Orakelsprecherinnen sind die

Abb.: Orakelsprecherin Zanaha

Abb. 1: Steinorakel : Die Orakelsprecherin bewegt die Steine auf ihren Körper zu. Je nachdem wie viele Steine zuletzt liegen bleiben – eins, zwei oder drei – ist die Antwort auf die gestellte Frage positiv, negativ oder unbestimmt. Diese Prozedur wird beliebig oft wiederholt.

Ausnahme) aufzusuchen, um nach der tieferen Ursache zu fragen.
Der Orakelsprecher stellt eine Frage an die transzendenten Kräfte und bewegt dann Steine oder Stäbchen, oder er lässt eine Krabbe in einer mit feuchtem Sand und Stäbchen gefüllten Tonschale wirken. Die Deutung der sich ergebenden Konstellationen ergibt in der Regel, dass hier transzendente Kräfte wirken. Krankheit kann durch Geister, durch Ahnen oder durch lebende Menschen, also durch Hexerei, verursacht werden. Indem ein Geistwesen oder ein Ahne eine Krankheit schickt, werden die für die Erd- und Ahnenopfer zuständigen Familienoberhäupter darauf hingewiesen, dass eines der regelmäßig zu den jahreszeitlichen Festen oder anlässlich der Zeremonien für die Verstorbenen zu bringenden Ziegen- oder Hühneropfer und auf jeden Fall ein Bieropfer fällig oder überfällig ist.
Krankheit und Siechtum, Unglück und Unwetter wird unabhängig davon ob ein Mann, eine Frau, ein Kind, das Vieh oder die Felder betroffen sind, als ein Angriff auf das Wohlergehen der Familie aufgefasst, dem nur das Familienoberhaupt

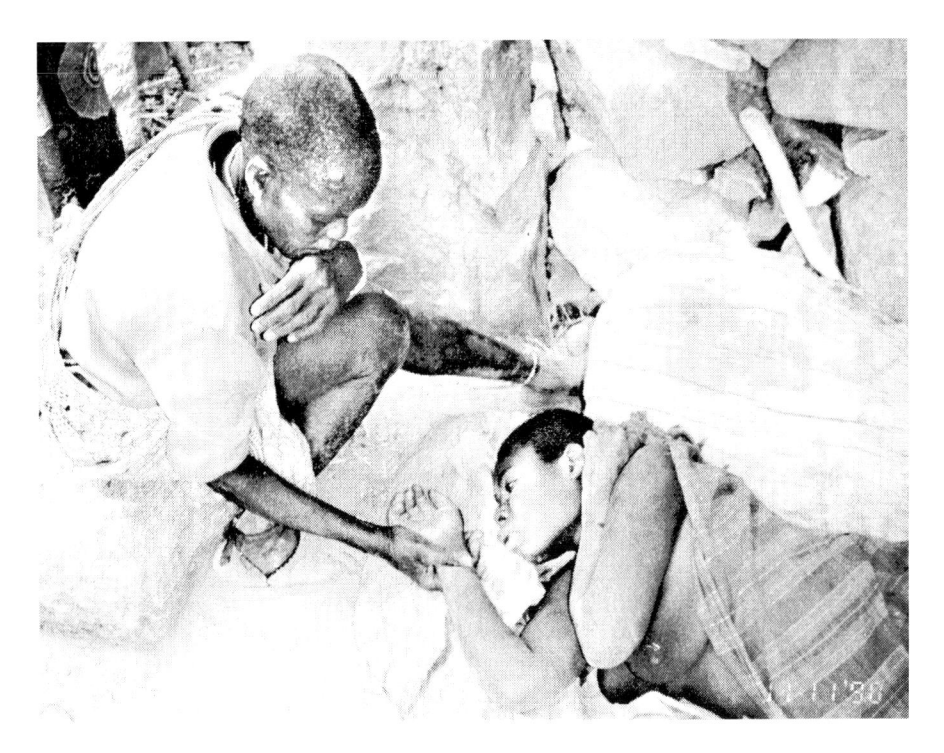

Abb. 2: Kranke Frau

entgegenwirken kann.
Wenn eine Familie besonderen hexerischen Angriffen ausgesetzt ist oder eine ungünstige Wetterlage den besonderen Schutz der Geister und Ahnen erforderlich macht, müssen zusätzliche Opfer gebracht werden, um Gesundheit und Fruchtbarkeit der Familie, des Viehs und der Felder zu gewährleisten oder wieder herzustellen. Je nachdem wie sehr sich die Geistwesen vernachlässigt gefühlt haben, zürnen sie minder oder stärker und verlangen entsprechend größere Opfer. Die Opfer der Menschen sind die Nahrung der Geister und Ahnen und der Tribut, der ihnen dafür gebührt, dass sie die Lebenden bis dato vor Krankheit und unnatürlichen Todesfällen sowie vor Zugriffen vonseiten der Hexer/n geschützt haben.
Die Mafa haben folgendes Konzept von Hexerei: Etwa sechzig Prozent aller Kinder werden mit Hexerkraft geboren. Diese Kraft kann vonseiten der Mutter oder des Vaters ererbt werden, wird aber erst im Laufe des Lebens entwickelt, und zwar entweder zum Guten - das ist als Fähigkeit zum Hellsehen, zum Erkennen von Hexern, zum Orakelsprechen oder zum Heilen - oder aber zum Bösen, um damit Menschen, Tieren, Pflanzen oder auch der Erde Schaden zuzufügen. Zwei Drittel der mit Hexerkraft Geborenen sind weiblichen Geschlechts.
Von zehn Hexe(r)n nutzt eine/r diese Kraft zum Guten, zwei von ihnen wenden ihre Kraft nicht an und drei sind "böse Hexer/n". Diese letzte Kategorie umfasst also dreißig Prozent der Bevölkerung. Auf welche Weise eine Person die

angeborene Hexerkraft entwickelt, hängt davon ab, welchen Einflüssen sie ausgesetzt ist. Bereits nach dem ersten Verzehr von "Menschenfleisch" (so bezeichnen die Mafa den Zugriff auf die Vitalkraft eines Menschen), ist die Person unfähig, je davon abzulassen, weitere Menschen zu schädigen. Sie muss sich von der Vitalkraft anderer nähren.

Fortan muss sie hexen, nicht unbedingt aus Bosheit, sondern weil sie sonst ihre eigene Vitalkraft verliert, und das bedeutet, dass sie krank wird oder gar stirbt. Andere Hexen/r verursachen allerdings Krankheit und Tod aus Neid, Missgunst, aus Konkurrenz oder ähnlichen Motiven. Dabei wird häufig der böse Blick eingesetzt oder Fremdkörper werden in den Leib des Opfers gehext, die stechende Schmerzen und ein allmähliches Abnehmen der Vitalkraft bewirken. Sehr verbreitet ist das Verstecken von *nkhè*, einer mit Schweiß, Urin oder Menstruationsblut getränkten Stofffaser, oder eines anderen Objektes, das in irgendeiner Weise mit dem Opfer in Berührung stand. Dadurch hat die/der Hexe/r ständigen Zugriff auf die Vitalkraft des Opfers.

Heilungskonzepte der *Mafa*

Um das Gleichgewicht im Kosmos sowie in der Familie und im Körper eines einzelnen wieder herzustellen, bedarf es verschiedener Hebel. Denn so wie eine

Abb. 3: Aussaugen durch den Heiler Matokwon
a) Matokwon spült den Mund aus
b) Matokwon saugt Fremdkörper aus dem Brustkorb des Knaben
c) Matokwon spuckt das Ausgesaugte in eine Tonscherbe

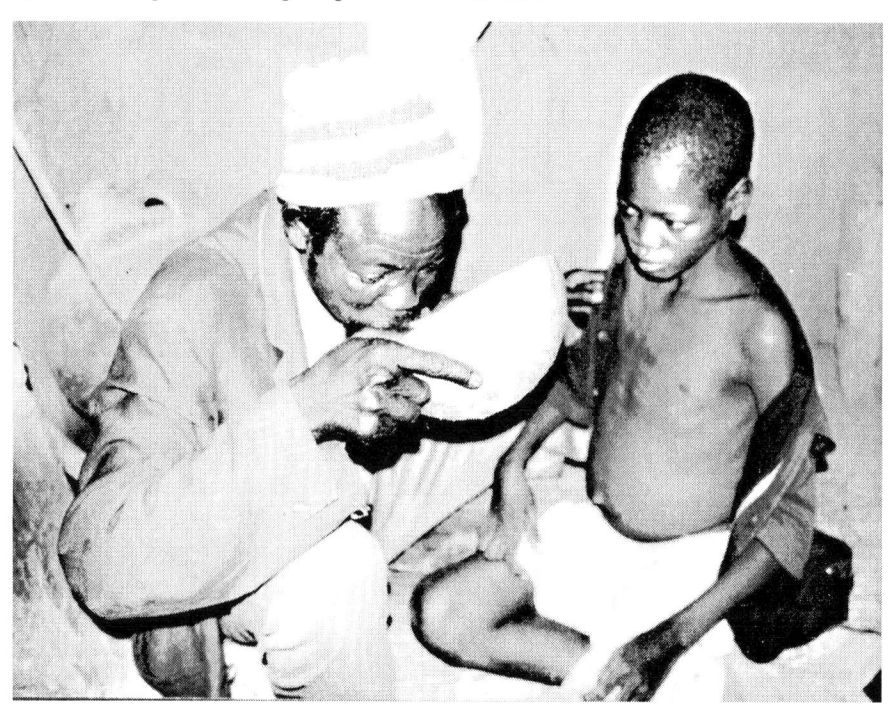

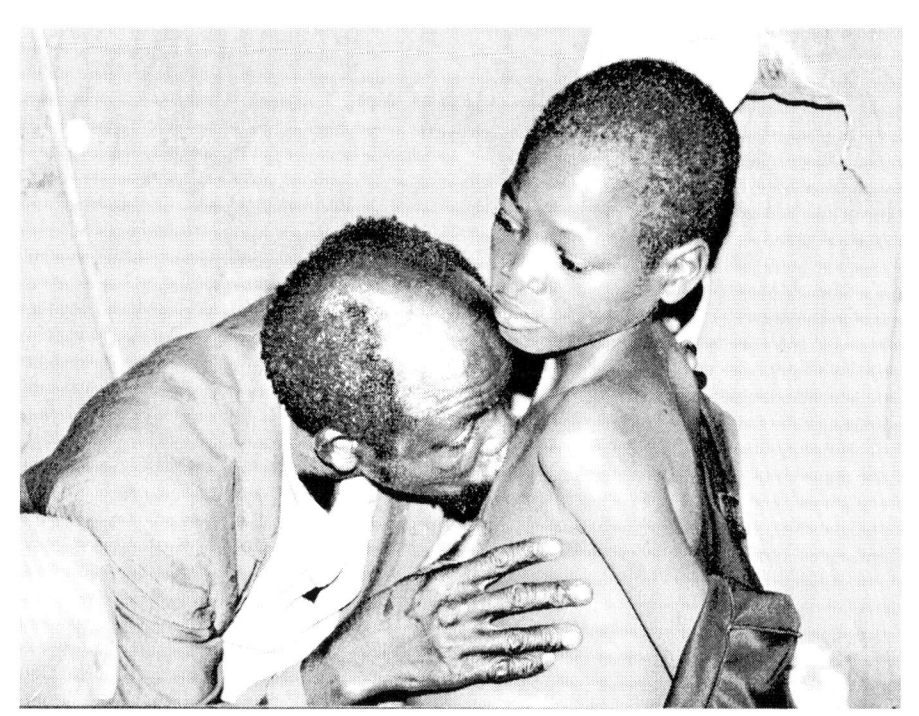

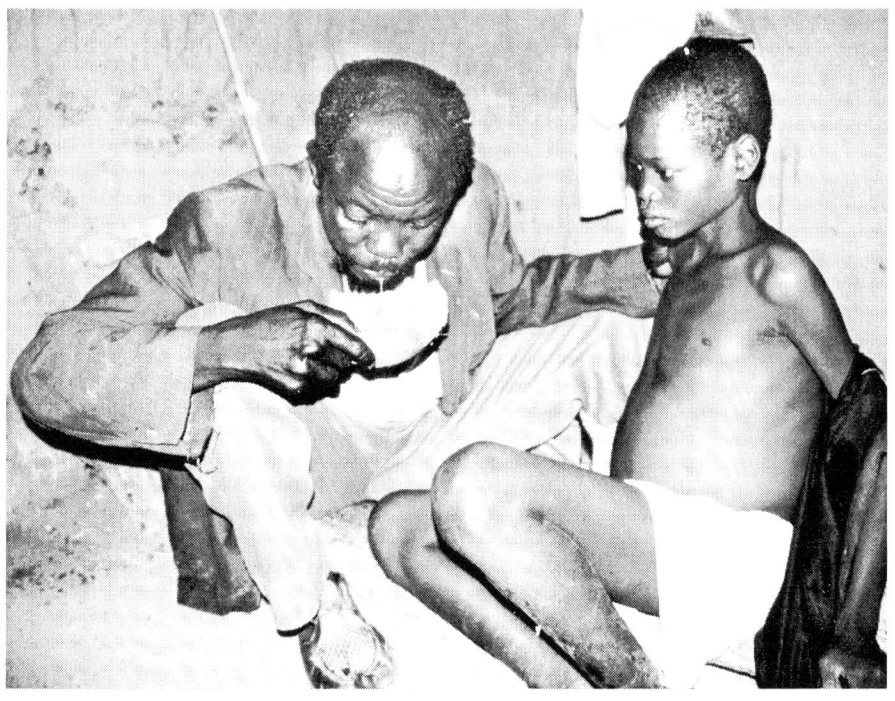

Die *Mafa* in Nordkamerun– ETHNOMED 2002

Krankheit nicht nur eine Ursache hat, so muss sie auch auf verschiedene Weisen behandelt werden. Die biochemischen, psychologischen und spirituellen Kräfte sind als Einheit im Menschen wirksam und können, wenn sie sich gegenseitig stärken, am ehesten den Zustand der Gesundheit wiederherstellen.

Die Mafa wenden sich an unterschiedliche HeilerInnen, je nachdem von welcher Krankheit sie heimgesucht werden. Bei den Mafa gibt es eine endogame Gruppe, die etwa 4 Prozent der Bevölkerung ausmacht, die *ngwozla*. *Ngwozla*-Männer sind Schmiede (sie haben in früheren Zeiten auch verhüttet) und Bestatter, *ngwozla*-Frauen sind Töpferinnen und Geburtshelferinnen. *Ngwozla*-Frauen und Männer sind HeilerInnen, wobei die Frauen sich mehr mit inneren Krankheiten und die Männer mit Knochenbrüchen und Verletzungen auskennen.

Die Behandlung einer kranken Person findet je nach Diagnose stets zugleich auf mehreren der folgenden Ebenen statt:

die strukturelle: Einrenken und Massagetechniken, im begrenzten Rahmen auch chirurgische Eingriffe, Aussaugen von Fremdkörpern,

die biochemische: Heilpflanzen (best. Wurzeln, Knollen, Sukkulentenarten, Blätter) werden gekaut oder als Sud verabreicht,

die elektromagnetische: Akupressur, Handauflegen,

die psychisch-emotionelle: Ortswechsel, der auch Veränderungen des

Abb. 3d) Matokwon massiert den Leib des Knaben nach der Behandlung
e) Wurzelstücke der maytenus senegalensis

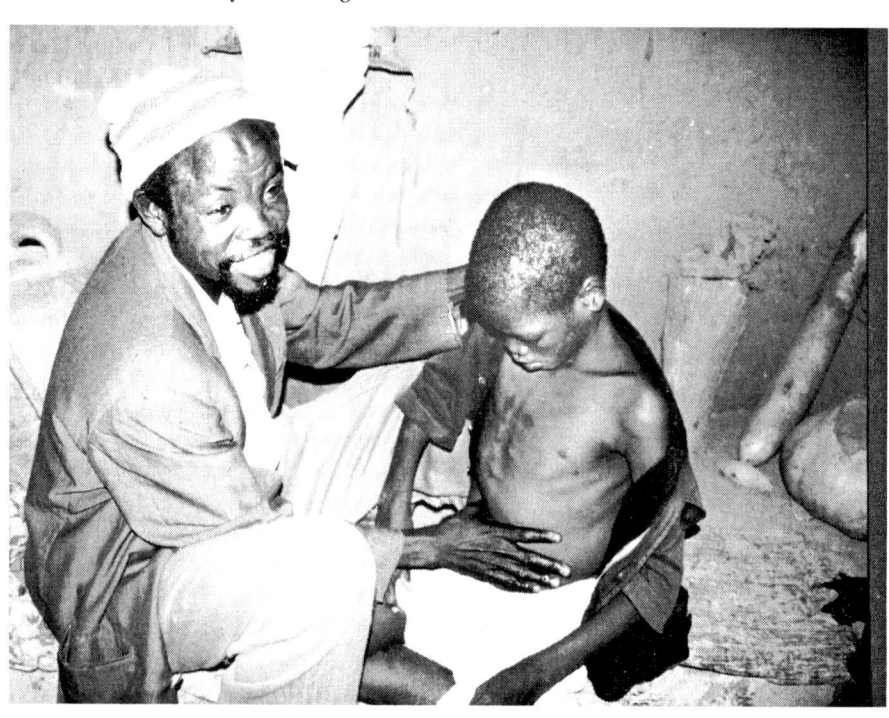

sozialen Umfeldes bedeutet,

die magische: Objekte wie kraftgeladene Steine oder mit Medizin gefüllte Amulette werden in Wasser gelegt, das dann getrunken wird,

die spirituelle: von Gebeten begleitete Opferhandlungen und Zeremonien.

Hat ein Mann durch das Orakel herausgefunden, dass er oder seine Familie von einem Hexer heimgesucht wird, dann kann er für sich und seine Kinder Amulette mit vom Orakelsprecher zu bestimmenden Medizinen von einem Heiler herstellen lassen, die um den Hals oder an der Hüfte getragen werden. Ein Betroffener kann auch bestimmte Pflanzen in der Nähe seines Gehöfts anbauen oder Medizinen vor seinem Hause anbringen. Wenn sich ein Hexer diesen Substanzen nähert, wird er unruhig und ergreift die Flucht.

Ein Hexer, der sein Opfer trotz der Schutzmaßnahmen am Körper oder im Haus heimsucht, muss sterben. Doch reicht bisweilen die Abwehr durch Amulette und Schutzpflanzen dennoch nicht aus, so zum Beispiel wenn sich die/der Hexe/r mit Gegenmitteln ausstattet. Dann muss das Familienoberhaupt resignieren oder aber den Kampf mit dieser/m mächtigen Hexe/r aufnehmen.

Dazu muss er einen Hexengegner finden, die sich dem Hexer gewachsen fühlt. Das ist nicht nur teuer, sondern für alle Beteiligten gefährlich, auch für die Hexengegner. Ehe die Zeremonie gemacht wird, die den Tod des Hexers zur Folge haben muss, werden verschiedene Ahnen- und manchmal auch Erdopfer gebracht um sich zu vergewissern, dass im Einklang mit den Ahnen gehandelt wird. Manche Hexer kommen dem GegnerIn zuvor und benutzen stärkere Mittel, um sie/ihn zu töten.

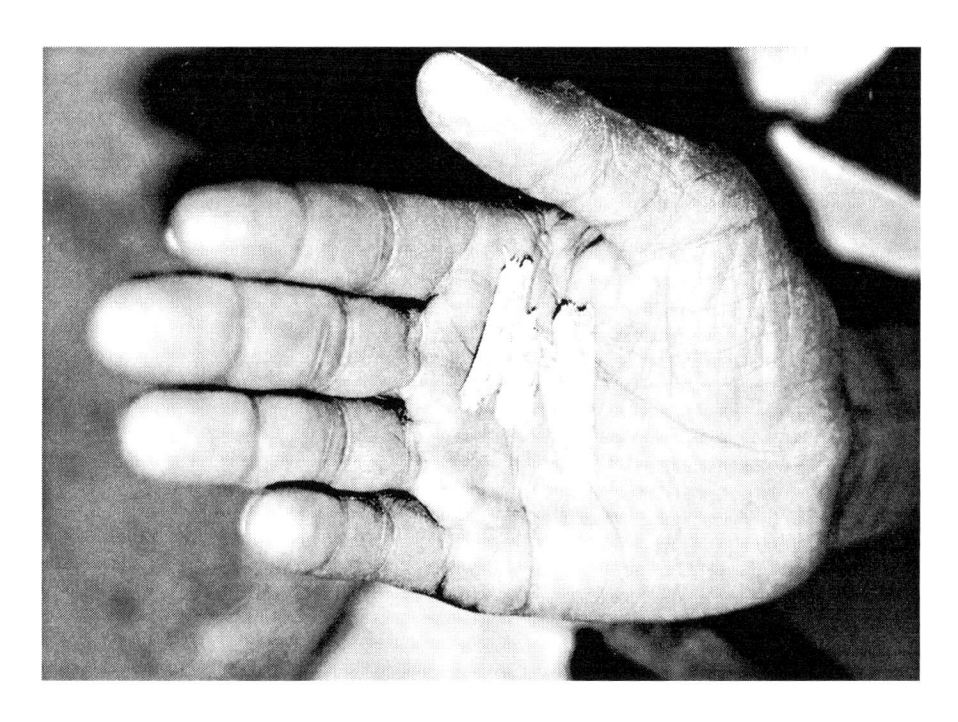

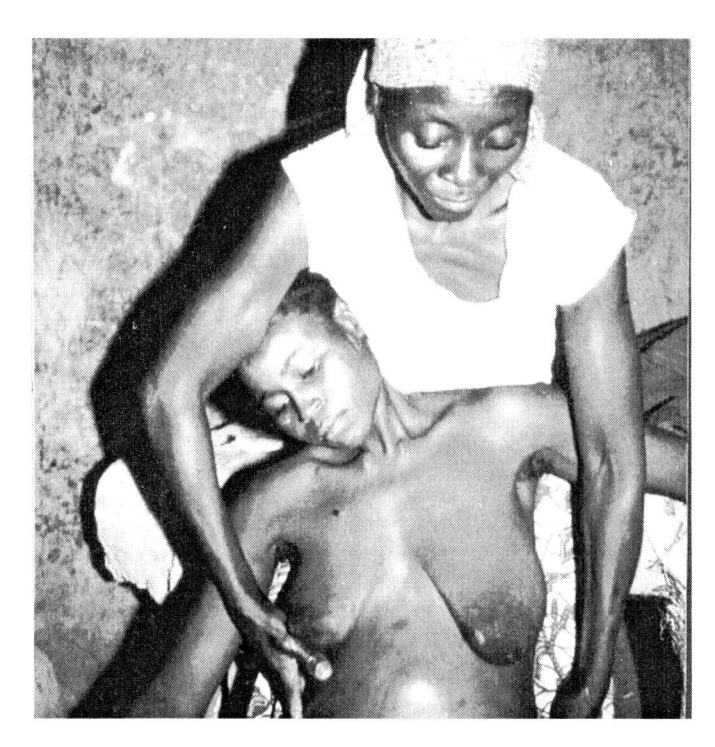

Abb. 4: Bèdèkwa bei der Behandlung einer Schwangeren

Behandlungen und Heilungszeremonien

Stofffetzen im Auge: Ein Mann mit kranken Augen suchte am 19. August 1990 die Heilerin Bèdèkwa in Guzda-Ula auf. Er hatte eine Frau heiraten wollen, die auch von einem anderen begehrt wurde. Sein Rivale beauftragte einen Hexer, diesem Mann einen Stofffetzen ins Auge zu zaubern.

Die Augen des Betroffenen schwollen rot an und tränten. Bèdèkwa bestrich seine Stirn, beide Schultern und die Herzpartie abwärts bis zu den Füßen mit einem blutigen Hähnchenschnabel. Dann nahm sie das Wasser in den Mund und fuhr mit ihrem Mund von den Augen abwärts den Körper entlang.

Danach hatte sie den Stofffetzen im Mund und spuckte ihn auf eine Tonscherbe. Diese legte sie unter einen Stein am Weg, der zum Hause des Hexers führte. Wenn der Hexer, der von dieser Zeremonie nichts weiß, dort vorbei kommt, wird der Stofffetzen in seinen Bauch eintreten. Er wird sofort Bauchschmerzen bekommen und sterben. "Könnte dieser Mann Bèdèkwa um Hilfe bitten um zu überleben?" frage ich. "Nein, denn wenn Bèdèkwa ihn berühren würde, müsste sie sterben. Auch jemand anderes kann ihm nicht mehr helfen, nicht einmal die Ärzte im Krankenhaus."

Fremdkörper im Leib: Muzai holt mich am 5. August 1997 zur zweiten Heilbehandlung ihres Enkelsohnes. Matokwon aus Ulad soll seinen Körper von den restlichen Fremdkörpern befreien, die ihm von einem unbekannten Hexer

Abb. 5: schwangerer weiblicher Geisttopf

zugefügt wurden.
Meine Assistentin Dabagai bestätigt noch einmal, wie schlecht es dem Jungen vor der ersten Behandlung gegangen war. Er war sterbenskrank und konnte nicht mehr laufen. Muzai hatte alle möglichen Behandlungen und auch Opferhandlungen versucht. Schließlich ergab ein Orakel, dass dem Jungen Fremdkörper ausgesaugt werden müssten, und zwar von einem mit dem Kind verwandten Heiler. Die Wahl fiel auf Matokwon, der sogleich durch Betasten des Kindes die Ursache herausfand.

Muzai sucht eine Tonscherbe und reinigt sie. Matokwon erhält eine Kalebasse mit heißem Wasser. Er nimmt einen Schluck, spült damit seinen Mund aus und spuckt ihn durch die offene Tür ins Freie. Er massiert den Bauch des Kindes. Dann nimmt er etwas Wasser in den Mund und saugt an dem Körper des Kindes.
Er spuckt weißen Schleim mit etwas Festem darin in die Tonscherbe. Wieder spült er seinen Mund gründlich aus und spuckt das Wasser in den Hof. Das Ganze wird neunmal wiederholt. Als Ergebnis des Saugens sehe ich: Einige Kubikzentimeter weißen Schleims mit einer faserigen Substanz darin, die als Brustbeerbaumrinde identifiziert wird. Muzai nimmt die Tonscherbe, um sie in ihrem Speicher zu verwahren. Nachts wird sie sie heimlich auf dem Hauptweg vergraben.
Wenn der Hexer, dessen Identität Matokwon aus Furcht vor den Konsequenzen nicht preisgibt, darüber schreitet, wird er sterben. Matokwon gibt Muzai drei

Stückchen der Wurzel des *maytenus senegalensis*, die sie dem Knaben zerstanzt in Hirsebier geben soll. Ich frage den Knaben nach seinem Befinden. Es ginge ihm gut. Vorher hätte er stechende Schmerzen gehabt und ihm sei heiß gewesen, nun fühle er sich richtig wohl. Das Saugen hätte ihm nicht weh getan, auch hätte er kein Stechen oder anderes schmerzhaftes Empfinden während des Saugens gefühlt, er hätte lediglich das Saugen gespürt.

Starke Menstruationsblutungen: Matokwon behandelt die Schwiegertochter Muzais. Sie hat starke Blutungen und wird nicht schwanger. Ihre *nswaltewa* (ein Körperteil, das je nach Gesundheitszustand als erbsen- bis hühnereigroß beschrieben wird und durch Umherwandern im Körper Krankheiten verursacht) ist verschoben. Eigentlich müsste eine Henne geschlachtet werden, doch das Blut, das an einer frisch gezogenen Feder haftet, tut es auch. Matokwon massiert den Bauch der jungen Frau mit Palmöl ein, in das er Halme von *madzaf nswaltewa (scoparia dulcis)* untergemischt hat. Ich sehe deutlich, wie er "etwas" unter der Haut vom Bauchraum an der Vulva vorbei das linke Bein entlang bis in den Fuß

Abb. 6: Krabbenorakel: Ein Orakelsprecher setzt die Krabbe in die Tonschale, in der er den sozialen Kosmos des Ratsuchenden mittels Stäbchen und Kalebassenstückchen aufgebaut hat. Je nachdem, was die Krabbe verrückt oder wo sie ein Loch gräbt bzw. einen Hügel aufwirft, weiß der Orakelsprecher zu deuten.

schiebt, wo es sich aufzulösen scheint. Diese Behandlung wiederholt er dreimal. Die Feder steckt dabei zwischen dem großen und dem benachbarten Zeh des linken Fußes.
Er massiert auch die Lenden und macht schließlich eine zeremonielle Geste, bei der er die Feder einen Kreis um den Kopf der Patientin führt. Anschließend muss die Patientin die Feder mit ihrem Mund berühren. Sie fühlt sich besser. Matokwon gibt ihr noch etwas *madzaf nsawaltewa* mit nach Hause, das sie bei Bedarf in Bier legen und trinken soll. Etwa ein Jahr später wurde die junge Frau schwanger.

Unfruchtbarkeit: Die Heilerin Zakali behandelt Frauen, die schwanger werden wollen. Dazu verabreicht sie eine Medizin aus *nsawalteva (scoparia dulcis)*. Diese Medizin hilft auch gegen die von einer Wunde im Bauch (Zyste?) verursachten Leibschmerzen. Wenn eine Frau nicht schwanger wird, lässt ihr Mann Hirsebier brauen und dann Zakali rufen. Der Mann legt eine Hacke und eine Axt nebeneinander auf den Boden, auf die sich die Frau kniet. Dann reicht der Mann Zakali eine Kalebasse Bier, in die sie einen in vier Teile geschnittenen *scoparia dulcis*-Halm wirft. Wenn zwei der Teile untertauchen und zwei obenauf schwimmen, wird der Frau das Bier zu trinken gegeben, wobei sie die Grashalmteile in der Kalebasse belässt. Nun kann sie getrost einer Schwangerschaft entgegensehen. Sinken allerdings alle vier Teile auf den Boden oder schwimmen alle oben, dann sind das schlechte Zeichen, denn dann wird die Frau nie schwanger werden.

Blutungen während der Schwangerschaft: Tengwocè bewahrt auf der Ablage über ihrem Bett einen Topf für einen weiblichen Himmelsgeist auf, der mit einer Vulva und einem Arm ausgestattet ist. Doch im Unterschied zu anderen weiblichen Himmelsgeist-Töpfen ist im Inneren auf dem Boden des Topfes noch ein kleiner weiblicher Topf samt Vulva und einem Arm angebracht, der, anders als die großen Töpfe, keinen Deckel hat. Als Tengwocè schwanger war und Blutungen hatte, musste sie insgesamt sechsmal das Orakel befragen, um herauszufinden, was sie gegen ihre Krankheit tun könnte.
Immer wieder hieß es, sie sollte einen weiblichen Himmelsgeist-Topf herstellen und ihm ein Bier- und Hühneropfer bringen lassen. Doch half das alles nichts. Endlich wurde durch das Steinorakel bestimmt, der Himmelsgeist-Topf müsste - wie sie - mit einer Maid schwanger sein. Erst als sie diesen Topf hatte herstellen lassen und beopfert hatte, wurde sie gesund. Sie gebar später eine gesunde Tochter.

Bauchschmerzen während der Schwangerschaft: Eine Gefahrenquelle während der Schwangerschaft ist *nsawalteva*. Bèdèkwa behandelte eine im fünften Monat schwangere Frau daraufhin. Sie litt unter ständigen Bauchschmerzen. Bèdèkwa massierte *nsawalteva* in den Rücken, wo sie keine Schmerzen mehr verursachte. Nach der Geburt des Kindes manipulierte sie *nsawalteva* wieder an ihren ursprünglichen Ort in der Blinddarmgegend zurück. Zwar schmerzt *nsawalteva* auch im Rücken noch, aber das ist weniger schlimm als im Bauch und schadet vor allem dem Kind nicht.
Bèdèkwa massierte bzw. pressierte die Frau auf eine Art und Weise, die von einem anwesenden deutschen Arzt als Akupressur identifiziert wurde. Die Frau fühlte sich anschließend besser.

Abb. 7:
Kinder mit Amuletten

a) Vierjähriges Mädchen mit Amuletten gegen Pocken und Bauchschmerzen um den Hals und mit *madzaf nkhè* gegen den Zugriff von Hexe(r)n um die Hüfte.

b) Neunjähriges Mädchen mit verschiedenen Amuletten gegen Krankheit und Hexerei

Autorin
Prof. Dr. phil. Godula Kosack
Privatdozentin für Völkerkunde an der Universität Marburg
Mehrjährige Feldforschung auch mit Familie bei den Mafa in Nordkamerun, Feldforschung in Georgien
Gegenwärtige Forschungsvorhaben:
- Vergleich der Konzeptionen von Hexerei in Europa zur Zeit der Hexenverfolgung und in Afrika heute
- Das Stierfest bei den Mafa in Nordkamerun (Filmprojekt)
Kontakt: E-Mail: G.Kosack@t-online.de

Literatur
- 1999: *Hexen – Gedenktage*, Escher-Verlag, Gehren/Thüringen.
- 2001: "*Die Mafa im Spiegel ihrer oralen Literatur. Eine Monographie aus der Sicht von Frauen*", Rüdiger Köppe Verlag Köln, 854 Seiten, ISBN3-89645-126-X
- 1992: Aus der Zeit der Sklaverei - alte Mafa erzählen, *Paideuma* 38: 177-194.
- 1994: Frauenforschung in einer anderen Kultur - Grenzen des Erfassens am Beispiel der Hexerei, in: Ilse Nagelschmidt (ed.): *Frauenforscherinnen stellen sich vor*, Universitätsverlag Leipzig: 152-164.
- 1995: Christianisierung - eine Chance zur Emanzipation? Die Bedeutung der Religion für die Mafa-Frauen (Nordkamerun), *Anthropos* 90-1995: 206-217.
- 1996: "Primitive Kulturen" und "magisches Weltbild", in: *Jahrbuch für Volkskunde* Neue Folge 19: 26-40.
- 1997: Das Wasser im Leben der Mafa, in: H. Jungraithmayr, D. Barreteau & U.Seibert (eds.): "*L'homme et l'eau dans le bassin du Lac Tchad*" Editions de l'Orstom, Paris: 297-304.
- 1997: Cived - das Leben einer Mafa-Frau, in in: Johanna Ludwig (ed.): *Was Frauen bewegte, was Fauen bewegt*, Sammlungen und Veröffentlichungen der Louise-Otto-Peters-Gesellschaft e.V. Leipzig: 87-94.
- 1999: Wird die Polygynie in der modernen Gesellschaft überleben? Überlegungen zur Mehrfrauenehe am Beispiel der Mafa in Nordkamerun, in: *Anthropos* 94-1999: 554-563.
- 1999: Warum wurden die Hexen verfolgt? Einige Bemerkungen zur männlichen Dominanz in Wissenschaft und Religion, in: Ulrike Krasberg (ed.): Religion und weibliche Identität. *Interdisziplinäre Perspektiven auf Wirklichkeiten*, Curupira Workshop Marburg: 224-246.
- 1999: "Ich habe dich im Himmel gesehen" Über Schamanismus bei den Mafa im nördlichen Mandara-Gebirge Nordkameruns, in: Alexandra Rosenbohm (ed.): *Schamanen zwischen Mythos und Moderne*, Militzke Verlag Leipzig: 120-134.
- 1999: L'idee que les femmes ont d'elles-mêmes illustrée par leurs contes sur la sorcellerie chez les Mafa du Nord-Cameroun, in: R. Carré, M. Dupré et D. Jonckers (eds.): *Femmes plurielles. La représentation des femmes, discours, normes et conduites*, Editions de la Maison des sciences de l'homme, Paris: 203-220.
- 2000: Rationalismus oder ganzheitliches Denken. Ein Rekurs auf die Hexereidiskussion. In: Ilse Nagelschmidt (ed.): *Frauenforscherinnen stellen sich vor*. Ringvorlesung Teil IV, Leipziger Universitätsverlag: 295-307.
- 2001: Hexen und Hexerei im Interkulturellen Vergleich,in: *Berichte von den Hexentagen vom 5.-7. November 1999 in Leipzig und Bad Düben*, LOUISEum 13, Sammlungen und Veröffentlichungen der Louise-Otto-Peters-Gesellschaft Leipzig: 26-33.
- 2001: Wie gehen die Mafa-Frauen (Nordkamerun) mit Krankheit um? in: *Curare* 23 (2000)1: 25-40.

THE MAFA IN NORTHERN CAMEROON*

by Godula Kosack

The traditional concept of health and illness of the *Mafa* in North Cameroon

For the *Mafa* health is the condition of harmony with the cosmos, i.e. with the spirits inhabiting the transcendental world and their ancestors. The spirits which inhabits the sky, the earth, the water, the ways, the rocks, the trees, the houses are generally favourable-minded towards the people for whom they are responsible, and they protect them from attacks from the outside.

Illness is a disorder in the cosmos directly surrounding humans. Rarely can an illness be explained by one cause only. If meningitis or yellow fever disease can afflict numerous children, it is well-known that the illness is caused by an infection, but nevertheless a divinator is asked to find out the more deeply lying reasons.

Why a family is affected by the illness in particular, compared to others, may be explained by male and female witches weakening the children or by angry ancestors or spirits. If disease or deaths accumulate in a family, if wounds do not want to heal or periodically appear again, if another misfortune happens, it will be time to visit an oracle-speaker (female ones are the exception) in order to ask for the deeper cause.

The oracle- speaker questions the transcendental forces and then moves stones or

Fig.: Oracle Speaker Zanaha
* Translated by Silke Tönsjost. Revised by Joy C. Green.

Fig. 1:
Stone- oracle: The oracle- speaker moves the stones towards her body. Depending on how many stones remain lying, one, two or three, the answer to the question is positive, negative or indefinite. This procedure is repeated arbitrarily often.

little sticks, or he lets a crab move about in a clay bowl filled with damp sand and little sticks. The interpretation of the given constellations usually shows that transcendental forces are working. Illness can be caused by spirits, by ancestors or by living humans, thus by sorcery.

By sending an illness, a spirit or an ancestor gives a hint to the family leaders (responsible for the earth- and ancestor-offerings) that an additionally beer offering is due or overdue.

These are regularly given at the seasonal celebrations or at the occasional ceremonies for the deceased in form of a goat or chicken- offering. Illness and infirmity, misfortune and tempest (independent of whether a man or a woman or a child, cattle or fields are concerned) is understood as an attack on the well-being being of the family, to which only the family head can answer.

If a family is exposed to special attacks by witches or unfavorable weather conditions, this requires the special protection of the spirits and ancestors: additional offerings must be given, in order to ensure or regain health and fertility

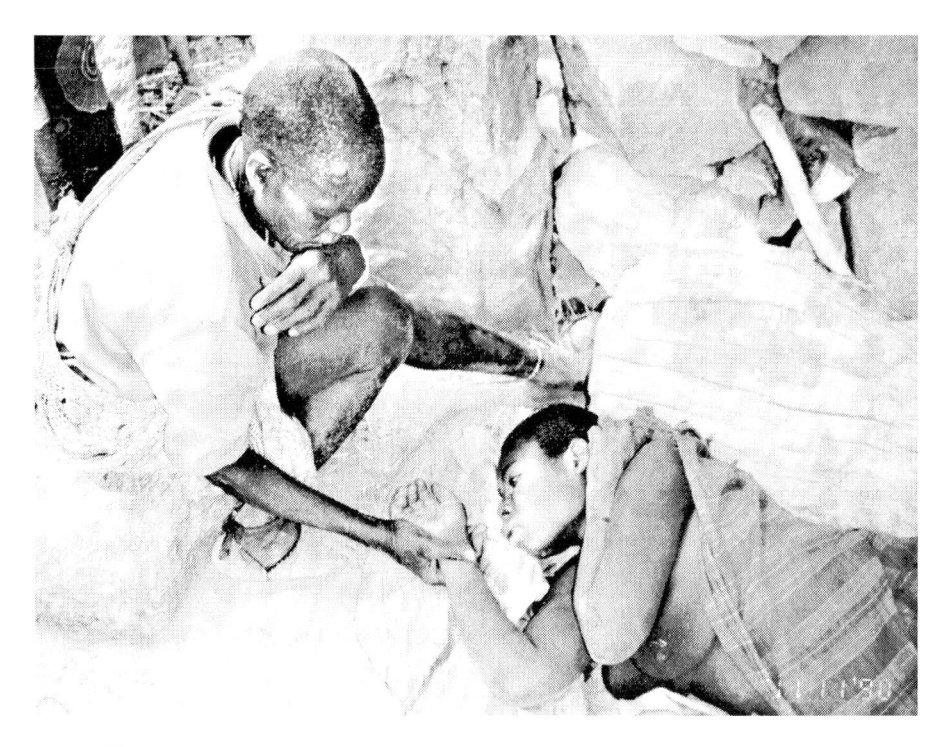

Fig. 2: Ill woman

of the family, the cattle and the fields. Depending on how much the spirits have been neglected, whether they are more or less angry and require bigger offerings. The sacrificial offerings humans give are the appreciation for the spirits and ancestors and tribute, for the fact that they have protected the living persons up to now against illness and unnatural deaths, as well as against accesses of witches.

The *Mafa´s* concept of sorcery

About sixty per cent of all children are born with witchcraft. This strength can be inherited from the mother or the father, it develops during life , either for good - which is as ability to be clairvoyant, to recognize witches, to interpret oracles or to heal - or however for the bad, in order to cause damage to humans, animals, plants or also to the earth. Two thirds of the children born with witchcraft are female. Out of ten witches one uses the strength for the good , two of them do not use it and three are "bad witches".

This last category covers thirty per cent of the population. In which way a person develops their innate witchcraft, depends on the influence he or she is exposed to. Already after the first consumption of "human flesh" (in such a way the Mafa designates the access to the vital strength of humans) the person is unable to stop damaging other humans. He/she must take from the vital strength of others. From now on he/she must practise witchcraft, not necessarily because of malice, but because he/she loses their own vital strength and that means that he/ she becomes ill or dies. Other witches cause illness and death out of envy, disfavor, competition or similar motives. Frequently the "evil eye" is used or items are brought into the victims body by magic, which causes stinging pain and gradually absorbs vital strength. Very common is the hiding of "*nkhè*", a material fiber, or another object, soaked with sweat, urine or menstrual blood, which had contact with the victim. Thus the witch has constant access to the vital strength of the victim.

The *Mafa`s* Concept of healing

For the family and the body to regain the balance of the cosmos, different approaches are required. Because an illness does not have one cause only, it must be treated in different ways. The biochemical, psychological and spiritual forces are effective together in humans and can re-establish the condition of health if they strengthen themselves mutually. The *Mafa* address different healers, depending on the type of illness they are afflicted with.

Part of the *Mafa* is an endogamous group, which constitutes about 4 per cent of the population called "*ngwozla*". *Ngwozla* men are black-smiths (they also have smelted in earlier times) and undertakers, *ngwozla* women are pot gutters and

Fig. 3: Draining by the healer Matokwon
a) Matokwon rinses the mouth
b) Matokwon sucks foreign elements from the boys thorax
c) Matokwon spits the exhaust into a clay piece

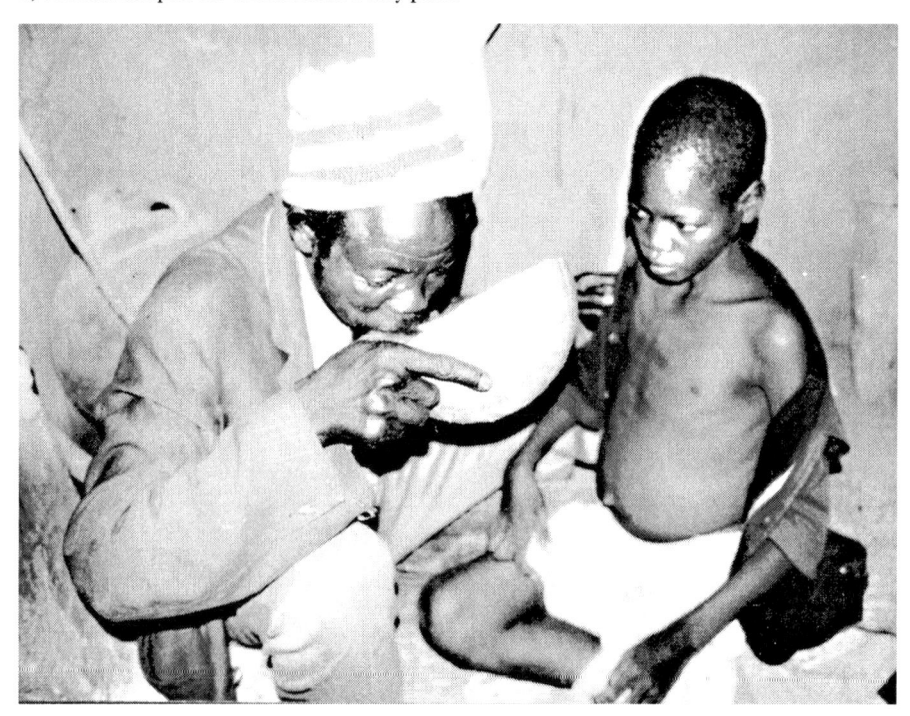

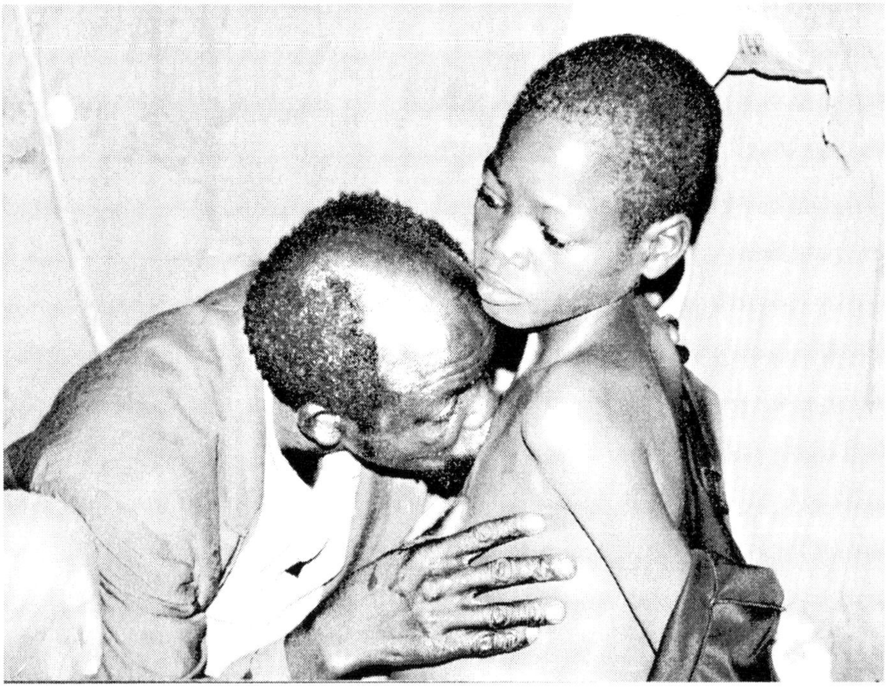

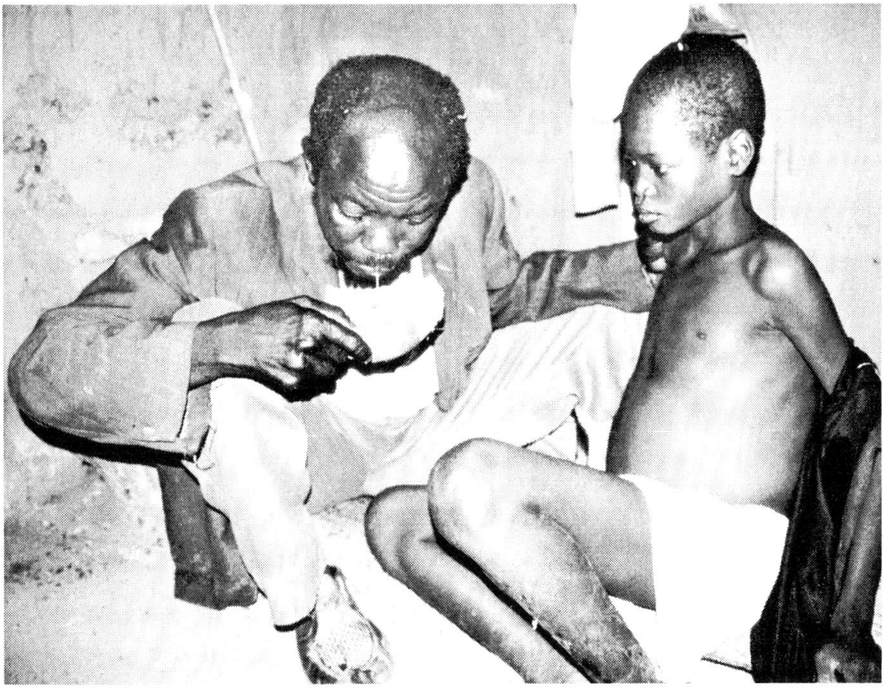

midwives. *Ngwozla* women and men are healers, whereby the women are versed more with internal diseases and the men with fractures and injuries.

The treatment of an ill person, depending on the diagnosis, always happens on several of the following levels at the same time:
the structural:
- straightening and massage, within the limited framework also surgical operations, exhausting foreign bodies;
- the biochemical: healing plants (stock roots, tubers, species of succulents, leaves) are chewed or given as an extract;
- the electromagnetic: akupressure, healing with hands;
- the psychological-emotional:change of place, which means also changes of the social surroundings;
- the magic: objects like energy stones or medicine filled amulets are put in water, which will be drunken;
- the magic ritual:sacrificial offerings and ceremonies accompanied by prayers.

If a man found out by the oracle that he or his family is afflicted by a witch, then he can get an amulet by the oracle-speaker for himself and his children. He determines the medicine needed and transfers it into the amulets, which are carried around the neck or on the hip.

The concerned patient can also cultivate certain plants in the proximity of his or her farmstead or attach a medicine in front of his/her house. If a witch aproaches

Abb. 3: Draining by the healer Matokwon
d) Matokwon massages the boys body after the treatment
e) Pieces of root maytenus senegalensis

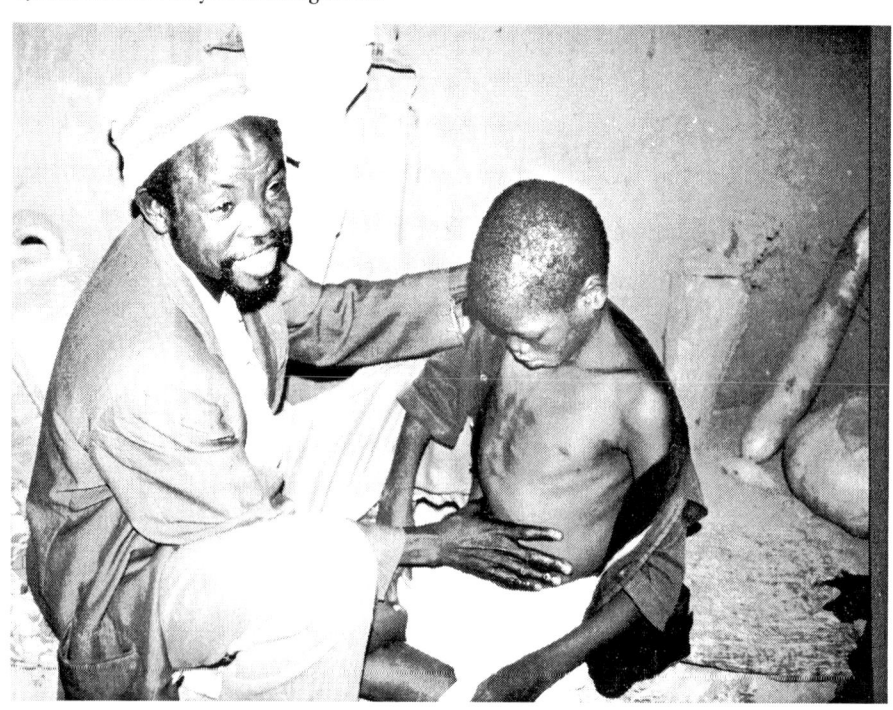

these substances, he/she becomes restless and flees. A witch, who receives his/her victim despite the preventive items at their body or in their house, will die. But sometimes the prevention by amulets and plants will not be sufficient, thus for example, if that witch equips himself with remedies.

Then the family head must resign or take up the fight with that powerful witch. In addition, he must find an antagonist to the witch who feels adequate to him/her. This is not only expensive, but dangerous for all involved, also for the antagonist. Before the ceremony, which must result in the death of the witch, different earth- and ancestor- offerings are brought, in order to ensure the conformity with the ancestors. Some witches forestall the antagonists and use stronger means, in order to kill them.

Treatments and healing ceremonies
Piece of cloth in the eye:
A man with ill eyes visited the healer Bèdèkwa in Guzda Ula on 19 August 1990. He had wanted to marry a woman who was desired by another, too. His rival assigned a witch, to put a piece of cloth in the eye of this man. The eyes of the patient swelled up redly and watered. Bèdèkwa smeared a bloody cockerel bill on its forehead, both shoulders and the heart portion downward up to the feet.

Then she took water into her mouth and drove her mouth from the eyes downward along the body. She had the piece of cloth in her mouth and spat it on a broken clay afterwards. She put it under a stone on the way that led to the witches house. If the witch, not knowing anything about this ceremony, passes that point, the piece of cloth will get into his belly. He will get belly pain immediately and die.

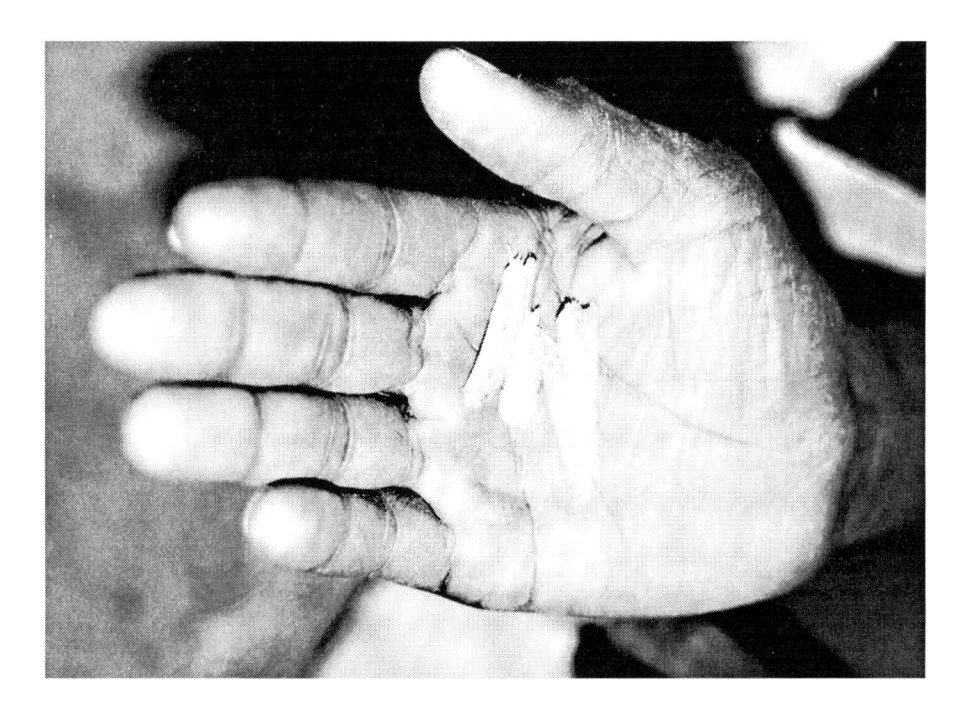

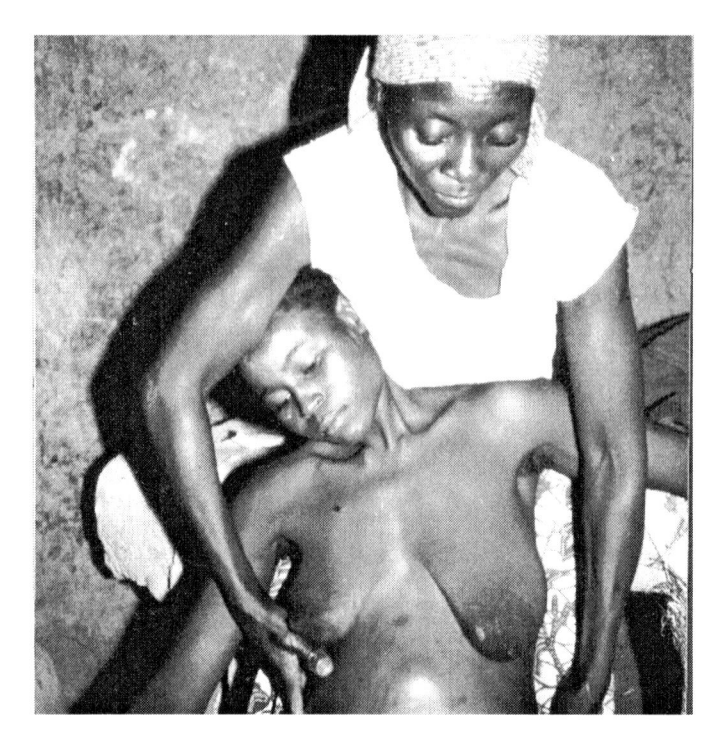

Fig. 4: Bèdèkwa at the treatment of a pregnant woman

"Could this man ask Bèdèkwa for assistance for surviving?" I ask. *"No, because if Bèdèkwa would touch him, she would have to die. Nobody else can help him any longer, not even the physicians in the hospital."*

Foreign body in the body:
Muzai gets me on the 5 th of August 1997 for the second treatment of her grandson. Matokwon from Ulad is to release his body from the remaining alien elements, which were added to him by an unknown witch. My female assistant Dabagai confirms again, how badly the boy had been before the first treatment. He was mortally ill and could not run any longer. Muzai had tried all possible treatments and also sacrifices. Finally an oracle said that the boy´s alien elements would have to be drained, in form of an relative-healer of the child. The choice fell on Matokwon, who found the cause immediately by touching the child.
Muzai looks for a broken clay piece and cleans it. Matokwon receives a calabash with hot water. He takes a sip, rinses his mouth out and spits it out through the open door into the free. He massages the belly of the child. Then he takes a little bit of water into the mouth and sucks at the body of the child. He spits white mucus with something firm inside into the broken clay piece. He rinses his mouth out thoroughly and spits the water into the yard.

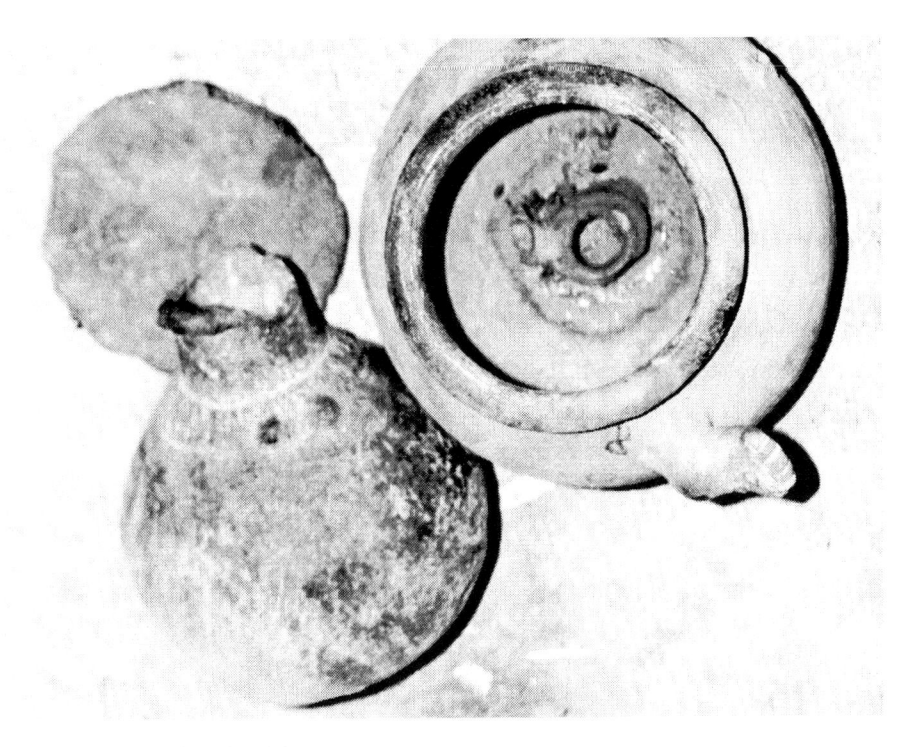

Fig. 5: Pregnant female spirit pot

This is repeated nine times. As a result of the sucking I can see: Some cubic centimeters white mucus with a fibrous substance therein, which is identified as Brustbeerbaum bark .Muzai takes the broken piece of clay in order to keep it in their warehouse. At night it is buried secretly on the aisle. If the witch, whose identity Matokwon wouldnt want to tell out of fear of the consequences, walks past it, he will die. Matokwon gives three bits of the root *maytenus senegalensis* to Muzai, which she is to give to the boy crushed in millet beer. I ask the boy for its condition. He was well. He had a stinging pain before and felt hot, now he feels well. The sucking didnt hurt him, he didnt feel a stinging or any other pain during the treatment, he only felt the sucking.

Strong menstrual bleeding:
Matokwon treats the daughter-in-law of Muzai. She has strong menstrual bleedings and does not become pregnant. Her *nswaltewa* (a part of the body, described as peasize upto the size of an egg floating in the body, causing diseases) is shifted. Actually a hen would have to be slaughtered, but the blood, which sticks to a freshly pulled feather, works also. Matokwon massages the belly of the young woman with palmoil, into which he mixed stems of *madzaf nswaltewa* (scoparia dulcis). I can see clearly, how he pushes "something" under the skin of the abdominal cavity to the vulva, along the left leg into the foot, where it seems to dissolve. He repeats this treatment three times. The feather is thereby between the

large and the neighbouring toe of the left foot. He massages also the lumbal region and finally makes a ceremonial gesture, he leads the feather in a circle around the head of the female patient. Subsequently, the female patient must touch the feather with her mouth. She feels better. Matokwon gives her some madzaf nsawaltewa to take home, it needs to be to put into beer and drunk if necessary. About one year later the young woman became pregnant.

Infertility:
The healer Zakali treats women who want to become pregnant. To support the fertility she gives a medicine out of *nsawalteva* (scoparia dulcis). This medicine helps also against stomach ache caused by a wound in the belly (cyst?).
If a woman does not become pregnant, her husband brews millet beer and then calls Zakali. The husband puts a heel and an axe next to each other on the soil, on which the woman kneels down. Then the man hands out a calabash filled with

Fig. 6:
Crab- oracle: An oracle- speaker sets the crab into the clay bowl, in which he constructed the social cosmos of the patient with little sticks and pieces of calabash. Depending on the movement of the crab or where it digs a hole or raises a hill, the oracle- speaker knows the interpretation.

beer to Zakali, into which she throws a scoparia dulcis stem cut into four parts.
If two of the parts submerge and two swim on top, the beer is given to the woman to drink, whereby she leaves the blade of grass parts in the calabash. Now she can expect a pregnancy confidently. However if all four parts sink onto the soil or if all swim above, then it is a bad indication,- the woman will never become pregnant.

Bleedings during the pregnancy:
Tèngwocè keeps a pot on the shelf over her bed for a female sky-spirit, the pot is equipped with a vulva and an arm. But in contrast to other female sky-spirit pots there is still another small female pot including Vulva and an arm on the inside on the soil of the pot, which, in contrast to the large pot, does not have a cover. When Tengwocè was pregnant and had bleedings, she had to ask the oracle six times, in order to find out what she could do against her illness.
Again and again it was said, she should manufacture a female sky -spirit pot and that she should let bring a beer and a chicken offering. But that did not help at all. Finally, determined by the stone-oracle, the sky-spirit pot should become pregnant - like her - with a girl. After she had let somebody manufacture that pot and had sacrificed with it, she became healthy. She gave birth to a healthy daughter later.

Belly pain during the pregnancy:
A source of danger during the pregnancy is *nsawalteva*. Bèdèkwa treated a five-month pregnant woman because of *nsawalteva*. She suffered from constant belly pain. Bèdèkwa massaged *nsawalteva* into the back, where it caused no more pain. After the birth of the child she manipulated nsawalteva again to its original place in the blind intestine area.
The *nsawalteva* hurts still in the back, but that is better than in the belly and it does not harm the child. Bèdèkwa massaged the woman in a way that was identified by a present german physician as acupressure. The woman felt better afterwards.

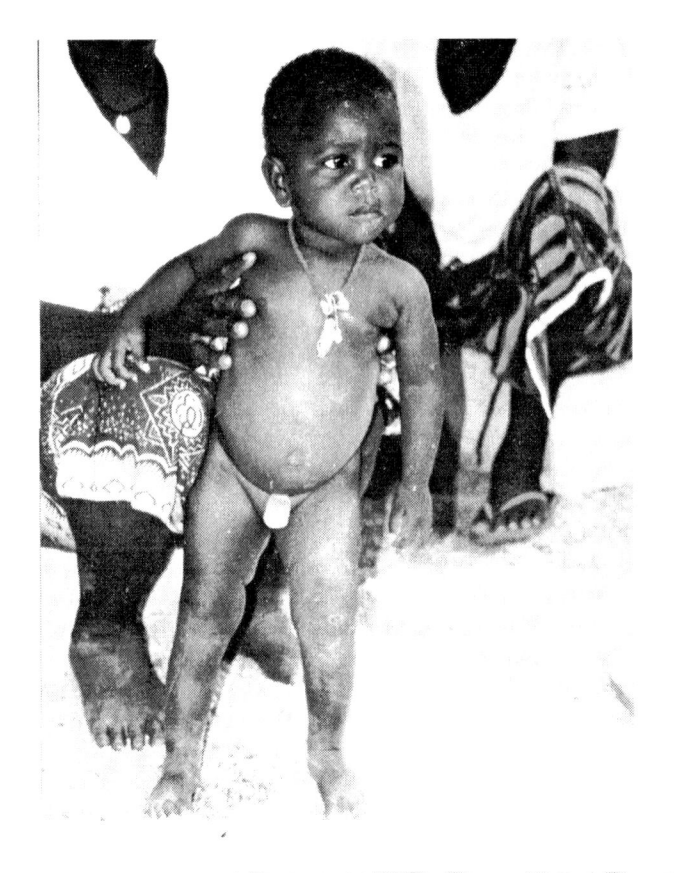

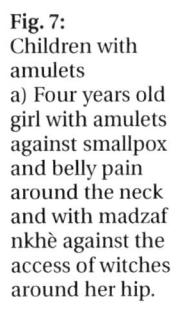

Fig. 7:
Children with amulets
a) Four years old girl with amulets against smallpox and belly pain around the neck and with madzaf nkhè against the access of witches around her hip.

b) Girl of nine years with different amulets against illness and sorcery.

Author
PROF. DR. PHIL. GODULA KOSACK,
Lecturer for Anthropology at the University of Marburg, Germany
- Field research of several years also with her family at the Mafa in north Cameroon - - field research in Georgien
- lecturer for ...at the University of Marburg
- Present research projects: comparism of the conceptions of sorcery in Europe at present witch pursuit and in Africa today
- the bull celebration at the Mafa in north Cameroon (film project)

Contact: E-Mail: G.Kosack@t-online.de

References
- 1999: *Hexen – Gedenktage*, Escher-Verlag, Gehren/Thüringen.
- 2001: "*Die Mafa im Spiegel ihrer oralen Literatur. Eine Monographie aus der Sicht von Frauen*", Rüdiger Köppe Verlag Köln, 854 Seiten, ISBN3-89645-126-X
- 1992: Aus der Zeit der Sklaverei - alte Mafa erzählen, *Paideuma* 38: 177-194.
- 1994: Frauenforschung in einer anderen Kultur - Grenzen des Erfassens am Beispiel der Hexerei, in: ILSE NAGELSCHMIDT (ed.): *Frauenforscherinnen stellen sich vor*, Universitätsverlag Leipzig: 152-164.
- 1995: Christianisierung - eine Chance zur Emanzipation? Die Bedeutung der Religion für die Mafa-Frauen (Nordkamerun), *Anthropos* 90-1995: 206-217.
- 1996: "Primitive Kulturen" und "magisches Weltbild", in: *Jahrbuch für Volkskunde* Neue Folge 19: 26-40.
- 1997: Das Wasser im Leben der Mafa, in: H. JUNGRAITHMAYR, D. BARRETEAU & U.SEIBERT (eds.): "*L'homme et l'eau dans le bassin du Lac Tchad*" Editions de l'Orstom, Paris: 297-304.
- 1997: Cived - das Leben einer Mafa-Frau, in in: JOHANNA LUDWIG (ed.): *Was Frauen bewegte, was Fauen bewegt*, Sammlungen und Veröffentlichungen der Louise-Otto-Peters-Gesellschaft e.V. Leipzig: 87-94.
- 1999: Wird die Polygynie in der modernen Gesellschaft überleben? Überlegungen zur Mehrfrauenehe am Beispiel der Mafa in Nordkamerun, in: *Anthropos* 94-1999: 554-563.
- 1999: Warum wurden die Hexen verfolgt? Einige Bemerkungen zur männlichen Dominanz in Wissenschaft und Religion, in: ULRIKE KRASBERG (ed.): Religion und weibliche Identität. *Interdisziplinäre Perspektiven auf Wirklichkeiten*, Curupira Workshop Marburg: 224-246.
- 1999: "Ich habe dich im Himmel gesehen" Über Schamanismus bei den Mafa im nördlichen Mandara-Gebirge Nordkameruns, in: ALEXANDRA ROSENBOHM (ed.): *Schamanen zwischen Mythos und Moderne*, Militzke Verlag Leipzig: 120-134.
- 1999: L'idee que les femmes ont d'elles-mêmes illustrée par leurs contes sur la sorcellerie chez les Mafa du Nord-Cameroun, in: R. CARRÉ, M. DUPRÉ et D. JONCKERS (eds.): *Femmes plurielles. La représentation des femmes, discours, normes et conduites*, Editions de la Maison des sciences de l'homme, Paris: 203-220.
- 2000: Rationalismus oder ganzheitliches Denken. Ein Rekurs auf die Hexereidiskussion. In: ILSE NAGELSCHMIDT (ed.): *Frauenforscherinnen stellen sich vor*. Ringvorlesung Teil IV, Leipziger Universitätsverlag: 295-307.

- 2001: Hexen und Hexerei im Interkulturellen Vergleich,in: *Berichte von den Hexentagen vom 5.-7. November 1999 in Leipzig und Bad Düben*, LOUISEum 13, Sammlungen und Veröffentlichungen der Louise-Otto-Peters-Gesellschaft Leipzig: 26-33.
- 2001: Wie gehen die Mafa-Frauen (Nordkamerun) mit Krankheit um? in: *Curare* 23 (2000)1: 25-40.

SÜDAFRIKANISCHE MEDIZINPFLANZEN IN DER ZULU-VOLKSMEDIZIN*

von John A. O. Ojewole

Einführung

Unter der zerstörerisch wirkenden kortikoiden Dysbalance, Epilepsie genannt, leiden Menschen beiderlei Geschlechts und aller Altersgruppen.

Gegenwärtige Schätzungen deuten darauf hin, daß über 6 Prozent der Weltbevölkerung an dieser Störung des zentralen Nervensystems (ZNS) leiden. Die "Epilepsie", gelegentlich auch als Zuckung oder Krampf bezeichnet, wird in dem Glauben aus alten Zeiten so gesehen, dass Menschen deren Körper von "bösen Geistern" besetzt waren, immer an dieser Krankheit litten.

Der Gebrauch der krampflösenden, einheimischen Heilmittel für Epilepsie, ist so alt wie die Krankheit selbst. Obwohl der Kräuterarzt kaum den detaillierten chemischen, biochemischen, pharmakologischen und ernährungsmäßigen Wert seiner medizinischen Behandlung erfassen kann. Jahrelange gründliche Beobachtung, praktische Langzeiterfahrung und Erfahrung mit Kräuterarznei, erbringen im Allgemeinen die Fähigkeiten des(r) wahren Heilers(in) in der erfolgreichen und effektiven Behandlung von Epilepsie.

Bei den in Südafrika lebenden *Zulus* wird die Behandlung und Kontrolle von Epilepsie durch den Gebrauch pflanzlicher Zubereitungen erreicht. Einige der krampflösenden Heilmittel werden in Seifenform verabreicht, mit der sich die Patienten waschen oder darin baden müssen. In manchen Zulugemeinschaften wird Epilepsie als ein Leiden betrachtet, das durch übernatürliche Mächte verursacht wird, z.B. durch Hexen, Zauberer und Geister der Ahnen. In solchen Fällen, werden die krampfartigen Störungen für gewöhnlich nicht nur mit

Abb.1: Eine Zulu "*izangoma*", auch genannt "*sangoma*", die eine krampflösende Substanz zubereitet

* Übersetzung aus dem Englischen: Birgit Neumann

Kräuterheilmitteln behandelt, sondern auch durch Exorzismus, Zaubersprüche und Beschwörungen.
In Heilriten oder Opferzeremonien wird das Wohlwollen der Ahnen erbeten und durch Anrufung der Hexen und Zauberer um Vergebung der Sünden gefleht. Die Opfer- und Heilzeremonien wirken normalerweise direkt auf den Körper und das Bewusstsein des krampfenden und zuckenden Patienten. Für gewöhnlich wird der Körper des Patienten mit krampflösenden Heilmitteln massiert.
Meistens werden die entkrampfenden Zubereitungen in Form von Abkochungen, Tinkturen, Infusionen, Pulver und Mixturen oral verabreicht. Gelegentlich werden Bäder in Kräutermixturen verschrieben.

In Südafrika werden seit vielen Jahrhunderten Pflanzen traditionsgemäß für medizinische Zwecke genützt. Mit über 30.000 Arten von Edelpflanzen (höher entwickelte Pflanzen) bilden medizinische Pflanzen den floristischen Wohlstand und ein wichtiges sozio-kulturelles Erbe Südafrikas. Die reichhaltige kulturelle und biologische Vielfalt Südafrikas, hat es ermöglicht nahezu 3000 Pflanzenarten zu medizinischen Zwecken zu nutzen. Unter diesen sind über 350 Arten der gebräuchlichsten und am häufigsten gehandelten Medizinpflanzen (VAN WYK et al. 1997).
Manche dieser Pflanzen wurden auch für magische, rituelle, spirituelle und symbolische Zwecke benutzt, zusätzlich zu ihrem medizinischen Wert und ihrer Nahrhaftigkeit.
Die bemerkenswerte kulturelle Vielfältigkeit Südafrikas spiegelt sich in den formalen und informalen medizinischen Systemen wieder, die ständig in verschiedenen Landesteilen praktisch angewandt werden.
Die informellen, oral-traditionellen medizinischen Systeme vieler Stämme, wurden bis jetzt noch nicht systematisiert, sondern werden mündlich von Generation zu Generation überliefert. Die Wurzeln dieser medizinischen Systeme mit ihrer spezifischen pflanzlichen, tierischen und mineralischen "Materia Medica" reichen bis zurück in die Altsteinzeit (Paleolithikum).

Zuerst sucht ein traditioneller afrikanischer Heiler immer nach der Ursache der Krankheit. Danach verabreicht er Behandlungen zusammen mit anderen Therapien, die sich an die erkannte Ursache der Krankheit richten, um die Symptome und Zeichen der Krankheit zu lindern.
Es gibt schätzungsweise 200.000 einheimische traditionelle Heiler in Südafrika und über 80 Prozent der Südafrikaner konsultieren noch diese Heiler, üblicherweise zusätzlich zu den gängigen, modernen, westlichen medizinischen Einrichtungen (WYK et al. 1997).

Traditionelle Heiler sind in Südafrika allgemein bekannt als "*izinyanga*" und "*izangoma*" (Zulu), "*ixwele*" und "*amaquira*" (Xhosa), "*nqaka*" (Sotho), "*bossiedoktor*" und "*kruiedoktor*" (West- und Nordkap).
Die *Zulu* Worte "*inyanga*" und "*isangoma*" wurden benutzt um respektvoll und ausschliesslich auf "Kräuterkundiger" (Herbalist) und "Geistheiler" (Diviner) hinzuweisen.
Heutzutage jedoch verwischen sich die Unterschiede, so praktizieren einige Heiler beide Arten (VAN WYK et al. 1997).
Bild 1 zeigt einen *Zulu* "*izangoma*" (Geistheiler), öfter als "*sangoma*" bezeichnet, bei der Zubereitung eines krampflösenden Heilmittels aus der Stammrinde einer

Medizinpflanze.
Außer den Kräuterkundigen und Geistheiler, von denen geglaubt wird, dass sie spirituell begabt und befähigt sind, gibt es auch traditionelle Geburtshelfer, Propheten, spirituelle Heiler, Intuitive und Träumer in Südafrika.
Die meisten alten Menschen auf dem Land verfügen über Wissen in Kräuterheilkunde und haben die Funktion als Erste-Hilfe-HeilerInnen, im Familienkreis mit altbewährten Hausmitteln aus der Kräuterheilkunde (VAN WYK, et al,. 1997).
Medizinpflanzen bilden die Verbindungsbrücke zwischen den verschiedenartigen traditionellen Heilern.
Diese Praktiker benutzen üblicherweise Pflanzenextrakte (in Form von Infusionen, Abkochungen, Mixturen, Tinkturen, Pulver, Seifen, etc.), hergestellt aus verschiedenen morphologischen Teilen der Pflanzen, speziell aus den Zweigen, Blättern, Stamm- oder Wurzelrinde, Holz, Früchten, Samen, Gummis, Nektar und so weiter, um ihre epileptischen Patienten zu behandeln.

Materialien und Methoden

Pflanzliche Materialien
Eine literarische Forschung an ausgewählten medizinischen Pflanzen wurde in dieser Arbeit erstellt, um deren chemische Zusammensetzung und zusätzlichen medizinischen Gebrauch zu untersuchen (WATT & BREYER-BRANDWIJK 1962; PUJOL 1990; HUTCHINGS ET AL. 1996; AND VAN WYK ET al 1997).
Eine Sammlung verschiedener einheimischer, antiepileptischer Pflanzen und Rezepte, Besuche bei traditionellen Heilern in Kwa *Zulu-Natal* und pharmakologisches Aussortieren der Pflanzenextrakte auf antiepileptische Eigenschaften hin, wurde im August 1998 begonnen und im Juli 2001 beendet. Die verschiedenen getesteten Pflanzenmaterialien wurden vom Kurator der Universität Durban-Westville, Botanische Fakultät, Südafrika und von Mitarbeitern des Natal Provinz Herbariums in Durban, Südafrika bioloisch bestimmt. Dort wurden die Beweisproben gelagert.

Ein Kilogramm der am häufigsten zu medizinischen Zwecken benutzten morphologischen Teile der Medizinpflanzen, die traditionell in der *Zulu*medizin zur Behandlung von Epilepsie und Krämpfen eingesetzt werden, wurden getrennt, in sauberem Leitungswasser gewaschen, getrocknet, in schmale Teile geschnitten und in einem Homogenisator homogenisiert.
Jedes Homogenat wurde im Soxhlet zwei mal extrahiert, bei jedem Durchgang wurden für 24 Stunden 2,5 Liter destilliertes Wasser bei einer Temperatur von 30 C0 (±1) geschüttelt.
Die kombinierten Extrakte wurden gefiltert und konzentriert und unter dem reduzierten Druck von 30 °C (±1) Celsius getrocknet.
Das endgültige Pflanzenextrakt wurde jedes Mal gefriergetrocknet und ergab Pulver oder Halbpulver, grobwässrige Extraktrückstände. Rückstandslos sich auflösende Portionen der wässrigen Extraktrückstände jeder der getesteten Pflanzen, wurden an jedem Experimenttag gewogen und in destilliertem Wasser zur Berechnung der krampflösenden Wirkung gelöst.

Tab. 1: Some South African Medicinal Plants Used as Anticonvulsant Remedies in Zulu Folk Medicine

Serial Number	Family, Species [and Zulu name]	Parts Used	Chemical Constituents	Medicinal Uses
1.	**Anacardiaceae** *Lannea discolor* (Sond) Engl. [isiganganyane]	Leaves/ Stem-bark/ Roots	Flavonoids, polyphenolics and tannins.	Convulsions and 'fits' diarrhoea, abscesses and boils, infertility, menorrhagia, sore eyes gonorrhea, swollen legs and whooping cough.
2.	**Apocynaceae** *Rauwolfia caffra* Sond. [umhlambamazi]	Stem-bark/ Root-bark/ Leaves	Indole and indoline alkaloids, rauvolfine, reserpine, yohimbine, ajmalicine and phytosterols.	Hypertension, malaria, fevers, colic pains, rheumatism, pneumonia, mental problems, insomnia and hysteria, rashes, convulsions, asthma, cough and other chest complaints.
3.	**Asteraceae** *Blumea alata* (D. Don) DC. [ugodide]	Roots/ Leaves	∝-Humulene, caryophyllene and squalene, minute amounts of cuathemone derivatives.	Fevers, convulsions, constipation, colic and abdominal pains, pneumonia, heart pains, headaches and leg pains, and *Trichomonas vaginalis* infection
4.	**Asteraceae** *Conyza scabrida* DC. [uhlabo]	Leaves/ Roots	Diterpenoids, hautriwaic acid, and clerodane derivatives.	Convulsions, colds and coughs, pleuritic pains, headaches, fevers, chest and heart complaints.
5.	**Asteraceae** *Vernonia neocorymbosa* Hilliard [uhlungu-lungu]	Leaves/ Twigs/ Roots	Squalene, vemolide and vemodalin, sesquiterpenoid lactones, flavonoids, pyridine, and diterpenoid alkaloids.	Epilepsy, abortion, stomachache, hysteria, irregular menstruation, dysentery and intestinal worm infestations
6.	**Bignoniaceae** *Kigelia africana* (Lam.) Benth. [umfongothi]	Fruits/ Stem-bark	Flavonoids, dihydroisocoumarin kigelin, naphthoquinone derivate lapachol, iridoid glycosides, cinnamic acid derivatives, stigmasterols and β-sitosterol.	syphilis, stomach ailments, dysentery, constipation, snakebite, wounds, boils and sores, gynaecological disorders, rheumatism, acne, pneumonia, convulsions, aphrodisia haemorrhoids and lumbago.
7.	**Bignoniaceae** *Tecomaria capensis* (Thunb.) Spach [lungana]	Stem-bark/ Leaves	Sterols and sterolins, tannins and terpenoids.	Fevers, pains, insomnia, chest complaints, diarrhoea, dysentery, bacterial infections, stomach pains, influenza, pneumonia and convulsions

8.	**Capparaceae** *Boscia albitrunca* (Burch.) Gilg & Ben [umvithi]	Roots/ Leaves/ Fruits	Phytosterols and sterolns.	Haemorrhoids, inflamed eyes, epilepsy.
9.	**Capparaceae** *Capparis tomentosa* Lam. [umabusane]	Roots/ Leaves	Oxindole compounds, alkaloid stachyurine, and sulphur oil.	Rheumatism, insanity, snakebite, jaundice, chest pains, malaria, headaches, pneumonia, coughs, asthma, constipation, eye problems and convulsions.
10.	**Celastraceae** *Maytenus senegalensis* (Lam.) Excell [isihlangu]	Roots/ Leaves	Polyphenolics, tannins and terpenoids	Haemoptysis, respiratory ailments, epilepsy, body pains, constipation, diarrhoea, night blindness, infertility, menorrhagia, mouth ulcers and wounds, sore throats, dysentery, microbial infections and schistosomiasis.
11.	**Commelinaceae** *Commelina africana* Linn. [idangabane]	Roots	Flavonoids, glycosides and anthocyanin derivatives.	Insomnia, infertility, epileptic 'fits', heart complaints, nervous ailments, venereal diseases, body pains, menstrual and bladder ailments
12.	**Crassulaceae** *Cotyledon orbiculata* Linn. [intelezi]	Leaves/ Leaf juice	Tyledoside and outadienolide-type cardiac glycosides such as orbicuside A, B, and C.	Corns and warts, toothache and earache, boils, inflammation, rheumatism, epilepsy, and syphilis.
13.	**Crassulaceae** *Crassula alba* Forssk. [isidwe]	Leaves/ Twigs	Polyphenolics and tannins.	Epilepsy, dysentery and diarrhoea, bloody stools, influenza, fevers, heartburn and hysteria
14.	**Cucurbitaceae** *Cucumis hirsutus* Sond. [intangazane]	Roots/ Fruits	Cucurmin, steroids and saponins	Coughs, constipation, abdominal pains, convulsions, abortion, penal and vulval sores.
15.	**Ebenaceae** *Euclea divinorum* Hiern [umhlangula]	Fruits/ Roots/ Stem-bark/	Naphthoquinones, diospyrin, lupeol and betulin, triterpenoids saponins, tannins and steroids	Convulsions, toothaches, constipation, schistosomiasis, chest pains, pneumonia, gastric disorders, infertility, swellings and inflammatory conditions, headaches and depressed fontanelles

	Family / Species	Part used	Constituents	Uses
16.	**Euphorbiaceae** *Croton gratissimus* Burch. [umahlabekufeni]	Stem-bark/ Roots/ Leaves	Alkaloids, flavonoids, saponins, cardenolides, monoterpenoids and diterpenoids, aromatic oils, crotonin, crotin and nucrierne	Fevers, bleeding gums, rheumatism, chest complaints, constipation and indigestion, oedema (dropsy), coughs, inflammation, insomnia, aphrodisia and epilepsy.
17.	**Euphorbiaceae** *Jatropha curcas* Linn. [inhlakuva]	Roots/ Seeds/ Leaves	Oil containing tiglian-type irritant diterpenoids, curcanoleic acid, toxic protein named curcin, cyanic acid, flavonoids, steroids, triterpenes and oleic acid.	Constipation, boils and wounds dropsy, sciatica, paralysis, skin diseases, sores, venereal diseases, angina, herpes, malaria, jaundice, fevers, diarrhoea, ringworm, rheumatism, convulsions and 'fits'
18.	**Fabaceae** *Abrus precatorius* Linn. [umkhokha]	Roots/ Leaves	Flavone, choline, trigonelline, precatorine, glycyrrhizin, abrin, abrusogenin, abrusosides, indole derivatives and abrine, saponins, anthocyaninsns and the steroids abricin and abridin.	Love and good luck charms, pleuritic chest complaints, eye ailments, contraception, convulsions, schistosomiasis, tuberculosis, warts and skin diseases, snakebite, intestinal worm infestations, aphrodisia, bronchitis, asthma and whooping cough, colds, fevers, and malaria
19.	**Fabaceae** *Acacia karroo* Hayne [umunga]	Stem-bark/ Leaves/ Gum	Polyphenols and tannins, uronic acid, galactan derivatives, and sulphated glycosides.	Diarrhoea and dysentry, conjunctivitis, haemorrhage, colds, oral thrush, stomach ache, osteomyelitis, dizziness, convulsions, venereal diseases and aphrodisia
20.	**Fabaceae** *Mimosa pudica* Linn [imbune]	Whole plant	Mimosine and norepinephrine.	Convulsions/epilepsy, dysmenorrhoea, heart palpitations, insomnia and nervousness.
21.	**Lamiaceae** *Leonotis leonurus* (Linn.) R. Br. [umunyane]	Leaves/ Stems/ Roots	Volatile oil, diterpenoids, labadane-type lactones, premarrubin and marrubiin.	Epilepsy, snakebite and insect stings, boils, eczema, skin diseases, itching, muscular cramps, influenza, coughs, colds, bronchitis and asthma, hypertension, partial paralysis, headaches and viral hepatitis.
22.	**Loganiaceae** *Nuxia floribunda* Benth. [ingobese]	Leaves/ Stem-bark	Polyphenolics and tannins.	Fevers, coughs, indigestion, influenza and infantile convulsions

	Family / Species [Zulu name]	Parts used	Chemical constituents	Uses
23.	**Meliaceae** *Melia azedarach* Linn. [umsilinga]	Leaves/ Root bark/ Heartwood	Oxidised triterpenoids known as limonoids, triterpenoid saponins, steroids, aromatic compounds, vanillic acid, azedarinic acid, melianoninol, coumarins, lignans and flavonoids.	Abdominal pains, helminthiasis, epilepsy, fits/convulsions, schistosomiasis, swollen legs, asthma, constipation, spasms and nervous pains, eczema, malaria, diuresis, rheumatism, gout and skin diseases.
24.	**Phytolaccaceae** *Phytolacca dodecandra* L'Hérit. [umhedeni]	Roots/ Leaves/ Berries	Steroidal triterpenoid saponins, endod saponoside, lemmatoxin and oleanonic acid derivatives.	Urinary complaints, snakebite, epilepsy, uterine tumors and fibroids, rheumatism, inflammatory conditions, fish poison, boils and wounds, spermicidal contraception, syphilis and other parasitic infections.
25.	**Polygonaceae** *Oxygonum atrigeanum* Meisn. [umaambane]	Roots/ Leaves	Triterpenoid saponins, oleasterol and flavonoids.	Abdominal pains, inflammatory conditions, schistosomiasis, convulsions, whooping cough, aphrodisia, diarrhoea and snakebite.
26.	**Rosaceae** *Rubus pinnatus* Willd. [amakonubi]	Roots/ Leaves	Polyphenolics and tannins, terpenoids.	Coughs and other respiratory complaints, toothaches, convulsions, chronic diarrhoea, abdominal cramps and rheumatism.
27.	**Rubiaceae** *Catunaregam spinosa* (Thunb.) Tirvengadum [isibhla]	Roots/ Leaves/ Fruits	Alkaloids, iridoids, ursolic acid-based saponins, oleanolic acid derivatives, triterpenoid saponins	Epilepsy and dizziness, fevers, aphrodisia, headaches, snakebite, nausea, respiratory and gynaecological ailments, rheumatism, emesis, diuresis, schistosomiasis, gonorrhoea and other bacterial infections.
28.	**Rubiaceae** *Gardenia ternifolia* Schumach. & Thonn [umkwakwane omkhulu]	Roots/ Twigs/ Fruits	Triterpenoids and tannins.	Malaria, protective charm against lightning and sorcery, sore eyes, headaches, madness, coughs, asthma, dysmenorrhoea, infertility chorea epilepsy and convulsions, earache, schistosomiasis, rheumatism, abdominal pains and fish poison.
29.	**Rutaceae** *Clausena anisata* (Willd.) Hook. f. ex Benth. [isinidu]	Roots/ Leaves/ Fruits	Sesquiterpenoids, fatty acids, umbelliferone, scopoletin, limonene, alkaloids clausanitine and mupamine, coumarins helietin and chalepin, limonoids and phenylpropanoids.	Convulsions, taeniasis and other parasitic infections, constipation, rheumatism, malaria and fevers, heart ailments, bad breath, abdominal pains and toothache, mental diseases, headaches, eye complaints, impotence and sterility, battle charms

30.	**Sapotaceae** *Englerophytum magalismontanum* Krause [umnqumabele]	Roots/ Fruits	Ascorbutic acid, tannin, steroids triterpenoids, oleanoic acid derivatives.	Epilepsy, headaches, abdominal pains, rheumatism and inflammatory conditions.
31.	**Solanaceae** *Datura stramonium* Linn. [iloyi]	Leaves/ Fruits/ Aerial Parts	Tropane alkaloids, atropine, hyoscine, and other atropine-like drugs, sesquiterpenoids	Asthma, bronchitis, coughs and many other respiratory conditions, rheumatism, gout, boils, abscesses and wounds, aphrodisia, motion sickness, sore throat and tonsilitis, visceral pains, epilepsy and Parkinsonism.
32.	**Solanaceae** *Withania somnifera* (Linn.) Dun [ubuvimbha]	Roots/ Leaves/ Aerial parts	Triterpenoid saponins, tropanol, sitoindosides, alkaloids, choline, steroidal lactones, withaferine A, withasomnine, withanolides, and flavonoids.	Fevers, sores, abscesses, wounds, syphilis, skin diseases, diarrhoea, proctitis, asthma, nausea, rheumatism, inflammation and pain, conjunctivitis, scabies and carbuncles, aphrodisia, sedation, epilepsy/convulsions.
33.	**Verbenaceae** *Clerodendrum glabrum* E. Mey. [umnukanbiba]	Leaves/ Roots	Steroidal saponins, flavonoids, and terpenoids	Fevers, intestinal parasites, childhood convulsions, colds, sore throats and chest complaints, fractured bones, toothaches, skin rashes, sedation and body pains
34.	**Verbenaceae** *Lippia javanica* (Burm. F) Spreng. [umsuzwane]	Leaves/ Twigs	Volatile oil, monoterpenoids, various organic acids and alcohols, iridoid glycosides and pentacyclic triterpenoids.	Coughs, colds, bronchitis, asthma and other chest ailments, malaria, fevers, stomach problems and headaches, convulsions, cataracts, diarrhoea, scabies and body lice.
35.	**V** *I Urdenuua* (Linn.) Wild & Drum. [isinwazi]	Roots/ Tubers/ Leaves	Proanthocyanins and flavanoids.	Epilepsy, dysmenorrhoea, safe delivery in pregnancy, renal complaints, menorrhagia infertility, stomach ailments, swellings, colds, wounds, boils and sores.

Tierische Materialien

Für jedes der getesteten Pflanzenextrakte wurden Mäuse (Mus domesticus) beiderlei Geschlechts im Test benutzt, die zwischen 25 – 30 g wogen. Die Mäuse wurden nach dem Zufallsprinzip in 3 Gruppen eingeteilt, nach "Test A", "Test B" und "Control C" Maus.

Jede Testgruppe setzte sich aus 8 Mäusen zusammen und eine gleiche Anzahl der Mäuse wurde immer als "Kontroller" benützt. Krampfartige Anfälle wurden chemisch in den Testtieren herbeigeführt, wie von OJEWOLE (2000) früher detailliert beschrieben wurde.

Pentylenetetrazol (i.e. Metrazol (PTZ – 90 mg/kg i.p.)) und Picrotoxin (PIC, 10 mg/kg i.p.) wurden benutzt um Anfälle in den Mäusen hervorzurufen.

Jedes der Kontrolltiere in der "Control C"- gruppe wurde mit destilliertem Wasser (2ml/kg i.p.) behandelt. Phenobarbitone (10 mg/kg i.p.) und Diazepam (0.5 mg/kg i. p.) dienten als Standardmittel im Vergleich zu den empfohlenen krampflösenden Drogen der genannten Pflanzenextrakte.

Ergebnisse

Unser ethnobotanischer Literaturüberblick zeigte, dass eine große Zahl medizinischer Pflanzen aus verschiedenen Gattungen und unterschiedlichen Familien in der traditionellen *Zulu*medizin zur Behandlung von Epilepsie eingesetzt werden.

Dies sind im Besonderen folgende Pflanzen: Asteraceae, Bignoniaceae, Fabaceae, Verbenaceae, Rubiaceae, Rutaceae, Commelinaceae, Meliaceae, Lamiaceae, Solanaceae, Apocynaceae, Euphorbiaceae, Myrtaceae, Polygonaceae, Rosaceae, Crassulaceae, Sapotaceae, Capparaceae, Vitaceae, usw. 35 der am häufigsten als antiepileptische Heilmittel in der *Zulu*medizin eingesetzten Heilpflanzen wurden gesammelt, verglichen, überprüft und authentisiert.

Die einheimischen (*Zulu*)-Namen der Pflanzen, die morphologischen Teile, die generell bei den traditionellen *Zulu*heilern als antiepileptische und krampflösende Heilmittel eingesetzt werden, ihre chemischen Zusammensetzungen und sonstiger medizinischer Gebrauch, ebenso ihre relativen krampflösenden Eigenschaften in chemisch hervorgerufenen (Schocks) Anfällen, sind in Tabelle 1 aufgeführt.

Die pharmakologische Auswertung der vielfältigen Pflanzenextrakte, sowie die empfohlenen antiepileptischen Arzneidrogen, die in dieser Studie benutzt wurden, zeigte, dass gemäß der Höhe der Dosis der Pflanzenextrakte (>800 mg/kg i.p.) entsprechend starke krampflösende Aktivitäten im beschriebenen Tierversuch produziert wurden. Phenobarbitone (10 mg/kg i.p.) und Diazepam (0,5 mg/kg i.p.) wirkten sehr stark und riefen krampflösende Effekte in den Mäusen hervor, sie boten 100prozentigen Schutz gegen durch Metrazol- und Picrotoxin hervorgerufene Anfälle (Bilder werden nicht gezeigt).

Der Prozentsatz an krampflösender Wirkung der verschiedenen Pflanzenextrakte wurde in Relation zu denen von Phenobarbitione und Diazepam gesetzt.

Die krampflösende Wirksamkeit der Pflanzenextrakte hatte eine große Spannbreite.

Außer in zwei Fällen, waren die Pflanzenextrakte generell wesentlich effektiver darin, die Tiere gegen durch Metrazol hervorgerufene Anfälle zu schützen als gegen die durch Picrotoxin induzierte.

Von den 35 getesteten Pflanzenextrakten, hatten 17 (i.e.,48,57 Prozent) eine stark

krampflösende Wirksamkeit gegenüber der durch Metrazol induzierten Anfällen (sie produzierten 62,5 - 87,5prozentigen Schutz gegen diese künstlich hervorgerufenene Anfälle in den Tieren).
Die verbleibenden 18 von 35 Pflanzenextrakten (i.e., 51,43%), zeigten milde bis schwach krampflösende Wirkung (12,50 - 50,00prozentiger Schutz der Tiere gegen durch Metrazol induzierte Anfälle).
Die maximale krampflösende Wirksamkeit der Pflanzenextrakte wurde bei Dosen von >800 mg/kg i.p., 15 bis 30 Minuten nach Verabreichung erreicht.

Diskussion und Schlussfolgerung

Die Ergebnisse der Tierversuche deuten an, dass die Gruppe der ausgewerteten Medizinpflanzen der *Zulu* krampflösende Eigenschaften besitzt. Schwach bis stark krampflösende Wirkungen wurden im Laborversuch erforscht, obwohl die Pflanzen zu verschiedenen Familien gehören und verschiedene chemische Zusammensetzungen beinhalten.
Die am häufigsten zitierten Pflanzen mit krampflösenden Eigenschaften sind: Asteraceae, Bignoniaceae, Fabaceae, Verbenaceae, Rubiaceae, Rutaceae, Commelinaceae, Meliaceae, Lamiaceae, Solanaceae, Sapotaceae, Apocynaceae, Euphorbiaceae, Myrtaceae, Polygonaceae, Rosaceae, Crassulaceae, Capparaceae, Vitaceae, etc. (HUTCHINGS et al. 1996).
Dies sind sehr weit verbreitete Pflanzenfamilien. Die phylogenetische Abstammungslinie zwischen den ausgewählten Pflanzenfamilien, kann ein aussagekräftiger Hinweis sein auf die vielfältige Erscheinungsweise/Natur ihrer aktiven chemischen Zusammensetzungen.

Unser ethnobotanischer Literaturüberblick hat dargelegt, dass 28 dieser 35 (i.e. 80 Prozent) der in der *Zulu* Medizin eingesetzten Medizinpflanzen zur Kontrolle oder Behandlung von Epilepsie, zum gleichen Zweck auch an völlig anderen Teilen der Welt in dortigen traditionellen Heilmethoden verabreicht wurden.

Der Literaturüberblick hat auch gezeigt, dass relativ wenig wissenschaftliche Untersuchungen unternommen wurden, den Gebrauch der in dieser Studie getesteten südafrikanischen Medizinpflanzen als krampflösende Heilmittel zu rationalisieren. 21 (i.e., 60 Prozent) dieser einheimischen krampflösenden *Zulu* – Heilmittel waren bereits an anderen Orten in der Welt auf ihre krampflösende Aktivität getestet worden.
Einheimische krampflösende Heilmittel sind in der richtigen Dosierung besonders im therapeutischen Einsatz recht nützlich. Von entscheidender Bedeutung sind die unterschiedlichen Verabreichungsformen. Alle indigenen, entkrampfenden Heilmittel als Abkochung, Tinktur, etc. zubereitet, werden generell oral eingenommen, manche auch als Badezusatz genutzt, aber nie über Injektionen verabreicht.
In der Zusammenarbeit von traditionellen Heilern, Photochemikern, organischen Chemikern, Pharmakologen und anderen medizinisch Praktizierenden wird größter Nutzen der "Neuen Drogen" erzielt, die aus traditionellen Heilmittel entwickelt wurden.
Mit dem weltweit zunehmenden Auftreten von Epilepsie in der Stadt- wie auch bei der Landbevölkerung, der Unfähigkeit gegenwärtiger moderner Therapien die Stoffwechseldefekte der Krankheit und ihre pathologischen Konsequenzen unter

Kontrolle zu bekommen, gekoppelt mit ernsthaft schädigenden Effekten und den enormen Kosten der modernen, konventionellen schulmedizinischen Behandlung, besteht eine große Notwendigkeit, neue, effektive, günstige, ungiftige, einheimische alternative Strategien in der Epilepsie-Therapie zu entwickeln.

Die Ergebnisse der Tierversuche haben gezeigt, dass die getesteten medizinischen Pflanzenextrakte schwache bis starke krampflösende Eigenschaften besitzen und somit der volkstümlichen Gebrauch der Pflanzen als antiepileptische Heilmittel in der traditionellen *Zulu*medizin bewiesen scheint.

Zusammenfassung

Gegenwärtige Schätzungen zeigen, dass wahrscheinlich 6 Prozent der Weltbevölkerung an Epilepsie leiden. Die Lebenserwartung wird bei dieser zerstörerischen gesundheitlichen Störung drastisch reduziert. Dies besonders in Entwicklungsländern, wo Epilepsie zusehend überhand nimmt und adäquate Behandlungen oft teuer oder nicht gegeben sind.

In vielen Entwicklungsländern verlassen sich noch Millionen von Menschen auf traditionelle Heiler und medizinische Pflanzen in ihrer täglichen Gesundheitsvorsorge.

Pflanzenprodukte gewinnen inzwischen sogar in westlichen Industrieländern an Popularität, als alternative und ergänzende Therapien.

Übergeordnetes Ziel dieser Studie ist es, einen Ausgangspunkt für afrikanische Programme zu schaffen, die zur Entwicklung einheimischer Pflanzen als günstige Quellen von wirkungsvollen, standardisierten, antiepileptischen pflanzlichen Rohstoffen führen. Ebenso zur Erforschung und Entwicklung von chemischen Zusammensetzungen neuer, sicherer und billiger krampflösender Drogen (pflanzlicher Arzneidrogen).

Keywords: Traditionelle Medizin; Südafrikanische Medizinpflanzen; Epilepsie; indigene (einheimische) krampflösende Heilmittel; Traditionelle *Zulu*medizin

Danksagung

Mein ganz besonderer Dank gehört den Mitarbeitern des Natal Provincial Herbariums in Durban, Südafrika, und den Mitarbeiter/innen des Departement of Botany, Faculty of Science, University of Durban-Westville, Durban, Südafrika, für die Identifizierung des in dieser Studie bearbeiteten Pflanzenmaterials.

Ebenso danke ich Frau Thembisa Jikwa für Ihre Unterstützung bei der Sammlung einiger der getesteten Pflanzen und Rezepte.

Meinen Dank aussprechen möchte ich auch Frau Patience Koloko (Direktorin der *KwaZulu-Natal* Traditional Healers Affairs) für ihre Unterstützung und Interesse an dieser Studie; Frau Dr. Esther K. Mutenda für ihre Assistenz im Extraktionsprozess;

Professor Clement O. Adewunmi, der mir unbegrenzten Zugang in sein Laboratorium gewährte, ebenso für seine konstruktive Kritik; und zuletzt dem Rat der Universität Durban-Westville, Durban 4000, Südafrika, für die Bereitstellung eines Forschungsstipendiums (R642) um einen Teil dieser Studie durchführen zu können.

Autor
JOHN A.O.OJEWOLE, DR.
Professor und Leiter des Ressorts, BPharm. (Hons.); M Sc (Clin. Pharm.); PhD (Pharmacology). Wissenschaftler beim Departement of Pharmacology, Fac. of Health Sciences, University of Durban-Westville, gegenwärtige Forschungsgebiete: Traditionelle Medizin/ Ethnomedizin, Ethnopharmacologie, Natural Products Pharmacology.
Kontakt: E-Mail: ojewole@pixxie.udw.ac.za

Literatur
HUTCHINGS, A., SCOTT, A.H., LEWIS, G. & CUNNINGHAM, A 1996. *Zulu Medicinal Plants - An Inventory.* University of Natal Press, Pietermaritzburg, Südafrika
OJEWOLE, J.A.O.2000. Anticonvulsant evaluation of the methanolic extract of Securidaca longipedunculata (Fresen.) (fam. Polyygalaaceae) root-bark in mice. 3. *Pharm. Pharmacol.*, 52 (Suppl.) : 286
PUJOL, J. 1990. *Naturafrica –The Herbalist Handbook* Jean Pujol Natural Heaker´s Foundation, Durban, Südafrika
VAN WYK, B. E., VAN OUDSHOORN, B. & GERICKE, N. 1997. *Medicinal Plants of South Africa.* Briza Publications, Pretoria, South Africa
WATT, J. M. & BREYER-BRANDWIJK, M. G. 1962. *The medicinal and poisonous plants of Southern and Eastern Africa.* 2. Ausgabe, E.&S.Livingstone, Edinburgh and London

SOUTH AFRICAN MEDICINAL PLANTS USED IN ZULU FOLK MEDICINE

by John A. O. Ojewole

Introduction

The devastating cortical disorder named epilepsy afflicts people of both sexes and of all age groups. Current estimates suggest that about 6% of the world's population suffer from this central nervous system (CNS) disorder. The term '*epilepsy*', sometimes referred to as '*convulsion*', derives from the belief that in the olden days, people whose bodies were possessed by 'evil spirits' always suffered from the disease.

The use of indigenous anticonvulsant remedies in the control of epilepsy is as old as when epilepsy itself was first recognized. Although the herbal doctor may not comprehend the detailed chemical, biochemical, pharmacological and nutritive values of his/her medications, years of committed observation, long-term practice and experience with herbal drugs usually prove valuable in the healer's ability to manage epilepsy successfully and effectively.

Among the *Zulu* people living in rural communities of South Africa, management and/or control of epilepsy is/are often achieved through the use of herbal preparations. Some of the anticonvulsant remedies are formulated in soap form, and patients suffering from the malady are made to wash and/or bath with the soap. In some communities, epilepsy is considered to be an affliction caused by supernatural powers, such as witches, wizards and/or ancestral spirits. In such cases, the convulsive disorders are usually not controlled with herbal remedies alone, but also with exorcisms, and/or incarnations. Curing rites or sacrifices are made to invoke the goodwill of the ancestors, and appeal to the witches and wizards for forgiveness of sins. The sacrifices are usually directed to the body and mind of the convulsing patient. The body of the patient is usually massaged with

Fig.1: A *Zulu* "*izangoma*", more often referred to as "*sangoma*", preparing an anticonvulsant remedy from the stem-bark of a medicinal plant

the anticonvulsant remedies. More often, concoctions, infusions, decoctions, tinctures or powders of the anticonvulsant preparations are administered orally. Baths in the herbal concoctions are sometimes prescribed.

In South Africa, plants have been used traditionally for medicinal purposes for many centuries. With over 30 000 species of higher plants, medicinal plants constitute the floristic wealth and an important socio-cultural heritage of South Africa. The rich cultural and bio-diversity of South Africa have made it possible to use approximately 3 000 plant species as medicines, out of which about 350 species are the most commonly-used and traded medicinal plants (VAN WYK et al. 1997). Some of the plants have also been used for magical, ritual, spiritual and symbolic purposes in addition to their medicinal and nutritive values. The remarkable cultural diversity of South Africa is reflected in the formal and informal systems of medicine that are currently being practised in different parts of the country. The informal, oral-tradition medical systems of many tribes in the country have not yet been systematised, and are only passed on by word of mouth from one generation to the other. These medical systems and their herbal, animal and mineral "materia medica" have ancient origins which may date back to palaeolithic times (VAN WYK et al. 1997).

First and foremost, an African traditional healer always seeks to know why a patient is ill. Thereafter, s/he administers treatment/s that will address the perceived cause/s of the illness, in addition to other specific therapies that s/he may administer to alleviate the signs and symptoms of the disease.

There are an estimated 200 000 indigenous traditional healers in South Africa, and about 80% of South Africans still consult these healers, usually in addition to using modern, Western medical services (VAN WYK et al. 1997). Traditional healers in South Africa are most commonly known and referred to as "*izinyanga*" and "*izangoma*" (*Zulu*), "*ixwele*" and "*amaquira*" (Xhosa), "*nqaka*" (Sotho), "*bossiedokter*" and "*kruiedokter*" (Western and Northern Cape). The *Zulu* terms "*inyanga*" and "*isangoma*" used to refer exclusively to "herbalist" and "diviner" respectively, however in modern times the distinction has become blurred, with some healers practicing both arts (VAN WYK et al. 1997). Figure 1 shows a *Zulu* "*izangoma*", more often referred to as "*sangoma*", preparing an anticonvulsant remedy from the stem-bark of a medicinal plant.

In addition to the herbalists and diviners who are believed to be spiritually endowed and empowered, there are also traditional birth attendants, prophets, spiritual healers, intuitives and dreamers in South Africa. Most elderly folks in rural areas of the country have knowledge of herbal lore, and function as first-aid healers with a family repertoire of herbal remedies or "*kruierate*" (van Wyk, et al., 1997). Medicinal plants constitute the link-pin of the various traditional healers. These practitioners usually employ galenicals (in the forms of infusions, decoctions, concoctions, tinctures, powders, soaps, etc), made from various morphological parts of plants, especially twigs, leaves, stem- and/or root- barks, wood, fruits, seeds, gums, nectar and so forth, to treat their epileptic patients.

Materials and Methods

Plant Material
A literature search (WATT & BREYER-BRANDWIJK 1962; PUJOL 1990; HUTCHINGS et al 1996; and VAN WYK et al 1997) on the medicinal plants examined in this study was

undertaken to determine their chemical constituents and accredited medicinal uses. Collection of the various indigenous antiepileptic plants and recipes, visits to traditional healers in *KwaZulu-Natal*, and pharmacological screening of the plant extracts for antiepileptic activities started in August 1998, and ended in July, 2001. The various plant materials tested were identified by the Taxonomist/Curator of the University of Durban-Westville's Department of Botany, Durban, South Africa; and/or by the staff of the Natal Provincial Herbarium in Durban, South Africa (where voucher specimens of the plants have been deposited). One kilogramme (1 kg) each of the most commonly-employed morphological parts of the medicinal plants (as used traditionally in *Zulu* folk medicine for the treatment of epilepsy/convulsion), were separately washed with clean tap water, dried, cut into smaller pieces and homogenized in a Waring blender.

Each homogenate was Soxhlet extracted twice, on each occasion with 2.5 litres of distilled water at a temperature of $30\pm1°C$ for 24 hours with shaking. The combined extracts were filtered and concentrated to dryness under reduced pressure at $30\pm1°C$. The resulting plant extract in each case was freeze-dried, finally yielding powdery or semi-powdery, crude aqueous extract residues. Aliquot portions of the aqueous extract residue from each of the plants examined were weighed out and dissolved in distilled water for anticonvulsant evaluation on each day of our experiment.

Animal Material

For each of the plant extracts examined, mice of both sexes (Mus domesticus) weighing 25 – 30 g were used. The mice were randomly divided into three groups of "Test A", "Test B" and "Control C" mice. Eight (8) mice were used for each "test" compound, and an equal number of mice were also used as "controls" in each case. Convulsive seizures were chemically-induced in the test animals as described in detail earlier by OJEWOLE (2000). Pentylenetetrazol [i. e., metrazol" (PTZ – 90 mg/kg i. p.)] and picrotoxin (PIC, 10 mg/kg i. p.) were used to induce chemoshock seizures in the mice. Each of the control animals in "Control C" group was treated with distilled water (2 ml/kg i. p.) only. Phenobarbitone (10 mg/kg i. p.) and diazepam (0.5 mg/kg i. p.) were used as standard, reference anticonvulsant drugs for comparison with the plant extracts.

Tab. 1: Some South African Medicinal Plants Used as Anticonvulsant Remedies in Zulu Folk Medicine

Serial Number	Family, Species [and Zulu name]	Parts Used	Chemical Constituents	Medicinal Uses
1.	**Anacardiaceae** *Lannea discolor* (Sond) Engl. [isiganganyane]	Leaves/ Stem-bark/ Roots	Flavonoids, polyphenolics and tannins.	Convulsions and 'fits' diarrhoea, abscesses and boils, infertility, menorrhagia, sore eyes gonorrhea, swollen legs and whooping cough.
2.	**Apocynaceae** *Rauvolfia caffra* Sond. [umhlambamazi]	Stem-bark/ Root-bark/ Leaves	Indole and indoline alkaloids, rauvolfine, reserpine, yohimbine, ajmalicine and phytosterols.	Hypertension, malaria, fevers, colic pains, rheumatism, pneumonia, mental problems, insomnia and hysteria, rashes, convulsions, asthma, cough and other chest complaints
3.	**Asteraceae** *Blumea alata* (D. Don) DC. [ugodide]	Roots/ Leaves	α-Humulene, caryophyllene and squalene, minute amounts of euathemone derivatives.	Fevers, convulsions, constipation, colic and abdominal pains, pneumonia, heart pains, headaches and leg pains, and *Trichomonas vaginalis* infection
4.	**Asteraceae** *Conyza scabrida* DC. [uhlabo]	Leaves/ Roots	Diterpenoids, hautriwaic acid, and clerodane derivatives.	Convulsions, colds and coughs, pleuritic pains, headaches, fevers, chest and heart complaints.
5.	**Asteraceae** *Vernonia neocorymbosa* Hilliard [uhlungu-lungu]	Leaves/ Twigs/ Roots	Squalene, vernolide and vernodalin, sesquiterpenoid lactones, flavonoids, pyridine, and diterpenoid alkaloids.	Epilepsy, abortion, stomachache, hysteria, irregular menstruation, dysentery and intestinal worm infestations
6.	**Bignoniaceae** *Kigelia africana* (Lam.) Benth. [umfongothi]	Fruits/ Stem-bark	Flavonoids, dihydroisocoumarin kigelin, naphthoquinone derivate lapachol, iridoid glycosides, cinnamic acid derivatives, stigmasterols and β-sitosterol.	Syphilis, stomach ailments, dysentery, constipation, snakebite, wounds, boils and sores, gynaecological disorders, rheumatism, acne, pneumonia, convulsions, aphrodisia, haemorrhoids and lumbago.
7.	**Bignoniaceae** *Tecomaria capensis* (Thunb.) Spach [lungana]	Stem-bark/ Leaves	Sterols and sterolins, tannins and terpenoids.	Fevers, pains, insomnia, chest complaints, diarrhoea, dysentery, bacterial infections, stomach pains, influenza, pneumonia and convulsions

#	Family / Species	Parts used	Chemical constituents	Uses
8.	**Capparaceae** *Boscia albitrunca* (Burch.) Gilg & Ben [umvithi]	Roots/ Leaves/ Fruits	Phytosterols and sterolins	Haemorrhoids, inflamed eyes, epilepsy.
9.	**Capparaceae** *Capparis tomentosa* Lam. [umabusane]	Roots/ Leaves	Oxindole compounds, alkaloid stachyurine, and sulphur oil.	Rheumatism, insanity, snakebite, jaundice, chest pains, malaria, headaches, pneumonia, coughs, asthma, constipation, eye problems and convulsions.
10.	**Celastraceae** *Maytenus senegalensis* (Lam.) Excell [isihlangu]	Roots/ Leaves	Polyphenolics, tannins and terpenoids	Haemoptysis, respiratory ailments, epilepsy, body pains, constipation, diarrhoea, night blindness, infertility, menorrhagia, mouth ulcers and wounds, sore throats, dysentery, microbial infections and schistosomiasis.
11.	**Commelinaceae** *Commelina africana* Linn. [idangabane]	Roots	Flavonoids, glycosides and anthocyanin derivatives.	Insomnia, infertility, epileptic 'fits', heart complaints, nervous ailments, venereal diseases, body pains, menstrual and bladder ailments
12.	**Crassulaceae** *Cotyledon orbiculata* Linn. [intelezi]	Leaves/ Leaf juice	Tyledoside and outradenolide-type cardiac glycosides such as orbicuside A, B, and C.	Corns and warts, toothache and earache, boils, inflammation, rheumatism, epilepsy, and syphilis.
13.	**Crassulaceae** *Crassula alba* Forssk. [isidwe]	Leaves/ Twigs	Polyphenolics and tannins.	Epilepsy, dysentery and diarrhoea, bloody stools, influenza, fevers, heartburn and hysteria
14.	**Cucurbitaceae** *Cucumis hirsutus* Sond. [intangazane]	Roots/ Fruits	Cucurmin, steroids and saponins	Coughs, constipation, abdominal pains, convulsions, abortion, penal and vulval sores.
15.	**Ebenaceae** *Euclea divinorum* Hiern [umhlangula]	Fruits/ Roots/ Stem-bark/	Naphthoquinones, diospyrin, lupeol and betulin, triterpenoids, saponins, tannins and steroids	Convulsions, toothaches, constipation, schistosomiasis, chest pains, pneumonia, gastric disorders, infertility, swellings and inflammatory conditions, headaches and depressed fontanelles

#	Family / Species	Part used	Constituents	Uses
16.	**Euphorbiaceae** *Croton gratissimus* Burch. [umahlabekufeni]	Stem-bark/ Roots/ Leaves	Alkaloids, flavonoids, saponins, cardenolides, monoterpenoids and diterpenoids, aromatic oils, crotonin, crotin and nucleterne	Fevers, bleeding gums, rheumatism, chest complaints, constipation and indigestion, oedema (dropsy), coughs, inflammation, insomnia, aphrodisia and epilepsy.
17.	**Euphorbiaceae** *Jatropha curcas* Linn. [inhlakuva]	Roots/ Seeds/ Leaves	Oil containing tiglian-type irritant diterpenoids, curcanoleic acid, toxic protein named curcin, cyanic acid, flavonoids, steroids, triterpenes and oleic acid.	Constipation, boils and wounds, dropsy, sciatica, paralysis, skin diseases, sores, venereal diseases, angina, herpes, malaria, jaundice, fevers, diarrhoea, ringworm, rheumatism, convulsions and 'fits'
18.	**Fabaceae** *Abrus precatorius* Linn. [umkhokha]	Roots/ Leaves	Flavone, choline, trigonelline, precatorine, glycyrrhizin, abrin, abrusogenin, abrusosides, indole derivatives and abrine, saponins, anthocyaninsns and the steroids abricin and abridin.	Love and good luck charms, pleuritic chest complaints, eye ailments, contraception, convulsions, schistosomiasis, tuberculosis, warts and skin diseases, snakebite, intestinal worm infestations, aphrodisia, orchitis, asthma and whooping cough, colds, fevers, and malaria
19.	**Fabaceae** *Acacia karroo* Hayne [umunga]	Stem-bark/ Leaves/ Gum	Polyphenols and tannins, uronic acid, galactan derivatives, and sulphated glycosides.	Diarrhoea and dysentry, conjunctivitis, haemorrhage, colds, oral thrush, stomach ache, osteomyelitis, dizziness, convulsions, venereal diseases and aphrodisia
20.	**Fabaceae** *Mimosa pudica* Linn [imbune]	Whole plant	Mimosine and norepinephrine.	Convulsions/epilepsy, dysmenorrhoea, heart palpitations, insomnia and nervousness.
21.	**Lamiaceae** *Leonotis leonurus* (Linn.) R. Br. [umunyane]	Leaves/ Stems/ Roots	Volatile oil, diterpenoids, labadane-type lactones, premarrubiin and marrubiin.	Epilepsy, snakebite and insect stings, boils, eczema, skin diseases, itching, muscular cramps, influenza, coughs, colds, bronchitis and asthma, hypertension, partial paralysis, headaches and viral hepatitis.
22.	**Loganiaceae** *Nuxia floribunda* Benth. [ugobese]	Leaves/ Stem-bark	Polyphenolics and tannins.	Fevers, coughs, indigestion, influenza, and infantile convulsions

#	Family / Species	Parts used	Chemical constituents	Uses
23.	**Meliaceae** *Melia azedarach* Linn [umsilinga]	Leaves/ Root bark/ Heartwood	Oxidised triterpenoids known as limonoids, triterpenoid saponins, steroids, aromatic compounds, vanillic acid, azedarinic acid, melianoninol, coumarins, lignans and flavonoids.	Abdominal pains, helminthiasis, epilepsy, fits/convulsions, schistosomiasis, swollen legs, asthma, constipation, spasms and nervous pains, eczema, malaria, diuresis, rheumatism, gout and skin diseases.
24.	**Phytolaccaceae** *Phytolacca dodecandra* L'Herit. [umdlebeleni]	Roots/ Leaves/ Berries	Steroidal triterpenoid saponins, endod saponoside, lematoxin and oleanonic acid derivatives.	Urinary complaints, snakebite, epilepsy, uterine tumors and fibroids, rheumatism, inflammatory conditions, fish poison, boils and wounds, spermicidal contraception, syphilis and other parasitic infections.
25.	**Polygonaceae** *Oxygonum atropurpureum* Meisn. [umambane]	Roots/ Leaves	Triterpenoid saponins, oleasterol and flavonoids.	Abdominal pains, inflammatory conditions, schistosomiasis, convulsions, whooping cough, aphrodisia, diarrhoea and snakebite.
26.	**Rosaceae** *Rubus pinnatus* Willd. [amakonubi]	Roots/ Leaves	Polyphenolics and tannins, terpenoids.	Coughs and other respiratory complaints, toothaches, convulsions, chronic diarrhoea, abdominal cramps and rheumatism.
27.	**Rubiaceae** *Catunaregam spinosa* (Thunb.) Tirvengadum [isibibha]	Roots/ Leaves/ Fruits	Alkaloids, iridoids, ursolic acid-based saponins, oleanolic acid derivatives, triterpenoid saponins	Epilepsy and dizziness, fevers, aphrodisia, headaches, snakebite, nausea, respiratory and gynaecological ailments, rheumatism, emesis, diuresis, schistosomiasis, gonorrhoea and other bacterial infections.
28.	**Rubiaceae** *Gardenia ternifolia* Schumach. & Thonn [umkwakwane omkhulu]	Roots/ Leaves/ Twigs/ Fruits	Triterpenoids and tannins.	Malaria protective charm against lightning and sorcery, sore eyes, headaches, madness, coughs, asthma, dysmenorrhoea, infertility chorea, epilepsy and convulsions, earache, schistosomiasis, rheumatism, abdominal pains and fish poison.
29.	**Rutaceae** *Clausena anisata* (Willd.) Hook. f. ex Benth. [isirudu]	Roots/ Leaves/ Fruits	Sesquiterpenoids, fatty acids, umbelliferone, scopoletin, limonene, alkaloids clausanitine and mupamine, coumarins heliettin and chalepin, limonoids and phenylpropanoids.	Convulsions, taeniasis and other parasitic infections, constipation, rheumatism, malaria and fevers, heart ailments, bad breath, abdominal pains and toothaches, mental diseases, headaches, eye complaints, impotence and sterility, battle charms.

30.	**Sapotaceae** *Englerophytum magalismontanum* Krause [umnqumabele]	Roots/ Fruits	Ascorbutic acid, tannin, steroids triterpenoids, oleanonic acid derivatives.	Epilepsy, headaches, abdominal pains, rheumatism and inflammatory conditions.
31.	**Solanaceae** *Datura stramonium* Linn. [iloyi]	Leaves/ Fruits/ Aerial Parts	Tropane alkaloids, atropine, hyoscine, and other atropine-like drugs, sesquiterpenoids	Asthma, bronchitis, coughs and many other respiratory conditions, rheumatism, gout, boils, abscesses and wounds, aphrodisia, motion sickness, sore throat and tonsilitis, visceral pains, epilepsy and Parkinsonism
32.	**Solanaceae** *Withania somnifera* (Linn.) Dun [ubuvimbha]	Roots/ Leaves/ Aerial parts	Triterpenoid saponins, tropanol, sitonosides, alkaloids, choline, steroidal lactones, withaferine A, withasomnine, withanolides, and flavonoids.	Fevers, sores, abscesses, wounds, syphilis, skin diseases, diarrhoea, proctitis, asthma, nausea, rheumatism, inflammation and pain, aphrodisia, scabies and carbuncles, aphrodisia, sedation, conjunctivitis, epilepsy/convulsions.
33.	**Verbenaceae** *Clerodendrum glabrum* E. Mey. [umnukambiba]	Leaves/ Roots	Steroidal saponins, flavonoids, and terpenoids	Fevers, intestinal parasites, childhood convulsions, colds, sore throats and chest complaints, fractured bones, toothaches, skin rashes, sedation and body pains
34.	**Verbenaceae** *Lippia javanica* (Burm. F.) Spreng. [umsuzwane]	Leaves/ Twigs	Volatile oil, monoterpenoids, various organic acids and alcohols, iridoid glycosides and pentacyclic triterpenoids.	Coughs, colds, bronchitis, asthma and other chest ailments, malaria, fevers, stomach problems and headaches, convulsions, cataracts, diarrhoea, scabies and body lice.
35.	**V** *I tridentata* (Linn. Willd & Drun. [isinwazi]	Roots/ Tubers/ Leaves	Proanthocyanins and flavanoids.	Epilepsy, dysmenorrhoea, safe delivery in pregnancy, renal complaints, menorrhagia infertility, stomach ailments, swellings, colds, wounds, boils and sores.

Results

Our ethnobotanical literature survey revealed that a large number of medicinal plants from various genera and diverse families (especially, Asteraceae, Bignoniaceae, Fabaceae, Verbenaceae, Rubiaceae, Rutaceae, Commelinaceae, Meliaceae, Lamiaceae, Solanaceae, Apocynaceae, Euphorbiaceae, Myrtaceae, Polygonaceae, Rosaceae, Crassulaceae, Sapotaceae, Capparaceae, Vitaceae, and so forth) are used in *Zulu* folk medicine for the control or management of epilepsy/convulsions. Thirty-five (35) of the medicinal plants frequently used as antiepileptic remedies in *Zulu* folk medicine were collated, reviewed, collected, and authenticated. Aqueous extracts of their most frequently-used morphological parts were pharmacologically screened for anticonvulsant activities in experimental, mammalian animal model. The local (*Zulu*) names of the plants, their morphological parts commonly used by *Zulu* traditional healers as antiepileptic and/or anticonvulsant remedies, their chemical constituents and accredited medicinal uses, as well as their relative anticonvulsant properties in chemically-induced seizures, are summarized in Table 1.

Pharmacological evaluation of the various plant extracts (and the reference antiepileptic drugs used in this study) showed that moderate to high doses of the plant extracts ($\geq$800 mg/kg i. p.) produced moderate to strong anticonvulsant activities in the mammalian experimental animal model used. On their own accord, phenobarbitone (10 mg/kg i. p.) and diazepam (0.5 mg/kg i. p.) produced very strong and pronounced anticonvulsant effects in the mice, offering 100% protections against metrazol- and picrotoxin-induced seizures respectively (figures not shown). The percentage anticonvulsant actions of the various plant extracts were calculated relative to those produced by phenobarbitone and diazepam.

The magnitude of the anticonvulsant effects of the plant extracts varied widely. Except in 2 cases, the plant extracts were generally more effective in protecting the animals against metrazol-induced seizures than in protecting the mice against picrotoxin-induced seizures. Of the 35 different plant extracts examined, 17 (i. e., 48.57%) produced moderate to strong anticonvulsant effects in metrazol-induced, chemoshock seizures (producing 62.50% – 87.50% protections against metrazol-induced seizures in the mice). The remaining 18 of the 35 (i. e., 51.43%) plant extracts showed weak to mild anticonvulsant activities (producing 12.50% – 50.00% protections against metrazol-induced seizures in the animals). Maximal anticonvulsant effects of the plant extracts were elicited at doses $\geq$ 800 mg/kg i. p., 15 – 30 minutes post administration.

Discussion and conclusion

The results of this experimental animal study indicate that the group of *Zulu* medicinal plants evaluated for anticonvulsant properties possess weak to strong anticonvulsant effects in the laboratory mammalian animal model used, despite the fact that the plants belong to diverse families, and contain different chemical constituents. The most frequently cited families of plants with anticonvulsant properties are Asteraceae, Bignoniaceae, Fabaceae, Verbenaceae, Rubiaceae, Rutaceae, Commelinaceae, Meliaceae, Lamiaceae, Solanaceae, Apocynaceae, Euphorbiaceae, Myrtaceae, Polygonaceae, Rosaceae, Crassulaceae, Sapotaceae, Capparaceae, Vitaceae, and so forth (HUTCHINGS et al. 1996). These are very large and widely distributed plant families. The phylogenetic distance between this select group of plant families may be a strong indication of the varied nature of their active chemical constituents.

Our ethnobotanical literature survey has revealed that 28 of these 35 (i. e., 80%) medicinal plants used in the control or management of epilepsy/convulsions in *Zulu* folk medicine have been used in traditional medicine in other parts of the world to manage epileptic seizures. The literature survey has also shown that although relatively very little scientific investigations have been undertaken to rationalise the use of the medicinal plants examined in this study as anticonvulsant remedies in South Africa, 21 (i. e., 60%) of these *Zulu* indigenous anticonvulsant remedies have had some experimental testing for anticonvulsant activity elsewhere in the world.

Indigenous anticonvulsant remedies will be more therapeutically useful if their right doses are known and used. The routes of administration of indigenous remedies are also crucially important. All indigenous anticonvulsant remedies prepared as concoctions, decoctions, etc, are usually taken orally, while some are used in bathing, but NEVER administered parenterally via the needle.

It is essential to involve traditional healers, phytochemists and organic chemists, pharmacologists, and medical practitioners working together to achieve the greatest benefit from new drugs developed from traditional remedies. With the increasing incidence of epilepsy in both urban and rural populations of the world, the inability of current modern therapies to control all the metabolic defects of the disease and their pathological consequences, coupled with the serious adverse effects and the enormous cost of modern, conventional pharmacotherapeutic agents; there is a dire need to develop new, effective, inexpensive, non-toxic, indigenous alternate strategies for epileptic therapy. Nevertheless, the results of this experimental animal study have shown that the medicinal plant extracts examined possess weak to strong anticonvulsant properties, and thus lend credence to the folkloric use of the plants as antiepileptic remedies in *Zulu* traditional medicine.

Abstract

Current estimates suggest that approximately 6% of the world's population suffer from epilepsy. Life expectancy may be drastically reduced by this crippling disorder, especially in developing countries of the world where its prevalence is increasing steadily, and adequate treatment is often expensive or unavailable. In many developing countries of the world, millions of people still rely on traditional healers and medicinal plants for their daily primary health-care needs, and plant products are now gaining popularity as alternative and complementary therapies even in industrialized, Western countries.

The overall aim of this study is to provide a starting point for African programmes leading to the development of indigenous plants as inexpensive sources of effective, standardized crude antiepileptic drugs, and for the discovery of lead compounds for new, safe and cheap anticonvulsant drug development. This study was undertaken to examine the anticonvulsant effects of some South African indigenous plants used as antiepileptic remedies in *Zulu* folk medicine.

Nevertheless, the results of this experimental animal study have shown that the medicinal plant extracts examined possess weak to strong anticonvulsant properties, and thus lend credence to the folkloric use of the plants as antiepileptic remedies in *Zulu* traditional medicine.

Keywords
Traditional Medicine; South African Medicinal Plants; Epilepsy; Indigenous Anticonvulsant Remedies; *Zulu* Folk Medicine.

Acknowledgements
I am indebted to the staff of Natal Provincial Herbarium in Durban, South Africa, and to the staff of the Department of Botany, Faculty of Science, University of Durban-Westville, Durban, South Africa, for the identification of the plant materials used in this study. The assistance of Ms Thembisa Jikwa in the collection of some of the plants and recipes examined in this study is gratefully acknowledged. I am grateful to Mrs. Patience Koloko (Director, KwaZulu-Natal Traditional Healers' Affairs) for her assistance and interest in this study; Dr. Esther K. Mutenda for her assistance in the extraction process; Professor Clement O. Adewunmi for granting me an unlimited access to the facilities in his laboratory, and also for his constructive criticisms; and to the Council of the University of Durban-Westville, Durban 4000, South Africa, for the provision of a Research Grant (R642) to carry out a part of this study.

Author
Professor and Head of Department, [BPharm. (Hons.); M Sc (Clin. Pharm.); PhD (Pharmacology). Scientist of the Dept. of Pharmacology, Fac. of Health Sciences, Univ. of Durban-Westville, Current Research Areas: Traditional Medicine / Ethnomedicine, Ethnopharmacology, Natural Products Pharmacology.
Contact: E-Mail: ojewole@pixie.udw.ac.za,
Tel: +27-31-204-4356, Fax: +27-31-204-4907

References
HUTCHINGS, A., SCOTT, A. H., LEWIS, G. & CUNNINGHAM, A 1996. *Zulu Medicinal Plants – An Inventory.* University of Natal Press, Pietermaritzburg, South Africa.
OJEWOLE, J. A. O. 2000. *Anticonvulsant evaluation of the methanolic extract of Securidaca longipedunculata (Fresen.) [family: Polygalaceae] root-bark in mice.* J. Pharm. Pharmacol., 52 (Suppl.) : 286.
PUJOL, J. 1990. *Naturafrica – The Herbalist Handbook.* Jean Pujol Natural Healers' Foundation, Durban, South Africa.
VAN WYK, B. E., VAN OUDSHOORN, B. & GERICKE, N. 1997. *Medicinal Plants of South Africa.* Briza Publications, Pretoria, South Africa.
WATT, J. M. & BREYER-BRANDWIJK, M. G. 1962. *The medicinal and poisonous plants of Southern and Eastern Africa*, 2nd edition, E. & S. Livingstone, Edinburgh and London.

VOLKSMEDIZIN BEI ORIENTALISCHEN JUDEN IN ISRAEL*

von Ofra Greenberg

Einleitung

Dieser Bericht konzentriert sich auf den Umgang mit der volkstümlichen Medizin in der modernen westlich orientierten Gesellschaft. Hierbei werden die Faktoren untersucht, die die Entscheidung einer Person bei der Auswahl einer Behandlungsmethode unter verschiedenen alternativen Behandlungsmethoden (hauptsächlich moderne westliche Schulmedizin oder traditionelle Heilmethoden - volkstümliche Medizin) beeinflussen.

Genauer gesagt, versucht diese Untersuchung herauszufinden, unter welchen Umständen volkstümliche Medizin neben herkömmlicher westl. Schulmedizin genutzt, bzw. ihr vorgezogen wird. In der heutigen pluralistischen Gesellschaft existieren verschiedene Behandlungsmethoden nebeneinander, jede nach ihren eigenen Regeln und Gesetzen.

Auf der einen Seite haben wir die etablierte westliche Schulmedizin und auf der anderen Seite eine wachsende Zahl vielfältiger Methoden, zusammengefasst als alternative Medizin. Diese Kategorie beinhaltet auch die Behandlungsmethoden, die man generell als "volkstümliche Medizin" bezeichnet, Behandlungen, die traditionell seit Generationen genutzt werden. Diese alternativen Heilmethoden werden in großem Ausmaß von einem großen Bevölkerungsanteil genutzt.

Das israelische Gesundheitswesen sieht diese volkstümliche Medizin als Überbleibsel der verschiedenen Kulturen, die hauptsächlich aus islamischen Ländern eingebracht wurden.

Unsere Forschungen haben ergeben, dass diese Art von Medizin ein integrierter Teil des lebendigen, sozialen und kulturellen Lebens in Israel ist, ganz besonders in den Einwanderungsgebieten. Das Hauptaugenmerk richteten wir auf den

---

* Übersetzung aus dem Englischen: Christine Granados Hughes

Entscheidungsprozess, in dessen Verlauf jemand eine bestimmte Methode der anderen vorzieht und den Faktoren, die diesen Prozess bestimmen oder beeinflussen.
Diese Studie wurde in einem israelischen Siedlungsgebiet mit 15.000 vorwiegend aus islamischen Ländern stammenden Einwohnern durchgeführt. Das Bildungsniveau ist im Verhältnis zur gesamten israelischen Bevölkerung sehr niedrig und das Einkommen relativ gering.
Die gesammelten Informationen beruhen auf anthropologischen Forschungsmethoden, besonders auf Beobachtungen der Teilnehmer, belegt durch unzählige spontane Interviews.

Die Untersuchungen erfolgten in einem Zeitraum von zwei Jahren (1981-82). In dieser Zeit lebten die Forscher in dem Wohngebiet dieser Bevölkerungsgruppe. Es wurden über 50 Patienten begleitet, die parallel Schulmedizin und Naturheilmedizin in Anspruch nahmen.
Zum besseren Verständnis dieser Fallstudien geben wir noch einige Informationen zum Gesundheitssystem in Israel und eine kurze Ausführung des Konzeptes des "bösen Blicks".
Im Prinzip wird nur westliche Medizin von den israelischen Gesundheitsbehörden und der Regierung anerkannt, während alternative Heilmethoden in privaten Händen liegen.

Das nationale Gesundheitssystem deckt fast alle schulmedizinischen Behandlungen ab und wird von einer Reihe von Krankenkassen getragen. Das Angebot umfasst aber auch Privatpraxen mit schulmedizinischen und/oder alternativen Heilmethoden. In den letzten Jahren haben die Krankenkassen begonnen, die Kosten für bestimmte alternative Heilmethoden zu übernehmen.

Der Glaube an den "bösen Blick" ist unter den Juden orientalischer Abstammung weit verbreitet. Er kann von wütenden oder eifersüchtigen Personen angerufen werden, um einer Person Schaden zuzufügen. Der "böse Blick" kann auf verschiedenen Ebenen schaden, körperlich als Krankheit oder Lähmung, wirtschaftlich mit dem Verlust des Eigentums, psychologisch, z. B. mit Depression und sozial, als vergebliche Partnersuche, um einige Beispiele zu nennen.
BILU (1978) untersucht in seiner umfassenden Erörterung die Merkmale des "bösen Blickes" unter den orientalischen Juden. Darüber hinaus glaubt diese Bevölkerungsgruppe an die Kraft und Existenz von bösen Geistern, die ähnliche physische und mentale Krankheiten als Bestrafung zur Folge haben.

Theoretische Einführung
Die Literatur über alternative Heilmethoden in der westlichen Gesellschaft beschäftigt sich selten mit volkstümlicher Medizin. Andererseits wurde viel über die verschiedenen Aspekte der gleichzeitigen Anwendung der volkstümlichen und westlichen Medizin in verschiedenen Entwicklungsländern geschrieben (GONZALES 1966, PRESS 1969, LIEBAN 1976, ALLAND 1977, FINKLER 1981, BISHAW, KAHANNA 1997) und über die Probleme, die sich bei der Annahme der Schulmedizin bei der Bevölkerung dieser Länder ergaben (WOODS 1977, CAMAZINE 1980, KUNITZ 1981).
Sowohl die öffentlichen Behörden als auch die Forscher kamen übereinstimmend zu dem Ergebnis, dass eine traditionell orientierte Bevölkerungsgruppe, die man

in eine moderne Gesellschaft bringt, sich rasch in die vorherrschenden Verhaltensmuster der neuen Umgebung integriert.
Wir dagegen sind durch unsere Studien zu dem Schluss gekommen, dass diese Integration eher langsam geschieht und oft mit großer Not verbunden ist.

Bei der Wahl einer bevorzugten Heilmethode stellen sich drei in Beziehung stehende Faktoren dar: *Alter* und *Bildung* der Patienten, die *Kenntnis* über das Angebot und dessen Verfügbarkeit sowie der *religiöse Hintergrund* haben, ausgehend von der Annahme, dass sich Ratsuchende mit Gesundheitsproblemen an Menschen gleichen Glaubens wenden und deren Empfehlungen eher befolgen.

Hat sich der Patient einmal für den Weg der volkstümlichen Medizin entschieden, muss er sich selbst eine bestimmte Heilmethode und den entsprechenden Heiler suchen.
Die folgenden zwei Fälle weisen einige der beschriebenen Faktoren bezüglich der Wahl der Behandlung und der gleichzeitigen Anwendung von volkstümlicher und Schulmedizin auf.

Hannah Azualai
Hannah Azualai ist 37 Jahre alt und gebürtige Irakerin. 1950 wanderte sie mit ihrer Familie nach Israel ein. Sie heiratete mit 17 und bekam 6 Kinder. Ihre Eltern und Brüder zogen vor einer Zeit in eine entfernte landwirtschaftliche Siedlung.
Ihr Ehemann, marokkanischer Herkunft, wuchs in der gleichen Stadt auf, ein Teil seiner Familie lebt noch dort. Er hat einen sicheren Arbeitsplatz als leitender Angestellter in einer großen Firma.
Zwei Jahre nahm ich mit meinen Beobachtungen an Hannah's Krankheitsgeschichte teil und erlebte so die Entwicklung sehr direkt. Die ersten Symptome erschienen vor fünf Jahren in Form von Schwellungen und Schmerzen in einem Bein. Sie suchte einen praktischen Arzt auf, der nach Blutuntersuchungen Rheumatismus diagnostizierte und ein Rezept für ein schmerzstillendes Mittel ausstellte.
Damit unzufrieden, konsultierte sie einen Chirurgen, der die gleiche Diagnose stellte. Sehr starke Schmerzen und lange Wartezeiten für eine orthopädische Untersuchung ließen Hannah einen bekannten Arzt in der Nachbarstadt aufsuchen.
Durch eine Röntgenuntersuchung stellte dieser Wucherungen im rechten Bein fest. Er empfahl eine Operation und überwies sie mit den ausgehändigten Röntgenbildern in ein regionales Krankenhaus. Hannah verbrachte dort 15 Tage auf der orthopädischen Station, während der Chefarzt, ein Psychologe und Psychiater, sie untersuchte. Ohne Befund wurde sie entlassen und blieb trotz Schmerzen ohne Behandlung.

Zwei Jahre nach den ersten Symptomen verschlechterte sich ihr Zustand. Sie unterzog sich einer orthopädischen Untersuchung und wurde mit einem Operationstermin einige Monate später in ein größeres Krankenhaus im Landesinneren eingewiesen. Zu dieser Zeit entschieden sich Hannah's verzweifelte Brüder zu einem Besuch bei einem jemenitischen Rabbi, der auch im Landesinneren lebte. (In der letzten Zeit tauchte dieser öfter in den Medien auf, durch Heilungen zahlreicher blinder Mädchen.)

Hannah's Brüder waren bereit, die Kosten für diesen Besuch zu übernehmen. Als sie dort ankamen erfuhren sie, dass eine Voranmeldung nötig gewesen wäre und erhielten von den Wächtern ausserhalb des Hauses einen Termin drei Monate später, für den eine Vorauszahlung fällig wäre. Der Termin des Krankenhausaufenthaltes fiel zufällig mit dem Besuchstermin bei dem Rabbiner auf den gleichen Tag.

Einer der Brüder fand einen Ausweg aus diesem Dilemma: Am frühen Morgen würden sie den Rabbi besuchen und danach entscheiden, ob sie mit der konventionellen Behandlung fortfahren würden. Dieser Plan wurde in die Tat umgesetzt. Nachdem der Rabbi Hannah einige Fragen über ihre Eltern gestellt hatte, diagnostizierte er als Krankheitsursache den "bösen Blick", der, beginnend in ihren Beinen, sich langsam in ihrem Körper ausbreitete.
Er gab ihr einen mit religiösen Versen beschriebenen schwarzen Stein und die Anweisung, ihn um den Hals zu tragen und nur während der Menstruation abzunehmen. Dazu sollte sie neunzig Tage lang ihren ganzen Körper mit einer Mischung aus Oliven- und Babyöl einreiben und vierzehn Nächte für ihre Füße Packungen aus einer Mischung von Henna (eine medizinische Pflanze zum Haare färben und für Rituale) Salz, Öl und Essig, vornehmen.
Als gläubige Frau hatte Hannah keinen Zweifel an der Wirksamkeit der vom Rabbi vorgeschriebenen Behandlung. Unterstützt von ihrem Ehemann befolgte sie die Anweisungen, trotzdem verschlechterte sich ihr Zustand. Sie entschied sich zur weiteren Behandlung im Krankenhaus und unterzog sich der operativen Entfernung der Wucherungen. Nach sechs Wochen kam sie wieder nach Hause, litt aber unter den Nebenwirkungen der Operation.
Über ihren schlechten Zustand schockiert, überwies sie ihr Hausarzt wieder zurück ins Krankenhaus. Sie blieb dort einen weiteren Monat mit weiteren Untersuchungen. Schließlich erfuhr Hannah, dass sie an einer unheilbaren Entzündung im Becken litt. Nur Physiotherapie könnte ihre Schmerzen ein wenig lindern. Aufrechtes Sitzen war für sie viel zu schmerzhaft, somit war Hannah zu diesem Zeitpunkt bettlägerig.
In einem Krankenhaus mit sehr gutem Ruf, diesmal in der Abteilung für rheumatische Krankheiten, erhielt sie Injektionen.
Der Chefarzt empfahl ihr eine Strahlentherapie und klärte sie über die möglichen Nebenwirkungen auf. Er empfahl ihr sich mit ihrer Familie zu beraten.
Hannah hatte Angst vor der Strahlentherapie. Aus Angst vor Schuldzuweisungen bei schädlichen Nebenwirkungen war es für die Familie schwierig, ihr einen Rat zu geben.
Die Krankenschwester der sozialen Nachbarschaftshilfe schlug vor, den lokalen Spezialisten zu fragen. Er war gegen die Bestrahlungstherapie, da es für ihn eine überholte Behandlungsmethode darstellte. Hannah beschrieb ihre Reaktion. Er dachte, im Krankenhaus bezeichneten sie die Bestrahlungstherapie als die letzte Möglichkeit, deshalb würde er die östlichen Heilmittel ausprobieren. So begann eine Reihe von Besuchen bei verschiedenen Volksheilern.
Ihr Bruder brachte sie zu einem Heiler irakischer Herkunft im Landesinneren. Sie besuchte ihn zweimal und führte seine Anweisungen, (Verzicht auf bestimmte Lebensmittel und Einnahme verschiedener, von ihm hergestellter Elixiere) sorgfältig aus. Aber vergeblich.– Hannah machte sich nicht die Mühe den Heiler zu informieren, dass die Behandlung nicht anschlug.
Während eines Besuches bei ihrer Schwester in einer anderen Stadt, circa sechs

Monate nach dieser Behandlung, hörte Hannah von einer Araberin "sheik's wife", die vielen Leuten geholfen hatte. Hannah's Bruder bot an sie hinzubringen, und so fuhren sie in Begleitung ihrer Schwester und deren Ehemann. Vor Beginn der Behandlung forderte Sheik's wife einen erheblichen Betrag. Ihr Bruder und ihre Schwester liehen ihr gerne diese Summe, da Hannah sie nicht aufbringen konnte. Um festzustellen, ob sie in der Lage war Hannah zu behandeln, stellte die Heilerin einige Fragen. Ihre Erklärung für die Krankheit war der "böse Blick".

Sie versprach in zwei Tagen eine Medizin fertigzustellen. Hannah blieb für diese zwei Tage bei ihrer Schwester und suchte zusammen mit ihrem Bruder, Schwager, ihrer Schwester und einer Nachbarin ihrer Schwester "sheik's wife" erneut auf. Dem Schwager wurde von der Heilerin aufgetragen einige Wildkräuter zu pflücken, die Hannah zerreiben und in zwei Liter Olivenöl kochen sollte. Nach der Filterung sollte sie ihren Körper mit dieser Flüssigkeit fünfzig Tage lang einreiben. Es wurde Hannah von der Heilerin verboten, während dieser Zeit das Haus zu verlassen, oder sich dem Wind auszusetzen. Ebenso erhielt sie einige Amulette.

Als die fünfzig Tage ohne Besserung ihres Zustandes vergingen, verlor Hannah jede Hoffnung und Glauben.

Hannah suchte noch zwei einheimische Heiler auf. Den einen kannte sie bereits seit ihrer Kindheit, als ihre Familien Nachbarn waren. Nachdem eine ihrer Freundinnen erfolgreich gegen Unfruchtbarkeit behandelt worden war, suchte sie ihn auf. Vergeblich verschrieb er ihr zwei mal einen Trunk. Der zweite Heiler, wieder ein Rabbi, führte ein Ritual mit Eiern aus und gab ihr ein Amulett, - wiederum ohne Erfolg. Neue Hoffnung fand Hannah im darauffolgenden Sommer. Ein Nachbar erzählte ihrer Tochter von einer Frau, die von einem muslimischen Scheich aus Haifa von Krebs geheilt wurde. Er berichtete von den ausserordentlichen Erfolgen des Scheichs, woraufhin in Hannah der Wunsch geweckt wurde, ihn aufzusuchen.

Von zwei Freunden wurde Hannah in Begleitung des Nachbarn dorthin gefahren. Nach Auskunft über ihr Alter, Krankheiten, Name ihrer Mutter, verkündete der Scheich nach einiger Zeit der Überlegung seine Diagnose: Hannah wurde von einem Geist bestraft, der sich darüber geärgert hatte, dass sie einige Gegenstände auf den Boden geworfen hatte. Er versicherte ihr, dass sie ihre Gesundheit innerhalb eines Jahres wiedererlangen würde, vorausgesetzt, sie würde all seinen Anweisungen folgen: tägliche Einreibungen mit von ihm verordneten Elixieren und Bädern in Pflanzenextrakten. Sein Honorar war beträchtlich, konnte jedoch in Raten abbezahlt werden.

Er versprach sogar die Rückzahlung, falls Hannah sich nicht erholen sollte. Dieses Honorar überstieg bei weitem Hannahs Möglichkeiten. Ein Teil wurde ihr von ihrem Bruder geschenkt, den Restbetrag erhielten sie als Darlehen von dem Arbeitgeber ihres Mannes, offiziell für eine Wohnungsrenovierung.

Vierzehntägig konnte die frische Medizin abgeholt werden. Diese Aufgabe teilten sich ihr Nachbar, ihr Ehemann und ihre Tochter. Abgesehen von einigen kurzen Unterbrechungen führte Hannah die Behandlung beharrlich fort. Anfangs setzte sie sich vor ihrer Wohnung in die Sonne, damit die Flüssigkeit besser einziehen konnte. Viele vorbeigehende Passanten und besonders die Nachbarn auf ihrem Einkaufsweg, erkundigten sich nach der Behandlung und zeigten großes Vertrauen in die Wirksamkeit dieser Behandlung.

Obwohl nach achtzehn Monaten noch keine Besserung eingetreten war, verlor Hannah die Hoffnung nicht. Sie vermutete sogar , dass es ihr wohl ohne die Behandlung des Sheicks schlechter gehen würde.

Susan
Susan wurde in Marokko geboren und ist ungefähr 45 Jahre alt. Sie emigrierte als Kind nach Israel, und wuchs in einem nördlich gelegenen Siedlungsgebiet auf.
Im Alter von 43 Jahren bekam Susan Depressionen mit gleichzeitigen, über den ganzen Körper verteilten, heftigen Schmerzen. Weitere Symptome waren Ohnmacht, Schlaflosigkeit, Händezittern und niedriger Blutdruck. Zuerst wandte sie sich an ihren Hausarzt, der ihr ein lokales Krankenhaus nannte, in dem jedoch keine Diagnose erstellt wurde. Zu dieser Zeit erkrankte Susan an einer Blaseninfektion. Der Hausarzt verschrieb Tabletten, die sie permanent einnehmen musste, da bei einer Unterbrechung die Infektion sofort wieder einsetzen würde.
Susan's Serie zahlreicher Besuche bei Volksheilern begann mit einem traditionellen Heiler aus einer Einwanderungsstadt im Landesinneren, von dem sie von Verwandten gehört hatte. Der Heiler diagnostizierte den "bösen Blick". Als die Behandlung (das Verbrennen von ihm gelieferter Zettelchen), ihren Zustand nicht besserte, wandte sich Susan an einen arabischen Scheich, eine Empfehlung ihrer Nachbarn. Laut seiner Diagnose rührte ihr Zustand vom Einfluss eines bösen Geistes her.
Auf den dritten Heiler, eine Frau, die ebenfalls im Landesinneren lebte, wurde sie von erfolgreich behandelten Patienten aus ihrer Stadt hingewiesen. In diesem Fall lautete die Diagnose "Furcht". Der nächste Heiler, erneut ein arabischer Scheich, wurde ihr von der Freundin ihres Sohnes aus einer Nachbarstadt genannt. Diese Behandlung, Abreibungen ihres Körpers mit Öl und Pflanzenextrakten, war wirksam. Susan verwies alle ihre kranken Freunde an diesen Scheich. Sie nahm die Gewohnheit an, Grabstätten von Heiligen in der Nähe aufzusuchen.
Während der ganzen Zeit besuchte Susan ihren Arzt und erhielt laufend Rezepte für schmerzstillende Mittel und Medikamente für andere allgemeine Störungen wie zum Beispiel Halsschmerzen. Der Hausarzt erfuhr nichts von ihren Besuchen bei anderen Heilern, da sie sich sicher war, dass er sie dafür verspotten würde, wenn er davon erführe.

Zusammenfassung
Volkstümliche Medizin existiert und breitet sich aus, trotz der von wenigen Ausnahmen abgesehen ablehnenden Haltung durch die Schulmedizin.
Dieses Resultat ist etwas überraschend, wenn wir die absolute Legitimität der westlichen Schulmedizin und die kostengünstige Gesundheitsvorsorge in Betracht ziehen.
Die Patienten tendieren dazu, einen Heiler nach dem anderen, manchmal sogar mehrere gleichzeitig, in Anspruch zu nehmen. Bei Beschwerden rein körperlicher Natur wendet sich der Patient im allgemeinen erst an einen westlich orientierten Arzt und wenn diese Behandlung nicht zur Heilung führt, an einen Heiler. Chronische Erkrankungen lassen viele Patienten parallel von Arzt und Heiler behandeln, ohne dass der eine von dem anderen erfährt.
Einige Patienten lassen sich bei einem Arzt eine Diagnose erstellen und entscheiden sich dann, je nach Schwere der Erkrankung, an wen sie sich für eine Therapie wenden.
Dieses Verhalten deutet auf eine Vorrangstellung des ärztlichen Status hin. Ein weiteres Indiz dieses Musters ist die Trennung der Behandlung, während der Bluthochdruck durch den Arzt eingestellt wird, wendet sich der Patient bei einer

Depression gleichzeitig an einen Heiler.

Eine Vielzahl von Faktoren trägt zu der Aufrechterhaltung der traditionellen Heilverfahren bei. Patient und Heiler teilen bezüglich der Krankheitsursachen das gleiche Glaubenssystem. Diese Menschen sind traditionell und religiös geprägt in dem Glauben, dass äußere Faktoren z.B. ein böser Geist oder eine Gottheit sich auf ihre Gesundheit oder Krankheit auswirken. Für sie ist es eine logische Konsequenz, sich an Rabbis und Scheich mit religiösem Hintergrund zu wenden, da diese Zugang zu übernatürlichen Kräften haben und die Mittel, diese zu beeinflussen.

In diesem Zusammenhang ist es interessant, dass Juden oft weise Moslems konsultieren, während Moslems bei jüdischen Experten Rat und Hilfe suchen.

Patient und Heiler teilen den Glauben, dass der "böse Blick" bei der Beeinträchtigung der Gesundheit eine zentrale Rolle spielt. Eine Auffassung die der Schulmedizin völlig fremd ist.

Das in sich geschlossene soziale Netzwerk von Nachbarn und Verwandten, normalerweise mit den gleichen Glaubensgrundsätzen, unterstützt und informiert die Patienten bei der Suche nach traditionellen Heilern. Viele Patienten wenden sich auch aus Enttäuschung über die moderne Schulmedizin und das technisch orientierte, unpersönliche Verhalten der westlichen Ärzte bewusst traditionellen Heilern zu, die sie zu Hause empfangen, keine Zeitbeschränkung setzen und ein persönliches, ganzheitliches Interesse zum Ausdruck bringen.

Im Jahre 2001, als dieser Bericht geschrieben wurde, gab es keine Anzeichen dafür, dass der Einsatz traditioneller Medizin abnimmt. Im Gegenteil, es kommt zu einer ständig zunehmenden sozialen Anerkennung. Die Menschen schämen sich nicht mehr, offen über ihre Besuche bei traditionellen Heilern zu sprechen und auch die Medien veröffentlichen wohlwollende Berichte über die Erfahrungen mit traditionellen Heilmethoden.

Autorin
DR. OFRA GREENBERG
Dozentin in Sozial- Antrophologie, spezialisiert in Medizinischer Antrophologie am Wetsren Galilee academic College.
Sie führte Untersuchungen in Volksmedizin und alternativer medizin durch. Ihre neuesten Untersuchungen betreffen den Umgang mit Nierenerkrankungen im Vergleich bei unterschiedlichen ethnischen Gruppen in Israel.
Kontakt: E-Mail: ofra_g@netvision.net.il

Literatur

ALLAND, A. 1977. Medical Anthropology and the Study of Biographical and Cultural Adaptation in D. Landy (ed.) *Culture, Disease and Healing,* New York: Macmillan, pp. 41-47.
ANDERSEN, R.M. 1995. Revisitng the Behavioral Model and Access to Medical Care: Does it Matter?, *Journal of Health and Social Behavior* 36 (1): 1-10.
BILU, Y. 1978. *Traditional Psychiatry in Israel,* (Unpublished Ph.D thesis), Hebrew University, Jerusalem (in Hebrew).
BISHAW, M. 1991. Promoting Traditional Medicine in Ethiopia, *Social Science and Medicine* 33 (2): 193-200.
CAMAZINE, S.M. 1980. Traditional and Western Health Care Among the Zuni Indians of New Mexico, *Social Science and Medicine* 14B (1): 73-80.
CHRISMAN, N.J. 1977. The Health Seeking Process: An Approach to the Natural History of Illness, *Culture, Medicine and Psychiatry* 1: 351-377.
FINKLER, K. 1981. A Comparative Study of Health Seekers or Why Some People Go to Doctors Rather than to Spiritualistic Healers, *Medical Anthropology* 5 (3): 383-424.
FURNHAM, A., C. VINCENT & R. WOOD. 1995. The Health Beliefs and Behaviors of Three Groups of Complementary Medicine and a General Practice Group of Patients, *Journal of Alternative and Complementary Medicine* 1 (4): 347-359.
GARRISON, V. 1977. Doctor, Espirista or Psychiatrist? Health Seeking Behavior in a Puerto Rican Neighborhood in New York City, *Medical Anthropology* 1: 65-180.
KAHANNA, S.K. 1997. Traditions and Reproductive Technology in an Urbanizing North Indian Village, *Social Science and Medicine,* 44 (2): 171-180.
KELNER, M. & B. WELLMAN. 1997. Health Care and Consumer Choice: Medical and Alternative Therapies. *Social Science and Medicine* 45 (2): 203-212.
KUNITZ, S.J., H. TEMKIN-GREENER, D. BROUDY & M. HAFFNER. 1981. Determinants of Hospital Utilization and Surgery on the Navajo Indian Reservation, *Social Science and Medicine* 15B (1): 71-79.
LATZER, Y. 1996. Intercultural Encounters and Mental Health: The Case of Moroccan Immigrant Women, in Y. KASHTI and R. EISIKOVITS (eds.) *Faces in the Mirror: Israeli Cultures in the 1990's,* Tel Aviv, Ramot.
LEE, B.P.L. 1996. Traditional Reaction to Modern Stress, Social Science and Medicine 42 (5): 639-641.
LIEBAN, R.W. 1976. Traditional Medical Beliefs and the Choice of Practitioners in a Philippine City, *Social Science and Medicine* 10 (6): 289-296.
McGUIRE, M. 1988. *Ritual Healing in Suburban America,* New Brunswick, Rutgers University.
NEW, P.K. 1977. Traditional and Modern Health Care: An Appraisal of Complementarity, *International Social Science Journal* 29 (3): 483-495.
PALGI P. 1981. Traditional Methods of Dealing with Mental Health Problems among Yemenite Immigrants in Israel, in U. AVIRAM & I. LEVAV (eds.) *Community Mental Health in Israel,* Tel Aviv, Cherikover, pp. 43-67 (in Hebrew).
PRESS, I. 1969. Urban Illness, Physicians, Curers and Dual Use in Bogota, *Health and Social Behavior* 10 (3): 209-218.
SHARMA, U. 1992. *Complementary Medicine Today: Practitioners And Patients,* London, Routledge.
SHOKEID, M. 1974. The Emergence of Supernatural Explanation for Male Barrenness among Moroccan Immigrants, in S. DESHEN & M. SHOKEID (eds.) *The Predicament of Homecoming,* New York, Cornell, pp.122-150.

FOLK MEDICINE AMONG ORIENTAL JEWS IN ISRAEL

by Ofra Greenberg

Introduction

This paper focuses on the use of folk medicine in modern Western society. It examines the factors that affect the individual's choice of treatment when faced with several alternatives (mainly a choice between modern and folk medicine). More specifically, it seeks to clarify under what circumstances folk medicine is utilized alongside conventional Western medicine, or even in preference to it.

In today's pluralistic society different health systems operate side by side, each with its own rules. On the one hand we have established Western biomedicine, and on the other, a growing number of various other methods, collectively termed 'alternative medicine'. This category includes the methods generally referred to as 'folk medicine': those methods of treatment that have been used traditionally for generations. To varying degrees, a considerable section of the population makes use of these alternative methods of cure.

The Israeli health establishment has generally viewed folk medicine as a remnant of traditional cultures imported from abroad, mainly from Islamic countries. Our research, however, has found this type of medicine to be an integral part of current Israeli social and cultural reality in general, and that of the immigrant town in particular. Our main topic of interest is the nature of the process whereby people choose a certain method in preference to others, and the factors that drive this process.

This issue was studied in an Israeli immigrant town, whose 15,000 inhabitants stem from predominantly Islamic countries. They have a low level of education relative to the general Israeli population, and are engaged in poorly paid occupations. The information used was gathered according to anthropological research methods, particularly the participant-observer technique, augmented by a number of unstructured interviews. The research was carried out over a period of two years (1981-1982), during which the researcher resided in the town under study. Over this period, the researcher and her assistant met with some fifty patients who had in parallel sought medical assistance from physicians and folk healers. Some basic information regarding medical services in Israel, as well as a short explanation of the concept of the *evil eye* is now presented as background to the case studies.

Western medicine is endowed with virtually exclusive legitimacy by the Israeli health authorities. For the most part, it is provided under government auspices, while alternative medicine is administered in private practice. Western medicine practiced in Israel is considered to be of a high international standard. The national health service covers most of the costs of biomedical treatment, which are administered by a number of governmental health funds. The market is also full of private practitioners, with biomedical and/or alternative qualifications. In recent years the governmental funds have begun to partially subsidize the cost of certain alternative forms of treatment in addition to the mainstream conventional forms. Belief in the power of the *evil eye* is prevalent among Jews of oriental origin. It can be invoked by angry or jealous individuals to harm the person towards whom they bear a grudge.
The *evil eye* can cause harm in a variety of forms, including physical injury, such as illness or paralysis, economic hardship (loss of property), psychological symptoms (depression) and social misfortune (inability to find a marriage partner). Bilu (1978) engages in an extensive discussion of the characteristics of the *evil eye* among oriental Jews. An additional belief prevalent among this population group is that in the power and existence of *evil spirits*, who inflict similar types of physical and mental illness as punishment for their own injury at the hands of human beings.

Theoretical Introduction
The literature dealing with the forms of alternative medicine practiced in Western society rarely touches on the use of folk medicine. On the other hand, much has been written about various aspects of the parallel use of folk and Western medicine in developing countries (Gonzalez 1966; Press 1969; Lieban 1976; Alland 1977; Finkler 1981; Bishaw 1991; Kahanna 1997), and about difficulties encountered in the adoption of modern medicine by the population of such countries (Woods 1977; Camazine 1980; Kunitz et al. 1981).
The assumption made both by public administrators and by many researchers is that a traditional population transplanted to a modern milieu would undergo rapid assimilation and accept the behavior patterns prevalent in its new surroundings. We are, however, able to deduce from research studies dealing with various aspects of immigrant communities that, as in other areas, the process of adopting new patterns of health-related behavior is not at all rapid, and is often fraught with many hardships.
Once the decision to try folk medicine has been made, the patient has to choose a particular healer or a type of healing that he or she wishes to undergo.
It portrays the process of choosing a specific health care method as a combination of three interrelated sets of determinants:
- **predisposing factors**, such as age and education;
- **enabling factors**, such as knowledge and accessibility of services, and

the underlying assumption is that people seek the advice of those who - **share their beliefs** regarding health and sickness, and are therefore predisposed to accept their recommendations.

Case Studies

The following two cases provide evidence of some of the factors discussed above, regarding choice of treatment and the simultaneous use of Western and folk medicine.

Hannah Azulai
Hannah Azulai, aged 37, was born in Iraq. She immigrated to Israel with her family in 1950. Married at the age of 17, she has six children. Her parents and brothers moved to a distant agricultural settlement some time ago. Her husband, of Moroccan origin, grew up in the same town, and some of his family still resides there. He has a secure job as a senior employee with a large public company. The history of her illness was related to me by Hannah, while developments over a two-year period were directly observed.

The first signs of a disorder appeared some five years previously, in the form of swelling and pain in one leg. Hannah approached a general practitioner, who diagnosed rheumatism after administering a blood test, and prescribed an analgesic. Not satisfied with this, Hannah consulted a surgeon, whose diagnosis was the same.

Faced with increasing pain and a long waiting list for an orthopedic examination, Hannah privately consulted a well-known physician in a nearby town, who, after having her legs X-rayed, diagnosed a growth on her right leg. He recommended that she undertake an operation, and referred her to the regional hospital sending the X-rays with her. Hannah spent fifteen days in the orthopedic ward, undergoing examinations by the head of the department, a psychologist and a psychiatrist. She was discharged with no pathological diagnosis.

The pain continued, but Hannah received no treatment. Some two years after her first symptoms her condition worsened. She underwent an orthopedic examination and was referred to a large hospital in the center of the country where she was given an appointment for surgery several months later.

Around this time, Hannah's brothers, despairing of conventional treatment, decided to take her to a rabbi of Yemenite origin who lived in the center of the country. (He had, of late, figured prominently in the media, following his curing of several blind girls.) Hannah's brothers were prepared to bear the expenses incurred by the visit. On arrival, it transpired that a prior appointment was required. Guards outside the rabbi's house set a consultation date three months hence, for which service payment was demanded.

The date set for Hannah's hospitalization coincided with her appointment with the rabbi. One of the brothers suggested a solution to the dilemma: they would visit the rabbi early that morning and then decide whether to proceed with the conventional treatment. This plan was indeed put into effect. After asking several questions about

Hannah's parents, the rabbi diagnosed her illness as 'evil eye', which, he said, had begun in her legs and subsequently spread throughout her body. He gave her a black charm inscribed with religious verses, instructing her to wear it around her neck and to remove it only during menstruation. She was also instructed to apply a mixture of pure olive oil and baby oil to all parts of her body over a ninety-day period. Finally, once a fortnight she was to mix henna (a medicinal herb in rituals, used to color hair), salt, oil, and vinegar, and rub this on her feet at night.

A religious woman, Hannah had no doubt that this treatment, prescribed by a rabbi, would effect a cure. Assisted by her husband she followed the instructions to the letter, but her condition worsened. She decided to resume treatment at the hospital, and underwent an operation to remove a growth on her leg. She returned home after six weeks, suffering from side effects of the operation.

A local specialist, shocked at her condition, demanded that she be re-admitted to hospital. She was referred to the same hospital for further examinations and remained there for another month. Hannah was eventually told that she was suffering from an inflammation of the pelvis, an incurable illness. Physiotherapy would be effective only in easing the pain.

By this stage Hannah found sitting upright too painful, and was mostly bedridden. She was referred to a different, prestigious hospital, where she received injections in the department of rheumatic diseases. The head of department recommended radiation therapy, but warned Hannah of the possible side effects, suggesting that she discusses the matter with her family.

Hannah was afraid of radiation therapy. Her family found it difficult to advise her, fearing they would be blamed should the treatment prove to have a damaging effect. The neighborhood primary-care nurse suggested that she sees the local specialist once again. He was against radiation therapy on the grounds that it was an outdated method of treatment. Hannah described her reaction: "I thought to myself, at the hospital they told me that (radiation therapy) was the last possible treatment. So I'll try the Eastern remedies." Thus began a series of consultations with various folk healers.

Her brother drove Hannah to a healer of Iraqi origin in the center of the country. She visited him twice and meticulously carried out his instructions (excluding certain foods from her diet and drinking various beverages that he gave her), but to no avail. Hannah did not bother to inform the healer that the treatment had failed.

Approximately six months after consulting this healer, wile visiting her sister in another town, Hanna heard about an Arab 'sheik's wife' from Nablus, who had helped many people. Hannah's brother volunteered to take her, and they were accompanied on their journey by the sister and Hannah's husband. The sheik's wife demanded substantial payment before beginning her treatment. Since Hannah could not afford this sum, her brother and sister bore the expense jointly. The healer asked a number of questions, and cast lots in order to determine whether she would be able to treat Hannah. Her explanation of the illness was 'evil eye'. She promised to prepare a medication that would be ready two days later. Hannah remained with her sister for two days, returning to the sheik's wife together with her brother, sister, brother-in-law, and her sister's neighbor. The healer instructed the brother-in-law to gather certain wild plants, which Hannah was ordered to grind and boil in two liters of olive oil. After straining, this liquid was to be applied to her body for fifty days. During this period Hannah was forbidden by the healer to leave her home, so as not to expose herself to the wind. She was also given several charms. When the fifty days passed without any improvement in her condition, Hannah lost hope and belief.

Hannah also consulted two local healers. She had known one of them since childhood, when their families had been neighbors. She went to see him after a friend of hers had been successfully treated for infertility. He twice prescribed a beverage, but to no avail. The second healer, a rabbi, performed a ritual in which he used eggs, and gave her a charm, again without success.

The following summer Hannah found new hope. A neighbor told her daughter of a local woman who had been cured of cancer by a Moslem sheik in Haifa. The neighbor recounted further stories of this sheik's extraordinary success, which awakened in Hannah the desire to consult him. Hannah was driven to the sheik by two friends, accompanied by the neighbor. The sheik's diagnosis was pronounced after receiving information about her age, illness and mother's name, and spending some time in seclusion: Hannah had been punished by a spirit that she had angered by throwing some object to the floor. He assured her that she would recover within a year, provided that she follow all his instructions: daily bodily application of liquids that he would provide, and bathing with a herbal essence. The sheik's fee was considerable, and was paid in installments. He promised to refund the payment if Hannah failed to recover. She would have to arrange to collect fresh medicine once a fortnight. It was agreed that this task would be shared by her neighbor, husband and daughter.

The fee was beyond Hannah's means. Part was paid by her brother, as a gift, while the remainder was obtained by her husband as a loan from his employer, ostensibly for renovating their apartment. Apart from a few short intervals, Hannah persisted with the treatment. In the beginning she took to sitting in the sun outside her apartment to facilitate absorption of the liquid. All the passersby, and particular neighbors on their way to the grocery, stopped to inquire about the treatment, expressing strong confidence and hope in its efficacy.

After continuing this treatment for 18 months there was still no marked change in her condition, but Hannah had still not lost hope. She conjectured that she may have been worse off without the sheik's treatment.

Susan

Susan is around 45 years old, born in Morocco. She immigrated to Israel as a child and grew up in the northern immigrant town under study.

At the age of 43 Susan began to suffer from depression, accompanied by severe pain in various parts of her body. Her symptoms included fainting, insomnia, trembling hands, and low blood pressure. At first she approached the family doctor, who referred her to the regional hospital, where no diagnosis was made. At this stage Susan began to suffer from a bladder infection. Her family doctor prescribed tablets, which she took on an ongoing basis, claiming that the infection returned when she stopped taking the medication.

Susan's series of visits to folk healers began with a traditional healer in an immigrant town in the center of the country, about whom she had heard from a relative. The healer diagnosed an '*evil eye*'. When the treatment he prescribed (burning pieces of paper supplied by him) failed to improve her condition, Susan approached an Arab sheik recommended by some of her neighbors. His diagnosis was that her condition was due to the intervention of an *evil spirit*.

She was introduced to the third healer, a woman who also resided in an immigrant town in the center of Israel, by former patients living in Susan's town who had been successfully treated by her. The diagnosis in this case was 'fright'.

The next healer was another Arab sheik from Haifa, to whom she was referred by her son's girlfriend, who lived in a neighboring village. The treatment, consisting of rubbing her entire body with oil and plant essences, was effective. Susan began to refer all her ill friends to this sheik. She also adopted the custom of visiting the graves of holy men in the vicinity.

During this period, Susan visited her doctor to obtain prescriptions for painkillers, and for treatment of other common disorders, such as a throat infection. The family doctor was told nothing of her visits to the other healers, since she was certain that he would deride her when hearing of them.

Summary

Folk medicine was found to exist and thrive in spite of the dismissive attitude towards it exhibited (with a few exceptions) by the medical establishment. This finding is somewhat surprising in view of the almost exclusive legitimacy enjoyed by Western medicine, and the subsidized nature of medical services.

Patients tend to try one healer after another, sometimes seeking help from two healers at the same time. If the complaint is a physical one, the patient generally approaches a Western doctor first, turning to a healer only after the conventional treatment has failed to effect a cure. Many patients suffering from chronic illnesses continue receiving treatment in parallel from both a doctor and a healer, without the former knowing about the latter.

Some patients first visit a doctor in order to receive a diagnosis, on the strength of which they decide to whom to turn for treatment. Such behavior points to the doctor's preferential status. Further evidence of this pattern is provided by a duality of treatment: while a certain ailment, such a s high blood pressure, once diagnosed, is treated by the doctor, the same patient's depression may be treated in parallel by the healer.

A number of factors contribute to the continuing existence of the system of traditional medicine. Patients and healers share the same belief systems regarding the causes of illness. These are traditional and religious people who believe that external elements, such as a divinity or an evil spirit, can affect one's health and illness. It is thus logical for them to turn to healers who have religious training, such as rabbis and sheiks (in this context it is interesting to note that Jews consult Moslem wise men, while Moslems seek help from Jewish experts), since they have access to these supernatural powers and the means to influence them. Patients and healers also share the belief that the *evil eye* plays a central role in harming one's health (an idea totally foreign to practitioners of modern medicine).

The close social network, comprising neighbors and relatives (who usually share the same beliefs), passes on information that encourages its members to approach traditional healers. Disappointment with modern medicine and with the technical, impersonal manner of many Western doctors also drives patients to turn to traditional healers who receive them in their home, set no time limit to the consultation, and express a personal, holistic interest.

Currently, in the year 2001, there is no sign that the use of traditional medicine is diminishing. On the contrary, it is steadily acquiring open social legitimacy. People are no longer ashamed to speak of their visits to traditional healers, and the media provide sympathetic coverage of individuals who recount their experiences of traditional treatment.

Author

DR. OFRA GREENBERG
Lecturer in social anthropology, specializing in Medical Anthropology at Western Galilee Academic College. Carried out research in folk medicine and alternative medicine. Recently investigated ways of coping with kidney disease among different ethnic groups in Israel.
Contact: Western Galilee Academic College, Acre 24121, Israel,
E-Mail: ofra_g@netvision.net.il

References

ALLAND, A. 1977. Medical Anthropology and the Study of Biographical and Cultural Adaptation in D. Landy (ed.) *Culture, Disease and Healing*, New York: Macmillan, pp. 41-47.

ANDERSEN, R.M. 1995. Revisitng the Behavioral Model and Access to Medical Care: Does it Matter?, *Journal of Health and Social Behavior* 36 (1): 1-10.

BILU, Y. 1978. *Traditional Psychiatry in Israel*, (Unpublished Ph.D thesis), Hebrew University, Jerusalem (in Hebrew).

BISHAW, M. 1991. Promoting Traditional Medicine in Ethiopia, *Social Science and Medicine* 33 (2): 193-200.

CAMAZINE, S.M. 1980. Traditional and Western Health Care Among the Zuni Indians of New Mexico, *Social Science and Medicine* 14B (1): 73-80.

CHRISMAN, N.J. 1977. The Health Seeking Process: An Approach to the Natural History of Illness, *Culture, Medicine and Psychiatry* 1: 351-377.

FINKLER, K. 1981. A Comparative Study of Health Seekers or Why Some People Go to Doctors Rather than to Spiritualistic Healers, *Medical Anthropology* 5 (3): 383-424.

FURNHAM, A., C. VINCENT & R. WOOD. 1995. The Health Beliefs and Behaviors of Three Groups of Complementary Medicine and a General Practice Group of Patients, *Journal of Alternative and Complementary Medicine* 1 (4): 347-359.

GARRISON, V. 1977. Doctor, Espirista or Psychiatrist? Health Seeking Behavior in a Puerto Rican Neighborhood in New York City, *Medical Anthropology* 1: 65-180.

KAHANNA, S.K. 1997. Traditions and Reproductive Technology in an Urbanizing North Indian Village, *Social Science and Medicine*, 44 (2): 171-180.

KELNER, M. & B. WELLMAN. 1997. Health Care and Consumer Choice: Medical and Alternative Therapies. *Social Science and Medicine* 45 (2): 203-212.

KUNITZ, S.J., H. TEMKIN-GREENER, D. BROUDY & M. HAFFNER. 1981. Determinants of Hospital Utilization and Surgery on the Navajo Indian Reservation, *Social Science and Medicine* 15B (1): 71-79.

LATZER, Y. 1996. Intercultural Encounters and Mental Health: The Case of Moroccan Immigrant Women, in Y. KASHTI and R. EISIKOVITS (eds.) *Faces in the Mirror: Israeli Cultures in the 1990's*, Tel Aviv, Ramot.

LEE, B.P.L. 1996. Traditional Reaction to Modern Stress, Social Science and Medicine 42 (5): 639-641.

LIEBAN, R.W. 1976. Traditional Medical Beliefs and the Choice of Practitioners in a Philippine City, *Social Science and Medicine* 10 (6): 289-296.

MCGUIRE, M. 1988. *Ritual Healing in Suburban America*, New Brunswick, Rutgers University.

NEW, P.K. 1977. Traditional and Modern Health Care: An Appraisal of Complementarity, *International Social Science Journal* 29 (3): 483-495.

PALGI P. 1981. Traditional Methods of Dealing with Mental Health Problems among

Yemenite Immigrants in Israel, in U. Aviram & I. Levav (eds.) *Community Mental Health in Israel*, Tel Aviv, Cherikover, pp. 43-67 (in Hebrew).

Press, I. 1969. Urban Illness, Physicians, Curers and Dual Use in Bogota, *Health and Social Behavior* 10 (3): 209-218.

Sharma, U. 1992. *Complementary Medicine Today: Practitioners And Patients*, London, Routledge.

Shokeid, M. 1974. The Emergence of Supernatural Explanation for Male Barrenness among Moroccan Immigrants, in S. Deshen & M. Shokeid (eds.) *The Predicament of Homecoming*, New York, Cornell, pp.122-150.

ALTORIENTALISCHE MUSIKTHERAPIE

von Gerhard Tucek

Altorientalische Musiktherapie (AM) stellt ein seit ca. eintausend Jahren dokumentiertes, empirisch bewährtes System praktisch therapeutischer, prophylaktischer und rehabilitativer Relevanz dar. Ihre Wurzeln reichen in die Zeit musikalischer Heilzeremonien zentralasiatischer Schamanen zurück, die, ähnlich der späteren islamischen Medizin, auf der Idee einer universell gültigen kosmischen Ordnung gründen, die sich durch Naturgesetzmäßigkeiten manifestiert.

Die mystische Dimension

Hafiz, einer der bedeutendsten persischen Dichter und Mystiker, schreibt über die Bedeutung von Musik: *"Viele sagen, das Leben sei mit Hilfe der Musik in den menschlichen Körper gelockt worden. Die Wahrheit ist aber, dass das Leben selbst Musik ist."*

Alles dreht sich im sufischen Denken, Fühlen und Handeln um ein zentrales *Hadith Qudsi*, (außerkor'anisches Gotteswort), welches lautet: *"ICH war ein verborgener Schatz und sehnte Mich, erkannt zu werden, deshalb schuf ICH die Welt"*. So entstand die Welt der Vielheit, durch die die Einheit sich selbst betrachtet. Menschliches Dasein ist aus dieser Sicht die "Pupille des Auges dieser Betrachtung". Somit liegt die Aufgabe des Menschen in der bewussten Hinwendung zum göttlichen Geliebten, bis man in IHM seine begrenzte Ichheit, auflösend in Liebe und Sehnsucht vergeht. Dieser Gedanke kommt in einem weiteren außerkor'anischen Gotteswort zum Ausdruck, in dem Gott ja versprochen hat, dass ER dem, der Ihm liebend naht, " *...zum Auge wird mit dem er sieht, zur Hand mit der er greift*". Die Metapher hierfür ist der Nachtfalter, der in der Flamme der Kerze verglüht und eins mit dem Feuer wird.

Islamische Mystiker sahen Musik und Tanz oft als einziges adäquates Mittel an die schöpferische Liebe annähernd zu verdeutlichen. So fand etwa der große Mystiker des 13. Jhdts., Dschalaleddin Rumi, auf den der im Westen als der Orden der "drehenden Derwische" bekannt gewordene Mevlevi Orden zurückgeht, in einer Nachdichtung durch Friedrich Rückert folgende Worte über Musik:

"Einstmals sprach unser Herr Dschalaleddin dieses:
"Die Musik ist das Knarren der Pforten des Paradieses!"
Darauf sprach einer von den dumm - dreisten Narren:
"Nicht gefällt mir von Pforten das Knarren!"
Sprach unser Herr Dschalaleddin drauf:
"Ich höre die Pforten, sie tun sich auf;
aber wie die Türen sich tun zu,
das hörst du!"

Altorientalische Musiktherapie erfreute sich in den frühen Asylen und Spitalskomplexen des Seldschuken- und späteren Osmanenreiches bei der Behandlung von Geisteskrankheiten großer Beliebtheit. Aber auch für die Mystiker war - auf einer anderen Ebene - die Musik eine Art der Therapie: Auf dem beschwerlichen und entbehrungsreichen Pfad der mystischen Gottessuche eröffnete sie den Suchenden und sich nach der "unio mystica" Sehnenden die Pforten des Paradieses.

Diese religiös motivierte Haltung hat nachhaltig das historische Gesundheitssystem geprägt. Schmerz , Krankheit und Leid werden aus dieser Sicht als für den Reifungsprozess unerlässliche Prüfungen angenommen und in diesem Sinne nicht als prinzipiell feindlich gesehen. Alle Methoden der Heilung - auch die sich in den "profanen Wissenschaften" begründenden - sind von dem Gedanken durchdrungen, dass letztlich alle Gesundheit und Krankheit vom Schöpfer selbst kommt und somit grundlegend angenommen werden. Kunst wurde als ein höheres Ordnungsprinzip verstanden, das die Aufgabe hat, die Beziehung des Menschen zur Welt zu klären und dem Geist zu helfen, *"von der unüberschaubaren Vielheit der Schöpfung auf die zu-grunde liegende Einheit aller Dinge zu schließen"* [1](vgl. BURCKHARDT 1955). Sie ist menschliche Ausdrucksform der harmonischen Gestaltung der Umwelt, welche "die göttliche Einheit" in Form universeller Gesetzmäßigkeiten bezeugt.

Ähnlich wie heutige Verhaltenstherapie die "gesunden" Persönlichkeitsanteile therapeutisch in den Mittelpunkt rückt, stellt AM auch heute noch das Bild des "heilen Menschen" in ihr Zentrum: die Entfaltung der Person zu der ihr wesenhaft zugrunde liegenden Essenz. Sie fordert den einzelnen Menschen auf, in sinnenhafter Offenheit zur Außen-, Innen- und transzendenten Welt, sein individuelles "Heilsein" (seine "Ganzheit") zu entwickeln. Dieser Erkenntnisprozess ist seinem Wesen nach offen und zieht keine scharfen Trennlinien zwischen physischen, psychischen und spirituellen Seins-Dimensionen. Therapie

---

[1] In der mittelalterlich - abendländischen Ästhetik gibt es bis Bonaventura nahezu idente Konzepte. Auch der Philosoph Boetius (480 - 524) vertritt in seinem Werk "De Musica" die Auffassung einer ästhetischen Theorie, die sich von einer göttlichen und kosmischen Ordnung herleitet.

zielt hier innerhalb ihres medizinischen Auftragsprofils wesentlich darauf ab, den Patienten zur Umsetzung von Lebensprinzipien als Konkretion eines höheren Ordnungsprinzips zu bewegen ("e-movere").

Dem religiösen Gebot der Mildtätigkeit folgend, stifteten die Herrscher und wohlhabende Menschen der Seldschuken- und Osmanendynastien Spitäler, in denen affektorientierte und naturwissenschaftliche Behandlungsmethoden gleichrangig und gleichwertig nebeneinander angewandt wurden. (Im heutigen Sinne ergänzen einander biomedizinische und beziehungsmedizinische Behandlungsmethoden) In den Spitälern jener Zeit setzten die Ärzte neben naturwissenschaftlich begründeten Behandlungsmethoden eine Vielzahl künstlerischer, ästhetisch ansprechender, affektiv wirkender Sinnesgenüsse ein. So galten diese Krankenanstalten sowohl als wissenschaftliche Bildungs- und Behandlungsstätten wie auch als Oasen der Stille und des Friedens.

Durch das Lauschen harmonischer Klänge - sei es Gesang, Poesie, oder das Plätschern von Wasser durch das Verweilen in Blumen- und Pflanzenhainen, umgeben von harmonischer Innenraumgestaltung und Architektur, durch harmonische Farbgestaltung, das Üben harmonischer, physischer Bewegungsabläufe (*Riyazed* vgl. TUCEK 2000), durch Wohlgerüche und gezielt eingesetzte, maßvolle Ernährung wurde versucht, die Grundlagen für die seelische und körperliche Genesung der Patienten zu schaffen.

Hierin scheint sich ein grundlegendes Moment des Menschlichen zu zeigen: wenn gegenwärtige psychologische Ästhetik nicht von getrennten ästhetischen Momenten des Sehens, Hörens etc. spricht, sondern von integrativen Sinnesakten des einen und des ganzen Menschen, dann ist der unübersehbare Trend zu künstlerisch integrativen Therapien sinnfällig - Therapieformen, die nicht paradigmatisch in Musiktherapie, Tanztherapie, Kunsttherapie etc. trennen, sondern die künstlerischen Medien und die ästhetischen Sinne aufeinander beziehen und als Gesamtes für einen therapeutischen Prozess nutzbar machen.

Die medizingeschichtliche Ebene der AM

Aus allen Epochen der arabischen und türkisch - islamischen Kulturgeschichte zeugen Berichte von der tiefgreifenden "pharmakologischen" Wirkung von Musik auf den Menschen. Man maß der theoretischen Betrachtung und Fundierung der musikalischen Effekte schon früh wichtige Bedeutung bei. Dieser historische Kontext sowie die musikalischen Heilzeremonien zentralasiatischer Bakseschamanen bildeten einen idealen Nährboden für die Entwicklung musiktherapeutischer Behandlungsmethoden.

Islamische Ärzte begriffen den Menschen als Mikrokosmos, der in sich die gesamte Schöpfung widerspiegelt. Ihr Verständnis der Schöpfung kommt sehr plastisch in dem Ausspruch *"al - insan ramz al - wujud"*: *"Der Mensch ist das Sinnbild der Schöpfung"* zum Ausdruck. So deuteten die islamischen Ärzte den menschlichen Körper als ein materialisiertes Abbild der Seele. Aus diesem Grund sahen sie die körperliche Disposition aufs Engste von geistig - mentalem und seelischem Geschehen bedingt. Mit anderen Worten sah die islamische Medizin den Menschen als innen- und außenbezogenes Wesen: Innenbezogen durch geistig - mentale und seelische Prozesse. Außenbezogen durch die verschiedenen Grade der makrokosmischen Hierarchien, die ihrerseits wieder Ausdruck universeller kosmischer Grundprinzipien waren.

Musik fand nicht nur in die von der islamischen Orthodoxie bisweilen angefeindete "wissenschaftliche Medizin" Eingang, sondern sogar in die "prophetische Medizin". So galt Musik dort als "Nahrung für die Seele.

Der berühmte Arzt und Philosoph Al Farabi (870 - 950 n.Chr.) prägte den für die weitere Entwicklung der AM grundlegenden Ausspruch: *"Der Körper ist krank, wenn die Seele geschwächt ist und er ist beeinträchtigt, wenn sie beeinträchtigt ist. Daher geschieht die Heilung des Körpers durch die Heilung der Seele, indem ihre Kräfte wieder hergestellt und ihre Substanz in die rechte Ordnung gebracht wird mit Hilfe von Klängen, die dies bewirken können und dafür geeignet sind."*

Ein weiteres historisches Beispiel des arabischen Arztes und Philosophen Ibn-Hindu aus dem 10. Jahrhundert beschreibt die der AM zugrunde liegende pharmakologische Wirktheorie von Musik (BÜRGEL 1972: 243f.): *"Was aber die Wissenschaft von der Musik anbetrifft, so gehört sie in einer bestimmten Hinsicht zur Medizin ... Wer die Musik ausübt, spielt nämlich geradezu mit den Seelen und Körpern ... denn wir wissen doch generell, daß es eine Art der Melodie und des Trommelns und des Blasens und des Rhythmus' gibt, die Trauer, eine andere, die Freude hervor-ruft, eine andere, die beruhigt und entspannt, eine andere, die beunruhigt und beklemmt, eine andere, die schlaflos macht, eine andere, die einschläfert; wir verordnen bei der Therapie von Melancholikern häufig die ihnen entsprechenden und für sie nützlichen tara'iq.*

Dieses Zitat zeugt u.a. auch von der Idee der Musiktherapie als eine die Wissenschaft und Kunst verbindende Disziplin.

Im Zuge der "Assimilation" der Medizin Zentralasiens und des Vorderen Orients übernahm der lateinische Westen vom 11./12. Jh. an diese heilende Funktion der Musik. Dies war unter anderem deshalb möglich, weil viele Texte, die meist in arabischer Sprache verfasst waren, ins Lateinische übersetzt wurden.

Für die historische Entwicklung von Musiktherapie hat demnach der islamische Raum wesentliche Bedeutung. Oruç Güvenç hat 1985 in seiner Dissertation das historisch gut dokumentierte Therapiesystem erstmals aus der Sicht einer praktisch- musiktherapeutischen Perspektive für die Türkei einer wissenschaftlichen Betrachtung und Aufarbeitung zugeführt.

Seither sind die therapeutischen Effekte und die transkulturelle Wirkung dieser Behandlungsmethode in weiteren Beiträgen für den europäischen Kulturraum von GUTJAHR, BRÜGGENWERTH, WILCKEN, MACHLEIDT, GÜVENÇ HINRICHS 1993; ÖZELSEL 1995; und TUCEK 1995, 1997, 1998, 1999, 2000B, 2001 TUCEK / MASTNAK 1998 diskutiert worden.

Aspekte therapeutischer Theoriebildung und Methoden der AM heute

Die klinische Anwendung der AM fußt gegenwärtig in Europa auf drei Grundgedanken:

- Hören ist von entscheidender Bedeutung für die Orientierung des Menschen in der Welt. Deshalb vermag auch der musikalische Klang als solcher heilsam zu wirken. Dieser Gedanke findet seine konkrete Anwendung in der *rezeptiven AM*.

- Selbst- und Welterkenntnis vermag über Sinnesverfeinerung durch ästhetischen Ein- bzw. Ausdruck gefördert werden. Dieser Gedanke findet seine konkrete Anwendung in der *aktiven AM*.

- Im therapeutischen Prozess gilt es auch den Menschen in seiner spirituell-geistigen Dimension zu erfassen. Dieser Gedanke findet seine konkrete Anwendung im *Beziehungsmodell der AM*.

Allen Methoden liegt ein primär nicht konfliktorientierter Behandlungsplan zugrunde, der - ähnlich den Ideen von Homöostase in der Psychosomatik, auf dem Prinzip des körperlichen und seelischen Ausgleichs beruht.

AM wird aktiv bzw. rezeptiv angewandt. Das Methodenrepertoire umfasst rezeptives tonartenspezifisches Musikhören, aktives Bewegen und Tanz, passives Bewegt - werden, Berührung, aktives gemeinsames Musizieren, geleitete & freie Imagination, Lehrgeschichten, Poesie, künstlerisches Gestalten (Ebru, Ornamentik), Arbeit mit Elementen (z.B. Wasser, Pferd, etc.), therapeutisches Gespräch. Die Haltung des Therapeuten mag in psychologischen, philosophischen oder auch religiös - spirituellen Konzepten ihren Ausgang haben Im Erkenntnisprozess des /der Therapeuten/in, spielen rationale wie intuitive Aspekte gemeinsam/interaktiv die zentrale Rolle.

Der therapeutische Effekt der *rezeptiven AM* beruht auf der Rezeption einer

Abfolge bestimmter Modi und Melodien. Ihr strukturell-intuitiver Weg unterscheidet sich dabei wesentlich von Musikstück-Sequenz-Plänen westlicher Musiktherapien, die einen mehr analog-heuristischen Ansatz vertreten. Sie ist "allopathisch" konzipiert, folgt also dem Prinzip des physiologischen und seelischen Ausgleichs von Defiziten oder Überschüssen durch Harmonisierung und Stärkung.

In der AM dienen Musik, Tanz und spezielle Bewegungsabfolgen dazu, einen bestimmten Affektzustand auszugleichen bzw. ihn aufzuheben. "Makamen" sind neunteltönig (d.h. dass ein Ganzton in neun Teiltonschritte geteilt wird) mikrotonal ausgerichtete Tonskalen, die mit spezifischen Klangstrukturen auf einem bestimmten Grundton aufbauen und somit nicht beliebig transponierbar sind. Gemäß historischer Literatur sehen wir Zuordnungen der Makamen zu Tierkreiszeichen, Elementen, den Mischungen der Körpersäfte, den Geschlechtern, Tageszeiten und sogar zu Wochentagen. In verschiedenen musiktherapeutischen Schulen des Orients wurde näher beschrieben, welche Makam welchem Körperorgan zugeordnet ist.

Historische Grundlage der Wirktheorie der *rezeptiven AM* ist die "Ethoslehre" in der Musik: Ihr Grundgedanke in der Musik ist die Theorie einer engen, auf dem Prinzip von Bewegung beruhenden Wechselbeziehung zwischen Klang und Rhythmus einerseits und dem menschlichen Gemütsleben andererseits. Auffallend ist hier die Beziehung zur Idee der heilenden Potenz von Musik wie sie Platon in seinem naturwissenschaftlichen Werk Timaios vertritt - ein Ansatz, der sich bis ins 20. Jahrhundert zieht: das naturgesetzhaft ontische (also auch humane) Ordnungsprinzip, in Klangform Gestalt geworden, als Agens, das in die Ordnungswirklichkeit des Menschen regulierend eingreift.

Islamische Gelehrte und Ärzte verknüpften die antike Lehre vom "Ethos" in der Musik mit dem Körper - Seele - Verständnis der Humoralmedizin und gliederten die Musik fest in die Diätetik und Therapie ein.

Das Konzept der *aktiven AM*, im modernen westlichen Sprachgebrauch als "Bewegungs-(Bewusstseins)therapie" beschreibbar, besteht aus einer Abfolge zunächst festgelegter Bewegungselemente, die später improvisatorisch vom Patienten erweitert werden. (vgl. TUCEK 2000) "Therapeutische" Bewegungen haben dabei nicht nur funktionalen Charakter, wie etwa physiotherapeutisch-rehabilitative Bewegungsübungen, sondern sind darüber hinaus auch Träger und Vermittler universeller geistiger Prinzipien.

Dieses Konzept fußt historisch auf sechs diätetischen Lebensregeln, die sich bereits in Galens "Ars medica" und später bei Ibni Sina, dem "philosophischen Arzt" (wenn dort auch nicht explizit, so aber doch ableitbar) finden (vgl. TUCEK 1997). Ziel des "Riyazed" ist es, den Übenden durch eine den "gesamten Menschen" in seiner physio- psychologisch - spirituellen Dimension meinenden Bewegung in einen Zustand größtmöglicher physischer und psychischer Ausgeglichenheit zu führen und zu stabilisieren. Das Prinzip, einen Ausgleich zwischen polaren Gegensätzen zu schaffen, um so verlorengegangene Harmonie wiederherzustellen, kann als zentraler Gedanke östlicher Heilkunst beschrieben werden.

Medizingeschichtlich dokumentierte Wirktheorien belegen den Einfluss von Bewegung (ebenso wie jenen des Klangs der Musik, des Worts oder des Geschmacks/Geruchs) auf die Wahrnehmung und das Denken des Menschen. "Rituellen" Bewegungen liegen dabei in der Natur beobachtbare Phänomene wesenhaft zugrunde. In Zentralasien und anderen östlichen Kulturen führte die

Beobachtung von Naturphänomenen zur Erkenntnis des Wesenhaften, das sich durch diese (Phänomene) vermittelt. Universelle Bewegungsmuster bleiben zwar, gleich Wind- oder Wasserströmung, ihrer Form nach unsichtbar, hinterlassen jedoch die ihnen eigenen Spuren. Wechselspiele von Naturgesetz und (nicht nur kognitiver) Erkenntnis, von physikalischem Prinzip und geistigem Phänomen legen innere Zusammenhänge mit der Evolutionären Erkenntnistheorie nahe.

Anthropologische und ethnologische Erkenntnisse legen die Bedeutung von im Menschen grundgelegten Bewusstseinskompetenzen nahe, die sich in Wachbewusstsein, Schlaf und VWB unterteilen lassen (vgl. MASTNAK 1994, TUCEK 2000). Die Evozierung von VWB (verändertes Wachbewusstsein) ist ein wichtiger methodologischer Faktor in der AM.

Das tranceinduzierende Moment (kinetische Trance / Ethnotrance) führt u.a. zu einer erhöhten Ausschüttung von Beta Endorphinen sowie die spezifische Reizung des Vestibularapparates, der hier als integrativer Teil des neuropsychologischen Sinnessystems zu verstehen ist (HOLLER 1991, S. 177, 182).

Nach WINKELMANN führen "magico - religiös" veränderte Bewusstseinszustände - wie etwa kinetische Trancen - zu erhöhter Suggestibilität, die - ähnlich wie bei Tranceprozessen im Sinne Ericksons - zur inneren Veränderung früherer Konditionierungen öffnet (WINKELMAN,1990, S. 192 / 193) Derartige Dekonditionierungen früherer Denk- und Verhaltensmuster sind im Sinne einer Balance evolutionär grundgelegter Bewusstseinsqualitäten (Wachbewusstsein, Schlaf und Trance, vgl. MASTNAK 1993, TUCEK 1997) eine wesentliche Voraussetzung für körperliche und seelische Gesundheit. AM legt, gerade unter diesem Wirkaspekt der verwendeten Musik, durchgehend hohen Wert auf die ethische Reflexion therapeutischer Interventionen.

Das heutige *therapeutische Beziehungsmodell* der AM lässt sich vielfach mit dem des Pädagogen MARTIN BUBER vergleichen. Beiden Konzepten ist gemeinsam, dass es um eine schrittweise Überführung des Wesens des anderen aus der Potentialität in die aktuelle Konkretion. *" ... Einflußwille bedeutet dann (wenn der andere in seinem Wesen bejaht wird) nicht die Bestrebung, den anderen zu ändern, ihm meine eigene "Richtigkeit" einzupfropfen, sondern die, das als richtig, als recht, als wahr Erkannte, das ja eben darum auch dort, in der Substanz des anderen angelegt sein muß, dort, eben durch meinen Einfluß, in der für das Individuation angemessenen Gestalt aufkeimen und erwachsen zu lassen ...."*. (BUBER M. 1960, S. 36f)

Die konkrete Umsetzung dieses Gedankens erfordert vom Therapeuten den Patienten in Seinsdimensionen zu begleiten, die er auch selbst lebt. Grundlage für diese Forderung ist - im Sinne BUBERS und der AM - die Idee, dass jede zwischenmenschliche Beziehung letztlich ihrem Wesen nach auf eine transzendente Beziehung Gott - Mensch verweist. BUBER knüpft ebenso wie die AM das Wesen dieses eigentlich gemeinten Ich - Du - Bezugs nicht primär an eine inhaltliche Mitteilung, sondern an die durchtönende transzendente Realität. Dieser Realität gilt es im therapeutischen Beziehungsprozess unmittelbar gewahr zu werden. Hier wird der Rahmen von rein zwischenmenschlich - kommunikationstheoretischen Ansätzen um eine transzendente Dimension erweitert.

Die Integration der AM in den Westen in Lehre und Praxis

Gegenwärtig befindet sich die AM in einem kreativen und lebendigen Diskurs zwischen tradierten orientalischen Sichtweisen von therapeutischer Lehre und heutigen europäischen Standards für die Ausbildung von Musiktherapeuten. Der schrittweise *Integrationsprozess der therapeutischen Lehre in den hiesigen Kulturraum* wurde von einem mehrjährigen universitären kulturwissenschaftlichen Praxisforschungsprojekt begleitet. Die Erkenntnisse aus diesem Projekt führten u.a. zu einem vertieften Bewusstsein der Notwendigkeit von interkultureller Verständnis- und Friedensarbeit.

Da sich zeigte, dass sich einzelne traditionelle Elemente der AM nicht 1:1 in den europäischen Lehr- und Klinikbetrieb übertragen lassen ging der Autor mit einem Team von Mitarbeitern dazu über, die AM vorsichtig an gegenwärtige hiesige Anforderungsprofile heranzuführen. Heutige klinische Anwendungsbereiche liegen in den Bereichen von psychosomatischen Störungen (z.B. im gastroenterologischen, onkologischen oder kardiologischen Bereich), akuter Schmerzsymptomatik, psychiatrischen Krankheitsbildern (z.B. Depression, Angst- und Zwangsstörungen), Burn-Out-, Erschöpfungs- und Stresssyndromen, geriatrischen Problemen sowie in der neurologischen Rehabilitation nach Schädel- Hirn -Trauma. Im Sinne ihres ganzheitlichen Menschenbildes betrifft der Anwendungsbereich der AM gleichermaßen Heilpädagogik und Psychohygiene, etwa als stützende Maßnahme bei Persönlichkeitsentwicklung, Lebenssinnfindung und der Bewältigung von Lebenskrisen. Die AM verfolgt dabei als Therapieziel eine Situationsverbesserung der Patienten auf vier Ebenen, nämlich der körperlichen, emotionalen, kognitiven Ebene und sozialen Ebene. Hierbei wird bei dem Begriff "Kognition" eine Differenzierung im Sinne von Gedächtnis, Konzentration, Wahrnehmung zu Reflexion vorgenommen.

Die einzelnen Ebenen sind im therapeutischen Prozess keine streng voneinander getrennten Entitäten, sondern durchdringen und bedingen einander.

Zur wissenschaftlichen Beantwortung der *Frage nach der praktischen therapeutischen Relevanz* der AM werden und wurden *klinische Studien* in Deutschland und Österreich und der Türkei durchgeführt. Dabei ließ sich u.a. zeigen, dass sich die vor Jahrhunderten beschriebenen Wirkeffekte der AM auch bei europäischen Patienten einstellten. Dies scheint ein Hinweis auf die transkulturelle Wirksamkeit der AM

Heutige klinische Anwendung der AM am Beispiel schwerer Schädel - Hirn - Verletzungen am Neurologischen Rehabilitationszentrum Meidling

Apallisches Syndrom
Neurologisches Zustandsbild nach Schädigung der Großhirnrinde oder seiner Verbindungen zu darunterliegenden Gehirnstrukturen, während der Hirnstamm und das aufsteigende retikuläre aktivierende System ("Wachheitszentrum") weitgehend intakt geblieben sind. Mittlerweile hat in der klinischen Arbeit AM einen unverzichtbaren Stellenwert und zeigt bislang drei deutlich beschreibbare Effekte:

- allgemeine Aktivierung (höherer Wachheitsgrad, Steigerung der Aufmerksamkeit)
- allgemeine Entspannung (z.B. Reduktion der Spasmen)
- allgemeine Motivationssteigerung und Verbesserung des Wohlbefindens durch Freude.

AM im Neurologischen Rehabilitationszentrum kann im Sinne obiger Überlegungen durchaus als eine Art basale Stimulation auf psychischer Ebene interpretiert werden. Sie will die Patienten in erster Linie über die Freude ermutigen und motivieren, den langen und beschwerlichen Weg zurück ins Leben in einer lebensbejahenden Grundhaltung zu beschreiten. AM bietet dabei durch ihre spezielle Wirkweise (a.a.O.) für diese Patienten zwei wesentliche Vorteile:

- Anfangs nur rezeptive Anwendung - d.h. ohne dass vom Patienten ein aktiver Beitrag geleistet werden muss, "ereignet sich etwas in ihm".
- Möglichkeit der speziellen Einwirkung auf bestimmte Organsysteme (ebenfalls a.a.O.)

Ein weiteres von uns als wesentlich erachtetes Therapieziel der AM ist eine lustvolle Seinserfahrung des Patienten an seiner langsam wachsenden Bewegungsfähigkeit im Zuge der therapeutischen Arbeit. Dabei geht es um spielerisches und lustvolles Wiederentdecken sinnenhaften Daseins. Der zuvor beschriebene Ansatz, den Menschen als physisch - geistige Einheit zu begreifen, und durch Förderung und Stärkung seelischer und geistiger Ressourcen indirekt auch die körperliche Natur des Menschen zu kräftigen, wirkt verblüffend zeitgemäß und deckt sich mit einer modernen Rehabilitationsphilosophie, die in ihren therapeutischen Zielen eine reduktionistische Besserung rein motorischer Störungen hinter sich gelassen hat.

Die Arbeit mit AM auf der körperlichen Ebene durch:
- Bewegungsübungen
- Rezeptives Musikerleben ausgewählter organ -bzw. körperzonenspezifischer Tonarten
- Aktives gemeinsames Musizieren von Therapeuten und Patienten
- Imaginative und sensorische Körpersensibilisierungsübungen zu Musik

Die Arbeit mit AM auf der emotionalen Ebene

Vor allem in einer frühen Behandlungsphase im Übergang von der Akut- zur Rehabilitationsphase erweist sich AM als ein den Patienten psychisch stabilisierender Faktor. Erfahrungen mit AM erlauben den Schluss, dass sich der Bewegungsaffekt über den auditiven Kanal besser, weil spielerisch leicht und ohne primären Leistungsanspruch an den Patienten, beeinflussen lässt. Musikhören ist ein psychischer Akt der nur bedingt der Willkür unterliegt und stimuliert per se Bewegung ohne Leistungsdruck.

Hierbei steht prozessorientiertes Vorgehen mit Bedachtnahme auf ein möglichst freudvoll - spielerisches Erleben des Patienten im Mittelpunkt. Dieser Prozess der Motivationssteigerung wird durch Evozierung von positiven, freudvollen Gefühlen eingeleitet. Dies geschieht in früheren Remissionsphasen durch die Auswahl spezieller Tonarten und Musikstücke durch die Musiktherapeuten. Von Beginn an wird gleichzeitig versucht, mit dem Patienten eine vertrauensvolle Beziehungsebene aufzubauen, die sich zunächst auf körpersprachlichem Ausdruck gründet.

Speziell in dieser Phase ist die Intuition des Therapeutenteams gefordert, da die Patienten über weite Strecken nicht in der Lage sind, ihre Gefühle und Wahrnehmungen zu verbalisieren. In einer späteren Remissionsphase wird versucht, den Patienten über assoziative Regression in eine positiv erlebte Emotionslage der Vergangenheit zurückzuführen. Es wird biographisch zu ergründen versucht, was dem Patienten in seinen "emotionalen Hochzeiten" wichtig und wertvoll war.

Vier Aspekte werden durch aktives Bewegen und Musizieren sowie rezeptives Musikhören auf der emotionalen Ebene gefördert:

- Die oftmals angstbesetzte Rückkehr des Patienten nach einem Schädel - Hirn- Trauma in das Alltagsbewusstsein wird durch spezielle Tonarten und Musikstücksequenzen begleitet. Musik hat hier beruhigende, schützende und vertrauensfördernde Funktion. Die vielfältigen Umweltimpulse (wie Geräusche, Gerüche, etc.) überfordern die psychischen Verarbeitungsmöglichkeiten des Patienten in frühen Remissionsphasen. So dauern Musiktherapien in den ersten Phasen oft nur wenige Minuten. Die einstimmige Musikstruktur der AM scheint hier auf den Patienten ordnend und beruhigend zu wirken.

- Wiedererweckung des Patienteninteresses an einer für ihn neu zu ordnenden und zu gestaltenden Umwelt.

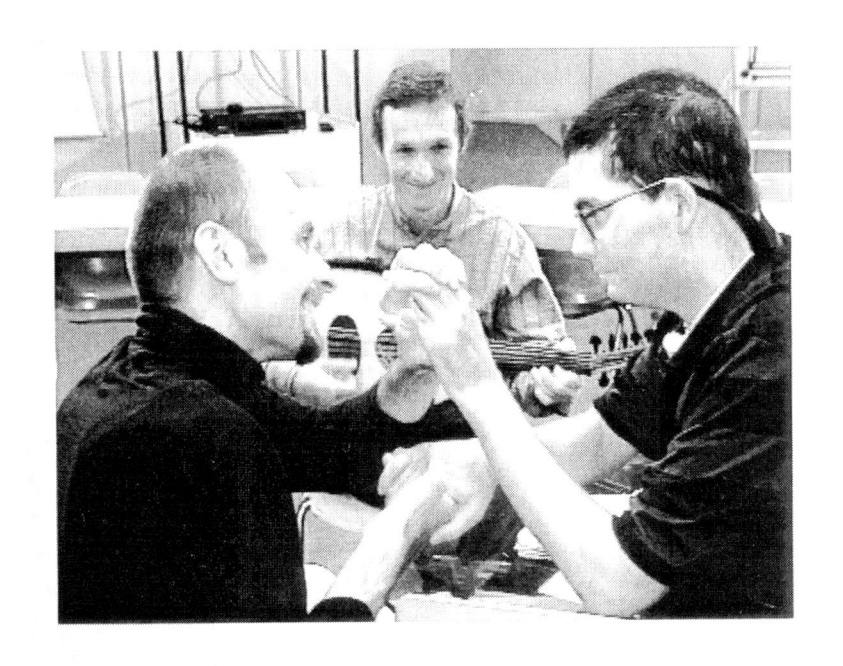

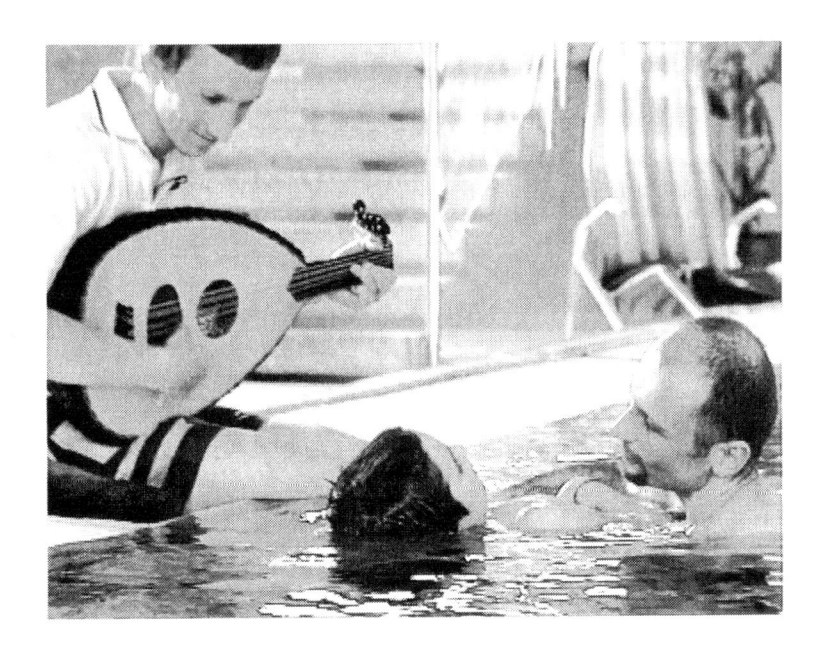

Altorientalische Musiktherapie – ETHNOMED 2002

- Emotionale Offenheit gegenüber der neuen Situation.
- Spielerisches Erforschen momentaner körperlicher Funktionskompetenzen, prozesshafte, positive Bezugsaufnahme zum Körper.

Aus der Psychoneuroimmunologie wissen wir, dass eine positive Emotionslage stärkend auf das Immunsystem wirkt und somit unspezifisch den Genesungsprozess fördert (vgl. SCHLEICHER 1997, S. 18, Abb. 4). Bei jenen Patienten, bei denen nach gegenwärtiger medizinischer Ermessenslage keine wesentliche Remission des Zustandsbildes zu erwarten ist, liegt das Therapieziel primär auf der Ebene einer Lebensqualitätsstabilisierung und -verbesserung.

Die Symbolebene

Als sehr inspirierend und förderlich zeigte sich bisher die Arbeit mit Patienten auf symbolsprachlicher Ebene. Hierbei wird vor allem die assoziative (bild- und sinnenhafte) Kompetenz des Patienten zusätzlich zur kognitiven Ebene gefördert.

- **Elementsymbolik** *Wasserklänge*: Der Patient oder Cotherapeut spielt mit Wasserschalen zu live gespielter Improvisationsmusik, indem er zwei kleinere Schalen in ein größeres mit Wasser gefülltes Becken taucht und auf diese Art das Geplätscher eines Springbrunnens imitiert. GEIER zeigte, dass sich beispielsweise eine körperliche Kontaktaufnahme zu autistischen Personen in einem mit Wasser gefüllten Becken leichter bewerkstelligen lässt. (1995)
- **Poesie und Lehrgeschichten** stellen ein Destillat aus den Gedanken vieler Jahrhunderte dar. Sie können mehrere Bedeutungsebenen haben, selbst wenn sie oberflächlich "nur" humorvoll zu sein scheinen. Wer kann z.B. lachen und innerlich angespannt bleiben? Hier schließt sich der Kreis zu einem als wesentlich erachteten musikalischen Wirkprinzip: Anxiolyse. Gleichzeitig vermag die Aussage der Geschichte in tiefere – vor- oder unbewusste – Bewusstseinsebenen vorzudringen und dabei den Raum für Perspektivenwandel vorzubereiten.
- **Imaginations- und Assoziationsarbeit zu Musik:** Zu Musikimprovisationen werden vom Therapeuten angeleitete und / oder vom Patienten frei assoziierte Imaginationsreisen in den eigenen Körper unternommen (in späteren Remissionsphasen). Dadurch soll eine Reintegration der geschädigten Körperzonen, Förderung der Akzeptanz des eigenen Schicksals sowie eine Körpersensibilisierung bewirkt werden.

Die Arbeit mit AM auf der kognitiven Ebene

Diese Ebene ist bei einer erheblichen Zahl unserer Patienten (Station der Schwerstversehrten) nicht bzw. kaum möglich, da sie in ihrem Remissionsprozess nicht kognitiv reflexionsfähig sind. Bei Patienten, bei denen diese Voraussetzung wenigstens zum Teil erfüllt ist, steht die Förderung kognitiver Verarbeitungs-

Abb. 4: Wasserklänge: Der Patient oder Cotherapeut spielt mit Wasserschalen zu live gespielter Improvisationsmusik, indem er zwei kleinere Schalen in ein größeres mit Wasser gefülltes Becken taucht und auf diese Art das Geplätscher eines Springbrunnens imitiert.

mechanismen durch ressourcenorientiertes therapeutisches Vorgehen im Vordergrund. Speziell in der Phase der bevorstehenden Entlassung des Patienten in sein gewohntes Umfeld rückt die therapeutische Bearbeitung der Frage in den Mittelpunkt, wie der Patient sein Lebensumfeld im Hinblick auf seine nunmehr veränderte Lebenssituation in Hinkunft subjektiv *sinnerfüllend* gestalten kann.

Die Arbeit mit AM auf der sozialen Ebene

Musiktherapeutische Einzel- und Gruppensitzungen verfolgen neben den bisher besprochenen Aspekten vor allem das Ziel, den Patienten durch den Prozess einer sozialen Wiedereingliederung zu begleiten. Gemeinsames Musizieren, rezeptives Musikhören und Körpersensibilisierungsübungen zu Musik sollen den Patienten in fortgeschrittenen Remissionsphasen aus einer häufigen Isolations- und reaktiven Depressionssymptomatik helfen. Wo immer es sinnvoll erscheint, bezieht AM Verwandte und Angehörige in den musiktherapeutischen Prozess mit ein.

Autor
GERHARD KADIR TUCEK, ÖSTERREICH
Leitung des Instituts für Ethnomusiktherapie, Österreich. Studium der Theologie und Psychologie in Wien, der angewandten Kulturwissenschaften in Klagenfurt und Wien und der Orientalischen Musiktherapie bei PD Dr. Oruc Güvenc, Istanbul. 1997 Entwicklung und Durchführung des interfakultären Hochschullehrgang-Pilotprojekts für Altorientalische Musiktherapie. Kooperationspartner: Hochschule für Musik in München und Marmara Universität Istanbul und Landesakademie Österreich.

Anschrift des Autors
INSTITUT FÜR ETHNOMUSIKTHERAPIE
A –3924 Schloß Rosenau
Niederneustift 66.
AUSTRIA
Tel:0043 / 2822 / 51248
Fax:0043 / 2822 / 5124818
E- Mail: ethno@Eunet.at
www.ethnomusik.com

Literatur
ANTONOVSKY, AARON. 1979. Health, Stress and Coping. Jossey - Bass, San Francisco
BLOCH ERNST. 1985. Das Prinzip Hoffnung. Frankfurt a.M. (Suhrkamp)
BUBER, MARTIN. 1997. Das dialogische Prinzip. Lambert Schneider Verlag, Heidelberg
BUBER, MARTIN. 1960. Urdistanz und Beziehung. Heidelberg
BÜRGEL, J.CHR.. 1972. Zur Musiktherapie im Arabischen Mittelalter. In: Geering-Festschrift. Bern/Stuttgart
BOURGUIGNON, ERIKA. 1973. (Hrsg) Religion, altered states of consciousness and social change. Ohio State University Press, Columbus
CAMPBELL, JOSEPH. 1996. Die Masken Gottes. Band 1 - 4, Deutscher Taschenbuch Verlag, München
DELMONTE, M.M.. 1984. Electrocortical activity and related phenomena associated with meditation practice: a literature review. International Journal of Neuroscience, 24 (3-4. 217-231
DIETRICH, ADOLF / SCHARFETTER, CHRISTIAN. 1987. (Hrsg) Ethnopsychotherapie, Psychotherapie mittels außergewöhnlicher Bewusstseinszustände in westlichen und indigenen Kulturen. Enke, Stuttgart
ELIADE, MIRCEA. 1990. Das Heilige und das Profane - Vom Wesen des Religiösen. Suhrkamp, Frankfurt / Main
ELIADE, MIRCEA. 1998. Die Religionen und das Heilige - Elemente der Religionsgeschichte. Insel Verlag, Frankfurt / Main und Leipzig
KLEIN FRANKE, FELIX. 1982. Vorlesungen über die Medizin des Islam. Franz Steiner Verlag, Wiesbaden
GADAMER, HANS GEORG. 1977. Die Aktualität des Schönen. Reclam, Stuttgart
GEBSER, JEAN. 1986. Gesamtausgabe Ursprung und Gegenwart. Band 1&2 Novalis,

Schaffhausen
GÜVENC, RAHMI ORUC. 1985. Geschichtlicher Abriss der Musiktherapie im Allgemeinen und im Besonderen bei den Türken. Band 1 der Studientexte der Schule f. Altorientalische Musik - und Kunsttherapie, Eigenverlag, A 3924 Schloss Rosenau, Niederneustift 66
HOLLER J. 1991. Das neue Gehirn. Bruno Martin, Südergellersen
HÖRMANN, KARL. 1988. Musik- und Tanztherapie - Situation und Perspektiven. In: HÖRMANN K. (Hrsg.) Musik- und Tanztherapie. Hettgen, Münster S. 7 - 20
IBN ARABI. 1994. Wer sich selbst kennt... . Eigenverlag Stiftung Chalice, Zürich
KROPIUNIGG, ULRICH. 1990. Psyche und Immunsystem. Springer Verlag, Wien
KÜMMEL, WERNER FRIEDRICH. 1977. Musik und Medizin, Ihre Wechselbeziehung in Theorie und Praxis von 800 bis 1800. Verlag Karl Alber, Freiburg
LEONARD G.. 1992. Der Pulsschlag des Universums. Scherz Verlag, München
LIPPE ZUR, RUDOLF. 1987. Sinnenbewusstsein. Grundlegung einer anthropologischen Ästhetik. Rowohlt, Hamburg
MASTNAK, WOLFGANG. 1993. Multidisziplinäres Integrationsfeld Musikpädagogik - Schnittflächen von Pädagogik und Therapie in einer polykulturellen Welt. Habilitationsschrift Universität Potsdam, Salzburg / Potsdam
MASTNAK W.. 1994. Sinne - Künste - Lebenswelten. Matus music Presov Slowakei
MASTNAK, WOLFGANG. 1995. Kultur - Abbild der Sinne; Sinne - Bild der Kultur. Zur evolutionären Not - Wendigkeit kultureller Bildung. In: Polyaisthesis Jahrbuch IV, Musikverlag Dr. Katzenbichler München - Salzburg S. 8 - 21
MIKETTA, GABY. 1992. Netzwerk Mensch. Trias Verlag, Stuttgart
NÖCKER RIBAUPIERRE, MONIKA. 2000. Vortrag anlässlich des Symposiums Musik- & Kunsttherapie Mai 1999 in Wien. In: Musiktherapie. Sammelband (in Vorbereitung, Facultas Wien)
PLATON. 1985. Politikos - Philebos - Timaios - Kritias. rororo Hamburg
POPPER, KARL R., ECCLES, JOHN C.. 1990. Das Ich und sein Gehirn. Piper
POPPER, KARL R.. 1984. Logik der Forschung. Verlag J.C.B. Mohr, Tübingen
SABOURIN, ME, CUTCOMB, SD, CRAWFORD HJ, PRIBAM K. 1990. EEG correlates of hypnotic susceptibility and hypnotic trance: spectral analysis and coherence. Int J Psychophysiol 10 (2. 125 - 42
SCHIPPERGES, HEINRICH, ENGELHARDT DIETRICH VON. 1980. Die inneren Verbindungen zwischen Philosophie und Medizin im 20. Jahrhundert. Wissenschaftliche Buchgesellschaft, Darmstadt
SCHLEICHER, P.. 1997. Grundzüge der Immundiagnostik und -therapie. Stuttgart: Hippokrates Verlag.
TUCEK, GERHARD. 1997. Ausgewählte Teilaspekte der Altorientalischen Musiktherapie. In Fitzthum, Oberegelsbacher, Storz (Hrsg.), Wiener Beiträge zur Musiktherapie. (S. 235 - 272). Wien: Edition Praesens.
TUCEK, GERHARD / MASTNAK, WOLFGANG. 1998. Musiktherapie der Türkvölker Zentralasiens. In: Christine E. Gottschalk- Batschkus & Christian Rätsch (Hrsg.) Curare Sonderband 14 / 98. VWB Verlag für Wissenschaft und Bildung, Berlin S. 97 - 100
TUCEK, GERHARD. 2000. Altorientalische Musik- und Tanztherapie. In . Hörmann (Hrsg.), Jahrbuch f. Transkulturelle Medizin und Psychotherapie 1996 / 97 Tanztherapie: Transkulturelle Perspektiven (S. 105 - 150). Berlin: VWB - Verlag für Wissenschaft und Bildung.
TUCEK GERHARD. 2000. Altorientalische Musiktherapie in der Diaspora - Die Begegnung mit dem kulturell Anderen erfahren und reflektiert anhand eines

Aktionsforschungsprojekts über den Implementierungsprozeß von Therapie- & Bildungsidealen der AM in Österreich. Diplomarbeit am pädagogischen Institut der Universität Klagenfurt

TUCEK GERHARD. 2001) Das Pädagogische Konzept der Altorientalischen Musiktherapie - Ein Praxisforschungsprojekt zur Frage "Spiritualität versus Wissenschaft?" Abschlußarbeit für den Universitätslehrgang PRAXEOLOGIE an der Universität Klagenfurt betreut von Univ. Prof. Eric Adam & Ass. Prof. Mag. Dr. Günther Stotz

TUCEK GERHARD. 2001) Qualitätsanforderungen in der Musiktherapie - reflektiert und erläutert an ausgewählten Beispielen der Altorientalischen Musiktherapie (AM). In: *Musik-, Kunst- und Tanztherapie - Qualitätsanforderungen in den künstlerischen Therapien*. Y. BERTOLASO (Hrsg.) Paroli- Verlag Münster

TUCEK GERHARD. 2001) Altorientalische Musiktherapie (AM) in Praxis, Forschung und Lehre. In: *Schulen der Musiktherapie* Hrsg. DECKER VOIGT. E. Reinhardt Verlag München

WINKELMAN M. & WINKELMAN C.. 1990. Shamanistic Healers an their Therapies - A Cross - Cultural Study. In: W. ANDRITZKY (Hrsg.), *Jahrbuch für Transkulturelle Medizin und Psychotherapie*. VWB, Berlin

WINKELMAN M.. 1990. Physiological, Social and Functional Aspects of Drug and Non - Drug Trance States. In: W. ANDRITZKY (Hrsg.), *Jahrbuch für Transkulturelle Medizin und Psychotherapie*, VWB.

ZIPS WERNER. 1998. Entprovinzialisierung der Moderne. In: *Ethnohistorie – Rekonstruktion und Kulturkritik - Eine Einführung*. WERNHART KARL R., ZIPS WERNER (Hrsg.) Verlag Promedia Wien S. 207 – 219

Fachzeitschriften, Magazine:

GUTJAHR, LEOPOLD, BRÜGGENWERTH, GÜNTHER, WILCKEN, CHRISTOPH, GÜVENC, ORUC, MACHLEIDT, WIELANT, HINRICHS, H.. 1994. Die Heilsame Wirkung der Musik – ein physiologischer Zugang. In: EEG - EMG Zeitschrift 1994 / 25 / 2 / S.126 - 129

JANTZEN, GÜNTHER. 1971. Osmanische Kranken- und Wohlfahrtspflege – Am Beispiel des Lehrkrankenhauses Bayezid II. aus dem 15. Jahrhundert. In: Sonderdruck aus Materia Medica Nordmark 1971 / 23 / 11 – 12 / S. 333 - 343

NEUBAUER, ECKHARD. 1990. Arabische Anleitungen zur Musiktherapie. Sonderdruck der Zeitschrift für Geschichte der arabisch-islamischen Wissenschaften. Band 6. Institut für Geschichte der Arabisch - Islamischen Wissenschaften an der Johann Wolfgang Goethe Universität Frankfurt / Main

ÖZELSEL, MICHAELA. 1995. Therapeutische Aspekte des Sufitums - Schamanisches und Islamisches. In: Ethnopsychologische Mitteilungen 1995 / 4 / 2 / S. 128 - 157

Tucek, Gerhard. 1995. Orientalische Musik- und Tanztherapie. In: Musik- Tanz- und Kunsttherapie 1995 /6 / 3 / S. 149 - 166

TUCEK, GERHARD. 1997. Das Menschenbild in der Altorientalischen Musiktherapie. In: Musik- Tanz- und Kunsttherapie. 1997 /8 / 3 / S. 21 - 34

TUCEK, GERHARD, AUER – PEKARSKY, ANN MARY, STEPANSKY, ROBERT. 2001. Altorientalische Musiktherapie bei Schädel - Hirn - Trauma. In: Musik- Tanz- und Kunsttherapie. 2000 / 12 / 4 / (in Druck)

TUCEK, GERHARD. 2000. in Druck Musiktherapie im Gesundheitssystem Grundlagen, Probleme, Richtungen, Perspektiven. Lehrgangsunterlage für den "Universitären Fernlehrgang für Integrative Heilkunde" der Wissenschaftlichen Arbeitsgemeinschaft für Integrative Heilkunde

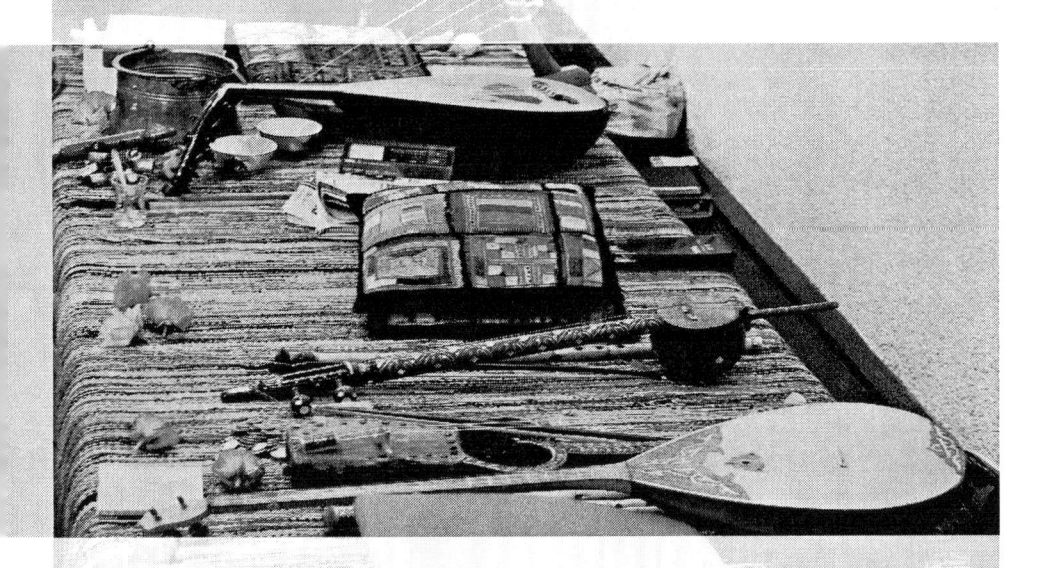

TRADITIONAL ORIENTAL MUSIC THERAPY

by Gerhard Tucek*

Traditional Oriental Music Therapy (AM) represents an empirically proven system of practical therapeutic, preventative and remedial relevance, which has been documented for approximately 1000 years.
Its roots can be found in the era of musical shamanic healing ceremonies of Central Asia, which, similar to the philosophy of later Islamic medicine, were based on the idea of a universal cosmic order manifest in the laws of nature.

The mystical dimension

Hafiz, one of the most significant Persian poets and mystics wrote about the meaning of music: *"Many people say that life was lured into the human body by the aid of music. But the truth is that life itself is music."*

Everything in Sufi thought, sentiment and conduct evolves around a central Hadith Qudsi (a non- Koranic spiritual maxim), which proclaims: *"I was a hidden treasure, longing to be recognized, therefore I created the world."*
And so the world of multiplicity came into being, thereby enabling the One-ness to reflect upon itself. From this perspective human existence can be considered the "pupil of the eye of this observation". Thus the task of humanity lies in the conscious devotion to the divine Beloved until the limited ego, dissolved in love

---

* Translated by Kat Morgenstern

and passion, merges with HIM. This idea finds expression in another non-Koranic maxim, in which God assures those who approach HIM with loving devotion 'will become the eye with which HE sees, the hand with which HE acts.' The metaphor for this image is the moth that glows as it burns in the candle's flame and thus becomes one with the fire.

Islamic mystics often considered music and dance the only adequate way to come close to elucidating the love of creation. Dschalaleddin Rumi, the great mystic of the 13th century and founder of the Mevlevi Order, which in the west became known as the order of the 'Whirling Dherwishes', made the following statement about music, poetically rephrased by Friedrich Rueckert:

Once upon a time our Lord Dschalaleddin spoke thus:
'Music is the creaking of the gates of paradise!'
Whereupon one of the ignorant fools replied:
'The squeaking of doors pleases me not'
Spoke thus the Lord Dschelaleddin:
'I hear the gates, they are opening;
But all you hear
Are the doors as they shut!'

In the early asylums and hospitals of the Seljuk Turks and the later Ottoman Empire, Traditional Oriental Music Therapy enjoyed great popularity as a treatment method for psychiatric patients. But, - on a different level - it also proved to be a kind of therapy for mystics: on the arduous and ascetic path of the mystical quest for God it unlocked the gates of paradise for those yearning for the 'unio mystica'.

This religiously motivated attitude has had a lasting impact on the historic health care system. Seen from this perspective, pain, sickness and suffering were accepted as unavoidable trials necessary for the development of character and were therefore not primarily regarded as hostile. All methods of healing, even those based on the 'profane sciences' are permeated by the idea that ultimately all health and disease is God given and must therefore be accepted in essence. Art was understood as a higher ordering principle with the task of elucidating the relationship between mankind and cosmos and thereby assisting the spirit in comprehending 'the inherent unity that underlies the unfathomable multiplicity of creation.' (see BURCKHARDT 1955). It is the human expression of a harmonically shaped environment, which bears witness to the 'divine unity' reflected in universal laws.

Similar to the way in which modern behavioural therapies place the 'healthy' parts of the personality in the therapeutic focal point, AM also still places the image of the 'whole (healthy) person' in its centre: the development of the person according to the inherent quintessential nature. It encourages each individual to develop their personal 'wholeness' by fostering a sensory openness towards outer, inner and transcendental realms. This process of realization is essentially open and does not draw sharp boundaries between physical, emotional and spiritual dimensions. The therapeutic intent, in terms of its medical purpose, aims at motivating the patient to implement principles of living as the tangible manifestations of a higher ordering principle ('e-movere').

Abiding by the religious commandment of compassion, the aristocracy and wealthy citizens of the Seljuk and Ottoman dynasties provided funding for hospitals which equally valued affect orientated and scientific treatment methods, both of which were being practiced parallel to each other. (In the modern sense, biomedical and relational treatment methods were complementing each other.) At that time, doctors utilized not only scientifically based treatment methods, but frequently also employed various artistic and aesthetically appealing, sensually affecting pleasurable delights.

Thus, such institutions were regarded as both, centres for education and healing, as well as sanctuaries of peacefulness and tranquillity. The object was to create the foundations of physical and emotional healing by means of listening to harmonic sounds, be it singing, poetry or running water, by resting in landscaped parks and flower gardens, being surrounded by harmonious interior designs and architecture, through creative self-expression with harmonically balanced colour designs, by practicing harmonically balanced sequences of physical movements (Riyazed see TUCEK 2000), as well as aromatic scents and a specifically designed moderate diet.

Apparently this demonstrates a fundamental part of human: when contemporary psychological aesthetics ceases to separate the aesthetic experiences of seeing, hearing etc. but instead speaks about interconnected sensory experiences of the one, whole person, then the trend towards artistically integrated therapies becomes obvious - therapy methods that are not separated into classical music therapy, dance therapy, art therapy etc. but instead relate the artistic media with the aesthetic senses and thus utilize the totality of the experience for the therapeutic process.

The medical history level of AM

Historic accounts from all periods of Arabic and Turkish-Islamic cultural history bear witness to the profound 'pharmacological' effectiveness of music on human beings. The theoretical conception and foundation regarding musical effects has long been considered extremely important. This historic context as well as the musical healing ceremonies of the Central Asian Bakse shamans formed an ideal breeding ground for the development of music therapy treatment methods.

Islamic doctors considered the human being a microcosm within whom all of creation is reflected. Their understanding of creation is aptly portrayed by the graphic aphorism: *"al - insan ramz al - wujud"* -" Man is the symbol of creation." Thus Islamic doctors interpreted the human body as a materialised image of the soul. Consequently they regarded the disposition of the physical body as closely dependent on mental and emotional events. In other words, Islamic medicine interpreted human beings as an organism that is both interoceptive and exteroceptive - interoceptive in terms of the inner mental and emotional processes; exteroceptive with regard to the various levels of macrocosmic hierarchies, which in turn were considered expressions of universal cosmic principles. Music was not only accepted by the 'scientific medicine', which at times was regarded with hostility by the Islamic orthodoxy, but was even accepted by the 'prophetic medicine'and considered as nourishment for the soul.

The famous doctor and philosopher Al Farabi (870 - 950 AD) coined the following fundamental dictum, which significantly contributed to the further development of AM: 'The body is sick when the soul is weakened and it is afflicted when the soul is afflicted. Thus, healing the body is achieved by healing the soul, by restoring its strength and returning its substance to proper order with the help of suitable soundsthat are capable of accomplishing this task.'

Another historical example regarding the Arabic doctor and philosopher Ibn-Hindu dates from the 10th century and describes the underlying principles of AM with reference to the theory of the pharmacological effect of music (BÜRGEL 1972: 243f.): *"As far as the science of music is concerned it should in some ways be considered an aspect of medicine...."*

Those who play music are in fact playing with souls and bodies...for it is generally known that there is a type of melody, a way of drumming and blowing and a type of rhythm that causes sadness, another that delights, one that calms and relaxes and another that agitates and frightens, one that causes sleeplessness and another that sedates; in therapy when treating depression we often use the *tara'iq'* most useful and appropriate. This quotation gives evidence to the idea of music therapy as a discipline that connects art and science.

From about the 11/12th century the Romanised Occident adopted the healing function of music as part of the process of 'assimilation' of the medical arts of Central Asia and Asia Minor.

This became possible when many manuscripts, originally written in Arabic, were being translated into Latin. Thus, the historic development of music therapy has been greatly influenced by the Arabic world. Oruç Güvenç in his dissertation in 1985 examined the historically well documented therapy system from the perspective of a practical musical therapy methodology for Turkey for the first time, submitting it to scientific examination and assessment. Since then further contributions concerning the therapeutic results and trans-cultural effects of this treatment method with regard to the European cultural sphere have been discussed by GUTJAHR BRÜGGENWERTH, WILCKEN, MACHLEIDT, GÜVENÇ, HINRICHS 1993; ÖZELSEL 1995; AND TUCEK 1995, 1997, 1998,
1999, 2000B, 2001 TUCEK / MASTNAK 1998.

Aspects of therapeutic theory formation and methods of AM today

The clinical application of AM in Europe is currently based on three principles

- Hearing is of fundamental importance to human beings with regard to their orientation in this world. Thus, a musical sound as such can have a healing effect. This principle finds its practical application in receptive AM.

- Refinement of sensual awareness via aesthetic impressions and expression can facilitate self- and world understanding. This principle finds its practical application in active AM.

- Furthermore, the therapeutic process also aims at recognizing the whole person including their spiritual-mental dimension. This principle finds practical application in the relationship model of AM.

All methods are based on a non-conflict orientated treatment plan, which, similar to the ideas of homeostasis in the psychosomatic model, is based on the principle of physical and emotional balance.

Fig. 1

AM can be applied actively or receptively. The repertoire of treatment methods comprises receptive listening utilizing music in specific keys, active movement and dance, passive 'being moved', touch, interactive shared music making, guided and independent visualization, parables, poetry, artistic expression, (Ebru, Ornamentic), work with elements (e.g. water, horse, etc.), counselling. The approach of the therapist may be based on psychological, philosophical or religious-spiritual concepts. In the exploratory process of the therapist both rational and intuitive aspects together/ interactively play the central role of importance.
The therapeutic effect of receptive AM is based on the reception of a certain sequence of particular modes and melodies. In comparison, AM's structural-intuitive way differs essentially from the method of sequencing pieces of music common in western music therapy, which has adapted a rather more analogue-heuristic approach. AM's concept is more allopathically conceptualised and

follows the principle of balancing physiological and emotional deficiencies or excesses through harmonisation and reinforcement.

AM follows an allopathic concept using music, dance and certain movement sequences to balance or counteract certain emotional states. The therapeutic effect of receptive AM is based on the sequence of certain modalities or melodies, known as '*Makamen*'. These are micro-tonally arranged scales based on a 'ninth tonality', (i.e. each full tone is divided into nine partial tones) with specific sound structures constructed on a particular base note and therefore can not easily be modulated. According to the historic literature the *Makamen* correspond with the signs of the zodiac, the elements, the combinations of bodily humours, the genders, the times of the day and even the days of the week. The different Oriental schools of music therapy have described the intricate correspondences between the *Makamen* and the various parts of the body in detail.

The historic basis of the theory of receptive AM is the "philosophy of ethos" in music: Its key notion in relation to music is the theory of a close interrelationship between sound and rhythm on one the hand and the human psyche on the other based on the principle of movement. Remarkable is the connection to the idea of a 'healing potency' of music as proposed by Plato in his scientific opus 'Timaios', an idea that has persisted up until the 20th century: the ontic (therefore also human) ordering principle based on natural laws, becomes manifest in the form of sound (Gestalt), and regulates the ordering faculty of man as a mediating force. Islamic scholars and doctors correlated the ancient doctrine of 'Ethos' in music with the body-soul concept of humoural medicine and firmly integrated music into dietetics and therapy.

The concept of active AM, which in modern terminology can be described as "movement- (consciousness) therapy", consists of a specifically prescribed sequence of movements that the patient progressively improvises and expands upon (see TUCEK 2000). Thus, therapeutic movements are not only functional in character as are for example physiotherapeutic rehabilitation exercises, but beyond that also act as agents and mediators of universal cosmic principles.

Historically this concept is based on six dietetic rules of living, which can be traced to Galen's 'Ars medica' and the later philosopher doctor Ibn Sina, (though not explicitly mentioned they are certainly inferred) (see TUCEK 1997). The aim of '*Riyazed*' is to guide the practitioner towards the greatest possible state of physical/emotional balance by stabilizing them through exercises that address the totality of the person in their physio-psychological dimension. The idea of balancing polar opposites in order to re-establish a lost harmony can be described as a key concept of oriental healing arts.

Medical history has documented the effect theories and attests to the influence of movement (as well as sound, speech, smell and taste) on the perception and thought processes of human beings. In essence, ritualised movements are rooted in observable natural phenomena. In Central Asia and other oriental cultures the observation of natural phenomena triggers the recognition of the essential nature revealed in such phenomena. Though they leave their distinctive traces, universal patterns of movement, just as air or water currents, remain invisible to the eye.

The interaction between natural law and (not only cognitive) comprehension of physical principles and spiritual phenomena suggest an inner connection with evolutionary epistemology.

Anthropological and Ethnological findings suggest the significance of inherent levels of awareness in human beings, which can be categorized as ordinary awareness, sleep and altered (awake) consciousness. (see MASTNAK 1994, TUCEK 2000). Methodologically, the evocation of altered states of consciousness is an important aspect of AM.

The trance-inducing event (kinetic trance/ethno-trance) causes increased levels of beta-endorphins as well as the specific stimulation of the vestibular apparatus, which in this context is understood as an integral part of the neuropsychological sensory system. (HOLLER 1991, S. 177, 182).

According to WINKELMANN, 'magico-religiously' altered states of consciousness, such as kinetic trance, produce a higher level of suggestibility, which, - similar to trance processes in the sense of Ericksons - opens the way to inner changes of previous mental conditioning. (WINKELMAN,1990, S. 192 / 193). Such de-conditioning of former thinking and behaviour patterns in relation to a balance between these underlying evolutionary qualities of consciousness (ordinary waking consciousness, sleep, trance, see MASTNAK 1993, TUCEK 1997) represents an essential prerequisite for physical and emotional health. Especially under this aspect of therapeutic intervention AM attaches great importance to ethical reflection concerning the effects of the music employed.
The present therapeutic relationship model of AM can in many ways be compared with that of the pedagogue MARTIN BUBER. Common to both concepts is the idea of facilitating a gradual shift of the essential nature from potentiality to actualisation. "The power to influence then, (the others' personality must be positively accepted), does not imply the attempt to change the other by imposing one's own 'righteousness', but instead to nurture the development of that, which has been recognized as correct, as true and virtuous, which therefore, by its nature, must also be potentially present in the essential substance of the other, and thus use my influence in accordance to the form most appropriate to the individuation process of the other, encouraging it to grow and develop there." (BUBER M. 1960, S. 36f)

The actualisation of such an idea demands the therapist to accompany the patient into dimensions of being, in which he lives himself. The basis of this idea, common to both Buber's and AM's philosophy, is the notion that all human relationships in their essence, refer to a transcendental relationship between God and mankind. Both BUBER and AM do not primarily tie the fundamental nature of this actually implied relationship (between the I and the other) to the communication content, but rather to the permeating transcendental reality. It is the aim of the therapeutic relationship process to become aware of this transcendental reality. Thus, a further, spiritual dimension expands the limits of an approach based on purely interpersonal communication theories.

Integration of AM in the West in theory and practice
AM is currently involved in a creative and lively dialogue between traditional oriental perspectives regarding the therapeutic teachings and current European

standards for the training of music therapists. The gradual process of integration of therapeutic teachings into the local cultural sphere has been accompanied by a practical sociological research project. Among other things, the insights resulting from this project have led to a deepened understanding regarding the need for intercultural awareness and peace work.

Since it was demonstrated that certain traditional elements of AM could not simply be transferred 1:1 to European educational- and clinical institutions, the author and a team of colleagues modified their approach to adapt AM carefully to current western requirements.

Current clinical applications fall into the department of psychosomatic disturbances (e.g. gastro-enteriological, oncologic or cardiological sector), pain symptomatology, psychiatric complexes, (e.g. depression, anxiety, obsession) burn out, exhaustion and stress, geriatric problems as well as neurological rehabilitation after cranial or cerebral trauma.

In accordance with its holistic treatment approach, AM is equally relevant to remedial education and psycho-hygiene, as a supportive measure for personality development, existentialist quests, and in dealing with life crises. The therapeutic aim of AM is to improve the situation of the patient on four levels: physical, emotional, cognitive and social. In the therapeutic process these levels are not to be understood as strictly separated entities, but rather as interdependent and interrelated spheres.

To answer the question regarding the practical therapeutic relevance of AM clinical studies have been, and are being conducted in Germany, Austria and Turkey. Among other things it was possible to demonstrate that the effects of AM, which had been described centuries ago, were also confirmed in European patients. This seems to be an indication of the transcultural efficacy of AM.

Current clinical applications of AM
eavy example: severe cranial -cerebral damage, Neurological Rehabilitation Centre, Meidling

Apallic Syndrom is a neurological symptom complex resulting from damage to the cerebral cortex or its connections to the underlying cerebral structures, while the brainstem and the reticular activating system have remained mostly intact.

AM has gained an indispensable position in terms of its clinical work and thus far can demonstrate three clearly definable effects:

- General stimulus (heightened awareness and increased attention span)
- General relaxation (e.g. reduction of spasms)
- Generally enhanced motivation and improvement of well being due to enjoyment

AM work at the neurological rehabilitation centre can in terms of the abovepoints

Fig. 2

be interpreted as a kind of base stimulation on the psychological level. Its primary aim is to encourage and motivate patients by means of joyful experiences to start the long and arduous return back to a normal life, with a positive, optimistic attitude. Due to its particular effects AM has two significant advantages to offer these patients:

- Initially only receptive application - i.e. the patient does not need to contribute actively and yet something happens within him/her
- Possibility to specifically affect certain organ systems

A further therapeutic aim of AM, which we consider to be of vital importance, is the pleasurable sensory exploration as the patients mobility slowly improves in the course of their therapeutic process. The aim is a playful and enjoyable rediscovery of the sensual aspects of life.

The previously described approach, to understand the human being as a physical-emotional unit and to indirectly affect the physical body by supporting and strengthening the mental and emotional resources, appears to be surprisingly modern and matches current models of rehabilitation theory. It has left behind the therapeutical aims of a reductionistic approach concerning the improvement of motorial dysfunctions.

The physical level of AM work through:

- Physical therapy (movement)
- Receptive musical experiences of specifically chosen tonal scales in correspondence with particular organs or body parts
- Active participatory music making of patients and therapists
- Imaginative and sensory body sensibilisation exercises accompanied by music

Emotional level of AM work

Especially in the early treatment stages, during the transition from the acute to the rehabilitation phase, AM proves to be a psychologically stabilising factor for the patients. Experiences with AM permit the conclusion that the movement stimulus can be influenced better and easier via the auditory canal, since it is handled playfully easy and without any achievement expectations of the patient.

Listening to music is a psychological activity, which is only partially compliant to the conscious will and stimulates movement impulses per se, without achievement pressure.

The focus is on a process-centred method with emphasis on creating as joyful and playful an experience for the patient as possible. Evoking positive, joyful feelings induces this process of enhanced motivation. In the earlier remission phases this is initiated by the therapist's choice of specific scales and pieces of music. Simultaneously, from the beginning the aim is to build the foundation of a trusting relationship, which at first is based on body-language expressions.

Specifically during this phase the intuition of the therapist-team is of vital importance, since the patients may not be able to verbalise their feelings and perceptions over long periods of time. In a later remission phase it is attempted to guide the patient by means of associative regression back to an earlier, positively experienced emotional foundation of the past. Attempts are made to biographically explore what had been important and precious to the patient during their previous emotional 'high times'.

Active movement and music making as well as receptive listening facilitate four aspects on the emotional level:

- The frequently fearful return of the patient to their everyday reality after a cranial-cerebral trauma is accompanied by specific tonalities and specially sequenced pieces of music. Music has a soothing, protective and trust building function. The many environmental impulses (e.g. noises, smells etc.) are too strenuous for the psychological assimilation process of the patient during the early remission phases. Thus, the initial phases of music therapy sessions may frequently only last a few minutes. The synchronous musical structure of AM appears to have an ordering and soothing effect on patients.
- Reawakening of the patient's interest in an environment that requires

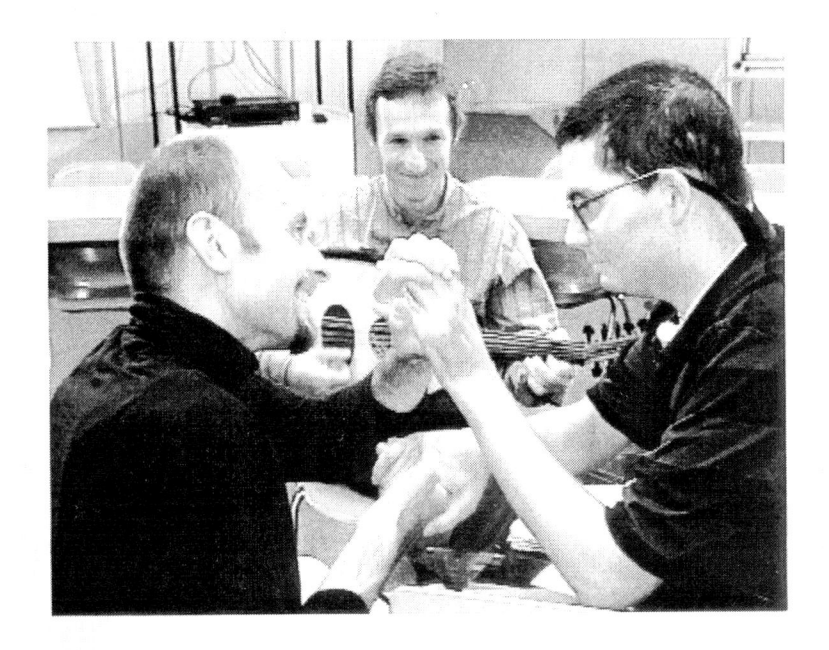

Fig. 3 a & b

to be newly ordered and re-created.
- Emotional openness towards the new situation
- Playful exploration of momentary bodily functional competences; process-orientated, positive relationship with the physical body

Psychoneuroimmunology asserts that a positive emotional attitude boosts the immune system and thereby supports the process of recuperation in a non-specific manner. (see SCHLEICHER 1997, S. 18, Abb. 4).
For patients who, according to present medical assessment capabilities cannot hope for a significant remission, therapy primarily aims at stabilizing and improving their life quality.

The symbolic level
Concerning the work with patients, the level of symbolic expression has been very inspiring and encouraging so far.
In addition to the cognitive level it is particularly the associative (imaginary and reflective) ability of the patient that is stimulated in this respect.

Elemental Symbolism
Watersounds: The patient or co-therapist plays with water bowls to improvised live music by immersing two small bowls into a larger basin filled with water, thus imitating the bubbly sounds of a fountain. E.g., GEIER has demonstrated that it is easier to establish physical contact with an autistic person in a water-filled pool (1995).

Poetry and Parables
represent a distillation of thought processes over many centuries. They can have many levels of meaning, though superficially they seem to 'only' be humorous. Who can laugh yet remains tense inside? This is where the circle closes and derives at a significant principle of musical effect theory: 'anxiolysis'. The message of a story can simultaneously reach deeper sub- or unconscious levels of awareness and thus prepare the ground for a change of attitude.

Imagination and association work in conjunction with music
Musical improvisations accompany the imaginary journeys into the body of the patient, which can be either freely associated or guided by the therapist (during later phases of remission.). The intention is to reintegrate the damaged body parts, to facilitate acceptance of one's own fate and to achieve body sensibility.

Cognitive work with AM
With many of our patients (intensive care unit) this level of work is often not at all or only barely possible as many are incapable of cognitive reflection in their rehabilitation process. With patients who at least partially meet this precondition the primary focus of the therapeutic process centres on facilitating the cognitive assimilation mechanisms using a resource orientated therapeutic approach.
Especially during the phase immediately preceding the patient's release into their normal environment the therapeutic process centers on the question of how the

Fig. 4: *Watersounds:* The patient or co-therapist plays with water bowls to improvised live music by immersing two small bowls into a larger basin filled with water, thus imitating the bubbly sounds of a fountain.

patient can re-create his environment and adapt it subjectively meaningfully in accordance to their now altered life situation.

Work with AM on the social level

Apart from the already mentioned aspects of AM, individual and group music therapy sessions primarily aim at assisting the patient with the process of social reintegration. Collective music making, receptive listening and body sensitive exercises in conjunction with music are intended to help the patient cope with isolation and the symptomatic reactive depression complex frequently encountered during later remission phases.

AM seeks to involve relatives and family members in the music therapy process wherever it seems appropriate and meaningful.

Author
GERHARD KADIR TUCEK
Director of the Institute for Ethnomusiktherapie, Austria. Study of Theology and Psychology at Vienna, Applied Anthropology at Klagenfurt and Vienna and Oriental Musiktherapy with PD Dr. Oruc Güvenc, Istanbul. 1997 Development and implementation of the interdisciplinary academic-Pilotproject for Traditional Oriental Musiktherapy. Co-operative associate: Academy of Musik in Munich and Marmara University, Istanbul.

Contact:
INSTITUT FÜR ETHNOMUSIKTHERAPIE,
A -3924 Schloß Rosenau, Niederneustift 66, AUSTRIA
Tel:0043 / 2822 / 51248
Fax:0043 / 2822 / 5124818
e- mail: ethno@Eunet.at
www.ethnomusik.com

References
ANTONOVSKY, AARON. 1979. Health, Stress and Coping. Jossey - Bass, San Francisco
BLOCH ERNST. 1985. Das Prinzip Hoffnung. Frankfurt a.M. (Suhrkamp)
BUBER, MARTIN. 1997. Das dialogische Prinzip. Lambert Schneider Verlag, Heidelberg
BUBER, MARTIN. 1960. Urdistanz und Beziehung. Heidelberg
BÜRGEL, J.CHR.. 1972. Zur Musiktherapie im Arabischen Mittelalter. In: Geering-Festschrift. Bern/Stuttgart
BOURGUIGNON, ERIKA. 1973. (Hrsg) Religion, altered states of consciousness and social change. Ohio State University Press, Columbus
CAMPBELL, JOSEPH. 1996. Die Masken Gottes. Band 1 - 4, Deutscher Taschenbuch Verlag, München
DELMONTE, M.M.. 1984. Electrocortical activity and related phenomena associated with meditation practice: a literature review. International Journal of Neuroscience, 24 (3-4. 217-231
DIETRICH, ADOLF / SCHARFETTER, CHRISTIAN. 1987. (Hrsg) Ethnopsychotherapie, Psychotherapie mittels außergewöhnlicher Bewusstseinszustände in westlichen und indigenen Kulturen. Enke, Stuttgart
ELIADE, MIRCEA. 1990. Das Heilige und das Profane - Vom Wesen des Religiösen. Suhrkamp, Frankfurt / Main
ELIADE, MIRCEA. 1998. Die Religionen und das Heilige - Elemente der Religionsgeschichte. Insel Verlag, Frankfurt / Main und Leipzig
KLEIN FRANKE, FELIX. 1982. Vorlesungen über die Medizin des Islam. Franz Steiner Verlag, Wiesbaden
GADAMER, HANS GEORG. 1977. Die Aktualität des Schönen. Reclam, Stuttgart
GEBSER, JEAN. 1986. Gesamtausgabe Ursprung und Gegenwart. Band 1&2 Novalis, Schaffhausen
GÜVENC, RAHMI ORUC. 1985. Geschichtlicher Abriss der Musiktherapie im Allgemeinen und im Besonderen bei den Türken. Band 1 der Studientexte der

Schule f. Altorientalische Musik - und Kunsttherapie, Eigenverlag, A 3924 Schloss Rosenau, Niederneustift 66
HOLLER J. 1991. Das neue Gehirn. Bruno Martin, Südergellersen
HÖRMANN, KARL. 1988. Musik- und Tanztherapie - Situation und Perspektiven. In: HÖRMANN K. (Hrsg.) Musik- und Tanztherapie. Hettgen, Münster S. 7 - 20
IBN ARABI. 1994. Wer sich selbst kennt... . Eigenverlag Stiftung Chalice, Zürich
KROPIUNIGG, ULRICH. 1990. Psyche und Immunsystem. Springer Verlag, Wien
KÜMMEL, WERNER FRIEDRICH. 1977. Musik und Medizin, Ihre Wechselbeziehung in Theorie und Praxis von 800 bis 1800. Verlag Karl Alber, Freiburg
LEONARD G.. 1992. Der Pulsschlag des Universums. Scherz Verlag, München
LIPPE ZUR, RUDOLF. 1987. Sinnenbewusstsein. Grundlegung einer anthropologischen Ästhetik. Rowohlt, Hamburg
MASTNAK, WOLFGANG. 1993. Multidisziplinäres Integrationsfeld Musikpädagogik - Schnittflächen von Pädagogik und Therapie in einer polykulturellen Welt. Habilitationsschrift Universität Potsdam, Salzburg / Potsdam
MASTNAK W.. 1994. Sinne - Künste - Lebenswelten. Matus music Presov Slowakei
MASTNAK, WOLFGANG. 1995. Kultur - Abbild der Sinne; Sinne - Bild der Kultur. Zur evolutionären Not - Wendigkeit kultureller Bildung. In: Polyaisthesis Jahrbuch IV, Musikverlag Dr. Katzenbichler München - Salzburg S. 8 - 21
MIKETTA, GABY. 1992. Netzwerk Mensch. Trias Verlag, Stuttgart
NÖCKER RIBAUPIERRE, MONIKA. 2000. Vortrag anlässlich des Symposiums Musik- & Kunsttherapie Mai 1999 in Wien. In: Musiktherapie. Sammelband (in Vorbereitung, Facultas Wien)
PLATON. 1985. Politikos - Philebos - Timaios - Kritias. rororo Hamburg
POPPER, KARL R., ECCLES, JOHN C.. 1990. Das Ich und sein Gehirn. Piper
POPPER, KARL R.. 1984. Logik der Forschung. Verlag J.C.B. Mohr, Tübingen
SABOURIN, ME, CUTCOMB, SD, CRAWFORD HJ, PRIBAM K. 1990. EEG correlates of hypnotic susceptibility and hypnotic trance: spectral analysis and coherence. Int J Psychophysiol 10 (2. 125 - 42
SCHIPPERGES, HEINRICH, ENGELHARDT DIETRICH VON. 1980. Die inneren Verbindungen zwischen Philosophie und Medizin im 20. Jahrhundert. Wissenschaftliche Buchgesellschaft, Darmstadt
SCHLEICHER, P.. 1997. Grundzüge der Immundiagnostik und -therapie. Stuttgart: Hippokrates Verlag.
TUCEK, GERHARD. 1997. Ausgewählte Teilaspekte der Altorientalischen Musiktherapie. In Fitzthum, Oberegelsbacher, Storz (Hrsg.), Wiener Beiträge zur Musiktherapie. (S. 235 - 272). Wien: Edition Praesens.
TUCEK, GERHARD / MASTNAK, WOLFGANG. 1998. Musiktherapie der Türkvölker Zentralasiens. In: Christine E. Gottschalk- Batschkus & Christian Rätsch (Hrsg.) Curare Sonderband 14 / 98. VWB Verlag für Wissenschaft und Bildung, Berlin S. 97 - 100
TUCEK, GERHARD. 2000. Altorientalische Musik- und Tanztherapie. In . Hörmann (Hrsg.), Jahrbuch f. Transkulturelle Medizin und Psychotherapie 1996 / 97 Tanztherapie: Transkulturelle Perspektiven (S. 105 - 150). Berlin: VWB - Verlag für Wissenschaft und Bildung.
TUCEK GERHARD. 2000. Altorientalische Musiktherapie in der Diaspora - Die Begegnung mit dem kulturell Anderen erfahren und reflektiert anhand eines Aktionsforschungsprojekts über den Implementierungsprozeß von Therapie- & Bildungsidealen der AM in Österreich. Diplomarbeit am pädagogischen Institut der Universität Klagenfurt

TUCEK GERHARD. 2001) Das Pädagogische Konzept der Altorientalischen Musiktherapie - Ein Praxisforschungsprojekt zur Frage "Spiritualität versus Wissenschaft?" Abschlußarbeit für den Universitätslehrgang PRAXEOLOGIE an der Universität Klagenfurt betreut von Univ. Prof. Eric Adam & Ass. Prof. Mag. Dr. Günther Stotz

TUCEK GERHARD. 2001) Qualtitätsanforderungen in der Musiktherapie - reflektiert und erläutert an ausgewählten Beispielen der Altorientalischen Musiktherapie (AM). In: *Musik-, Kunst- und Tanztherapie - Qualtitätsanforderungen in den künstlerischen Therapien.* Y. BERTOLASO (Hrsg.) Paroli- Verlag Münster

TUCEK GERHARD. 2001) Altorientalische Musiktherapie (AM) in Praxis, Forschung und Lehre. In: *Schulen der Musiktherapie* Hrsg. DECKER VOIGT. E. Reinhardt Verlag München

WINKELMAN M. & WINKELMAN C.. 1990. Shamanistic Healers an their Therapies - A Cross - Cultural Study. In: W. ANDRITZKY (Hrsg.), *Jahrbuch für Transkulturelle Medizin und Psychotherapie.* VWB, Berlin

WINKELMAN M.. 1990. Physiological, Social and Functional Aspects of Drug and Non - Drug Trance States. In: W. ANDRITZKY (Hrsg.), *Jahrbuch für Transkulturelle Medizin und Psychotherapie*, VWB.

ZIPS WERNER. 1998. Entprovinzialisierung der Moderne. In: *Ethnohistorie – Rekonstruktion und Kulturkritik - Eine Einführung.* WERNHART KARL R., ZIPS WERNER (Hrsg.) Verlag Promedia Wien S. 207 – 219

Journals:

GUTJAHR, LEOPOLD, BRÜGGENWERTH, GÜNTHER, WILCKEN, CHRISTOPH, GÜVENC, ORUC, MACHLEIDT, WIELANT, HINRICHS, H.. 1994. Die Heilsame Wirkung der Musik - ein physiologischer Zugang. In: EEG - EMG Zeitschrift 1994 / 25 / 2 / S.126 - 129

JANTZEN, GÜNTHER. 1971. Osmanische Kranken- und Wohlfahrtspflege – Am Beispiel des Lehrkrankenhauses Bayezid II. aus dem 15. Jahrhundert. In: Sonderdruck aus Materia Medica Nordmark 1971 / 23 / 11 – 12 / S. 333 - 343

NEUBAUER, ECKHARD. 1990. Arabische Anleitungen zur Musiktherapie. Sonderdruck der Zeitschrift für Geschichte der arabisch-islamischen Wissenschaften. Band 6. Institut für Geschichte der Arabisch - Islamischen Wissenschaften an der Johann Wolfgang Goethe Universität Frankfurt / Main

ÖZELSEL, MICHAELA. 1995. Therapeutische Aspekte des Sufitums - Schamanisches und Islamisches. In: Ethnopsychologische Mitteilungen 1995 / 4 / 2 / S. 128 - 157

Tucek, Gerhard. 1995. Orientalische Musik- und Tanztherapie. In: Musik- Tanz- und Kunsttherapie 1995 /6 / 3 / S. 149 - 166

TUCEK, GERHARD. 1997. Das Menschenbild in der Altorientalischen Musiktherapie. In: Musik- Tanz- und Kunsttherapie. 1997 /8 / 3 / S. 21 - 34

TUCEK, GERHARD, AUER – PEKARSKY, ANN MARY, STEPANSKY, ROBERT. 2001. Altorientalische Musiktherapie bei Schädel - Hirn - Trauma. In: Musik- Tanz- und Kunsttherapie. 2000 / 12 / 4 / (in Druck)

TUCEK, GERHARD. 2000. in Druck Musiktherapie im Gesundheitssystem Grundlagen, Probleme, Richtungen, Perspektiven. Lehrgangsunterlage für den "Universitären Fernlehrgang für Integrative Heilkunde" der Wissenschaftlichen Arbeitsgemeinschaft für Integrative Heilkunde

VOLKSGLAUBE UND PSYCHIATRIE – PATIENTEN TÜRKISCHER HERKUNFT

von Hans-Jörg Assion

Heilinstanzen der türkischen Volksmedizin

Bis heute sind in südeuropäischen, vorder- und zentralasiatischen Ländern und auch in der Türkei traditionelle Krankheitsvorstellungen verbreitet. Diese haben vorzugsweise in ländlichen Regionen Bedeutung [16]. Dennoch sprechen Menschen mit magischen Erklärungen außerhalb ihrer gewohnten sozialen Umgebung nur ungern über dieses Weltverständnis und ihre Vorstellungen. Besonders schwer fällt das im Zusammenhang mit psychischer Erkrankung: Sie befürchten, ausgelacht oder missverstanden werden [17].

Zudem sind volksheilkundliche Praktiken von offizieller staatlicher Seite nicht gestattet. Bereits 1925 wurden sie durch den damaligen Staatspräsidenten *Mustafa Kemal Pascha* - auch "*Atatürk*" ("Vater der Türken") genannt - gesetzlich explizit unterbunden [7].

Mit der orthodoxen islamischen Lehre sind volkstümliche Praktiken ebenfalls nicht zu vereinbaren. Die offizielle Lehrmeinung verbietet nämlich ausdrücklich die Auseinandersetzung mit magischen, übernatürlichen oder außerirdischen Vorstellungen. Lediglich Gottes Wille soll die wesentliche und einzige Erklärung für Krankheit sein, in die es sich zu fügen gilt.

Dennoch ist die Volksheilkunde trotz dieser restriktiven Vorgaben vielfältig: So gibt es einen reichhaltigen Glauben, dass übernatürliche Ursachen - wie magische oder animistische Kräfte (z.B. Geister oder ‚der Böse Blick') - bei der Entstehung von Krankheiten bedeutsam sind, ebenso auch Einflüsse der Umwelt. Typischerweise werden im traditionellen Verständnis Krankheiten auf von außen

einwirkende Kräfte zurückgeführt, die den Körper ganzheitlich befallen. Auch ein Durchbrechen von Tabus oder unreine Verhaltensweisen sollen krankheitsauslösend sein [8, 14].
Zum Schutz vor diesen übernatürlichen Kräfte wenden Heiler eine Vielzahl von Heilpraktiken an, ohne eine scharfe Trennung der verschiedenen Heilverfahren. Demnach gibt es Gemeinsamkeiten bei den Erklärungsmodellen und Vorgehensweisen der jeweiligen Heilinstanzen.

Abb. 1.1: Spektrum volksmedizinischer Angebote

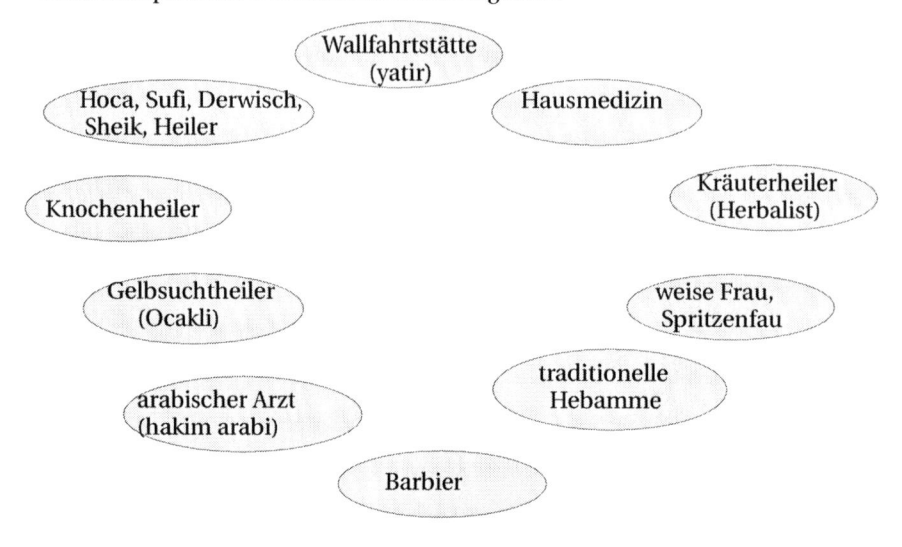

- Wallfahrtstätte (yatir)
- Hoca, Sufi, Derwisch, Sheik, Heiler
- Hausmedizin
- Knochenheiler
- Kräuterheiler (Herbalist)
- Gelbsuchtheiler (Ocakli)
- weise Frau, Spritzenfau
- arabischer Arzt (hakim arabi)
- traditionelle Hebamme
- Barbier

(nach Koen [9], Ostermann [14], Öztürk [16])

Traditionelle Krankheitsvorstellungen
"Nazar" - "der Böse Blick"
Entsprechend der weitreichenden historischen und kulturellen Bedeutung dieser magischen Vorstellung gibt es in zahlreichen Sprachen Begriffe für den "Bösen Blick": In der deutschen Sprache erinnern Bezeichnungen wie "Böses Auge", "Augenzauber", "Zauber-", "Wunder-" oder "Basiliskenblick" daran, ebenso Redewendungen, wie "jemanden mit giftigem Blick ansehen" oder "wenn Blicke töten könnten".
Im Englischen gibt es die Ausdrücke "evil eye", "bad eye" oder "ill eye", im Italienischen Begriffe wie "*malocchio*" oder "*occhio cattivo*" [1, 3, 22].
Im Arabischen und Türkischen ist das Wort "*nazar*" verbreitet, was sowohl lediglich "Blick" als auch in magischem Verständnis "Böser Blick" bedeuten kann [11, 22].
In den "Heiligen Schriften" des Koran (113. Sure) steht auf den "Bösen Blick" bezogen geschrieben: "*Ich suche Zuflucht beim Herrn ... vor dem Unheil eines Neiders, wenn er neidisch ist*" [4, 7].
Der als "*nazar*" bezeichnete Glaube an den "Bösen Blick" ist regional und in verschiedenen Bevölkerungsschichten bis in die heutige Zeit verbreitet, besonders bei Menschen mit niedrigem Bildungsstand und geringer Urbanisation [16]. Einer

der ersten deutschen Berichte aus der Türkei darüber stammt von STERN (1903) [24].
Besonders Personen mit blauen Augen und hellen Haaren wird die Fähigkeit des "Bösen Blicks" zugesprochen [8]. In dem Komplex "Neid-Bewunderung-Feindschaft" existiert dabei erstaunlicherweise auch die Vorstellung, dass gerade die nächste und engste Bezugsperson durch einen bewundernden Blick Schlechtes bei seinen Verwandten auslösen kann.
So gibt es Leute, die dem Glauben anhängen, dass eine Mutter das eigene Kind nicht mit Bewunderung und Stolz anschauen oder lobend hervorheben soll, um es vor Gefahren zu bewahren. Schädigende Einflüsse sollen dabei nicht nur visuell, sondern auch verbal vermittelt werden können [4, 16].
Der Glaube an den "Bösen Blick" geht davon aus, dass er Auswirkungen auf soziale Beziehungen hat und eine Trennung eines Ehe- oder Liebespaars bewirken kann. Er wird als Erklärung für verschiedenste Erkrankungen angesehen, wie Kopfschmerzen, Erkältungen, Übelkeit, Müdigkeit, Schwindel, Konzentrationsstörungen, Ruhelosigkeit, Kinderkrankheiten, sogar schwere Krankheit und Tod werden darauf zurückgeführt [14].
Um von einem neidvollen Blick abzulenken, wird (mehrfach) das Wort "*Mashallah*" ausgesprochen, was "Gottes Wille" oder "Gott soll es schützen" bedeutet. Auch (dreimaliges) Ausspucken, das Herausstrecken der Zunge oder Abschirmen des Blicks mit erhobener rechter Hand wird zur Abwehr böser Einflüsse praktiziert. Gegenstände werden in dem Glauben einer schützenden Wirkung besonders mit blauer Farbe bemalt. Die am häufigsten praktizierte Möglichkeit ist das Tragen eines von einem Heiler gefertigten Amuletts [4, 14, 16].

"Weiße" und "Schwarze Magie"
Seit Jahrtausenden sind im Volksglauben zahlreicher Völker zum einen die "positive", "heilige" oder "weiße Magie" und zum anderen die "negative" oder "schwarze Magie" bekannt [13].
Bei der "weißen Magie" wird mittels magischer Handlungen Schutz vor den Einflüssen von bösen Mächten gesucht. Sie wird eingesetzt, um die Familie, Beziehung oder Ehe vor unheilvollen Einflüssen zu bewahren [8].
Im Gegensatz dazu steht die "schwarze Magie" ("*büyü*"), die zum Ziel hat, jemandem bewusst Schaden zu bereiten [4].
Zahlreiche Praktiken sind bekannt, um "schwarze Magie" anzuwenden. So werden Amulette versteckt, magische Knoten geknüpft oder magische Texte gelesen. Es gibt auch den Glauben, dass dies von Zauberern ausgeht.
Die "schwarze Magie" dient in der Volksmedizin als vielfältiges Erklärungsmodell (für Missernten, Beziehungskonflikte, Unfälle und verschiedenste Erkrankungen); auch psychische und neurologische Krankheiten werden darauf zurückgeführt [14].
Zum Schutz vor magischen Einflüssen werden Rituale als "Gegenmagie" durch einen Heiler durchgeführt (*büyüyü cözmek* – ‚die Magie wieder aufmachen') oder auch Amulette (*muscas*) getragen [9, 16].

"Geister" - "Djinnen" - "Cinler"
Es ist davon auszugehen, dass der Prophet Mohammed (569-632) seiner Zeit gemäß an die Existenz von Geistern, an Magie und Zauberei geglaubt hat. Geister *(Djinnen, Cinler)* haben nämlich in mehreren Koransuren Bedeutung [7]:
"Er hat den Menschen aus einer Trockenmasse wie dem Töpferton erschaffen.

Und Er hat die Djinn aus einer Feuerflamme erschaffen."
(55. Sure, Vers 14, 15)

Djinnen sollen nach islamischer Auffassung "intelligente", aber für die menschlichen Sinne nicht wahrnehmbare "Wesen aus Dampf oder Feuer" sein, die verschiedene körperliche Gestalten annehmen können. Angeblich sind sie befähigt, sich in menschen- oder tierähnlicher Form zu zeigen (z. B. als Adler, Schlange, Skorpion oder als Wind) [6, 7].

Es gibt im Volksglauben "gute *Djinnen*" und "böse *Djinnen*", die unsichtbar und sowohl männlichen als auch weiblichen Geschlechts sein sollen und sich als schnell bewegliche Wesen während des Tags im Dunkeln, in Abfall, in Wäldern, Höhlen, schmutzigen Gewässer, verlassenen Häusern und nachts auf Friedhöfen, im öffentlichen Bad (*hammam*) etc. aufhalten.

Daraus leitet sich das Gebot ab, nicht in Müllhaufen zu stochern oder in Wasserpfützen zu urinieren, um keine (aggressiven) *Djinnen* aufzuschrecken. Flüche, Vergehen bei den rituellen Waschungen (insbesondere nach dem Geschlechtsverkehr oder autoerotischen Handlungen), Zurückweisungen der Eltern oder Verstöße gegen göttliches Gebot können den Unmut und Zorn von *Djinnen* wecken. Auch bei alltäglichen Aktivitäten, beim Ausschütten von Schmutzwasser oder beim Urinieren werden ritualisierte Entschuldigungen ausgesprochen, um sich vor ihrem Einfluss zu schützen [14, 16].

In der traditionellen Überlieferung wird den *Djinnen* nachgesagt, dass sie essen, trinken und sich fortpflanzen. Sie sollen sogar sexuelle Beziehungen untereinander haben, Kinder bekommen und in der Lage sein, Menschen zu einer sexuellen Beziehung zu verführen.

In der türkischen Sprache gibt es mehrere Ausdrücke, die mit dem Wort "*cin*" in Verbindung stehen: "*Cin carpmasi*" ("vom *Cin* befallen") meint das Eindringen eines *Djinn* in einen Menschen, um ihn krank zu machen oder "*cinler basima üsüstü*" ("*Cinler* haben sich auf dem Kopf gesammelt") für "sehr nervös" oder "überfordert"; "*Cinnet getimek*" ("bis zum Verrücktwerden").

Cinler werden schließlich häufig mit psychischen Krankheiten in Verbindung gebracht. Schizophrene Erkrankungen, wahnhafte Depressionen, Manien oder Angststörungen werden auf den Einfluss von *Cinler* zurückgeführt. *Cinler* (*Djinnen*) sollen auch die Fähigkeit haben, schweres Leid zuzufügen und den Lebensgeist zu nehmen. Schließlich werden sie sogar als befähigt angesehen, einen Menschen töten zu können [8, 14].

Demgegenüber stehen Aussagen zahlreicher muslimischer Gelehrter, die Dämonen und Geister als Aberglaube, deren Austreibung als Scharlatanerie und Angaben darüber in den Rechtsbüchern als Fehlentwicklung ansehen. Einige Koran-Interpretationen betrachten *Djinnen* dagegen wiederum als medizinische Phänomene und versuchen sogar Parallelen zu Mikroben oder Bakterien in dem Bemühen herzustellen, einen realen, nachvollziehbaren Bezug zu wissenschaftlich gesichertem Wissen zu bekommen [7].

Traditionelle Heilmethoden
Diätetische Maßnahmen
Die auf eine unzureichende oder fehlerhafte Ernährung zurückzuführenden Erkrankungen sollen durch eine bestimmte Diät, die Aufnahme oder das Meiden bestimmter Lebensmittel zu einer Linderung oder gar einer Heilung führen.

Eine besondere Bedeutung kommt dem Wasser zu, das in der Vorstellung muslimischer Menschen einen wichtigen Platz auch bei der religiös-rituellen

Reinigung hat. Ein Zuviel oder Zuwenig an Wasser oder die Aufnahme von 'schlechtem Wasser' werden durchaus als Erklärungen für Erkrankungen angegeben [8].

Bereits Hippokrates (460-370 v. Chr.) hob die Bedeutung der Lebensführung und deren Bedeutung für das körperliche Wohlergehen hervor. Er empfahl Ruhezeiten und Maßhalten beim Essen, Schlafen und Beischlafen [21]. Bis heute prägen Regeln zur Lebensführung den Alltag eines gläubigen Muslim [7].

Volksheilkundliche Methoden zum Erkennen und Behandeln von Krankheit
Es gibt eine Vielzahl unterschiedlicher Vorgehensweisen traditioneller Heiler, um eine magische Beeinflussung zu erkennen. Dabei können ähnliche Praktiken eine individuelle Ausprägung und Modifikation erfahren.

Zumeist besteht die "Diagnostik" in einem Orakel-Ritual, bei dem der Heiler durch einen Blick in den Koran, in heilige Schriften oder auf einen Gegenstand (z.B. ein Glas Wasser) die Ursache der Erkrankung zu erkennen versucht. Häufig werden dabei meditative Gebete gesprochen [9, 14, 19].

Zur "Behandlung" und Linderung von Beschwerden werden verschiedene magische Praktiken durchgeführt, wobei insbesondere das Lesen heiliger Schriften, Inkorporieren krafttragender Substanzen (Inhalieren von Rauch, das Essen oder Trinken geheiligter Essenzen), Reinigen des Körpers und Verbrennen von Dingen mit magischer Bedeutung (Buchseiten aus heiligen Schriften, Einstreuen von Salz, etc.) praktiziert wird.

Das Wort eines 'Schriftgelehrten' und das Lesen in heiligen Schriften hat im islamischen Kulturkreis aus historischen Gründen einen hohen Stellenwert. Meistens liest daher der Heiler (*Hoca*) in ritueller Weise Suren aus dem Koran oder aus anderen heiligen Schriften des Islam.

Bedeutung hat die Inkorporation von Lebensmitteln, denen während der magischen Zeremonie eine Heilkraft beigemessen wird. So bespricht der Heiler z.B. Früchte, die dann vom Ratsuchenden verzehrt werden müssen. Weitverbreitet ist auch die Praktik, Worte aus dem Koran mit Tinte auf einen Zettel zu schreiben, diesen in ein Glas Wasser oder Tee zu geben, aufzulösen und schließlich zu trinken ("Tee mit Gebet").

Mit Suren beschriebene Zettel werden verbrannt, damit der "koranhaltige Rauch" eingeatmet wird (*tütsüleme*). Bei anderen Ritualen bläst der Heiler Rauch eines verbrannten Koranpapiers ins Gesicht des Ratsuchenden, haucht oder pustet den Hilfesuchenden an.

Wasser (mit darin getauchten, beschrifteten Zettel) dient auch zur Waschung und Reinigung. Die rituelle Waschung (*kirklama*) hat als präventive Maßnahme zum Schutz vor magisch ausgelösten Erkrankungen ebenfalls Bedeutung.

Meist werden als krafttragende Gegenstände Amulette (*muscas*) empfohlen, wie im Folgenden dargestellt wird.

Amulette
Ein Amulett bezeichnet einen meist leicht tragbaren, krafterfüllten Gegenstand, dessen Kraft dort wirksam werden soll, wo er aufgehängt oder befestigt wird.

Die Kraft eines Amuletts wird entweder durch das Material selbst, durch die aufgezeichneten Bilder, Worte, Zahlen, durch Berühren geweihter Gegenstände oder durch eine magische Handlung eines Heilers (magisches Besprechen) verliehen.

Verschiedenste Gegenstände können zu einem Amulett werden (Haare, Knochen,

Steine, etc.) und in Form und Aussehen vielfältig variieren. Bestimmte Motive sind häufig, wie Augen-, Hand- und Mondamulette. Zu erwähnen sind die geschriebenen Amulette (Himmelsbriefe, Gichtzettel, magische Quadrate, etc.), wobei der Glaube an die magische Kraft von Buchstaben, Zahlen oder Wörter entscheidend ist.

Die in der islamischen Kultur und bei türkischen Heilern verbreiteten Amulette werden in einem rituellen Akt angefertigt. Die Hauptbestandteile des Amuletts sind üblicherweise in Stoff oder Leder eingenähte, mit Koransuren, Texten aus heiligen Schriften oder magischen Wörtern beschriftete Zettel, die entsprechend einer symbolträchtigen Zahl (z.B. drei- oder siebenmal) gefaltet werden. Die Amulette selbst haben oft eine Dreiecksform.

Amulette werden am Brautbett eingenäht, um Glück und Fruchtbarkeit zu bringen, am Körper eines Säuglings, einer Schwangeren oder eines Kranken getragen, um Dämonen oder Krankheiten abzuwehren.

Ein weiterer Brauch zum Einverleiben der Kraft eines Amuletts ist das Essen eines solchen ("Esszettel"). Entweder werden diese Amulette pulverisiert eingenommen oder in Wasser getaucht, das dann getrunken wird.

Amulette sollen dem Schutz oder der Abwehr vor bösen Kräften ("*Djinnen*", dem "Bösen Blick", "schwarzer Magie") dienen und somit zur Heilung verhelfen. [4, 9, 11, 14].

Blei- und Zinngießen

Das Ausgießen von erhitztem Blei oder Zinn in Wasser (*kursun dökme*) wird im Rahmen eines rituellen Aktes als Methode zum Erkennen von schädigenden Einflüssen, Bestimmen der Ursachen von Krankheiten und Fernhalten oder Vertreiben von 'bösen Kräften' eingesetzt. Es besteht die Vorstellung, dass dadurch *Djinnen* ferngehalten, der 'Böse Blick' abgewehrt, '*Büyü*' neutralisiert und Zauberei abgewehrt werden können. Die Riten sind regional unterschiedlich. Meist erfolgt eine Deutung der im Wasser erstarrten Bleiformen [8].

Eigene Untersuchung

Die von uns durchgeführte Erhebung an 105 Patienten türkischer Herkunft, die sich in ambulanter oder stationärer psychiatrischer Behandlung befanden, ging der Frage nach, welche Bedeutung die dem Volksglauben entlehnten Heilinstanzen haben. Es sollte die Inspruchnahme traditioneller Heilkundiger evaluiert und die volksmedizinischen Krankheitskonzepte und -vorstellungen erfragt werden.

Die Befragung erfolgte als semistrukturiertes Interview und berücksichtigte verschiedene Themenbereiche (Soziodemographische Daten, Angaben über Familie, Herkunft und Migration, Religiosität, psychische Erkrankung, Krankheitsvorstellungen und -konzepte, volksheilkundliche Inanspruchnahme).

Ergebnisse

Es wurden jeweils gleich viele Frauen wie Männer befragt, der Altersdurchschnitt betrug 36,5 Jahre (17 bis 69 Jahre). Die Mehrzahl wurde in der Türkei geboren und wuchs auf dem Land auf (66%), nur ein Zehntel lebte von Geburt an in Deutschland. Die Mehrzahl der Patienten hatte eine Volks- oder Hauptschulbildung (61%); sie waren meist verheiratet (70%) und bekannten sich überwiegend zum Islam (82%).

Der Erstkontakt zu Heilern erfolgte überwiegend auf Anraten der Familie oder der

Abb. 1:
Amulette
in
Dreiecksform

näheren Verwandtschaft (60%); besonders häufig kam die Empfehlung von der Mutter, dem Lebensgefährten oder Ehepartner.
Häufig hatten die Patienten zwei bis fünf Kontakte zu einem Heiler, ein Viertel sogar öfter. Männer suchten dabei weniger häufig als Frauen einen Heiler auf. Die häufigste Begründung dafür war die psychische Erkrankung, aber auch Ehe- und Familienprobleme, die Erwartung, die eigene Zukunft vorausgesagt zu bekommen oder Sorgen bezüglich der Treue des Partners.
Dabei hatte ein Viertel aller Patienten eine positive Meinung über traditionelle Heilverfahren, mehr als ein Drittel eine neutrale Einstellung, doch ein Drittel eine negative Haltung dazu. Nach der Einschätzung der Patienten war die Einstellung der Volksheiler zur "westlichen Medizin" eher neutral oder positiv, nur ein Zehntel bewertete deren Haltung als negativ. Die Patienten gingen davon aus, dass Volksheiler der Einnahme von Medikamenten eher aufgeschlossen gegenüber stehen, und nur wenige Patienten vermuteten eine negative Haltung der Volksheiler zu medikamentöser Behandlung (8%).

Ritualisierte Handlungen der Volksheiler
Nach den Berichten der Patienten war das Vorgehen der Volksheiler zum Erkennen von magisch-mystischen Einflüssen unterschiedlich. Meist erfolgte zunächst ein Gespräch, dann wurde in Stille oder laut ein religiöser Text (Koran, heilige Schrift) verlesen oder ritualisierte Aussprüche getan. Es wurde auch heißes, flüssiges Blei ausgegossen und die Formen zur Deutung herangezogen. Einige Patienten berichteten über komplexe ritualisierte Zeremonien, bei denen verschiedene Gegenstände eingesetzt wurden.

Volksmedizinische Empfehlungen
Die Ratschläge der Volksheiler waren vielfältig. Am häufigsten wurde empfohlen, ein Amulett zu tragen (62%), "geweihtes Wasser" einzunehmen oder im Koran, oder in den heiligen Schriften zu lesen. Es wurden auch seltene oder individuelle Ratschläge gegeben: Tragen oder Aufbewahren eines oder mehrerer Amulette, Einnahme oder Applikation von "geweihtem Wasser", Lesen von Korantext, Gebet, Besuch einer Moschee, Riechen an ausgesuchten Körnern oder Gräsern, Tee heilbringender Pflanzen, Einnahme von "geweihtem Zucker", Tragen eines "geweihten Fadens", Überqueren einer bestimmten Brücke, Aufsuchen eines heiligen Grabes, Erde von der Stelle besorgen, an der Geister in den Patienten eindrangen, Güsse mit Meerwasser, Verschnüren von Haaren, Aufenthalt in der Türkei, etc.
Die meisten Patienten befolgten die Empfehlungen der Volksheiler (76%) und nur wenige unterließen dies vollständig. Die volksheilkundlichen Ratschläge wurden meistens durch Geldgaben entgolten.

Kasuistik: "Magisches Ritual"
Aus dem Bericht einer 58-jährigen Frau mit rezidivierenden depressiven und manischen Episoden, die seit 8 Jahren in nervenärztlicher Behandlung ist und mehrfach stationär behandelt wurde:
Sie habe schon sehr oft einen *Hoca* wegen zeitweiser trauriger Stimmung aufgesucht. Dann habe sie aber auch Phasen mit verändertem Zeitgefühl und gehe bereits früh am Morgen, gegen 4.00 Uhr durch die Stadt, um Leute zu besuchen. Von den *Hocas* habe sie ein Amulett, aber auch "geweihtes" Wasser und verschiedene Pflanzen bekommen. Einmal habe sie zusammen mit drei anderen Frauen über mehrere Tage in einer Moschee übernachten müssen. Dabei sei ein Ritual praktiziert worden, bei dem man ein Tablett mit Brot, Salz Zwiebel, Kamm und Spiegel, sowie eine Schüssel mit Leitungswasser benötigt habe. In das Wasser sei geschmolzenes Metall gegossen worden, um aus den Formen den Ursprung der Erkrankung zu erkennen. Davon habe der *Hoca* abgeleitet, dass sie sich beim Monduntergang erschrocken habe, was ein *Cin* (Geist) bewirkt habe.
Amulett und Wasser seien aber bisher nicht hilfreich gewesen und auch der Arzt helfe ihr nicht.

Diskussion

Die türkische Bevölkerungsgruppe ist die größte ausländischer Herkunft in Deutschland und hat somit eine große gesundheitspolitische und sozialmedizinische Bedeutung [15]. Daraus ergibt sich, dass auch die Auseinandersetzung mit transkulturellen und migrationsspezifischen Fragen für eine verständnisvolle ärztliche, psychologische und soziale Versorgung wichtig ist.
Auffällig ist, dass bei somatischen Krankheiten eher schulmedizinische Therapeuten aufgesucht werden, bei psychischen Störungen hingegen häufiger Heiler, Heilpraktiker und traditionelle Heilinstanzen [26]. Koptagel-Ilal erklärte das mit der Schwierigkeit, sich bei einer psychischen Erkrankung zu öffnen und sich "aufzuschließen" [10].
So nahmen in einer von ÖZTÜRK veröffentlichten Erhebung an der Universitätsklinik von Ankara/Türkei 60 von 100 psychiatrischen Patienten einen volksmedizinischen Heiler in Anspruch. Ungefähr die Hälfte suchten diese wiederum mehrfach auf [16].

In einer anderen Untersuchung am Stadtrand von Istanbul berichtete KOEN über Binnenmigrantinnen (36 Frauen eines "*Gecekondu*"), dass 77% dieser Frauen mindestens einmal einen "*Hoca*", Wallfahrtsstätten (63%), Knochenheiler (25%) oder Gelbsuchtheiler (22%) aufgesucht hatten. Die westliche Medizin wurde meistens parallel dazu (von zwei Drittel der Patientinnen) in Anspruch genommen [9].

Die beiden in der Türkei durchgeführten Erhebungen lassen vermuten, dass auch in Deutschland lebende türkische Migranten traditionellen Vorstellungen anhängen und Volksheiler aufsuchen. Bisher gibt es darüber aber nur wenige Untersuchungen, die wissenschaftlichen Beiträge beschränken sich auf kasuistische Darstellungen oder wenige, meist retrospektive Erhebungen [6, 18].

RUHKOPF & ZIMMERMANN wiesen in ihrer Untersuchung daraufhin, dass türkische Migranten zwischen "*Hoca*-" und "Ärztekrankheit" unterscheiden, als Ausdruck dafür, wer am ehesten als geeignet angesehen wird, die betreffende Erkrankung zu behandeln, ohne dass diesen Begriffen ein definiertes Konzept zugrunde liegt. Zu den "*Hoca*-Krankheiten" zählen (wahllos) verschiedene - meist psychische - Erkrankungen [20].

RÖDER & OPALIC stellten am Beispiel von vier Patienten "das Ausmaß und die Vielschichtigkeit der *Hodschas*" dar. Anhand dieser Berichte verdeutlichten sie die unterschiedlichen Möglichkeiten einer Einflussnahme durch türkische Heiler und das durchaus hohe Ansehen, das sie bei den Patienten und deren Familien genießen. Heiler haben für Patienten eine nicht zu unterschätzende subjektive Bedeutung und Einfluss auf deren Meinungsbildung. Die Intensität der Beziehung spiegelt sich dabei auch in der Häufigkeit der Kontakte zum Heiler wieder. Doch auch bei wenigen Kontakten kann eine starke (emotionale) Bindung zu einem Heiler bestehen und dessen Einfluss groß sein.

In einem weiteren Beitrag berichtete RÖDER über 20 psychisch kranke Patienten türkischer Abstammung, von denen "mindestens elf einmal einen *Hoca* in der Bundesrepublik" aufgesucht hatten [19].

Die Schwierigkeiten, über traditionelle Praktiken Informationen zu erhalten und die Notwendigkeit geeigneter Fragen über den Volksglauben - sofern man solche Einflüsse nicht übersehen will -, wird aus der Untersuchung von KROEGER (1986) deutlich: Von 288 befragten türkischen Arbeiterfamilien im Rhein-Neckar-Kreis gab lediglich eine Person an, bei einem Heiler (*Hoca*) gewesen zu sein [12].

Zu anderen Ergebnissen kommt dagegen eine Befragung durch einen in Deutschland tätigen türkischen Arzt, nahezu alle der 52 befragten (psychiatrischen) Patienten türkischer Herkunft hatten Kontakt zu einem Heiler und trugen ein Amulett [6].

RUHKOPF & ZIMMERMANN (1987) befragten 76 türkische Eltern über deren Krankheits- und Therapieverständnis bezüglich ihres Kindes während einer Behandlung in der pädiatrischen Klinik der Universität Freiburg. In dieser dreiteilig angelegten Untersuchung wurden u.a. auch die Einstellungen zu volksmedizinischen Therapiekonzepten und die persönlichen Erfahrungen mit Volksheilern erfragt.

Ein Drittel der Eltern gab an, wegen der Krankheit ihres Kindes volksmedizinische Heilmethoden - besonders solche mit magischem Charakter - in Anspruch genommen zu haben. Von den Autoren wurde dieser Anteil wegen der bekannten Scheu der Eltern, sich über traditionelle Vorstellungen zu äußern, noch höher vermutet [20].

Bei den 105 Patienten der vorliegenden Untersuchung war auffällig, dass überwiegend Angehörige oder Bekannte das Aufsuchen eines Heilers anregten. Bekanntlich hat das soziale Umfeld bei der Symptomwahrnehmung eine herausragende Bedeutung. Krankheit wird dabei im Rahmen des kulturellen Konzepts gesehen. Bei vermuteter magischer Auslösung wird somit die Aufforderung nachvollziehbar, dass Eltern und Familienangehörigen einen Heiler empfehlen.

OSTERMANN berichtete in diesem Zusammenhang: "Dort, wo die westliche Medizin keine Erfolge zeigt - wie im Falle chronischer oder psychosomatischer Erkrankungen - gewinnen die traditionell geprägten Krankheitsvorstellungen wieder an Bedeutung." [14]

Begünstigt wird dies durch das prinzipielle Vorgehen in der Volksheilkunde, den familiären Kontext zu bewahren und in die Behandlung einzubeziehen.

Harding wies in diesem Zusammenhang auf das traditionelle Erklärungsmodell, dass geistige oder psychische Krankheiten als eine Störung des Erkrankten zu seinem sozialen Umfeld oder der belebten Natur (mit Geistern und Dämonen) versteht. Aus dieser Vorstellung resultiert, dass eigentlich nicht die Erkrankung einer Behandlung bedarf, sondern Ausdruck einer gestörten Wechselwirkung zur Umwelt ist, die es zu korrgieren gilt [2].

Damit wird die Erkrankung ebenso zu einer Angelegenheit für die Familie oder Gemeinde, wie für den Symptomträger. Türkische Migranten sehen sich dabei "sehr stark als Teil der Gemeinschaft und der sozialen Struktur" [14].

Über Dreiviertel der Patienten kamen in unserer Untersuchung den volksheilkundlichen Ratschlägen vollständig oder zumindest teilweise nach. Dabei bestand eine erstaunliche Diskrepanz zwischen der generellen Einstellung gegenüber den Heilmethoden und der Bereitschaft, diese Ratschläge tatsächlich zu befolgen, denn nur ein Viertel hatte eine eindeutig positive Meinung über traditionelle Heilmethoden.

Dabei war die Einstellung der (meist älteren) Familienangehörigen zu traditionellen Heilmethoden deutlich positiver als die der (jüngeren) Patienten. Hieran lässt sich ein Wandel in der Bedeutung traditioneller Vorstellungen erkennen.

Bei der jüngeren Generation werden diese Vorstellungen durch den besseren Zugriff auf moderne schulmedizinische Angebote und die Einflüsse der westlichen Kultur zurückgedrängt, bei der älteren - noch mehr mit den Traditionen des Heimatlands vertrauten - Generation sind die volksmedizinischen Bezüge dagegen stärker. Allerdings wird besonders bei psychischen oder neurologischen Störungen wiederum auch in der jüngeren Generation auf traditionelle Verfahren zurückgegriffen, besonders, wenn wegen eines chronischen Verlaufs schulmedizinisch keine vollständige Heilung erreichbar oder eine zufriedenstellende Besserung möglich ist [20].

Angesichts einer gewissen Anzahl von Heilern mit einer ablehnenden Haltung gegenüber der westlichen Medizin wäre eine Interferenz mit der schulmedizinischen Behandlung zu erwarten. Demgegenüber steht aber die praktische Erfahrung, dass türkische (psychiatrische) Patienten die ärztlich verordneten Therapien - bis auf wenige Ausnahmen - bereitwillig akzeptieren und durchführen.

Folglich sollte die gleichzeitige Inanspruchnahme volksmedizinischer Heilmethoden neben der ärztlichen Behandlung toleriert werden. Es ist zudem

Fakt, dass viele Patienten parallel zur Schulmedizin traditionelle Verfahren in Anspruch nehmen [6, 19].

Volksheiler kommen dabei dem Patienten entgegen, weil sie Erkrankungen auf vertraute, herkömmliche Erklärungsmuster außerhalb des Verantwortungsbereichs des Patienten zurückführen (*djinnen, nazar,* etc.), während Ärzte andere, für den Patienten weniger nachvollziehbare Erklärungsmodelle haben und biologische Prozesse oder Verhaltensweisen des Patienten als ursächlich ansehen.

Autor
PRIV.- DOZ. DR. MED. HANS-JÖRG ASSION
Westfälisches Zentrum für Psychiatrie und Psychotherapie Bochum, Universitätsklinik
Arzt für Neurologie, Psychiatrie und Psychotherapie, Ärztliche Tätigkeiten an den Universitäten Bonn und Bochum; seit 1998 Oberarzt am Westfälisches Zentrum für Psychiatrie der Ruhr-Universität Bochum. Oberärztliche Leitung des Akutbereichs und der rehabilitativen Stationen. Wissenschaftliche Arbeiten über transkulturelle Psychiatrie, schizophrene Psychosen und psychopharmakologische Themen.
Kontakt: E-Mail: WZfPP-Bochum@wkp-lwl.org

Literatur
1. FOULKS, E., FREEMAN, D., KASLOW, F., MADOW, L.: THE ITALIAN EVIL EYE: MAL OCCHIO. J *Operational Psychiat* 8,2 (1977) 28-34.
2. HARDING T.W.: *Traditional healing methods for mental disorders.* WHO Chronicle 31 (1977) 436-440.
3. HAUSCHILD, Th.: *Der Böse Blick.* Verlag Mensch und Leben, Berlin 1982.
4. HOVORKA, O.V., KRONFELD, A.: *Vergleichende Volksmedizin. Eine Darstellung volksmedizinischer Sitten und Gebräuche, Anschauungen und Heilfaktoren, des Aberglaubens und der Zaubermedizin.* Von STRECKER & SCHRÖDER, Stuttgart 1908.
5. HUGHES, Th. P.: *Lexikon des Islam.* Fourier, Wiesbaden 1995.
6. KARTAL, R.: Probleme und Besonderheiten bei der Akut- und Langzeitbehandlung türkischer Patienten. In: HEINRICH K (Hrsg.) *Leitlinien neuroleptischer Therapie.* Springer, Berlin-Heidelberg-New York 1990, 173-183.
7. KHOURY, A.T., HAGEMANN, L., HEINE, P., et al.: *Islam-Lexikon. Geschichte-Ideen-Gestalten.* Herder, Freiburg-Basel-Wien 1991.
8. KOEN, E.: *Die Bedeutung des informellen medizinischen Sektors und traditionellen Krankheitsvorstellungen in der Türkei.* Med. Dissertation. Heidelberg 1986.
9. KOEN, E.: Krankheitskonzepte und Krankheitsverhalten in der Türkei und bei Migrantinnen in Deutschland: ein Vergleich. *Curare* 9 (1986) 129-136.
10. KOPTAGEL-ILAL, G.: Behandlung der eingewanderten Türken in Westeuropa. *Curare* 9 (1986) 155-160.
11. KRISS, R., KRISS-HEINRICH, H.: Volksglaube im Bereich des Islam. Band II - *Amulette, Zauberformeln und Beschwörungen.* Otto Harrassowitz, Wiesbaden 1962.
12. KROEGER, A., KOEN, E., WEBER, W., STREICH, K.: *Der Umgang mit Krankheit in*

türki-schen und deutschen Arbeitnehmerfamilien. Heidelberg 1986.
13. LEHMANN, A.: Aberglaube und Zauberei. *Von den ältesten Zeiten an bis in die Ge-genwart.* Ferdinand Enke, Stuttgart 1925.
14. OSTERMANN, B.: *Wer versteht mich? Der Krankheitsbegriff zwischen Volksmedizin und High Tech.* Verlag für Interkulturelle Kommunikation, Frankfurt 1990.
15. ÖZELSEL, M.: *Gesundheit und Migration. Eine psychologisch-empirische Untersuchung an Deutschen sowie Türken in Deutschland und der Türkei.* München 1990.
16. ÖZTÜRK, O.M.: Folk treatment of mental illness in Turkey. In: A. KIEV (ed.): *Magic, Faith & Healing.* Free Press Glencoe, London (1964) 343-363.
17. PORTERA, A.: Psychotherapeutische und beraterische Interventions-möglichkeiten bei italienischen Klienten mit magischen Vorstellungen. In: JAEDE, W., PORTERA, A. (Hrsgg.) *Ausländerberatung: Kulturspezifische Zugänge in Diagnostik und Therapie.* Lambertus, Freiburg 1986.
18. RÖDER, F., OPALIC, P.: Der Einfluss des Hodschas (magischer Heiler) auf türkische psychiatrische Patienten in der Bundesrepublik - Eine Auswertung klinischer Fallbei-spiele. *Psychiat Prax* 14 (1987) 157-162.
19. RÖDER, F.: Die Bedeutung der Hodschas für die Betreuung türkischer psychiatrischer Patienten. In: JÄDE, W., PORTERA, A. (Hrsgg.) *Ausländerberatung. Kulturspezifische Ansätze in Diagnostik und Therapie.* Lambertus, Freiburg (1986) 127-137.
20. RUHKOPF, H., ZIMMERMANN, E., BARTELS S.: Das Krankheits- und Therapieverständnis türkischer Migranten in der Bundesrepublik Deutschland. In: NESTMANN, F., NIEPEL, T. (Hrsg.): *Beratung von Migranten. Neue Wege der psychosozialen Versorgung.* VWB, Berlin 1993.
21. SCHOTT, H.: *Die Chronik der Medizin.* Chronik Verlag, Dortmund 1993.
22. SELIGMANN, S: *Der böse Blick und Verwandtes. Ein Beitrag zur Geschichte des Aberglaubens aller Zeiten und Völker.* Barsdorf, Berlin 1910.
23. SEN, F., GOLDBERG, A.: *Türken in Deutschland. Leben zwischen zwei Kulturen.* C.H. Beck, München 1994.
24. STERN, B.: *Medizin, Aberglaube etc. in der Türkei.* Berlin 1903.
25. SUZUKI, P-T.: Social Work, Culture-Specific Mediators, and Delivering Services to Aged Turks in Germany and Aged Chinese in San Francisco. *Int Soc Work* 21 (1978) 19.
26. WEBER, W., STREICH, K., KROEGER, A.: Die Inanspruchnahme von Gesundheitsdiensten durch türkische und deutsche Arbeiterfamilien in einem süddeutschen Landkreis. *Curare* 9 (1986) 171-178.

ETHNIC BELIEF AND PSYCHIATRY – PATIENTS OF TURKISH ORIGIN*

by Hans-Jörg Assion

Healing categories of the turkish ethnomedicine

Traditional conceptions of illness are wide spread in south European and middle Eastern/ Central Asian countries, as well as in Turkey.

Nevertheless, people with magical explanations do not like to speak about their world view and their ideas outside their social environment. This is particularly difficult in connection with mental disease.

This is particularly difficult in connection with mental disease. People fear to be misunderstood or to be laughed at. [17] Moreover ethnopharmacological methods are not allowed by the government.Already by 1925 they were legally stopped by the state president Mustafa Kemal Pascha (also called "*Atatürk*"=Father of the Turks) already. [7] Traditional methods are not to be agreed upon with orthodox islamic teachings as well. The official doctrine explicitly forbids discussion of magical, supernatural or extraterrestial conceptions.

Only gods will should be the substantial and the only explanation for illness, into which needs to be accepted.. Nevertheless ethnopharmacology practiced widly despite of these restrictive specifications. It is often believed that supernatural causes like magic or animistic forces (e. g. spirits or the "*evil eye*") , as are environmental influences, are significant for the emergence of diseases.

In the traditional belief diseases are traced back to an outer force that strikes the

---

* Translated by Dominik Schweizer. Revised by Joy C. Green.

entire body. To break a taboo or unchaste behavior can cause diseases for example. In order to protect people from these supernatural forces, healers use a huge number of healing treatments, without a sharp separation between different methods. Therefore the explanation models and healing procedures of the different healing pracctitioners are overlapping.

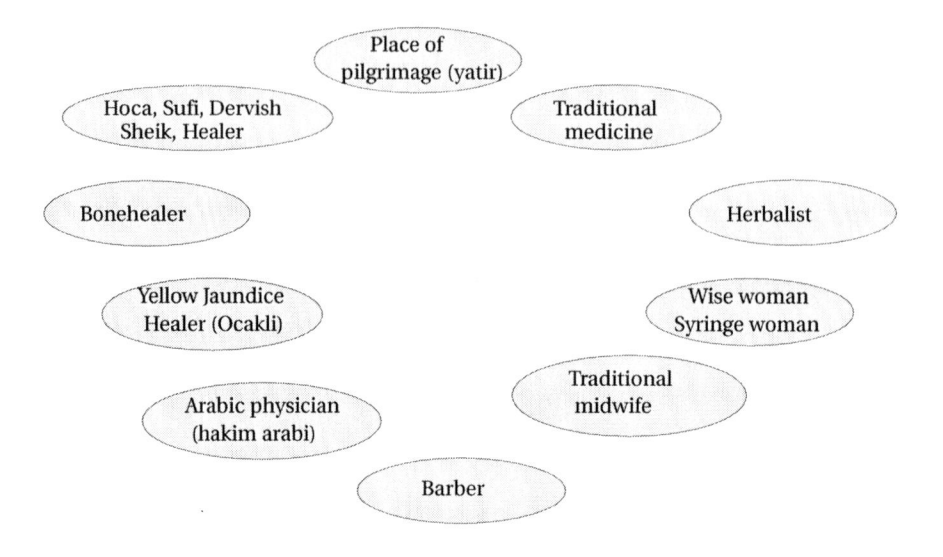

- Place of pilgrimage (yatir)
- Hoca, Sufi, Dervish Sheik, Healer
- Traditional medicine
- Bonehealer
- Herbalist
- Yellow Jaundice Healer (Ocakli)
- Wise woman Syringe woman
- Arabic physician (hakim arabi)
- Traditional midwife
- Barber

Fig. 1. 1: Spectrum of ethnomedical offers according to (KOEN [9], OSTERMANN[14], ÖZTÜRK[16])

Traditional conceptions of illness

"Nazar"- the "evil eye"

Corresponding to the far-reaching historical and cultural meaning of this magical conception, numerous languages have terms for the "evil eye":
in the German language descriptions like "*böses Auge*" (evil eye), "*Augenzauber*" (eye magic), "*Zauber-*" (magic), "*Wunder-*" (miracle) or "*Basilikenblick*" (basilic look), as well as idioms like "*jemand mit giftigem Blick ansehen*" (to give somebody a bad look) or "*wenn Blicke töten könnten*" (if looks could kill).
In English you find sayings like "*evil eye*", "*bad eye*" or "*ill eye*", in Italian "*malocchio*" or "*occhio cattivo*" (1,3,22). In Arabic or Turkish the word "*nazar*" is used, which can only mean "look" as well as "*bad look*". (11,22)
In the wholy writings of the koran (113,Sure) you find about the "evil look": "I search for shelter in GOD....befor the harm of an envier, when he is envious." (4,7)
The belief in the evil look ("*nazar*") is widly spread in certain social populations, especially those with less education and in rural areas.(16) One of the first German reports from Turkey about this subject is to be found by STERN (1903) (24). Particularly persons with blue eyes and fair hair are said to have the ability of the "*evil eye*". [8]

You find people that believe a mother should not look upon her own child with pride or admiration to protect it from danger.And that negative influences are not only caused visually but also verbally.(4,16) The belief in the "*evil eye*" assumes that it has effects on social relations and can cause for example a separation of a couple.It is regarded as an explanation for various symptoms like headache, cold, nausea, tiredness, swindles, concentration disturbances, restlessness, teeth troubles, even severe illness and death. [14]

In order to divert an envious look the word "*Marshallah*" is spoken out loud several times, which means "gods will" or "god protect it". Also spitting three times, sticking out the tongue or screening through raising the right hand is practiced to ward off bad influences. Objects are painted particularly with blue colour to provide a protecting effect. The most frequent practice is wearing an amulet made by a healer. [4, 14, 16]

"White" magic and "Black" magic

For thousands of years , the "positive" or "white" magic on the one hand and the "negative" or "black" magic on the other hand is known in the ethnic belief of various folks. [13]

The "white" magic, protection against the influence of evil forces, is searched for through magical actions. It is practiced to protect family, relationships or marriage from bad or evil influence. [8] On contrary we find the "black" magic ("*büyü*"), that aims to damage someone consciously. [4] Numerous practices are known in order to use "black" magic. Amulets are hidden, magic knots are tied or magical texts are read. All this is believed to come from sorcerers.

Black magic served as an explanation for a lot of incidents (bad harvest, relation conflicts, accidents, several diseases); also psychical and neurological diseases are traced back to it. As a protection against magical influences rituals are carried out by a healer *(büyüyü cözmek-* 'reopen magic') or amulets (*muscas*) are being carried.

"Spirits" "Djinns" "Cinler"

It is assumed that the prophet Mohammed (569-632), in accordance with his time, believed in the existence of spirits, magic and sorcery. In several soures of the Koran , spirits (*Djinns, Cinler*) have a meaning. [7] "He has made man from dry matter like clay. And he has made the *Djinns* from a flame. " (55th sure, verse 14, 15). From an islamic view *Djinns* are "intelligent" beings of steam or fire, not perceptible to human senses, which can appear in different physical shapes. They are capableappearing in forms similar to humans or animals. (e.g. as an eagle, snake, scorpion or as wind)[6, 7].

In the ethnic belief, "good *Djinns*" and "bad *Djinns*" exist. Invisible, of both, male and female, these fast moving beings stay in the dark during the day, in waste, in the forests, in caves, dirty waters and abandoned houses, on cemeteries, in public bathes (*hammam*) etc. during the night. The command not to poke in garbage heaps and to urinate in water puddles has derived, in order to not frighten up (aggressive) *Djinns*. Curses, offences during ritual washings (especially after sexual intercourse or autoerotic actions), rejection of the parents or violations of divine rules can provoke the displeasure and the anger of *Djinns*. Also along with everyday activities while pouring out wastewater or urinating, ritualised apologies

are spoken, in order to protect oneself from their influence. [14, 16]
In the traditional deliveryit is said that *Djinns* eat, drink and reproduce: They even have sexual relationships between each other, bear children and are able to seduce humans to a sexual relation. In the Turkish language a lot of expressions are related to the word "*cin*":" *Cin carpmas*i" (stroke by a *djinn*), meaning a *Djinn* stroke upon a human to make him sick or "*cinler basima üsüstü*" (*cinler* assembled on the head) for somebody very nervous or overstressed; "*Cinnet getimek*" (until insanity).
Cinler are very often related to psychical diseases. Schizophrenia, insane depression, mania or fear are traced back to *cinler*. They have the ability to cause heavy harm and take away the life spirit. They are even considered to be able to kill a person.Contrary to this we find statements of several well educated muslims who consider demons and spirits as misbelief and the exorcism as a quackery. Some koran- interpretations look upon the *Djinns* as a medical phenonemon and search for parallels to microbes and bacterias to achieve a real, sensible relation to scientifically proved facts.

Traditional healing methods

Dietary measures

Diseases caused by insufficient or poor nutrition, can be relieved or even cured, by certain diets or the input, respectively, of the avoidance, of certain food. A central position has water, that plays an important role with religious cleaning ritual in the beliefs of Muslims.
Too much or too little water or the input of bad water are used to explain diseases. [8]
Hippokrates (460- 370 b.C) emphasised the meaning of the daily life routine and its importance for the physical well being already. He recommended rest periods and well measured eating, sleeping and sexual activities. (21) Until today these ideas regulate the life of a believing Muslim.(7)

Ethnopharmacological methods for diagnosing and treating illness

Meditative prayers are spoken frequently. [9, 14, 19]
For the treatment and relief of diseaes various practices are used, especially: reading of holy writings, incorporation of energetic substances (inhaling of smoke, eating or drinking of sacred essences), cleaning of the body, burning of itmes with magical meaning (pages of holy books, spreading of salt).
The word of a scribe and the reading out of holy writings has a very strong position in the islamic culture out of historical reasons. The incorporation of food, to which healing powers are attached during the magical ceremony is of importance. Thus the healer talks about fruits for example, which have to be eaten by the advice-seeking person afterwards. A widespread practice also is to write words from the Koran on a piece of paper with ink , then put it into a glass of water or tea to dissolve it and finally drink it ("tea with prayer").
Pieces of paper with sures written on them are burned and the "Koran-containing smoke" is inhaled (*tütsüleme*). In other rituals the healer blows or breathes the smoke of burned Koran-paper into the face of the help-seeking person. Water (with

Fig. 1: Amulets in triangle form

pieces of marked paper in it) serves for washing and cleaning. The ritual washing (*kirklama*) as a preventive measure to protect from illness caused by magic is likewise of importance. Usually, amulets as energetic objects are recommended, as shown in the following.

Amulets

An amulet is usually an easily portable, power-filled object. Amulets used in the islamic culture and by turkish healers, are made in a ritual ceremony.
The main components of the amulet are usually pieces of paper marked with sures of the Koran, texts from holy writings or magic words, folded corresponding to a symbolic number (e. g. three or seven times) and sewed in material like leather.
The amulets itselves often have a triangle form. Amulets are sewed into in the bed of a couple, to bring luck and pregnancy, or are worn by babies, pregnant women or sick persons, in order to refuse bad spirits or diseases.
Another custom for incorporating the strength of an amulet is to eat one (eating-paper). Either this amulet is taken pulverized, or dipped in water which then is drunk. Amulets serve as the protection or the defence from evil forces ("*Djinns*", the "*evil eye*", "*Black magic*") and thus help to bring healing. [4, 9, 11, 14]]

Lead and Tin-pouring

Within a ritual act, the pouring of heated lead or tin into water (*kursun dökme*) is used as a method to detect harmingful influences, to determine the cause of a

disease and to keep away or drive away "evil forces".
Within a ritual act, the pouring of heated lead or tin into water (*kursun dökme*) is used as a method to detect harming influence, to determine the cause of a disease and to keep away or drive away "evil forces".
The idea is that, *Djinns* can be kept away, the "*evil eye*" or sorcery can be repulsed and "*Büyü*" can be neutralized this way. These rites are regionally different. Usually an interpretation of the leadform, solidified in water, takes place.(8)

Investigation
Our survey with 105 patients of turkish origin, who were in ambulatory or stationary psychiatric treatment, pursued the question what importance healing authorities have coming from ethnic belief. The use of traditional healers and the ethnomedical conceptions were to be inquired and evaluated.

Results
Patients often had 2 to 5 contacts with a healer, twentyfive percent of the patients more frequently. Men went to see a healer less frequently than women. The main reason was one's own mental condition, also marriage and family problems, anxiety about one's future or worries concerning the faithfulness of the partner.

Ethnomedical recommandations

The advice of the healers varied. The most frequent recommendations were to wear an amulet (62%), to drink sanctified water or to read in the Koran or in holy writings. Also rare or individual advices were given: wearing or keeping one or several amulets, input or application of "blessed" water, reading texts from the Koran, prayer, going to a mosque, smelling at certain grains or plants, tea of healing plants, intake of "blessed sugar", wearing a "blessed string", crossing a certain bridge, going to a holy grave, getting earth from the place where spirits penetrated the patient, bathings in sea water, tying up hair, a stay in Turkey, etc.
Most patients followed the recommandations of the healers (76%) and only few omitted them completely. The ethnopharmacological advices were mostly payed for by money contributions.

Casuistry: "Magic ritual"

The report of a 58 years old woman with repetitious depressive and manic episodes, who is in psychiatric treatment since 8 years and who has been in in-patient treatment several times:
She had already seen a *Hoca* very often because of temporary sad moods. Additionally she had phases with an altered sense of time and would go through the town early in the morning, towards 4 o'clock, in order to visit people.
From the *Hocas* she had got an amulet, as wll as "sanctified" water and various plants.
Once she had to stay overnight in a mosque for several days together with three other women. Thereby a ritual was practiced, where each one needed a tray with bread, salt, onion, comb and mirror as well as a dish with tap water.
Melted metal had been poured into the water , in order to detect the origin of the

illness by form. The *Hoca* devined that she had frightened herself by moon fall, which a *Cin* (spirit) had caused. However, amulet and water had notso far been helpful. The physician also could not help her.

Discussion

The Turkish population is the largest of foreign ethnic groups in Germany, and thus has great sociomedical importance. [15]

Consequently the discussion of inter-cultural and migration-specific questions is important for an understanding in medical, psychological and social health systems of this ethnic. In their investigation RUHKOPF & ZIMMERMANN pointed out, that turkish migrants make a distinction between "*Hoca*"-Diseases- and "Doctor"-diseases, as an indication of the choice, who is most suitable to treat the disease, without a defined Western concept underlying these terms. Various mental diseases (at random) are among the "*Hoca*" diseases. [20]

RUHKOPF & ZIMMERMANN (1987) asked 76 turkish parents about their understanding of illness and therapy , concerning their children, during a treatment in the pediatric clinic of the university in Freiburg. Among other things, the attitude towards ethnomedical therapy concepts and the personal experiences with traditional healers were asked for in this tripartite investigation.

One third of the parents stated to have taken up ethnomedical treatments, particularly with magical character, because of the illness of their child. Because of the well-known shyness of parents to talk about traditional concepts, the authors assumed this share to be higher. [20]

Although it might be expected that, given the fundamental differences between traditional, Moslem-based Turkish practices and Western medicine, our research showed a general acceptance of both systems by Turkish patients.

Therfore the simultaneous demand for ethnomedicalpractices apart from Western medical treatment should be tolerated. Traditional healers thereby come to meet patients, because they explain diseases by familiar, traditional patterns of explanation beyond the responsibility of the patient (*Djinns, Nazar*), while physicians have other, less understandable explanations and regard biological processes or behaviors of the patient as the cause.

Author
Westfälisches Zentrum für Psychiatrie und Psychotherapie Bochum, Universitätsklinik. Physician for Neurology, Psychiatry and Psychotherapy; medical activities at the Universities of Bonn and Bochum; since 1998 Assistant Medical Director at the Westfälisches Zentrum für Psychiatrie und Psychotherapie Bochum.
Supervision as Assistant Medical Director of the emergency and the rehabilitation wards. Scientific work over cross-cultural psychiatry, schizophrenic psychosis and psychopharmacological topics.
Contact: E-Mail: WZfPP-Bochum@wkp-lwl.org

References
1. FOULKS, E., FREEMAN, D., KASLOW, F., MADOW, L.: The Italian Evil Eye: Mal Occhio. J *Operational Psychiat* 8,2 (1977) 28-34.
2. HARDING T.W.: *Traditional healing methods for mental disorders.* WHO Chronicle 31 (1977) 436-440.
3. HAUSCHILD, Th.: *Der Böse Blick.* Verlag Mensch und Leben, Berlin 1982.
4. HOVORKA, O.V., KRONFELD, A.: *Vergleichende Volksmedizin. Eine Darstellung volksmedizinischer Sitten und Gebräuche, Anschauungen und Heilfaktoren, des Aberglaubens und der Zaubermedizin.* Von STRECKER & SCHRÖDER, Stuttgart 1908.
5. HUGHES, Th. P.: *Lexikon des Islam.* Fourier, Wiesbaden 1995.
6. KARTAL, R.: Probleme und Besonderheiten bei der Akut- und Langzeitbehandlung türkischer Patienten. In: HEINRICH K (Hrsg.) *Leitlinien neuroleptischer Therapie.* Springer, Berlin-Heidelberg-New York 1990, 173-183.
7. KHOURY, A.T., HAGEMANN, L., HEINE, P., et al.: *Islam-Lexikon. Geschichte-Ideen-Gestalten.* Herder, Freiburg-Basel-Wien 1991.
8. KOEN, E.: *Die Bedeutung des informellen medizinischen Sektors und traditionellen Krankheitsvorstellungen in der Türkei.* Med. Dissertation. Heidelberg 1986.
9. KOEN, E.: Krankheitskonzepte und Krankheitsverhalten in der Türkei und bei Migrantinnen in Deutschland: ein Vergleich. *Curare* 9 (1986) 129-136.
10. KOPTAGEL-ILAL, G.: Behandlung der eingewanderten Türken in Westeuropa. *Curare* 9 (1986) 155-160.
11. KRISS, R., KRISS-HEINRICH, H.: Volksglaube im Bereich des Islam. Band II - *Amulette, Zauberformeln und Beschwörungen.* Otto Harrassowitz, Wiesbaden 1962.
12. KROEGER, A., KOEN, E., WEBER, W., STREICH, K.: *Der Umgang mit Krankheit in türki-schen und deutschen Arbeitnehmerfamilien.* Heidelberg 1986.
13. LEHMANN, A.: Aberglaube und Zauberei. *Von den ältesten Zeiten an bis in die Ge-genwart.* Ferdinand Enke, Stuttgart 1925.
14. OSTERMANN, B.: *Wer versteht mich? Der Krankheitsbegriff zwischen Volksmedizin und High Tech.* Verlag für Interkulturelle Kommunikation, Frankfurt 1990.
15. ÖZELSEL, M.: *Gesundheit und Migration. Eine psychologisch-empirische Untersuchung an Deutschen sowie Türken in Deutschland und der Türkei.* München 1990.
16. ÖZTÜRK, O.M.: Folk treatment of mental illness in Turkey. In: A. KIEV (ed.): *Magic, Faith & Healing.* Free Press Glencoe, London (1964) 343-363.
17. PORTERA, A.: Psychotherapeutische und beraterische Interventionsmöglichkeiten bei italienischen Klienten mit magischen Vorstellungen. In: JAEDE, W., PORTERA, A. (Hrsgg.) *Ausländerberatung: Kulturspezifische Zugänge in Diagnostik und Therapie.* Lambertus, Freiburg 1986.
18. RÖDER, F., OPALIC, P.: Der Einfluss des Hodschas (magischer Heiler) auf türkische psychiatrische Patienten in der Bundesrepublik - Eine Auswertung klinischer Fallbei-spiele. *Psychiat Prax* 14 (1987) 157-162.
19. RÖDER, F.: Die Bedeutung der Hodschas für die Betreuung türkischer psychiatrischer Patienten. In: JÄDE, W., PORTERA, A. (Hrsgg.) *Ausländerberatung. Kulturspezifische Ansätze in Diagnostik und Therapie.* Lambertus, Freiburg (1986) 127-137.
20. RUHKOPF, H., ZIMMERMANN, E., BARTELS S.: Das Krankheits- und Therapieverständnis türkischer Migranten in der Bundesrepublik Deutschland.

In: NESTMANN, F., NIEPEL, T. (Hrsg.): *Beratung von Migranten. Neue Wege der psychosozialen Versorgung.* VWB, Berlin 1993.
21. SCHOTT, H.: *Die Chronik der Medizin.* Chronik Verlag, Dortmund 1993.
22. SELIGMANN, S: *Der böse Blick und Verwandtes. Ein Beitrag zur Geschichte des Aberglaubens aller Zeiten und Völker.* Barsdorf, Berlin 1910.
23. SEN, F., GOLDBERG, A.: *Türken in Deutschland. Leben zwischen zwei Kulturen.* C.H. Beck, München 1994.
24. STERN, B.: *Medizin, Aberglaube etc. in der Türkei.* Berlin 1903.
25. SUZUKI, P-T.: Social Work, Culture-Specific Mediators, and Delivering Services to Aged Turks in Germany and Aged Chinese in San Francisco. *Int Soc Work* 21 (1978) 19.
26. WEBER, W., STREICH, K., KROEGER, A.: Die Inanspruchnahme von Gesundheitsdiensten durch türkische und deutsche Arbeiterfamilien in einem süddeutschen Landkreis. *Curare* 9 (1986) 171-178.

SCHAMANINNEN IN ZENTRAL ASIEN: ANPASSUNG AN EINE LANDSCHAFT IM WANDEL*

von Eva Jane Neumann Fridman

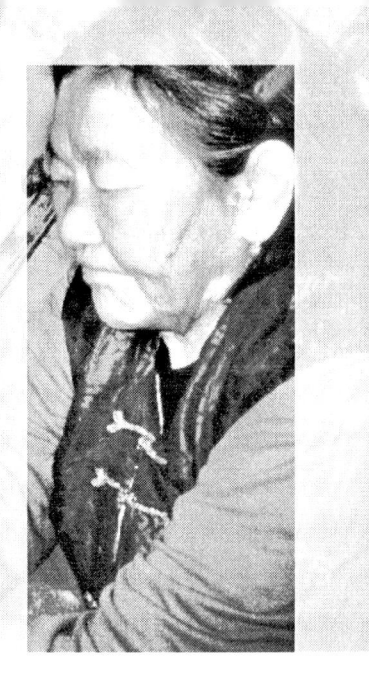

Einleitung

Seit dem Niedergang der Sowjetunion hat der Schamanismus in der Mongolei und Russland eine gewaltige Erneuerung erlebt. In vielen Fällen sind traditionelle Formen des Schamanismus, überlagert mit neuen und anderen kulturellen Zusammenhängen, wieder aufgetaucht. Die Schamanen berichten aber auch, dass sie Kräfte ihrer schamanischen Vorfahren aus der Zeit vor der Revolution (vor 1920) heute nicht mehr in sich tragen.

Die jahrzehntelange Unterdrückung aller religiöser Aktivitäten in der UDSSR und der Mongolei hat die schamanistische Arbeit ständig beeinflusst, trotz der Möglichkeit, offen zu praktizieren. Die politische Unterdrückung schuf nicht nur ein Klima der Angst, in Hinsicht auf die Möglichkeit beim Ausüben jedweder schamanistischer Rituale gesehen zu werden, sondern brachte auch auch Verluste von in religiösen Traditionen erfahrener Stammesältester mit sich.

Manche Schamanen, die ihre Fähigkeiten in einem Klima der Unterdrückung entwickelten, benutzen bis heute nicht ihr schamanisches Wissen. Sie arbeiten als Heiler ohne Geistwesen zur Hilfe zu rufen. In anderen Fällen konnten Schamanen die Praktiken ihrer Vorfahren, teilweise verändert oder um neue Elemente ergänzt, fortführen. Verwirrung über die Frage, ob jemand als Schamane, als Buddhist oder sogar im Sinne psychotherapeutischer Prinzipien arbeiten solle, kam auf.

Dieser Text wird anhand der Betrachtung von sechs Heilerinnen aus der Mongolei und der ehemaligen UDSSR das sich wandelnde Gesicht zentralasiatischen Schamanismus zu erläutern versuchen. Jede dieser Schamaninnen repräsentiert Aspekte der neuen Präsenz des Schamanismus in all seinen Variationen, der sich

---

* Übersetzung aus dem Englischen: Arne Frercks

sowohl auf die Geister der oberen Welt, als auch auf die Geister unserer inneren Welt beruft, vom traditionellen Heiler, bis zur "neoschamanischen Suche".

Schamanismus, ein altes Glaubenssystem der zentralasiatischen Welt, entwickelte sich im Zusammenhang einer Gesellschaft aus Jägern und Sammlern, in der das Jagen von Wild und die ausreichende Versorgung mit Nahrung von essentieller Bedeutung war. Schamanen waren die Menschen, die auf Grund ihrer besonderen Fähigkeiten, mit der Geistwelt zu sprechen, die Vermittler für andere Stammesmitglieder waren, die auf Jagdglück und Schutz vor den Kräften der Natur angewiesen waren. Der Schamane besaß Kenntnisse darüber, wie man sich diesen Gottheiten der geistigen Welt nähert, seien es die Herren der Berge, der Flüsse und Seen oder des Tieres, das gejagt werden sollte – das "Master Being", der mystische Kopf einer ganzen Spezies, der Entscheidungen für alle treffen kann. Aus Respekt vor dem gejagten und getöteten Tier entstanden Rituale, Formeln und Tabus, um seinen "spirit" nicht zu verärgern.
Betrachtet man die schamanischen Praktiken in noch nördlicheren Gegenden wie dem äußersten Nordosten Sibiriens (die *Chuckchee, Koryak, Eskimo* und die *Ainu* Stämme auf der japanischen Hokkaido Insel), stellt man fest, dass deren rituelle Formeln und Tabus, was das Fangen von Tieren, die Behandlung getöteter Tiere und die damit zusammenhängender Aktivitäten angeht, noch strenger sind. Ohne Zweifel sind die extremen Jagdbedingungen in diesen Gegenden der Grund dafür. Diese unbedingte Notwendigkeit, die geistige Welt gnädig zu stimmen, um eine Wiederkehr der Tiere für alle Zeiten zu bewirken, war der eigentliche Antrieb, etwas wie Schamanismus zu entwickeln, mit seiner Kosmologie und seinem Stammesschamanen, der die Verbindung zur Geistwelt herstellen konnte. Die Versorgung seines Stammes war abhängig von seiner Macht und Fähigkeiten. Die Welt des Schamanen ist dementsprechend von folgenden Faktoren bestimmt:

- seine inneren Fähigkeiten durch einen veränderten Bewusstseinszustand mit einer anderen Welt in Berührung zu kommen,
- seinen Stamm/Gesellschaft für die er die Verbindung herstellt
- und die natürliche Welt der Geister, Gottheiten, Herrscher der Berge und der Wasser.

Der Verlust von Gebieten, Plätzen, Stammesstrukturen und Familienmitgliedern kann verheerend für das Fortbestehen des Schamanismus in Zentralasien sein, weil dieses Glaubenssystem in sich so abhängig von seinen spezifischen Orten und Gesellschaftsstrukturen ist. Aus diesem Grund stellten die Spaltungen in der Zeit der Sowjetunion, mit ihrer Unterdrückung von Religion, dem Töten von Religion praktizierenden Menschen, der Zwangsumsiedelung nomadischer Völker in Dörfer, dem verschleppen wichtiger Stammesmitglieder in *Gulags* und, im extremsten Fall , der Umsiedelung einer ganzen Stammesbevölkerung - den *Kalmyks* - ins äußerste Sibirien, das Überleben von Schamanismus sehr in Frage.

Diese besondere Bindung an Stamm und Ort bedeutete aber auch, dass die Menschen nach Aufhebung der Zwänge der Sowjetzeit zu ihren Wurzeln zurückfinden und der Schmanismus neu erblühen konnte. Nach 70 Jahren Untergrund brachen schamanische Praktiken sowohl in traditioneller als auch in

Abb. 1: Tsedenpil– eine Heilung. Mongolei 9/9/99.

neuer Gestalt hervor. Der Schamanismus in Zentralasien ist keine Jagdmagie mehr. Die Welt hat sich verändert, auch in der sibirischen und mongolischen Wildnis. Neue Anforderungen brachten einerseits Not und Chaos, andererseits aber auch neue Möglichkeiten. Der Schamanismus gedeiht als ein Heilberuf, der sich mit sowohl physischer als auch psychischer Not befasst. Selbst Weissagen, das Vorhersehen der Zukunft, wurde ein wichtiger Aspekt des Heilens für Menschen auf der Suche nach dem richtigen Weg in ihr "postsowjetisches Leben". Seit in der modernen Welt die Jagd als elementarer Lebensbestandteil verschwunden ist und sich die Heilung ausschließlich auf Individuen und Stammesgemeinschaften bezieht (3), sind überdies Frauen als Schamanen sehr beliebt geworden. Schamaninnen scheint es, zumindest in der jüngeren Geschichte Zentralasiens immer gegeben zu haben. Sowohl in Zusammenhang mit den oben erwähnten wirtschaftlichen Veränderungen und sozialen Brüchen, als auch mit der gezielten Unterdrückung männlicher Schamanen während der Sowjetzeit, erkennt man zur Zeit eine schillernde Vielfalt weiblicher Schamanen.

Heilerinnen
Beobachtungen und Gespräche mit all diesen Schamaninnen stammen aus meiner Feldarbeit in Russland und der Mongolei 1996, 1999 und 2000.
Tsedenpil, 82 Jahre alt, lag in eine Steppdecke gehüllt auf dem Bett in ihrer Jurte,

umgeben von drei Generationen ihrer Familie und rauchte ihre Pfeife. "Ich arbeite nicht mehr schamanisch" informierte sie uns sofort. Tatsächlich hat sie seit 1945 weder ihr Schamanenkleid getragen, noch praktiziert. Aus Angst vor Unterdrückung verbrannte sie 1945 ihre Schamanenkleidung und Trommel, die vorher von ihrem Bruder versteckt gehalten wurden. Tsedenpil gehört dem Stamm der *Hotgoid* an, der in der Steppe im Südwesten der mongolischen Provinz Hövsgöl lebt. Sie stammt aus einer sowohl schamanischen als auch einer lamaischen Familie, was für Menschen in Tuva oder der Mongolei nichts ungewöhnliches ist.

Sie hatte einen Lama Vorfahren mütterlicherseits, dessen Sohn und Enkel Boozaarins (Schamanen) waren. Ihre Kräfte habe sie von ihrer mütterlichen Seite geerbt, bemerkt sie, aber auch ihr Vater, in den 1890er Jahren geboren, war ein Schamane. Tsedenpil begann 1931, mit 14 Jahren, ihre schamanischen Fähigkeiten zu entwickeln, als sie krank wurde. Sie wollte keine Schamanin werden, weil sie fürchtete, so nicht heiraten zu können, aber es waren sehr schwere Zeiten, viele ihrer Tiere starben und ihre Mutter ermutigte sie, Schamanin zu werden. Ihre erste Lehrerin war eine *Udagan*, eine Schamanin, *Ammbaa*.

Sie hatte zwei schamanische und einen Lama Lehrer. Die Zeiten waren so grausam, sagt sie, dass die Leute Angst hatten, sie zu bitten, schamanisch für sie zu arbeiten. Zudem hatte sie noch wenig Übung, also praktizierte sie nur für sich und ihre Familie. Sie begab sich in einen bewusstseinsveränderten Zustand, in dem sie ihren Geistern begegnete, die ihr halfen, die Krankheit einer Person zu erkennen und zu behandeln. Sie trug die typische Schamanenkleidung der Hövsgöl Gegend und eine aus Rehlederhaut gefertigte Trommel mit einem Pferdekopf und zwei sich gegenüberstehenden Drachen, "Hüter der Himmelsgeister", die darauf gemalt waren. Ihre Schamanenkleidung enthielt 88 Schlangen mit den Köpfen auf ihren Schultern und 88 Stoffstreifen. Wie gesagt, hielt ihr Bruder Trommel und Kleidung versteckt, bevor er 1945 alles verbrannte, weil dies, wie sie sagt, die sozialistische Zeit war und sie sich fürchteten. Zu ihrer Angst kam noch die Tatsache, dass all ihre vier Brüder Lamas waren und drei von ihnen Ende der 30er Jahre Repression erfahren hatten.

Nachdem Tsedenpil aufgehört hatte, schamanisch zu arbeiten, wurde sie Heilerin. Sie liest buddhistische Mantras wenn sie behandelt. Kontakt zu Geistern hat sie nicht, sie kommen nicht zu ihr und sie versucht auch keinen Kontakt zu ihnen aufzunehmen. Sie benutzt Massagen und Pulsdiagnose um die gesunden Körperfunktionen zu fühlen und herauszufinden, wodurch sie gestört wurden. Sie beschrieb Fälle, in denen sie Nierenleiden mit Hilfe von Mantras und Mehlpackungen heilen konnte. Trotz alledem ist ihre Arbeit eine synkretische Mischung aus Buddhismus und Schamanismus. Über ihrem Altar mit buddhistischen Artefakten hängen 13 *Ongons*. *Ongons* können sowohl Darstellungen von Geisthelfern, als auch deren Behausung sein.

Hat sie sich wirklich komplett von ihren Geistern getrennt oder haben sich diese während der sozialistischen Zeit nach innen zurückgezogen? Was die Zukunft angeht, meint sie, so könnte der kleine Sohn ihres ältesten Sohnes ein *Zaarin* werden, sie hat eine Kraft in ihm gesehen, aber vielleicht wird es auch nie passieren, da die Zeiten sich geändert haben. Der Sohn ihrer jüngsten Tochter ist ein Lama und er wird ihre 13 *Ongons* weihen, was ihm deshalb erlaubt ist, weil einer ihrer Lehrer ein Lama war. Die Mischung aus Schamanismus und Lamaismus (Tibetanischer Buddhismus) ist sehr bezeichnend für die Bräuche der Heiler in Kalmykia. Kalmykia, eine russische Republik in der Nähe des Kaukasus

Abb. 2: Lyubov Gavrilovna– Schamanen im Zelt. Kalmykia 10/30/96.

zwischen den Flüssen Don und Wolga, wurde im 17. Jahrhundert von den Oirat Mongolen besiedelt.

Die Form des Schamanismus, die sie mitbrachten, war durch die Unterdrückung des Schamanismus durch den Lamaismus in der Mongolei im frühen 17. Jahrhundert stark vom Buddhismus überlagert. Der landschaftliche Wechsel von einem unglaublich schönen Bergland, in dem die Geister der Natur allgegenwärtig waren in eine flache Steppe mit weit weniger Orten der spirituellen Resonanz und Verbindung, mag auch einen entmutigenden Einfluss auf den Schamanismus ausgeübt haben.

Die beiden kalmykischen Heilerinnen Alexandra Semenova und Lyubov Gavrilovna benutzen viele buddhistische Elemente in ihrer Arbeit als Heilerinnen. Alexandra, die sehr aktiv als Heilerin arbeitet, erbte diese Berufung von ihrer Mutter und begann zu heilen, nachdem sie selbst mehrere Jahre an Krankheiten litt, ein typisches Muster bei Schamanen.

Sie hat Geisthelfer, unter ihnen den "alten weißen Mann", den *"Buddha Maitrea"*, die "Grüne Tara" (hilfreich für Frauen und Kinder), den "Medizin Buddha" und die "Weisse Tara". Sie benutzt sowohl Massagen und Berührung, als auch schamanische Werkzeuge um Patienten zu heilen, so zum Beispiel einen Hartgummistift, den sie in Massagen einsetzt, ein kupfernes 5 Kopeken Stück, mit dem sie heilen kann und eine silberne Münze von 1925, die beim Reinigen von

Krankheiten wirksam ist. Während der Heilung rezitiert sie ein buddhistisches Meditationsgebet, das ihr hilft, sich eigener schlechten Energien zu entledigen. Sie kommuniziert mit ihren eigenen persönlichen Geistern, um das Wesen der Krankheit ihres Patienten zu verstehen, und die richtige Heilung für ihn zu finden, die sie dann weitergibt.

Sie sagt, sie sehe soviele Dinge, von denen sie aber nicht sprechen könne und dürfe, weil die Leute sie sonst für verrückt halten würden.
Lyobov Gavrilovnas Arbeit besitzt, neben vielen buddhistischen Elementen, auch einige sehr intensive schamanische Eigenschaften. Sie liest buddhistische Gebete in der Sprache der *Kalmyk*, sie heilt Kinder, massiert Herzen und besitzt spezielle Mantras, die sie zur Heilung des Herzens rezitiert. Sie steht um 5 Uhr Morgens auf um eine Stunde buddhistische Gebete zu lesen, dasselbe um 9 Uhr Abends. Fünfmal täglich entzündet sie ihre kleinen buddhistischen Lampen. Ihre speziellen Gottheiten sind der "Alte weise Mann", die "Grüne Tara" und die "Schwarze Tara". Ihre Familie rettete während der Zeit des Exils in Sibirien (1943 - 1957) den 150 Jahre alten Gebetskranz, den sie benutzt, ebenso ein paar buddhistische Tankas (Bilder buddhistischer Gottheiten).

Obwohl der Buddhismus in ihren Heilritualen und im täglichen Leben eine große Rolle spielt, kennt sie auch viele schamanische Rituale und hat bei einer mächtigen Schamanin studiert. Sie benutzt schamanische Elemente, wenn sie heilt. Sie wendet Nadeltherapie und Berührungstherapie an und kann weiße und schwarze Mächte herbeirufen.
Ihre Tochter sagt, dies sei eine Heilmethode über die sie nicht spreche. Sie habe auch geheime schamanische Gebete von ihrer Lehrerin Aka gelernt, die sie erst auf ihrem Sterbebett offenbaren dürfe. Mit 11 Jahren wurde sie sehr krank und es wurde ein spezielles Ritual für sie abgehalten bei dem der "Alte Weisse Mann " gebeten wurde, in ihren Kopf zu kommen. Es folgte eine Zeremonie für die "Weiße Tara". Nach diesem Ritual musste sie 49 Tage lang auf einer speziellen Gebetsmatte sitzen, es war ihr verboten, Butter oder Fleisch zu essen. Sie saß und betete in einem besonderen weißen Zelt, dabei trug sie eine weiße Jacke, ein Hemd und ein Kleid in rot, grün, gelb oder weiß, jenachdem welche Gottheit gerade über sie wachte.

Margarita Danchinova, eine Schamanin aus *Buryat*, die in der Gegend von Kurumkan (nordöstliche Seite des Baikalsees, Bryatia) lebt, veranschaulicht in vielerlei Hinsicht die heute in Buryatia verbreiteten schamanischen Praktiken. Als eine Buddhistin aus einer *Khori* Familie versuchte sie ursprünglich, ihre Berufung als Schamanin zu verleugnen. Aber schließlich beginnt sie 1992, nach einem Ritual mit den Ahnen ihres Mannes, das all ihre Krankheiten heilte, als Schamanin zu arbeiten. Sie betet zu den Ahnen, zu den Wesen, die die Herren des Ortes um Kurumkan und zu *Barhim-baba*, einem mongolischen *Tengri* (Gottheit), der zu dem Teil der Mongolei gehört, aus dem ihre Familie stammt. Sie heilt Krankheiten des Geistes wie Schizophrenie und behandelt oft Menschen, die unter einem Fluch (witchcraft) leiden, den jemand anderes über sie verhängt hat. Mit Segnungen und

Abb. 3: Margarita Danchinova überträgt ihre Energien auf die Hand. Kurumkan Region, Buryatia. 3/9/99.
Abb. 4: Valentina Baldakhinova bestreicht ein Schaf mit Butter. Buryatia 28/8/99.

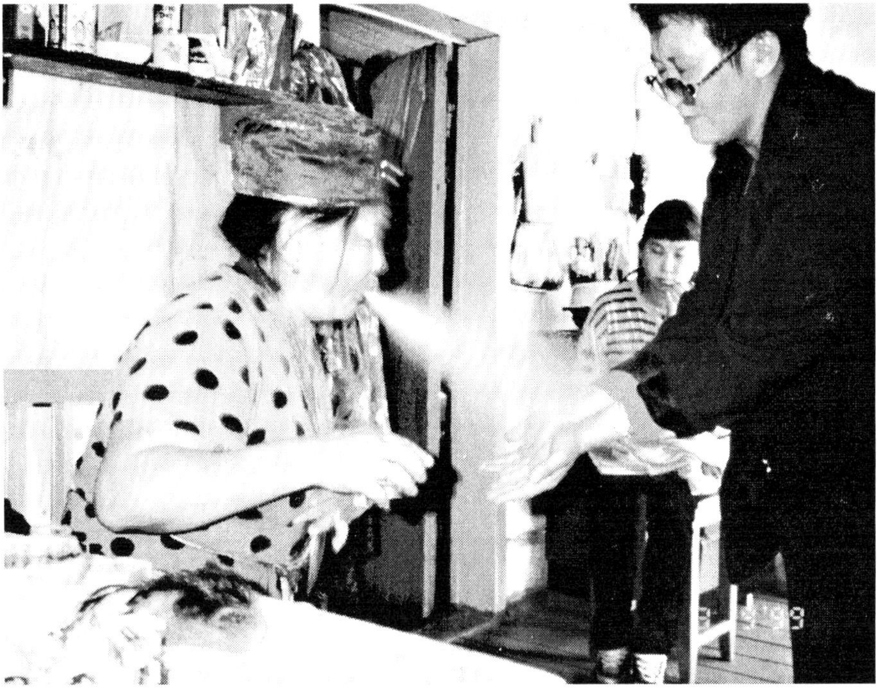

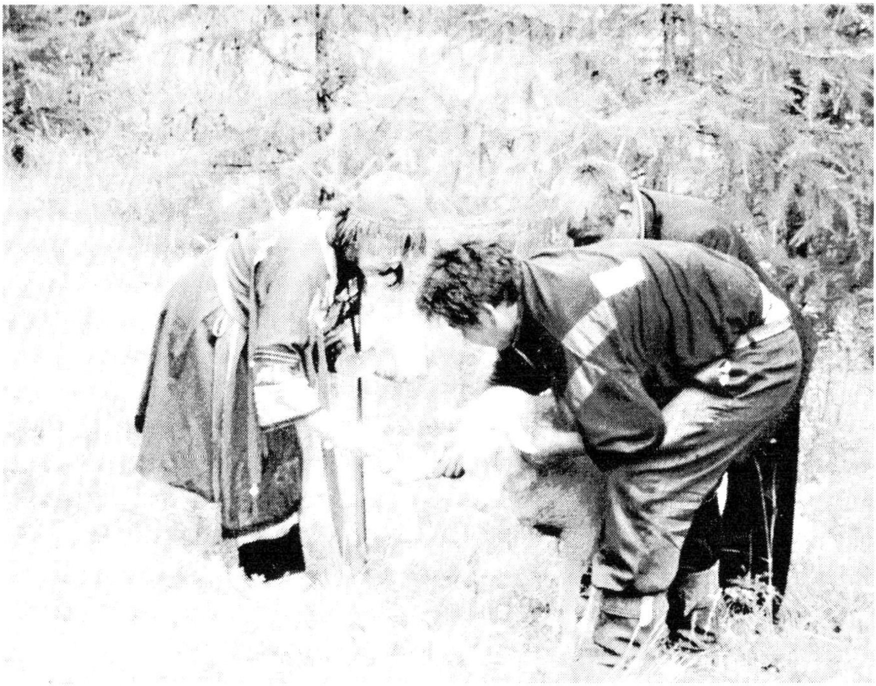

Gebeten kann sie den Fluch abwenden. Sie erzählte mir von einem Mann, der zu ihr kam, weil einer seiner Nachbarn einen Fluch über ihn ausgesprochen hatte. Weil sein Großvater einst die Beerdigung eines mächtigen Schamanen gestört hatte, war die persönliche Aura dieses Mannes beschädigt, so dass er keinen Schutz hatte und es ein Leichtes war, ihn weiter mit Zauberei zu verletzen. Margarita heilte ihn, indem sie ihre Ahnen und die Tengris um Hilfe bat, seine Seele zurückzubringen.
Sie kann die Gesuche der Menschen beantworten, indem sie drei Streichhölzer entzündet, diese in Wasser hält, dann das Wasser mit dem Messer schneidet und die Bilder, die sie dabei sieht, deutet. Im Sommer 1999, als ich sie wieder besuchte, hatte sie einen Hut, sowie einen Schamanenspiegel und Glocken hinzugefügt. Sie sang, hielt den Puls des Patienten und läutete Glocken über seinem Kopf. Dieser Mann, ein Freund, kam wegen Problemen bei der Arbeit zu Margarita. Sie reinigte ihn von Kälte und schlechter Energie. Er saß mit geöffneten Händen da um eine Segnung zu erfahren. Von einer Flasche Wodka stieg Wärme auf und Margarita trank Wodka aus einer Tasse und blies ihn in die Hände des Patienten, der die Wärme jetzt fühlen konnte. Margarita selbst fühlte sich, nachdem sie ihn zum ersten Mal geheilt hatte, sehr kalt und hatte zwei Tage lang Verdauungsstörungen.

Ein anderes Beispiel für Heilung war der Fall einer jungen Frau, die wegen schlimmer Magenkrämpfe zu ihr kam. Für diese Heilung saß Margarita vor ihr und machte Greif- und Ziehbewegungen mit ihrer rechten Hand, als ob sie etwas schwarzes aus dem Magen zöge. Sie sah schwarze Fäden herauskommen und die Patientin fühlte ihren Magen, der anfangs eiskalt gewesen war, wärmer und wärmer werden. Margaritas rechte Hand schien dunkel zu werden, nachdem sie die Fäden hervorgezogen hatte und nachdem die Prozedur wiederholt worden war, fühlte sich die Frau wesentlich besser und die Krämpfe traten nicht mehr auf. Margarita betrachtete das schwarze "Zeug" als Folge eines schlechten Einflusses oder Fluchs, der auf der Patientin lastete, vielleicht hervorgerufen durch eine zufällige, unangenehme Begegnung mit einer Frau in einem Zug.

Auch Valentina Baldakhinova, eine weitere schamanische Heilerin mit großer und viel besuchter Heilpraxis in Ulan-Ude, arbeitet mit Praktiken zur Behandlung diverser Formen von schlechten Einflüssen, zeitgenössischen Problemen wie Stress, situativen und emotionalen Problemen. Ihre Arbeit gleicht in vielerlei Hinsicht der westlicher Psychotherapie, nur dass sie als Schamanin mit einer weit zurück reichenden schamanischen Herkunft schamanische Methoden der Behandlung und Heilung einsetzt.
Sie behandelt zudem auch körperliche Störungen, wobei sie kosmische Methoden und Wissen um Akupunkturpunkte nutzt, die es ihr möglich machen, aus der Distanz zu heilen. Schamanistische Rituale zum Wohle einer Gemeinde sind ein weiterer wichtiger Aspekt des buryatischen Schamanismus und Valentina wird oft darum gebeten, Rituale dieser Art zu vollziehen, um einer speziellen Gruppe von Menschen Gesundheit und spirituelle Segnung zukommen zu lassen.
Im Spätsommer 1999 wurde sie gebeten, in der Mykhorshibirski Region des südlichen Buryatias ein Ritual für den *Tsaagantan Khori* Stamm durchzuführen. Als wir morgens am Lager ankamen, hatte sich eine große Gruppe von Menschen versammelt und war damit beschäftigt, Holz, einen großen schwarzen Kessel sowie ein zusammengebundenes Schaf zum auserwählten Platz zu bringen. Nachdem jeder mit einem Wacholderzweig geweiht wurde, wurden den

Mitgliedern des Stammes Bänder verliehen, die sie an einer Birke befestigten. Dieser Baum wurde gefällt und wieder in den Boden eingepflanzt, wodurch er zu einem symbolischen fliegenden Pferd wurde und zudem zu einem Befestigungspfahl für die Pferde der Götter, wenn sie zu diesem Ort kommen.
Es folgten Gebete zu den Geistwesen und Valentina fragte nach den Namen bestimmter Vorfahren, um sich entsprechend direkt an sie wenden zu können und um ihren Segen für diesen Stamm zu bitten.

Dann wurde das Schaf vorbereitet, den Geistern des Stammes geopfert zu werden. Sie gab ihm Milch und salbte seinen Kopf, Rücken und jede Klaue mit Milch, gefolgt von einer ähnlichen Salbung mit Butter. Das Schaf wurde rituell geschlachtet, gehäutet und zerteilt, wobei eine alte Frau den Männern Anweisungen gab, wie dies zu geschehen hatte. Die Frau hatte das traditionelle Wissen, ihr war es jedoch nicht erlaubt, das geheiligte Fleisch zu berühren. Die Beine und der Kopf des Schafs wurde als eine Gabe an die Götter verbrannt. Als Schlussakt des zeremoniellen Rituals wurde die Haut, gefüllt mit den Knochen des Schafes auf einen Holzhaufen gebreitet, und die Birke, mit den daran befestigten Zierbändern darauf plaziert. Das Ganze wurde in Flammen gesetzt, das Schaf ein Opfer an die Götter, geehrt durch seinen Geist, der in den Flammen gen Himmel geschickt wird. Die Geister nehmen das Schaf und geben den Menschen als Gegengabe Erfolg zurück.
Dieser Tausch, ein Tier aus der Herde des Stammes den Göttern zu opfern, geht auf die ursprünglichen Jagdopfer der Schamanen zurück. Dort wurden Kopf, Haut und Pfoten des geschlachteten Tieres mit besonderem Respekt behandelt.
Die Entwicklung einer Art von Neo-Schamanismus kann auch unter jüngeren Schamanen beobachtet werden, die versuchen, eine schamanische Praxis von Bedeutung in der postsowjetischen Ära wiederzuerschaffen.
Ein typisches Beispiel ist die tuvanische Schamanin Rosa Nasyk-Dorjou, die 1961 in der Bai-Khaakh Region direkt südlich der tuvanischen Hauptstadt Kyzyl geboren wurde. Sie wuchs in Mongun-Taiga, der westlichen Steppe Tuvas, unter dem Einfluss einer starken schamanischen Tradition, sowohl väterlicher - als auch mütterlicherseits, auf. Bereits im Jugendalter begann sie, befremdliche Visionen zu haben, begann jedoch mit dem Heilen bzw. der Tätigkeit als Schamanin erst 1991 als sie den Geist des Berges bei Arzan Shivilig, einer heiligen Quelle westlich von Teeli, sah.
Ihre Berufung ist, das individuelle Heilen, sowie die traditionellen sieben Tage und neunundvierzig Tage Rituale nach dem Tod von Personen durchzuführen. In ihren individuellen Heilungen nutzt sie eine Mischung aus Schamanismus, Buddhismus und modernen psychotherapeutischen Behandlungsprinzipien. Wenn sie schamanisch arbeitet, trägt sie eine besondere seidenumsäumte Vlieseste (keine traditionelle Schamanen-Tracht) und benutzt Trommel und Schlegel, um sich in andere Bewusstscinszustände zu versetzen, die jedoch nur wenige Minuten andauern. Bemerkenswert sind vor allem die neo-schamanischen Elemente in ihrem etwas eklektischen Heilungsansatz, aber auch die kurze Dauer ihrer Trancezustände. Viele Elemente der reichhaltigen Bilder, die sie sieht, sowie der Rituale, die sie durchführt, sind traditioneller Natur.
Trotz ihrer Stärke als Heilerin, hegte sie jedoch diverse Zweifel, ob nicht die Prinzipien des Buddhismus oder jene westlicher Psychotherapieformen eventuell wirksamere Heilmethoden seien. Wir können daher das Wiederaufleben schamanischer Heilweisen nicht als ein Wesen (des Schamanismus) betrachten,

sondern vielmehr als äußerst facettenreiche Ansammlung von Praktiken. Sie basieren auf einer schamanischen Weltanschauung, welche Menschen mit Naturgewalten verbindet, insbesondere mit geographisch lokalen, verwandschaftlichen Verbindungen und Gottheiten, aber auch mit Stammesgeistern, die Menschen sowohl als Individuen als auch als Stammesangehörige stützen und stärken können.

Sowohl Elemente traditioneller schamanischer Praktiken, sogar Spuren umgewandelter Jagdrituale, buddhistische Überlagerungen von Artefakten und Gebeten als auch neue Kontakte zu westlichen Philosophien, die das Wissen um psychotherapeutische Heilmethoden mit einbeziehen, sind letztlich alle Teil der heutigen schamanischen Heilpraxis Zentralasiens geworden. Zudem hat der Neo-Schamanismus der westlichen Welt - mit seinem Schwerpunkt auf der persönlichen spirituellen Gedankenreise im Kontrast zu einem immer am Wohl einer Gemeinschaft und deren Individuen orientierten Schamismus – Einzug in den Schamismus Zentralasiens erhalten und in der Tat begonnen, diesen zu infiltrieren. Gewisse Elemente bleiben jedoch weiterhin erhalten.

"Ich habe Rosa gefragt, warum es so viele Schamanen in Tulva gibt. Sie sagte, es gibt so viele, weil dort so viele Geister sind. Menschen können diese Geister immer treffen. Wenn Menschen Schafe hüten, so können sie die niederen Geister der Erde und der Natur treffen. Es gibt viele Geister der Erde und der Berge und wenn, was des öfteren der Fall war, viele Rituale vollzogen werden, um die Berge um Hilfe zu bitten, so werden die Geister stark. Wenn Geister um Hilfe gebeten werden, bedeutet dies, dass die Person an diese Geister glaubt, und dieser Glaube, sagt Rosa, macht Geister stark, verleiht ihnen Kraft" (FRIDMAN, 1998:266-267).

Autorin
DR. EVA JANE NEUMANN FRIDMAN, PH.D.
Brown University. Absolvierte den B.A. cum laude an dem Radcliffe College, Harvard University in Geschichte und Literatur. An der Simmons School of Social Work empfing sie den M.S. in psychiatrischer Sozialarbeit und arbeitete als Psychotherapeutin in der Psychiatrie, seit 1964 auch in eigener Praxis. An der Harvard University absolvierte sie den M.A. in Anthropologie und Archäologie. Ihren Ph.D. (1997) an Brown University, Abteilung für Anthropologie, behandelte die Ethnographie und Anthropologie des Mittleren Ostens, Eurasia und Zentralasien mit dem Schwerpunkt auf Nomadentum und Glaubenssysteme.
Ihre Feldforschung führte sie in der früheren USSR, in Sibirien und Kalmykia durch. Sie lehrte an der Harvard- und Brown University. Sie ist co-editor-in-chief der "Encyclopedia of Shamanism" (ABC-CLIO, Inc. (in progress). Als Senior Fellow am Center for the Study of World Religions, Harvard Divinity School, Harvard University (2000-2001), unterrichtet sie einen Kurs über "Schamanismus - Osten und Westen" an der Brown University. Kontakt: E-Mail: joneva@worldnet.att.net

Literatur
FRIDMAN, EVA JANE NEUMANN 1998 *Sacred Geography: Shamanism in the Buddhist Republics of Russia*. Ann Arbor: UMI

WOMEN SHAMAN HEALERS IN INNER ASIA: ADAPTATIONS IN A CHANGING LANDSCAPE

by Eva Jane Neumann Fridman

Introduction
Since the demise of the Soviet Union, shamanism in the Inner Asian world of Russia and Mongolia has undergone an almost exploding revival. In many instances traditional forms of shamanism have reemerged, but now overlaid with new and different cultural contexts. Shamans also say that they no longer contain within themselves the strength and power of their shaman ancestors from pre-Revolutionary (pre-1920) times.
The suppression of all religious activity, including shamanism, for many decades both in the USSR and in Mongolia has affected the practice of shamanism currently – despite the opportunity to practice openly. Political repression not only created an environment of fear with respect to being seen practicing any kind of shamanic ritual, but also brought about losses of clan elders versed in religious traditions. Some shamans, having grown to maturity in a repressive environment, remain unwilling to use shamanic knowledge and only work as healers without calling upon the spirits to help them. In other instances, shamans have been able to continue the shamanic practices of their ancestors, and have also changed and added elements. Confusion over whether one should practice as a shaman, or a Buddhist, or according to psychotherapeutic principles even, has taken hold.
As illustrative of the changing face of healing and shamanism in Inner Asia today, this paper will consider the experiences of six women healers from Mongolia and the former USSR. Each of these shamans represents aspects of the renewed presence of shamanism, in all its current variations from traditional healer to neo-shamanic quest calling upon not only the spirits of the Upper World, but also the spirits residing within us in our Inner World.
Shamanism, an ancient belief system in the Inner Asian world, was developed within the context of a hunting and gathering society living in a somewhat marginal environment, in which the taking of game and the sufficiency of (wild)

food supplies was crucial. Shamans were those people who had special abilities to speak to the world of the spirits and hence to be the intercessors for other members of their clan or group who needed protection from the elements of nature and good fortune for hunting. Moreover, the shaman had knowledge of how to approach these deities in the spirit world, whether they were masters of the mountain or of the river or lake, or they were Masters of the animal to be hunted – the Master being that chief (mythical) head of all that species, who could make the decisions for all. Hence, rituals, formulae, and taboos arose with respect to the treatment of the animal when caught and killed, so that its spirit would not be offended. If we look at shamanic practices in even more northern environments, such as extreme northeastern Siberia (the *Chuckchee, Koryak,* Eskimo and *Ainu* groups on Hokkaido Island in Japan), it can be noted that these ritualistic formulae and taboos respecting animal capture, treatment of the dead animal and related activities become even more stringent due no doubt to the extreme constraints on hunting dictated by the very marginality of the environment.

This need to appease and propitiate the spiritual world so that there would be an eternal return of animals was the initial impetus to the development of shamanism with its cosmology and its clan shaman, a person who could make that connection to the spirit world. The welfare of his community depended upon his skill and powers.

The world of the shaman is therefore bounded by these factors: his inner ability to reach another world (through entering an altered state of consciousness), his clan or community for whom he is making the appeal and the connection, and the natural world of spirits, deities, masters of the mountains and the waters. Loss of territory, place, clan structure, and family members can be almost totally devastating for the continuance of shamanism in Inner Asia because this belief system is so interdependent with its specific locale and community.

For this reason, the disruptions of the Soviet Period with its suppression of religion, killing of religious practitioners, moving of peoples from nomadic clan emplacements into villages, removal of more substantial members of clans into gulags, and (in the extreme case) the removal of an entire population – the *Kalmyks* – to the further reaches of Siberia, made the survival of shamanism quite doubtful. However, those particular attachments to clan and locale also meant that once the constraints of the Soviet Period were lifted and people were able to reconnect to their roots, shamanism was free to flourish again. After 70 years underground, shamanic practices have burst forth in both traditional and new guises.

Shamanism in Inner Asia is no longer hunting magic. Even in the wilds of Siberia or Mongolia, the world has changed. New demands, as well as disruptions from the dying out of the old order, have brought distress and chaos as well as opportunities. In response, shamanism is flourishing as a healing profession, dealing with both psychic and physical distress.

Divination, the foretelling of the future, has also become an important aspect of healing, as people search to find the right directions for their new post-Soviet lives. Moreover, with the disappearance of hunting as an important lifeway in the modern world, and the exclusive focus on healing of individuals or clan communities, women have become very prominent as shamanic practitioners. In the Inner Asian world, there seem to have always been women shamans, at least in the more recent historical times. However, due to the economic changes and social

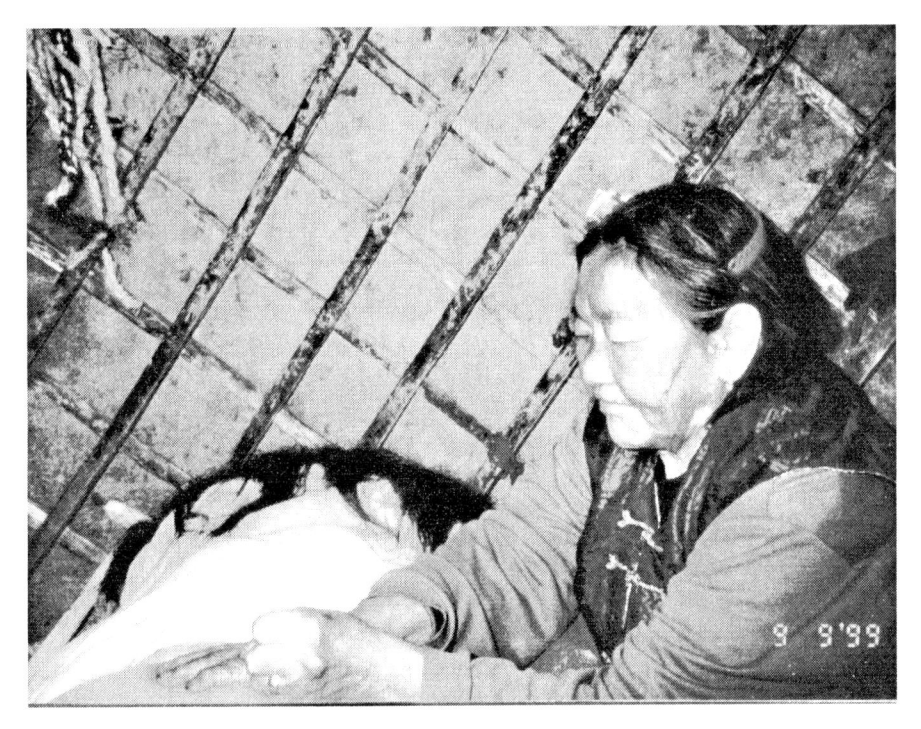

Fig. 1: Tsedenpil– Healing. Mongolia 9/9/99.

disruptions mentioned above, as well as to the patterns of somewhat selective repression of male shamans during the Soviet Period, we can see a fluorescence presently of many women shaman practitioners.

Women healers

Observations of and discussions with all these women shaman healers occurred during my fieldwork conducted in Russia and Mongolia in 1996, 1999 and 2000.

Tsedenpil, age 82, was lying in her yurt on her bed wrapped in a quilt, smoking her pipe and surrounded by three generations of her family. She immediately informed us "I don't shamanize anymore". In fact she has not put on shaman clothes or practiced as a shaman since 1945 when she became so frightened of repression that she burned her drum and shaman outfit, which had already been hidden by her brother. Tsedenpil is a member of the *Hotgoid* tribe, living in the steppe in the southwest corner of *Hövsgöl* province in Mongolia. She comes from both lama and shaman lineage, not unusual for people in Tuva or Mongolia. On her maternal side she had a lama ancestor whose son and grandson were *boozaarins* (shamans). She stated that she inherited her shamanic powers from her mother's line but her father, born in the 1890s, was also a shaman.

Tsedenpil started to shamanize in 1931 when she was fourteen and became ill. She didn't want to become a shaman because she was afraid she would not get married but it was a very difficult time since many of their domestic animals were dying, and her mother encouraged her to become a shaman. Her first teacher was an *udagan,* (a female shaman) a woman, Ammbaa. She had two shaman and one lama teachers. Times were so cruel, she said, that people were scared to ask her to shamanize and she had little shamanic practice, so she only shamanized for herself and her family. She would go into an altered state and her spirits, whom she encountered in this state, helped her to know which disease a person had and how to treat that illness. She wore a typical outfit for shamans in the Hövsgöl area which included a drum made from wild deerskin with a horse head and two opposing dragons, protectors of the sky spirit, painted on it. Her shaman clothes had 88 snakes with their heads on her shoulders and 88 strips of cloth. As noted, prior to 1945 her brother hid her drum and shaman clothes and in 1945 she burnt everything because she said this was the socialist period and she was afraid. Adding to her fears was the fact that all her four brothers were lamas and three of them were repressed at the end of the 1930s.

Having stopped shamanizing, Tsedenpil became a healer. When she heals she reads Buddhist mantras (prayers). She has no contact with spirits; they don't come to her and she doesn't try now to contact them. She uses massage and pulse to diagnose the patient which helps her to sense normal functions and what has happened to disturb them. She described cases where she healed kidney malfunctions by use of mantras and administrations of flour poultices. Nevertheless, her practice shows a syncretic mix of Buddhism and shamanism; over her altar with Buddhist artifacts she has 13 *ongons* hanging. *Ongons* may be representations of spirit helpers and also dwellings for the spirit helpers to reside in.

Did she really divorce herself completely from her spirits or did they migrate inwards and underground during socialist times? As for the future, she says the small son of her oldest son could become a *zaarin* – she has seen some power in him – but maybe this will never happen because times have changed. The son of her youngest daughter has become a lama and he will sacrilize her 13 shaman *ongons,* which is possible for him to do because one of her teachers was a lama.

The syncretic mix of shamanism and Lamaism (Tibetan Buddhism) is very marked in the practices of healers in Kalmykia. Kalmykia, a republic of Russia located near the Caucasus between the Don and Volga rivers, was settled by the Oirat Mongols in the 17th. century. They arrived with a form of shamanism already strongly overlaid with Buddhism, due to the suppression of shamanism by Lamaism in the early 17th. century in Mongolia. The change in landscape, from an incredibly beautiful mountainous country where the spirits of nature are ever-present to a flat steppe with less points of connection with natural sites strong in spiritual resonance may also have played a role in discouraging shamanism. Both *Kalmyk* healers, Alexandra Semenova and Lyubov Gavrilovna, use many elements of Buddhism in connection with their healing practices.

Alexandra, who has a very active practice as a healer, inherited her calling as a healer from her mother and began healing after suffering illnesses herself for many years, a typical pattern for a shaman. She has spirit helpers, among them the Old White Man, the Buddha *Maitrea,* the Green Tara (helpful for women and children), the medicine Buddha, and the White Tara. She uses massage and touch in healing patients, and also shamanic implements such as an ebonite pencil used for

Fig. 2: Lyubov Gavrilovna– shamans in tent. Kalmykia 10/30/96.

massage, a copper 5-kopek piece good for healing, and a silver 1925 coin efficacious for cleansing from illnesses. During the process of healing she recites a Buddhist meditation prayer which helps her to take off the bad energy from within herself. She communicates with her own personal spirits in order to understand the nature of the patient's problem and the necessary cure, which she then transmits to the patient.
She says she sees so much but she cannot and does not tell all because if she told everything she saw, many people would believe she was not sane.

Lyubov Gavrilovna uses many Buddhist elements in her practice but has many very intensive shamanic attributes. She reads Buddhist prayers only in the Kalmyk language, heals children, massages hearts and has special mantras she reads to heal the heart. She rises at 5 a.m. and reads Buddhist prayers at that hour and also at 9 p.m.
She lights her small Buddhist lamps five times a day. Her special deities are the Old White Man, the Green Tara and the Black Tara. During the period of exile in Siberia (1943-1957) her family saved the 150 year old prayer beads she uses and also some Buddhist *tankas* (images of Buddhist deities). However, despite strong evidence of Buddhism in her daily life and healing rituals, she had studied with a powerful shamaness and knows many shamanic rituals. She uses shamanic elements in her healing, doing needle therapy, touch therapy and can call upon white and black

powers. Her daughter said that this is a method of healing which she does not discuss and that she also has secret shamanic prayers she learned from Aka, her shaman teacher, which she may only reveal on her death-bed. When she was 11 years old she became very ill, so that a special ritual was done for her, asking the Old White Man to come into her head. This was followed by a ritual for the White Tara. After this ritual she had to sit on a special mattress for prayers for 49 days and was not allowed to eat butter or meat. She sat and prayed in a special white tent wearing a white jacket, a chemise and a dress in red, green, yellow or white depending on the deity who is protecting her at that moment.

Margarita Danchinova, a *Buryat* shaman-healer who lives in the Kurumkan region (north-east side of Lake Baikal, Buryatia), exemplifies in many ways the forms of shamanistic practice now prevalent in Buryatia. As a Buddhist from a Khori kinship, she originally sought to deny her calling to become a shaman, but finally, after she made a ritual to the ancestors of her husband, which cleared away all disease away from her, she started a healing practice as a shaman in 1992. She prays to ancestors, to masters of the locality and masters who are around Kurumkan where she lives, and to Barhim-baba, a Mongolian *tengri* (deity) who belongs to the part of Mongolia her family comes from.

She heals mental diseases such as schizophrenia and often treats people suffering from witchcraft thrown on them by other people. She can turn this witchcraft away with blessings and prayers. She told me about a man who came to her because one of his neighbors threw witchcraft on him. His grandfather had disturbed the burial of a powerful shaman, and due to this the man's personal aura was damaged and he did not have any protection, so that it was easy to hurt him further by the use of witchcraft. Margarita healed him by bringing back his soul, asking for help from her ancestors and from the *tengris*.

She may answer peoples' requests by lighting three matches, putting them into water, then cutting the water with a knife and interpreting the image she sees in the water. In the summer of 1999 when I visited her again, she had added a hat and a shaman mirror and bells, she sang and held the patient's pulse and rang bells over the patient's head. This patient, a friend, came to Margarita because of problems at work. Margarita's procedure was a cleansing of coldness and bad energy from the patient.

The patient sat with open hands to receive a blessing. Warmth rose from a bottle of vodka and then Margarita drank vodka from a cup and blew it on the patient's hands, and now the patient could feel the warmth. Margarita herself felt very cold after the first curing of this patient and had indigestion for two days. Another example of healing was the case of a young woman who came to her for help for bad stomach cramps. In this healing, Margarita sat in front of her and with her right hand made grabbing and pulling motions towards and from the patient's stomach, as if pulling black matter from her stomach.

She saw black threads coming out and the patient felt her stomach which was ice cold at first, get warmer and warmer. Margarita's right hand appeared to turn dark after these threads were pulled out, and after the procedure was repeated the

Fig. 3: Margarita Danchinova blowing shaman´s warmth on hands. Kurumkan Region, Buryatia. 3/9/99.
Fig. 4: Valentina Baldakhinova annointing sheep with butter. Buryatia 28/8/99.

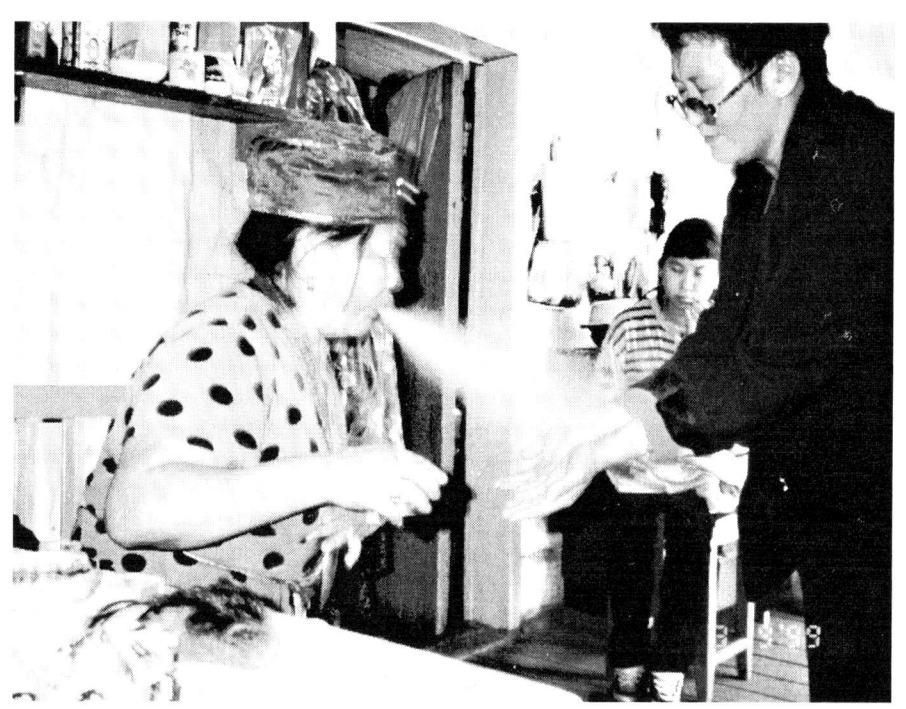

Woman Shaman Healers in Inner Asia – ETHNOMED 2002

patient felt much better and her cramps did not reoccur. Margarita understood this black stuff to come from a bad influence or a witchcraft laid on the patient by a chance unpleasant encounter with a woman on a train.

Valentina Baldakhinova, another shaman-healer with a very extensive and busy healing practice in Ulan-Ude, also deals with many instances of bad influences, contemporary problems of stress, emotional and situational problems - a practice in many ways resembling western psychotherapy - except that she is a shaman, of long shaman heritage, and uses shamanistic methods of treatment and healing. She also treats many physical disorders, using cosmic methods and knowledge of acupuncture points to enable her to do healing from a distance. Shamanistic rituals for the benefit of a community are also an important aspect of Buryat shamanism and Valentina is called upon to do many rituals of this type for the purpose of bringing well-being and spiritual blessing to a particular group of people.

In the late summer of 1999, she was asked to do a ritual in the Mykhorshibirski region of southern Buryatia for the *Tsaagantan Khori* clan. When we arrived at the site in the morning, a large group of people had gathered and were occupied with carrying wood and a large black kettle, as well as a trussed sheep, to the chosen spot. After each person was sanctified with *artish* (juniper branch) the members of the clan were given ribbons which they attached to a birch tree. This tree was cut and planted into the ground, changing the tree into a symbolic flying horse, a tree which also became the hitching post for the horses of the gods when they come to this place. Prayers and libations to the spirits followed with Valentina asking the names of specific family ancestors so she could address them appropriately and ask for their blessings for this clan.

The sheep was then prepared for sacrifice to the clan spirits. She gave it milk to drink and anointed it with milk on its head, back and each foot, followed by a similar anointing with butter. The sheep was ritually cut, then skinned and divided into parts, with the old women advising men how to do it. The women had the traditional knowledge, but were not permitted to touch sacred meat. The skin, legs and head of the sheep were burnt as an offering to the gods. As a the conclusion of the ceremonial rite, the skin of the sheep was laid over a woodpile filled with the bones of the sheep and the birch tree with its ribbons was placed on top. The whole was set aflame - the sheep a sacrifice to the gods, honored by being cremated as its spirit is sent up to the sky. The spirits take the sheep and give success to people instead. This exchange of the domestic animal taken from the flocks of the clan and offered to the deities harkens back to the original hunting offerings by shamans of the slain wild animal with its respectful treatment of head, paws and skin.

The development of a type of neo-shamanism can also be noted among younger shamans who are seeking to recreate a meaningful practice for the new post-Soviet period. A typical example is the Tuvan shaman, Rosa Nasyk-Dorjou, born in 1961 in Bai-Khaakh region, directly south of Kyzyl, the capitol city of Tuva. She grew up in Mongun-Taiga (western steppe of Tuva) with a strong shaman lineage from both sides of her family. She first began to have strange visions when she was an adolescent, but did not begin to heal and work as a shaman until 1991 when she saw the spirit of the mountain at Arzan Shivilig, a sacred spring west of Teeli. She is called to do individual healing as well as the traditional seven day and forty-nine day rituals after the death of a person. In her individual healing she uses a mixture of Shamanism, Buddhism, and modern psychotherapeutic principles in treating people. She wears a special fleece vest lined with silk when she shamanizes (not a traditional shaman garb) and uses her drum and beater to go into an altered state of consciousness, which however lasts only a few minutes. The Neo-shamanic elements are noticeable in her somewhat eclectic approach to healing, and also the brevity of the trance-state.

Much of the rich imagery she sees and the rituals she conducts are traditional in nature. However, she despite her strengths as a healer, she has expressed many doubts as to whether principles of Buddhism or (western) psychotherapy might not be more efficacious in healing.

We therefore cannot see the revival of shamanic healing as a single entity but rather as a multifaceted practice which is based on a shamanic world view relating human beings to natural forces, particular geographic locale, kinship ties and deities as well as to ancestral spirits who can support and sustain humans both individually and as members of an extended clan. Elements of traditional shamanic practices – even traces of transformed hunting rites, Buddhist overlays of artifacts and prayers, and new contacts with western philosophies bringing in knowledge of psychotherapeutic methods of healing have all become a part of shamanic healing in Inner Asia today. In the western world, neo-shamanism with its emphasis on the personal spirit-journey as contrasted with a shamanism always connected to the welfare of the community and its individuals, has held sway and has indeed begun to infiltrate into the shamanism of Inner Asia also. However, certain matters remain constant.

"I asked Rosa why there are so many shamans in Tuva. She said there are so many shamans because there are so many spirits. People can meet these spirits all the time. When people herd sheep, they can meet the low-level spirits of earth and nature. There are many spirits of the earth and mountains and when, as has been the case, many rituals are done asking the mountains for help, then the spirits become strong. When spirits are asked for help, it means the person believes in these spirits, and this belief, says Rosa, makes spirits strong, gives them strength " (FRIDMAN 1998:266-267).

Author

DR. EVA JANE NEUMANN FRIDMAN, PH.D.

Brown University, received her B.A. cum laude from Radcliffe College, Harvard University in the field of History and Literature; specializing in England, France and Germany, she wrote her thesis on the French poet, Guillaume Apollinaire. After earning an M.S. from Simmons School of Social Work in psychiatric social work, she began to work as a psychotherapist, in psychiatric hospitals and mental health clinics; since 1964 she has had a continuing private practice in psychotherapy. She received her M.A. from Harvard University in the field of Anthropology and Archaeology (Master's thesis: Of domestication, dog-husbands and dog-feasts: human-canine interaction in Native North America). Her Ph.D. (1997) at Brown University, Dept. of Anthropology, was focused on the ethnography and archaeology of the Middle East, Eurasia, and Inner Asia with a special focus on nomadism and belief systems.

Her fieldwork was done in the former USSR, in Siberia and Kalmykia. Her dissertation: Sacred Geography: Shamanism in the Buddhist Republics of Russia was followed by a number of papers on various topics of shamanism, religious syncretism in the former USSR, ethnic identity, and current adaptations of Old Believers in Tuva. She has actively been teaching and lecturing in the field of anthropology and psychology at Columbia, Harvard, and Brown University. She is co-editor-in-chief of The Encyclopedia of Shamanism (ABC-CLIO, Inc. (in progress). A Senior Fellow at the Center for the Study of World Religions, Harvard Divinity School, Harvard University (2000-2001), she is currently teaching a course on Shamanism-East and West at Brown University.

Contact: E-Mail: joneva@worldnet.att.net

References

FRIDMAN, EVA JANE NEUMANN 1998 *Sacred Geography: Shamanism in the Buddhist Republics of Russia*. Ann Arbor: UMI.

Abb. 1

VON DER URZEIT LERNEN - BAAWAI, SCHAMANE DER MONGOLEI

von Amélie Schenk

> Wir sind vom Himmel und vom Wasser geborene, sind daraus hervorgegangene und in diese Welt verpflanzte Wesen, und was es damit auf sich hat, ergründet der Schamane. Ja, das Schamanentum ist schon eine Wissenschaft für sich.
>
> ZEREN BAAWAI,
> burjat-mongolischer Schamane

Aus dem schwarzen Himmel kamen einst sechs mächtige Schwarze herunter. Und unter ihnen war auch einer, der hieß Düdger Waantschig, der Himmlische, und so wie sein Himmel, war auch er: schwarz. Es war ein unberechenbarer, ungebildeter schwarzer Himmlischer. Er machte sich schließlich daran, den Weltenberg so wild zu schlagen, wie man Stutenmilch nach landesüblicher Art schaumig schlägt, auf dass sie schneller gärt und zum leicht berauschenden Getränk Kumys wird. Daraus bildete sich ein Wesen, das oben aussah wie eine Frau und unten wie eine Schlange. Dieses Schlangenweib stieg vom Grund des Ozeans empor. Daraufhin tat sich der himmlische Schwarze mit diesem weiblichen Wesen zusammen, und kurz darauf gebar sie aus beiden Seiten je ein Kind. So kamen die ersten Nachfahren des himmlischen Schwarzen in diese Welt. Das ist die Geschichte der Erzeugung des ersten Menschen.

Abb. 2

Diese Geschichte hörte ich von Zeren Baawai, Schamane der Burjaten in der nordöstlichen Mongolei. Ich habe sie in dem Buch "Herr des Schwarzen Himmels" festgehalten. Diese und ähnliche Geschichten erzählen von den Himmeln und ihren Bewohnern, die kamen, um hier auf der Erde etwas anzurichten, das Folgen für das Leben hatte, schließlich kulturstiftend war. An diese einstigen Taten erinnern uns die Schamanen immer wieder: in ihren Zeremonien und ihren Gesängen, wenn es in den Eingangsanrufungen heißt: "*In weiter Ferne, in nordöstlicher Richtung, im Reich am Rande der Welt...*" Epen und Legenden sprechen von alten Zeiten, und so heißt es: *"als die goldene Welt noch schimmerte, die Welt noch jung und grün und feucht war."*

Rituale von der Geburt bis zum Tod

Schamane Zeren Baawai ist also angebunden an die Urzeit, die den Ursprung besingt und feiert, an die Vergangenheit, welche die Herkunft der Schamanen selbst und damit auch die der Menschen kennt. Das ist die Grundlage der Rituale, die an die urzeitlichen Ereignisse erinnern und dadurch den Menschen anbinden an die Vergangenheit, die derart hineinreicht in die Gegenwart, und immer wieder von neuem herbeigerufen und erzeugt wird, auf das sie weiterlebe und uns belebe. Ganz nach dem Grundsatz: Wer sich erinnert, kennt seinen Ursprung, kann seiner ursprünglichen Bestimmung entsprechend leben. Wer sein Woher kennt, wird auch sein Wohin verstehen, ist Reisender, der seinen Anfangspunkt kennt und auch sein Ziel. Menschen sind Reisende durch die Zeit: von Geburt zu Tod und

Abb. 3

weiter zu Geburt und wieder zum Tod und so fort. Um sich an diesen Kreislauf zu erinnern, in ihn einzugehen, ihn in vollem Bewusstsein für die Ganzheit zu leben, bindet der Schamane uns in die Rituale ein. Das wirkt lebensrettend, lebensfördernd in einer Zeit, in der die Vergangenheit und ihre Ahnen vergessen werden und alles auf eine graue Zukunft zujagt, nach mehr und größerem.

In den Ritualen rückt alles zusammen: die Dinge, die Menschen, die Geistwesen, die Ereignisse der Vergangenheit, mit denen einer kommenden Zeit. Im Ritual ist es, wie wenn alles, was geschieht, einem das selbstverständlichste von der Welt ist. Das, was von großer Ferne und aus der Zeit jenseits unserer Lebenszeit kommt, und die eigenen Bewegungen und Bestrebungen laufen ineinander. So wirkt das Ritual.

Prüfung der Schamanen

Es geht hier um die Prüfungen, denen sich ein Schamane zu unterziehen hat und um alle, die in seinem Umkreis leben. *Tschanar* heißt dieses Ritual bei den Burjaten der Mongolei, und es bedeutet: Überprüfung der Fähigkeiten, Qualitätsprüfung. *"Der Tschanar ist das große Buch des Schamanischen, in dem es gilt, lesen zu lernen. Als Weihe ist er dicht, gehaltvoll, fast unergründlich, sein weit verzweigtes Muster lässt die Ereignisse der Urzeit wieder aufleben.*
Da sind die Neun, die, einer Legende nach, die neun Söhne des Himmelsschmieds waren, die herabkamen und den Menschen das Metallhandwerk, diese seine

himmlische Fähigkeit, übermittelten. Der Himmelsschmied selbst ist ein Schamane. Bei den Burjaten können Schmied und Schamane ein- und dieselbe Person sein. Die Neun schützen den Tschanar vor Feindlichem, allein schon durch die Tatsache, dass sie gegenwärtig sind. Einst vom Himmel heruntergekommen, machen sie uns glauben, sie stiegen mit jedem Tschanar erneut herab. Und so, wie sie einst zusammen auftraten, tun sie es auch jetzt wieder: sich an den Händen haltend, ohne auseinander zu gehen. So wirken sie mit vereinten Kräften, die Himmelskinder. Urzeit und Jetztzeit fallen zusammen."

Bedeutung der Bäume

Der Birkenwald, der für dieses Ritual gepflanzt wird, wirkt wie ein großes Feld voller Antennen, die sich zum Himmel hin ausstrecken. Die Bäume streben der Verbindung von unten nach oben, zum Ort der Herkunft entgegen. An der Spitze der aufgesteckten Birken steht eine Lärche. Es ist der Nestbaum, der drei Nester trägt, in dem je drei Eier liegen. Dahinter ragen zwei große Birken empor: eine ist der Mutterbaum, der andere der Vaterbaum.

Das am Anfang stehende Eine wird aufgespalten in das Weibliche und das Männliche. Und diese beiden bringen alle anderen Bäume, die dahinter aufgereiht stehen, hervor. Aus dem Baum mit den Nestern und Eiern geht die Zweiheit hervor, Mutter- und Vaterbaum, und diese bringen die Vielheit hervor. Die Baumreihen, mit je neun Birken, vermehren sich mit jeder Prüfung, die abzulegen ist. Beim ersten *Tschanar* sind es neun Birken, beim zweiten achtzehn und beim letzten, dem dreizehnten sind es dreizehn mal neun, also einhundertsiebzehn Birkenbäumchen, die den Wald aus lauter Antennen ausmachen.

"Das Tschanar-Feld ist nach den Himmelsrichtungen hin ausgerichtet und steht für die Fülle der Möglichkeiten. Steht doch jede Richtung für einen Himmlischen und gleichzeitig für eine Vielzahl von Himmlischen, neunundneunzig Himmlische im Norden, fünfundfünfzig gute im Westen, vierundvierzig böse im Osten und siebenundsiebzig im Süden. Und aus all diesen Richtungen kommen sie auch, nicht aber, ohne von dem silbernen und goldenen Faden, der über alle Bäume bis zum Nestbaum läuft, gelenkt zu werden, heißt es auch im Gesang, und weiter: Sie kommen herbeigewirbelt. Dieser Faden ist die Geisterleitung, der Draht von oben nach unten.

Er gibt den Weg von oben nach unten vor, stellt die Verbindung zwischen Himmel und Erde, zwischen Geistern der Verstorbenen sowie körperlosen Wesenheit und Energiewesen her. Es verknüpft alles, was miteinander in Kontakt treten kann: der große Lebensfaden, der, wie der berühmte rote Faden, das Leben im Großen wie im Kleinen durchzieht."

Es heißt bei den Burjaten: *"Als die Himmlischen einst herabkamen, zeugten sie uns, die menschlichen Wesen, gaben uns Leben ein, verpflanzen uns also von dort nach hier. Und so erinnert auch der Tschanar in seiner Gesamtheit an die Schaffung der Welt und bringt damit gleichsam die Welt von neuem hervor: hier und jetzt."*

Ritual des Schamanen

"Durch den Aufbau des Tschanar-Feldes, die Reinigungsrituale, die Anrufungen, das Kommen der Himmlischen, der Ahnen- und Schamanengeister der vorhergehenden Generationen wird eine Atmosphäre erzeugt, die Urzeit, Jenseits und Diesseits

Abb. 4

einander zudrängt, den zu weihenden Schamanen immer heftiger ergreift, ihn trägt und ihn eintreten lässt in die Nichtzeit, in den Nichtraum, in das Wissen des Nichtwissens, was ihn nur sein lässt, leibhaftig, lodernd. Das ganze Ritual gipfelt in einem Sprung in den Baum. Je heftiger der Schamane den Baum angeht, je höher er hinaufgelangt, desto tiefer und echter erscheint seine Trance. Je weiter er sich von der Erde hin zum Himmel bewegt, desto mächtiger wird er eingestuft."

Letztlich ist dieses Ritual eine öffentlich Angelegenheit, an der alle mitwirken. *"Das ist der tiefere Sinn. Der Tschanar schafft den Raum und die Zeit, indem alles aufgeht und in die Mitte rückt, für alle Anwesenden und Mitwirkenden, vor allem aber für den Schamanen selbst, der erweckt und angesteckt von den Jenseitigen, letztlich eingeweiht wird, um sich auf ihrer Ebene, in jener Welt hinter der Welt, bewegen und dort wirken zu können. Und das mit jedem weiteren Tschanar von neuem."*

Das Eingehen ins Ganze, hier durch die Durchführung des Rituals, macht ganz, heil. Das Ritual des *Tschanar* erneuert die Anbindung an die Urzeit, bindet alle Menschen in der Zeit, die das Ritual anhält, darin ein und lässt sie wirklich leben, indem sie aufleben.

Alle Zitate aus: *Herr des Schwarzen Himmels. Zeren Baawai - Schamane der Mongolei.*

Autorin

DR. PHIL. AMELIE SCHENK
Ethnologin mit Schwerpunkt der Heilweisen der Stammeskulturen. Sie lebte bei den Indianern Nordamerikas, später in Indien mit Lehrauftrag an der Benares Hindu University mit Forschungsreisen in den Himalaya. Derzeitiger Schwerpunkt ist die Mongolei. Ihr Anliegen ist es, die Vermittlung des Wissens und der Kulturtechniken der alten Völker zu fördern. Sie ist Mitgründerin der "Freunde der Altai e.V." und eines Ost-West-Zentrums in der Mongolei, wo sie zur Zeit lebt.
Kontakt: E-Mail: freundedesaltai@hotmail.com

Literatur

SCHENK, A.. 2001. Ich reise mit dem Wind – Schamanen in der Mongolei. In: *Die Mongolei. Aspekte ihrer Geschichte und Kultur,* hrg. VON JOHANNES GIEßAUF, Grazer Morgenländische Studien, Bd. 5, Graz 2001: 119-126.
SCHENK, A.. 2001. Orakel und Heiler in Westtibet. Die Berufung und ihre Verweigerung. In: *Zeitschrift für Ethnologie* 126, Berlin 2001: 63-92.
SCHENK, A.. 2000. Herr des schwarzen Himmels. Zeren Baawai – Schamane der Mongolei, O.W. Barth im Scherz Verlag, Bern, München, Wien.
SCHENK, A.. & H. Kalweit 1998/99. Schamanische Heilung durch Reisen ins Totenreich. In. KRIPPNER, STANLEY & HOLGER KALWEIT (Hgg.): Mythologie, Medizin und Heilung: Transkulturelle Perspektiven. *Jahrbuch für Transkulturelle Medizin und Psychotherapie* 1998/99, Berlin: 103-123.
SCHENK, A.. 1996. Was ist Schamanentum? *Der Grüne Zweig* 192, Löhrbach.
SCHENK, A.. 1994. *Schamanen auf dem Dach der Welt. Trance, Heilung und Initiation in Kleintibet,* Graz.

Abb. 1

LEARNING BY THE PRIMEVAL TIMES-
BAAWAI, SHAMAN OF MONGOLIA*

by Amélie Schenk

> We are born out of the sky and water,
> we are creatures which are
> transplanted into this world and the
> shaman explores what this is about.
> Well, shamanism is a science itself
> ZEREN BAAWAI,
> Shaman of Burjat-Mongolia

At that time, six mighty black creatures descended from the sky. One among them was called Düdger Waantschig, the divine, and he was as black as his own sky. He was an unpredictable, uneducated black divine. Finally, he started to beat the mountain of the world as wild as you usually beat mare milk in our country to make it ferment into the lightly intoxicating drink "Kumys". By doing this, a creature arised, looking like a woman on top and like a snake on the bottom. This snake woman arised from the bottom of the ocean. In answer to it, the black divine joined this female creature and a short time later she beared one child on each side. So the first descendants of the black divine came into this world. This is the tale of the creation of the first human being.

---

* Translated by Katharina Scholz

Abb. 2

I heard this tale from Zeren Baawai, shaman of the *Burjat* in north eastern Mongolia and I put it down in the book *Herr des schwarzen Himmels*. This tale and similar ones tell about the skies and people who came to initiate something here on earth with consequences for our life and cultures. The shamans always remind us of these former acts: in their ceremonies and songs, when they recite their invocations beginning with: "*Far away, in the northeast, in the kingdom at the edge of the world ......*".

Epic poems and legends are talking about former times saying "*When the golden world was still shining, when the world was young and green and fresh*".

Rituals from birth to death

Therefore, shaman Zeren Baawai is connected to the primeval times, that sing about and celebrate the origin; to the past that knows the origin of the shaman himself and of all human beings. This is the base of the rituals that remind us of the events of primeval times and thereby bond the human being to its past . It reaches into the present, is called and renewed again and again so it can live on and stimulate us. According to the principle: those who remember know their origin and can live according to their original destination. Those who know their "where from" will also understand their "where to", and is a traveller that knows the starting point and also the destination". People are travellers through time: from birth to death and further on to birth and death again and so on. To remember this circle, to melt into it and to live it with full consciousness for the whole, the shaman

Abb. 3

ties us up into the rituals. This saves and encourages life in times where the past and the ancestors are forgotten and everything is a chase after a grey future for "more and bigger".

Within the rituals, everything moves up close together: things, people, spirits and the events of the past get together with those of a future time. Within the ritual, everything that happens is the most normal thing in the world. Things arising from far away and from times beyond our lifetimes and the own movements and intentions intermesh. That is the effect of the ritual.

Initiation of the shaman

This is about the initiation the shaman has to go through and in which every person in his environment participates. The Burjat in Mongolia call this ritual "*Tschanar*" and that means "test of the skills, quality check".

"The Tschanar is the great book of shamanism which you have to learn to read. As an inauguration it is profound, rich in content, nearly inscrutable and its wide ramifications revive the events of primeval times. There are the Nine who were, according to the legend, the nine sons of the divine black smith who descended and handed down to the people the metal working, his divine skill. The divine black smith himself is a shaman. At the Burjat, a black smith and a shaman can be the same person. The Nine protect the Tschanar against enemies just with their presence. Once descended from the sky, they make us believe they always descend

again with each *Tschanar*. And like they once performed together, they do again right now : taking each others hand without separating. So they work with their united strength, children of God. Primeval time and nowadays coincide.

The meaning of the trees
The birch wood, which is planted for this ritual, looks like a big field of antennas that stretches into the sky and strives for the connection from earth to sky, to the place of their origin. On top of the prepared birches stands a larch, the "nest tree" that carries three nests with three eggs each. Behind it, two big birch trees rise above: one is the mother tree, the other one the father tree.

The original ONE is divided in the female and the male at the beginning. These two produce all the other trees that are lined up behind them. Out of that tree with the nests and eggs arises the duality mother and father tree and those create the plurality. The rows of trees with nine birches each, increase with every test that has to be passed. In the first *Tschanar* there are nine birches, in the second one 18 and in the last one, the 13th *Tschanar*, there are 13 x 9 = 117 small birches which create the field of antennas.

The song tells: *"The Tschanar field is built to the four cardinal directions and signifies the multitude of possibilities, as any direction stands for one divine and in the same time for a plurality of divines: 99 divines in the north, 55 good ones in the west, 44 bad ones in the east and 77 in the south. And they all come from these four directions but not without being guided by the silver and golden thread that connects all the trees up to the nest tree."* and further on:

"They arrive swirling. The thread is the spiritual bonding, the wire from above to below. It leads the path from above to below, it connects sky and earth as well as the spirits of the dead and corpeless spirits and energy spirits. It connects everything that is able to get in contact with each other: the great life thread that passes through everything in life like the famous red thread. "

The Burjat tell: *"When once the divines descended, they created us, the human beings, they gave life to us and transplanted us from there to here. Thus the whole Tschanar reminds us of the creation of the world and thereby also creates the world once again: here and now."*

The shaman s ritual
"Through building the Tschanar field, the purification rituals, the invocations, the arrival of the divine and the spirits of the ancestors and shamans of former generations, an atmosphere is created in which the primeval time, the beyond and this life merged together. The shaman who is being initiated is involved more and more, the atmosphere carries him away and makes him enter into the non- time, the non- space, into the knowing of the not- knowing that only makes him be passionate, burning.
The whole ritual peaks in a jump into the tree. The more vehement the shaman gets onto the tree, the higher he goes up, the deeper and more real his trance appears. The further he moves from earth to sky the mightier he is said to be."
This ritual is an open ceremony where everybody can participate.

Abb. 4

"This is the deeper sense. The Tschanar creates the space and the time in which everything opens up and comes to the centre for everybody present and participating, but especially for the shaman himself. He is awoken and inspired by the participants, finally is being initiated in order to act and work on their level, within their world behind the world. And this process starts again with every new Tschanar."

The entrance into the whole through the ritual heals and unites. The ritual of the *Tschanar* renews the connection to primeval times, ties people up during the time of the ritual and makes them live entirely by livening them up.

Author

DR. PHIL. AMÉLIE SCHENK
Ethnologist with emphasis on healing treatments within tribe cultures. She lived with the North American Indians, later in India teaching at the Benares Hindu University with expeditions to the Himalaya. She now concentrates the emphasis of her work on Mongolia in order to impart the know-how and the cultural techniques of ancient folks. She founded the "Friends of the Altai e.V. and an East-West-Centre in Mongolia where she is living presently.
contact : freundedesaltai@hotmail.com

References

SCHENK, A.. 2001. Ich reise mit dem Wind – Schamanen in der Mongolei. In: *Die Mongolei. Aspekte ihrer Geschichte und Kultur,* hrg. VON JOHANNES GIEßAUF, Grazer Morgenländische Studien, Bd. 5, Graz 2001: 119-126.

SCHENK, A.. 2001. Orakel und Heiler in Westtibet. Die Berufung und ihre Verweigerung. In: *Zeitschrift für Ethnologie* 126, Berlin 2001: 63-92.

SCHENK, A.. 2000. *Herr des schwarzen Himmels. Zeren Baawai – Schamane der Mongolei,* O.W. Barth im Scherz Verlag, Bern, München, Wien.

SCHENK, A.. & H. Kalweit 1998/99. Schamanische Heilung durch Reisen ins Totenreich. In. KRIPPNER, STANLEY & HOLGER KALWEIT (Hgg.): Mythologie, Medizin und Heilung: Transkulturelle Perspektiven. *Jahrbuch für Transkulturelle Medizin und Psychotherapie* 1998/99, Berlin: 103-123.

SCHENK, A.. 1996. Was ist Schamanentum? *Der Grüne Zweig* 192, Löhrbach.

SCHENK, A.. 1994. *Schamanen auf dem Dach der Welt. Trance, Heilung und Initiation in Kleintibet,* Graz.

DHRUPAD – HEIL UND HEILUNG IM KLASSISCHEN GESANG NORDINDIENS

von Dierk Tietze

Abb. 1

Geschichte des Dhrupad-Gesangs

Klang gilt in Indien als die Grundlage der Schöpfung (*nada-brahma* = das Göttliche ist Klang). Das Weltall ist aus dem Urlaut *Om* entsprungen, der in der ganzen Natur erklingt. Musik wird, nicht nur in Indien, eine besondere Kraft zugeschrieben. *Krschna* soll Vögel und Tiere durch den Klang seiner Flöte bezaubert haben, Orpheus schmolz Felsen mit seinem Gesang.

Gesang wird als höchste Ausdrucksform der indischen klassischen Musik angesehen, da er mit dem Atem unmittelbar als Ausdruck der Seele verbunden ist. Die Stimme drückt unmittelbar unsere Gefühle aus. In alter Zeit dienten Instrumente lediglich zu ihrer Begleitung und auch heute versuchen die Melodieinstrumente noch, sie möglichst gut nachzubilden.

Dhrupad gilt als der älteste überlieferte klassische Gesangstil Nordindiens.

Er ist aus der religiösen Musik entstanden, die als Weg zur Verbindung mit dem Göttlichen betrachtet wird (*Nada-Yoga*). Das Wort *Dhrupad* ist aus den *Samskrt*-Worten *Dhruva* (fest) und *Pada* (Fuß, Versmaß) gebildet und bezeichnet musikalische Kompositionen, in denen Text, Melodie und Rhythmus in einem festen Verhältnis zueinander stehen. Einzelne Zeilen dienen als Grundlage der Improvisation. Als Grundlage der Improvisation dienen im *Dhrupad* Klangsilben, die als *Mantras* ("Sprüche", meist *vedische* Rezitationen, die als heilige Laute gelten) abgeleitet sind.

Dhrupad entstand im 13-15 Jhdt. im Rahmen der *Krschna* Verehrung in Mathura / in Vrindavan und wurde am Hof von Raja Man Singh Tomar (1468-1525) in Gwalior sehr gefördert. Seinen Höhepunkt erreichte *Dhrupad* mit Tansen, Musiker am Hof

Abb. 1: Ustad Ziya Fariduddin Dagar

des Groß-Moguls Akbar (1542-1605). Er ermutigte auch eine Ablösung von der Gelehrtensprache *Samskrt* hin zur Volkssprache *Bhraj*.

Über Tansen gibt es zahlreiche Legenden, die den religiösen Hintergrund und die magischen Wirkungen illustrieren. Eine besagt, dass der Großmogul so entzückt über die Kunst seines Musikers war, dass er dachte, wie gut dann dessen Lehrer sein müsse, und diesen durch einen Boten an den Hof riefen ließ. Der Bote kehrte unverrichteter Dinge heim und berichtete Tansens Lehrer Swami Haridas lasse ihm ausrichten er singe nur für Gott. Daraufhin kleidete sich Akbar in das Gewand eines einfachen Mannes und machte sich mit Tansen auf den Weg zur Einsiedelei von Haridas am Ufer der Yamuna in Vrindavan. Dort wiederholte er seinen Wunsch, erhielt aber die selbe Antwort.

Auch vielfaches Bitten von Tansen half nicht weiter. Daraufhin stimmte Tansen ein Stück an, dass er von Swami Haridas gelernt hatte. Nach einer Weile sang er bewusst eine falsche Note. Als Swami Haridas dies hörte konnte er nicht an sich halten und korrigierte diese umgehend und setzte das Stück, zu Akbars großem Entzücken, einige Phrasen lang fort. Nur so war es Akbar möglich Swami Haridas Singen zu hören.

In einer anderen Legende sang Tansen den Regen-*Raga* inmitten einer Dürreperiode, wonach ein heftiger Regenguss einsetzte. Als er den Feuer-*Raga* sang, entzündeten sich alle Fackeln im Raum. In einer Variante verstarb Tansen durch das innere Feuer, in der anderen fing er an zu qualmen und sprang in den nächstgelegenen Brunnen.

Die Schule von *Darbhanga* führt sich direkt auf Tansen zurück.Die *Dagar*-Schule aus Rajastan enstand aus *Brij Chand* aus *Dagar*, die in direkter Linie auf Swami Haridas zurückführt. Sie waren Brahmanen bis Baba Gopal im 18 Jhundert den Islam annahm und als Baba Imam Khan Dagar bekannt wurde. In den Kompositionen dieser Schule sind beide Religionen vertreten.

Raga und *Tala*

Die indische Musik ist einstimmig und basiert auf *Ragas*. Wörtlich wird der Begriff *Raga* im Samskrt als das definiert, was färbt *(ranjayati iti ragaha)*. Mit diesem Begriff werden Skalen mit fünf bis sieben Tönen, zwei Schwerpunkttönen (*vadi & samvadi*) sowie spezifischen Verzierungen und Sequenzen bezeichnet.

Ausgangs- und Bezugspunkt jeder Darbietung ist der Grundton. Er erklingt auf der Langhalslaute *Tambura*, dessen Saiten (meist vier) leer mit der rechten Hand angespielt werden.

Der Resonanzraum des *Tambura* besteht aus einem Hohlhals und einem Kalebassenkürbis. Zusätzlich zum Grundton erklingt die Quinte, Quarte oder Septime. Durch die besondere Bauweise des Stegs (aus Horn oder Elfenbein) verschmilzt der Klang seiner Saiten in einen sanft surrenden, von Obertönen funkelnden Teppich, auf dem die Melodie sich entfaltet.

Im ersten Abschnitt (*Alap*) setzt der Künstler die Töne des *Raga* nacheinander in Beziehung zum Grundton. Der Raum zwischen zwei Tönen wird mit langsam gezogenen Gleitbewegungen geöffnet. Einzelne Töne und kurze Phrasen werden zu einer Melodielinie aneinander gereiht. Hierbei schreitet er nach einer

Exploration der unteren Oktave voran zur mittleren und oberen Oktave. Nach diesem Abschnitt mit freiem Rhythmus folgt ein leicht pulsierender mittleren Tempos (*Jod*), der seinen Höhepunkt in einem schnell pulsierenden Teil (*Jhalla*) findet.
Grundlage der Darbietung sind Klangsilben. Sie wurden abgeleitet aus dem *Mantra* (Sinn-, Zauberspruch) *Hari Om Narayana tu hi ant tarana ananta hari Om* das auf den *Samaveda* (3. Jahrhundert v. Chr.) zurückgeführt wird.
Im Schlussteil wird ein zwei- oder mehrstrophig vertontes Gedicht religiösen oder weltlichen Inhalts mit vier Zeilen pro Strophe rhythmisch auf der Grundlage von *Talas* ausgestaltet.
Beim *Tala* handelt es sich um eine zyklische, rhythmische Struktur, die in Einheiten von zwei bis vier Schlägen unterteilt ist. Melodie, Stimme und Rhythmusinstrument treffen sich stets auf dem ersten Schlag, zu dem hin die Spannung ständig steigt und sich dort explosionsartig entlädt. Beim sogenannten "leeren Schlag" (*khali*) wird völlige Entspannung erreicht, wonach eine erneute Steigerung einsetzt. Viele Kompositionen liegt der *Cau-Tala* mit zwölf Zählzeiten (4/4/2/2) zugrunde, ein weiterer gebräuchlicher Tala ist *Dhamar* mit vierzehn Zählzeiten (2/3/2/3/4).
Im *Dhrupad* wird zur rhythmischen Begleitung der *Phakavaj* eingesetzt, eine doppelseitig bespannte Doppelkonustrommel, deren hohe Saite auf den Grundton gestimmt wird, während auf der tiefen Saite Oktave, Quinte oder Quarte erklingen. Nordindische *Ragas* werden traditionell nur zu bestimmten Tages- oder Jahreszeiten vorgetragen. Diese Zuordnungen werden in langjähriger Hörpraxis von Kindesbeinen an durch Assoziationen von tageszeitbedingten Stimmungen mit *Ragas* erlernt.

Praktische Übungen beim Erlernen des *Dhrupad*

1. Grundton

Die beste Zeit zum Üben des Grundtones ist der frühe Morgen vor Sonnenaufgang. Bei Männern ist der entspannteste Ton der tiefste, bei Frauen liegt er eine Quint oder Oktave höher.
Er soll musikalisch einwandfrei klingen und mindestens 15-30 Minuten gesungen werden, wobei er von einem *Tambura* oder anderen *Bordun*instrumenten mit konstanter Tonhöhe begleitet wird. So vertieft sich der Atem, durch die Schwingung setzt eine Tiefenentspannung ein.

2. Einzeltöne

Die Töne werden einzeln ohne Verzierung und Bewegung lange aufeinander angehalten. Die Lage des Tones ist wie eine Messerschneide, auf der man wie ein Seiltänzer balancieren muss, um die Lage stabil beizubehalten und ohne Zittern oder Schwanken felsenfest auf einem Ton zu stehen.

3. Silben

Langsam wird eine Silbenfolge zunächst auf einem Ton erarbeitet, später auf drei und auf fünf Tönen.

4. Phrasen / Komposition

Der Lehrer singt / spielt vor, der Schüler ahmt nach, bis die Phrasen korrekt wiedergegeben werden.

Wirkung der Übungen auf die Gesundheit

Es kommt zu einer allgemeinen Entspannung der Sprechstimme, einer Vertiefung des Stimmvolumens und einer Präzisierung der Aussprache. Beim Singen tritt eine Tiefenentspannung auf, die meist angstlösend und schmerzlindernd wirkt. Durch die verschiedenen Vokale werden unterschiedliche Resonanzräume zum Schwingen angeregt.

Vokal	Resonanzbereich
I	Kopf
E	Kehle
A	Brust
O	Bauch
U	Becken

Dhrupad und *Kundalini-Yoga*

Die Resonanzbereiche entsprechen im tantrischen *Kundalini-Yoga* verschiedenen psychischen Zentren (*Cakras*), die sich als Bewusstseinspotentiale auf der Wirbelsäulenachse befinden. Durch sie muss die *Kundalini*-Energie aufsteigen, um sich mit dem Göttlichen, genannt *Shiva* ("Glanz") zu vereinen. Es ist das reine Bewusstsein, das das ganze Universum durchdringt. Das *Samskrt*wort *Kundalini* bedeutet "aufgerollt". Die aufgerollte *Kundalini* wird als die weibliche Energie bezeichnet, die verborgen in jedem Atom des Universums existiert. Die *Kundalini* liegt beim Menschen aufgerollt im Halbschlaf um die Wurzel der Wirbelsäule. Die *Kundalini* wird als Beginn des Urklangs betrachtet. Das Wurzel*cakra* wird daher auch als "Geburtsort aller Klänge" bezeichnet.

Zentren

Name des Zentrums	Bedeutung	Lage
Muladhara Cakra	(Wurzelzentrum)	am Steißbein/Damm
Svadisthana Cakra	(Zentrum des guten Stands)	am Venushügel
Manipura Cakra	(Edelsteinzentrum)	am Bauchnabel
Anahata Cakra	(Zentrum, das unangeschlagen klingt)	auf Herzhöhe
Visuddha Cakra	(Reinheitszentrum)	am Kehlkopf
Ajna Cakra	(Kontroll-, Koordinationszentrum)	zwischen den Augenbrauen
Sahasrara Cakra	(tausendfältiges Zentrum)	vier Finger breit über dem Scheitel

Als notwendige Bedingung für den Aufstieg der *Kundalini*-Energie wird der Rückzug der Sinne durch Konzentration auf einen Punkt bezeichnet, bis die Gedankentätigkeit eingestellt ist.

Durch tiefes, volles Atmen wird ein Maximum von Energie (*Prana*) aufgenommen. Ein ständig wiederholtes *Mantra* zentriert das Gehör. Gesten begleiten es. So wird die Aufmerksamkeit auf einen Punkt fokussiert. Während des Aufstieges werden psychische Bereiche, die verschleiert oder unterdrückt waren schrittweise geöffnet und ins Bewusstsein gehoben. Jeder Knoten, jede Blockade muss so bearbeitet werden, um die Bindungen an die allgemeine Meinung der Realität zu lösen.

Musik und Religion aus mystischer Sicht
Wie manche Dichter der *Bhakti*-Tradition Musik und Religion als ineinander verwoben empfinden, zeigt das folgende Gedicht des Webers Kabir (1440-1518):

Die Flöte der Unendlichkeit spielt fort und fort,
und ihr Ton heißt Liebe:

Wenn Liebe alle Grenzen überspringt,
erreicht sie die Wahrheit.

Wie weit sich der Duft verbreitet!
Er verströmt ununterbrochen, nichts hindert ihn.

Die Gestalt dieser Melodie ist
hell wie eine Million Sonnen:
unvergleichlich tönt die Vina,
die Vina der Musik der Wahrheit.

(Übersetzung Martin Kämpchen)

Autor
DIERK TIETZE, DIPL. PSYCH.
Studium der Indologie in Tübingen, mehmonatige Studienaufenthalte in Indien (Musikakademie Bhopal) bei Ustad Ziya Fariduddin Dagar. Langjähriges Vorstandsmitglied der Deutsch-Indischen Kulturgesellschaft e.V. Tübingen. Tätigkeiten in Bildungsforschung, Familienberatung, Psychiatrie (Musik, Gespräch und Entspannungstherapie) sowie Krebs- und Suchttherapie, derzeit freiberuflich tätig als Psychotherapeut.
Kontakt: E-Mail: Dierk_Tietze@web.de

Literatur

HAMEL, PETER M 1980. *Durch Musik zum Selbst*, München
INAYAT KHAN >HAZRAD< 1987. *Musik und kosmische Harmonien aus mystischer Sicht*, Heilbronn
KÄMPCHEN, MARTIN. 2002. *Krishnas Flöte - religiöse Liebeslyrik aus Indien*, Freiburg i. Br.
MENON, RAGHAVA R 1988. *Abenteuer Raga*, Leimen
MOOKERJEE, AJIT 1984. *Kundalini-Die Erweckung der inneren Energie*, Bern
NEUHOFF, HANS 1992. Klassische Musik in Indien /Nordindische Musik In : *Haus der Kulturen der Welt* (Hrsg.), *Klassische Indische Musik*, Berlin
PANNKE, PETER 1987. *Discographie of EP-LP Recordings of Dhrupad Music*, Benares

Schallplatten-Auswahl

Pandit Ram Chatur Mallik
Inde du Nord / Chant Dhrupad et Dhamar:
Raga Darbari Kanada, Raga Multani — Playa Sounds PS 33513/SF 202
The king of Dhrupad: Ram Chattur Mallik — Wergo SM 1076-50 (1988)
in Concert (ed.PANNKE, PETER)

Ustad Siya Ram Tiwari
Doyen of Darbhanga Gharana:
Raga Darbari, Raga Bageshvari, Raga Adana — HMV/EMI India ECSD 2771

Asad Ali Khan (Rudra Vina)
Raga Miyan ki Todi, Raga Desh — HMV/EMI India ECSD 2533
String Instruments: an anthology of — BM 30 SL 20152
North Indian Classical Music, — Bärenreiter/Musicaphon
Vol. II Raga Vasant

Ustad Ziya Mohiuddin Dagar (Rudra Vina)
Musique classique de l´Inde: Raga Mangeyabushan — Disques Alvarez LD 114
Rudra Veena Recital: Raga Chandrakauns — HMV India ECSD 2736
Raga Pancham Kosh — Auvidis AV 4514 / AD 038

Ustad Rahimuddin Khan Dagar
Dhrupad: Raga Todi, Raga Malhar — HMV 7 EPE 1206
Dhamar: Raga Kedar, Raga Bihag — HMV 7 EPE 1218

Ustad Rahim Fahimuddin Dagar
Dhrupad: Masters of Raga — Wergo (1990)

Ustad Nasir Moinuddin Dagar und Ustad Nasir Aminuddin Dagar
The Music of India III Dhrupad: Raga Asavari, — BM 30 L 2018
Raga Bhairavi — Bärenreiter/Musicaphon
North India: Dhrupad and Khyal: Raga Kamboji — Phillips 6586 003
Dagar Brothers: Raga Darbari Kanada, Raga Adana — HMV/EMI India EALP 1291

Ustad Nasir Aminuddin Dagar und Ustad Ziya Fariduddin Dagar
Alap, Dhrupad and Dhamar: Raga Bhimpalasi,
Raga Yaman **Concert Hall SVS 2793**

Ustad Nasir Zahiruddin Dagar und Ustad Nasir Fayazuddin Dagar
The younger Dagar Brothers, Raga Jayjayvanti **Odeon S MOAE 181**
Vocal Music/ Alap-Dhamar-Khyal-Thumri: Raga **BM 30 SL 2051**
Ahir Bhairav **Bärenreiter/Musicaphon**

Dhrupad: Dagar Brothers: Raga Darbari Kanada,
Raga Adana, Raga Bihag, Raga Kedar **Loft Stereo 1006**

Ustad Ziya Fariduddin Dagar
Raga Chandrakauns **Origo 1002**
Le chant Dhrupad: Raga Bhimpalasi **ESP 8413/SF 16**
SonoDisc/DisquesEsperance

Filme

Kaul, Mani. 1982. *Dhrupad*, Mumbay/Pune, Hindi mit englischen Untertiteln (vgl. Indienfestspiele)
Pannke, P. 1994. *Dagarwani: Musik aus Nordindien* - (VHS 55min, Mitschnitt Arte)

DHRUPAD-HEALING IN THE TRADITIONAL SINGING OF NORTHERN INDIA*

by Dierk Tietze

History

In India sound is regarded to be the base of the creation (*nada brahma* : the devine is sound). The universe came into being from the devine music that fills the whole nature.

Not only in India music is ascribed to a special power. *Krshna* would charm the birds and animals with the enchanting sound of his flute, Orpheus melted rocks with his singing.

Singing is regarded as the highest form of expression in Indian classical music because it originates like *prana* (breath) directly from the soul. The voice is a direct expression of our emotions.

In former times instruments were only used for its accompaniment. Until today the instruments are still trying to imitate the human voice as well as possible.

The *Dhrupad* style is regarded to be the oldest classical music style of northern India. The word '*Dhrupad*' is buildt of the *Sanscrit* words *Dhruva* (solid) and *Pada* (foot, metrum) and means musical compositions in which text, melody and rhythm are bond to each other in a solid relation.

It developed in the 13th- 15th century in the context of the *Krshna* devotion in *Mathura, Vrindava* and was supported a lot at the court of Raja Man Singh (1468-1525) in Gwalior. *Dhrupad* reached its peak with Tansen, a musican at the court of the great- mogul Akbar (1542-1605). He also encouraged the exchange from the *brahmin* language *Samscrt* to the peoples' language *Bhraj*.

Fig. 1: Ustad Ziya Fariduddin Dagar
* Translated by Ingo Armbruster & Joy C. Green

There exist numerous legends about Tansen. They say that the great-mogul was so delighted about the art of his musician that he considered Tansen´s teacher to be a master and sent a messenger to bring this man to the court. The messenger could not achieve anything and told Tansen, his master Swami Haridas let him know that he only sings for God. So Akbar dressed in a simple suit and went down the way to the herimitage of Haridas next to the Yanuma in Vrindavan with Tansen. He repeated his wish, but got the same answer.

Also the numerous pleadings of Tansen would not help. Then Tansen started to sing a composition which he had learned from Swami Haridas. After a while he consciously sang a wrong tone. When the Swami heard this he could not stay calm, corrected the mistake and continued singing for some phrases, for the delight of Akbar. This was the only way possible for Akbar to hear Swami Haridas' singing.

Another legend tells that Tansen sang the rain-*raga* in the middle of a drought, whereafter a strong rain started. When he sang the fire-*raga* all the torches in the room would enflame. In one version Tansen died of his inner fire, in another his body started smoking and he jumped into the next water fountain.

The school of *Darbhanga* goes back in the direct line to Tansen. The *Dagar* school from Rajastan stands in the line of *Brij Chand* from *Dagar*, who is in the tradition of Swami Haridas. They were *brahmins* until Baba Gopal Das converted to the Islam in the 18th century and got known as Baba Imam Khan Dagar. In the compositions of this school both religions are represented.

Raga and *Tala*

Indian music is of one voice and is based on ragas. The expression raga is defined in *Samscrt* with "the one giving colour"(*ranjayati iti ragaha*). The expression is used for scales with 5- 7 notes, two tonic keynotes (*vadi* and *samvadi*) as well as specific additions and sequences.

The tonic keynote is the basis and the reference point of every session. It is played by the *Tambura*, whose strings (mainly four) are played only with the right hand. The resonance- space of the *Tambura* contains the hollow neck and a calebass-pumpkin. Additional to the keynote the quint, quart or septime is to be heard. Due to the special way of the construction of the bridges (from horn or ivory) the sound of its strings melts into a gently swinging sound carpet, sparcling with overtones, on which the melody enfolds.

In the first part (*Alap*) the artist sets a relation between the notes of the *raga* and the keynote. The space between two notes is opened with slowly bending slide movements. Single notes and short phrases are bond together into a melody line. He proceeds, after an exploration of the lower octave, to the middle and upper octaves. After the part with a free rhythm a slightly pulsating mid tempo follows (*Jod*) which reaches its climax in a fast pulsating part (*Jhalla*). Base of the performance are sound syllabels. They come from the *mantra* (magic spell)

Hari OM Narayana tu hi ant tarana ananta hari OM." rooted in the Samaveda (3rd century B.C.).

In the last part a poem with one or several verses, with religious or worldly content, four lines per verse, is rhythmically sung on the base of the *Talas*. The *Tala* is structured into units of 2 to 4 beats. Melody, voice and rhythm instrument always meet on the first beat, up to which the tension is permanently increasing and explosivly unloads at that point. In the so-called "empty beat" (*khali*) complete relaxation is achieved, whereafter a new cycle follows. Many compositions are based on the *Cau-tala* with 12 beats (4/4/2/2), another usual *tala* is *Dhamar* with 14 beats (2/3/2/3/4).

In *Dhrupad* the *Phakavaj* is used for the rhythmical accompaniment, a double-face stringed konus-drum, whose high string is tuned to the keytone, whereas the octave, quint, or quart is to be found on the low string.

Northern Indian *ragas* are traditionally played on special times of the day and year only. These traditions are learned through listening for many years from childhood on, associating daytime-depending moods with certain *ragas*.

Dhrupad in practice

1. Keytone

The best time to rehearse the keytone is early in the morning before sunrise. The most relaxed tone of men is their lowest note, women are a quint or octave higher. It needs to by musically blameless and should be sung at least 10- 15 minutes, accompanied by a *Tambura* or another bordun instrument with a constant tone pitch. Breath is deepened and a great relaxation is achieved through the vibrations.

2. Single tones

Single tones are sung without any movement for a long time. The position of the tone is like the edge of a knife on which you have to balance, like a rope- dancer, to keep a steady tone without trembeling or wavering.

3. Syllables

Slowly a syllabel following will be developed . First on a single tone then on 3 and 5 tones.

4. Phrasing / Composition

The teachers sings/plays and the pupil imitates him until he can repeat the phrase correctly.

Effects

A general relaxation of the voice is achieved, deepening of the voices' volume and precision of the articulation. Deep relexation is achieved through singing, relieving fears and pain. Different vowels reach specific resonance areas in the body, motivating vibrations in them.

vowel	resonance center
I	head
E	throat
A	chest
O	stomach
U	pelvis

The resonance centers correspond to the different psychical centers (*chakras*), consciousness potentials along the spine, found in the *kundalini yoga*. The *kundalini* energy has to raise through it to unite with the godly *Shiva* ("splendor"). It is the real consciousness that prevails in the whole universe. The *samskrt* word for *kundalini* means: unrolled. The unrolled *kundalini* is seen as the female energy, hidden in every atom of the universe. The *kundalini* lies unrolled, half asleep at the root of every person´s spine. *Kundalini* is said to be the origin of sound. The *root cakra* is named to be the place of birth for all sounds.

Chakras

Muladhara Chakra	root chakra	at the coccyx
Svadisthana Chakra	center of position/good stand	mons pubis
Manipura Chakra	gem center	navel
Anahata Chakra	vibrates untouched	heart level
Visuddha Chakra	purity center	pharynx level
Ajna Chakra	control/coordination	between eye-brows
Sahasrara Chakra	thousandfold center	4 fingers wide above the forehead

Nececssary condition to allow the raise of *kundalini*- energy is the retreat of senses through concentration to the point where thinking is stopped.
Through full, deep breathing a maximum of energy (*Prana*) is taken in. Steady repetition of the mantra trains the hearing. Gestures go along with it. So the concentration is focussed on one point. During the raise psychical areas that were hidden or suppressed are opened up step by step, brought forward into consciousness. Every knot, every blockage must be worked on to release the bonding to the average meaning of reality.

Author

DIPL. PSYCH. DIERK TIETZE

Studies of indology at the University of Tübingen. Field studies for several months in India (music acadamy Bhopal). Member in the board of direction in the German-Indian-cultural Society e.V. Tübingen.

Activities in educational research, family therapy, psychiatry (music-, conversation and relaxation therapy) as well as cancer and drug addict therapy.

Works as an independant psychiatrist at the present time.

Contact: E-Mail: Dierk_Tietze@web.de

References

HAMEL, PETER M 1980. *Durch Musik zum Selbst*, München
INAYAT KHAN >HAZRAD< 1987. *Musik und kosmische Harmonien aus mystischer Sicht*, Heilbronn
KÄMPCHEN, MARTIN. 2002. *Krishnas Flöte - religiöse Liebeslyrik aus Indien*, Freiburg i. Br.
MENON, RAGHAVA R 1988. *Abenteuer Raga*, Leimen
MOOKERJEE, AJIT 1984. *Kundalini-Die Erweckung der inneren Energie*, Bern
NEUHOFF, HANS 1992. Klassische Musik in Indien / Nordindische Musik In :
Haus der Kulturen der Welt (Hrsg.), *Klassische Indische Musik*, Berlin
PANNKE, PETER 1987. *Discographie of EP-LP Recordings of Dhrupad Music*, Benares

Records

Pandit Ram Chatur Mallik
Inde du Nord / Chant Dhrupad et Dhamar:
Raga Darbari Kanada, Raga Multani   **Playa Sounds PS 33513/SF 202**
The king of Dhrupad: Ram Chattur Mallik **Wergo SM 1076-50 (1988)**
in Concert (ed.Pannke, Peter)

Ustad Siya Ram Tiwari
Doyen of Darbhanga Gharana:
Raga Darbari, Raga Bageshvari, Raga Adana **HMV/EMI India ECSD 2771**

Asad Ali Khan (Rudra Vina)
Raga Miyan ki Todi, Raga Desh   **HMV/EMI India ECSD 2533**
String Instruments: an anthology of   **BM 30 SL 20152**
North Indian Classical Music,   **Bärenreiter/Musicaphon**
Vol. II Raga Vasant

Ustad Ziya Mohiuddin Dagar (Rudra Vina)
Musique classique de l´Inde: Raga Mangeyabushan **Disques Alvarez LD 114**
Rudra Veena Recital: Raga Chandrakauns   **HMV India ECSD 2736**
Raga Pancham Kosh   **Auvidis AV 4514 / AD 038**

Ustad Rahimuddin Khan Dagar
Dhrupad: Raga Todi, Raga Malhar   **HMV 7 EPE 1206**
Dhamar: Raga Kedar, Raga Bihag   **HMV 7 EPE 1218**

Ustad Rahim Fahimuddin Dagar
Dhrupad: Masters of Raga   **Wergo (1990)**

Ustad Nasir Moinuddin Dagar und Ustad Nasir Aminuddin Dagar
The Music of India III Dhrupad: Raga Asavari,   **BM 30 L 2018**
Raga Bhairavi   **Bärenreiter/Musicaphon**
North India: Dhrupad and Khyal: Raga Kamboji   **Phillips 6586 003**
Dagar Brothers: Raga Darbari Kanada, Raga Adana   **HMV/EMI India EALP 1291**

Ustad Nasir Aminuddin Dagar und Ustad Ziya Fariduddin Dagar
Alap, Dhrupad and Dhamar: Raga Bhimpalasi,
Raga Yaman   **Concert Hall SVS 2793**

Ustad Nasir Zahiruddin Dagar und Ustad Nasir Fayazuddin Dagar
The younger Dagar Brothers, Raga Jayjayvanti   **Odeon S MOAE 181**
Vocal Music/ Alap-Dhamar-Khyal-Thumri: Raga   **BM 30 SL 2051**
Ahir Bhairav   **Bärenreiter/Musicaphon**

Dhrupad: Dagar Brothers: Raga Darbari Kanada,
Raga Adana,   Raga Bihag, Raga Kedar   **Loft Stereo 1006**

Ustad Ziya Fariduddin Dagar
Raga Chandrakauns   **Origo 1002**
Le chant Dhrupad: Raga Bhimpalasi   **ESP 8413/SF 16**
    SonoDisc/DisquesEsperance

Movies
KAUL, MANI. 1982. *Dhrupad, Mumbay/Pune*, Hindi mit englischen Untertiteln (vgl. Indienfestspiele)
PANNKE, P. 1994. *Dagarwani: Musik aus Nordindien* - (VHS 55min, Mitschnitt Arte)

Abb. 1

PFLANZENMEDIZIN IN ZENTRAL-INDIEN*

von Ranjay K. Singh, B.S. Dwivedi, Ashish K. Sharma

Region Baatar, Chhatisgarh

Die Kaktusart *Nagphani* (*Opuntia vulgaris mill*) wird zu **Abtreibung**szwecken genutzt. Die wildwachsende Opuntie wird von den Dornen befreit und das Innere herausgenommen, mit Weizenmehl vermahlen und zu Tabletten geformt.

Jeweils morgens und abends nimmt die Frau dann über vier Tage hinweg je zwei Tabletten mit Wasser ein. Die Dosis kann eventuell erhöht werden. Diese Tabletten dürfen höchstens bis zum 4. Oder 5. Monat eingenommen werden, sonst kann die Medizin für die Frau schädlich sein. In 90 Prozent der Fälle wird der Embryo ausgestoßen.

Der Volksstamm *Gond* in Jalpur

Die Frauen der *Gond* nutzen die Samen einer Pflanze namens *Ghanghchi* (*Glycyrrhiza globera*) um die **Einnistung eines Eis** zu verhindern. Diese Kletterpflanze rankt hohe Bäume empor und produziert rot schwarz gepunktete Samen, die im März geerntet und für den Hausgebrauch gelagert werden.

7-8 Samen werden mit Weizenmehl vermahlen und zu 6g Tabletten geformt. Frauen, die nicht schwanger werden wollen, nehmen nach jeder Menstruation drei Tabletten mit Wasser ein. Die Erfolgsrate ist 80 Prozent.

---

* Übersetzung aus dem Englischen: Adelheid Ohlig
Abb. 1: *Nagphani* (*Opuntia Vulgaris mill*) für Abtreibungszwecke

Ost-Jalpur, Zentralindien

Gegen **Malaria** nutzen Volksstämme in diesem Gebiet die Pflanze *Garaine* (*Caesalpina crista*). Diese Pflanze beansprucht wenig Wasser, oft wird sie als Ackerbegrenzung angebaut, um wilde Tiere von den Feldfrüchten abzuhalten, denn *Gataine* ist haarig und dornig. Von den Haaren befreit wird die Frucht mit Salz und Pfeffer gemischt und etwa eine Stunde lang abgelutscht und gekaut. Diese Medizin muss zehn Tage lang morgens auf nüchternen Magen genommen werden und hat eine Erfolgsrate von 70 Prozent.

Gegen **Gelbsucht** wird diePflanze *Hazardana* genutzt. Sie wächst auf relativ trockenem Boden und gilt als Unkraut. Die Pflanze wird gewaschen, gereinigt und mit Weizenmehl vermahlen zu 12g Tabletten geformt. Einen Moment lang werden jeweils morgens und abends je vier Tabletten zur Heilung von Gelbsucht eingenommen. Während dieser Zeit sollten scharfe und fette Speisen gemieden werden. Diese Medizin hat in 80% aller Fälle gewirkt.

Durchfall bei Kindern bekämpfen die Einheimischen mit *Chhoti Dudhi* (*Euphorbia thymifolia*). Dieses Unkraut wächst in der regenreichen Winterzeit. Aus der Pflanze wird ein Brei bereitet und mit Wasser auf 60ml verdünnt, 8g Salz und 12g Zucker werden hinzugefügt. Das Kind erhält diesen Trank während drei bis vier Tagen viermal täglich. Es wirkt in 80% aller Fälle erfolgreich.

Abb. 2a:
Ghonghchi-Samen oder *Mulhati* (*Glycyrrhiza blabra L.*)
Samen um eine Einnistung zu verhindern

Abb. 2b:
Ghonghchi oder *Mulhati*-Holz (*Glycyrrhiza glabra L.*) zur Schwangerschaftsverhütung

Abb. 3:
Gataine
(Caesalpinia Crista)
gegen Malaria

Abb. 4:
Hzardana (Phyllanthus niruri L.)
gegen Gelbsucht

Abb. 5:
Chhoti Duddhi
(Eurphorbia spp.)
gegen Durchfallerkrankungen
bei Kindern

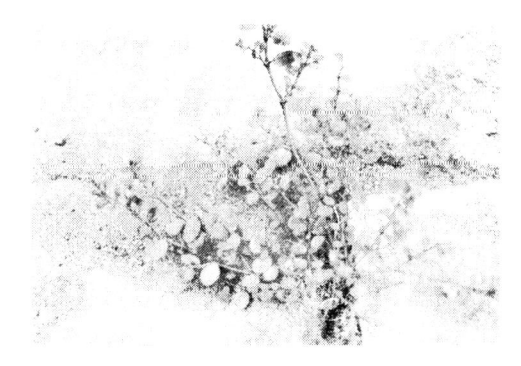

Arthritis bekämpft die Dorfbevölkerung mit der Rinde von *Amerbel* (*Cassytha filiformis L.*). Diese Pflanze rankt an hohen Bäumen in der Wildnis und wird von den LandbewohnerInnen gesammelt.

Ein Kilo Rinde wird mit drei Litern Wasser zu einem Sud aufgekocht, gefiltert und die verbleibende Paste auf schmerzende Stellen aufgetragen und einmassiert. Bis zu 70% der Betroffenen berichten, dass sie schmerzfrei wurden.

Autor
Ranjay K Singh
B.Sc.(Ag) Student JNKVV
Geb. 1974 in Indien, Dr. Agrarwissenschaften , Projektarbeit in Dörfern zur Entwicklung der Landwirtschaft, Forschung zu Weiterbildungsbedürfnissen der ländlichen Bevölkerung, Untersuchungen in Zusammenarbeit mit UNESCO und anderen internationalen Einrichtungen zu traditionellem Wissen und alten Techniken einheimischer indischer Bauern, Veröffentlichungen zu verschiedenen Pflanzen und deren Nutzung in der Behandlung von Mensch und Tier, Mitarbeit bei Zeitungen und Rundfunk.
 Kontakt: Consultant Participatory Developement and Expert Indigenous Knowledge System, C-2, Krishi Nagar Colony, Jabalpur MP-482004, India
E-Mail: ranjay_jbp@rediffmail.com

ETHNOMEDICINE IN CENTRAL INDIA

by Ranjay K. Singh, B.S. Dwivedi, Ashish K. Sharma

Ethnomedicine and abortion

Galloping population growth has posed a major threat to the health and hygiene in India as well as in other developing countries. The majority of resource-poor and tribal people have no allopathic drugs as remedial measures to cope with these problems.

They have developed their own indigenous ways of ethnomedicine as remedial measure for many diseases. In reality, when women acquire an undesired embryo then, for tribal women, it is very difficult to take costly allopathic drugs due to poor economic situations.

But it is very much necessary to feticide the embryo, because the dignity of women is at the stake. One major is abortion. An indigenous way to do abortion is studied by using participant-observation approach at Bastar district of Chhatisgarh in India. For the purpose of abortion a plant named *Nagphani* (Opuntia vulgaris mill) is gathered from a wild area.

First of all, its thorns are removed from the stem and the pulp of stem is then taken out. This pulp is later ground and is mixed with wheat flour, later tablets of 10 gm. are formed. Daily, the patient consumes two tablets in the morning and same amount again at night, with water. Dose can be increased depending on the time from conception. This procedure goes on for the four days. Care should be taken that this medicine is used for abortion only up to 4-5 months of pregnancy. If taken later, then, it may harm the female body. One of the astonishing facts about this ethnomedicine is that its efficiency is more then 90 per cent.

Keywords: Poor people, Ethnomedicine, Abortion, Efficacy.

Fig. 1: *Nagphani (Opuntia Vulgaris mill)* used for abortion

Gond ethnomedicine for inhibiting the women embryo formation

It's quite rubbish to think that poor tribal people can afford costly allopathic drugs for family planning. Due to poor socio-economic conditions and positive beliefs towards native plants, tribal rely on their skills for the family planning. To cope with this problem, a tribe named *Gond* of Jabalpur in India has developed an indigenous ethnomedicine to inhibit embryo formation. Effort have been made to understand the ethnic methodology of this ethnomedicine. Participant-observation was made at this tribe. It was found that tribal people used seeds of *Ghonghchi*, (*Glycyrrhiza globera*), commercial name *Mulhati*, for preventing unwanted embryo formation. This is a kind of climber plant that survives with the help of tall trees by the climbing on the trees. It is well developed under the well-drained land and produces a red and black spotted seed. The seeds of this plant are harvested in the month of March and then stored.

For the purpose of inhibiting the women embryo 7-8 seeds are grounded and mixed with wheat flour to make tablets of 6 gm. Married women generally take 3 tablets a day, at night, along with water usually after each menstrual cycle. Care should be taken to prevent an overdose. It's really exciting to note that the efficiency of this ethnomedicine is about 80 per cent. It takes about one month before embryo formation can occur in the women after stop taking this ethnomedicine. The tribal people are habituated to cultivate part of this plant for its sustainable use.

Keywords: Gond tribe, Economic Conditions, Ethnomedicine, Women Embryo Inhibition

Fig 2a:
Ghonghchi seed or *Mulhati* (Glycyrrhiza blabra L.) seed is used for inhibeting women conception

Fig. 2b:
Ghonghchi or *Mulhati* Stem (Glycyrrhiza glabra L.) Inhibition of women conception

Ethnomedicine for malaria

For health and hygiene we have to combat many diseases and one of them is malaria. Those areas where the medical services are not good and illiteracy, as well as unawareness about preventive measures for malaria is extensive, peoples of those region suffer highly with the germs of malaria. There is a direct relationship between illiteracy and unawareness about health and hygiene with the occurrence of malaria.

An effort has been made to explore the knowledge of resource poor peoples about remedial measures against the malaria disease. During the participant learning expert team has found that, in the eastern part of Jabalpur district, Central India, the malaria problem was raising its head so the people of that region have discovered that the fruit locally called *Gatine* (*Caesalpinia crista*) can be an effective medicine to control malaria. The positive result of this ethnomedicine was found after a trial and error basis done by the local people within the two years for deciding the appropriate doses. *Gataine* is the mesophytic plant, survives best in well-drained soil. There are large number of epidermal hairs on the stem and fruits of the plant.

Some times resource-poor people grow it in areas surrounding of their agricultural farms as fencing busy plants to save the crop from the wild animals. For controlling malaria, *Gataine* fruit is taken and its epidermal hairs are removed. Later this fruit is mixed with table salt and black pepper. After this, the mix it is taken inside of mouth, which is later licked and chewed for about one hour. One should make sure that the medicine is taken on an empty stomach in the morning. This dose is continued for 10 days. Interestingly its efficacy level is found to be 70 per cent against malaria.

Keywords: Resource-poor people, Ethnomedicine, Malaria Disease, Efficacy Level

Fig. 3:
Gataine (Caesalpinia Crista)
used for control of malaria

Ethnomedicine for the jaundice

Poverty leads to unhygienic conditions and among this stagnant water poses a basic problem for many diseases under the poor socio-economic conditions. This problem paves the way for jaundice usually among the developing societies. The people in the eastern part of Jabalpur district in Central India are facing this problem and these resource-poor people have developed an indigenous approach to control jaundice.

An effort has been made by using the participatory rural appraisal (PRA) to find out the ethnomedicine used by resource-poor people used the plant locally called *Hazardana* for controlling the jaundice. This annual herbaceous mesophytic plant grows as a weed in the cropping area and requires well-drained soil. Firstly the plant is taken, then properly washed and cleaned. Later it is properly ground and it is mixed with wheat flour for the formation of near about 12 gm of tablets. The daily dose of this medicine consists of taking four tablets in the morning and the same dosis at the night. This dose is continued for the period of one month for a complete cure of jaundice. Care should be taken to avoid taking spices and oily foods during its dosal period. It is quite interesting to find that the efficacy level of this ethnomedicine was found to be more than 80 per cent.

Keywords: Resource-Poor people, Ethnomedicine, Jaundice, Efficacy.

Fig.4:
Hzardana (Phyllanthus niruri L.) used for control of jaundice

Ethnomedicine for dysentery among children

Impoverished conditions are surely posing a major threat to the health of children. Poverty leads to illiteracy and illiteracy paves the way for unhealthy and unhygienic conditions among the children of resource-poor peoples. It's very difficult for resource-poor people to have easy access to costly medical treatment because they live far away from the medical and health services. Illiterate contributes to their unawareness and lack of mission mode programs from the government side. Therefore, they totally depend on their local resources and have developed their ethnic way to control dysentery among children.

One of the effective medicines used for this purpose around the eastern part of Jabalpur district Central India is the essence of *Chhoti Dudhi* (Euphorbia thymifolia) This herbaceous weed mainly grows in rainy, winter seasons usually under moist conditions. The result pertaining study was recorded by using the participatory approach. It was found that resource-poor people take the herb of *Chhoti Dudhi*, about 30 gm and after proper cleaning it is ground well and a paste is formed. It is then mixed with water to form a solution of 60 ml. After this, about 8 gm common salt and about 12 gm sugar are added in this solution. This dose is given to a child 4 times a day. This practice is continued for 3-4 days for the complete cure of dysentery. Interestingly the efficacy level of *Chhoti Duddhi* against control of jaundice among children was found to be more than 90 per cent among children of 8 years old.

Keywords: Resource-Poor people, Ethnomedicine, Dysentry, Children, Efficacy.

Fig. 5:
Chhoti Duddhi
(Eurphorbia spp.)
used for treatment of
child dysentery

Ethnomedical pain killer for arthritis

With increasing age, synovial fluid and synobial cavity are affected. This produces pain in the bones due to the stiffness of joints. It is hard to imagine that the resource-poor people can afford costly medicines from the market for getting the relief from arthritis. They are socio-economically poor and face a lot of the problem with their health management due to poor medical and health services.
Alternatively they have developed their local knowledge, on a trail and error basis, to utilize the natural resources available to them from their local surroundings.
Poor people of eastern Jabalpur, Central India use the locally called *Amerbel bark (Cassytha filiformis L.)* to get relief from the horrible pain of arthritis. *Amerbel* thrive, basically, tall trees around the woody. For the preparation of medicine against arthritis 1 kg of *Amerbel* bark is collected from a wild area and is boiled with the 3 liters of water till one-liter decoction is left.
Later it's filtered. The solution so obtained is applied over the arthritis affected bones. Proper massage of this decoction is done for up to the 25 minutes. It's wonderful to note that this medicine gives 65-70 per cent relief from pain.

Keywords: Resource-Poor people, Ethnomedicine, Arthritis, Efficacy.

Author
RANJAY K SINGH
B.Sc.(Ag) Student JNKVV
born in 1974 in India, doctor in agricultural science; field works in villages for "development of agriculture"; reaearch about needs of development of rural population; inquiries (in cooperation with UNESCO and other International institutions) about traditional knowledges and old techniques of native, indian farmers. Publications about various plants and their applicability in treatments of humans and animals. Cooperation with newspapers and radio stations.
Contact: Consultant Participatory Developement and Expert Indigenous Knowledge System, C-2, Krishi Nagar Colony, Jabalpur MP-482004, India
E-mail: ranjay_jbp@rediffmail.com

GEISTER-BESESSENHEIT UND GEISTER-AUSTREIBUNG IN INDIEN IM TRADITIONELLEN UND WESTLICHEN VERSTÄNDNIS

von Traute Dattenberg-Holper

Vorbemerkung: Was ist Besessenheit?
Der Glaube, dass fremde Wesen den Menschen in Besitz nehmen können, ist in allen Kulturen zu finden. Diese Vorstellung bietet sich als Erklärung an, wenn sich der Mensch verändert fühlt. Die abendländische `Besessenheit´ im christlichen Kontext war besonders negativ durch den `Teufel´ geprägt.
In Indien ist das religiöse Phänomen der Besessenheit weit verbreitet und hat an sich keinen Krankheitswert, sondern wird als Verbindung zur Transzendenz aufgefasst. So ist die Besessenheit durch Götter erwünscht, jedoch die durch Geister unerwünscht, weil sie krank machen kann.

Bei der indischen Besessenheit handelt es sich um Phänomene einer ekstatischen Religion (LEWIS), denn sie ist mit Trance-Zuständen verknüpft. Entsprechende westliche Bezeichnungen sind: Exstase, Hypnose, Dissoziation und außergewöhnliche Bewusstseinszustände: altered states of consciousness = ASC. Die Trance kann induziert werden durch Tanz, Musik, verstärktes Atmen (Hyperventilation) und Phantasien, besessen zu sein (Autosuggestion).
Es werden in Indien dazu keine Drogen benutzt. Während bei uns Trance kaum bekannt ist, ist sie in traditionellen Kulturen (Afrika, Südamerika, Japan, Haiti) die am weitesten verbreitete psychotherapeutische Technik überhaupt.

In welcher Beziehung steht die Geister-Besessenheit zur indischen Kultur?

Den kulturellen Hintergrund für den Glauben an Geister in Indien bildet der Hinduismus in seiner volkstümlichen Form. Die Geister-Besessenheit ist ein religiöses und soziales Phänomen, sie spiegelt die Machtstrukturen von Glaubensüberzeugungen und gesellschaftlichen Realitäten wider. Was die religiöse Seite betrifft, gehören die Geister zur bunten Vielfalt von transzendenten Kräften. Der Gläubige kann sich eingebettet fühlen in eine kosmische Hierarchie von Göttern, Geistern und Dämonen. Dabei sind die Götter die mächtigsten, dann folgen die Dämonen, darunter stehen die Geister. Jedoch sind die Machtverhältnisse unter den transzendenten Kräften nicht starr und diese Mächte sind nicht eindeutig gut oder böse, sondern die Ordnung muss immer wieder neu errungen werden. Das geschieht beispielsweise dadurch, dass die Götter gegen die Geister zu kämpfen haben.

Nach hinduistischer Sicht handelt es sich bei den Geistern um Verstorbene, die durch unglückliche Umstände nicht gleich wiedergeboren werden können und sich stattdessen in lebende Körper einnisten wollen, um ihre Bedürfnisse nach Hunger, Sexualität und Macht zu befriedigen. Es gibt drei Gründe dafür, dass Verstorbene zu Geistern werden:

    Der vorzeitige Tod, z.B. von Kindern

    Der gewaltsame Tod, z.B. Mord, Selbstmord, Unfalltod

    Ein unsittliches Verhalten, z.B. sexuelle Verfehlungen zu Lebzeiten

So handelt es sich bei den Geistern überwiegend um solche Verstorbene, die man für böse oder unglücklich hält. Daraus wird für die Gläubigen erklärbar, dass Geister von bösen, aber vor allem von unbezähmbaren Wünschen getrieben sind und gegen die Ordnung von Menschen und Göttern agieren.

Die westlichen Wissenschaftler deuten die Geister als abgespaltene Persönlichkeits-Anteile der Besessenen, d.h. als Symbole für unterdrückte Wünsche wie sexuelle Begierde, Wut, Neid und Hilflosigkeit. Die Menschen seien besessen von ihren unbewussten Konflikten, die sie nach außen projizierten.

Die Gesellschaft in Indien ist durch das Kastensystem (vier Hauptkasten mit jeweils hunderten von Unterformen) geordnet. Prinzipiell haben höhere Kasten mehr Macht über untere, man ist aber auch gegenseitig abhängig voneinander und deswegen um Zusammenhalt bemüht. In eine Kaste wird man geboren und in ihr wird man verheiratet. Mit Angehörigen anderer Kasten sind Berührungen zu meiden, z.B. ein gemeinsames Essen ist tabu.

Der religiöse Hintergrund der Kasten-Ordnung zentriert sich um Reinheitsvorstellungen. Es handelt sich um eine spirituelle oder rituelle, keine materielle, Reinheit. Diese kann schon in früheren Leben durch gute Taten (*karma*) angesammelt worden sein oder durch Geburt in eine bestimmte Kaste mitgegeben werden oder ist auch durch gottgefälligen Lebenswandel zu erwerben. Nur den wenigen, die den höchsten Grad von Reinheit erreichen, kann es gelingen, den Kreis der Wiedergeburten zu unterbrechen und in ein göttliches Paradies einzugehen. Die Geister sind sehr weit von diesem Ziel entfernt, denn sie gelten als besonders unrein.

Der Grad der rituellen Reinheit geht in etwa parallel zum gesellschaftlichen

Ansehen der Person. Menschen aus den höheren Kasten, wie der Priester- und Kriegerkaste besitzen sowohl mehr rituellen wie sozialen Status als die aus den Händler- und Bauernkasten. Die niedrigsten sind die Kastenlosen (`Unberührbare´).
Die gesellschaftliche Ordnung für Männer und Frauen beruht ebenfalls auf Vorstellungen von Reinheit und Hierarchie. Die Frauen gelten als grundsätzlich unreiner, was mit der weiblichen Menstruation assoziativ verknüpft wird. Die in den Traditionen befangenen indischen Frauen sind spezifischen sozialen Repressionen ausgesetzt: In allen Lebensphasen ist die Frau einem Mann zugeordnet, der über sie Gewalt hat: dem Vater, dem Ehemann und nach dessen Tod dem Sohn. Ein Großteil der indischen Frauen wird von den Eltern verheiratet und bleibt rituell und ökonomisch abhängig vom Mann. Der Generationenwechsel Tochter – Ehefrau –Witwe ist oft verbunden mit einem traumatischen Identitätswechsel. Die Braut muss ihre Familie und ihr Dorf verlassen, um zu den Angehörigen des Ehemannes zu ziehen. Als Witwe hat sie auch im Haus nichts mehr zu sagen, es bestimmt jetzt der Sohn. Die Sexualität der Frau unterliegt einer starken Kontrolle. Wenn sie nicht keusch und treu ist, bringt sie nicht nur sich selbst, sondern auch ihre Familie und ihre Kaste in Unehre. Insbesondere sind sexuelle Beziehungen zu einem Mann unterer Kasten tabu.

Aus dem Konzept der Reinheit – Unreinheit wird nun verständlich, dass die unreinen Geister bevorzugt bei den unreineren Frauen vermutet werden und bei Angehörigen der niederen Kasten. Tatsächlich findet man die Geister-Besessenheit überwiegend in niederen Kasten und zu etwa zu 70 Prozent bei Frauen , während es nur die reineren Männer sind, die von göttlichen Kräften besessen werden können. Denn die Götter sind rein und mächtig. So gibt es Männerkulte in Indien, die die Göttinnen-Besessenheit zur Stärkung ihres rituellen und sozialen Status suchen. Dagegen wird die Besessenheit bei Frauen immer als Geister-Besessenheit und damit als Unglück oder Krankheit verstanden.

Was hat Geister-Besessenheit mit dem *Ayurveda* zu tun?
Die zweitausend Jahre alten Vorstellungen von Gesundheit, Krankheit und Heilung in Indien beruhen auf der hinduistischen Lehre des *Ayurveda* (Das Wissen vom Leben). Eine seiner acht Fachrichtungen hat die Geister-Lehre (*bhutavidya*) zum Inhalt. Die heutige Ausprägung des *Ayurveda* wird von den *Ayurveda*-Heilern (*Vaids*) vertreten und spielt neben der in Indien akzeptierten westlichen Medizin eine wichtige praktische Rolle. Viele Inder fahren heute zweigleisig mit westlichen und *ayurvedischen* Ärzten.
Ayurveda ist eine Mischung aus religiöser und rational-empirischer Medizin. Nach seiner ganzheitlichen Auffassung zeigt sich jede Störung sowohl im körperlichen wie im seelischen Bereich. Krankheiten werden als eine Disharmonie der drei Körpersäfte (*tridoshas*) verstanden. Sie können aber auch durch astrologische, karmische und andere übermenschliche Kräfte wie Götter und Geister verursacht sein, die dann wieder das Ungleichgewicht der Säfte hervorrufen. Die ayurvedischen Ärzte behandeln Geisteskranke mit Ermahnungen, Tröstungen und körperlichen Medizinen. Nur Männer dürfen als rituelle Spezialisten (Exorzisten) Geister-Austreibungen durchführen.
Die Ursache für die Geister-Besessenheit ist also nach der ayurvedischen Lehre eine Unausgewogenheit der Körpersäfte, die gleichzeitig eine kosmische

Unordnung zeigt. Der Geist wird gesehen als ein metaphysischer Feind, der in den Körper eindringt. Schuld hat der Geist und damit hat die Krankheit eine äußere Ursache. Die Besessene und ihre Familie haben nur eine Teilschuld durch Übertreten sozialer Verbote.
Dementsprechend ist der Exorzismus ein Heilungsritual, das den metaphysischen Feind bekämpft, die Schuldigen bestraft, die sozialen Tabus erneut einsetzt und das Gleichgewicht der Säfte und der kosmische Ordnung wieder errichtet.

Da westliche Schulmediziner nicht an Geister glauben, geben sie den Geister-Besessenen gern die Diagnosen `Hysterie´, `Angstneurose´ oder `Psychose´ und meinen damit exaltierte Gefühle, starke Suggestibilität und phantastische Einbildungen bis zum Wahn. Da die Geister-Besessenheit aber nicht eine Krankheitseinheit im westlichen Sinne darstellt, sollte man sie gar nicht übersetzen oder sehr breit als `Leiden´ oder `Störung der Befindlichkeit´ begreifen.

Wie ist die Geister-Austreibung in Indien zu verstehen?
Vor allem ist sie ein Heilungsritual, das mal mehr einem Gerichtsverfahren, mal mehr einer Theater-Aufführung gleicht.
Die Geister- Austreibung ist ein Reinigungsritus. Denn eine Geister-Besessenheit ist eine gefahrvolle Verunreinigung für den Betroffenen, das Haus und die Angehörigen.
Die grundlegende Struktur eines Exorzismus ist folgende: Zuerst ist eine Diagnose zu stellen. Aus den Symptomen Zittern und Schütteln ist die Furcht der Befallenen vor ihrem Geist zu erschließen. Wenn die Opfer bewusstlos werden oder in Trance geraten und mit fremder Stimme sprechen, ist die Diagnose zwingend. Offenbar kann aber jede Art von Störung einen Verdacht auf Geister-Besessenheit aufkommen lassen. Dann diskutieren Verwandte mit einem Wahrsager oder Exorzisten solange, bis alle von der Geister-Besessenheit überzeugt sind. In der Folge wird ein exorzistisches Ritual notwendig. Es findet im Haus der Betroffenen, auf einem öffentlichen Dorfplatz oder in einem Heiltempel statt, zu dem die ganze Familie pilgert.
Dort beginnt der eigentliche Exorzismus mit der Anrufung von Göttern. "Kommt und helft, denn nur Eure Macht ist wirksam" wiederholt in rituellen Gesängen der Exorzist. Dann wendet er sich dem Opfer (also der Frau) zu und das Ritual der Befragung des Geistes beginnt: "wer bist Du"? Dies ist der wichtigste und für uns befremdendste Teil des Rituals: Das Opfer muss sich meist bemühen, in Trance zu kommen, denn nur dann kann mit dem Störenfried verhandelt werden. Wenn der sich sträubt, wird er von allen Beteiligten bedrängt, verbal oder auch handgreiflich: die Geister-Besessene wird an den Haaren gezogen und auf die Knie gezwungen. Endlich wird sich der Geist geschlagen geben, indem er durch den Mund der Frau spricht. Er wird gestehen, wie er heißt, warum er kommt, was er will. Zum Schluss hat er zu versprechen, dass er wieder weggeht. Um ihn zu vertreiben, können alle Kampfmittel eingesetzt werden: streiten, lächerlich machen, bedrohen, schlagen, bestrafen oder schlichten. Dieser Kern der Zeremonie kann bis zu mehreren Stunden dauern.

Zur Illustration berichte ich aus der Krankengeschichte des Mädchens Shakun, 19 Jahre, die sich in einem indischen Heiltempel mit Mutter und drei Brüdern den

Austreibungsriten unterzog (KAKAR 1984: 71).

Mit 16 Jahren wurde sie erstmalig vom Geist der toten Tante ergriffen. Shakun hatte angstvoll geschrieen, denn sie sah vor dem Einschlafen, wie sich ihr eine lachende Frau näherte, auf ihrem Kopf herumtanzte und ihr heftige Kopfschmerzen verursachte. Seitdem litt Shakun unter Angstanfällen und Kopfschmerzen, wenn die Frau sie in regelmäßigen Abständen besuchte. Der Geist der Tante entsprach den typischen Geister-Vorstellungen, denn sie war ehebrecherisch gewesen und hatte sich umgebracht.

Folgende Szene veranschaulicht die Atmosphäre im Heiltempel (Bharatpur, nördlich von Delhi)

"Im Hof drängen sich die Menschen. Die meisten sind junge Frauen; viele von ihnen sitzen oder liegen in wunderlicher Stellung am Boden. Ein junges Mädchen, vielleicht 18 Jahre alt und ziemlich attraktiv, aber von einer unnatürlichen Blässe des Gesichts, liegt auf dem Rücken. Das offene Haar fliegt ihr um den Kopf, den sie heftig hin und her schüttelt, während ihr Gesicht von Schmerz verzerrt ist. Sie bewegt die Lippen in einem unhörbaren Flüstern, doch dann bricht wieder ein überlauter Schrei aus ihrer Kehle: `Baba, Baba, ich will nicht weg! Ich will nicht weg!´ - es ist ein bhuta (Geist) (ein männlicher bhuta, nach dem Klang der Stimme und der Verbalform zu urteilen), der sich sträubt, ihren Körper zu verlassen. Ein anderes junges Mädchen…..kniet am Boden, die Arme nach hinten gestützt, und bewegt aufreizend die Hüften und das Becken, wie um einen unsichtbaren Angreifer einzuladen und gleichzeitig abzuwehren. `Geh weg! Geh weg! Lass mich los` ruft sie mit lauter Stimme. Dann entringen sich ihr tiefe Seufzer: Oh Baba, Oh Baba`, während ihre fest geschlossenen Augen die Außenwelt von ihrem einsamen Kampf mit dem Geist, der sie besessen hat, fernhalten" (KAKAR 1984: 64).

Das Tempelpersonal besteht hier aus Priestern, die die rituelle Verbindung zum Affengott *Hanuman* herstellen. Mit den Opferspeisen, die die Familie mitgebracht hat und die aus Kokosnüssen, Reis und Geld bestehen, wird das Gottesbild berührt. Man glaubt, dass dadurch göttliche Kraft in den Patienten eingeht und den Geist zwingt, zu erscheinen: dieser soll durch den Mund des Mädchens sprechen. Mit Spannung erwartet die Tempelgemeinschaft, dass die Frau in den erkennbaren Besessenheits-Zustand fällt. Dann wird sie mit der Stimme des Geistes antworten, tanzen, weinen, klagen, in Wutausbrüche oder Obszönitäten verfallen. Nach der Zeremonie wird sie keine Erinnerung mehr daran haben. Amnesie nach Trance ist ein häufiges Phänomen.

Das Tempelritual gleicht hier einem Gerichtsprozess: in strengem Ton stellt der Priester den Geist zur Rede. Im Verhör soll sich der Geist zu erkennen geben: wer er ist, an was er leidet, warum er das Mädchen besitzen will, was er fordert, damit er für immer verschwindet? Oft wird ihm etwas Verlockendes in Aussicht gestellt, z.B. Süßigkeiten oder ein schöner roter Stoff. Manchmal muss die Familie dem tobenden Geist versprechen, das Mädchen nicht mehr zu schlagen oder nicht zur Heirat zu zwingen. Zum Schluss entgeht der Geist aber nicht der Strafe, diese muss allerdings die Besessene ertragen: sie wird sich selbst Schmerzen zufügen oder sich fesseln oder sich in schmutzige Abwässer setzen.

Frauen überwiegen nicht nur als Besessene, sondern Mütter, Tanten und Töchter begleiten auch ihre Angehörigen zu den Heiltempeln, in denen die Familie oft Wochen und Monate verweilt und die Rituale wiederholt, wenn die Besessenheit nicht verschwindet. Frauen in Indien sind besonders verantwortlich für die Gesundheit der Familie.

Für die Exorzisten ist es dann ein Heilungserfolg, wenn unreine und böse Geister von den reinen und guten Göttern verdrängt wurden. Dazu dienen die Rituale, sie müssen nur richtig ausgeführt werden.
Die Wirkungen einer Austreibung im westlichen Sinn (Effektivität) sind nie gemessen worden, jedoch berichten die Forscher glaubhaft von Erleichterungen und Heilungen.

Acht ethnologische Autoren haben in den letzten 40 Jahren auf Grund teils jahrelanger Feldforschungen in Indien ihre Interpretationen zur Geister-Besessenheit entwickelt. Die Rituale können von Ort zu Ort sehr unterschiedlich sein. Die Forscher ergänzen sich in ihren Beobachtungen, aber widersprechen sich in ihren Deutungen der Rituale. Die Widersprüche in diesen Theorien scheinen dadurch zustande zu kommen, dass jeweils einzelne Aspekte des komplexen Geschehens besonders hervorgehoben werden. Denn Gegensätze sind im Austreibungs-Ritual essentiell, wenn kulturell erwartet wird, dass antisoziale Emotionen mit der traditionellen Ordnung kämpfen.

Hier folgen Beispiele aus den wissenschaftlichen Theorien:
Die Amerikanerin NABOKOV, die in Südindien (*Tamil Nadu*) forschte, vertritt die Unterdrückungs-Theorie: Das Ritual fördere die Repression der Frauen. Diese würden, wenn sie von zu Hause weggelaufen sind, durch die Geister-Austreibung öffentlich gezüchtigt und zur Konformität als Ehefrauen gezwungen. Den engen Verwandten ermögliche das Ritual, ihre Autorität innerhalb der häuslichen Ordnung wieder herzustellen.

Dagegen verficht die deutsche Medizin-Ethnologin PFLEIDERER, die in Nordindien (*Gujarat*) das Ritualgeschehen dokumentierte, die Kompensations-theorie: Die Art des dortigen Exorzismus biete eine hilfreiche Kompensation für die unterdrückten Frauen. Im Ausnahmezustand der ekstatischen Raserei könnten sie ihren Protest, ihre Wut und Ohnmacht, ihre unsittlichen Wünsche und seelischen Verletzungen wie auf einer Bühne ausleben. Das führe zu einer Stärkung der Person. Die Gemeinschaft erlebe die exorzistischen Aufführungen mit ihrem spielerischen Unterhaltungscharakter wie eine befreiende Kunstform (PFLEIDERER 1994, KAPFERER 1983).

Der indische Psychoanalytiker KAKAR hat die psychotherapeutischen Wirkungen der Austreibungsrituale differenziert und dabei den Aspekt der Familientherapie hervorgehoben:

> Die Kranke erhält Aufmerksamkeit von ihrer Familie, der Tempel-gemeinschaft und den göttlichen Kräften.
>
> Zweitens wird ihr geholfen, ihrem Leiden, dem Geist, ins Gesicht zu sehen, wodurch der Schrecken gemildert wird.
>
> Drittens kommt es zu einer Reinigung von krankmachenden Affekten, wobei verbotene Impulse ausagiert werden - ermutigt durch die anfeuernden Zuschauer.

Viertens wird die Patientin gleichzeitig die Verantwortung für ihre Ausbrüche dem bösen Geist zuschieben dürfen (Projektion) und selbst schuldlos bleiben.

Fünftens wird versucht, die belastenden Lebensumstände zu lindern, indem man die Familienangehörigen nötigt, sich mit den Forderungen der Kranken auseinanderzusetzen.

Sicher ist das indische Heilungsritual der Geister-Austreibung nicht anwendbar in der westlichen Welt. Es ist in Indien verwurzelt. Dort wird es auch heute noch durchgeführt.

Autorin
DR. MED. TRAUTE DATTENBERG-HOLPER
Psychoanalytikerin, Psychotherapeutin, M.A. der Ethnologie, Ethnologin.
Kontakt: E-Mail: dattenberg-holper@freenet.de

Literatur
KAKAR, SUDHIR, 1984: *Schamanen, Heilige und Ärzte. Psychotherapie und traditionelle Indische Heilkunst.* München: Biederstein. (Original: 1982: Shamans, Mystics and Doctors)
KAPFERER, Bruce, 1983: *A Celebration of Demons. Exorcism and the Asthetics of Healing in Sri Lanka.* Washington: Indiana Univ. Press
LEWIS, ION, M., 1971: *Ecstatic Religion. An Anthropologic Study of Spirit Possession and Shamanism.* Harmondsworth: Pinguin Books
NABOKOV, ISABELLE, 1997: Expel the Lover, Recover the Wife: Symbolic Analysis of a *South Indian Exorcism.* J. Roy. Anthrop. Inst. 3: 297-316
PFLEIDERER, BEATRIX, 1994: *Die besessenen Frauen von Mira Datar Dargah. Heilen und Trance in Indien.* Unter Mitarbeit von VIRCHAND DHARAMSEY. Frankfurt/ M., New York: Campus

SPIRIT OBSESSION AND EXORCISM IN INDIA IN TRADITIONAL AND WESTERN TERMS*

by Traute Dattenberg-Holper

Preliminary remark: what is obsession?

The belief that foreign entities can take possession of a human is found in every culture. This image serves as a good explanation when people feel changed. The occidental "obsession" in christian terms was negatively marked by the devil. In India the religious phenomenon of obsession is widespread and not regarded as illness-related but as a connection to transcendency. The obsession by gods is desired, the obsession by spirits is not desired, because that can cause a person to be sick.

The Indian obsession is a phenomenon of an ecstatic religion (LEWIS) because it is linked with states of trance. The trance can be induced by the use of dance, music, heavy breathing and phantasies of being posessed. To reach this altered state no drugs are used in India. Trance is hardly known in our culture, whereas in traditional cultures it is the most widespread psychotherapeutic technique.

What connection can be found between spirit obsession and Indian culture?

Hinduism in its traditional form serves as a cultural background for the belief in spirits in India. Obsession is a religious and social phenomenon which reflects the

---

* Translated by Björn Lehmann

power structure of belief systems and social realities. In religious terms, spirits are part of the colourful diversity of transcendental powers. The believer can feel himself embedded in a cosmic hierarchy of gods, spirits and demons. The gods are the most powerful, followed by the demons; the spirits are the weakest. However, the balance of power within the transcendental vigours is not rigid and these powers are not obviously good or evil, but the order must be established newly every time. This can be achieved by a fight of the gods against the spirits, for example.

In hinduistic belief, spirits are deceased bodies who cannot be reborn immediately due to unfortunate circumstances, but instead want to intrude into living bodies to satisfy their needs for food, sexuality and power. There are three reasons why deceased ones will become spirits in this world: Untimely death, e.g. of kids, death under the influence of direct force, e.g. murder, suicide, accident; immoral behaviour, e.g. sexual misconduct in one´s life.

That's the explanation for the believer that spirits are driven by evil, but above all, indomitabale wishes and act against the orderliness of humans and gods.
Western scientists interpret spirits as schismatic personality portions of the obsessed, i.e. as symbols for supressed wishes such as sexual desire, anger, envy and helplessness. The people are obsessed by their unconscious conflicts which are projected out.

The society in India is divided into a system of castes (four main castes each with hundreds of subtypes). Higher castes have more power over lower ones generally, however, each one depends upon the other and therefore looks out for a good understanding and communication. One is born into a caste and within it one will be married. One should avoid contact with members of other castes, e.g. sharing a meal is taboo. The religious background of the caste system focuses on principles of purity. It deals with spiritual or ritual purity. This purity can be achieved by good deeds in prior lives (*karma*) or by birth into a specific caste or by god-pleasing moral conduct. Only the few who reach the highest level of purity can break the circle of reinkarnations and enter into a divine paradise. Spirits are far away from reaching this goal because they are considered as very impure. The level of ritual purity goes along with the social prestige of the person. People from higher castes, such as the priest and warrior caste are of a higher ritual and social status compared to the ones from the merchants and farmer caste. The lowest are the outcastes ("untouchables"). The social order for men and women is also based on principles of purity and hierarchy. Women are generally considered as impurer, something which is associated with the menstruation. Being caught in traditions, Indian women are exposed to specific social repression: in all stages of her life, a woman is assigned to a man who has power over her: the father, the husband and after his death, his son. Most of the Indian women get married according to her parents wishes and are ritually und economically dependent on the husband. The alternation in generations (daughter, wife, widow) is often connected to a traumatic change of identity. The bride must leave her family and her village to live with the family of the husband. Being a widow, the son is in charge .

The sexuality of women is heavily controlled. If she is not modest and faithful she brings dishonour not only to herself but her family and her caste as well.

Especially sexual relations to a man of a lower caste are taboo.
Following the concept of purity and impurity it is now understandable that the impure spirits are suspected to be primarily within impurer women and members of the lower castes. In fact, spirit obsession is mainly found in lower castes and among approximately 70% of the women, whereas only the purer men can be possessed by divine powers. Because the gods are pure and powerful. There are male cults in India whose members seek for goddess obsession to strengthen their ritual and social status. In contrast, the obsession of women is always understood to be a spirit obsession and thus, as misfortune or illness.

What does obsession have to do with *ayurveda*?
The two thousand year old beliefs of health, sickness and healing in India are based on the hinduistic teachings of *ayurveda*. The content of one of its eight fields of study is the spirit teaching (*bhutavidya*).
Today´s occurrence of *ayurveda* is represented by the *ayurveda*-healers (*Vaids*) and plays an important practical role in India along with the accepted western medicine. Many Indians are visiting western as well as *ayurvedic* doctors at the same time. *Ayurveda* is a mixture of religious and rational-empirical medicine. Due to its holistic concept every defect shows physically as well as mentally. Illnesses are regarded as a disharmony of the three bodyfluids (*tridoshas*). However, the sickness can also be caused by astrological, *karmic* and other supernatural powers like gods and spirits who then again induce the imbalance of the juices. *Ayurvedic* doctors treat mentally sick people with admonition, with consolation and medicine. Only men as ritual specialists (exorcists) are allowed to apply exorcism. Considering the *ayurvedic* teachings, the reason for spirit obsession is an imbalance of the bodyfluids simultaneously showing a cosmic disorder. The spirit is regarded as a metaphysical enemy which enters the body. The origin is the spirit and therefore the illness has an external cause. The obsessed and her family are only partially guilty by violating social regulations. Correspondingly, exorcism is a healing ritual that fights the enemy, punishes the culprit, re-establishes the social taboos and the balance of juices and the cosmic order.

Because western doctors do not believe in spirits, they like to diagnose the obsessed with hysteria, anxiety neurosis or psychosis and refer to eccentric feelings, strong suggestibility and phantastic imagination up to delusion. Since spirit obsession is not an element of illness in western understanding, we should not translate it but rather understand it in a wide sense as "suffering" or a "disorder in the well- being".

What does exorcism in India look like?
Mainly it is a healing ritual, which may appear like a court procedure or a theater performance. Exorcism is a cleaning rite because obsession is a dangerous impurity for the victim, the house and the relatives. The basic structure of exorcism follows these guidelines: first a diagnosis is issued. Symptoms like shivering and shaking indicate the fear of the victims versus their spirit. If the victims become unconscious or get into trance and speak with an alienated voice, then the diagnosis is stringend. Obviously, however, every kind of malfunction can lead to suspicions of spirit obsession. In this case, relatives discuss this matter with a

fortune teller or exorcist until everyone is convinced of the obsession. In consequence, an exorcistic ritual becomes necessary.
It takes place in the house of the victim, a public place in the village, or in a (healing) temple, a place to where the whole family pilgrimages. There the actual excorcism begins with the invocation of the gods. The exorcist repeats in ritual chant "Come and help because only your power is effective". Then he turns to the victim (the woman) and the ritual of the questioning of the spirit begins. *"Who are you?"*

This is the most important and - for us - strangest part of the ritual:
the victim must try to get into trance, because only then it can be negotiated with the intruder. If the invader is reluctant, it will be pressed by all the attendees, verbally or even by the use of force: they pull the obsessed victim´s hair or force her onto her knees. Finally, the spirit will surrender by speaking through the mouth of the woman. It will confess its name, why it is here, what it wants. At the end, it must promise to leave again. All types of fighting can be used to expel it: argueing, ridiculing, threatening or pacifying. The main part of the ceremony can last up to several hours.

To illustrate the above I will tell the story of the girl Shakun, 19 years of age, who underwent an exorcism rite with her mother and her three brothers in an Indian (healing) temple (KAKAR 1984: 71).
At the age of 16 she was seized by the spirit of the dead aunt for the first time. Shakun had screamed frightfully, since she saw a laughing woman approaching, dancing on her head and causing severe headaches, before falling asleep. Since then, Shakun suffered from anxiety attacks and headaches when the woman visited her in regular intervals. The spirit of the aunt corresponded to the typical image of spirits, since she had been adulterous and had killed herself.

The following scene illustrates the atmosphere in the temple (Bharatpur, north of Delhi): people are crowding in the yard. Most of them are young women. Many are sitting or lying in peculiar positions on the floor. A young girl, probably 18 years old and rather attractive but of an unnatural paleness of the face is lying on her back. Her hair is flying around her head as she shakes it vigorously to the left and to the right while she grimaces with pain. She moves her lips and whispers inaudibly - but then a loud scream from her throat *"Baba, Baba, I don´t want to go! I don´t want to go!"* ´ it is a *bhuta* (spirit) (a male *bhuta* judging the tone of the voice and the verbal form) which resists to leave her body. Another young girl kneels on the ground, arms propped up backwards and moves her hips and pelvis provocatively as if to invite an invisible opponent and to reject him at the same time. *"Go away! Go away! Leave me!"* she screams with a loud voice. Then a deep sigh is heard *"Oh Baba, oh Baba"* while her tightly closed eyes keep the outer world away from her lonesome fight against the spirit which has posessed her (KAKAR 1984: 64).

Here the temple staff consists mainly of priests who establish a ritual connection to the ape-god (*Hanuman*). The image of the god is touched with sacrificial offerings such as coconuts, rice and money which the family brought along. It is a general belief that thereby godly power enters the patient and forces the spirit to appear: it shall speak through the mouth of the girl. Anxiously the temple community waits for the woman to fall into the recognizable state of obsession.

Then she will answer with the voice of the spirit, dance, cry, moan, become angry or use obscenities. After the ceremony she will not be able to remember this. Here the ritual in the temple resembles a law-suit in court: the priest questions the spirit with a harsh voice. The spirit is to show its identity during the interrogation: who it is, what it is suffering from, why it wants to own the girl, what it demands so that it disappears forever. Often, something tempting is offered to the spirit, e.g. sweets, or beautiful red cloth. Sometimes the family must promise the raging spirit not to hit the girl anymore or not to force her into marriage. In the end, the spirit nevertheless has to be punished, however, this must be endured by the obsessed: she will hurt herself or enchain herself or place herself in dirty sewage. Women not only outweigh the men in numbers as obsessed ones but also mothers, aunts and daughters accompany their relatives to the healing temples in which the family often stays for weeks or months and repeats the rituals if the obsession does not disappear.

For the exorcist it is a success when the impure or evil spirits are driven out by the good gods. For this sake, rituals are applied; they only have to be carried out properly. The impact of exorcism in western terms has never been measured, but researchers are giving credible accounts on reliefs and healings.

Eight ethnological authors have generated their interpretations on spirit obsession based on fieldwork (sometimes for years) in India in the past 40 years. Rituals can differ greatly from place to place. The researchers complement one another in their observations but are contradictory regarding the interpretation of the rituals. The inconsistencies seem to evolve from the fact that each researcher emphasizes single aspects of the complex event in particular. When it is culturally expected that antisocial emotions fight with the traditional order, contradictions are an essential part of the exorcism rite.

The following are examples from scientific theories: the American scientist NABOKOV who researched in South-India (*Tamil Nadu*) holds the theory of suppression: the ritual supports the repression of women. As a result of the spirit exorcism the clients are punished in open and forced into conformity as wives , when they had run away from home. For close relatives the ritual is a possibility to re-establish their authority within the family order. In contrast, the German medicin-ethnologist PFLEIDERER who documented the ritual practice in North-India (*Gujarat*) believes into the theory of compensation: the type of exorcism which is practiced there provides a helpful compensation for the suppressed women. In the exceptional state of ecstatic furiousness they can express their protest, their anger and powerlessness, their unmoral wishes and mental injuries as if they were on a stage. This leads to a strengthening of the person. The community experiences the exorcistic performance with its playful character of entertainment like a liberating form of art (PFLEIDERER, KAPFERER).

The Indian psychoanalyst KAKAR differs the psychotherapeutic effects of the rituals and thereby emphasized the aspect of family therapy:

> First of all the sick person gets attention from the family, the temple community and the godly powers.
>
> Secondly she is being helped to face her suffering and the spirit directly

and that smoothens her fright.

Thirdly, a clearing of sickening affects is achieved, forbidden impulses are lived out ´, all encouraged by shouting spectators.

Fourthly, the patient is allowed to shift the blame and responsibility for her outbursts over to the evil spirit (projection) and remain unblamable.

Fifthly is an attempt to smooth the stress factors of life by forcing the family relatives to deal with the demands of the sick person.

Certainly, the Indian healing ritual of spirit exorcism is not applicable in the western world. Its roots are found in India and it is still practiced there until today.

Author
DR. MED. TRAUTE DATTENBERG-HOLPER
Psychoanalyst, psychotherapist, M.A. of Ethnology, Ethnologist.
Contact: E-Mail: dattenberg-holper@freenet.de

References
KAKAR, SUDHIR, 1984: *Schamanen, Heilige und Ärzte. Psychotherapie und traditionelle Indische Heilkunst*. München: Biederstein. (Original: 1982: Shamans, Mystics and Doctors)
KAPFERER, Bruce, 1983: *A Celebration of Demons. Exorcism and the Asthetics of Healing in Sri Lanka*. Washington: Indiana Univ. Press
LEWIS, ION, M., 1971: *Ecstatic Religion. An Antropologic Study of Spirit Possession and Shamanism*. Harmondsworth: Pinguin Books
NABOKOV, ISABELLE, 1997: Expel the Lover, Recover the Wife: Symbolic Analysis of a South Indian Exorcism. J. Roy. Anthrop. Inst. 3: 297-316
PFLEIDERER, BEATRIX, 1994: *Die besessenen Frauen von Mira Datar Dargah. Heilen und Trance in Indien*. Unter Mitarbeit von VIRCHAND DHARAMSEY. Frankfurt/ M., New York: Campus

VOLKSMEDIZIN BEI DEN ZEME NAGAS IN INDIEN*

von Babul Roy

Einführung

Zeme ist einer der wenig bekannten *Naga* Stämme, der hauptsächlich die Gebiete von Nagaland, Manjour und Assam (N.C. Gebirgs Region) in der Indian Union bewohnen. Sie praktizieren wechselnden Ackerbau auf Bergabhängen und sind dadurch relativ unabhängig.

Sie haben eine reiche indigene Tradition von Heilverfahren. Die Substanzen, die als Medizin genutzt werden, bestehen hauptsächlich aus biologischen Bestandteilen, zum einen pflanzlicher und zum anderen tierischer Herkunft. Die Auffassung der *Zeme* von Medizin beruht auf analogem Denken. Dieses symbolische oder magische Weltbild jedoch heißt nicht, dass die moderne Pharmazie und all ihre therapeutischen Möglichkeiten verleugnet oder verweigert werden. Dieses Kapitel enthält zum ersten Mal einen Einblick in die Medizin der *Zeme* und ihren basierenden Prinzipien.

Traditionelles Wissen der *Zeme Nagas*

Der Wald der nordöstlichen Region in Indien umfasst die sieben Staaten der Indian Union und ist ein ursprüngliches Gebiet mit reichhaltigen biogenetischen Resourcen (KURUP 1974; RAO 1974).

---

* Übersetzung aus dem Englischen: Judith Beyer

In Assam, dem Zwei-Hügel-Distrikt, (Viz. Karbi Anglong und North Cachar Hills) gibt es ein großes Waldgebiet. In den Distrikt North Cachar Hills ist eine Fülle von wertvollem alten Waldbestand zu finden (siehe auch DUTTA 1979), der derzeit die Heimat des bedeutenden mongolischen *Naga* Stammes *Zeme* ist. Der Stamm *Zeme* zählt etwa 9000 Stammesmitglieder.

Diese Region ist von der Zivilisation immer noch weitgehend abgeschnitten. Dies erfordert von seinen Bewohnern eine unanbhängige Lebensweise und Selbstversorgung basierend auf ihrem traditionellem Wissen und Fertigkeiten.

Die Moderne Medizin, die in dieser Region Anfang des 20.Jahrhunderts eingeführt wurde, konnte jedoch das traditionelle Wissen der Einwohner nicht ersetzen. Sie konnte bis heute nicht für mehr als 20% der Bevölkerung zugänglich gemacht werden.
Dennoch hatte die Einführung der modernen Medizin Auswirkungen auf das bestehende traditionelle System. Überall sind die alten Systeme auf Grund der Entwicklungspolitik und ökonomischer Faktoren gefährdet (BENZ et al. 2000; CANIAGO & SIEBERT 1998; MYER 1984).

Die Rodung der Wälder wirkt sich auf das traditionelle System der Medizin aus, das immer noch stark von den Ressourcen der Wälder abhängig ist. Obwohl die *Zeme Naga* bis heute größtenteils ihrer Tradition treu bleiben, beeinflussen sie die Veränderungen in gewissem Maße doch. Für die Veränderungen gibt es Gründe wie z.B. der Einfluss der Modernisierung, Zivilisierung wie auch der Christianisierung mit Anteilen des Hinduismus.
Auch auf Grund ihrer eigenen sozio-religiösen Reform durch die *Heraka*-Bewegung unterliegt ihre Kultur Veränderungen (ROY 1995; YONUO 1982).

Die Wälder dezimieren sich in einem bedrohlichen Ausmaß und aufgrund der sich ausbreitenden Kultivierung viel zu schnell.
Diese Veränderungen werden früher oder später ihr indigenes Medizinsystem gefährden. Diese Studie dokumentiert die verschiedenen Substanzen, die von den *Zeme Nagas* als Medizin angewandt werden.
Das grundliegende therapeutische Erklärungsmodell einer solchen medizinischen Nutzung wurde ebenso untersucht. Die hier dargestellten Daten sind aus erster Hand und stammen aus Feldforschungsarbeiten im nördlichen Cachar-Gebirge in Assam 1992 und 1995.

Tabelle 1: Einige nutzbare Pflanzen, Tier- und Vogelarten bei den *Zeme Nagas* und ihre entsprechende Bedeutung

ARTEN (NAMEN)	1. CHARAKTERE 2. NUTZUNG 3. BEDEUTUNG
Adler	1. Der Adler fliegt kreisend hoch am Himmel. 2. Das Fleisch des Adlers wird konsumiert um Kopfschmerzen und Schwindel zu behandeln. 3. Die analoge und homöopathische Bedeutung ist klar. Der Adler fliegt hoch kreisend; unser Kopf ist anatomisch am höchsten Punkt unseres Körpers. Aufgrund dessen haben folglich der Adler und der Schwindel die gleiche Bedeutung. Homöopathisch ähnliche Dinge verursachen gleichartige Beschwerden.
Hegatangpui (Selten Art der Krabben)	1. Es handelt sich um eine seltene Krabbenart mit haarigen Beinen/Antennen. Sie macht Geräusche wie *krack...krack...* 2. Um Magenbeschwerden zu behandeln, bei denen der Magen ähnliche Geräusche macht, wird diese zuvor in Wasser gekocht und dann gegessen. 3. Die Geräusche der Krabbe und der Magenbeschwerden sind dieselben. Die Analogie zwischen Krabbe und dem Leiden ist gegeben. Nach homöopathischähnlicher Lehre kann man ähnlche Dinge mit ähnlichen Verfahren heilen.
Helung (Wildes Schaf)	1. Es kann von einem steilen Hang springen ohne sich eine Verletzung der Gliedmaßen zuzuziehen. Auch wenn es sich etwas bricht kann es die Wunde heilen indem es ein wenig *Helungmau* frisst. Dies ist eine weiche, schwarze, muskulöse Masse unter seinen Hufen. 2. Die *Zeme* benutzen *Helungmau* um Beschwerden durch Verrenkung oder Brüche zu heilen. 3. Im Falle der Analogie kann bei gleichen Beschwerden heilsam für den Menschen sein, was für ein Tier heilsam ist.
Hemeube (Schildkröte)	1. Sie ist eine langsame und scheue Kreatur. Sie versteckt ihren Kopf unter ihrem Schild bei der geringsten Störung. Wird nicht von den jungen *Zeme* verzehrt, die ihr ganzes Leben vor sich haben. 2. Wenn eine Person sie isst, könnte sie die langsamen und scheuen Eigenschaften des Tiers annehmen, welche die *Zeme* nicht mögen. 3. Homöopathisch gleiches führt zu gleichem Resultat.

Heinei (Fuchs)	1. Der Fuchs ist das cleverste aller Tiere. Er wird selten in einer Falle gefangen. 2. Wenn man Fuchsfleisch oder Blut konsumiert, erhält man Immunität gegenüber magischen Fallen der Hexerei und Zauberei. 3. Analoge und homöopathische Erklärungen sind klar. Durch Hexerei und Zauberei kann eine Person gefangen werden. Der Fuchs ist das einzige Tier, das schwer gefangen werden kann. So kann eine Person, indem sie Fuchsfleisch isst, so clever wie ein Fuchs werden und so kann sie nicht so leicht von Hexereien oder Zaubereien eingenommen werden.
Hepobei (Wurzel einer Zinginber Art)	1. Es ist eine der Zinger ähnliche Pflanze. Das spitze Ende des Zingers der unterirdischen Wurzel ähnelt der Brustwarze. 2. Der Zinger wie die Wurzel wird verwendet, um die Milchproduktion bei stillenden Müttern einzuleiten. 3. Die analogen und homöopathischen Vergleiche sind klar. Die Spitze der Wurzel sieht aus wie die Brustwarze. Deshalb sind die Wurzel und die weibliche Brust gleich im Bezug auf die Analogie. Und homöopathisch gleiches führt zu gleichem Ergebnis.
Heradi (Tiger)	1. Der Tiger ist die energiereichste, kraftvollste und agilste Kreatur. 2. Alle Teile des Tigers werden für nützliche Medizin gehalten. Es ist klar, da der Tiger das kraftvollste Tier ist, dass jeder Teil des Tigers, wenn er gegessen wird zu gleichen Fähigkeiten für den Konsumenten führen kann. 3. Die homöopathische Logik ist klar. Das traditionelle Erklärungsmuster besagt, dass gleiches zu gleichen Effekt führt.
Hethei (Schakal)	1., 2., 3. Wie Fuchs
Hingkuipau (Langsame Loris)	1. Es handelt sich um ein nachtaktives Tier. Während des Tages ist es sehr träge und versteckt stets sein Gesicht unter seinem Körper. 2. u. 3. wie die Schildkröte.
Kepe (Gibbon)	1. Es ist ein sehr lebhaftes Tier, dessen Knochen sehr biegsam sind. Es kann weit springen. Beim Springen und Hüpfen stürzt es auch, aber es verletzt sich niemals und seine Knochen brechen seltent. 2. Der Knochen dieses Tieres, so glaubt man, besitzt magische Kräfte. Deshalb wird jemand, der einen Knochen als Armulett trägt, immun gegen verschiedene Beschwerden wiez.B. Gelenkbeschwerden (Arthritis) und Knochenbrüche. 3. Homöopathisch gleiche Dinge produzieren das gleiche Resultat.

Keram (Otter)	1. Er schluckt lebendige Fische ohne sich dabei im Hals zu verletzen. 2. Wenn jemand einen Keran tötet, indem er ihm sein Genick bricht, erhält er magische Kräfte. Solche Personen können ganz einfach eine Gräte, die im Hals steckt, mit bloßen Händen, entfernen oder Verletzungen der Kehle heilen. Dazu massieren sie einfach den Hals mit der Hand die das Tier getötet hat. 3. Die analoge und homöopathische Bedeutung ist so hergeleitet. Man erhält die Eigenschaften des Kerams, der einen lebenden Fisch schlucken kann ohne sich eine Verletzung durch eine Gräte zuzuziehen.
Mbachi (Mangifera sp.)	1. Das spitze Ende der Frucht sieht wie ein Brustwarze aus. Die Frucht wird für stillende Mütter verwendet. 2. u. 3. Wie *Hepobei*.

Author
BABUL ROY, MSc, PH.D.
Ph.D in Medizinischer Anthropologie, ODI Livelihoods Options Project, Arera Colony. Während der letzten 10 Jahre ausgedehnte Feldforschung bei indigenen Stämmen u.a. in der nördlichen Gegend der Cacher Berge (Assam), Zentral-Himalaya, Zentral Indien bei Madhya Pradesh. Die Forschungsschwerpunkte liegen auf Themen der Ethnomedizin, Ethno-Ökologie, struktureller und symbolischer Anthropologie. Derzeit arbeitet er im Team des Overseas Development Institute (U.K) in Madhya Pradesh, Indien.

Kontakt: Babul Roy, Fatashil G. S. Colony, Guwahati - 781009 (Assam: India)
E-Mail: babul_roy@hotmail.com

Literatur
BENZ, BRUCE F., J. CEVALLOS E., FRANCISCO SANTANA M., JESUS ROSALES A., & S GRAF M. 2000: Losing knowledge about plant use in the Sierra De Manantlan Biosphere Reserve, Mexico. *Economic Botany* 54(2): 183-191.
BORDOLOI, B.N. & G.C. SHARMA-THAKUR 1988: *Tribes of Assam*, Part II, Guwahati: Tribal Research Institute, Assam.
BOWER, GRAHAM U.V. 1945: Cycle-migration of the Zeme-Nagas, North Cachar Hills, Assam. *Man in India* XXVI: 50-52.
BOWER, GRAHAM U.V. 1950: *Naga Path*. John Murray, 50 Albemarle St., London.
CANIAGO, IZEFRI & STEPHEN F. SIEBERT 1998: Medicinal plant ecology, knowledge and conservation in Kalimantan, Indonesia. *Economic Botany* 52(3): 229-250.
DAS, S.T. 1986: *Tribal life of North Eastern India*. Gian Publishing House (Delhi: India).
DUTTA, K.N. (Ed.) 1979: *Assam District gazetteers*, U.M & N.C. Hills District. Govt. of Assam (India).
DUTTA, P 1993 *The Zeme Nagas of Assam Hills: A Short Profile*. Assam Institute of

Research for Tribal and Scheduled Castes, (Guwahati, Assam: India).

KABUI, GANGMUMEI 1994: The Zeliangrong religion: its theology and philosophy - some observations. *Journal of Indian Anthropological Society* 29(1-2): 173-78.

KAMKHENTHANG, H. 1984: "A note on religious belief of the Northern Chin (Zemi)", in SEBASTIAN KAROTEMPREL, Ed., *The tribes of North East India*. Vendrame Missological Institute: Shillong.

MYERS, NORMAN 1984: "Disappearing cultures", in EDMUND HILLARY, Ed., *Ecology 2000*. Michael Joseph Ltd., London.

ROY, BABUL 1998: *Socio-Cultural and Environmental Dimensions of Tribal Health: A Study among the Dimasa Kacharis and the Zeme Nagas of North Cachar Hills in Assam*. PhD Thesis (Unpublished), Gauhati University, Guwahati – 781014 (Assam: India).

ROY, BABUL 1995: An anthropological peep at Zeme religion. *Bulletin of the Department of Anthropology*, Gauahti University (Assam) IX: 51-60.

ROY, BABUL & A.N.M.I. ALI 1997: "Shifting cultivation and forest in North East India", in K.C. MAHANTA, Ed., *People of the Himalayas: Ecology, Culture, Development and Change*. pp. 135-143. Kamla-Raj Enterprises: Delhi.

SAHA, N. 1988: "Ethnographic study of the Zeliangrong tribe of North East India", in SEBASTIAN. KAROTEMPREL, Ed., *The Tribes of North East India*. Vendrame Missological Institute: Shillong.

YONUO, A 1982: *Nagas Struggle against the British Rule Under Jadonang and Rani Gaidinliu 1925-1947*. Leno Printing Press: Kohima (India).

FOLK MEDICINE AMONG THE ZEME NAGAS OF INDIA

by Babul Roy

Introduction

Zeme is one of the little known *Naga* tribes mainly inhabiting the states of *Naga*land, Manipur and Assam (North Cachar Hills district) of the Indian Union. They practice shifting cultivation in hill slopes and live relatively independent. They have a rich indigenous tradition of curative practices. The substances that are used as medicine consist mostly of biological materials of both plant and animal origins. Analogical thinking is often the basic structure in the *Zeme* perception of medicine. Such a symbolic or magical interpretation, however, does not suggest an absence of pharmaceutical values all of their therapeutic ingredients.

This paper is the first account of *Zeme* medicines and their underlying folk principles.

Indigenous knowledge of the *Zeme Nagas*

The forest in the northeastern part of India, comprising the seven states of Indian Union, is a repository for most of the regional biogenetic resources (KURUP 1974; RAO 1974). In Assam, the two hill districts, viz. Karbi Anglong and North Cachar Hills, have a large number of forests.

The district of North Cachar Hills (240 58' - 250 47' N and 920 32' - 930 28' E) is filled with varieties of valuable forest resources (see DUTTA 1979), which is the current homeland of an important Mongoloid *Naga* tribe called *Zeme* numbering some 9,000 souls (for ethnography see BORDOLOI & SHARMA-THAKUR 1988; BOWER 1945,

1950; Das 1986; Dutta 1993; Kabui 1994; Kamkhenthang 1984; Roy 1995, 1998 and Saha 1988). This region is still relatively cut off from the mainstream, requiring its inhabitants to lead, to a large extent, a self-sufficient existence based on their own indigenous knowledge.

However, modern medicine, which was introduced to this region in the early 20th century, could not replace the existing of indigenous knowledge of the people, and is still not accessible to more than 20% of the population. Nevertheless, introduction of modern medicine has brought several changes to the existing indigenous system.

Indigenous systems are endangered everywhere through the impact of modern forces and the market economy (Benz et al.2000; Caniago & SieBert 1998; Myer 1984). Reduction of the forest affects the traditional system of medicine, which is always heavily depending on the forest resources.

The *Zeme Nagas*, though still mainly conservative, are undergoing change. Change is happening under the impact of various modernization factors and forces of development like conversion to Christianity, indirect influences of Hindu India, and also because of their own socio-religious reforms through the *Heraka* movement (Roy 1995; Yonuo 1982). The forest of this region is diminishing rapidly, primarily because of shifting development too extensively (Roy & Ali 1997). These changes will affect perceptibly their indigenous medical system sooner or later. This study documents the different substances used by the *Zeme Nagas* as medicine. The underlying therapeutic logics of such medicinal uses of ingredients have also been explored. First hand data used here was collected through intensive fieldwork conducted in North Cachar Hills of Assam through several field trips during the period of 1992 through 1995.

Tab. 1: Some useful (or prohibited) plant, animal & bird species among the *Zeme Nagas* and their analogical reasoning

SPECIES NAME	1. CHARACTERS 2. UTILITY 3. ANALOGICAL REASONING
Eagle	1. The eagle flies high in the sky in a circular path. 2. The meat of eagle is consumed to cure headache and head reeling complaints. 3. The analogical and homeopathic logics are clear. The eagle flies high in a circular path; our head anatomically is rested on the top of our body. Thus by the reason of analogy the eagle and head reeling all are same. And a homeopathically similar thing produces a similar result.
Hegatangpui (A rare sp. of crab)	1. It is a rare sp. of crab with hairy tentacles/antennae. It makes a sound like *krake krake* 2. To cure stomach complaint in which case the stomach makes similar sound it is consumed on being boiled in water. 3. The sounds of the crab and of the stomach complaint are the same. Therefore, by the reason of analogy the crab and the ailment are the same. And a homeopathically similar thing can cure a similar complaint.
Helung (Wild sheep)	1. It can jump from a steep peak without causing any injury to its limbs. Even if it breaks its limbs it can cure the wound by consuming a small bit of *helungmau*, which is a soft black muscular mass underneath its nails. 2. The *Zemes* use *helungmau* to cure complains like bone displacement and fracture. 3. By the reason of analogy, for similar complaints, whatever is useful to an animal could also be useful to man.
Hemeube (Tortoise)	1. It is a slow and shy creature. It keeps its head under its shell when getting slight disturbance. 2. This is not to be consumed by the young *Zemes* who still have to live a long life. By consuming it a person may acquire the slow and shy qualities of the creature, which the *Zemes* don't like. 3. Homeopathically similar thing produces a similar result.
Henei (Fox)	1. Fox is the cleverest of all animals. It rarely gets caught in a trap. 2. Eating of fox's meat and blood give immunity against magical trap of witchcraft and sorcery. 3. Analogical and homeopathic logics are clear. Through witchcraft and sorcery a person is understood to be a trap. The fox is the only animal that rarely gets trapped. So by eating fox's meat a person can become clever like a fox and as such not to be easily trapped by witchcraft or sorcery practices.

Hepobei (Rhizome of a Zinginber sp.)	1. It is a zinger like plant. The terminal pointed end of the zinger like underground rhizome looks like the nipple. 2. The zinger like rhizome is taken to induce milk for a breast-feeding woman. 3. The analogical and homeopathic logics are clearly derivable. The tip of the rhizome looks like the nipple. Therefore, the rhizome and the female breast are same by the reason of analogy. And homeopathically similar thing induces similar effect or result.
Heradi (Tiger)	1. Tiger is the most energetic, powerful and agile creature. 2. All parts of the tiger are considered to be useful as medicine. It is stated that since the tiger is the most powerful, any part of it if consumed can induce similar quality to its consumer. 3. The homeopathic logic is clearly derivable from the folk explanations that a similar thing induces similar effecst.
Hethei (Jackle)	1. Same as fox. 2. Same as fox. 3. Same as fox.
Hingkuipau (Slow Loris)	1. It is a nocturnal creature. During the day it is very lethargic and always keeps its face hiding under its body. 2. Same as tortoise. 3. Same as tortoise.
Kepe (Gibbon)	1. It is a highly agile creature whose bones are very flexible. It can jump over a long gap. During leaping and jumping even if it falls down, it never gets hurt and its bone hardly ever break. 2. The bone of this animal is believed to have magical values. Therefore, if somebody takes it as an amulet he becomes immune against different complaints like bone-joint-pain (arthritis) and bone-fracture. 3. Homeopathically a similar thing produces similar results or effects.
Keram (Otter)	1. It swallows living fishes without causing any injury to its throat. 2. If a person kills a keram by breaking its neck, he acquires a magical power. Such a person can heal spike injuries in a throat by simply doing some massaging with his hand, that he had once used to kill the animal with . 3. The analogical and homeopathic logics are derivable: As a man acquires the quality of a keram by which can swallow living fish without getting any spike inserted.
Mbachi (Mangifera sp.)	1. The pointed end of the fruit looks like the nipple. 2. The fruit is used for breast- feeding women. 3. Same as *Hepobei*.

Author
BABUL ROY, MSc, PH.D.
Ph.D in Medical Anthropology, ODI Livelihoods Options Project, Arera Colony
During the last decade did extensive fieldworks among several primitive tribes in North Cachar Hills (Assam), Central Indian Himalayas and in Central Indian State of Madhya Pradesh (particularly in eastern region), etc.
Primary research interests are in ethno-medicine, ethno-ecology, structural and symbolic anthropology, etc.
Currently working as team members with Overseas Development Institute (U.K) in a developmental policy research project in Madhya Pradesh (India).
Contact: Babul Roy, Fatashil G. S. Colony, Guwahati - 781009 (Assam: India)
E-mail: babul_roy@hotmail.com, livelihoods@satyam.net.in

References

BENZ, BRUCE F., J. CEVALLOS E., FRANCISCO SANTANA M., JESUS ROSALES A., & S GRAF M. 2000: Losing knowledge about plant use in the Sierra De Manantlan Biosphere Reserve, Mexico. *Economic Botany* 54(2): 183-191.

BORDOLOI, B.N. & G.C. SHARMA-THAKUR 1988: *Tribes of Assam*, Part II, Guwahati: Tribal Research Institute, Assam.

BOWER, GRAHAM U.V. 1945: Cycle-migration of the Zeme-Nagas, North Cachar Hills, Assam. *Man in India* XXVI: 50-52.

BOWER, GRAHAM U.V. 1950: *Naga Path. John Murray*, 50 Albemarle St., London.

CANIAGO, IZEFRI & STEPHEN F. SIEBERT 1998: Medicinal plant ecology, knowledge and conservation in Kalimantan, Indonesia. *Economic Botany* 52(3): 229-250.

DAS, S.T. 1986: *Tribal life of North Eastern India*. Gian Publishing House (Delhi: India).

DUTTA, K.N. (Ed.) 1979: *Assam District gazetteers*, U.M & N.C. Hills District. Govt. of Assam (India).

DUTTA, P 1993 *The Zeme Nagas of Assam Hills: A Short Profile*. Assam Institute of Research for Tribal and Scheduled Castes, (Guwahati, Assam: India).

KABUI, GANGMUMEI 1994: The Zeliangrong religion: its theology and philosophy - some observations. *Journal of Indian Anthropological Society* 29(1-2): 173-78.

KAMKHENTHANG, H. 1984: "A note on religious belief of the Northern Chin (Zemi)", in SEBASTIAN KAROTEMPREL, Ed., *The tribes of North East India*. Vendrame Missological Institute: Shillong.

MYERS, NORMAN 1984: "Disappearing cultures", in EDMUND HILLARY, Ed., *Ecology 2000*. Michael Joseph Ltd., London.

ROY, BABUL 1998: *Socio-Cultural and Environmental Dimensions of Tribal Health: A Study among the Dimasa Kacharis and the Zeme Nagas of North Cachar Hills in Assam*. PhD Thesis (Unpublished), Gauhati University, Guwahati – 781014 (Assam: India).

ROY, BABUL 1995: An anthropological peep at Zeme religion. *Bulletin of the Department of Anthropology*, Gauahti University (Assam) IX: 51-60.

ROY, BABUL & A.N.M.I. ALI 1997: "Shifting cultivation and forest in North East India", in K.C. MAHANTA, Ed., *People of the Himalayas: Ecology, Culture, Development and*

Change. pp. 135-143. Kamla-Raj Enterprises: Delhi.

SAHA, N. 1988: "Ethnographic study of the Zeliangrong tribe of North East India", in SEBASTIAN. KAROTEMPREL, Ed., *The Tribes of North East India.* Vendrame Missological Institute: Shillong.

YONUO, A 1982: *Nagas Struggle against the British Rule Under Jadonang and Rani Gaidinliu 1925-1947.* Leno Printing Press: Kohima (India).

CHAKMA TALIKA CIKITSA - DAS THERAPEUTISCHE SYSTEM DER CHAKMA IM CHITTAGONG HILL TRACT VON BANGLADESH*

von Mahmud Tareq Hassan Khan

Einleitung

Der Chittagong Hill Tract (CHT) in Bangladesh ist die Heimat zwölf verschiedener Stammesgemeinschaften, der *Chakma, Arakani, Rakhain, Mogh (Marma), Murang* und anderer Stämme. Die *Chakma* sind der größte dieser Stämme. Etwa 1,1 Millionen Menschen leben gegenwärtig in einem Gebiet von 1,32 Millionen Hektar Grundfläche. Die meisten von ihnen betreiben Jhum-Anbau. Der CHT mit einer Größe von 13191 Quadratkilometern liegt zwischen 21'' 25' und 23'' 45' nördlicher Breite und 91'' 45' und 92'' 50' östlicher Länge und befindet sich im Südosten von Bangladesh. Er umfasst drei Berggebiete: Rangamati, Khagrachari und Bandarban. Er umfasst 76% der Berggebiete des Landes; 90% seiner Grundfläche sind gebirgig, 4% sind Ansiedlungen, Flüssen, Seen und Sumpfland und nur die restlichen 6% sind für intensive Landwirtschaft geeignet (CHAKMA et al., 2000) Im Gebiet herrscht tropisches Monsunklima mit einer durchschnittlichen jährlichen Niederschlagsmenge von 2553 mm. Die Jahresdurchschnittstemperatur beträgt 25,2°C und die durchschnittliche Luftfeuchtigkeit 79,3%. Die Vegetation dieses Gebietes ist schein-immergrün bis tropisch-immergrün und wird von großen Bäumen der Arten Dipterocarpaceae, Euphorbiaceae, Lauraceae, Leguminosae und Rubiaceae überragt.

Das therapeutische System der *Chakma*

Unzweifelhaft bildet die Fülle der vorkommenden Pflanzen eine reiche Quelle an Rohmaterialien zur Herstellung der vom Beginn der Zivilisation dieses Subkontinentes an gebräuchlichen ayurvedischen Heilmittel. Die Eingeborenen des CHT verfügen über reiches lokales Wissen. Ihre traditionelle Klassifikation der

---

* Übersetzung aus dem Englischen: Paul Baumann

Arten, die nahe verbunden ist mit dem Ökosystem, der Flora und Fauna, unterscheidet verschiedene Kategorien und beschreibt das Aussehen, den Lebensraum und die Nützlichkeit von Pflanzen. Die bevorzugte Verwendung von Pflanzenarten variiert entsprechend der Gegebenheiten. Die Ernte der natürlichen Ressourcen steht im Zusammenhang mit Umgebungsbedingungen und Jahreszeiten, so dass eine verträgliche Nutzung gewährleistet ist. Die Pflanzenkenntnis der weiblichen Stammesmitglieder ist umfassender (ALAM et al. 2000). Im therapeutischen System der Chakma gibt es viele Arten der Behandlung von Krankheiten. Da gibt es *tantro-mantro-jhar-funk-tabij-kabach-bali-utsharga* (Behandlung durch magische und andere übernatürliche Kräfte) und Behandlungen unter Zuhilfenahme verschiedener Arten von Drogen, hauptsächlich pflanzlichen, aber auch tierischen Ursprunges.

Früher wurden Behandlungen von den ältesten Familienmitgliedern wie den Großeltern als Familienärzte durchgeführt. In diesen Fällen verwendeten sie verschiedene pflanzliche und mineralische Produkte sowie im Haushalt vorrätige Produkte. Diese wurden in der Umgebung ihres Wohnplatzes eingesammelt, was sehr einfach war. Heutzutage bestimmen professionelle traditionelle Heiler die Medikation. Diese verwenden bestimmte Formeln von bestimmten Verzeichnissen von Krankheiten, nachdem sie die Anzeichen und Symptome beobachten, genauso wie in der modernen Medizin.

Chakma Talik

Im medizinischen System der *Chakma* wird dieses Verzeichnis von Krankheiten und Formeln zu deren Behandlung "*Chakma Talik*" genannt. Vermutlich kommt das Wort "*Talik*" vom bengalischen Wort "*Talika*", das "Liste, Verzeichnis" bedeutet; zum Beispiel wird das Verzeichnis der Krankheiten, ihrer Behandlungen und der Anweisungen für die Medikation "*Talik*" genannt. Der "*Talik*" bestand aus *Chakma*-Handschriften, und traditionelle Heiler führten diese immer mit sich. Die Zahl dieser *Taliks* (Verzeichnisse) ist unzählbar.

Professionelle Heiler sammelten diese *Taliks* von ihren alten Lehrern während der letzten Jahrzehnte. Jetzt enthält der "*Talik*" eine Vielzahl von Rezepturen. Die neuen professionellen Heiler vereinten auch Taliks verschiedener Personen aus unterschiedlichen Epochen. Diese unterscheiden sich nicht nur im Namen, sondern auch in ihren medizinischen Schlussfolgerungen. Für die Behandlung ein und derselben Krankheit geben zwei Taliks zwei verschiedene Beschreibungen.

Vier Arten der medizinischen Behandlung sind im *Talik* enthalten (KISHNA 1996).
Es sind dies
1. "Passaries"
2. Produkte tierischer Herkunft oder tierische Sekrete
3. Übernatürliche oder magische oder spirituelle Produkte
4. Heilkräuter.
Davon sind eine Vielzahl in der traditionellen Kultur enthalten.

1. "Passaries"
Passaries oder Medizinen, die aus ayurvedischen Quellen entwickelt wurden. Diese stammen hauptsächlich von Ayurveda (Ayurvedisches Medizin-System) und werden hauptsächlich in "Passary-Shops" verkauft. Daher werden sie Passaries genannt. Sie sind hauptsächlich in getrockneter Form erhältlich. *Aloe vera* (Fam.

Liliaceae), Piper longum Linn. (Fam. Piperaceae), etc. gehören zu dieser Gruppe. Andere getrocknete Hölzer und Wurzeln, die nicht im Lande wachsen, wie *Acanthus ilicifolius Linn.* (*Fam. Acanthaceae*), weißes und rotes Sandelholz (*Pterocarpus santalinus*), Himalayische Zeder (Cedrus deodar), Withania somnifera Dunal (Fam. Solanaceae), etc. werden von auswärts importiert und sind ebenfalls in Passary-Shops erhältlich.

Einige Mineralsalze, wie Steinsalz, Amalgum, rotes Quecksilbersulphid sind ebenfalls in Passary Shops zu finden, ebenso werden Verbindungen ("Aschen") verschiedener Metalle wie Gold, Silber, Quecksilber, Blei etc. verwendet.

2. Produkte tierischer Herkunft oder tierische Sekrete

Zuerst sollen die Gallenblase und Gallensalze als Produkte tierischer Herkunft erwähnt werden. Aufgrund des Gehaltes an Verdauungssäften (Pankreassekreten) werden Gallensekretpräparate bei verschiedenen Erkrankungen des Magens und der Eingeweide eingesetzt. Im *Chakma*-medizinischen System werden 15 Arten von Galle verwendet. Die Große Python liefert die beste Galle (im Sinne von Qualität), danach kommt die Schildkrötengalle. Nach der Schlachtung von Tieren oder Vögeln werden die Gallenblasen dem Körper entnommen, gesammelt, getrocknet und zur künftigen Verwendung gelagert.

Horn, Zähne, Blut und Klauen vom Rhinozeros sind sehr wichtig und entsprechend teuer. Sie werden für die Zubereitung vieler wichtiger Medikamente für unterschiedliche Beschwerden verwendet. Es wird geglaubt, dass, wenn Rhinozeroshorn einige Tage in starken Whisky oder Wein und in tödliches Gift eingetaucht wird, dass sich dann der Whisky und das Gift in ungiftige Flüssigkeit verwandeln, zu Wasser werden. Die Zähne von Schwein, Tiger, Elefant (der *Chakma*-Name ist "*Heth-Rangma*" werden häufig zur Behandlung verschiedener Leiden verwendet. Echsen fressen junge Schildkröten. Nachdem diese Echsen getötet werden, werden die un- oder halbverdauten Schildkröten getrocknet und dienen zur Herstellung von Medizin. Tote Spinnen werden in der *Chakma*-Medizin verwendet. Pfauenfedern werden gegen das Erbrechen eingesetzt. Die Fette und Öle verschiedener Tiere helfen gegen Rheumatismus. Diese Fette stammen von Krokodil, Schwein, Huhn, Python, Echse etc. Der Urin von Stieren wird ebenfalls im *Talik* verwendet und auch im *Ayurvedischen* Medizinsystem.

3. Übernatürliche oder magische oder spirituelle Produkte

Manche *Ojihas*, eine Art übernatürlicher Heiler, verwenden magische oder übernatürliche Kräfte zur Behandlung unterschiedlicher Beschwerden. Viele mentale und/oder psychologische Störungen werden in der *Chakma*-Medizin dem Hauch ("*Baiuu*") von Phantomen oder Geistern zugeschrieben.

Sie werden alle mit magischen Produkten behandelt, die in der *Chakma*-Medizin beschrieben sind. Beispiele dafür sind Gewehrkugeln, mit der zuvor drei verschiedene Tiere getötet wurden, Holzasche von der Verbrennungsstelle menschlicher Leichen, Donner des Himmels (ein Mineralstein), Feuerstein (letzterer wird zur Heilung von Schlangenbissen eingesetzt. Man glaubt, dass dieser Stein das Gift aus der Bisswunde saugt) etc.

4. Pflanzliche Produkte, Heilkräuter

Eine große Anzahl von Heilkräutern wächst in der Hill Tract Region. Praktisch alle Gräser, Kräuter, Büsche, Kriechpflanzen und Bäume werden als Medizin verwendet. Keines von ihnen ist nutzlos. Heutzutage werden Heilkräuter auch

häufig in der modernen Welt eingesetzt. Manche Wissenschaftler und Ärzte glauben, dass in Zukunft pflanzliche Heilstoffe eingesetzt werden bei Beschwerden und Erkrankungen aller Art, von der kleinen Schnittwunde bis zu verschiedenen Krebsarten und AIDS. Es muss aber noch viel Forschungsarbeit geleistet werden, um die exakte Molekülstruktur oder Analogien zu finden, welche die Krankheiten treffen können. Wir hoffen, dass uns eines Tages dieser *Chakma Talik* dabei helfen wird, diese Moleküle und Analogien zu finden.
Verschiedene Teile von Kräutern, Büschen, Bäumen etc. werden im *Talik* verwendet. Wurzeln, Stamm, Rinde, Fruchthülsen, Blätter, Knospen, Blüten, Samen etc. werden verwendet. Wenn bei einer Pflanze kein bestimmter Teil im *Talik* angegeben wird, dann ist es immer die Wurzel. Frischer Brei oder Saft von Pflanzen oder auch die ganze Pflanze werden eingesetzt.

Wurzel: Frische oder getrocknete Wurzeln werden zur Behandlung unterschiedlicher Beschwerden eingesetzt. In manchen Fällen werden unter Berücksichtigung der klimatischen Bedingungen nur die Wurzeln auf der westlichen Seite der Pflanze genommen. Manchmal wird eine Paste aus Wurzeln verwendet, manchmal Pillen, die aus dieser Paste hergestellt wurden. Bestimmte Wurzeln werden eine Zeitlang mit Fäden an Arme und Beine gebunden.

Rinde: Es wird angenommen, dass die aktivsten Bestandteile der Pflanzen in der Rinde gegenwärtig sind. So wird Rinde mit Wasser gewaschen, zu Brei verarbeitet und mit anderen Zutaten vermischt und eingenommen oder zu kleinen Tabletten verarbeitet, in der Sonne getrocknet und gemeinsam mit anderen Materialien, wie Wasser, Honig, Milch etc. geschluckt. Das ist je nach Erkrankung unterschiedlich.

Holz: Pasten werden von verschiedenen Pflanzen zubereitet wie weißem und rotem Sandelholz und Holz von der Himalaya-Zeder. Dann werden sie als Heilmittel verwendet.

Blätter: Blätter werden meist als Paste oder als Saft verwendet. Manchmal werden Blätter zuerst getrocknet, mit anderen Materialien vermischt und zu Pillen geformt. In anderen Fällen wird frischer Brei von Blättern über Schnittwunden oder Verletzungen gerieben. Manche Blätter werden gekocht und der Dampf wird für die Behandlung verwendet (in diesem Fall wird der Körper des Patienten mit Tüchern bedeckt, der Dampf kommt von dem Gefäß, in dem die Blätter kochen, so dass er am Körper außen entlang streicht und der Patient heftig schwitzt). Manchmal werden Schnittwunden und Verletzungen auch mit ganzen, frischen Blättern bedeckt.

Andere Teile von Pflanzen wie Fruchthülsen, Zweige, Blüten, Früchte, Samen, Wurzelstock etc. werden ebenfalls zur Therapie verschiedener Erkrankungen auf verschiedene Art und Weise verwendet.

Im *Talik* werden an die 250 Pflanzen erwähnt, davon sind 132 bestimmt und der Rest (etwa 118) noch nicht identifiziert, die gewöhnlich von den Chakmas und den traditionellen Heilern verwendet werden. Bestimmt wurden bereits folgende

Pflanzen:
Achyranthus aspera Linn.
Acorus calamus Linn.
Aegle marmelos
Allium cepa Lam.
Allium sativum Lam.
Alocacia indica
Aloe indica
Aloe vera
Alpina nigra
Alpinia malaccensis Rose
Amaranthus gangeticus
Amaranthus spinosis Linn.
Amaranthus viridis
Ananas comosus Merr.
Annona reticulata Linn.
Anthocephalas chinensis Lamk.
Aristolochia indica Linn.
Artocarpus heteophyllus
Artocarpus lakoocha Roxb.
Asterocantha longifolia Ness.
Azadirachta indica
Bauthinia malabarica Roxb.
Benincasa hispida
Bramssica napus
Broussonetia paperifera Linn.
Cajanus indicus
Calamus viminalis
Calotropis gigantia
Calotropis procera
Canabis sativa
Capsicum annum
Carica papaya Linn.
Cassia alata
Cassia siamca Linn.
Centella asiatica Linn.
Centipeda minimal Linn.
Chicrassia tabularis Jubs.
Citrus maxima Linn.
Citrus medica Linn.
Cleodendrum viscosum
Coccinia cordifolia
Coccinia medica
Colocasia esculentus Linn.
Corchorns capsularis Linn.
Coriandrum sativum Linn.
Cucumis sativa Linn.
Curcuma amada Roxb.
Curcuma caesia Roxb.
Curcuma domestica
Curcuma longa Linn.
Cuscuta reflexa Roxb.
Datura fastuosa Linn. var. D. alba
Datura metel Linn.
Dehasia kurzi King
Dillenia indica Linn.
Diospyros peregrina Linn.
Dipterocarpus alatus
Dipterocarpus gracilis
Dipterocarpus turbinatus
Elaeocarpus rugosus Roxb.
Emblica officinalis Gaertn.
Erythrina variegata Linn.
Ficus racemosa Linn.
Fleurya interrupta
Glycosmis pentaphylla Retz.
Hibiscus esculentus Linn.
Hordeum vulgare Linn.
Hydnocarpus kurzii
Ilex godajam
Ipomoea reptans Linn.
Lageneria siceraria
Lagerstroernia speciosa Linn.
Lannea coromondelica
Lathyrus sativus Linn.
Licuala pellata Roxb.
Lunnea grandis
Mallotus albus
Mangfera indica Linn.
Mesua ferrea Linn.
Momordia charantia
Momordia muricata
Morinda anguistifolia Roxb.
Moringa oleifera
Musa ornata Roxb.
Musa paradisiacal Linn. sub sp. sylvestris
Musa sapientum Linn.
Nardostachys jatamansi Dc.
Nicotiana tobactim Linn.
Nymphaea nouchali
Ocimum basilicum Linn.
Ocimum gratissimum Linn.
Oroxylum indicum Linn.
Oryza sativa Linn.
Pandanus lectonis
Piper bettle Linn.
Piper chaba Linn.
Plantago ovata Forst.
Polygonatrum cirrhifolium Royle
Polygonatrum oppositifolium

Polygonum hydropiper
Psidium guyava Linn.
Punica granatum Linn.
Rawalfia serpentina
Ricinus communis Linn.
Rununculus seleratus Linn.
Saccharurn officinarum Linn.
Samalia insignis
Santalum album Linn.
Saraca indica Linn.
Seasamum indicum D.C.
Sida cordata
Sida orientalis Cav.
Sida rhombitolia Linn.
Solarium melongena Linn.
Spondias magnifera
Spondias pinnata

Stendnera virosa Prain
Strychnos nuxvomica
Tabernae montana divericata Linn.
Tamarindus indica Linn.
Terminalia belerica Retz.
Terminalia chebula Retz.
Tragia involucrata Linn.
Tribulus terrestris Linn.
Tricosanthes tricuspidata
Xeromphis spinosa
Zingiber casumumum
Zingiber officinalis
Zingiber purpureum
Zinziber rubens Roxb.
Zizyphus jujuba
Zizyphus sativa

Schlussfolgerung

Untersuchungen in Ethnoepidemiologie und Ethnoökologie können erbracht werden, indem die ethnoempirischen und ethnotheoretischen Perspektiven erforscht werden, wie ortsansässige oder eingeborene Menschen die Ursachen von, den Schutz vor und die Ökologie menschlicher und tierischer Erkrankungen wahrnehmen.

Dies kann nützlich sein bei menschlichen Parasitenerkrankungen und Zoonosen, vom Standpunkt aus, wie krankheitsübertragende Insekten und Tiere als Zwischenwirte die Übertragung menschlicher Infektionskrankheiten beeinflussen. Forschungen über die wechselseitigen Beziehungen zwischen der Gesundheit des Ökosystems und der menschlichen Gesundheit müssen von einem multidisziplinären Team von Experten, die Disziplinen repräsentieren wie klinische Humanmedizin, Epidemiologie, Systemische Ökologie, Zoologie, Insektenkunde und Ethnobiologie, erbracht werden.

Diese Studien gewinnen an Bedeutung durch die Zusammenarbeit mit der lokalen eingeborenen Bevölkerung und das Erlernen ihrer Sichtweise der Wechselbeziehungen zwischen der Ethnoökologie von Ökosystemen und der Ethnoepidemiologie menschlicher und tierischer Erkrankungen. Achtsame Forschung kann die ethnoempirischen und ethnotheoretischen Perspektiven erhellen, die von ortsansässigen Eingeborenen entwickelt wurden und ihre Anschauung steuern, wie die Ökologie des Ökosystems die Ursachen von, die Vorbeugung gegenüber und die Ökologie von menschlichen und tierischen Erkrankungen beeinflussen.

Diese ethnobiologischen und Medizinökologischen Untersuchungen können aufzeigen, wie ökosystemische Veränderungen wie Rodungen, Veränderungen im Wasserhaushalt und Schwankungen der Witterung die menschliche Gesundheit beeinflussen. Die Umwelt betreffende, ökologische und kulturelle Veränderungen können ihrerseits Luft, Wasser, Boden, Ökosystem, Nahrungsquellen und menschliche Aktivitäten in einer Weise verändern, die Auswirkungen auf die

menschliche Gesundheit hat. Bevölkerungswachstum und -wanderung intensivieren die menschliche Interaktion mit den ökologischen Systemen, wodurch biotische Störungen sich in einer Zunahme menschlicher Infektionskrankheiten manifestieren können. Grundregulierungen und die räumliche Beziehung zwischen Mensch und Tier können Seuchenübertragung beeinflussen. Die Veränderung des menschlichen Lebensstils vom Hirten und Bauern zu einer sesshaften urbanen Umwelt bringt eine Erhöhung der Bevölkerungsdichte mit sich, wodurch wieder der Anteil mikrobiologisch verunreinigten Wassers steigt und die Übertragung infektiöser Erkrankungen.
Diese Veränderungen bewirken auch eine Veränderung der Ernährung und ein mehr sitzender Lebensstil wird die Raten von Fettleibigkeit, Erwachsenendiabetes, Bluthochdruck und Herzerkrankungen ansteigen lassen. Gemeinsame Projekte von Ökologen, Zoologen, Naturschützern, Ethnobotanikern, Ärzten und Epidemiologen in Zusammenarbeit mit der lokalen Bevölkerung werden Programme ermöglichen zum besseren Verständnis dafür, wie die Gesundheit des Ökosystems und die menschliche Gesundheit miteinander verbunden sind. Die lokale, eingeborene Bevölkerung und die Gemeinden können in regionale Gesundheitsprogramme eingebunden werden, deren Schwerpunkt die Epidemiologie und die Kontrolle menschlicher Erkrankungen, speziell des Ausbruches von Krankheiten und Epidemien darstellt (THOMAS, 2000).

Das *Chakma Talik Cikitsa* (Medizinsystem) ist eine sehr reiche Quelle an Informationen über den Stamm der *Chakma*, ihre traditionelle Medizin und ihre Kultur. Eine große Anzahl der Pflanzen, die im *Talik* verwendet werden, muss erst noch identifiziert werden. Diese Bestimmung und Klassifikation muss mittels wissenschaftlicher Evaluierungsverfahren geschehen.

Autor
MAHMUD TAREQ HASSAN KHAN
arbeitet als Forschungsassistent an der University of Karachi, Bangladesh. Er veröffentlichte etwa 50 Beiträge in verschiedenen Fachzeitschriften. Die letzten 7 Jahre arbeitet er an der Pharmakologie und Toxikologie von Naturprodukten in verschiedenen Medizinsystemen, wie z.B. Ayurveda, Unani etc.
Kontakt: Pharmakologisches Forschungslabor, Pharmazeutisch- Wissenschaftliche Fakultät, Universität für Wissenschaft und Technologie,75270- Karachi, 56/E, Jamal Khan Road, Chittagong-4000, Bangladesh.
E-Mail: mthkhan2002@yahoo.com

References

ALAM, K.M. & KHISA, S.B. 2000. *Indigenous Knowledge of Upland People For Bio-Diversity Management and Land Use Planning in Chittagong Hill Tracts, Bangladesh.* VII International Congress of Ethnobiology: Ethnobiology, Benefits Sharing and Biocultural Diversity, p. 31.

CHAKMA, T.K.; NAHAR, N.; SHAHRIAR, M.; ALAMGIR, M.; & CHOUDHURI, M.S.K. 2000. Studies on the prospect of medicinal plant resources of the Chittagong Hill Tracts, Bangladesh *J Integr Med*, 1(1), 23-29.

KHISHA, B. 1996. *Chakma Talik Cikitsa, Herbal Medicine Center Committee*, First edition, pp. 13-120.

THOMAS, C. 2000. *Contributions of Ethnomedical Knowledge To Public Health.* VII International Congress of Ethnobiology: Ethnobiology, Benefits Sharing and Biocultural Diversity, p. 48.

CHAKMA TALIKA CIKITSA - THE THERAPEUTIC SYSTEM OF THE CHAKMA TRIBE CHITTAGONG HILL TRACT OF BANGLADESH

by Mahmud Tareq Hassan Khan

Introduction

The Chittagong Hill Tracts (CHT) in Bangladesh is the homeland for twelve different tribal communities, e.g., *Chakma, Arakani, Rakhain, Mogh (Marma),* and *Murang,* etc. The *Chakma* is the largest tribe among them. About 1.1 million people currently live in an area of 1.32 million hectar, and 90% of them are involved in Jhum cultivation. The CHT with a territory of 13191 sq. km. lies between 21" 25' and 23" 45' north latitude and 91" 45' and 92" 50' east longitude and is situated to the southeast of Bangladesh. They are comprised of three hill districts: Rangamati, Khagrachari and Bandarban. It constitutes 76% of the total hilly regions of the country; of which 90% are hilly area, 4% covers villages, rivers, lakes and marshes and only the remaining 6% is suitable for intensive agriculture (CHAKMA et al. 2000). The area has tropical monsoon climate with yearly average rainfall of 2553 mm. Average annual temperature of the region is 25.2°C and average relative humidity is 79.3%. The main features of the vegetation are semi-evergreen to tropical evergreen, dominated by tall trees belonging to Dipterocarpaceae, Euphorbiaceae, Lauraceae, Leguminosae and Rubiaceae. Unmistakably the abundance of the floristic composition offers a vast source of raw materials for the preparation of Ayurvedic medicines, which has been the custom from the very early age of civilization in this subcontinent.

Chakma therapeutic system

The local knowledge of indigenous peoples of CHT is very rich. Their folk-taxonomy, closely linked with the ecosystem, flora and fauna delimits different taxa and indicates the habit, habitat and utility of plants. The preference of plant species for different uses varies extensively covering a range of habitats. The harvest of resources relates to the environment and seasonality that helps sustainable management of resources. The tribal women's knowledge of plants is more comprehensive (ALAM et al. 2000).

In the *Chakma* therapeutic system, there are many ways for the treatment of diseases. They are - *tantro-mantro-jhar-funk-tabij-kabach-bali-utsharga* (magical and some other super-natural powers) and treatments with the administration of different kinds of drugs, mainly from plants and some animal-derived materials. Previously, treatments were done by the most aged members of the family like grandfather or grandmother as family physician. In these cases they used different herbal and mineral products and previously stored products within the family. These were collected from the surrounding areas of their home. It was very easy for them to collect. Nowadays professional traditional healers give the medications. However, they use certain formulas from a list of diseases after observing the signs and symptoms, just like modern medicine. In the *Chakma* system of medicine, this list of diseases with treatment and formulas of medications is called "*Chakma Talik*". Probably, the word '*Talik*' came from the Bengali word '*Talika*', which means "List", i.e., the list of diseases, their treatments and formulas of the medications are called "*Talik*". The '*Talik*' was written in *Chakma*-hand written scripts and the traditional healers always kept these with them. The number of such kind of *taliks* (lists) are uncountable. Professional traditional healers collected these *Taliks* from their ancient teachers throughout the last several decades. Just now this '*Talik*' contains a lot of formulas. They also brought together the *Taliks* from different persons in different epochs. They are distinctive, not only by their names, but diversified also with medicinal consequences. For the treatment of the same disease, two *Taliks* give two different kinds of prescriptions. Four types of medications are available in the *Talik* (KHISHA 1996).

1. Passaries,
2. Animal-derived products or materials secreted from animal bodies,
3. Supernatural, magic or spiritual products,
4. Herbals.

These types are in large number and contain the traditional culture.

1. Passaries

Passaries or medicines are derived from *Ayurvedic* sources. These came mainly from *Ayurveda (Ayurvedic* system of medicine) and are sold mainly in the passary shops. So these are called passaries. These are sold mainly in dry forms. *Aloe vera* (Fam. Liliaceae), Piper longum Linn. (Fam. Piperaceae), etc. fall into this group. Some other dry woods and roots, which are not available in this country, such as, Acanthus ilicifolius Linn. (Fam. Acanthaceae), white and red sandal (Pterocarpus santalinus) wood, Cedrus deodar, Withania somnifera Dunal (Fam. Solanaceae), etc., are imported from abroad and found in the passary shops.

Some mineral salts, such as, rock-salt, amalgum, red mercuric sulphide, etc. are also found in the passary shops. Ashes of different metals, such as, gold, silver, mercury, lead, etc., are used.

2. Animal-derived or materials secreted from an animal body

At first the gall bladder and bile salt should be discussed for animal-derived products. Due to the presence of digestive (pancreatic) juice, the bile secretions are used for the treatment of different types of gastric and intestinal disorders. In the *Chakma* system of medicine, 15 kinds of biles are used. These are basically categorized on the basis of their sources. Large python is the best type of bile (in sense of quality). Second best is turtles' bile. After birds or other animals have been slaughtered, their gall bladder is collected, dried and then stored for future use. The horns, teeth, blood and nails of rhinoceroses are very important and expensive. These are used for the preparation of many important medicines for different diseases. It is believed that if the horn of rhinoceros is submerged in strong whisky or wines and in deadly poisons for several days, then the whisky or poison is converted to non-poisonous or non-toxic liquids, becomes water. The teeth of swine, tiger and elephant (*Chakma* name is "*Heth-rangma*") are frequently used for treating different diseases. The lizard swallows the small turtles. After killing these lizards, the undigested or semi-digested turtles are collected, dried and are used for the preparation of some medicines.

The dead bodies of spiders are used in *Chakma* medicines. A peacocks´s feather is used as an antivomiting agent. The fats and oils collected from different animals are used in rheumatism. These fats are collected from crocodiles, pigs, chickens, pythons, lizards, etc. The urine of bull is also used in the *Talik*, which is also mentioned in the *Ayurvedic* system of medicine.

3. Supernatural or magic or spiritual products

Due to lack of modern knowledge, some magic or spiritual ways of treatment are used. Some *Ojhhas*, a kind of supernatural practitioner, use magical or supernatural powers for the treatment of different diseases. Many of the mental and/or psychological disorders are designated in *Chakma* medicine as due to the air ("*Baiuu*") of phantoms or ghosts. All of these are treated with magical products described in *Chakma* medicine. These are for example the same bullet collected from three different dead bodies of animals, ash collected from the firewood used to burn the human dead body, thunder of the sky, a kind of stone collected from mineral, fire-stone used for the treatment of snake bite. It is supposed to suck the snake poison from the wound, etc.

4. Herbal products

A very large number of herbal recources grow in the hill tract region. Practically all grasses, herbs, shrubs, creepers, trees are used as medicine. None of them are useless. Nowadays, herbal medicines are frequently used in the modern world. Some scientists and physicians believe that medicines for the treatment of a small cut up to different kinds of cancers and AIDS will come from the herbal medicines. The only requirements are vast searches to find out and pin point the exact molecule or analogue that causes the diseases. We hope one day this *Chakma Talik* will help us to find that exact molecule or analogue.

Different parts of herbs, shrubs, trees, etc. are used in the *Talik*. Root, stem, bark, pod, leaves, buds, flowers, fruits, seeds, etc. are used. If there was a part of some specific plants not mentioned in the *Talik*, it would be the root. Fresh paste or juice of plants or the whole plants are taken.

Root: Fresh and dried roots are used for the treatment of different diseases. Some times, taking consideration of climatic conditions, the roots of the western side of the plant are used. Sometimes a paste of the roots is taken and sometimes tablets prepared from the paste from the roots are taken. For a time the specific roots are tied up on the hand or leg with threads.

Bark.The bark is supposed to contain the most active ingredients of the plants. Therefore, a paste is made of washed bark mixed with water and other ingredients.

From this paste you can also shape small tablets and let them dry in the sun. Depending on the disease, these tablets are taken with other materials such as water, honey, milk, etc.

Wood: Pastes from different plants are prepared, such as white and red sandalwood, and wood from the Cedrus deodar. Then they are used as medicine.

Leaves: Leaves are mostly taken as paste or as juice. Sometimes the paste from the leaves are dried, mixed with other materials and tablets are prepared. Sometimes the fresh paste of leaves is rubbed over the cut skin or injury. Some leaves are boiled, the vapor then used for treatment (in this case the body of the patient is covered with cloths and then the vapor is taken from the pan, where the leaves are boiling. The vapor can flow round the body and the patient severely sweats). Sometimes the cuts or injury are just covered with the full fresh leaves.

Other parts from plants such as pod, branches, flowers, fruits, seeds, rhizomes, etc., are also used for therapy of different diseases in different ways.

In the *Talik* about 250 plants have been mentioned, of which about 132 are identified and the rest (about 118) of the plants have not yet been identified, which are habitually used by the Chakma peoples and the traditional practitioners. The identified plants are:

Achyranthus aspera Linn.
Acorus calamus Linn.
Aegle marmelos
Allium cepa Lam.
Allium sativum Lam.
Alocacia indica
Aloe indica
Aloe vera
Alpina nigra
Alpinia malaccensis Rose
Amaranthus gangeticus
Amaranthus spinosis Linn.
Amaranthus viridis
Ananas comosus Merr.
Annona reticulata Linn.
Anthocephalas chinensis Lamk.
Aristolochia indica Linn.
Artocarpus heteophyllus
Artocarpus lakoocha Roxb.
Asterocantha longifolia Ness.
Azadirachta indica
Bauthinia malabarica Roxb.
Benincasa hispida
Bramssica napus
Broussonetia paperifera Linn.
Cajanus indicus
Calamus viminalis
Calotropis gigantia

Calotropis procera
Canabis sativa
Capsicum annum
Carica papaya Linn.
Cassia alata
Cassia siamca Linn.
Centella asiatica Linn.
Centipeda minimal Linn.
Chicrassia tabularis Jubs.
Citrus maxima Linn.
Citrus medica Linn.
Cleodendrum viscosum
Coccinia cordifolia
Coccinia medica
Colocasia esculentus Linn.
Corchorns capsularis Linn.
Coriandrum sativum Linn.
Cucumis sativa Linn.
Curcuma amada Roxb.
Curcuma caesia Roxb.
Curcuma domestica
Curcuma longa Linn.
Cuscuta reflexa Roxb.
Datura fastuosa Linn. var. D. alba
Datura metel Linn.
Dehasia kurzi King
Dillenia indica Linn.
Diospyros peregrina Linn.

Dipterocarpus alatus
Dipterocarpus gracilis
Dipterocarpus turbinatus
Elaeocarpus rugosus Roxb.
Emblica officinalis Gaertn.
Erythrina variegata Linn.
Ficus racemosa Linn.
Fleurya interrupta
Glycosmis pentaphylla Retz.
Hibiscus esculentus Linn.
Hordeum vulgare Linn.
Hydnocarpus kurzii
Ilex godajam
Ipomoea reptans Linn.
Lageneria siceraria
Lagerstroernia speciosa Linn.
Lannea coromondelica
Lathyrus sativus Linn.
Licuala pellata Roxb.
Lunnea grandis
Mallotus albus
Mangfera indica Linn.
Mesua ferrea Linn.
Momordia charantia
Momordia muricata
Morinda anguistifolia Roxb.
Moringa oleifera
Musa ornata Roxb.
Musa paradisiacal Linn. sub sp. sylvestris
Musa sapientum Linn.
Nardostachys jatamansi Dc.
Nicotiana tobactim Linn.
Nymphaea nouchali
Ocimum basilicum Linn.
Ocimum gratissimum Linn.
Oroxylum indicum Linn.
Oryza sativa Linn.
Pandanus lectonis

Piper bettle Linn.
Piper chaba Linn.
Plantago ovata Forst.
Polygonatrum cirrhifolium Royle
Polygonatrum oppositifolium
Polygonum hydropiper
Psidium guyava Linn.
Punica granatum Linn.
Rawalfia serpentina
Ricinus communis Linn.
Rununculus seleratus Linn.
Saccharurn officinarum Linn.
Samalia insignis
Santalum album Linn.
Saraca indica Linn.
Seasamum indicum D.C.
Sida cordata
Sida orientalis Cav.
Sida rhombitolia Linn.
Solarium melongena Linn.
Spondias magnifera
Spondias pinnata
Stendnera virosa Prain
Strychnos nuxvomica
Tabernae montana divericata Linn.
Tamarindus indica Linn.
Terminalia belerica Retz.
Terminalia chebula Retz.
Tragia involucrata Linn.
Tribulus terrestris Linn.
Tricosanthes tricuspidata
Xeromphis spinosa
Zingiber casumumum
Zingiber officinalis
Zingiber purpureum
Zinziber rubens Roxb.
Zizyphus jujuba
Zizyphus sativa

Conclusion

Investigations on ethnoepidemiology and ethnoecology can be brought about by researching the ethnoempirical and ethnotheoretical perspectives of how local or indigenous peoples perceive the causes, deterrents, and ecology of human and animal diseases. Particularly this can be useful in the study of human parasitic diseases and zoonoses from the stance of how insect vectors and animal hosts influence the transmission of human infectious diseases. Research has been accomplished on the interrelationships of ecosystem health and human health assistances from a multidisciplinary team of experts representing disciplines including human clinical medicine, epidemiology, ecosystem ecology, zoology, entomology, and ethnobiology. These studies are further enhanced by collaborating with local or indigenous peoples and learning about their perceptions on the interrelationships of ethnoecology of ecosystems and ethnoepidemiology of human and animal diseases. Careful research can enlighten the ethnoempirical and ethnotheoretical perspectives developed by the local/indigenous peoples that steer their understanding of how ecosystem ecology influences the causes, deterrents, and ecology of human and animal diseases. These ethnobiological and medical ecological studies can discover how ecosystem changes such as deforestation, changes in water systems, and oscillations in weather can influence human health. Environmental, ecological, and cultural changes can alter air, water, soil, ecosystems, food sources, and human activity in such ways that impact human health. Population growth and movement intensifies human interactions with ecological systems that may potentiate biotic disease resulting in the spread of human infectious diseases. Land use patterns and the spatial relationship of humans to animals can influence disease transmission. Human lifestyle transition from a pastoral/agrarian environment to a more sedentary urban environment results in increased population density that results in increased rates of microbiologically polluted water and infectious diseases. This transition also results in a change in diet and a more sedentary lifestyle with increased rates of obesity, adult diabetes, hypertension, and cardiac disease. Unified projects with ecologists, zoologists, conservationists, ethnobotanists, physicians and epidemiologists collaborating with local peoples enable programs to better research and understand issues of how ecosystem health and human health are interrelated. Local peoples and communities can be integrated into regional public health programs that focus on epidemiology and human disease monitoring, particularly of emerging diseases (THOMAS, 2000). This *Chakma Talik Cikitsa* is a very rich source of information on the *Chakma* tribe, their traditional medicines as well as their culture. A large number of plants that are used in the *Talik* have yet to be identified. They must be identified and justified with scientific evaluationary processes.

Author

MAHMUD TAREQ HASSAN KHAN
Pharmacology Research Laboratory, Faculty of Pharmaceutical Sciences, University of Science and Technology Chittagong, Chittagong, Bangladesh
Contact: International Center for Chemical Sciences, H.E.J. Research Institute of Chemistry, University of Karachi, Karachi-75270, Pakistan. E-Mail: mthkhan2002@yahoo.com

References

ALAM, K.M. & KHISA, S.B. 2000. *Indigenous Knowledge of Upland People For Bio-Diversity Management and Land Use Planning in Chittagong Hill Tracts, Bangladesh.* VII International Congress of Ethnobiology: Ethnobiology, Benefits Sharing and Biocultural Diversity, p. 31.
CHAKMA, T.K.; NAHAR, N.; SHAHRIAR, M.; ALAMGIR, M.; & CHOUDHURI, M.S.K. 2000. Studies on the prospect of medicinal plant resources of the Chittagong Hill Tracts, Bangladesh *J Integr Med*, 1(1), 23-29.
KHISHA, B. 1996. *Chakma Talik Cikitsa, Herbal Medicine Center Committee,* First edition, pp. 13-120.
THOMAS, C. 2000. *Contributions of Ethnomedical Knowledge To Public Health.* VII International Congress of Ethnobiology: Ethnobiology, Benefits Sharing and Biocultural Diversity, p. 48.

JHARPHUK - EINE SCHAMANISCHE HEILBEHANDLUNG IN NEPAL

von Andreas Reimers

Kultureller Hintergrund

Unter den 38 Volksgruppen Nepals sind schamanische Heilrituale weit verbreitet. Nach neueren Untersuchungen gibt es ca. 600.000 Schamanen (Nepali: *jhankri, dhami*), die neben ihrem eigentlichen Broterwerb für die Gesundheit von durchschnittlich fünfzig Personen zuständig sind und zu deren Heilung Trance- und Heilrituale durchführen. Obwohl ein Großteil der medizinischen Versorgung in den ländlichen Bereichen von den Schamanen geleistet wird, fand eine angemessene Berücksichtigung ihrer Tätigkeit im westlich geprägten staatlichen Gesundheitssystem Nepals bisher nicht statt (HITCHKOCK & JONES 1994, MILLER 1987, SHRESTA 1980).

Die vorliegende Studie bezieht sich auf Untersuchungen, die in der Zeit von 1993 bis 2001 bei den *Tamang* und *Gurung* in Zentralnepal durchgeführt wurden. Diese Bergvölker gehören tibetischen Sprachgruppen an, benutzen aber im Alltag und in ihren Ritualen auch Nepali. Obwohl sie sich offiziell zum Buddhismus bekennen, besitzen sie eine reiche schamanische Tradition (EIGNER 1990).

Abb. 1: Maile Lama, Schamanin der *Tamang* aus Nepal.

Werdegang der Schamanen

In Nepal gibt es drei Wege, um Schamane zu werden:
    a) durch die persönliche Berufung
    b) durch die Familientradition
    c) durch die Lehre bei einem Lehrer

Für alle drei Wege ist die eigene Erfahrung und der Kontakt mit den verborgenen seelischen und kosmischen Kräften notwendig. Wenn sich die schamanische Kraft manifestiert, kommt es häufig zu Visionen und auffälligen Verhaltensmustern. Die zukünftigen Schamanen springen z.B. ins Feuer, sagen ungewöhnliche Dinge voraus, rennen von ihrer inneren Stimme getrieben in die Wildnis und verschwinden für mehrere Tage und Wochen in den Wald oder in Höhlen, wo sie in einer inneren Schau in der schamanischen Heilkunst unterrichtet werden.

Über den Prozess der eigenen Heilung und Ganzwerdung gewinnt der Schamane die Kraft und die Hilfsgeister, die ihm später das Heilen ermöglichen. Die endgültige Approbation erfolgt über den Unterricht bei einem anerkannten Schamanen, der die Erfahrungen als schamanische Berufung anerkennt und dem Initianten hilft, sie zu integrieren und therapeutisch nutzbar zu machen, indem er ihn in die kulturspezifischen Traditionen einführt. Im Schamanenkostüm, den Gesängen und Paraphernalien wird diese Erfahrung in den Heilsitzungen immer wieder neu inszeniert. Er übernimmt die Verpflichtung, jedem Hilfesuchenden jederzeit mit seinem Wissen zu helfen, wobei die Höhe des "Gehalts" keine Rolle spielt. Demzufolge übt der Schamane neben seiner Heiltätigkeit noch einen Beruf aus, wobei die Belastung oftmals so groß wird, dass in Nepal viele Schamanen versuchen, ihrer Berufung aus dem Weg zu gehen.

Heilpraxis

Die Heilung des Patienten kann eine Reihe verschiedener Behandlungsmethoden erforderlich machen. So kann auf der physischen Ebene die Behandlung in der Anwendung von Massagetechniken und Pflanzenpräparaten bestehen.

Was aber die eigentliche Kraft des Schamanen ausmacht, ist seine Fähigkeit, willentlich in Trance zu gehen und zwischen der Alltagswirklichkeit und der Welt der geistigen Kräfte zu vermitteln. Um veränderte Bewusstseinszustände herbeizuführen, benutzen die Schamanen verschiedene Methoden wie Fasten, Reizdeprivation, Schlafentzug, Hyperventilation, Halluzinogene und in Nepal vor allem die Reizintensivierung (Trommeln und Singen).

Durch die Rezitation der kulturspezifischen Mythen und Mantren wird eine metaphorisch-symbolische Dimension eröffnet, die im Kranken die zentralen archetypischen Kräfte evoziert. Es entsteht ein dynamischer Prozess, der zu einer intensiven emotionalen Bindung zu sich selbst, der Gemeinschaft und dem Universum führt. Die Herstellung dieser ursprünglichen Einheit ist ein heilsamer Vorgang, der die blockierten Energien in uns wieder in Fluss bringt (Q̦uekelberghe 1996).

Kosmologie

In der Kosmologie der nepalesischen Schamanen hat die Welt eine dreigeteilte Struktur (Nepali: *tintriloka*). Diese besteht aus der oberen Welt der Götter (Nepali: *akasha*), der mittleren Welt der Menschen (Nepali: *dhariti*) und der unteren Welt der Schlangenkräfte (Nepali: *patala*). Shiva, der höchste Gott, unterwies den ersten Schamanen (Nepali: *bonjhankri*) in der Kunst des Heilens. Auf diesen Urahn gehen in einer langen Reihe von Meistern und Schülern alle heutigen Schamanen

zurück. Aufgabe der Schamanen ist es, das Unheil und die Krankheiten, die durch die negativen Kräfte und die Hexen in die Welt kamen, zu vertreiben. Die transzendenten, metaphysischen Ursachen der Krankheiten werden in einer Reihe von Mythen ausführlich dargestellt. Dabei werden einzelne Krankheitsbilder auf das Einwirken bestimmter Geister zurückgeführt.
Diese werden von dem Schamanen identifiziert und in einem Heilritual besänftigt. Alle im Ritual verwendeten Paraphernalien verweisen auf den Mythos. Im Altar (Nepali: *than*) verschmelzen der Makrokosmos und der Mikrokosmos zu einer Einheit, in der die Mitte der Welt (axis mundi) und des Menschen zusammenfallen (MÜLLER-EBELING et al. 2000).

Aufbau der Heilrituale
Einem typischen Heilritual (Nepali: *chinta*) liegt folgender Aufbau zugrunde:
Auf die Diagnosestellung folgt das Rufen der Kräfte und die Induktion der Trance. Der Höhepunkt des Rituals ist die rituelle Heilung, die durch den Dank an die Kräfte abgeschlossen wird. Es folgen weitere Anordnungen für den Alltag.

> 1. Zur Diagnosestellung, (Nepali: *jokhana*) gibt es eine Reihe von Methoden. Als Beispiel seien die Trancereisen, das Pulsfühlen und das Reiszählen genannt. Bei der Trancereise reist der Schamane über neun Stufen zu den Göttern der Oberwelt oder über sieben Tunnel in die Unterwelt, die von den Schlangenkräften bewohnt wird, um nach der Krankheitsursache zu fahnden und den verantwortlichen Geist zu identifizieren (s. Abb. 1).

Abb.1:
Maile Lama in der diagnostischen Trance. In Trance erfahrene Realitätsebenen bei den *Tamang* in Nepal.

Beim Pulsfühlen erfühlt der Schamane Veränderungen des Pulses, während er mögliche Krankheitsursachen abfragt. Beim Zählen des Reises ergibt die Zahl der zufällig aufgenomenen Reiskörner ebenfalls Hinweise auf die Ursache.

2. Beim nächsten Schritt werden die spirituellen Kräfte aller drei Welten einschließlich der höchsten Gottheit (*Mahadev*), die für Allmacht, Kraft und Harmonie steht, angerufen. Die geistigen Kräfte werden sowohl als intrapsychisch als auch kosmisch wirksame Kräfte verstanden. Dabei ist die Grundhaltung nicht bestimmend, manipulativ, sondern eher dankbar, hingebungsvoll, um Segen bittend.

3. Durch bestimmte Trommelrhythmen, das Singen von Mantren, Räuchern und rituelle Handlungen wird ein Trancezustand eingeleitet, der alle Beteiligte in einen intensiven Prozess einbezieht. Die Gegenwart der spirituellen Kraft wird durch ein Zittern des Körpers sowie ein verändertes Verhalten des Schamanen, das jedoch kontrolliert bleibt, signalisiert.

4. In der rituellen Heilung holt der Schamane den verlorenen Seelenanteil zurück oder extrahiert den negativen Einfluss. Die alte Ordnung wird wieder hergestellt. Der Kranke erhält seinen Platz in der menschlichen Gesellschaft und im Kosmos zurück. Spezifische Heilrituale sind z.B. "die Seelenrückholung" bei Seelenverlust, "das Durchtrennen der Lebenslinien" bei Schicksalsschlägen und "die Erhebung des Kopfes" bei Depressionen.

5. Die Heilzeremonie schließt mit dem Dank an die Kräfte ab. Es werden Reis- Blumen-, Tier- und andere Opfer dargebracht. Der Geheilte bekommt als Ausdruck des stattgefundenen Reframings einen neuen Sitzplatz zugewiesen. Zum Abschluss folgen Anordnungen und Richtlinien zum Verhalten im Alltag.

6. *Jharphook*

Es gibt in Nepal eine große Anzahl verschiedener, differenziert ausgestalteter Heilrituale. Diese lassen sich im wesentlichen zwei Gruppen zuordnen:

a) Extraktion von negativen Krankheitsursachen

b) Rückholung von verlorenen Seelenanteilen

Bei allen verwendeten Methoden spielt die Besänftigung der geistigen Kräfte durch Opfer eine zentrale Rolle. Heilen heißt opfern. Im Opfer werden der verletzten oder erzürnten Kraft Aufmerksamkeit und Respekt gezollt. Werden z.B.

Reisfelder bestellt, so muss zuvor *Jangeli*, der Göttin des verdrängten Waldes, geopfert werden. Werden ihre Gesetze verletzt, kommt es zu verschiedenen typischen Krankheiten.
Je nach Erkrankung gibt es kleinere Heilrituale von mehreren Minuten Dauer und nächtelange Heilsitzungen (*Chinta*), die sehr komplex aufgebaut sein können. Bereits die Vorbereitungen erfordern dann einen nicht unerheblichen Beitrag des Kranken.

Jharphook stellt die spirituelle (*Jhar*) Behandlung durch Luft (*Phook*) dar. Sie ist eine spezielle Blasetechnik, die in verschiedenen Varianten eingesetzt wird, um in Akutsituationen mit Hilfe des Atems negative, krankheitserzeugende Einflüsse im Menschen zu extrahieren und umzustimmen und den geschwächten Bereich energetisch aufzuladen (d.h. *shakti* zu übertragen). Dazu werden verschiedene Hilfsmittel wie Reis, Asche von Räucherstäbchen, der *Phurba* oder ein Besen aus *Kusha*gras verwendet.
Nach der Diagnose erfolgt die Heilbehandlung, bei der in höchster innerer Sammlung und Konzentration unter Wiederholung der spezifischen *Mantren* (Heilgesänge) die entsprechenden bedeutungsgeladenen Ritualobjekte in ritualisierten Bewegungsabläufen zum Körper und an diesem vorbei geführt werden. Mit Reis und dem *Phurba* werden häufig neben der betroffenen Körperpartie die Schläfen, die Schultern und die Fußsohlen berührt. Danach wird Asche auf die Stirn gedrückt. Der Besen wird häufig dazu benutzt, den ganzen Körper abzustreifen und damit zu reinigen.

In dem verwendeten Mantra wird auf den hingebungsvollen Affengott *Hanuman* Bezug genommen, der versprach, Gott *Rama* in seinem Kampf gegen die Dämonen zu unterstützen. Eilfertig brachte er einen ganzen Berg mit Heilkräutern aus dem Himalaya zu dem Schlachtfeld in Südindien, um die verwundeten Helden wieder zu heilen. Dann werden die schädigenden Kräfte und Geister aufgefordert, den Patienten zu verlassen. Diese Aufforderung wird mit einem dreifachen Blasen besiegelt.

Die auch bei uns verbreitete Sitte, Kindern bei einer Verletzung unter Wiederholung eines Spruches auf die betroffene Stelle zu blasen, erscheint wie ein ferner Abglanz der hier beschriebenen Technik, die sehr differenziert ist und in sich das ganze tradierte Weltbild verlebendigt. Dies wird unter anderem in der Struktur der Mantren und dem Aufbau des *Phurba* deutlich. Die Mantren nehmen Bezug auf den tradierten, sinnstiftenden Mythos und werden so zu einem mächtigen, Heilung kreierenden Impuls. Der *Phurba*, der Donnerkeil Gottes, enthält die Dreiteilung der Welt in eine obere, mittlere und untere Sphäre, die Schöpfungsdynamik in der göttlichen Dreiheit, sowie den Kampf des mythischen Vogels *Garuda* gegen die Schlangenkräfte (*Nagas*). In vielen Heilsitzungen konnte ich miterleben, wie durch die *Phukne*-Behandlung die aktuelle Symptomatik (z.B. Kopfschmerzen, Magen-Darm-Beschwerden und Gliederschmerzen, sowie Ängste und Depressionen) gelindert wurden oder verschwanden.

Wirkmechanismen in schamanischen Heilritualen

In einem solchermaßen gestalteten Heilritual finden wir eine Reihe unterschiedlicher therapeutischer Interventionen miteinander verquickt.

FRANK hat bei seinem Vergleich traditioneller Heilmethoden mit westlicher Medizin und Psychotherapie unspezifische Wirkfaktoren (common factors) herausgearbeitet. (FRANK 1961). Von anthropologischer, religionswissenschaftlicher und psychologischer Seite wurden Heilrituale auf ihre Wirkfaktoren auf sozialer, kognitiver und affektiver Ebene untersucht. Es würde den Rahmen dieser Darstellung sprengen auf einzelne Konzepte einzugehen, so dass hier nur eine grundsätzliche Zusammenschau der Wirkfaktoren erfolgen soll (PFEIFFER 1994, ACHTERBERG 1985, ANDRITZKI 1990).

1. Der Schamane zeigt zumeist eine intensive Anteilnahme, eine emotionale Wärme sowie ein echtes und kongruentes Verhalten. Dabei steht jedoch nicht so sehr die reale Person als vielmehr die typische Gestalt des Heilers als Repräsentant einer höheren Macht im Vordergrund.

2. Die Heilsitzung findet meistens im Kreise der Familie, der Freunde und der Nachbarn statt. Dem Kranken wird Zeit und Aufmerksamkeit gewidmet. Er wird ernstgenommen und erfährt soziale Zuwendung und Unterstützung. Dadurch erfolgt eine Korrektur gestörter Beziehungsmuster entsprechend dem Leitbild der tradierten Ordnung.

3. Durch Anrufen der kosmischen Kräfte entsprechend den kulturgebundenen Mythen wird die Verbindung mit der kosmischen Ordnung wieder hergestellt. Das individuelle Leiden erhält Ort und Sinn im überindividuellen, tradierten Zusammenhang des Mythos, der zugleich die Leitlinie zur Überwindung des Leidens bietet.

4. Der Schamane versetzt sich in veränderte Bewusstseinszustände, die andere Wirklichkeitsebenen zugänglich machen und eine heilsame Wirkung entfalten. Der Kranke partizipiert an der Trance des Schamanen und es kommt zu einer Veränderung seines Bewusstseins mit einer Schwächung der rationalen Anteile der Abwehr und einer Fokussierung auf das Ritualgeschehen. Durch geeignete Stimuli und die geschickte Verwendung von kulturell validierten Symbolen werden archetypische Bilder in dem kollektiven Unbewussten des Kranken geweckt und die damit assoziierte hohe psychische Energie für die Heilung aktiviert. (BOURGIGNON 1973, DITTRICH 1987, GROF 1985, SCHARFETTER 1986, 1996, WILBER 1987).

Abb. 2 und 3:
Maile Lama beim *Jharphook*.

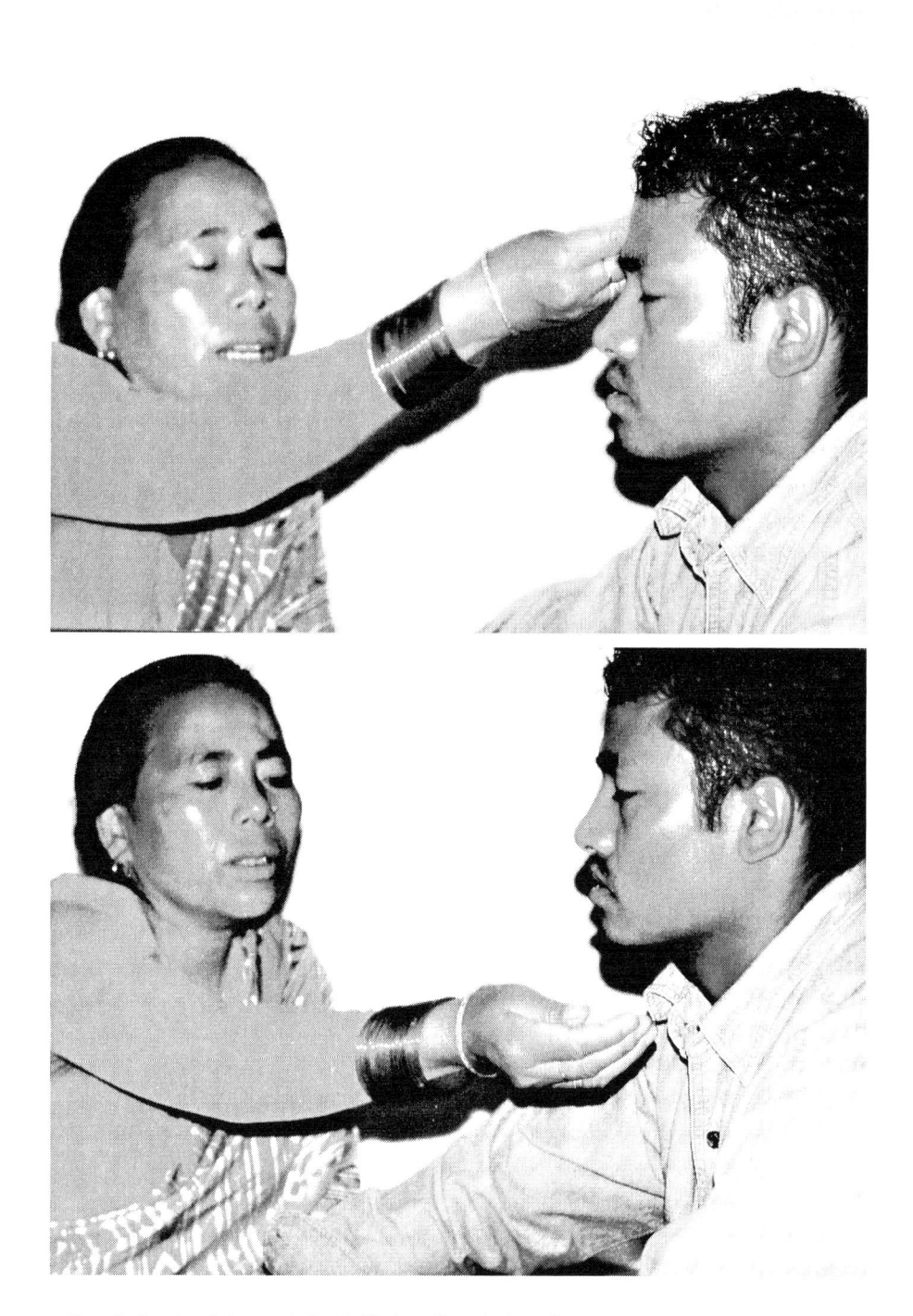

Jharphuk - eine Schamanische Heilbehandlung in Nepal – ETHNOMED 2002

5. Die Krankheitssymptome und inneren Konflikte des Patienten werden von dem Schamanen spirituell gedeutet und auf einer imaginativen Ebene inszeniert und einer Lösung zugeführt. Zum Teil werden Verhaltensweisen ausgelebt, die im Alltag tabuisiert sind. Dadurch kann die Heilsitzung zu einem kathartischen Erleben führen. Konflikte und aufgestaute Emotionen können sich lösen und der Patient findet wieder Kontakt zu seiner inneren Lebensenergie (HOLZ & ZAHN 1995).

6. Durch die neugewonnene positive Ausrichtung werden über psychoneuroimmunologische Wirkmechanismen die Selbstheilungskräfte aktiviert und die Krankheitssymptome spezifisch beeinflusst (QUEKELBERGHE 1996, UEXKÜLL 1990).

Der ganze Ritualverlauf folgt nicht starren Regeln, sondern ist der jeweiligen Situation angepasst und wird durch Prozess-bezogene Interventionen (process task) gesteuert. Sie setzen bei typischen Situationen oder Ereignissen ein, die durch bestimmte Merkmale (processmarker) gekennzeichnet sind (z.B. haben rituelle Handlungen zur Vorhersage des Heilungserfolges die Einleitung entsprechender Maßnahmen zur Folge).

Während in den modernen Psychotherapien neben einem erhöhten Ausmaß seelischer Funktionsfähigkeit im emotionalen und sozialen Bereich die Entwicklung einer angemessenen Ich-Stärke und sozialen Kompetenz sowie eines positiven Selbstbildes als Ziel angesehen wird, betonen traditionelle, schamanische Heilsysteme eher die Rückgewinnung des Platzes in der sozialen Gemeinschaft und in der kosmischen Ordnung. Anders als in der Gestalttherapie, dem Psychodrama und anderen erlebnisorientierten Therapieformen übernimmt nicht der Patient, sondern vorwiegend der Schamane selbst die Rolle, Gefühle, Träume und Konflikte darzustellen, zu verkörpern und zu personifizieren. Der Patient partizipiert häufig lediglich an der Musik, dem Tanz und den kulturell vorgegebenen Imaginationen des Schamanen und überlässt sich damit dem Therapieprozess, wodurch das Lernen am Modell sowie einer direkte Kraftübertragung stärker in den Vordergrund rückt. Im Gegensatz zu Roger´s Klientenzentrierten Gesprächstherapie sowie nicht direktiven psychoanalytischen Interventionen, arbeitet der Schamane direktiver und im westlich modernen Sinne nicht einsichtsorientiert. Vielmehr wird im Rahmen der tradierten Denk- und Verhaltensregeln der Mythos als gegenwärtig erfahren, so dass das individuelle Leiden in ihm Aufnahme und Heilung findet.

Schlussfolgerung

Die hier dargelegten Ansätze erlauben es, schamanische Heilmethoden wie das *Jharphuk* als ein sinnvolles, effizientes Handeln zu verstehen. Es ist zu erwarten, dass die neueren Forschungen der Psychologie, der Psychoneuroimmunologie sowie der Physik weitere Zusammenhänge aufzeigen werden. Ein tieferes Verständnis wird sich allerdings immer an den schamanischen Deutungen selbst orientieren müssen (REIMERS 2000).

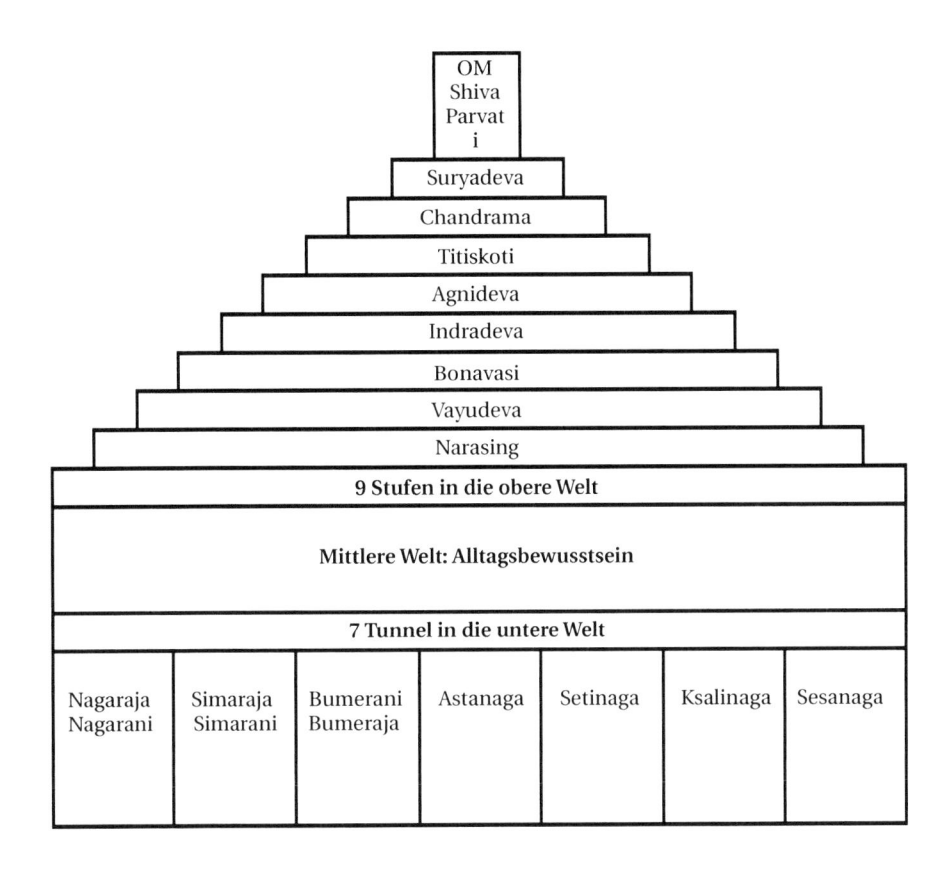

			OM Shiva Parvati			
			Suryadeva			
			Chandrama			
			Titiskoti			
			Agnideva			
			Indradeva			
			Bonavasi			
			Vayudeva			
			Narasing			
9 Stufen in die obere Welt						
Mittlere Welt: Alltagsbewusstsein						
7 Tunnel in die untere Welt						
Nagaraja Nagarani	Simaraja Simarani	Bumerani Bumeraja	Astanaga	Setinaga	Ksalinaga	Sesanaga

Autor

DR. MED. DIPL.-BIOL. ANDREAS REIMERS ist als Nervenarzt und Psychotherapeut in eigener Praxis tätig. Im Rahmen seiner wissenschaftlichen Tätigkeit befasst er sich mit veränderten Bewusstseinszuständen in Meditation, Mystik und Schamanismus. Sein ethnologischer Schwerpunkt ist der Schamanismus bei den Bergvölkern Nepals. An der Universität Münster leitete er das Projekt "Krankheit und Heilung im kulturellen Kontext". Ein Schwerpunkt seiner therapeutischen Tätigkeit ist die Begleitung von spirituellen Krisen. Er ist Präsident der AGEM (Arbeitsgemeinschaft für Ethnomedizin) und Mitglied beim ECBS (Europäisches Collegium für Bewußtseinsstudien).

Literatur

ACHTERBERG, J. 1985: *Imagery Healing: Shamanism and Modern Medicine.* Boston.

ANDRITZKI,W. 1990: Konzepte für eine Kulturvergleichende Therapieforschung. Probleme der Effektivität, der Vergleichbarkeit und Übertragbarkeit ethnischer Heilmethoden. In: *Jahrbuch für transkulturelle Medizin und Psychotherapie.* Internationales Institut für Kulturvergleichende Therapieforschung, Berlin.

BOURGIGNON, E. (ed.) 1973: *Religion, altered states of consciousness, and social change.* Ohio.

DITTRICH, A. 1987. Bedingungen zur Induktion außergewöhnlicher Bewusstseinszustände. In: A. DITTRICH & C. SCHARFETTER (eds.), *Ethnopsychotherapie. Psychotherapie mittels außergewöhnlicher Bewusstseinszustände in westlichen und indigenen Kulturen.* Stuttgart.

EIGNER, D. 1999: Die Kraft der Götter. Tamang Schamanentum in Nepal. In: *Zeitschrift für Ethnomedizin,* Sonderband 13. Braunschweig/Wiesbaden.

ELIADE, M. 1951. *Le chamanisme, et les techniques archaiques de l`extase.* Paris.

FRANK, J.D. 1961. *Persuasion and healing: a comperative study of psychotherapy.* Baltimore/London.

GOTTSCHALK-BATSCHKUS, C & D. REICHER. 2000. *Wanderer zwischen den Welten.* Murnau.

GROF, S.T. 1985. *Geburt, Tod und Transzendenz.* München.

HOLZ, K. & C. ZAHN 1995. Rituale und Psychotherapie. Transkulturelle Perspektiven. *Forschungsberichte zur Transkulturellen Medizin und Psychotherapie,* Band 1. Berlin

HITCHCOCK, J.T & R.L. JONES 1994. *Spirit Possession in the Nepal Himalayas.* New Delhi.

MILLER, C. J. 1987. *Faith-healers in the Himalayas.* Kathmandu.

MÜLLER-EBELING, C., RÄTSCH C.& SHAHI S. 2000: *Schamanismus und Tantra in Nepal.* Aarau.

PFEIFFER, W.M. 1994: *Transkulturelle Psychiatrie. Ergebnisse und Probleme.* 2. Auflage, Stuttgart/New York.

QUEKELBERGHE, R. VON 1996: Schamanisches Heilen: Vom fragmentierten zum integrierten Bewusstsein. In: ders. (ed.), *Ethnomedizinische Mitteilungen.* Forschungsstelle für Ethnomedizin der Universität Landau. Band 5, Heft 1.

REIMERS, A. 2000: Auf den Spuren der Urschamanen. In: GOTTSCHALK-BATSCHKUS C. &

SCHARFETTER, C. 1995: Welten des Bewusstseins und ihre Kartographen. In: *curare* 18. Arbeitsgemeinschaft für Ethnomedizin, Berlin.

SCHARFETTER, C. 1986: *Schizophrene Menschen.* München-Weinheim.

SHRESTA, R.M. 1980: *Faith-healers: a force of change.* Kathmandu.

TART, C.T. (ed.) 1969: *Altered States of Consciousness.* New York.

UEXKÜLL, TH. VON. *Psychosomatische Medizin.* 4. Auflage, München/ Wien/ Baltimore.

WILBER, K. 1987. *Das Spektrum des Bewusstseins.* Bern/München/Wien.

JHARPHUK - A SHAMANISTIC HEALING RITUAL IN NEPAL*

by Andreas Reimers

Cultural Background

In Nepal there exists an unbroken shamanistic tradition of healing, which goes back to the distant past and is interwoven with *Yoga* and *Tantric* traditions. At the present time there are approximately 600 000 of shamans still practising. During a healing ceremony, the shamans are using different methods to put themselves into trance.

This enables them to connect with the cosmic powers and brings the disorder back into balance using certain traditionally established rituals. The progress of the healing rituals has a definite structure, which reflects the inner healing process. The analysis of the healing procedure shows clearly in which way the altered states of consciousness and ritual actions are used for therapeutic purposes. The myths, the songs, the robes a shaman is wearing, and the altar can be described as the symbolic representation of the inner experience.

Among the 38 different native tribes shamanistic healing rituals are widely spread. Recent inquiries show that approximal 600.000 shamans (Nepali: *jhankri, dhami*), are responsible to take care of the health of about 50 people each- next to their

---

* Translated by Joy C. Green
Fig. 1: Maile Lama, Shaman of the Tamang in Nepal.

regular professions- and proceed trance- and healing rituals. Even though the main part of medical care in rural areas is provided by shamans, adequate recognition of their work has not been shown yet by the state health care system of Nepal which is strongly influenced by the western medicine. (HITCHKOCK & JONES 1994, MILLER 1987, SHRESTA 1980)

The present study relates to field works in the years 1993 through 2001 in the centre of Nepal among the Tamang and Gurung folks. These mountain tribes belong to the tibetanian language group, but use *Nepali* in their every day work and in the rituals. Though they confess themselves to buddhism they own a rich shamanistic tradition (EIGNER 1990).

Becoming a shaman

There are 3 possibilities to become a shaman in Nepal:

1. personal call
2. family tradition
3. studies with a teacher

All three options require personal experience and the connection with hidden psychical and cosmical energies. When the shamanistic powers take over, visions and odd behaviors often appear.

For example future shamans jump into a fire, predict unusual things, run off into the wilderness driven by an inner voice and dissapear in the wilderness or in caves for days or weeks. Within an inner cleaning process they are tought the shamanistic healing.

Through the process of their own healing the shaman develops his powers and experiences the spirits necessary to be able to heal. The final approbation is achieved through lessons with a well- known shaman. One that understands personal calls and helps the shaman to use his newly won experiences by teaching him specific cultural traditions.

In the shamanistic robe, with the songs and the paraphernalies this experience is repetitiously put on stage in the healing rituals. A shaman has to take the responsibility to help every help- seeking individual irrespective to financial compensation.

Therefore a shaman has to work next to his healing sessions, so that a lot of times the burden is becoming so much that a lot shamans try to avoid their calls in Nepal.

Healing practice

The healing of a patient might ask for a combination of healing methods. On the physical level treatments with massaging techniques and herbs may take place.

But the real power of shamans must be seen in his skill to willingly fall into trance and mediate between the daily reality and the world of spiritual powers.

To achieve these changed consciousness levels shamans use different methods,- like: dieting, stimulus deprivation, sleep deprivation, hyperventilation, drugs and – more than anything else – stimulus intensifying (drumming & singing) is used in Nepal.

Through recitation of myths and mantras a methaphoric- symbolistic dimension is entered that avokes central archetypical energies in the patient.
A dynamical process arises, leading to an intensive emotional bonding within the patient, with the group and the unsiverse. The rebalancing of this original unit is a healing process that frees blocked energies within ourselves. (QUEKELBERGHE 1996)

Cosmology

The cosmology of the nepal shamans describes a world structure of three levels (Nepali: *tintriloka*):
- the upper world of the gods (Nepali: *akasha*),
- the middle world of the humans (Nepali: *dhariti*) and
- the under world of snake energies (Nepali: *patala*).

Shiva, the highest god of all, tought the first shaman (Nepali: *bonjhankri*) the art of healing.
A long line of teachers and students up until today leads back to this ancestors.
The shamans work is to expel the evil and the diseases that come to the world through negative forces and witches. The transcendential, metaphysical causes of a desease is represented by several myths comprehensively.
Certain deseases are clearly connected to certain spirits. Shamans will identify them and appease them in a healing ritual. All paraphernalies used in a ritual leads to the myth. On the altar (Nepali: *than*) macro - and microcosmos melt together into a union, in which the axis of the world (*axis mundi*) and the human fall into place (MÜLLER- EBELING et al. 2000).

Fig. 1:
Maile Lama in diagnostic trance.

Structure of the rituals

A typical healing ritual (Nepali: *chinta*) shows the following structure: after diagnosis was made, the call upon the powers and induction of the trance status follows. The peak of the ritual is the healing of the patient, finished with gratitudes for the spirits. In addition directions for every day are given to the patients.

1. For diagnosis we find a couple of methods.

Examples are: trance visions, pulse diagnosis and rice counting.

- in a trance vision the shaman travels over nine steps to the gods of the upper world or through seven tunnels to the under world of the snakes to find the cause of the desease and identify the responsible spirit (Fig. 1).

-pulse diagnosis shows the shaman changes in the pulse while questioning the patient

-while counting the rice, the number of accidentially picked rice corns also delivers hints of the possible cause.

2. In the next step the spiritual forces of all three worlds are called upon, as well as *Mahadev* (highest god), symbol for omnipotence, power and harmony.

The spiritual powers are understood as intrapsychical as well as cosmical powers. Whereas the shamans attitude is not demanding or manipulating rather than thankful, devoting and praying for blessing.

3. Through certain drum rhythms, singing of mantras, fumigation and ritual actions a state of trance is initiated, where all persons participating are intensively involved. The presence of the spiritual forces is shown by a trembling of the body as well as a changed attitude of the shaman, that, however, remains controlled.

4. In the ritual healing the shaman regains the lost part of the patient´s soul or extracts the negative influences of the spirit. The old order is reinstalled. The sick patient regains his place in the human society and in the cosmical order. Specific rituals are for example: "regain of the soul" after its loss; "the cut of the life line" after a heavy blow; "the elevation of the head" in a state of depression.

5. The healing ceremony ends with the gratitude towards the spirits. Offerings like rice, flowers, animals and others are prepared. The healed patient gets a new seat in the group as an expression of the reframing process. He receives recommendations and informations for his future everyday behavior.

6. *Jharphook*

In Nepal there exist a great amount of various, highly different rituals. They are mainly to be divided into two groups:

a) extraction of negative desease causes

b) regain of a lost soul

Essential is the soothing of the spiritual forces through offerings in all used methods. Healing means offering. In the offering procedure the hurt or maddened spirit is shown respect and attention. When a rice field is going to be cultivated for example, the god of the displaced forest (*Jangeli*) must be offered to. When these rules are disregarded, various typical deseases appear.

Depending on the disease there are smaller rituals of only a few minutes and rituals lasting a whole night long (*Chinta*) that are extremely complex. Preparations require a considerable contribution of the patient.

Jharpook is the spiritual treatment (*Jhar*) with air (*phook*). It is a special blowing technique, used in various forms. In an acute situation, with the help of breath, negative, diseasing influences are extracted, changed and weakened areas are energetically recharged (*shakti* is transferred). Different auxiliaries like rice, ashes, *Phurba* or a broom made from *kushagras* are used.

After the diagnosis the healing treatment follows. In the highest state of composure and concentration specific mantras are repeticiously sung and significant ritual objects are moved along the body in ritual procedures. Often rice and phurba are used to touch the temple, the shoulders and the sole of the foot beside the concerned body part. Then ashes are pushed onto the persons fore-head. The broom is often used to cast off and clean the entire body.

In the used mantras the devoted monkey god *Hanuman* is mentioned, who promised to support god *Rama* in his fight against demons. He had brought a large amount of herbs from the Himalaya to the battle field in South India to heal the wounded heroes. The harming forces and spirits were asked to leave the patients. This request is sealed with a three- times- blowing.

Even in our culture we have customs to blow on childrens injuries, repeating consolidating words of comfort. The mantras reflect the traditions of old myths and become a mighty, healing impulse.

In many shamanistic rituals I was able to experience how a *phukne* treatment brought releaf or complete healing to patients with symptoms of headaches, intestiny problems, fears, depressions and body aches.

Mechanism in the healing rituals

In such a structured ritual a few different therapeutical interventions are interwoven with each other. FRANK has sorted out unspecific factors in his comparison of traditional healing methods with western medicine and psychotherapy. (FRANK 1961) From anthropological, religious and psychological perspectives the effectivness of healing rituals were analyzed on social, cognitive and affective levels. It would exceed the frame of this pamphlet to explain the concepts in detail, therefore I will only give a summary of the factors. (PFEIFFER 1994, ACHTERBERG 1985, ANDRITZKI 1990).

1. The shaman shows an intense interest, emotional warmth and real, congruent behavior. However, we rather find a representative- the healer as a typical body of a higher power- than the real person.

2. The healing rituals usually take place in the company of the family, friends and neighbours. The patient receives time and attention. He is taken seriously and gets social support. A correction of disbalanced relation patterns in the traditional order is achieved.

3. Through calling upon the cosmical powers in the form of traditional myths connection with the cosmical order is being set. The individual burden finds its sense and place in the traditional context of the myth, that gives the clue to overcome the burden.

4. The shaman transfers himself into a changed consciousness, finding a different level of reality and unfolding a healing effect. The patient participates in the healer´s trance, his consciousness changes, rational defences are weakened and the focus can be set on the ritual. Adequate stimuli and experienced use of symbols activate unknown, high effective psychical energies for the healing process. (Bourgignon 1973, Dittrich 1987, Grof 1985, Scharfeter 1986, 1996, Wilber 1987)

5. The symptoms and inner conflicts of the patient are read spiritually by the healer, put into a play in the imagination and led to a solution. Sometimes behaving patterns are used that are taboo in everyday life. Conflicts and blocked emotions can be solved and the patient can find his way back to his inner energies. (Holz & Zahn 1995)

6. With the newly won positive direction psycho-neuro-immunological mechanisms are activated and symptoms of deseases can be specifically influenced (Quekelberghe 1996, Uexküll 1990).

The whole ritual is not pressed into fix rules but depends strongly on the present situation and is directed by the process interventions (process task). They happen at typical situations or incidents, clearly marked by the ritual.
While modern psychotherapy is aiming for a higher grade of psychical abilities in the emotional and social area, the development of an adequate ego-strength and

Fig. 2 & 3:
Maile Lama at *Jharphook*.

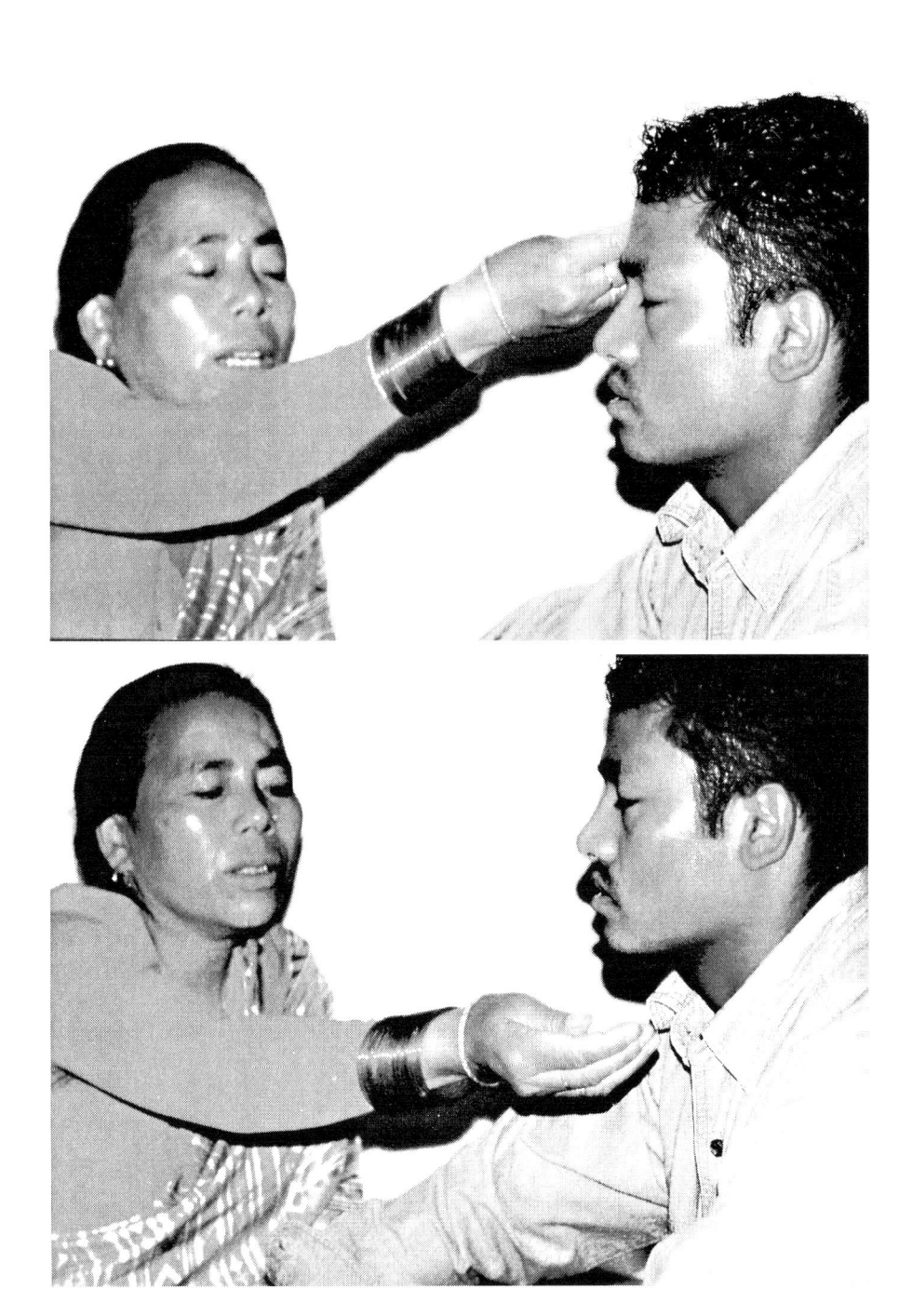

Jharphuk - a Shamanistic Healing Ritual in Nepal – ETHNOMED 2002

social competence as well as a positive self- confidence, the traditional, shamanistic healing system emphasises the regain of the place in the social community and in the cosmical order. Different than in the shape therapy, the psycho drama and other event-oriented therapies, we rather find the shaman in the role to imbody feelings, dreams and conflicts instead of the patient. The patient only participates in the music, the dances and the cultural imaginations and gives himself up to the therapy process entirely. The focus is set strongly on learning by the model and the transfer of energies. In contrary to ROGERS client concentrated conversation therapy, the shaman works very direct and not at all sensible oriented. Rather traditional thinking- and behaving patterns of the myths are experienced as present, so that individual suffering finds acceptance and healing within them.

Conclusion

The given examples allow to accept shamanistic healing methods- like *Jharpuk*- as reasonable, effectful treatents. It is to be expected that modern research in psychology , psycho-neuroimmunology as well as physics will show even further aspects. A better understanding however, will always depend on the individual shamanistic interpretations. (REIMERS 2000)

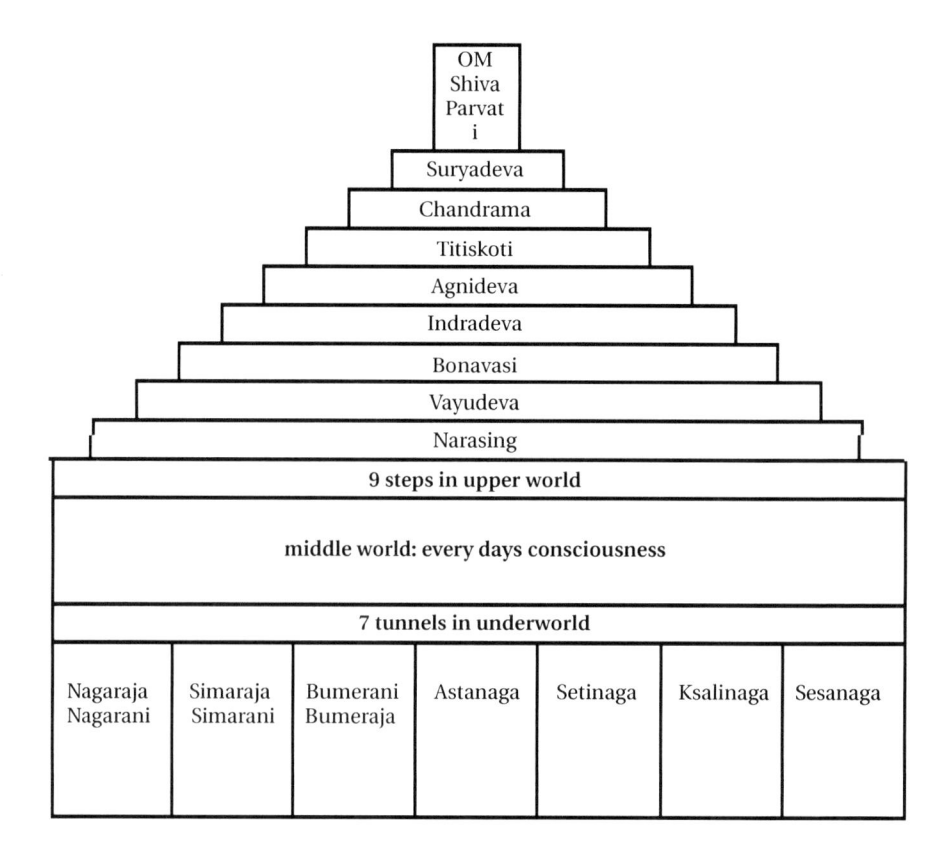

			OM Shiva Parvati			
			Suryadeva			
			Chandrama			
			Titiskoti			
			Agnideva			
			Indradeva			
			Bonavasi			
			Vayudeva			
			Narasing			
9 steps in upper world							
middle world: every days consciousness							
7 tunnels in underworld							
Nagaraja Nagarani	Simaraja Simarani	Bumerani Bumeraja	Astanaga	Setinaga	Ksalinaga	Sesanaga

Author

DR. MED. ANDREAS REIMERS
Doctor med. and biologist, he works in his own practice as a psychiatrist and psychotherapist. His research contains changed consciousness levels in meditation, myths and shamanism. His ethnological focus is the shamanism in the mountain areas in Nepal. He leads the project "desease and healing in the cultural context " at the Universitiy of Münster, Germany.
The focal point in his therapeutical work is the guidance of patients through spiritual crises. He is president of the AGEM and he is a member of the ECBS (european college for consciousness studies)

References

ACHTERBERG, J. 1985: *Imagery Healing: Shamanism and Modern Medicine*. Boston.
ANDRITZKI,W. 1990: Konzepte für eine Kulturvergleichende Therapieforschung. Probleme der Effektivität, der Vergleichbarkeit und Übertragbarkeit ethnischer Heilmethoden. In: *Jahrbuch für transkulturelle Medizin und Psychotherapie*. Internationales Institut für Kulturvergleichende Therapieforschung, Berlin.
BOURGIGNON, E. (ed.) 1973: *Religion, altered states of consciousness, and social change*. Ohio.
DITTRICH, A. 1987. Bedingungen zur Induktion außergewöhnlicher Bewusstseinszustände. In: A. DITTRICH & C. SCHARFETTER (eds.), *Ethnopsychotherapie. Psychotherapie mittels außergewöhnlicher Bewusstseinszustände in westlichen und indigenen Kulturen*. Stuttgart.
EIGNER, D. 1999: Die Kraft der Götter. Tamang Schamanentum in Nepal. In: *Zeitschrift für Ethnomedizin*, Sonderband 13. Braunschweig/Wiesbaden.
ELIADE, M. 1951. *Le chamanisme, et les techniques archaiques de l`extase*. Paris.
FRANK, J.D. 1961. *Persuasion and healing: a comperative study of psychoterapy*. Baltimore/London.
GROF, S.T. 1985. *Geburt, Tod und Transzendenz*. München.
HOLZ, K. & C. ZAHN 1995. Rituale und Psychotherapie. Transkulturelle Perspektiven. *Forschungsberichte zur Transkulturellen Medizin und Psychotherapie*, Band 1. Berlin
HITCHKOCK, J.T & R.L. JONES 1994. *Spirit Possession in the Nepal Himalayas*. New Delhi.
MILLER, C. J. 1987. *Faith-healers in the Himalayas*. Kathmandu.
MÜLLER-EBELING, C., RÄTSCH C.& SHAHI S. 2000: *Schamanismus und Tantra in Nepal*. Aarau.
PFEIFFER, W.M. 1994: *Transkulturelle Psychiatrie. Ergebnisse und Probleme*. 2. Auflage, Stuttgart/New York.
QUEKELBERGHE, R. VON 1996: Schamanisches Heilen: Vom fragmentierten zum integrierten Bewusstsein. In: ders. (ed.), *Ethnomedizinische Mitteilungen*. Forschungsstelle für Ethnomedizin der Universität Landau. Band 5, Heft 1.
REIMERS, A. 2000: Auf den Spuren der Urschamanen. In: GOTTSCHALK-BATSCHKUS C. & REICHERT, D.:*Wanderer zwischen den Welten*. Murnau.

Scharfetter, C. 1995: Welten des Bewusstseins und ihre Kartographen. In: *curare* 18. Arbeitsgemeinschaft für Ethnomedizin, Berlin.
Scharfetter, C. 1986: *Schizophrene Menschen*. München-Weinheim.
Shresta, R.M. 1980: *Faith-healers: a force of change*. Kathmandu.
Tart, C.T. (ed.) 1969: *Altered States of Consciousness*. New York.
Uexküll, Th. von. *Psychosomatische Medizin*. 4. Auflage, München/ Wien/ Baltimore.
Wilber, K. 1987. *Das Spektrum des Bewusstseins*. Bern/München/Wien.

Abb. 1

TRADITIONELLE HEILVERFAHREN IN DER KULTUR DER ALTEN ORDNUNG DER AMISH*

von Sharyn Buccalo & J. Keim

Einführung
Die Alte Ordnung der *Amish* (Old Order Amish, Mennoniten) ist eine ethnoreligiöse Gruppe, die in den Vereinigten Staaten und in Kanada lebt. Diese Gruppe hat eine funktionelle Anschauung von Gesundheit und Krankheit, und die Dienste des traditionellen Heilers werden nur dann in Anspruch genommen, wenn Beschwerden oder Krankheit die Arbeitsfähigkeit einschränkt.

Der Zweck dieser ethnomedizinischen Studie war, die Reichweite der traditionellen Anwendungen zu entdecken, wie sie von einem Heiler der *Amish* der Alten Ordnung praktiziert werden. Sie umfassen den Gebrauch von Hilfsmitteln, Kräutern und Homöopathie, sind aber nicht darauf beschränkt. Resultierende Erkenntnisse werden hier einschließlich ihrer Folgerungen für die Praxis dargestellt.

Der Heiler
Dieses Dokument ist eine Studie der naturheilkundlichen Praxis eines Heilers aus der Alten Ordnung der *Amish*. J.K. ist ein Mann, der seit zwanzig Jahren in einer konservativen Gemeinschaft der Alten Ordnung der *Amish* im mittleren Westen der Vereinigten Staaten als Heiler praktiziert. Er berät und behandelt Patienten, die ihn in seiner Praxis besuchen und auch solche, die ihn schriftlich kontaktieren. Diese letzte Gruppe Patienten, sowohl Englischsprechende (nicht-*Amish*) als auch *Amish*, stammt meist aus den Vereinigten Staaten und Kanada. Der Heiler, mit dessen Praxis sich diese Studie beschäftigt, hat wie alle *Amish* der Alten Ordnung

---

Abb.1: Die Heilpflanze *Klette* mit herzförmigen Blättern und rotvioletten Blütenköpfen. Die Blätter werden als Umschlag bei Verbrennungen, Geschwüren und Wunden verwendet.

* Übersetzung aus dem Englischen: Paul Baumann

eine achtjährige Schulausbildung erhalten. J. K. hat sein Wissen über die Werte, der in seiner Heimat vorkommenden natürlichen Hilfsmittel von seinen Vorfahren und anderen Mitgliedern seiner Gemeinde erhalten.

Er ist ein Landwirt der *Amish*, der seit zwanzig Jahren traditionelle Heilverfahren praktiziert. Wenn er sich nicht mit seiner alltäglichen Arbeit beschäftigt oder sich seinen Patienten widmet, findet man ihn beim Studium von Artikeln über verschiedene Arten natürlichen Heilens. Als ein Mann seiner Kultur erlernte J.K. den Beruf des Hufschmiedes. Er und sein Vater waren die Schmiede ihrer Gemeinde, und er lernte, sich auch um kranke und verletzte Tiere zu kümmern.

Er begann mit menschlichen Patienten zu arbeiten, als ihn ein Mann mit mehrfachen Frakturen des Unterschenkels um Hilfe bat. Das Bein dieses Mannes war für den nächsten Tag zur Amputation vorgesehen. J.K. verwendete Informationen von anderen und seine eigenen Erfahrungen und konnte dadurch das Bein retten. Er stellte die Ernährung des Patienten um und fügte zusätzliche Nahrungsmittelergänzungen hinzu.

Natürliche Medizin in der Kultur der Alten Ordnung der *Amish*

Traditionelle Medizin oder wie die *Amish* sie nennen, natürliche Medizin, basiert auf unkonventionellen Vorstellungen von Gesundheit, Erfahrungen und lokalen Traditionen. Seit dem 16. Jahrhundert praktizieren die Amish natürliche Medizin, die stark beeinflusst ist von kulturellen Normen und Werten. Im 16. Jahrhundert wurden die in Städten lebenden *Amish*-Gläubigen, Studenten und Intellektuelle aus den Städten vertrieben und gezwungen, sich in versteckten, ländlichen Gebieten anzusiedeln. Hier, ohne Zugang zu Ärzten, mussten sie lernen, ihre Kranken und Verwundeten selbst zu versorgen. Diese und andere traditionelle Heilpraktiken blieben bis zum heutigen Tag erhalten.

Es gibt viele kulturelle Einflüsse auf die Wahl der Gesundheitspflegepraktiken. Sie umfassen Krankheit, Krise oder Nichtkrise; wie die "Freundshaft" (das erweiterte Familiennetzwerk) die Krankheit deutet und glaubt, dass sie behandelt werden sollte; ferner hohe Kosten der medizinischen Behandlung, ein Vertrauen auf Gottes Willen im Bereich der Gesundheit und der Krankheit, ein begrenztes Bauernhof- oder Hausindustrieeinkommen und das Fehlen einer Gesundheitspflegeversicherung.

Die *Amish* kennzeichnen einen wünschenswerten Praktiker als einen, der zuhört, Bezahlung annimmt, aber nicht verlangt, und der ihre eigene Sprache versteht. Andere Eigenschaften sind Integrität und Interesse, beides Eigenschaften, die in dieser hohen Kontextkultur (HUNTINGTON 1994) hoch geschätzt werden. Der Einsatz und die Art des Praktikers sind unterschiedlich je nach Gemeinschaft.

Einige Beispiele für Praktiker sind der *Bee Man* (Imker, Bienenkundler), Iridologist (Augendiagnostiker), Reflexologist (Reflexzonenkundige), Herbalist (Kräuterkundige) oder ein Heiler, der eine Kombination dieser Ansätze verwendet. Der *Bee Man* wie er in der *Amish* Gemeinschaft, in der er praktiziert, genannt wird, verwendet die Produkte der Biene. Ihr Gift für nicht-heilende Geschwüre und Wunden und ihren Honig, der als natürliches antibakterielles Mittel in Salben weithin bekannt ist. Der Iridologist kann Leiden bestimmen, in dem er die Iris des Auges betrachtet und beurteilt. Basierend auf seiner Diagnose, verschreibt er Nahrungszusätze und Vitamine, um die Leiden zu heilen.

Amish kennen auch Reflexologisten, die Nerven und Zonen an den Füßen massieren, die mit bestimmten Körpersystemen korrelieren. Die so behandelten

Abb. 2: Ein Feld mit Kletten auf dem Hof eines *Amish* Heilers

Patienten berichten von Beschwerdeerleichterungen des Kopfes, des Rückgrades und des Magens, sowie anderer Systeme des Körpers.
In der beobachteten Amish-Gemeinschaft ist J.K. ein natürlicher Heiler, er besucht Patienten und berät andere Patienten per Post. Er betreibt einen Laden, der Vitamine, Nahrungsergänzungen und Kräuter verkauft, damit er die Möglichkeit hat, seine Patienten mit ihren Gesundheitsproblemen zu unterstützen und das passende Heilmittel verschreiben zu können. Es gibt Faktoren in J.K.'s Praxis, die sich zu dem einer schulmedizinischen Praxis deutlich unterscheiden. Er fordert keine Bezahlung für seine Dienstleistungen, aber er nimmt Zuwendungen an.
Seine angekündigten Dienststunden sind von 8 Uhr morgens bis 6 Uhr abends. Aber er besucht auch routinemäßig Patienten bis 1 Uhr morgens, wenn er um Mitternacht in ein Haus gerufen wird. Während der Dienststunden verbringt er üblicherweise eine Stunde oder mehr mit dem Patienten und dessen Familie, in der er lehrt und erklärt.
Diese traditionelle Heilpraxis basiert auf Glaubenssätzen, die in dieser Kultur lange vor der Entwicklung und Verbreitung der westlichen Medizin existiert hat. Diese traditionelle Heilpraxis ist so grundlegend mit den vielfältigen Glaubenssystemen verwoben, dass jede Form des Heilens, die diese Vorstellungen ignoriert, sowohl psychologisch unbefriedigend als auch für den Patienten nicht akzeptabel wäre. Das zeigt an, wie die westliche Medizin von der Einbeziehung traditionell heilender Modalitäten in ihrer Praxis profitieren könnte, wenn sie auf Patienten anderer Kulturen trifft.

Beispiele der Heilung einer bestimmten Krankheit oder Störung

J.K. erklärt die Grundbestandteile (der natürlichen Medizin, Anm. d. Übers.) so: Honig, der die Basis bildet, ist ein weithin bekanntes, heilendes Mittel, das die Narbenbildung minimiert. Er reduziert auch den Schmerz und die Blasenbildung. Weizenkeimöl liefert Vitamin E, das ebenfalls die Heilung fördert und die Narbenbildung reduziert. Aloe vera hat Eigenschaften, die wirkungsvoll Schmerzen stillen. Olivenöl enthält reichlich die Vitamine A, D, E und K und daneben auch noch andere Vitamine und Mineralien. Es wird leicht durch die Haut absorbiert und trägt die Kräuterbestandteile der Salbe. Eibischwurzel hat erweichende und beruhigende Eigenschaften.

Weiße Eichenrinde ist ein leistungsfähiges pflanzliches Adstringenz und wirkt antiseptisch. Dieses Kraut entlastet vom Juckreiz, festigt das Gewebe und beruhigt gereizte Haut. Wermut erleichtert Verspannungen. Beinwell fördert die Zellproduktion. Lobelia lindert Muskelschmerzen. Pflanzliche Glycerine dienen als Konservierungsmittel gegen Schimmelbildung und Bakterienwachstum in der Kräutermischung. Bienenwachs ist eine natürliche Beimengung, um die Öle in eine Salbenform zu bringen, damit sie selbst bei heißer Witterung oder durch Körperwärme nicht vom Körper des Patienten abfließen.

Heilende Substanzen oder Pflanzen:
Klette (amerik: *Lesser Burdock*, lat. *Arctium*):
Holländischer Name: Gletta
Familie: Compositae
Verbreitungsgebiet: gesamte USA
Höhe: Ein Meter
Bauplan: ein zweijähriges Unkraut, das an Straßenrändern und Schutthalden wächst, fleischige Pfahlwurzel, große, herzförmige Blätter und rotviolette Blütenköpfe, die von zahlreichen mit Widerhaken Korbblättern umgeben sind
Blütezeit: Juni bis Herbst
Standort: Halden, Waldränder, Straßenränder, entlang von Hecken
Bodenbeschaffenheit: Feuchter Boden
Verwendung in der Naturmedizin: Klette ist ein ausgezeichnetes Entgiftungsmittel. Die Pflanze wirkt bakterientötend, pilztötend und enthält lindernde, schleimbildende Eigenschaften. Die Blätter werden als Umschlag bei Verbrennungen, Geschwüren und Wunden verwendet.

Wegerichblätter (amerik: *Plantain leaves*)
Allgemeiner Name: Breitwegerich
Holländischer Name: Sow-ear
Familie: Plantaginaceae
Verbreitung: gesamte USA
Höhe: Bis zu 20 cm (8 inches)
Bauplan: Am Boden ausgebreitet in Rosettenform, elliptisch bis breit eiförmig, stark gerippt und wächsern
Blütezeit: Juni bis September
Vorkommen: Wiesen und Weiden
Bodenbeschaffenheit: Feuchter Boden
Verwendung in der Naturmedizin: Zerriebene Blätter können als Verband zur Schmerzstillung verwendet werden.

Heilbeispiele
Diese Publikation stellt natürliche Hilfsmittel bei Verbrennungen und Wunden vor, die auf der 20jährigen Erfahrung und den Bemühungen J.K.'s in der Behandlung von Patienten beruhen. Dieser Heiler gibt zu, dass er nicht nach den Regeln und Gepflogenheiten der orthodoxen Medizin geschult wurde. Er sagt: *"Ich habe das Wissen um die Werte der heimatlichen und natürlichen Hilfsmittel von meinen Vorfahren und anderen Mitgliedern unserer Gemeinde übernommen."* Er hat nach natürlichen, ungiftigen Heilmitteln gesucht, wenn Behandlungen weniger erfolgreich waren oder sich schmerzvoll in die Länge zogen. Seine Methode ist es immer, ungiftige natürliche Substanzen zu verwenden und Komplikationen oder teure Medikamente zu vermeiden. J.K. ist überzeugt davon, dass der Schöpfer für alle Menschen effektive Heilmittel zur Verfügung stellt, speziell für die Armen.
Seine Arbeit als Ernährungsberater hat ihn gelehrt, dass wir alle reines Wasser und Nahrung benötigen, um gesund zu bleiben.

Abb. 3: J.K. ist Besitzer eines Ladens. Er verkauft Vitamine, Hilfsmittel, Homöopathische Medizin und Heilkräuter

Falldarstellungen

Als der Sohn J.K.'s zwei Jahre alt war, verbrühte er sich sehr schlimm. Er wandte die damals übliche Behandlung an, aber das Wechseln der Verbände verursachte seinem Sohn unerträgliche Schmerzen. In Verbindung mit den Briefen, die J.K. empfangen hatte von Verwandten, deren Kinder ebenfalls einmal Verbrühungen erlitten hatten, war das mehr als ein Vater ertragen konnte. J.K. ging hinaus in die Natur, um nachzudenken und zu beten. Er dachte darüber nach, wie Gott die Welt erschaffen hatte. Und darüber, wie arme und einsame Menschen imstande sein sollten, das Notwendige für ihre Bedürfnisse zu finden. Er erinnerte sich an eine Girlande aus glänzenden Blättern , und wie sehr die Blätter glänzten und wie er dachte, sie würden nicht an einer Wunde kleben bleiben.Zu diesem Zeitpunkt ging er und sah viel Breitwegerich (Plantain). Da erkannte er, dass dies dem ähnelte, was er gesucht hatte.

Er sammelte einen Hut voll Blätter ein. Wieder zuhause, bedeckte er die Brandwunde mit BFC-Salbe (eine Brandsalbe) und einer einfachen Schicht aus Breitwegerichblättern. Diese Prozedur wurde zwei mal täglich wiederholt. Binnen fünf Tagen hatte sich neue Haut über der Wunde gebildet. Das Bemerkensweste für den Vater aber war, dass der Wechsel der Verbände ohne Schmerzen möglich war. Zusammen mit der neuen Verbandsauflage reicherte er außerdem die Diät mit extra Obst und Gemüsesaft an. Wichtige Faktoren waren die Verfügbarkeit von entsprechenden Nahrungsmitteln, die Zubereitung und die unterstützende Arbeit mit dem Patienten.

Seit über zwei Jahrzehnten, in denen J.K. die besagte Brandsalbe und die beschriebene Verbangsauflage anwendet, nimmt er den vorliegenden Fall als Beispiel dafür, wie und auf Lösungen in seinen Behandlungen stößt.

Er erzählte weiter von einem Krebspatienten, der zu ihm wegen Schmerzen und der Schwellung seines Beins nach einer Strahlentherapie kam.

Die Patientengeschichte:
der Patient hatte einen Tumor an seinem Bein. Dieser wurde chirurgisch entfernt. Der Patient erhielt dann Strahlentherapien und das Bein schwoll an. Zu dieser Zeit ersuchte der Patient J.K.um Hilfe. Er hatte große Schmerzen und Angst das Bein zu

verlieren. Das Bein war geschwollen, der Patient hatte große Schmerzen und die Haut über der schmerzenden Stelle war aufgebrochen. Der Geruch war wie der einer toten Kuh auf dem Misthaufen, auf den die Sonne schien.
Der Geruch war so extrem, dass J.K.'s Frau, den Raum verlassen musste. J.K. begann die Behandlung auf zwei Ebenen: erst einmal die Ausleitung der Giftstoffe und dann die Schmerzerleichterung.
Mit einem Kaffesatzeinlauf erreichte er die Anregung und Auswaschung der Eingeweide.
Die Formel des Einlaufes entsprach 2 Teelöffeln starken Kaffees auf 2 Quarts Wasser. Dies wurde zweimal täglich verabreicht. Der Einlauf sollte 10 Zoll über dem Körper hängen. Der Einlauf wurde langsam und vorsichtig verabreicht. Wenn der Patient Krämpfe bekam, so wurde die Behandlung für 15 Minuten unterbrochen. Das Abdomen konnte zum Austausch der Flüssigkeiten unterstützend massiert werden. J.K. verwand auch Umschläge aus Klettenblättern.
(Zu diesem Zeitpunkt des Jahres musste er getrocknete Klettenblätter verwenden.)

Die Vorgehenweise:
Die Blätter werden nach J.K..s Vorschrift, fern einer Straße wegen der Verunreinigung, gesammelt. Die jüngeren Blätter sind zu bevorzugen, da sie nicht so viele Querverbindungen enthalten, die ausgeschnitten werden müssen. Dann werden die Blätter auf Zeitungen in einzelnen Lagen ausgelegt. Nun bringt man sie an einen trockenen, kühlen Platz.
Wenn sie benötigt werden, wird ein großer Topf mit Wasser auf den hölzernen Kochofen aufgesetzt und das Wasser erhitzt.
Die Blätter werden hineingelegt bis das Wasser seine Farbe verändert.
Die Blätter werden entnommen und das überschüssige Wasser wird aus ihnen entfernt, was zum Abkühlen der Blätter beiträgt. Nun wirde die B&W Salbe in einer dünnen Schicht auf die Wunde aufgetragen und mit den behandelten Klettenblättern abgedeckt.

Autor
Sharyn Buccalo
Magister in Transcultural Nursing (Kulturenübergreifende Betreuung von Kranken) an der Universität Duquesne. Durch ihre Zusammenarbeit mit der Amish Gemeinschaft entwickelte sie Interesse an der Naturheilkunde, wie sie von den Amish praktiziert wird und an ihren Gesundheitsüberlieferungen und -traditionen. Sie hat 16 Jahre lang in der alte Ordnung Amish Gemeinschaft gearbeitet, in der J. K. praktiziert. Als sie eine gute Vertrauensbasis gefunden hatten, erlaubte J.K. ihr, in seiner Praxis zu beobachten und zu assistieren.
Die Patienten zeigten der Autorin gegenüber eine große Bereitschaft mit ihr Ihre Krankheiten und die Behandlungsweisen zu diskutieren und zu klären.
Kontakt: E-Mail: sbuccalo@crosslink.net

Literatur
Huntington, G.E. 1993, *Health Care in the Amish and the State*, Donald Kraybill ed pp 163- 190

THE APPROACH OF TRADITIONAL HEALING IN THE OLD ORDER AMISH CULTURE

by Sharyn Buccalo and J. Keim

Introduction

The Old Order *Amish* are an ethnoreligious group found in the United States and Canada This group has a functional view of health and illness and the services of the traditional healer is sought only when illness or disease interfere with work activities.

The purpose of this ethnonursing study was to discover the range of traditional interventions as practiced by an Old Order Amish healer: they included, but were not limited to, use of supplements, herbs and homeopathy. The discoveries that resulted are presented including implications for practice.

The Healer

This paper is a case study of the natural healing practice of an Old Order *Amish* healer. J.K. is an Old Order Amish male who has practiced in this mid western conservative Old Order *Amish* community for twenty years. Treatments are available to patients that consult him at his office and those that contact him via letters. This latter population encompasses patients, both English (non-*Amish*), and *Amish* from most of the United States and Canada.

The Old order Amish healer, whose practice is profiled in the case study, has been educated, as all Old Order *Amish* are, with an eighth grade education. J. K. is an Old Order *Amish* person who has knowledge of the values of home and natural remedies from his ancestors and other members of his community. He is an *Amish* farmer who has practiced traditional healing for twenty years. He can be found,

---

Fig.1: Healing Plant *Burdock* with heart- shaped leaves and red violet flower heads. The leaves are poulticed onto burns, ulcers and sores.

when not involved in day-to-day life or caring for his patients, studying articles and learning about the various modalities of natural healing.

As a male in the culture J.K. learned the trade of blacksmithing. He began to work with his father as the blacksmith in his community and was taught to care for sick and injured animals. He began his work with human patients when a man with multiple fractures of the lower leg begged for help. This man was scheduled for an amputation of his leg the next day. J.K. utilized information form others and his own results obtained from time to time, with success of saving the leg, by adjusting his diet and added supplements for extra nourishment.

Natural Medicine in the Old Order *Amish* Culture

Traditional medicine, or as it is defined by the *Amish*, Natural Medicine, is made up of inofficial health beliefs, practices and local traditions. Since the 1500s, the Amish have practiced Natural Medicine, strongly influenced by cultural norms and values. In the 1500s the town-dwelling *Amish* faithful, students and intellectuals, were forced from the towns into hiding in rural areas. Here, with no access to physicians, they were forced to learn how to care for their sick and wounded. These and other traditional healing practices have carried over to the present day.

There are many cultural influences on the choice of health care practitioners. They include illness, crisis or non-crisis, how the *Frieundshaft* (extended family network) interprets the illness and feels it should be treated, high cost of medical care, a reliance on God's will in the area of health and illness, a limited farm or cottage industry income, and no health care insurance.

The *Amish* identify a desirable practitioner as one who listens, accepts donations but not charge a fee, and is able to communicate in their own language. Other attributes include integrity and a sense of concern, both of which are highly valued in this high context culture (HUNTINGTON 1994).

The use and type of practitioner vary by community. Some examples of practitioners are the bee man, Iridologist, Reflexologist, herbalist, or a healer that uses a combination of approaches. The bee man, as he is known in the *Amish* community, where he practices, utilizes the by-products of the bee, its sting for non-healing ulcers and wounds, and honey, well known as natural antibacterial, in ointments. The Iridologist is one who is able to diagnose ailments by looking at and evaluating the iris of the eye. Based on a diagnosis, he will prescribe supplements and vitamins to heal the ailment. *Amish* also utilize Reflexologists, who massage nerves and zones in the feet correlating with certain systems of the body. Recipients of this type of therapy verbalize relief from ailments of the head, spine, and stomach as well as other systems of the body.

Experienced in the *Amish* community, J.K., a natural healer, sees patients, communicates with and advises other patients via mail and operates a store that sells vitamins, supplements and herbs, so that he is able to assist his patients with their health problems and prescribe the appropriate herb. There are other factors in J.K.'s practice that make his approach different from a biomedical practice. He does not charge for his services but will accept donations. His posted office hours are from 8:00AM to 6:00 PM. But he will routinely see patients up to 1:00pm, then make a house call at midnight. During office hours he also will routinely spend an hour or more with the patient and family, teaching and explaining.

Fig. 2: A field of Burdock on the farm of the *Amish* healer

Traditional healing practices are based on beliefs, which have existed in this culture long before the development and spread of Western medicine. The traditional healing system is so fundamentally interwoven into many belief systems that any form of healing that ignores these beliefs can be both psychologically unsatisfactory and unacceptable to the patient. This indicates Western Medicine could benefit from interpolating traditional healing modalities into their practices when interacting with patients of other cultures.

Examples of the healing of a certain disease or disorder

J.K. gives the rationale for the ingredients; honey, which forms the base, is a well-known healing agent that minimizes scarring. It also relieves the pain and blistering. Wheat germ oil provides Vitamin E, which also promotes healing and reduces scarring. *Aloe vera* has properties that make it efficacious for reducing pain. Olive oil has an abundant supply of vitamins A, D, E, and K besides other vitamins and minerals; easily adsorbed through the skin it carries the herbal ingredients of ointment. Marshmallow root has softening and soothing properties. White oak bark is a powerful vegetable astringent and antiseptic.

This herb will relieve itching, firms up tissue and soothes irritated skin. Wormwood relieves soreness. Comfrey root promotes rapid production of cells. Blessed lobelia will soothe muscle soreness. Vegetable glycerine will act as a preservative to inhibit mold and bacterial growth in the herbal mixture. Beeswax is a natural ingredient used in the salve to keep the oils firm enough so that hot climes and body heat do not cause the salve to run off the body of the patient

Healing substances or plants

Lesser burdock
Common name: burdock, Dutch name gletta
Family: compositae
U.S. distribution: throughout
Height: one meter
Foliage: a biennial weed of waste places and roadsides
   grows from a fleshy taproot and produces large,
   heart- shaped leaves and red violet flower heads
   surrounded by numerous hooked brackets that
   form a bur-like cup.

Bloom time: June through autumn
Habitat: waste ground, edges of woods, roadsides, and hedgerows
Soil: moist soil
Alternate health use: burdock is an excellent detoxifying herb. The plant is antibacterial, antifungal and has soothing mucilaginous properties. The leaves are poulticed onto burns, ulcers and sores

Plantain leaves
Common name: Broadleaf plantain, (Dutch name sow-ear)
Family: plantaginaceae
U.S. distribution: throughout
Height: up to 8 inches
Foliage: alternate in rosettes, all basal, elliptic to broadly ovate, strongly ribbed and waxy
Bloom time: June to September
Habitat: pastures lawns and meadows
Soil: moist soil
Alternate health use: crushed leaves can be applied as a poultice to relieve pain

Healing examples
The publication presents natural remedies for burns and wounds based on J.K.'s effort and experience in treating patients for over twenty years. This healer admits he has not been schooled in the procedures of western medicine. He states "*I do have knowledge of the values of home and natural remedies from my ancestors and other members of our community.*" He has searched for the natural nontoxic, remedies when he has had treatments that proved less than successful or painfully prolonged. His methods are to attempt to use the nontoxic substances and exclude complicated or expensive remedies. It is J.K.'s idea that the creator gave consideration to have effective remedies available to all, especially the poor.
His work as a nutritional consultant taught him that we all need pure water and food to stay healthy.

Case stories
When J.K.'s two year old son was badly scalded, he used the popular treatment of the day but it caused his son unbearable pain, when removing the bandages. Combined with the letters this healer had been receiving from relatives with burned children of their own, it was too much for a father. J.K. went out to be alone to think and pray. He thought of how God had created the earth. And how the poor and isolated people should be able to find the necessities for their needs, leaves and other growing plants.

He remembered about a shiny leafed wreath and how shiny the leaves were and how he thought they would not stick to a wound. At the time he was walking through a heavy patch of plantain (sow-ear in Dutch) leaves. It struck him that they were similar to what he was looking for. He gathered a hatful of leaves. Upon reaching home, BFC salve (a burn salve) and a single layer of plantain leaves was applied to his son's burns. This procedure was repeated twice daily. Within five days the burn was covered with new skin. The most remarkable and satisfying

Fig. 3: J.K. is the owner of a store. He sells vitamins, supplements, homoeopathy drugs, and herbs, and all general treatment nodarities

thing as a father was the lack of pain associated with the dressing changes. Along with the dressings he supplemented the diet with extra fruits and juiced vegetables. Factors addressed were availability of the foods suitable for juicing, time and help needed for food preparation and assistance with the patient.
In over two decades of using the burn salve and leaves as dressings J.K. utilizes past cases to illustrate his thinking process related to how he handles cases.

He spoke about a cancer patient who came to him because of pain and swelling of his leg post-radiation treatments.
Patient history: the patient had a tumor on his leg. It was removed; the patient then received radiation treatments, which caused the leg to swell. It was at this point the patient came to J.K. seeking help. He was afraid he would lose the leg and he was in great pain. The leg swelled, the patient had a great amount of pain and the area on the leg broke open. The smell was like a dead cow on the barn-heap with the sun shining upon it. The smell was so foul that J.K.'s wife, his helper, had to leave the room. J.K. started treatment on two fronts: first was removal of toxins which was achieved by coffee enemas in the bowel system, and second pain relief.

The formula is two tablespoons of strong coffee placed in two quarts of water. Give this enema twice daily. The enema should hang 10 inches above the body; administer slow and easy; if the patient experiences cramping, hold the enema for 15 minutes. Also the abdomen can be massaged to change the water. J.K. also made poultices of burdock leaves. The season was such that they were utilizing dried burdock leaves.

The procedure: the leaves are gathered to J.K.'s specifications, not near a road because of pollution, the younger leaves are better, not so many ribs that must be cut off the leaf. Then the leaves are laid on newspaper in a single layer. Then placed in a dry cool place. When needed, a large pan of water is placed on the wood cook stove, the water heated then the leaves are placed in the water until the water changes color. The leaves are removed and the excess water is removed. This part of the process cools the leaves. The B&W salve was then applied in a thin layer to the wound, then the burdock leaves.

Author

SHARYN BUCCALO is a Post Masters student in Transcultural Nursing at Duquesne University. Through her interactions with this Amish community she became interested in Natural Health as practiced by the Amish and their health care beliefs and practices. She has worked in the Old Order Amish community where J. K. has practiced for sixteen years. When a level of trust was established, J.K. allowed her to observe and assist in his practice. The patients were very open to discuss and educating the author about their perceptions of health and illness.

Reference

HUNTINGTON, G.E.1993. *Health Care in The Amish and the State.* DONALD KRAYBILL ed pp.163-190.

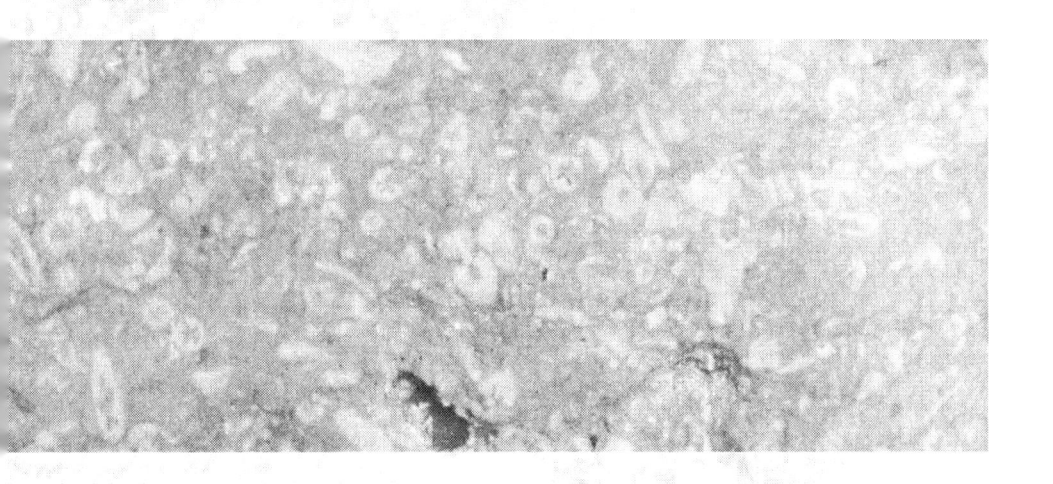

DIE THERAPEUTISCHE SEITE DER HAITIANISCHEN RELIGION VODOU IN NEW YORK CITY

von Bettina E. Schmidt

Kultureller Hintergrund

Vodou ist eine Religion, die in Haiti aus der Vermischung mehrerer Religionen unter dem Druck der Sklaverei entstand. Sie enthält Elemente verschiedener westafrikanischer Religionen, des Katholizismus sowie Aspekte indianischer Religiosität, aber auch Bezüge zum Widerstand gegen die Sklaverei. Da während der Sklaverei alles, was an Afrika erinnerte, verboten war, versteckten die versklavten Afrikaner ihre Religion unter dem Mantel des Christentums, insbesondere der volkstümlichen Heiligenverehrung. Durch diese Praxis konnten zahlreiche afrikanische Kulturelemente bis heute in Amerika überdauern. Im Mittelpunkt der Verehrung stehen die *loas*. Die meisten von ihnen gehen auf afrikanische Götter zurück, aber auch einige *marrons* (entflohene Sklaven) und indianische Geister werden im *Vodou* verehrt.

Das Heilsziel ist auf die Gegenwart gerichtet, die für die Gläubigen erträglicher gestaltet werden soll. Um dieses zu erreichen, müssen die *loas*, die das Schicksal der Menschen beeinflussen, mit bestimmten Opfergaben oder Zeremonien wohlwollend auf den Bittsteller eingestimmt werden.

Das heißt, sie müssen überredet werden, ihr Verhalten zu verändern. Daher steht die Divination, die Kommunikation mit den *loas*, im Mittelpunkt der Religionsausübung. Über einen Priester kann ein Gläubiger die *loas* über ein Orakel befragen. Außerdem ist es möglich, die *loas* direkt anzusprechen, wenn sie sich in den Körpern von Gläubigen manifestieren, z.B. während einer Feier zu Ehren eines *loas*. Diese oft als »Besessenheit« stigmatisierte religiöse Manifestation steht im Mittelpunkt der religiösen Praxis im Vodou und dient der direkten Kommunikation mit den *loas*.

Bei beiden Kommunikationsweisen sind die Priester unentbehrlich, da sie darin ausgebildet sind, die *loas* zu verstehen und mit ihnen zu verhandeln. Obwohl *Vodou* über keine institutionelle Struktur (d.h. keine Kirche) verfügt, dominieren die Priester die Ausübung der Religionen. Sie können von allen Gläubigen konsultiert werden (oftmals gegen Bezahlung). Die meisten Priester leiten einen eigenen Tempel mit einem festen Kreis von Mitgliedern, die regelmäßig Feiern zu Ehren bestimmter *loas* abhalten. Als Priester sind sie für die Mitglieder, vor allem die von ihnen in die Religion eingeführt wurden, verantwortlich wie für ein enges Familienmitglied. Diese Eltern-Kind-Beziehung steht im Mittelpunkt der therapeutischen Seite von *Vodou*.

Von Haiti aus breitete sich die Religion im 20. Jahrhundert immer weiter aus. Seit den 1980er Jahren steigt auch die Präsenz von *Vodou* in New York City, anfangs vor allem durch die haitianischen Migranten. Heute allerdings hat sich die Religion auf andere Gruppen ausgebreitet, sowohl auf Migranten von anderen karibischen Inseln als auch auf Amerikaner europäischer und afrikanischer Herkunft. Die genaue Zahl von Gläubigen ist nicht zu ermitteln, da sich die Tempel in der Regel nicht im Kirchenregister eintragen lassen und sich viele Gläubigen scheuen, ihre Religion offen zu praktizieren.

Noch immer leidet *Vodou* unter dem negativen Bild, das von dieser Religion verbreitet ist. Diese negative Betrachtung basiert zum Teil darauf, dass *Vodou* eine zentrale Rolle im Kampf gegen die Sklaverei und in der Unabhängigkeitsbewegung Haitis im 19. Jahrhundert zugeschrieben wurde. Entflohene Sklaven beriefen sich oftmals auf die Macht von *Vodou*, die sie angeblich unverwundbar für die Waffen der Sklavenfänger mache. Auch der Aufstand, der letztendlich zur Unabhängigkeit Haitis 1804 führte, soll 1796 mit einer *Vodou*-Zeremonie – unter Leitung eines *Vodou*-Priesters – ihren Anfang genommen haben. *Vodou* gilt seitdem auch außerhalb Haitis als machtvoll und gefährlich. Aus Angst vor der Ausbreitung des Unabhängigkeitskampfes wurde *Vodou* als »schwarze Magie« oder gar als »Aberglaube« stigmatisiert. Dennoch gewinnt *Vodou* heute – vor allem durch die therapeutischen Angebote – kontinuierlich mehr Anhänger, auch in New York City.

Therapeutische Aspekte von Vodou

Die Priester übernehmen eine zentrale Rolle im therapeutischen Angebot von *Vodou*. So schließt die Ausbildung zum Priester auch die Anleitung in unterschiedliche Therapieformen mit ein, wie beispielsweise die Phytotherapie, d.h. die Anwendung von Heilpflanzen, die als Bad, Tinktur, Duftwasser oder Tee bei der Behandlung verabreicht werden. Wichtiger ist allerdings die Diagnose, da zahlreiche physische und psychische Leiden religiöse Ursachen haben können. In einem holistischen Konzept wird der ganze Mensch und nicht nur sein körperlicher Aspekt von dem Priester behandelt.

In zahlreichen privaten und äußerst vertraulichen Gesprächen wird über Orakel (siehe Abbildung 1: Konsultationsraum) die Ursache der Probleme ermittelt, ob es sich nun um gesundheitliche Probleme, um familiäre Schwierigkeiten oder um Probleme handelt, die im weiteren sozialen Umfeld existieren. Neben dem persönlichen Rahmen ist für den Patienten wichtig, dass seine Probleme ernst genommen werden und die Ursache der Schwierigkeit und nicht nur die Symptome ermittelt werden. Auch die Schuldzuweisung an andere (oftmals

Abb. 1: Konsultationsraum in einem *Vodou*-Tempel in New York City (1999)

übernatürliche) Wesen hat eine große Bedeutung für die Therapie, denn die Ursache liegt dann nicht mehr bei der erkrankten Person, sondern bei jemand anderem, der nun überredet werden muss, die Krankheit zurückzunehmen.
Daneben ist wichtig, dass der Patient aktiv an seiner Heilung mitarbeiten muss, sei es mit Versöhnungsgeschenken an seinen *loa* (z.B. mit einem Opfer oder mit der finanziellen Beteiligung bei der Ausrichtung einer Feier zu Ehren des *loa*) oder mit bestimmten Sühnetaten nach einem Tabubruch (z.B. Verzicht auf bestimmte Konsumgüter). Mitunter wird eine Erkrankung auch als Aufforderung der *loas* interpretiert, sich in die Religion initiieren zu lassen. Durch eine Ausbildung zum Priester wird der Patient letztendlich selbst gestärkt und damit befähigt, sich und später andere zu heilen.
Dieses geschah auch im Fall einer Priesterin, die ich kurz vorstellen möchte. Marie S. erfuhr bereits als Kind von 11 Jahren in Haiti das erste Mal am eigenen Körper die Manifestation eines *loa*. Nachdem ihr Körper noch weitere Male von *loas* «geritten», das heißt von ihnen kurzzeitig in Besitz genommen wurde, konnte sie seit dem Alter von 14 Jahren Nachrichten von den Geistern empfangen. Damit begann sie bereits im jugendlichen Alter, anderen Personen zu helfen. So sieht sie beispielsweise, wenn jemand verflucht ist und vermag dann einzugreifen und den Fluch zu brechen.
Seit 1982 lebt sie in New York, wo sie anfangs auf ein College ging. Dann allerdings wurde sie erneut von den Geistern gerufen. Sie kämpfte dagegen an, aber ihre

Probleme häuften sich. Dann verlor sie sogar noch ihre Arbeit. Schließlich floh sie vor ihren Problemen zu ihrer Familie nach Haiti und ließ sie sich letztendlich in *Vodou* initiieren. Seit ihrer Rückkehr nach New York arbeitete sie als Priesterin. Dafür gründete sie einen eigenen Tempel, deren Mitgliederzahl seit Mitte der 1990er Jahre immer mehr anwächst. Der Tempel befindet sich im Keller ihres Wohnhauses in einer ruhigen Wohngegend in Brooklyn. Der Boden im Keller ist nicht betoniert, sondern verfügt über einen Lehmboden, um den Kontakt zur Natur zu bewahren (in Haiti finden die Feiern in der Regel im Freien statt, was in New York nicht möglich ist). Die weiß gekalkten Wände sind mit farbenfrohen Bildern von katholischen Heiligen dekoriert, welche die wichtigsten *loas* symbolisieren (siehe Abbildung 2). Am Kopfende befindet sich ein langer Tisch, der während der Feste als Altar für die Gaben dient. Im Zentrum des Raumes steht ein mit drei Trommeln verzierter Pfosten, der den *poteau-mitan* symbolisiert, über den die loas auf die Erde kommen. Neben diesem zentralen Raum gibt es noch kleinere Kammern als Aufbewahrungsraum für religiöse Objekte, als Konsultationsraum für Patienten, als Umkleidekammer während der Feste und als Raum für die Initianden in ihrer mehrtägigen Abgeschiedenheit.

Für die Heilung sind zwei Aspekte von zentraler Bedeutung: zum einen die Beziehung zur Priesterin und zum anderen die Beziehung zu den *loas*. Die Priesterin verfügt über eine große Autorität über ihre Gemeindemitglieder, welche durch die regelmäßigen privaten Konsultationen immer wieder gestärkt wird. Die Menschen kommen nach Angaben der Priesterin aus den unterschiedlichsten Gründen zu ihr, denn sie hat für jedes Problem eine Antwort bzw. weiß stets, an welchen *loa* sie sich wenden muss: "If someone tries to hurt you and you want to stop it, ... if your child is sick, if someone keep a curse on you ..., if you look for treatment, ... I have a charm." Dieses Angebot macht einen Großteil der Attraktivität von *Vodou* aus, denn sie wird häufig von Außenstehenden konsultiert. *Vodou* bietet Hilfe bei Krankheiten und Problemen, wo andere Systeme scheitern. Aber diese Arbeit zehrt nach der Kraft der Priesterin, die Tag und Nacht für die Mitglieder ihres Tempels ansprechbar ist. Während der Konsultationen behandelt Marie S. nicht nur Probleme, sondern ihre Gemeindemitglieder lassen regelmäßig ihre individuelle Beziehung zu den *loas* und den Totengeistern untersuchen. Alle wichtigen Lebensentscheidungen werden erst nach Beratung mit der Priesterin getroffen, denn eine falsche Entscheidung könnte die *loas* verärgern. Alle Gläubigen müssen die Beziehung zu den *loas* regelmäßig überprüfen lassen, um sich vor Strafen wie z.B. Krankheiten zu schützen. Außerdem haben die Gläubigen zu Hause einen privaten Altar aufgebaut, wo sie täglich der *loas* und der Toten gedenken.

Auch die Einbindung in eine Gemeinschaft kann für die Heilung unter Umständen eine gewisse Rolle spielen, und sei es nur, damit der Patient merkt, dass auch andere unter ähnlichen Problemen leiden und dass er nicht alleine ist. Außerdem symbolisiert *Vodou* in New York für viele Haitianer ein Stück Heimat in der Fremde. Besonders während der Feste herrscht durch die Geräusche und den Geruch eine fast haitianische Atmosphäre. Für einige Stunden entsteht eine Welt, in der sich die Migranten aus ihrem Alltag lösen können. Die Gemeinschaft bietet Familienersatz, besonders bei fehlenden Verwandten in der Region. Durch rituelle Verbindungen werden lebenslange Netzwerke gewoben, die den Migranten nicht nur bei religiösen Problemen helfen, sondern auch bei häuslichen oder finanziellen Sorgen.

Aber noch wichtiger ist das Herauslassen der eigenen Gefühle und Probleme nach

Abb. 2: Vodou-Tempel im Keller eines Wohnhauses in Brookley, New York (1999)

außen, besonders in der von allen akzeptierten Manifestation der *loas* im Körper der Gläubigen. Der Patient geht plötzlich in die Mitte des Kreises und wirbelt herum, verändert sein Verhalten und lebt seine geheimen Träume und Wünsche aus. Diese Verwandlung, die in den Zeremonien nicht nur akzeptiert, sondern vielmehr erwünscht und gefördert wird, wirkt wie ein Katalysator für angestaute Zwänge. Gleichzeitig werden Priester darin ausgebildet, die *loas* zu beherrschen und damit die eigenen Gefühle zu kontrollieren.

Alle Therapieformen schließen die aktive Mitarbeit des Patienten in die Behandlung ein. Nur zusammen mit dem Patienten kann die Priesterin die Ursache des Problems entdecken und ihn auf den Weg der Heilung führen. Die Mitarbeit bewirkt gleichzeitig die Stärkung der eigenen Person: aus einem willenlosen Opfer der übernatürlichen Wesen wird eine Person, die ihr Schicksal selbst in die Hand nimmt und die *loas* überreden kann, sie in Ruhe zu lassen. Gerade in der heutigen Zeit ist diese Seite von großer Bedeutung, besonders in einer so unpersönlichen Stadt wie New York City.

Zusammenfassung

Seit den 1980er Jahren verbreitet sich die haitianische Religion *Vodou* immer stärker in New York. Dabei wächst die Zahl der Nicht-Haitianer, die sich *Vodou* vor allem aus therapeutischen Gründen annähern. In den *Vodou*-Gemeinschaften und in den Konsultationen mit den Priestern finden sie Hilfe bei Problemen, bei denen kein Schulmediziner helfen konnte. Gerade das holistische Körperkonzept, in dem die Seele gleichzeitig mit dem Körper behandelt wird, wirkt erfolgreich bei der Behandlung physischer und psychischer Probleme. Außerdem befreit das Ausleben des eigenen Körpers in der Trance von Ängsten und Spannungen. Der Beitrag stellt nach einer Einführung in *Vodou* und der haitianischen Geschichte die therapeutischen Ebenen von *Vodou* vor. Im Mittelpunkt steht dabei eine haitianische mambo, d.h. eine *Vodou*-Priesterin, die in Brooklyn einen *Vodou*-Tempel leitet. Anhand ihrer Person werden die unterschiedlichen Heilungsweisen sowie die Bedeutung von *Vodou* in New York verdeutlicht.

Autorin
SCHMIDT, BETTINA E.
Privatdozentin am Fachgebiet Völkerkunde der Philipps-Universität Marburg
Studium der Völkerkunde, Afrikanistik und Religionswissenschaft in Marburg. 1989 Magister über traditionelle Heilpflanzen bei den Purhépecha in Mexiko; 1995 Dissertation über Santeria und Spiritismus in Puerto Rico; 2001 Habilitation mit einer Arbeit über karibische Religionsgemeinschaften in New York, Mitglied der AGEM seit 1990.
Kontakt: E-Mail: bschmidt@mailer.uni-marburg.de

Literatur
BRODWIN, PAUL. 1996. *Medicine and morality in Haiti: the contest for healing power.* Cambridge: Cambridge Univ. Press.
BROWN, KAREN MCCARTHY. 1991. *Mama Lola: a Vodou priestress in Brooklyn.* Berkeley/Los Angeles: Univ. of California Press.
BROWN, KAREN MCCARTHY. 1997. The power to heal: Haitian women in Vodou. In: *Daughters of Caliban: Caribbean women in the twentith century,* hrsg. von CONSUELO LÓPEZ Springfield. Bloomington/London: Indiana Univ. Press. S. 123-142.
HURBON, LAËNNEC. 1972 *Dieu dans le Vaudou haitien.* Paris: Payot.
LAGUERRE, MICHEL S. 1996 (1984). *American Odyssey: Haitians in New York City.* Ithaca/London: Cornell Univ. Press.
MCALISTER, ELIZABETH. 1992 Serving the spirits across two seas: Vodou culture in New York and Haiti. In: *Aperture* (San Francisco, Cal.), 126: S. 40-47.
1992/1993. Sacred stories from the Haitian dispora: A collective biography of seven Vodou priestess in New York City. In: *Journal of Caribbean Studies* (Lexington, Ky), Vol. 9, No. 1&2: S. 11-27.
MÉTRAUX, ALFRED. 1993 *Voodoo in Haiti.* Merlin Verl.
MINTZ, SIDNEY & MICHEL-ROLPH TROUILLOT. 1994 The social history of Haitian Vodou. In: *Secret arts of Haitian Vodou,* hrsg. von DONALD COSENTINO. Los Angeles: UCLA Fowler Museum of Cultural History. S. 123-147.
SCHMIDT, BETTINA E. [in Druck] Mambos, Mothers and Madrinas in New York City: Religion as a Means of Empowerment for Women from the Caribbean. In: *Wadabagei: A Journal of the Caribbean and its Diaspora* (New York), Vol. 5.
SOMMERFELD, JOHANNES. 1995 *Körper, Krise und Vodou: eine Studie zur Kreolmedizin und Gesundheitsversorgung in Haiti.* Münster/Hamburg: Lit.

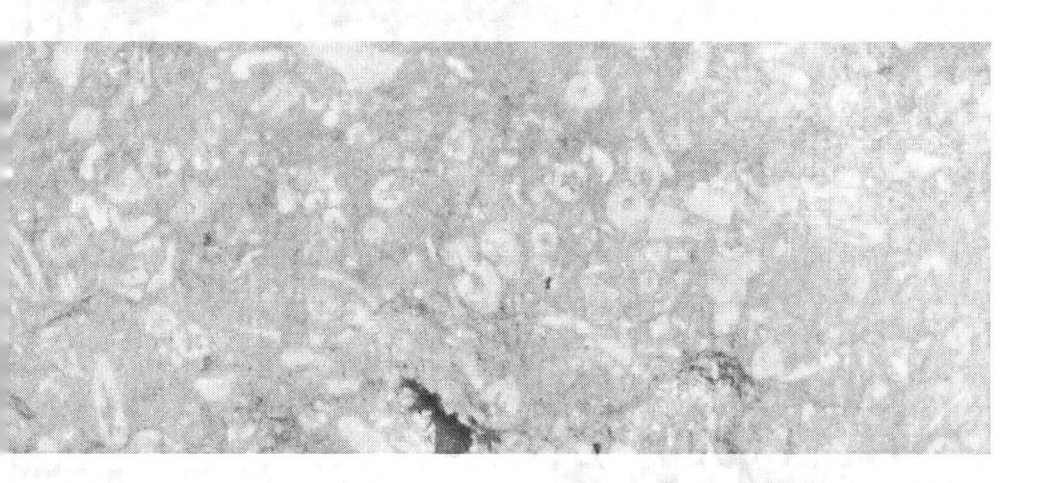

THERAPEUTIC ASPECTS OF VODOU IN NEW YORK CITY*

by Bettina E. Schmidt

Cultural background
Vodou is a religion created in Haiti from various religions that co-mingled under the pressures of slavery. It contains elements of west-african religions, of catholicism as well as aspects of Indian religiosity and is interrelated with the resistance-movement against slavery. African slaves were hiding and preserving their religion beneath the surface of christian religiosity especially traditional veneration of saints- as everything cultural of Africa had been forbidden during the period of slavery. Several elements of african religion survived in America by this custom. In the centre of worship are
the *loas*.
Most of them originate from african gods, but also some *marrons* (slaves that succeeded to flee) and Indian spirits are given reverence.
The religious focus is to make the present situation more bearable. As the *loas* have a strong influence on human fate, they have to be given certain sacrificial gifts or ceremonies to help the petitioners.
That means they have to be persuaded to change their behaviour, and divination, the communication with the *loas*, is most important. With the help of a priest, the believer is able to question the *loas* as an oracle.
It is also possible to address the *loas* directly, when they manifest in the body of a

---

* Translated by Sylvia Peipe

believer, e.g. during the celebrations to honour a special loas. These religious manifestations, often stigmatised as "being possessed [by a spirit]", are the centre of *Vodou* practice and enable direct communication with the *loas*.

Priests are skilled in both ways of communication, they have to understand the *loas* and negotiate with them. Although *Vodou* has no institutionalized structure (so to say, no church), priests dominate religious practice. All believers can consult them (often paying a certain fee). Most priests lead their own temple with a fixed circle of members, that regularly do ceremonies in honour of a certain *loas*.

Priests take over responsibility for the members, especially for those they had been initiating into the religion. Strong ties almost resembling those of families are created. Those parent-child-relationships are most important taking in account the therapeutic aspects of *Vodou*.

Originating in Haiti, the *Vodou*-religion spread out more and more in the 20th century. In New York City since 1980 *Vodou* became more and more popular, in the beginning mostly practised by migrants from Haiti. Today followers of *Vodou* can be found in several cultural groups - migrants from other carribean islands as well as Americans of european and african origin belong to *Vodou* temples. It is difficult to figure out the concrete number of believers as most temples normally do not register in church-indexes. Also many believers are afraid to live their religion in public.

Vodou-religion is suffering from the negative image circulating in the minds of society. Partly this negative view is based on the fact that *Vodou* is said to have played a central role in the struggle against slavery and in the independence-movement in Haiti in the 19th century. Slaves that had succeeded to flee often referred to the power of *Vodou* and claimed that it made them invulnerable to the weapons of the slave-hunters. Also the revolt in 1796, that finally led to the independence of Haiti in 1804, is said to have started with a *Vodou*-ceremony headed by a *Vodou*-priest. *Vodou* since then is regarded as strong and dangerous also outside Haiti. Fearing a possible proliferation of the independence movement, *Vodou* was stigmatised as "black magic" or even as "superstition". Nevertheless *Vodou* today gets increasingly popular, in New York as well, mainly due to offers in the therapeutic sector.

Therapeutic aspects of *Vodou*

Looking at *Vodou* priests play a central role in matters of therapy. Being educated as a priest contains a training in several therapeutic disciplines such as phytotherapy using medicinal plants for creating baths, tinctures, odorous waters or teas for treatment. Diagnosis is more important, because several physical and psychic problems might have a religious source. In a holistic concept the human as a whole is treated by the priest, not only his body.

In numerous private, often intimate conversations, the origin of problems is found through oracles (see Fig. 1: consultation-room), no matter whether the client has health-problems, difficult family-life or problems, that exist in a broader social context. Apart from the more intimate atmosphere, it is important to the client that his problems are regarded as serious and that more attention is given to the cause of his difficulties than to mere symptoms. Directing guilt to other (often supernatural) beings is of great importance in therapy. The ill person is no longer responsible for having caused problems. Ssomebody else is in charge of it and now has to be persuaded to take back the illness.

Fig. 1: Consultation-room in a *Vodou*-Temple in New York City (1999)

It is essential that the client actively co-operates in his recovery, be it through offering reconciliation-presents to his *loa* (e.g. through an offering or through the donation of money for giving a party in honour of the *loa*) or through certain actions of expiation after breaking a taboo (e.g. to dispense with consumer goods). Occationally, an illness also is interpreted as the *loas*´ call to become initiated into the religion. Having been educated as a priest, the patient himself becomes stronger and therefore able to heal himself as well as others.

This happened to a priestess from Haiti, I want to introduce. At the age of eleven, Edeline Saint Armand had contact with a *loa* for the first time that manifested itself in her body.
When she was fourteen she experienced further short-time possessions by *loas* and could receive messages from the spirits. Back then she started to help others using her skills: when e.g. a curse is put upon somebody she is able to see it and intervenes to break it. Since 1982 she has been living in New York, where she attended college. Again the spirits called upon her. She fought against them, but her problems multiplied, she even lost her work. In the end she ran away from her problems and returned to her family in Haiti, where she was initiated into *Vodou*. She has been working as a priestess in her own temple since she returned to New York. Since 1980 the number of members has been increasing continually. The temple is situated in the basement of her house in a peaceful area of Brooklyn. No

concrete was used to build the basement-floor because only through clay is contact to nature possible (in Haiti celebrations are held outside, a custom that cannot be realized in New York).
The whitewashed walls are decorated with colourful pictures of saints which symbolize the most important *loas* (see Fig. 2). At the head of the room you can find a long table used as an altar for offerings during the celebrations. In the centre of the room a stake with three drums is located, symbolizing the poteau-mitan that the *loas* use for approaching the world of humans. Next to this room there are smaller chambers that serve as consultation-rooms, dressing-rooms during the celebrations, as a space for members in the process of initiation, or just to store religious objects.
The two most important aspects in healing are, on the one hand, the relationship between priestess and client, on the other hand the relationships with the *loas*. The authority of the priestess in the parish is high, constantly strengthened by the regular practice of private consultations.
According to the priestess she has to deal with people´s various problems and questions, she is able to offer an answer and solution to each of them, at least she knows which *loas* to address:
If someone tries to hurt you and you want to stop it,
... if your child is sick,
... if someone keeps a curse on you,
... if you look for treatment,
... I have a charm.

This is one explanation for *Vodou´s* attractiveness because the priestess is often consulted by people from outside the parish. *Vodou* is offering help where other systems fail. However, this work is also very exhausting. The priestess is accessible day and night for the members of her temple. During consultations Edeline Saint Armand does not only deal with problems, the members of the parish also have her check their individual relationships with the *loas* and the spirits of the deceased. All important decisions in life are undertaken only after a consultation with the priestess, because a wrong decision would make the *loas* angry. All believers have to have their relationships with the *loas* checked regularly to protect themselves from punishments like illnesses. Often believers build a private altar at home where they daily think of the *loas* and the deceased.

Becoming a part of a parish can support the healing process in certain cases and showing the client that he is not alone or that others suffer from similar problems. For many migrants from Haiti in New York, *Voudo* became a taste of home abroad. During the celebrations the sounds and smells create an almost Haiti-like atmosphere. For some hours a world is created in which the migrants can loosen the ties to their everyday-life. The community is a kind of family-substitute, especially filling the places of relatives. Through ritual interrelations, networks are woven that might last a whole life long and help the migrants not only in religious contexts but also with their financial worries or family-problems.
Even more important is the fact that they can release and express their feelings, especially during the *loas* manifestation in the believer´s body. Suddenly the client moves to the centre of the circle, whirling and changing his behaviour, living his secret dreams and wishes. This transformation, which is not only accepted but requested and supported during the ceremonies, works as a catalyst for

Fig. 2: Vodou-Temple in the basement in Brookley, New York (1999)

constraints, hidden inside the person. At the same time priests are taught to rule the *loas* and to control their own feelings.

In all kinds of therapies, clients´ active support is crucial. Only with the client´s help is the priest able to guide him to the path of healing. Working together with the priest makes the client´s personality even stronger: a victim of supernatural powers, somebody without own will becomes a person that takes over responsibility for his fate and is able to convince the *loas* to leave him in peace. These days this becomes more and more important, especially in a big and impersonal city like New York City.

Abstract
Since the 1980ies, the *Vodou*-religion from Haiti has spread more and more into New York. The number of Non-Haitians approaching *Vodou* for therapeutic reasons is growing. In *Vodou*-communities and through consultations with priests, they get help presenting problems, that no normal doctor could manage. The holistic body-concept which treats body and soul equally, is successful when treating physical and psychic problems. The possibility of freely reacting during the trance liberates the body from fears and tensions.

The text introduces *Vodou* and the haitian history as well asdescribing the therapeutic levels of *Vodou*. The focus is on a haitian *mambo*, a *Vodou*-priestess, heading a temple in Brooklyn. Different healing-methods, as well as the meaning of *Vodou* in New York, are explained using her as a reference example.

Author
PD Dr. phil. Bettina E. Schmidt
private lecturer in Ethnology at the Phillips University of Marburg, studies of ethnology, africanology and religion in Marburg 1989 master term paper about traditional healing plants of the Purhépecha in Mexico
1995 dissertation about Santeria and spiritism in Puerto Rico
2001 habilitation paper about caribean religion groups in NYC
contact: email: bschmidt@mailer.uni-marburg.de

References
Brodwin, Paul. 1996. *Medicine and morality in Haiti: the contest for healing power.* Cambridge: Cambridge Univ. Press.
Brown, Karen McCarthy. 1991. *Mama Lola: a Vodou priestress in Brooklyn.* Berkeley/Los Angeles: Univ. of California Press.
Brown, Karen McCarthy. 1997. The power to heal: Haitian women in *Vodou.* In: *Daughters of Caliban: Caribbean women in the twentith century,* hrsg. von Consuelo López Springfield. Bloomington/London: Indiana Univ. Press. S. 123-142.
Hurbon, Laënnec. 1972 *Dieu dans le Vaudou haitien.* Paris: Payot.
Laguerre, Michel S. 1996 (1984). *American Odyssey: Haitians in New York City.* Ithaca/London: Cornell Univ. Press.
McAlister, Elizabeth. 1992 Serving the spirits across two seas: *Vodou* culture in New York and Haiti. In: *Aperture* (San Francisco, Cal.), 126: S. 40-47.
1992/1993. Sacred stories from the Haitian dispora: A collective biography of seven *Vodou* priestess in New York City. In: *Journal of Caribbean Studies* (Lexington, Ky), Vol. 9, No. 1&2: S. 11-27.
Métraux, Alfred. 1993 *Voodoo in Haiti.* Merlin Verl.
Mintz, Sidney & Michel-Rolph Trouillot. 1994 The social history of Haitian Vodou. In: *Sacret arts of Haitian Vodou,* hrsg. von Donald Cosentino. Los Angeles: UCLA Fowler Museum of Cultural History. S. 123-147.
Schmidt, Bettina E. [in Druck] Mambos, Mothers and Madrinas in New York City: Religion as a Means of Empowerment for Women from the Caribbean. In: *Wadabagei: A Journal of the Caribbean and its Diaspora* (New York), Vol. 5.
Sommerfeld, Johannes. 1995 *Körper, Krise und Vodou: eine Studie zur Kreolmedizin und Gesundheitsversorgung in Haiti.* Münster/Hamburg: Lit.

DAS KALLAWAYA HEILUNGSSYSTEM AUS DEM ANDENGEBIET*

von Stanley Krippner

Die traditionelle Sicht der *Kallawayas* von Gesundheit und Krankheit

Die Heiler der *Kallawayas* haben eine sehr alte Tradition. Sie kann bis vor die Zeit der spanischen Eroberung, dem *Inka* Imperium, den Zeitaltern verschiedener Prä-*Inka*-Kulturen bis zur legendären *Tiahuanaco* Kultur (400-1145 C.E.) zurückverfolgt werden.

Bolivianische *Kallawaya*-Praktiker sind in Gebieten von Argentinien, Chile und Peru anzutreffen. Sie reisen immer in kleinen Gruppen, ungern alleine. Sie sprechen *Aymara*, *Quecha* und/oder Spanisch.

Die Heiler unterteilen sich in verschiedene Kategorien: Heilkräuterkundige (*herbalarios*) sammeln Pflanzen, Kräuterheiler (*yerbateros*) bereiten die Pflanzen zu und Medizinmänner (*curanderos*) wenden die Kräuter und andere Substanzen an.

Yatiris sind die spirituellen Heiler und *partidas* nennt man Hebammen. Im Laufe der Zeit begannen die *Kallawaya*-Praktiker mehr als eine Funktion auszuüben. Aufgrund dessen wurde diese traditionelle Aufteilungen weniger starr. Alle Praktizierenden vermitteln zwischen der Umgebung und dem Patienten. In manchen Fällen wird die gesamte Gemeinschaft einbezogen.

In der Volkstradition der Anden wird jemand als krank definiert, der "unfähig ist zu arbeiten". Unter den *Kallawayas* wird der Körper eines Patienten als ein Mikrokosmos der natürlichen Umgebung gesehen. Es ist die Pflicht eines *Kallawaya*-Heilers eine genaue Diagnose zu erstellen, und dann die Entscheidung zu treffen, ob der Patient zu einem Schulmediziner überwiesen werden soll oder nicht.

Ein übliches Diagnose-Werkzeug ist das "Werfen" (*casting*) von Coca-Blättern.

Abb.1: Pharmazeut mit Kallawaya Kräuterzubereitungen, Tambillo Krankenhaus.

* Übersetzung aus dem Englischen: Simone Siahdodoni

Einige dieser Blätter hält der *Kallawaya* weit über seinen Kopf und wirft diese dann auf den Boden oder auf eine Zeremonial-Mesa (ein Tuch, welches spirituelle Kraft besitzt, und auf dem verschiedene Gegenstände aufgestellt sind).

Viele *Kallawayas* untersuchen den Puls und Blutdruck des Patienten und begutachten die Zunge, Augen, Atmung, Urin und die Ausscheidungen. Ein unregelmäßiger Puls ist ein Zeichen von Disharmonie.

Die Farbe der Zunge und der Iris werden genauso sorgfältig untersucht wie die Pupillenweite.

Ein traditionelles Diagnoseverfahren wird mit einem Meerschweinchen durchgeführt. Das Verfahren beginnt, indem man das Meerschweinchen in der Gegend des Magens oder der Niere an den Patienten anbindet. Ein vorbereitetes Coca-Blatt wird über den Kopf des Patienten platziert.

Dann folgt ein gemeinsames Gebet, das den Glauben an das Verfahren bekräftigt. Anschließend wird das Meerschweinchen wieder abgebunden und aufgeschnitten, so dass man die inneren Organe untersuchen kann. Eine Abnormalität der inneren Organe wird als eine Darstellung der Krankheit des Patienten angesehen.

Ungeachtet der Diagnose ist es wichtig, das der *Kallawaya* und der Patient zu einer Übereinstimmung kommen. Familienmitglieder sind oftmals anwesend, wenn die Diagnose verkündet wird, und es gibt häufig vorgegebene Aufgaben, die es zu erfüllen gilt.

Die Patienten und ihre Familien werden umfassend informiert und werden angehalten die Diagnose mit der ganzen Gemeinschaft zu teilen - außer im Fall von *kharisiri* oder Zauberei, die verschwiegen behandelt wird, um den Patienten nicht zu beunruhigen.

Im Allgemeinen sind Leber-, Magen- und Atemwegsprobleme die am häufigsten diagnostizierten. Aber die *Kallawayas* diagnostizieren und behandeln auch viele andere körperliche wie psychische Krankheiten, die in der Schulmedizin bekannt sind.

Dazu befassen sie sich auch mit spirituellen Problemen, wie z.B "susto" (Schrecken) - der Verlust des Geistes (spirit), den man sich als lebenswichtige Flüssigkeit vorstellt.

Die Ursache einer Krankheit wird in einer Störung der Harmonie zwischen dem Patienten und seiner Gemeinschaft und/oder der natürlichen Umgebung gesehen. Außer in den Fällen, bei denen ein übernatürlicher Angriff vorliegt, wie bei *kharisiri*.

Susto (Schrecken) hat verschiedene mögliche Krankheitsursachen, z.B. Zauberei, Traumata, Schockzustände oder ein starker Wind, der den Geist eines Babys geraubt hat (aufgrund dessen finden Geburten im Haus statt).

Das *Kallawaya*-Heilungssystem lehrt seinen Praktizierenden zwischen dem kranken Körper des Patienten und der Umgebung zu vermitteln und die verlorengegangene Balance wieder herzustellen.

Kallawaya-Praktizierende sind hauptsächlich Kräuterheilkundige und Ritualkundige. Ihre implizite Theorie erkennt die Wichtigkeit des Glaubens an ihre Verfahren, genauso wie die Überlegenheit der natürlichen Methoden.

Das Ziel des *Kallawaya*-Systems ist es, harmonische Beziehungen unter den Gemeinschaftsmitgliedern, der Gemeinschaft als Ganzes und der natürlichen Umgebung herzustellen und zu erhalten. Als Vorbeugung dient die Praxis der Mäßigung im täglichen Leben und das Vertrauen unter den Mitgliedern einer Gemeinschaft.

Abb. 2:
Kräuterladen mit Lamaskeletts (gebraucht in der Volksmedizin) und Elixiere in Flaschen, LaPaz

Der Ansatz der traditionellen *Kallawaya*-Heilung

Das Ergebnis einer Behandlung oder Prognose ist von vielzähligen Faktoren abhängig - der Krankheit selbst, ihres Stadiums und der Kooperation der Patienten und ihrer Familien. Das Vertrauen und der Glaube sind Schlüsselfaktoren, da eine Kräuterbehandlung ein langsamer Prozess ist und viel Geduld erfordert. Der Glaube ist nötig, um die für die Genesung fundamentalen Selbstheilungsmechanismen zu aktivieren. Der Erfolg der Behandlung wird an der

Arbeitsfähigkeit des Patienten gemessen.

Der Behandlungsrahmen ist von der Beweglichkeit des Patienten abhängig - ist der Patient nicht dazu in der Lage zum Heiler zu gehen, kommt dieser zu ihm. Weibliche *Kallwaya*-Praktizierende jedoch verlassen normalerweise nicht ihr Zuhause, der Patient muss zu ihnen kommen. Es gibt Kliniken, in denen Patienten einen männlichen *Kallawaya*-Praktiker aufsuchen können. Die Patienten bevorzugen normalerweise den Hausbesuch, weit weg von dem Einfluss feindseeliger Geister und fremder Umgebung und in der Nähe von vertrauten Tieren, Pflanzen und ihrem Land.

Krankenhäuser werden gefürchtet, zum Teil wegen ihrer weißen Farbe, welche mit dem Tod und dem Begräbnis von Säuglingen assoziiert ist. Eine Behandlung ist individuell ausgerichtet. Es müssen aber auch allgemeine Regeln eingehalten werden wie z.B. eine ausgeglichene Ernährung als vorbeugend gegen Krankheit. Den Patienten wird geraten, Nahrung aus dem Gebiet und der Saison zu essen. *Kallawaya*-Praktiker kennen mehr als 1000 medizinischen Pflanzen. Ein Drittel davon haben eine nachweisbare Wirksamkeit und ein weiteres Drittel wird als "wahrscheinlich" wirksam eingestuft.

Diese Pflanzen werden den drei verschiedenen "Wettern" zugeordnet, die *Pachamama* (Mutter Erde) und *Tataente* (Vater Sonne) den Menschen gegeben haben: heiß, mild und kalt.

Coca spielt in vielen Heilprozessen eine große Rolle, da die Pflanze zwischen der Welt der Menschen und der Welt der Geister wächst. Eine Coca- und Chinin-Mixtur wird benutzt um Malaria zu behandeln - weltweite Aufmerksamkeit brachte ihnen die Geschichte der erfolgreichen Malaria-Behandlung im Graben des Panama-Kanals.

Ein Pilz, der an Getreide oder Bananen wächst und eine penizillinähnliche Substanz produziert, ist bekannt. Dieser wird für lokale Infektionsherde eingesetzt. Systemische Infektionen werden mit einer Zubereitung behandelt, die dem Tetramycin ähnlich ist. Dieses wird aus fermentierter Erde gewonnen. Die Zubereitung wird auch bei Geschwüren auf der Haut und chronischen Krankheiten angewendet.

Kallawaya-Medizin wird von Ritualen begleitet, die Gebete, Amulette und eine *Mesa* mit einbeziehen. Der Fötus eines Lamas wird für die Vorbereitung einer *Mesa* benutzt. Das Lama gilt als heiliges Tier. Amulette werden auf die *Mesa* gelegt, oder der Patient trägt diese um den Hals. Sie sollen ihm Vertrauen und spirituelle Kraft bringen, insbesondere wenn der Patient sich über bestimmte Arten von Enthaltsamkeiten beklagt.

Verschieden Amulette repräsentieren Gesundheit, Liebe, Wohlstand oder ein Gleichgewicht mit *Pachamama* und *Tataente*. *Mesas* werden angewendet um Krankheiten oder Ungleichgewicht vorzubeugen, häufig für die gesamte Gemeinschaft.

Es gibt auch Kräuterzubereitungen in Verbindung mit einer "Dampfbox" oder Anwendungen ohne Kräuter, z.B. Heilgesänge – insbesondere zum Heilen von Schlaflosigkeit. Tänze sollen beispielsweise den Patienten mit Energie versorgen. Besonders gefürchtet ist der Misserfolg einer Behandlung. Der *Kallawaya* zieht dann manchmal einen Suizid vor, denn der Tod eines Patienten schadet dem Ansehen der Familie.

Dem Tod jedoch kann man mit Wagemut begegnen. Das Glaubenssystem der *Kallawayas* besagt, dass jeder zwei Geister (spirits) besitzt, und einer oder beide vereinigen sich nach dem Tod wieder mit *Pachamama*.

Abb. 3:
Heilungsschrein,
Umland von LaPaz

Beispiele

Während unseres Besuches in Bolivien interviewten wir vier bekannte Praktizierende: Walter Alvarez, Gualberto Chambilla, Mario Vargas und Juan Villa. Wir haben auch Victor Morales interviewt, einen Psychologen, der *Kallawaya*-Prinzipien anwendet, aber selbst kein Heiler ist. Ebenso Luisa Aeschbacher und Luisa Balderrama, zwei Heilerinnen, welche im Gebiet von La Paz arbeiten.

Zur Zeit unserer Interviews war Alvarez Präsident der "Sociedade Boliviano de Medicina Tradicional", und Chambilla war Präsident der "Asociacion de Yatiris Tradicionales de La Paz" d.h. der "La Paz Association of Traditional Spiritual Kallaway Practitioners".

Die zuerst genannte Gruppe hat mehrere Tausend Mitglieder (über die Hälfte sind Frauen), während die Letztere eine angeschlossene Gruppe ist. Jeder vierte der Kallawaya-Männer ist ein Kräuterspezialist, aber nur ein paar Hundert werden als gut geschulte Praktizierende angesehen.

Wir waren glücklich Zeuge bei Gualberto Chambillas "Werfen" (casting) von Coca Blättern sein zu dürfen. Seine Klientin war eine junge gesunde Frau. Zu Beginn kaute Chambilla einige Coca Blätter. Er glaubt, dass diese Praxis ihm hilft zu einer Einheit mit der Pflanze zu finden und so die Informationen der Blätter direkt zu ihm fließen. Dann warf Chambilla die Coca-Blätter. Er hielt sich erst einige Blätter über dem Kopf und warf sie dann unvermittelt auf die Zeremonial-*Mesa*. Chambilla erklärte uns, dass jeder Aspekt des Blattes lehrreich sei, z.B. welche Seite nach oben liegt, die Ausrichtung des Blattes, seine Ähnlichkeit mit dem christlichen Kreuz und seine Position im Bezug zu den anderen Blättern.

In diesem Fall lag die glatte Seite der Blätter oben. Dies wurde als positives Zeichen gewertet, d.h. der Patient wurde als gesund diagnostiziert. Lägen jedoch mehrere Blätter mit der dunklen Seite nach oben, würde man dies als schlechtes Zeichen interpretieren, und weitere Diagnosen wären notwendig.

Kräuterzubereitungen werden normalerweise eingenommen, aber gelegentlich auch in Verbindung mit einer "Dampfbox" verwendet: Der nackte Patient begibt sich in eine Dampfbox. Diese ist mit dem Dampf aus der medizinischen Mixtur gefüllt. Die aktiven Bestandteile der Kräuter dringen in die Poren des Patienten ein und gleichzeitig verlassen Gifte über den Schweiß den Körper.

Wir haben einen Patienten von Walter Alvarez in einer dieser Dampfboxen im Tambillo-Krankenhaus außerhalb von La Paz beobachtet. Zusätzlich zu den Dampfboxen und ihren Reinigungstherapien war das Krankenhaus mit mehreren hundert Kallawaya-Kräuterzubereitungen ausgestattet, alle sehr sorgfältig beschrieben, gewogen und den Patienten mit einer genauen Anweisung verabreicht.

Nach der *Kallawaya*-Theorie gibt das Verhalten der Patienten einen wichtigen Hinweis auf die Diagnose und die Behandlung. Alvarez nimmt an, dass im Allgemeinen ein ruhiger Patient gesund ist, während Weinen und Schreien ein Hinweis auf den Verlust des Geistes sein kann. Die Symptome von "*susto*" variieren, sie beinhalten Depression, Besorgnis, Faulheit, Appetitlosigkeit, Zittern, Fieber, Übelkeit, Ohrengeräusche und Blähungen.

Der Patient, den wir beobachtet hatten, war mittleren Alters und zeigte keine Symptome von "*susto*", aber er wurde präventiv in einer Dampfbox behandelt. Alvarez, ein Gynäkologe und Chirurg wie auch *Kallawaya* Heiler, war maßgeblich an der Organisation einer Klinik in La Paz beteiligt. Dort sind Ärzte und Kräuterspezialisten beschäftigt. Er erzählte uns, dass die biomedizinischen Techniken ihren Weg in die *Kallawaya* Praxis gefunden hätten, ohne den Verlust der traditionellen, einmaligen Identität, insbesondere der Kräutermedizin und der Rituale. Alvarez bemerkte, dass die traditionellen *Kallawaya* drei Anordnungen folgen: *ama swa* - nicht stehlen; *ama llulla* - nicht lügen; *ama khella* - nicht faul sein. Die *Kallawaya* glauben an ein Prinzip der Natur, das sie als das "Boomerang Gesetz" bezeichnen: wenn du andere verletzt, werden bösartige Taten zu dir zurückkehren. Diese Lebensprinzipien werden als grundlegend dafür angesehen, Harmonie in einer Gemeinschaft aufzubauen und zu erhalten.

Alvarez meinte abschließend, dass ein maßvolles Leben in Frieden und Harmonie im Einklang mit den *Kallawayas* stehen und ein dynamisches Gleichgewicht für eine gesunde Balance wichtig ist.

Autor

STANLEY KRIPPNER, PH.D.

Professor an der Saybrook Graduate School and Research Center, San Francisco, California. Er hat Schamanen aus Nord- und Südamerika, Europa, Asien und Afrika beobachtet und mit ihnen gearbeitet. Seine Ergebnisse sind in dutzenden von Artikeln und in dem Buch "Spiritual Dimensions of Healing: From Tribal Shamanism to Contemporary Health Care" zu finden.
Kontakt: E-Mail: skrippner@saybrook.edu

Literatur
(siehe bitte S. 442)

THE KALLAWAYA HEALING SYSTEM OF THE ANDES

by Stanley Krippner

The traditional *Kallawaya* view of health and illness

Kallawaya practitioners trace their tradition back to the legendary *Tiahuanaco* cultures of 400-1145 C.E., continuing through the eras of other pre-*Inca* cultures, the *Inca* Empire, and the Spanish conquest, to present times. Bolivian *Kallawaya* practitioners often travel to parts of Argentina, Chile, and Peru, but always in small groups rather than alone. *Kallawaya* practitioners are members of the *Kallawaya* ethnic group; members of this group speak *Aymara, Quechua,* and/or Spanish. Their practitioners represent various skills and functions: *Herbalarios* collect plants; *yerbateros* prepare plants; *curanderos* apply the herbs and other medicines; *yatiris* are spiritual healers; *partidas* are midwives. Over time, *Kallawaya* practitioners began to perform more than one function, hence many of these traditional divisions have become less rigid. All practitioners mediate between the environment and the patient, and, in some cases, the community-at-large.

Folk tradition in the Andes defines "being sick" operationally, as someone who is "unable to work." Among the *Kallawaya*, a patient's body is seen as the microcosm of the natural environment. It is the task of the *Kallawaya* practitioner to make an accurate diagnosis, then a decision must be made as to whether or not the patient should be referred to an allopathic physician. A common diagnostic tool is the "casting" of coca leaves in which the practitioner holds several leaves high above his or her head, dropping them onto the ground or onto a ceremonial *mesa* (i.e., a cloth that purportedly has spiritual powers, and on which various objects are displayed). Many practitioners take their patients' pulse and blood pressure, and make direct observations of the tongue, eyes, breath, urine, and feces. Irregular

Fig.1: Pharmacist with Kallawaya herbal remedies, Tambillo Hospital.

pulse is an immediate sign of disharmony. The color of the tongue and iris are observed carefully as well as the dilation of the patient's pupil. A common folk method of diagnosis utilizes a guinea pig. The procedure begins with tying the guinea pig to the patient's stomach or kidney area. A coca leaf preparation is placed over the head of the patient followed by a joint prayer affirming belief in the procedure. The guinea pig is removed and cut open so that its internal organs can be observed. Any anomaly of these internal organs is regarded as a representation of the patient's illness.

Regardless of the diagnosis, it is important that the practitioner and patient come to an agreement. Family members often are present when the diagnosis is announced and are often given tasks to perform. The patients and their families are fully informed and are advised to share the diagnosis with the entire community -- except in the case of *kharisiri* or sorcery, which the practitioner might treat privately so as to not alarm the patient. In general, liver, stomach, and respiratory problems are the most commonly diagnosed sicknesses, but *Kallawaya* practitioners also diagnose and treat most other conditions known to allopathic medicine, both physical and psychological. In addition, they work with spiritual problems such as susto, the loss of one's spirit, often conceptualized as a vital fluid that animates each human being.

The cause of illness is seen as a disintegration of harmony between the patients and their community and/or natural environment, except in cases where there is a direct supernatural intervention, as in *kharisiri*. *Susto* has several possible etiologies, e.g., sorcery, traumas or shocks, an inclement wind that captures a baby's spirit (which is why the birth process occurs indoors). The *Kallawaya* healing system trains its practitioners to mediate between the sick person's body and the environment, attempting to restore the balance that has been lost. *Kallawaya* practitioners are basically herbalists and ritualists. Their implicit theory recognizes the importance of faith in their procedures, as well as the superiority of natural methods. A life of moderation, peace, and harmony is in accord with the *Kallawaya* maxims, and a dynamic equilibrium is needed to produce a healthy balance.

The goal of the *Kallawaya* system is to maintain and restore the harmonious relationship of community members, the community as a whole, and the natural environment. Prevention involves the practice of moderation in daily life, and the maintenance of trust among members of the community.

The approach of traditional *Kallawaya* healing

The anticipated outcome of treatment, or prognosis, is dependent on a number of factors -- the sickness itself, its severity, and the cooperation of patients and their families. The confidence and the faith of the patient are key factors because herbal treatment is a slow process that requires a great deal of patience. Belief is felt to activate the self-healing mechanisms that are fundamental to recovery. The basic outcome measure is the patient's ability to return to work. The treatment setting depends on the patient's mobility; if the patient can not go to the practitioner, the practitioner will go to the patient. However, female *Kallawaya* practitioners typically do not leave their homes, thus their patients must come to them. There are clinics where patients can visit a male *Kallawaya* practitioner. However, the patient's preference usually is home visitation, far from the influence of hostile spirits and unfamiliar surroundings and near to familiar animals, plants, and land.

Fig 2: Herbal supply shop with llama skeletons (used in folk healing), and bottled elixiers, LaPaz

Hospitals are dreaded, in part because the color white is associated with the death and burial of infants.

Treatment is highly individualized but a balanced diet is needed to prevent sickness. Patients are advised to "eat food from the area and during its season." Kallawaya practitioners employ more than one thousand medicinal plants, about one third of which have demonstrated their effectiveness by Western biomedical standards, and another third of which have been judged to be "likely" effective.

These plants are divided according to the three distinct "weathers" which *Pachamama* (Mother Earth) and *Tataente* (Father Sun) have given to human beings, namely hot, mild, and cold.

Coca plays a major role in many of the healing procedures because the plant grows between the world of human beings and the world of the spirits. A coca and quinine mixture has been used to treat malaria -- most notably, as *Kallawaya* enthusiasts tell the story, during the digging of the Panama Canal, a triumph that brought them to world-wide attention. The fungus of corn or bananas produces a substance similar to penicillin that is used for local infections. More serious infections are treated by a preparation similar to tetramycin yielded by fermented soil; this preparation is also used for ulcerated skin and chronic illnesses.

Kallawaya medicine generally is accompanied by rituals involving prayers, amulets, and *mesas*. Llama fetuses are commonly used in the preparation of *mesas* because the llama is a sacred animal. Amulets are placed on the *mesa* or worn around the patient's neck, giving him or her confidence and spiritual power, especially when a patient complains of some type of deprivation. Different amulets represent health, love, wealth, or equilibrium with *Pachamama* and *Tataente*. *Mesas* are often used to prevent sickness or imbalance, often for the entire community. Sometimes, herbal preparations are used in conjunction with a "steam box." There is an armamentarium of procedures that do not involve herbs, e.g., healing songs, especially for treating insomnia, and dances, particularly to renew the patient's supply of energy.

If the treatment does not work, or if the patient's condition can not be successfully treated, the result may be death. There are few suicides among the Kallawaya, as this would bring dishonor to the family. Death, however, is a natural process that can be prepared for and confronted with valor. The *Kallawaya* belief system hold that each person has two spirits; after death, one or both of these spirits rejoins *Pachamama*.

Examples

During my visit to Bolivia, I interviewed four noted practitioners: Walter Alvarez, Gualberto Chambilla, Mario Vargas, and Juan Villa. I also interviewed Victor Morales, a psychologist who uses Kallawaya principles but is not a healer himself, and Luisa Aeschbacher and Luisa Balderrama, two eclectic healers who work in the La Paz area. At the time of our interviews, Alvarez was president of the *Sociedade Boliviano de Medicina Tradicional,* i.e., the Bolivian Society of Traditional Medicine, and Chambilla was president of the *Asociacion de Yatiris Tradicionales de La Paz*, i.e., the La Paz Association of Traditional Spiritual *Kallawaya* Practitioners. The former group has thousands of members (about half of them women) while the latter is an affiliated group. About one out of every four *Kallawaya* men are herbalists but only a few hundred are regarded as well-trained practitioners.

I was fortunate to witness Gualberto Chambilla initiate a "casting" of coca leaves. His client was a young woman who had come to thim for a "check-up" despite the fact that she reported no symptoms that might indicate a health problem. Initially, Chambilla chewed coca leaves, a practice he believed help him to attain "unity" with the plant, allowing the information to "flow" to him directly from the leaves. Following this procedure, Chambilla "cast" the coca leaves, holding several leaves high above his head. Suddenly, he dropped them onto a ceremonial *mesa*.

Fig. 3: Healing shrine, outskirts of LaPaz

Chambilla told us that each aspect of the leaf is instructive. e.g., the side of the leaf exposed, the orientation of the leaf, its resemblance to the Christian cross, its relative location to other leaves. In this case, the leaves' clear side was exposed; this was seen as a positive sign, and the patient was considered to be in good health. However, if the dark side of one of more leaf had been exposed, this would have been interpreted as a negative sign, and further diagnosis would have been necessary.

Herbal preparations usually are ingested but occasionally are used in conjunction with a "steam box"; the naked patient enters the receptacle, and it is been filled with steam created from the medicinal mixture. The active ingredients of the herbs enter the pores of the patient at the same time as the sweat cleanses the toxins. I observed a patient of Walter Alvarez in one of these steam boxes in the Tambillo Hospital we visited on the outskirts of La Paz. In addition to the steam boxes and their cleansing therapy, the hospital was replete with hundreds of *Kallawaya* herbal preparations, all carefully prescribed, measured, and given to patients with explanatory procedures. According to *Kallawaya* theory, the patient's behavior provides important clues for diagnosis and treatment. Alvarez assumes that, in general, a calm patient is healthy; crying and screaming may be signs of spirit loss. The symptoms of *susto* vary, but include depression, anxiety, laziness, loss of appetite, shaking, fever, nausea, hearing noises in the ears, and passing gas.

The patient I observed was a middle aged man who showed none of the symptoms of *susto*, but who had been given the steam box treatment for preventive purposes. Alvarez, a gynecologist and surgeon as well as a *Kallawaya* healer, was instrumental in organizing a clinic I visited in La Paz, staffed by both a physician and a herbalist. He told me that biomedical techniques are finding their way into *Kallawaya* practice without a loss of the tradition's unique identity, most notably its reliance on herbal medicines and rituals. Alvarez noted that traditional *Kallawaya* follow three injunctions: *ama swa*, do not steal; *ama llulla*, do not lie;

ama khella, do not be slothful. The *Kallawaya* also believe in a principle of nature they refer to as the "boomerang law": if you harm others, malevolent acts will return to you. Living by these precepts is felt to be fundamental in establishing and maintaining harmony within the community. Alvarez concluded that a life of moderation, peace, and harmony is in accord with the *Kallawaya* maxims, and a dynamic equilibrium is needed to produce a healthy balance.

Author
STANLEY KRIPPNER, PH.D.
Professor of Psychology at Saybrook Graduate School and Research Center, San Francisco, California. He has observed and worked with shamans in North and South America, Europe, Asia, and Africa, presenting his findings in dozens of articles and in the book Spiritual Dimensions of Healing: From Tribal Shamanism to Contemporary Health Care. Contact: E-Mail: skrippner@saybrook.edu

References
BASTIEN, J.W. (1987). *Healers of the Andes: Kallawaya herbalists and their medicinal plants*. Salt Lake City: University of Utah Press.
BASTIEN, J.W. (1992). *Drum and stethoscope: Integrating ethnomedicine and biomedicine in Bolivia*. Salt Lake City: University of Utah Press.
FONTANA, B.L. (1974). Foreword. In D.M. BAHR, J. GREGORIO, D.I. LOPEZ, & A. ALVAREZ. *Piman shamanism and staying sickness* (pp. ix-xi). Tucson: University of Arizona Press.
FRANK, J.D. (1973). *Persuasion and healing (rev. ed.)*. Baltimore: Johns Hopkins University Press.
HUFFORD, D. (1995). Cultural and social perspectives on alternative medicine: Background and assumptions. *Alternative Therapies in Health and Medicine*, 1(1), 53-61.
KRIPPNER, S. (2000). Epistemology and technologies of shamanic states of consciousness. In J. ANDRESEN & R. K. C. FORMAN (Eds.), *Cognitive models and spiritual maps* (pp. 93-118). Bowling Green, OH: Philosophy Documentation Center, Bowling Green State University.
KRIPPNER, S., & GLENNEY, E.S. (1997). The Kallawaya healers of the Andes. The Humanistic Psychologist, 25, 212-229.
KRIPPNER, S., & WELCH, P. (1992). Spiritual dimensions of healing: From tribal shamanism to contemporary health care. New York: Irvington.
LEVIN, D.M., & SOLOMON, G.F. (1990). The discursive formation of the body in the history of medicine. *Journal of Medicine and Philosophy*, 15, 515-537.
LEVI-STRAUSS, C. (1955). The structural study of myth. *Journal of American Folklore*, 78, 428-444.
MAHLER, H. (1977, November). The staff of Aesculapius. *World Health*, p. 3.
O'CONNOR. B.B. (1995). *Healing traditions: Alternative medicine and the health professions*. Philadelphia: University of Pennsylvania Press.
O'CONNOR, B., CALABRESE, C., CARDE A, E., EISENBERG, D., FINCHER, J., HUFFORD, D.J., JONAS, W.B., KAPTCHUCK, T., MARTIN, S.C., SCOTT, A.W., & ZHANG, X. (1997). Defining and describing complementary and alternative medicine. *Alternative Therapies in Health and Medicine*, 3 (2), 49-57.
STEWART, C. (1997). Fields in dreams: Anxiety, experience, and the limits of social constructionism in modern Greek dream narratives. *American Ethnologist*, 24, 877-894.
VALENSTEIN, E.S. (1986). *Great and desperate cures: The rise and decline of psychosurgery and other radical treatments for mental illness*. New York: Basic Books.

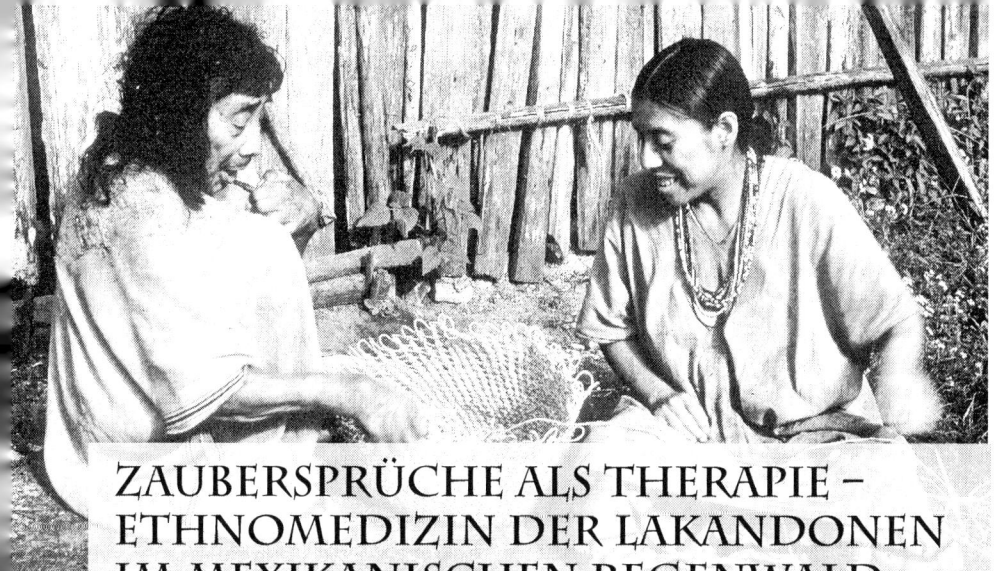

ZAUBERSPRÜCHE ALS THERAPIE – ETHNOMEDIZIN DER LAKANDONEN IM MEXIKANISCHEN REGENWALD

von Christian Rätsch

Die *Lakandonen* aus dem Regenwald im mexikanischen Bundesstaat Chiapas haben ein eigenes, sehr komplexes medizinisches System. Da sie keine medizinischen Spezialisten haben ist jeder Mann ein Heiler. Das Wissen über die Struktur des Menschen und über die Geschehnisse in der unsichtbaren Welt bilden die Grundlage für das Erkennen und Behandeln von Krankheiten. Beides ist sehr mit sozialen Interaktionen der gesamten Dorfgemeinschaft gekoppelt.

"Der Ethnologe geht ein Schülerverhältnis zu dem Schamanen ein, womit er die klassische Wissenschaftlerrolle transzendiert, seine forscherische Neugierde auf ein neues Niveaus hebt und Lernen und aktives Reflektieren zu kombinieren versucht."
(KALWEIT 1984:249)

Kulturanthropologie und Ethnomedizin

Die Kulturanthropologie ist die Wissenschaft vom Menschen als kulturelles Wesen. Ihr Forschungsgegenstand ist die Kultur des Menschen. Zur ihr gehört die Ethnographie, die Beschreibung fremder Völker. Die Formen der Ethnographie pendeln zwischen Kolonialismus und Verständigung. Viele Ethnographen, die bei einem fremden Volk Forschung betrieben haben, bemühen sich, dieses Volk zu verstehen und ihre Kultur von innen heraus zu erfassen und darzustellen. Der

---

Abb.1: Ein *Lakandonen*paar, der inzwischen mit ca. 110 Jahren verstorbene Chan K´in Ma´ax mit seiner jüngsten Frau Koh K´en´en, beim Flechten eines Tragenetzes aus Baumrindenzwirn. In der anarchisch, d.h. partnerschaftlich organisierten Kultur der *Lakandonen* von Naha´ gibt es keine spezialisierten Schamanen oder Heiler. Jeder Mann und jede Frau verfügen in unterschiedlichem Maße über schamanisches Wissen, z.B. in Form der Zaubersprüche (*kunyah*). Die *Lakandonen*kultur ist schamanisch, denn die Techniken stehen jedem zur Verfügung. Das ist ein ethnologischer Sonderfall, der offensichtlich selten ist oder in der kognitiven Anthropologie bisher nicht berücksichtigt wurde. (Naha´, Chiapas, Mexiko; 8/1988)

Ethnograph versucht, den Standpunkt des Fremden einzunehmen. Auf diese Weise bleibt die Ethnographie keine oberflächliche Beschreibung, sie wird der Zugang zur Perspektive des Fremden. Der Ethnograph schlüpft sozusagen in den Kopf des Fremden und sieht durch seine Augen die Welt, seine Lebenswirklichkeit. So schrieb dann auch ein Anthropologe zur Theorie des ethnographischen Interviews, "...*ethnography means learning from people.*" (SPRADLEY 1979, S. 3). Der Forscher erlernt die Kultur, die er erforscht; er hat Anteil daran.
Zu den kulturellen Systemen eines jeden Volkes gehört die Medizin. Ein besonderer Zweig der Ethnographie, die Ethnomedizin, beschäftigt sich mit medizinischen Systemen fremder Völker, aber auch mit der landeseigenen Volksmedizin (vgl. HAUSCHILD 1977). Dabei können vom Forscher verschiedene Herangehensweisen betrieben werden. Er kann feststellen, an welchen Krankheiten die Fremden leiden, und beobachten, was sie dagegen unternehmen. Er kann aber auch seinen eigenen Standpunkt aufgeben und das fremde medizinische System erlernen. Er wird zum Lernenden, die Kundigen des fremden Volkes werden zu seinen Lehrern. Dazu muss er zunächst das fremdkulturelle medizinische System als Alternative akzeptieren.
Ich habe seit 1979 ein mehrjähriges Forschungsprojekt zur Ethnomedizin der *Lakandonen* von *Naha´* in Südmexiko durchgeführt. Dabei habe ich die Rolle des Schülers, des Auszubildenden eingenommen. Mein Ziel war es, die *lakendonische* Medizin selbstständig auszuüben, also fremdkulturelles Verhalten anzunehmen und so anwenden zu können.

Dabei stellte ich fest, dass die *Lakandonen* gelegentlich an Krankheiten erkranken, die der westlichen Schulmedizin unbekannt sind, und erfuhr am eigenen Leib die Wirksamkeit der einheimischen Medizin. Die Medizin der *Lakandonen* ist ein sehr effektives System zu Gesunderhaltung und Krankenheilung in ihrer Lebenswelt. Dort wo unsere Tropenmedizin nicht mehr helfen kann, beginnt die *lakandonische* Medizin wirksam zu werden.
Besonders beeindruckte mich die Umgehensweise der *Lakandonden* mit Kranken, die soziale Betreuung und interaktive Anteilname. Während bei uns die Sprechzeiten bei den Ärzten immer kürzer werden (vgl. BALINT & NORBELL 1975) und die Krankenpfleger immer anonymer, sorgt sich in einem ernsteren Krankheitsfalle das ganze Dorf um den Erkrankten.

Die Welt der *Lakandonen*

Die *Lakandonen* nennen sich selbst *hach winik*, "Echte Menschen", und ihre Welt, den Regenwald des mexikanischen Bundesstaates Chiapas, schlicht *k'ax*, "Wald". Ihre kulturellen Wurzeln reichen bis weit in die vorspanische Zeit zurück und haben direkt mit dem Volk der *Maya* zu tun.
Heute leben ca.460 *Lakandonen* verteilt auf drei Dörfer. Zwei dieser kleinen Siedlungen tief im Regenwald fielen protestantisch-absolutistischen Sekten zum Opfer: brutal missioniert, zerfiel ihre traditionelle Kultur (vgl.MA'AX & RÄTSCH 1984, S.16-18).
In *Naha'*, der Ansiedlung am gleichnamigen See, sind die alten Götter noch lebendig, die traditionellen Gewänder werden noch von allen getragen, und die Männer haben noch lange Haare. Und auch sonst hat sich wenig am täglichen Leben verändert. Die Männer gehen zur Jagd, legen Brandrodungsfelder an und beten zu den Göttern. Die Frauen bereiten die Speisen zu, hauptsächlich

Abb. 2: Der über 70jährige *Lakandone* Antonio, der ebenfalls Chan K´in Ma´ax heißt, bei einem Heilritual im Götterhaus (*yatoch k´uh*). Er opfert den berauschenden *Balche´*-Trank (eine Art 2-4%iges Honigbier mit Lonchocarpus violaceaus) und *pom*, "Weihrauch" (Pinienharz), den Göttern und Göttinnen. Diese Opfergaben werden als *yoch k´uh*, "Speisen der Götter"klassifiziert. Durch das Ritual, begleitet durch Gebete (*t´ani k´uh*) und Zaubersprüche (*kunyah, hach k´ay*), werden die "Seelen" der Opfergaben zu den Göttern geschickt. Dort manifestieren sie sich als köstliche Getränke, an denen sich die Götter laben. Dadurch erfreut, senden sie ihre Heilkräfte zu den Kranken und Notleidenden, für die das Ritual durchgeführt wird. (Naha´, Chiapas, Mexiko; 2/1995)

Maisfladen, schwarze Bohnen, gelegentlich Affen- oder Papageienfleisch, pflegen die kleinen Kinder und kümmern sich um die Haustiere: Hühner und Truthähne. Eine politische Hierarchie gibt es nicht, ein "Häuptling" ist ihnen unbekannt. Ihre Gesellschaft ist anarchisch, jede Familie bestimmt über sich selbst. Einstimmig sind sie in Bezug auf Fremdbestimmung, z.B. durch die mexikanische Regierung. Chan K'in Ma'ax, der achtundneunzigjährige Dorfälteste von *Naha'* sagt immer wieder lächelnd :
"*Alle Regierungen lügen!*" Tuxtla Gutiérrez, die Landeshauptstadt von Chiapas, nennt er *tusta'* , "Volle Scheiße", denn das war alles, was sie bisher den *Lakandonen* bescherte. Von dort aus wurde die Abholzung des Waldes, der die Welt der *Lakandonen* war, abgesegnet. Neuerdings wird am Usumacinta, dem Grenzfluss nach Guatemala ein Staudamm gebaut, der dem Wald den Garaus machen wird. Für die *Lakandonen* wird das das Ende der Welt – und nicht nur ihrer – werden (vgl. RÄTSCH 1983).

Drei Wissensbereiche der *Lakandonen*

Die *lakandonische* Medizin ist neben der Subsistenz der zentralste Komplex ihrer Kultur. Die Subsistenz dient dem Lebenserhalt; die Medizin ordnet und gestaltet die dazu gewünschte Lebensform.

Die *Lakandonen* bezeichnen den Zustand eines Menschen als uts, wörtlich "gut, okay, in Ordnung", wenn dessen Bewusstsein gut ist, wenn er weder von Gedanken, Sorgen und Ängsten gequält wird, wenn seine Seele in seinem Herzen ruht und wenn er keine Schmerzen spürt.

Dieser gewünschte und angestrebte Zustand kann durch Krankheiten, Verletzungen, Hexerei oder Erlebnisse (z.B. Schrecken) gestört werden: dann ist der Mensch *ma'uts*, "nicht gut, nicht okay, nicht in Ordnung", d.h. krank.

Um den guten, also gesunden Zustand wieder herzustellen, gibt es mehrere Methoden, die zur Anwendung kommen können. Das medizinische System der *Lakandonen* setzt sich so aus drei Wissensbereichen zusammen:
- dem Wissen über die Struktur des Menschen und den damit verbundenen Zuständen (Ethnoantomie)
- dem Wissen über die zustandsverändernden Faktoren, die zum Krankheitszustand führen (Ätiologie und Nosologie)
- dem Wissen über die zustandsverändernden Faktoren, die zum Gesundheitszustand zurückführen bzw. ihn erhalten (Therapie und Prävention).

Bei den *Lakandonen* gibt es keinen medizinischen Spezialisten, keinen Profi, Schamanen, Medizinmann, Zauberer oder Priester. Jeder *Lakandone* besitzt medizinisches Wissen, kennt Zaubersprüche, kann Heilzeremonien durchführen, Heiltees herstellen und (neuerdings) auch Injektionen verabreichen.

Die drei Wissensbereiche der *lakandonischen* Medizin sind jedem *Lakandonen* verfügbar. Allerdings kann der Wissensstandard variieren. So können ältere Leute meistens mehr Zaubersprüche zur Krankenheilung als jüngere; aber auch das ist keine Regel.

Ethnoanatomie – die Struktur des Menschen

In der Urzeit formte *Hachäkyum*, Unser Wahrer Herr, Menschen aus farbig bemaltem Ton. Er setzte ihnen Maiskörner als Zähne in den Mund. Er, der Gott, pustete seine Geschöpfe der Erde an und dachte sie zum Leben. Durch diesen göttlichen Zauber ist aus Lehm, Farbe und Mais das komplexe Gebilde, das die *Lakandonen* Mensch nennen, geworden.

Nach dem Wissen der *Lakandonen* besteht der Mensch aus einem fleischlichen Körper, der Seele, die im Herzen wohnt, den vier Geistern, die im Puls und Knöchel pochen, dem Bewusstsein, das sein Zentrum ist, dem Denken und dem Tiergeist. Der Körper besteht aus Knochen, Fleisch, Blut, Haut, Haaren und Horn. In ihnen sind die Organe tätig, die alle in einer Verbindung zum Herzen und zur Galle stehen.

Im Herzen wird das Blut versammelt und in den Körper verteilt. Ist das Herz schwach oder die Galle vergiftet (z.B. durch einen Schlangenbiss), sinkt das Blut ab, "es geht dahin". Dann wird die Haut gelb, die Muskeln werden schwach. Im Herzen wohnt die Seele des Menschen. Sie ist sein nicht-stoffliches Duplikat, das des Nachts den Körper verlässt und in der gewöhnlich unsichtbaren Welt, in der fast alles spiegelverkehrt ist, agiert. Die Erlebnisse seiner Seele nimmt der Mensch

als Traum wahr. Die Seele kann aber auch in Krankheitszuständen den Körper verlassen und anderen Menschen sichtbar in Erscheinung treten. Wenn der Mensch stirbt, geht die Seele in die Unterwelt ein.
An den Puls- und Knöchelstellen pocht das Blut vom Herzen. Dort sitzen vier weitere nicht-stoffliche, unsichtbare Duplikate des Menschen. Sie verlassen bei seinem Tod seinen Körper und spuken in der Nacht herum. Bewohner der Unterwelt, die den Menschen nach seinem Leben trachten, um sich seiner Seele dienstbar zu machen, versuchen immer wieder, den Lebenden einer dieser Geister zu entlocken, denn dann müssen sie sterben.

Das Bewusstsein sitzt im Kopf, genau dort, wo das Gehirn ist. Das Bewusstsein ist der Fokus aller Gefühle und aller Körpervorgänge. Jedes Gefühl wird als ein besonderer Zustand des Bewusstseins ausgedrückt. Das Bewusstsein kann gewaltsam aus dem Körper vertrieben werden, (z.B. durch Schrecken): dann wird der Betroffene krank.

Ebenfalls im Gehirn sitzt das Denken. Das Denken ist der einzige Teil des Menschen, der nicht von Geburt an vorhanden ist. Das Denken entsteht im Laufe der Sozialisation und wird den Pubertierenden in Form von Kürbiskernen bei der Initiation verliehen. Wenn jemand denkt, verhält er sich der Lakandonen-Kultur adäquat. Gleichzeitig produziert das Denken aber auch Sorgen und Trauer. Beides führt zu unerwünschten Krankheitszuständen.
Außerdem ist der Mensch mit einem Tier des Waldes schicksalhaft verbunden. Man kann diesen Tiergeist, etwa einen Spinnenaffen, ein Wildschwein oder Reh im Traum sehen. Zeigt der Tiergeist irgendwelche Symptome, wird der mit ihm verbundene Mensch im Wachzustand daran leiden. Jede Desintegration in der Struktur des Menschen führt zwangsläufig zu einer Krankheit. Dann gilt es, die Krankheit und die damit verbundene Desintegration zu erkennen. Mit den dafür geeigneten Therapiemethoden wird der Mensch in seiner Struktur wieder integriert, er wird gesund.

Die Krankheiten

Es gibt drei Klassen von Krankheiten, die von den drei Schöpfergottheiten erschaffen und belebt wurden. *Hachäkyum*, Unser Wahrer Herr, hat die Echten Krankheiten des Waldes geschaffen, weil ein Urahne der *Lakandonen* aus blindem Eifer heraus den Götterboten *Äkinchob* erschlagen hatte. Die Echten Krankheiten sind:

- Winde, die in den Körper eindringen und seine Funktion stören

- Eigenschaften bestimmter Tiere, die sich durch die Wahrnehmung von ihnen im Körper des Menschen manifestieren

- die unsichtbaren Seelen einiger Reptilien und Raupen, die den Seelenkörper des Menschen anfressen

- die Essenzen giftiger Tiere (Schlangen, Zecken, Nesselraupen, Wespen)

- Verletzungen (Schnittwunden, Knochenbrüche), die als von den Göttern befohlen gelten

- Hexerei.

Mänsebäk, der Pulvermacher (vgl. RÄTSCH 1984), hat die Krankheiten der *Kah*, derjenigen, die eng zusammenwohnen, erschaffen:
- Parasiten (Wanzen, Läuse, intestinale Würmer)
- unsichtbare Krankheitskörper, die von einem Menschen zum nächsten übergehen.

Äkyantho´, der Gott der Nichtindianer, der Gott der Weißen, hat in der Urzeit für seine Geschöpfe Krankheiten aus Ton erschaffen, die gegen ein allzu gewaltiges Bevölkerungswachstum ankämpfen sollten. Diese Krankheiten sind gewöhnlich unsichtbar. Sie sind allesamt männlich, ca. 90 cm hoch, haben glühende Augen und tragen Pfeil und Bogen mit sich herum. Wen sie treffen, den machen sie mit ihrem Giftpfeil krank. Sämtliche epidemische Krankheiten (alle Arten von Erkältungen und Grippe, Kinderkrankheiten, Amöbenruhr, Cholera, Gelbsucht, usw.) aber auch Malaria und Syphilis gehören zu den Krankheiten des *Äkyantho´*. Diese drei Schöpfergötter haben für ihre Geschöpfe aber auch Heilmethoden erschaffen. *Hachäkyum* gab den *Lakandonen* das Wissen um die Zaubersprüche zur Heilung der Echten Krankheiten. *Mensäbäk* lehrte seinen Geschöpfen den Gebrauch von Heilpflanzen. *Äkyantho´* überreichte dem Weißen die Fähigkeit, chemische Mittel gegen Krankheiten herzustellen. Von der Art der Krankheit hängt die Therapie ab. Die Echten Krankheiten können nur durch Zaubersprüche geheilt werden. Die Krankheiten der *Kah´* und der Weißen werden auch mit deren Heilmitteln behandelt. Allerdings heilen sie nur die Götter, die bei entsprechenden Zeremonien angerufen werden. Der alte Chan Kín sagt über die Heilmittel der Weißen: "*Sie helfen, aber heilen tun nur die Götter!*"

Wenn ein Mensch erkrankt, muss sofort versucht werden, die Krankheit zu erkennen, damit man sie in der ihr angemessenen Weise behandelt. Dazu werden herangezogen:
Gespräche mit dem Kranken, Traumdeutung, Divination und Vorzeichendeutung.

Der Kranke wird genau nach äußerlich sichtbaren Symptomen abgesucht, nach seinen Erlebnissen kurz vor der Erkrankung gefragt und dazu ermuntert, über den Zustand seines Bewusstseins, seines Denkens, seines Fleisches und Blutes zu sprechen. Wichtig sind die Träume des Kranken, denn in ihnen können sich Symbole zeigen, die den wahren Grund der Erkrankung entschlüsseln helfen. Aber auch die Trauminhalte aller anderen Dorfbewohner werden zu Rate gezogen. Da die Krankheiten aus der unsichtbaren Welt kommen, gibt auch die im Traum wahrgenommene unsichtbare Welt Botschaften über die Krankheit an das Wachbewusstsein. Zur Traumdeutung treffen sich die Männer jeden Morgen im Götterhaus und sprechen über ihre eigenen Träume und die ihrer Frauen und Kinder. Gemeinsam wird das des Nachts Geschaute gedeutet und daraus wird das Verhaltenskonzept des neuen Tages abgeleitet. Wenn man im Traum eine brennende Zigarre sieht, wird man im Wachzustand von einer Schlange gebissen werden. In diesem Fall verlässt der Träumer nicht sein Haus und betet zu den Göttern.

Die *Lakandonen* haben verschiedene Divinationsmethoden, mit denen sie den Rat der Götter einholen. In einem Lied fragen sie die Götter nach Ursprung, Verbreitung und Auswirkung einer Krankheit und was dagegen zu tun sei. Ein eingerolltes Palmenblatt zwischen den Händen bewegt sich an bedeutungsvollen Passagen des Liedes und zeigt so an, welche Aussagen auf die Krankheit zutreffen. Die Götter werden auch danach befragt, welche Opferspeisen sie sich wünschen, um dann die Krankheit zu heilen.

Die Therapiemethoden

Nachdem die Krankheit erkannt ist, beginnt eine Veränderung im Verhalten aller Dorfbewohner. Es werden sämtliche zur Verfügung stehenden Verhaltensweisen und Medikamente eingesetzt, um den gesunden Zustand des Kranken wieder herzustellen. Die Krankenbehandlung wird eine gemeinsame Aktion der Dorfgemeinschaft, die Heilung ist das Ergebnis der durch die Aktion bewegten unsichtbaren Mächte. Vier Therapiemethoden bilden zusammen die Aktion; ihre Formen und Funktionen sollen im folgenden dargestellt werden.

Die Zaubersprüche

Wenn der Erkrankte an einer Echten Krankheit leidet, muss er von einem Wissenden mit einem Zauberspruch (*kunyah*) besprochen werden. Der Wissende setzt sich vor den Kranken, pustet ihn dreimal an und bespuckt ihn: damit wird die Verbindung zwischen der sichtbaren und der unsichtbaren Welt hergestellt. Dann trägt der Wissende im Flüsterton den Spruch vor: wenn ein Dritter den Spruch erlauscht, wird er die Krankheit, die der Spruch heilen soll, auf sich ziehen. Am Ende des Vortrags wird der Kranke wieder bepustet und bespuckt: die Wirksamkeit des Zaubers ist besiegelt.

In dem Zauberspruch wird metaphorisch die unsichtbare Welt beschrieben und der Prozess der Heilung so dargestellt, als sei er bereits geschehen. Leidet der Kranke an einem durch die Seelen einer Raupenart ausgelösten blutigen Durchfall, wird eine unsichtbare Höhle, an deren Wänden die Raupen knabbern, beschrieben. Die Höhle ist der Bauch des Kranken. Der Wissende beschreibt in dem Spruch dann die Handlungen seiner eigenen Seele: die Seele des Wissenden verlässt seinen Körper, verwandelt sich in einen Adler, fliegt in die Höhle hinein, zerbeißt und tötet die Raupen - die Krankheitsursache ist beseitigt, der Kranke wird wieder gesund. Derartige Zaubersprüche dienen der Wirklichkeitsveränderung, und zwar in einer gewünschten Form.

Bei anderen Zaubersprüchen werden dem Kranken Eigenschaften anderer Wesen verliehen, die ihn gegen die Krankheit resistent machen. Das geschieht z.B. bei dem Zauberspruch zur Heilung der Fiebererkrankung, die von einer roten Zeckenart übertragen wird:

Dort erhebt sie sich (die Zecke/ihre Krankheit)
Das ist der Hals des Rehs
Dort erhebt sie sich / beim Reh
Das ist das dicke Leder an seinem Hals / dort erhebt sie sich
Dort unter seinem Fleisch / dort an seinem Hals
Den Tapir / hat sie gebissen
Dort erhebt sie sich / das ist sein Fleisch
Dort erhebt sie sich / das ist der Rücken seiner Ohren
Das sind die Ohren / des Rehs / des Hirsches
Dort erhebt sie sich / beim Reh
Das ist der Hals des Rehs / dort am Reh erhebt sie sich
Das ist meine Haut / dort erhebt sie sich
Das Reh / das ist sein großes Fleisch / das ist seine Wirbelsäule
Seine Haut / nicht hat sie den Schmerz gespürt
Dort erhebt sie sich (die Zecke)
Sie trinkt meinen Saft
Dort erhebt sich / das Baumhuhn
Da hat sie sich festgesaugt / an seinem Hals

Dort erhebt sie sich
Das Pferd / der Goldhase
Dort erhebt sie sich
Der Hund / das echte Wildschwein
Dort erhebt sie sich / da hängt sie an ihnen
Ich habe das Brennen mit meinen Händen gekühlt
Ich habe den Sud meiner Zigarre daraufgepustet
Sein Duft ist verströmt
Das ist der Herr (der Zecke) / dort erhebt sie sich
Es kommt unsere Mutter (= der Mond)
Das ist ihre Herrin / dort erhebt sie sich
Dort erhebt sie sich / da hat sie sich festgesaugt
Da zieht sie / durch den Wald
Das ist ihr Nest
Dann kehrte ich zurück (und zauberte)
Dort erhebt sich (der Schmerz) / ich habe ihn abgekühlt
Versteckt in ihrem Nest / dort verwandelt sie sich / spinnt sich ein
Dort im Walde / dort erhebt sie sich
Beim trockenen Laub / dort erhebt sie sich
Die Blätter der roten Fächerpalme / die Blätter der pahok-Palme
Dort erhebt sie sich / an ihnen sitzt sie fest
An den Armen der Bäume / der bä´ch´ich-Bäume
Dort sitzt sie fest / an den Blättern, am Laub
Da kroch sie hinein und begräbt sich selbst
Ich habe den (Schmerz) abgekühlt
Ich gab ihr das Innerste meiner Zigarre
Ich habe sie alle (die Zecken) mit meiner Hand herausgezogen
Die xukibil-Taube / dort erhebt sie sich

Die in diesem Spruch genannten Tiere (Reh, Hirsch, Tapir, Pferd, Hund, Goldhase, Wildschwein, Baumhuhn, Taube) sind immun gegen die Krankheit der Zecke. Die Seele des Erkrankten wird in die genannten Tiere verwandelt und macht ihn so ebenfalls immun gegen die Krankheit : er wird wieder gesund. Gleichzeitig wird die Bisswunde mit der unsichtbaren Essenz des Tabaks (i.e. "das Innerste meiner Zigarre", "Sud des Tabaks") entgiftet und kann sich wieder schließen (RÄTSCH 2002). Nach der empirischen Erfahrung der *Lakandonen* wirkt dieser Spruch immer. Wird die Krankheit der roten Zecke nicht mit ihm behandelt, kann der Krankheitsverlauf ein tödliches Ende nehmen. Die *Lakandonen* kennen über dreißig Zaubersprüche zur Krankenheilung. Mit allen wird die unsichtbare Welt der Seelen verändert. Dadurch verändern sie die mit der sichtbaren Welt innigst verknüpfte sichtbare Wirklichkeit. Bei der Zaubersprzuchbehandlung wird auch eine soziale Interaktion angestrebt : am wirksamsten ist ein Spruch, wenn er von einer gesunden Person angewendet wird. Denn die gesunde Person ist in ihrer Struktur integriert und gibt mit ihrem guten Zustand das Vorbild des erwünschten Zustandes für den Kranken.

Heilungszeremonien

Sobald eine Person erkrankt, ganz gleich an welcher Art von Krankheit, geht der ihr am nächsten stehende Verwandte in das Götterhaus und verbrennt in seinen Götterschalen unter Gebeten Weihrauch für die Götter. Der Rauch des verbrannten Harzes hat eine Seele, die durch die Himmelsschichten zu den Göttern emporsteigt. Dort verwandelt sie sich in den allerköstlichsten Trunk. Und gerade diesen Trunk lieben die Götter besonders. Dadurch zeigen sie sich geneigt, einen Kranken mit ihrem Zauber zu heilen, sie können ihn damit gesund denken. Der Mann, der den Weihrauch verbrennt, hält ein eingerolltes Palmenblatt in den aufsteigenden Rauch und fängt ihn und etwas seiner Seele ein. Das geschwärzte Blatt trägt er anschließend zur Lagerstatt des Kranken. Die Götter können dann sehen, wohin sie ihre heilenden Zauberkräfte lenken sollen.

Bei den Gebeten zum Weihrauchverbrennen verspricht der Mann den Göttern weitere Opfer, wenn sie den Kranken heilen. Ist der Kranke wieder gesund, versammelt sich das ganze Dorf zu einer Dankzeremonie, bei der ein berauschender Ritualtrunk (*balche´*) und mit Affenfleisch oder Bohnen gefüllte Maisspeisen den Göttern dargebracht werden. Die Seelen der Opfer ziehen in den Himmel und laben die Götter, die zurückgebliebenen Hüllen werden gleichmäßig an die Dorfbewohner verteilt: es gibt einen wahren Festschmaus (RÄTSCH 1987).

Die Seelen der ungeborenen Kinder
Wenn eine Person des Dorfes krank wird und darniederliegt, kommen alle menstruationsfähigen Frauen zu Besuch und binden dem Kranken einen handgesponnenen Baumwollfaden um den Hals. Bei einer Verletzung von Arm oder Bein binden sie ihn um das Handgelenk oder den Knöchel.

Der Grund dafür: menstruationsfähige, also gebärfähige Frauen tragen die unsichtbaren Seelen ungeborener Kinder in sich. Diese Seelen können den Körper der Mutter verlassen. Sehen sie einen Krankheitsherd in einer Person, wissen sie nicht, um was es sich dabei handelt und beginnen neugierig darin zu spielen. Dadurch wird die Krankheit für den Kranken noch schmerzender, noch unerträglicher. Ist dem Kranken aber ein Baumwollfaden umgebunden, wird dieser dünne Faden von den Seelen der ungeborenen Kinder als Lederpeitsche wahrgenommen. Vor der Peitsche haben sie Angst und fliehen zurück in den Mutterleib. So lassen sie aus Angst von dem Kranken ab. Wenn es eine Frau unterläßt, dem Kranken einen Baumwollfaden umzubinden, kann sie ihm dadurch indirekt großen Schaden zufügen. Jedes pubertierende Mädchen bekommt im Laufe der Initiationszeremonie von ihrer Mutter oder einer nahen Verwandten eine Spindel aus dem Holz des Lebensbaumes und aus einer Schildpattscheibe verliehen. Gleichzeitig wird sie über die Seelenreisen ihrer ungeborenen Kinder aufgeklärt und in dem damit zusammenhängenden sozialen Verhalten unterwiesen. Mit der Spindel soll sie fortan die Fäden für die Kranken spinnen.

Materia medica
Obwohl aus dem Regenwald, in dem die *Lakandonen* zu Hause sind, viele international anerkannte, begehrte und angezeigte Heilpflanzen stammen (vgl. SCHENDEL 1968), haben die Götter den Urahnen nur sehr wenig über materielle Mittel, die eine Krankheit heilen oder einen Schmerz stillen können, verraten. So wissen die *Lakandonen* nur von den heilenden Kräften weniger Pflanzen: z.B. Magnolienblüten gegen Diarrhoe, Schachtelhalmtee als Tonikum und Aphrodisiacum, Lianensäfte gegen Mundfäule, Ingwer gegen Magenverstimmung, Tabak gegen äußere Parasiten, Rindenextrakt des Kaugummibaumes als Mittel gegen blutige Darmerkrankungen, Geflechte aus Fächerpalmenblättern gegen Hautbeulen usw. (RÄTSCH 1994). All diese Mittel werden nur selten benutzt, denn

sie heilen nicht, sie helfen nur, sie unterstützen lediglich den durch Zaubersprüche oder Zeremonien eingeleiteten Heilprozess.

Ganz anders sieht der Gebrauch westlicher Medikamente aus. Handelt es sich um eine Krankheit der Weißen, wollen die *Lakandonen* möglichst auch die Heilmittel der Weißen benutzen. Denn den Weißen wurde das Wissen der medikamentösen Therapie von ihrem Gott, *Äkyantho´*, verliehen. Folglich müssen ihre Methoden die für ihre Krankheit relevante Heilverfahren sein. So haben die *Lakandonen* schnell akzeptiert, dass sie sich bei Grippeepidemien, die früher meist tödlich endeten, Penicillin spritzen lassen. Sie haben auch den Wert von Schutzimpfungen bei Krankheiten, die sie nicht kennen und gegen die sie keinerlei körpereigene Abwehrstoffe besitzen, erkannt. Sie haben ihr medizinisches System so der derzeitigen Situation angepasst und ihre Chance vergrößert, in einem von europäischen Krankheiten verseuchten Regenwald weiterhin zu überleben.

Autor
Dr. phil. Christian Rätsch

Ethnopharmakologe und Altamerikanist. Er lebte fast drei Jahre mit den *Lakandonen-* Indianern im mexikanischen Regenwald und bereiste seither viele Orte in der äußeren und inneren Welt. In Publikationen wie z.B. "Indianische Heilkräuter", "Rituale des Heilens", "Die Steine der Schamanen" und vor allem der "Enzyklopädie der psychoaktiven Pflanzen" ist seine jahrzehntelange Forschung der Öffentlichkeit zugänglich.

Kontakt: E-Mail: ethnomedizin@web.de

Literatur
Balint & J.S. Norell (Hg.). 1975. *Fünf Minuten pro Patient: Eine Studie über die Interaktionen in der ärztlichen Allgemeinarztpraxis.* Suhrkamp, Frankfurt, M.

Boremanse, D. 1981. Una forma de clasificatión simbólica: Los encantamientos al balche´ entre los lacandones, *Jounal of Latin American Lore* 7(2): 191-214.

Hauschild, T. 1977. Zur Ideengeschichte der Ethnomedizin. in: *Ethnomedizin* 4, S. 357-68.

Kalweit, H. 1984. *Traumzeit und innerer Raum.* Bern/ München/ Wien.

Ma´ax, K´ayum / Rätsch, C. 1994. *Ein kosmos im Regenwald: Mythen und Visionen der Lakandonen-Indianer,* Diederichs (Gelbe Reihe DG 48), 2.Aufl., Köln.

O.W. Barth Ma´ax, K´ayum & C. Rätsch. 1984. *Ein Kosmos im Regenwald: Mythen und Visionen der Lakandonen-Indianer.* Diederichs, Köln.

Rätsch, C. 1983. Wenn es keinen Wandel mehr gibt, kommt das Ende der Welt. *Trickster* 11, S. 14-15.

---. 1984. Toniná - das alte Haus des Pulvermachers. *Mexicon* 6 (6).

---. 1985a. *Das Erlernen von Zaubersprüchen: Ein Beitrag zur Ethnomedizin der Lakandonen von Naha´,* EXpress Edition, Berlin.

---. 1985b. *Bilder aus der unsichtbaren Welt: Zaubersprüche und Naturbeschreibung bei den Maya und Lakandonen,* Kindler, München.

---. 1987. Alchemie im Regenwald - Dichtung, Zauberei und Heilung. *Salix* 2(2): 44-64.

---. 1988. Das Bewußtsein von der Welt: Mensch und "Umwelt" im lakandonischen Kosmos, in: Peter E. Stüben (Hg.), Die neuen "Wilden" (Ökozid 4): 166-171, *Focus,* Giessen (Reprinted in *Politische Ökologie* 24: 51-53, 1991).

---. 1992. Their Word for World is Forest: Cultural Ecology and Religion Among the Lacandone Maya Indians of Southern Mexico, in: *Jahrbuch für Ethnomedizin und Bewußtseinsforschung* 1:17-32, VWB, Berlin.

---. 1994. Ts´ak: Die Heilpflanzen der Lakandonen von naha´, in: *Jahrbuch für Ethnomedizin und Bewußtseinsforschung* 2:43-93, VWB, Berlin.

---. 2002. *Schamanenpflanze Tabak.* Nachtschatten Verlag, Solothurn.

Schendel, G. 1968. *Medicine in Mexico.* University of Texas Press. Austin, London.

Spradley, P. 1979. *The Ethnographic Interview.* Holt, Rinehart and Winston, New York.

MAGIC SPELLS AS THERAPY – ETHNO-MEDICINE OF THE LACANDON INDIANS OF THE MEXICAN RAIN FOREST*

by Christian Rätsch

The *Lacandon* Indians from the rain forest of the Mexican State of Chiapas have their own, highly complex medical system. As they do not have any medical specialists, every man is a healer. The knowledge of the human structure and the events of the invisible world form the basis for the recognition and treatment of illnesses. Both are closely related to the social interaction of the entire village community.

"The ethnologist enters a student relationship with the shaman. Through this, he transcends the classic role of the scientist, raises his scientific curiosity to a new level, and attempts to combine learning and active reflection."
KALWEIT (1984: 249)

Cultural anthropology and Ethno-Medicine

Cultural anthropology is the science of man as a cultural being. The object of research is the culture of man. This includes ethnography, i.e. the description of foreign people. The different forms of ethnography vary between colonialism and understanding. Many ethnographers who conducted research among foreign people have attempted to understand these people and to comprehend and

Fig.1: A *Lakandian* couple Chan K´in Ma´ax and his youngest wife Koh K´en´en plaiting a carrying-net from bark thread (Chan K´in Ma´ax has passed away in the meantime at the age of 110 years). In the anarchical, means partnership oriented community of the *Lakandonian* von Naha´ you won´t find specialized shamans or healers. Every man and every women own shamanistic knowledge to a certain level, f.e. magic spells (*kunyah*). The culture of the *Lakandons* is shamanistic since their techniques are open to be used by everybody. This represents a special category in ethnology, obviously, very seldom or never taken into consideration in the cognitive anthropology. (Naha´, Chiapas, Mexico; 8/1988)

* Translated by Gert Venghaus, Kat Morgenstern, Christine Granados Hughes

portray their culture from within. The ethnographer tries to adopt the point of view of the foreigner. This way, ethnography does not limit itself to being a superficial description but becomes the entry point to the foreign perspective. The ethnographer slips, so to say, into the head of the foreigner and sees the world and lifes´ realities through his eyes.

An anthropologist wrote about the theory of the ethnographic interview:
".... *ethnography means learning from people.* " (SPARDLEY 1979, pg. 3) The scientist adapts the culture he studies, he takes part in it.

Medicine is a part of every persons' cultural system. As one particular branch of ethnography, ethno-medicine does not only deal with the medical systems of foreign people, but also with the popular medicine (see HAUSCHILD 1977). In doing so, the scientist can try different approaches: He can identify the illness, the foreigner is suffering from, and observe the treatment that is applied. Alternatively, he can also surrender his own point of view and learn about the other, foreign medical system. He takes on the role of the student, and local experts of the foreign culture become his teachers. To achieve this, it is essential to accept the foreign medical system as an alternative.

Since 1979, I have conducted a research project on the ethno-medical system of the *Lacandon* Indians of Naha in the South of Mexico over several years. For this research, I have taken on the role of the pupil, the traineé. My aim was to practice *Lacandon* medicine independently. This meant accepting the foreign behaviour and being able to apply it.

During my research, I noticed that the *Lacandon* Indians occasionally fell ill suffering from diseases unknown to our Western orthodox medicine. I also experienced the effectiveness of local medicine for myself. The medical system of the *Lacandon* Indians is highly effective, maintaining health and treating illnesses within their environment. In areas where our conventional tropical medicine fails, the medicine of the *Lacandon* Indians begins to take effect.

I was particularly impressed by the way the *Lacandon* Indians handled their ill people, by the social caring, and by the interactive sympathy. While in our medical systems the consultation time of physicians is getting increasingly shorter (see BALINT & NORELL 1975) and nursing care becomes more and more anonymous, the entire *Lacandon* village community will care for a seriously sick patient.

In this article, I would like to depict the medical system of the *Lacandon* Indians in the way I have learned it, at my time being there. It is clear that some parts can only be described briefly, due to the brevity of the pamphlet. The research project was funded mainly by the German Academic Exchange (DAAD). I would like to express my thanks to this institution and its teachers.

The *Lacandon* Indians

The *Lacandon* Indians call themselves *hach winik*, "True People" , and their world the rain forest of the Mexican State Chiapas - simply *k´ax*, "Forest". Their cultural roots reach back far to the pre-Hispanic era and show direct links to the *Mayans*.

Today, some 460 *Lacandon* Indians live in three villages. Two of these small settlements deep in the rain forest fell pray to protestant-absolutist sects and were brutally proselytised. This resulted in the complete disintegration of their traditional culture. (see MA´AX & RÄTSCH 1984, pg. 16-18).

In *Naha´*, the settlement on shore of the lake with the same name, the old Gods are still alive, the traditional dress is still worn by all, and the men still have long hair.

Fig. 2: Ober 70years-old *Lakandonian* Antonio, also named Chan K´in Ma´ax, at a healing ritual in the Gods-house (*yatoch k´uh*). He sacrifices the intoxicating drink *Balche´* (a kind of 2-4% honey beer with Lonchocarpus violaceaus) und *pom*, "incense" (Pinienharz), to the Gods. These sacrifices are also classified as *yoch k´uh*, "Foods of the Gods". Through the ritual, accompanied by prayers (*t´ani k´uh*) and magic spells (*kunyah, hach k´ay*), the souls of the sacrifices are sent to the Gods. There they manifest as tasty drinks, the Gods refresh themselves with. Pleased by that, they send their healing forces to the sick and needy, whom the ritul was carried out for. (Naha´, Chiapas, Mexico; 2/1995)

Life has largely remained unchanged. The men go hunting, work the fields using slash-and-burn cultivation, and pray to the Gods. The women prepare the food (mainly flat corn bread, black beans, occasionally meat of monkeys or parrots), care for the infants, and look after the domestic animals (chicken and turkeys). There is no political hierarchy, a tribal chief is unknown. Society is anarchic and each family determines their own life, takes their own decisions. Unanimity exists on one issue only: external regulation, e.g. by the Mexican government.

Chan K´in Ma´ax, the ninety-eight year old village elder of *Naha´* always says smilingly: "*All governments lie* !" He calls Tuxtla Gutiérrez, the regional capital of Chiapas, *tusta* "bull shit" , for this was all the *Lacandon* Indians had received from there so far. From there, the logging of the forests was sanctioned, the very forest that represents the world for the *Lacandon* Indians. Recently, a dam is being constructed on the Usumacinta, the border river to Guatemala. This dam will finally destroy the forest. For the *Lacandon* Indians this will be the end of the world, and not only theirs. (see RÄTSCH 1983)

Three areas of knowledge

Besides subsistence, the *Lacandon* medicine is the most central complex of their culture. Subsistence serves to sustain life; medicine organises and forms the desired way of life. The *Lacandon* Indians describe the conditions of a man as *uts* (literally "good, ok, in order") when the consciousness is good, when he is not tortured by thoughts, sorrows or anxiety, when his soul rests in his heart, and when he does not suffer any pain.

When this desired state is disturbed by illnesses, injuries, witchcraft or events such as shock or fright, the person is *ma´uts*, ("not good, not ok, not in order"), in other words: the person is ill. A variety of methods exist, however, to restore the good, healthy state. The medical system of the Lacandon Indians is made up of three fields of knowledge:

- the knowledge of the structure of man and the related states (ethno-anatomy)
- the knowledge of those factors that can change states and create illness (ethiology and nosology)
- the knowledge of those factors that can change states and restore or maintain health (therapy and prevention)

Among the *Lacandon* Indians, there are no medical specialists, no medical professionals, no shamans, medicine men, magicians or priests. Each *Lacandon* Indian possesses medical knowledge, knows magic spells, can conduct healing ceremonies, prepares healing teas and, recently, can give injections.

The three fields of knowledge of *Lacandon* medicine are available to each one in the community. However, it is possible for the actual level of knowledge to vary. Although this is not always the rule, many older people know more spells to heal the sick than younger ones.

Ethno-anatomy – The structure of man

In ancient times, *Hachakyum*, Our True Lord, formed men from clay. He painted them brightly and paced grains of corn as teeth in the mouth. He, God, blew upon the creatures on the earth and thought them to life. Through this Godly magic, the complex creature developed from clay, paint and maize into the being which the *Lacandon* Indians call Man.

To the knowledge of the *Lacandon* Indians, the man consists of an own fleshy body, a soul that resides in the heart, the four spirits that throb in the pulse and in the ankles, the consciousness, the thinking, and the animal spirit.

The body consists of bones, flesh, skin, hair and horn. Inside, all organs are at work. They are constantly connected with the heart and the gallbladder. Blood is collected in the heart and then pumped out into the body. If the heart is weak or the bile is poisoned (e.g. by a snake bite), the blood "sinks", it "disappears". Then, the skin turns yellow, and muscles grow weak.

The soul of man resides in the heart. The soul is a non-material duplicate that leaves the body at night and mainly acts in the invisible world where almost everything is turned into a mirror image. Man perceives the experiences of the soul

as dreams. However, the soul can also leave the body in times of illness and appear visibly to other people. When man dies, his soul descends into the Underworld.
The blood throbs at the ankles and on the pulse. You find four non-material, invisible duplicates of man there. They leave his body in the moment of death and spook around at night. Inhabitants of the Underworld who are after someone´s blood to enslave his soul, continuously try to elicit these spirits from people who, as a result, will die.

Consciousness resides in the head, exactly where the brain is located. Consciousness is the focal point of all feelings and all bodily functions. Each feeling is being expressed as a particular state of consciousness. Consciousness can be evicted by force, e.g. fright, resulting in the death of the affected.
Thinking also resides in the brain. Thinking is the only part of man that is not present at the time of birth. Thinking develops through the process of socialisation and, at the age of puberty, becoming adolescents, is received in form of pumpkin seeds during their initiation. If someone thinks, he acts adequately according to *Lacandon* culture. Simultaneously, thinking also produces sorrow and grief. Both lead to undesired states of illness.
In addition, man is tightly hooked to an animal of the forest by fate. These animal spirits, such as a Woolly Spider Monkey, a boar, or a deer can be seen in dreams. If the animal spirit shows any signs of illness, the person hooked to the spirit will develop the symptoms of this disease when he awakes.
Any disintegration in the structure of man inevitably results in illness. It is, therefore, essential to recognize the illness and the related disintegration. Suitable therapeutic measures can be applied to reintegrate the human structure he recovers and regains his health.

The illnesses
There are three classifications of illnesses that were created and brought to life by three creator Gods:

Hachakyum, Our True Father, created the real diseases of the forest, because one of the forefathers of the *Lacandon* Indians killed the Godly messenger *Akinchob* in the heat of the moment. The real diseases are:
- Winds that enter the body and disturb its functions;
- Attributes of specific animals that manifest themselves inside the human body;
- The invisible souls of some reptiles and caterpillars that eat away the soul of the person;
- The essences of poisonous animals (snakes, tics, caterpillars, wasps);
- Injuries (cuts, fractures) that are regarded as ordered by God;
- Witchcraft.

Mensabak, the maker of powder (see RÄTSCH 1984) created the diseases of *Kah*, the diseases of those who live together closely:

- Parasites (bugs, lice, intestinal worms);
- Invisible disease particles that pass from one person to another.

In ancient times, *Akyantho* the God of the Non-Indians, the God of the Whites, formed diseases for all his creatures from clay, in order to fight an unwanted, massive population growth. These diseases are usually invisible. They are all male, approximately 45 inches tall, have glowing eyes and carry bow and arrows. With their poisoned arrows, they will cause illness to whomever they encounter. All epidemics (all kinds of colds, influenza, children s diseases, amoebic dysentery, cholera, yellow fever, etc.) but also malaria and syphilis belong to the diseases of *Akyantho*.

However, these creator Gods also created healing methods for their creatures. *Hachakyum* gave the Lacandon Indians the knowledge of the magic spells to heal real diseases. Mensabak taught his creatures the use of medical plants. Akyantho presented the whites with the ability to develop chemical remedies to cure diseases. The therapy depends on the kind of disease. The real diseases can only be cured by magic spells. The diseases of *Kah* and those of the whites are being treated with their appropriate remedies. However, the true healers are the Gods themselves, who will be called upon with the respective ceremonies. Regarding the remedies of the whites, the old Chan´K in says: "*They cure, but only the Gods can heal*".

When a person has become sick, an immediate attempt to diagnose the illness must be made to ensure that the disease is being treated appropriately. The diagnosis is found with the help of:

- Talks with the patient;

- Interpretations of dreams;

- Divination and omen interpretation

The sick person is carefully searched for any externally visible symptoms, thoroughly asked about any experiences or events right before the illness appeared and encouraged to talk about the state of his consciousness, his thoughts, his flesh and his blood. Particular importance is given to dreams since they can reveal symptoms that could be the key to diagnosing the real reason for the disease. Also, the contents of the dreams of all other members of the village community are being consulted. Since the diseases originate from the invisible world, the very same invisible world experienced in dreams can give clues for the reason of the illness.

For the interpretation of dreams, the men meet in the God house and discuss their own dreams and the ones of their wives and children every morning. All that was seen by night is being interpreted to derive various concepts of action for the day. If, for example, one sees a burning cigar in a dream, the person is endagered to be bitten by a snake when awake. In this case, the dreamer will not leave the house and pray to the Gods instead.

The *Lacandon* Indians possess a variety of divination methods which they can apply to consult the Gods. In a song they ask the Gods for the origin, the spreading and the effect of the disease as well as for the appropriate treatment. A rolled up palm leaf between the hands moves during passages of the song, thus indicating which statement relates to the diseases. The Gods are also being asked which sacrificial foods they desire to heal the diseases.

Therapy methods

Once the disease has been recognized, the behaviour of the villagers starts to change. All available behaviour patterns and medicines are employed to re-establish the health condition of the patient. The treatment becomes a collective process; the cure is the result of invisible forces that have been set in motion by this process. Four therapy methods collectively constitute this procedure; the following is a presentation of their structures and functions:

Magic Spells

If the diseased person suffers a real disease a magic spell (*kunyah*) must be cast upon him. The wise person sits down in front of the patient, blows at him three times and spits at him: this establishes the connection between the visible and the invisible world. The wise person whispers the spell. After the recital the patient is once again blown and spit at. The efficacy of the spell is sealed. The spell metaphorically describes the invisible world and portrays the healing process as if it had already taken place.

If the patient suffers from bloody diarrhoea caused by the soul of a caterpillar species, the description depicts an invisible cave, the walls of which are being gnawed at by the caterpillars. Next the wise persons´ spell describes the actions of his own soul: His soul leaves his body and transforms into an eagle, it flies into the cave and catches and kills the caterpillars. The cause of the illness is eliminated and the patient recovers. These kinds of spells are intended to change reality according to a specific ally desired outcome. Other spells endow the patient with the powers of other beings in order to make him resistant to the disease. This is the case for example with a spell used against a feverish condition, transmitted by a red tick species:

There it rises (the tick/ it disease)
There is the neck of the deer
There it rises / in the deer
There is the thick leather of its neck / there it rises
There, beneath its flesh/ there, in its neck
The Tapir/ it has bitten him
There it rises / that is his flesh
There it rises/ that is the back of his ears
There are the ears/ of the deer/ of the stag
There it rises/ in the deer
That is the neck of the deer/ there it rises in the deer
That is my skin/ there it rises
The deer/ that is his big flesh/ that is his spine
His skin/ it did not feel the pain
There it rises (the tick)
It drinks my juice
There it rises / the forest turkey
There it has sucked itself tight / in his neck

There it rises
The horse / the gold rabbit
There it rises
The dog / the wild pig
There it rises/ there it clings to them
I have cooled the burning of my hands
I have blown the suds of my cigar at it
Its aroma has spread
He is the master (of the tick)/ there it rises
Our mother is coming (the moon)
She is its matron/ there it rises
There it rises/ there it has sucked itself tight
There it roams through the forest
There is its nest
Then I returned (to cast the spell)
There it rises (the pain) / I have cooled it down
Hidden in its nest / there it transformed / spun a tangled web
There in the forest / there it rises
Among the dry leaves of the red fan palm, the leaves of the Pahok palm
There it rises/ there it clings to them
On the arms of the trees/ of the bae ck ich trees
There it clings to them / on the leaves / in the foliage
There it crawled and dug itself in
I have cooled off my pain
I gave it the essence of my cigar
I have pulled them all off (the ticks) with my hand
The Xukibil-pigeon / there it rises

The animals referred to in this spell (deer, stag, tapir, horse, dog, gold rabbit, wild pig, turkey, pigeon) are immune against the disease transmitted by the tick. The soul of the patient is transformed into the cited animals, which bestows immunity to him also: he returns to good health.

At the same time the bite is purified with the invisible essence of the cigar , so it can close up and heal (RÄTSCH 2002)l. According to the empirical experiences of the *Lakandons* this spell is always effective. If the disease of the red tick is not treated, it can result in death. The *Lakandons* know more than 30 spells used for healing, all of which change the invisible world of the soul. Thus, a change is also affected in the visible world, which is closely linked to the invisible world. The spell treatment also involves a social interaction. The spell is most effective when conducted by a healthy person. The healthy person is structurally integrated and his good condition serves as a good example or pattern for the condition desired for the patient.

Healing ceremonies

As soon as a person gets sick, no matter what disease it is, the person closest to the patient goes to the God-house, burns incense for the Gods and prays. The smoke released by the burnt resin has a soul, which rises through the heavenly layers to the Gods. There it transforms into the most delicate nectar. It is this nectar that the Gods love the most. Thus they are inclined to help the patient with their magic.

They use their thoughts to make him well. The man burning the fank incense is holding a rolled palm-leaf into the ascending smoke to catch it and parts of its soul. Then he takes the blackened leaf to the sick person, so the Gods might see, where to bring their healing powers. While burning incense, the person offers more gifts to the gods, if they will heal the sick person. After the recovery of a sick person, the whole village is gathering to hold a thanksgiving ceremony, offering an intoxicating ritual drink ("*balche*") and corn dishes filled with ape meat or beans to the gods. The spirits of these offerings move back to heaven and nourish the gods, while the remains are equally divided among the villagers, they are celebrating a big feast (RÄTSCH 1987).

The souls of the unborn children

When one of the villagers turns sick and has to stay in bed, all menstrual women come for a visit and bind a hand-spun cotton thread around the patient's neck. Is an arm or leg injured, the thread is bound around the wrist or ankle. The reason for this is that all menstrual women can give birth and are carrying the invisible souls of unborn children. These souls can leave the mother's body. If they detect a disease in a person, they have no idea what to do and start playing with it. That brings even more pain and misery to the sick patient. But if the patient has been given a cotton thread, that would turn into a leather wip.
Since the souls are afraid of the wip, they go back to their mother's womb. Out of fear, they leave the sick person alone. If a women fails to bring the cotton thread, she eventually brings great harm to the sick person.
In the process of her initiation ceremony, each girl in puberty receives a spindle by her mother or a close relative. The spindle is made of wood of the arbor vitae, the tree of life, or of a tortoise shell. At the same time she is informed about the journeys of the souls of her unborn children, and instructed on all correlated aspects of her social behaviour. From that day on she will have to spin the threads for the sick.

Materia medica

Although many internationally accepted, demanded and indicated medical plants originate from the rainforest (see SCHENDEL 1968), where the *Lacandonians* live, the gods of the ancestors have told them little about the material use to cure a disease or to ease the pain. The Lakandonians only know about the healing effect of a few plants. Like: magnolia flowers against diarrhoea, horse-tail or shavegrass infusion as a tonic and aphrodisiac, the juice of the liana against stomatitis, ginger against gastritis, tobaccco against external parasites, root-extract of the rubber-tree as cure against colitis, lichen of the sabal palmetto leaves against skin affections etc. (RÄTSCH 1994)
All these remedies are rarely used, since they cannot heal, they can only help by supporting the actual healing process, induced by magic words or ceremonies. The use of Western medication, however, is a different story. If someone comes down with a disease of the white man, the *Lakadonians* prefer to use a White man's remedy. For the White man's knowledge about medication and therapy was given to them by their god *Äkyantho* and so their methods have to be the suitable cures to heal those diseases. The *Lakandon* Indians have quickly accepted a shot of penicillin at the merge of an influenza epidemic, whereas in former times most of

those epidemias ended mortally. They have accepted the importance of vaccinations against diseases they have no natural immunization for. They have adapted their medical system to the current situation, to improve their chance to survive in a rainforest polluted with European diseases.

Author
DR. PHIL. CHRISTIAN RÄTSCH
Ethnopharmacologist and Cultural Anthropologist. He lived with the *Lakandon* Indians for almost three years in the mexican rain forest and visited a lot of places in the inner and outer world ever since. In publications like "Indian healing plants", "Ritual healings", "The stones of the shamans" and especially the "Encyclopedia of psychoactive plants" his decades of research is accessible to the public.
Contact: E-Mail: ethnomedizin@web.de

Literatur
BALINT & J.S. NORELL (Hg.). 1975. *Fünf Minuten pro Patient: Eine Studie über die Interaktionen in der ärztlichen Allgemeinarztpraxis.* Suhrkamp, Frankfurt, M.
BOREMANSE, D. 1981. Una forma de clasificatión simbólica: Los encantamientos al balche´ entre los lacandones, *Jounal of Latin American Lore* 7(2): 191-214.
HAUSCHILD, T. 1977. Zur Ideengeschichte der Ethnomedizin. in: *Ethnomedizin* 4, S. 357-68.
KALWEIT, H. 1984. *Traumzeit und innerer Raum.* Bern/ München/ Wien.
MA´AX, K´AYUM / RÄTSCH, C. 1994. *Ein kosmos im Regenwald: Mythen und Visionen der Lakandonen-Indianer,* Diederichs (Gelbe Reihe DG 48), 2.Aufl., Köln.
O.W. BARTH MA´AX, K´AYUM & C. RÄTSCH. 1984. *Ein Kosmos im Regenwald: Mythen und Visionen der Lakandonen-Indianer.* Diederichs, Köln.
RÄTSCH, C. 1983. Wenn es keinen Wandel mehr gibt, kommt das Ende der Welt. *Trickster* 11, S. 14-15.
---. 1984. Toniná - das alte Haus des Pulvermachers. *Mexicon* 6 (6).
---. 1985a. *Das Erlernen von Zaubersprüchen: Ein Beitrag zur Ethnomedizin der Lakandonen von Naha´,* EXpress Edition, Berlin.
---. 1985b. *Bilder aus der unsichtbaren Welt: Zaubersprüche und Naturbeschreibung bei den Maya und Lakandonen,* Kindler, München.
---. 1987. Alchemie im Regenwald - Dichtung, Zauberei und Heilung. *Salix* 2(2): 44-64.
---. 1988. Das Bewußtsein von der Welt: Mensch und "Umwelt" im lakandonischen Kosmos, in: Peter E. Stüben (Hg.), Die neuen "Wilden" (*Ökozid* 4): 166-171, *Focus,* Giessen (Reprinted in *Politische Ökologie* 24: 51-53, 1991).
---. 1992. Their Word for World is Forest: Cultural Ecology and Religion Among the Lacandone Maya Indians of Southern Mexico, in: *Jahrbuch für Ethnomedizin und Bewußtseinsforschung* 1:17-32, VWB, Berlin.
---. 1994. Ts´ak: Die Heilpflanzen der Lakandonen von naha´, in: *Jahrbuch für Ethnomedizin und Bewußtseinsforschung* 2:43-93, VWB, Berlin.
---. 2002. *Schamanenpflanze Tabak.* Nachtschatten Verlag, Solothurn.
SCHENDEL, G. 1968. *Medicine in Mexico.* University of Texas Press. Austin, London.
SPRADLEY, P. 1979. *The Ethnographic Interview.* Holt, Rinehart and Winston, New York.

DIE HEILTRADITION DER HUITOTOS IN KOLUMBIEN*

von Fabio Alberto Ramirez

Einleitung

Der kolumbianische Südosten entlang des Flusses Caquetá ist die Heimat der *Huitotos*. Östlich von der Anden liegt ihr Habitat in einer Urwaldflussebene unweit der peruanischen Grenze. Obwohl dieses indianische Volk noch im Einzugsgebiet des Amazonas lebt, bildet es eine eigenständige ethnische Gruppe mit einer speziellen Ausrichtung der Heiltradition: der *Yagé*-Schamanismus. Er besitzt bislang keinen besonderen Stellenrang im Amazonas, weckt aber durch seine Wissensfülle, Komplexität und Spiritualität Interesse und regt zu neuen Formen der Anwendung an. Die Mythologie besagt, dass *Yagé* von den ersten Stufen des Kosmos komme, die Kenntnisse hierüber seien heilig. Einbezogen in dieses Wissen wird durch eine langjährige Ausbildung der Medizinmann (‚*Curandero*' oder ‚*Sanador*'), der in der Gruppe eine tragende Rolle einnimmt.

Die *Huitotos*

Die *Huitotos* leben in mehren Clans verstreut über ein Gebiet, das so groß ist wie das Bundesland Bayern. Gründe dieser Verstreuung liegen in den Auswirkungen des Kolonialismus wie auch endogener Sozialstrukturen.
In einer typischen Siedlung nimmt die ‚*Maloca*' eine zentrale Stellung ein. Sie ist eine Art Versammlungshaus, das vielseitig genutzt wird. Traditionelle Feste wie

---

* Überarbeitung von Guido Terlinden

auch rituelle Treffen finden hier statt. ‚*Maloca*' ist ein Begriff der Weißen. Das Wort der Indios dafür ist ‚*Ayoco*' und es bedeutet großes Haus. Es stellt die Mutter beim Gebären dar. Die Eingangstür ist die Scheide, die vier Säulen sind die unteren und die oberen Glieder. Andere Strukturen stellen die Adern dar.

Die *Maloca* ist der Ort, wo sich Medizinmänner, die Weisen und andere Männer mit entscheidenden Positionen treffen. Mit ‚*Mambeodero*' bekommt die *Maloca* noch einen speziellen Namen, der dann zutrifft, wenn ‚*Mambeo*' praktiziert wird. Es handelt sich um ein zentrales Ritual, bei dem Männer unter Einfluss von Tabak und Koka, den ganzen Tag reden, diskutieren, die Stammesgeschichte erzählen oder ihre Ahnen anrufen (*Duca*).

Dieses Ritual darf man sich aber nicht als eine Unterhaltung im üblichen Sinne vorstellen, sondern es ist eine Methode, transzendente Sphären zu erreichen. In diesem Zustand nimmt der ‚sitzende Mann', der spricht und der das `Blatt der Weisheit` einnimmt, das Koka-Blatt, die Stelle des Wissenden ein. Er steht im Mittelpunkt der Natur, ist Beauftragter des Schöpfers und habe Gewalt über seine Umwelt. Der Ort in der *Maloca*, wo der *Mambeo* stattfindet, ist heilig und repräsentiert den Mutterleib, wo das Kind aufwächst.

Heilige Pflanzen - Heilpflanzen der *Huitotos*

Der Tabak und das Koka sind die Heilpflanzen der *Huitotos* aus Araracura, einer Region um die gleichnamige Stadt am Fluss Caquetá. Sie stehen für das weibliche (Tabak) und das männliche (Koka) Prinzip. Diese heiligen Pflanzen haben in der Mythologie wie auch im täglichen Leben ihren festen Platz.

Die Tabakpflanze ist den Indianern ein Sinnbild für die Familienstruktur. An ihr verdeutlichen sich Wachstum, Gesundheit und Krankheit; so steht ein gebrochener Zweig für ein Kind, das erkrankt ist oder stirbt.

Die Tabakpflanze (*Nicotiana tabacum*) gehört zur Familie der Nachtschattengewächse. Sie wird bei den *Huitotos* zu *Ambil*, einem Tabaksirup, verarbeitet. Man lässt einen Tee mit Tabaksblättern köcheln bis er die Konsistenz von Sirup hat und fügt alkalisches Salz hinzu, das man aus der Asche einiger Pflanzen gewinnt. Das dicke *Ambil* wird mit dem Finger oder einem Stock auf das Zahnfleisch gestrichen; vermengt mit Speichel wird es allmählich heruntergeschluckt.

Als Koka bezeichnet man die getrockneten Blätter des zu den Storchenschnabelgewächsen gehörenden Kokastrauches (*Erythroxilon coca*). Beim Kauen der Blätter wird Kokain freigesetzt, das einen Rauschzustand bewirkt. Das Kokablatt gehört aber auch zur alltäglichen Ernährung. Es deckt einen Großteil des täglichen Kalziumbedarfs ab, enthält außerdem die Vitamine A und C, Mineralstoffe wie Kalium, Zink, Magnesium, Mangan, Eisen u. a. Der Gebrauch von Koka ist seit 1000 Jahren bekannt.

Bei rituellen Zeremonien wie dem *Mambeo* wird das *Mambe* als instrumentelles Mittel verwendet. Es handelt sich hierbei um eine Mischung von *Ambil* und gerösteten Kokablättern bzw. grünem Kokapulver, die eine dicke Paste ergibt. Zusätzlich vermengte man es noch mit der Asche der Yarumo-Palme.

Yagé ist eine weitere sakrale Heilpflanze, die der Schamanismus-Richtung auch den Namen gibt. Es handelt sich hierbei um eine Liane namens *Banisteriopsis caapi*, deren Rinde äußerst psychoaktive Substanzen enthält (*Telepathin* und das Alkaloid *Harmin*). Neben starken Wahrnehmungsveränderungen und Halluzinationen soll die Einnahme des Lianengebräus es möglich machen, in telepathischen Kontakt mit Mitmenschen, Geistern und Göttern zu treten.

Alle drei Pflanzen weisen Alkaloide auf, was biochemisch von Bedeutung ist, da diese Substanzen auf die Neurotransmitter bzw. die Erregungsleitung im Nervensystem im Menschen wirken.

Spirituelle Entwicklung der *Huitotos*

Die Erziehung der Kinder bei den *Huitotos* beginnt im fünften Lebensjahr. Ab diesem Alter gibt man dem Nachwuchs kleine Mengen *Ambil* (Tabaksirup).

Den Kindern wird beigebracht, wie sie mit ihrer Umwelt umgehen müssen. Sie lernen Flüsse, Blumen, Pflanzen und Tiere mit Respekt zu begegnen. Die enge Verbundenheit und darüber hinaus die Abhängigkeit von Mensch und Natur soll ihnen über mythologische Erzählungen nahe gelegt werden. Diese wurden ihnen vor allem nachts erzählt, um die Lehren vom Unbewussten, Traum und Imagination der Kinder prägen zu lassen, bevor sie bei Tageslicht reell werden. Ab dem zehnten Lebensjahr werden sie in das Ritual des *Mambeo* und des *Duca* (Vorfahrenanrufung) eingeführt. Dabei wird ihnen Mambe verabreicht, das sie möglichst lange im Mund behalten sollen.

Duca, so heißt es, gebe den Wörtern Kraft. Es sei eine Bibliothek, es vereinige die Lehren der Vorfahren mit dem Gegenwärtigen.

Ambil sei das Wort, Koka die Zunge. *Mambeo* – oder *Duca* – ist dem Kind bereits vertraut, da es ab dem fünften Lebensjahr während des Rituals anwesend sein darf.

Die *Huitotos* meinen, dass sich die Eltern, um ein Kind zu bekommen, schon fünfzehn Jahre davor vorbereiten müssen. Sie müssen lernen, *Mambeo* zu machen.

Mit dem Kind offenbart sich, wieviel der Vater in Wirklichkeit gelernt hat. Das Kind weint und da es nicht sprechen kann, muss der Vater sich über die möglichen Ursachen des Unwohlseins Gedanken machen und entsprechen reagieren. Wenn ein Kind eine Frage stellt, dann muss sich der Vater 'fest mit den Zehen in der Erde verankern', um eine plausible Antwort zu haben.

In der Mythologie des *Enokaye*-Clans, einer von vielen Clans bei den *Huitotos*, ist die Rede von der Existenz dreier Welten. Die erste Welt ist die der Schöpfung, die Welt des Ursprungs. Die Kenntnis über diese Welt ist heilig und es braucht sechs Jahre, um sie zu verstehen. Die zweite Welt ist die, zu der wir hinreisen, wenn wir schlafen oder auch die, in der wir verweilen nach unserem Tode. Der Tod als Leere oder Nichts existiert sozusagen in dieser Anschauung nicht. Stirbt ein Mensch, so leben seine Lehren in den Verbliebenen weiter und durch das *Ambil* und das Koka ist es sogar möglich, in Kontakt zu treten. Der Verstorbene mag vielleicht erscheinen und gegenwärtige Geschehnisse wahrsagen.

Die dritte Welt ähnelt der zweiten. Es ist die Welt, in der wir leben. Allerdings ist die zweite Welt ruhiger und heller. Dort gibt es keinen Kummer und keine Sorgen. Es ist auch die Welt, in die sich der *Curandero* begibt, um sich zu bestimmten Behandlungen inspirieren zu lassen. Er gewinnt sozusagen seine therapeutischen Kenntnisse aus dieser Welt.

Die zweite Welt, die Totenwelt, ist die Ruhe für den Körper, die dritte Welt, in der wir leben, die Vernunft. Zwischen der dritten und der zweiten Welt gibt es eine Gasse, in der sich Dunkles und Böses ansammelt. Zauberer im Indianervolk besuchen diesen Raum, von hier wirken sie. Das unterscheidet einen Zauberer grundsätzlich von dem *Curandero*, da er nur mit der 'hellen' Seite arbeitet.

In der Mythologie wird *Araracura* als Mittelpunkt der Welt und die *Huitotos* als Menschen des Zentrums angesehen. Die Stadt ist der Ursprung der Welt, in der es

am Anfang zwei Menschen gab: den Weißen und den Dunkelfarbigen. Der Weiße wanderte in den Norden aus und bildete die weiße Rasse, die indianischen Rassen stammen von dem Dunkelfarbigen ab.
Ihm schenkte der Schöpfer den Tabak. Die Indianer, die nach Nordamerika ausgewandert sind, hatten die Gabe, den Tabak zu rauchen und den aufsteigenden Rauch für ihre 'Wissenschaften' wie Astronomie und Kalendariographie zu nutzen. Die Indianer von *Araracura* bekamen vom Schöpfer den Auftrag, das Land zu beschützen.

Der *Curandero*

Dem *Curandero* wird in seiner Ausbildung beigebracht, dass das Böse und das Gute als solches nicht existieren. Es gibt Licht und Schatten, Sonne und Mond. Die rechte Seite der Menschen leuchtet, die linke Seite ist dunkel. Nahe am rechten Ohr sitzt ‚*Joria*' und gibt Rat über das, was zu tun ist. Nahe am linken Ohr ist ‚*Jana*', Wesen des Schattens, das den Menschen zu verwirren versucht. *Jana* symbolisiert den Tod, der näher am Menschen ist als das Leben.
Die menschenkundliche Betrachtung stellt einen weiteren Teil der Ausbildung dar. Wesentlich für die Gesundheit des Menschen ist das In-Balance-sein und Sich-in-der-Mitte befinden zwischen den Extremen. In der Mitte zu sein heißt, wie am innersten Punkt einer Uhr zu stehen, bewegungslos und doch am Ursprung der Bewegung. Der Mittelpunkt des Menschen ist der Nabel, eine besondere Kraftquelle. Das "Ich" des Menschen ist laut dem *Curandero* wie eine Flasche, es leuchtet im Zentrum.
Der *Curandero* sieht im Patienten den Mikrokosmos. Sein wichtigstes Heilwerkzeug ist der *Logos*. Er stellt fest, wie die Krankheit entstanden ist: war der Grund ein Blitz oder ein Regen, war es Geisterwanderung oder Feuer? Anschließend versucht er eine Vertrauensbasis zum Patienten herzustellen, um dem Heilungsprozess seinen Lauf zu lassen.

"*Deine Krankheit entstand durch Feuer, aber du selber bist Feuer geworden. Dein Feuer ist freundlich, dein Feuer beschützt dich. Dein Feuer kann das schädliche Feuer ausgleichen*".

Es werden im Menschen sechs Sinne erkannt, die als sechs Personen dargestellt werden:
- Der Gehörsinn, der uns das Hören verleiht. Erlernt werden muss das genaue Hinhören, das Kennen der Geräusche des Urwalds
- Das Herz
- Das Gehirn
- Die Augen, die uns sehen lassen – 'richtiges Sehen' geht noch tiefer.
- Der Mund, der mit den Augen und dem Herzen verbunden ist, alles fließt durch den Mund herein – mit dem was herausgeht, ist Vorsicht geboten. Wörter und Gebete verlassen den Mund. Dadurch verleihen sie den Medikamenten und Pflanzen eine besondere Beziehung zum Mund bzw. dem verbalen Element.
- Der Geruchssinn ist die letzte Person.

Es gibt spirituelle Heilungssprüche oder Gebete, die man gezielt anwendet, allgemeine Gebete sind nicht üblich. So gibt es Gebete, um einen Schlangenbiss zu heilen und Glück beim Fischen zu haben. Auch *Yagé* und *Mambe* nimmt man mit einem Gebet ein. Es ist unmöglich für einen *Huitoto*, *Yagé* zu trinken, ohne zu wissen, mit welchem Gebet, Beschwörung oder Gesang es eingenommen werden muss.

Der *Curandero* lernt auch etwas über allgemeine Maßnahmen zur Kräftigung der Lebhaftigkeit. Das Wasser ist hierbei ein wichtiges Element. So ist es gesundheitsförderlich, sich morgens im Fluss, bevor der weiße Schmetterling das Wasser drei Mal berührt und bevor die Krabbe ihren Arm ausstreckt, zu baden. Man solle sich so ins Wasser werfen, dass der Körper kräftig auf die Wasseroberfläche aufschlägt. Mit Luft und Nahrung müsse man vorsichtig sein.

Bevor der *Curandero* mit seinen heilenden Behandlungen anfangen kann, muss er sich bestimmten Diäten unterwerfen. Für eine gewisse Zeit muss er den Kontakt mit Frauen vermeiden. Der Geist '*Horia*' am Ohr der *Curanderos* ist warm und weiblich. Nähert sich ihm eine Frau, könnte ihre Wärme '*Horia*' an sich ziehen.

Jede Krankheit ist Ausdruck von Unglück. Diese Tatsache muss von jedem Patienten erkannt werden und ihn anregen, sich mit den inneren Prozessen auseinanderzusetzen. Unterbleibt dies, hat es nachteilige Auswirkungen für den Heilungsprozess. Der Therapeut stößt häufig auf Barrieren, die nicht nur von den Patienten ausgehen, sondern auch gesellschaftlicher Art sind.

Ganzheitliche Therapien, wie die *Unicista*-Homöopathie verlangen häufig große Bereitschaft seitens der Patienten wie auch des Arztes. Die ärztliche Begleitung während des Heilungsprozesses ist wesentlich für den Erfolg der Therapie.

Anwendung in der modernen Therapie

Man versucht zusammen Geist, Körper und Seele in Einklang zu bringen und die Wurzeln der Erkrankung zu erkennen. Chronischen Erkrankungen liegen zum Beispiel oft unverarbeitete innere Konflikte zu Grunde. Diese und andere krankmachenden Prozesse gilt es deutlich anzuschauen.

In Kolumbien war es möglich, Gruppenbehandlungen durchzuführen, bei denen traditionell mit *Mambeo* oder *Duca* – also mit *Mambe* (Koka-*Ambil*-Gemisch) gearbeitet wurde. Allerdings untersagt ein internationales Gesetz die Behandlung mit der Kokapflanze, also auch die Behandlung mit dem potenten *Mambe*. Dabei sei es in der traditionellen Anwendung noch nie zu Suchterkrankungen bei Indianern gekommen. Man habe sogar Drogenabhängige mit *Mambe* therapiert.

Dennoch eröffnet das ‚legale' *Ambil* große Behandlungsmöglichkeiten für den modernen Therapeuten. Dabei werden kleine Mengen in den Mund verabreicht und nicht geschluckt, sondern im Mund behalten. Dann wird der Patient dazu angeregt, über seine Sorgen und Ängste zu reden.

Ambil besitzt keine spezifisch pharmakologische Wirkung, dennoch ist es sehr wirksam und heilend, indem es das innere Orakel zum Ausdruck kommen lässt. Das *Ambil* öffnet das Bewusstsein, das für eine Neuordnung sozialer und energetischer Aspekte notwendig ist.

Die Behandlung mit *Ambil* wird oft ergänzt mit traditionellen oder alternativen medizinischen Maßnahmen. Da der Tabak nur einmalig eingesetzt wird, sind andere Ansätze kurz- und langfristig gefragt. Letztendlich sind für eine erfolgreiche Behandlung das direkte Erleben und Verarbeiten der inneren Prozesse entscheidend.

Autor
DR. MED. FABIO ALBERTO RAMINEZ
Arzt in eigener Klinik nahe Bogota, Kolumbien. Er verbindet die moderne Medizin mit Ritualen des amazonischen *Yagé*-Schamanismus. Er ist Schüler der bekannten Schamanen Isayas Mavisoy des Inka-Volkes. Durch ihn wurde er zum Ritual-Leiter ausgebildet. Nach dem ethnopharmakologischen Studium in sakralen Zeremonien bei *Huitotos* Meistern begann er vor 8 Jahren die Integration von archaischen Ritualen und schulmedizinischen Therapieformen.
Kontakt: E-Mail: framirez@cable.net.co

Weiterführende Empfehlungen, Nachschlagewerke
JÜRGEN FALBE, MANFRED REGNITZ (Hrsg.). 1999. *Römpp Lexikon Chemie*, Bände 1-6, 10. Auflage, Georg Thieme Verlag

http://galeon.hispavista.com/culturasamerica/Huitotos.htm
http://www.sacharuna.com/Shamanism.html
http://www.reichertorga.de/konferenz00/schamanen/schaman.html
http://www.warwick.ac.uk/society/PILAS/1999/ForTEMP
http://www.biopark.org/peru/mapacho.html
http://www.mamacoca.org/feb2002/art_constantino_posibles_impactos_fusarium_fr.html

HEALING TRADITION OF THE HUITOTOS IN COLUMBIA*

by Fabio Alberto Ramirez

Introduction

The home of the *Huitotos* is found in the south- east of Columbia along the river Caquetá. Their Habitat is situated east of the Andes in a river valley of the jungle close to the Peruanian border. Even though this indigenious folk is living in the area of the Amazonas, they represent an independant ethnic group with a specific type in their healing tradition:

the *yagé* shamanism. It does not have a special ranking in the Amazonas area, yet arises interest through its wide knowledge, complexity and spirituality and initiates new structures of treatments. The myth says *yagé* comes from the first step of the cosmos and knowledge about it is sacred.vThe medicine man ("*Curandero*" or " *Sanador*") is introduced to this knowledge through years of education and plays an important role in his society.

The *Huitotos*

The *Huitotos* live in clans spread over an area as big as the State Bavaria in Germany. Reasons for this separation can be found in colonization and endogenian social structures. In a typical village the "*Maloca*" plays a central role. This is a type of meeting house used in various forms. Traditional festivals as well as ritual meetings take place in it. "*Maloca*" is the white people's word . The Indian

---

* Revised by Guido Terlinden. Translated by Joy C. Green

word for it is "*Ayoco*" and means "big house". It represents the mother giving birth. The entrance represents the vagina, the four pillars are the upper and lower extremities. Other structures are meant to be the veins.
The *Maloca* is the place where medicine men, the wise and men in important positions meet. A *Maloca* receives a special name - *Mambeodero* - when people meet to pratice *Mambeo*. This is a important ritual where men, under the influence of tobacco and *koka* (coke), talk the whole day, discuss, memorize their ancestors' traditional stories and call upon the ancestors (*Duca*).

We must not mistake this ritual as a conversation in the regular meaning but as a method to reach into higher spheres. In this condition, the "sitting man" that talks and consumes "the leaf of knowledge" (the *koka* leaf), holds the position of the wise man. He is the focus of the nature, the mediator of the creator and holds the power over his environment. The place in the *Maloca* where *Mambeo* happens is sacred and respresents the mothers' womb, where the fetus grows.

Holy plants - healing plants of the *Huitotos*
Tobacco and *koka* are healing plants from the region Araracura by the river Caquetá. They represent the female (*tabacco*) and male (*koka*) principle. These holy plants are firmly established both in myth and in daily live. The tabacco plant symbolizes the family structure in the thinking of the Indians. It shows growth, health and illness; a broken branch stands for a child that has become sick or dies. Botanically the tabacco plant (*nicotiana tabacum*) belongs to the family of *solonaceae*. The *Huitotos* process it into ambil, a tabacco syrup. Tea is cooked until it simmers down to the consistency of syrup and alcaline salt is added, which is won out of the ashes of various plants. The thick *ambil* is applied to the gum with a finger or a stick; mixed with spittle it is swollowed gradually.
The dried leaves of the *koka* bush (*Erythroxilon coca*) are named *koka*. Through chewing the leaves cocain is released that initiates intoxication. But the koka leaf is part of the daily food as well. It covers a main part of the daily calcium requirement, contains the vitamins A and C as well as minerals like potassum, zinc, magnesium, mangan, ferrum a.o. The use of *koka* has been known for 1000 years. At ritual ceremonies, like the *Mambeo*, the *mambe* is used as an instrument. A mixture of *ambil* and roasted koka leaf or green *koka* powder, results in a thick paste. Additionally, ashes of the *yaruma* palm is mixed into it. *Yagé* is a sacred healing plant that has given its name to this type of shamanism. We find a climbing plant named *Banisteriopsis caapi*, bark of which contains very psycho-active substances (telepathin and the alcaloid harmin).

Beside strong changes in the perception and hallucinations taking this mixture is supposed to make telepathic contact with people, spirits and gods possible.
All three plants contain alcaloids, which is of biochemical importance since these substances affect the neuro transmitter in the human nervous system.

Spiritual development of the *Huitotos*
The education of the children of the *Huitotos* starts when they are five years old. From this age on small doses of ambil are given to them. The children are tought how to live with their environment. They learn to respect rivers, flowers, plants

and animals. The close connection and foremost the interdependence of human and nature is brought home to them through mythological narrations. They are mainly told at night, so that the unconsciousness, dream and imagination will influence the children before daylight makes the stories real. From their tenth year on the ritual of the *mambeo* and duca is introduced to the children. They receive *mambe*, which they are supposed to keep in their mouths as long as possible. *Duca* is said to strengthen words. It is meant to be a library and unite the myths of the ancestors with the present. *Ambil* should be the word, *koka* the tongue. *Mambeo* - or *duca* is known by the children, since they are allowed to attend the rituals from the age of five on.

The *Huitotos* think parents have to prepare themselves fifteen years before they can have a child.
They have to learn how to prepare *Mambeo*. The child reveals how much the father has really learned. The child cries and since it cannot speak, the father has to think about the possibilities of the indisposition and react adequately.
When a child asks a question the father has to have his feet on the ground to give good answers. One of the many clans of the *Huitotos*, the *Enokaye*, have a mythology that refers to the existence of three worlds.
The first world is the one of the creation, the world of the origin. The knowledge about this world is holy and it takes six years to understand it. The second world is the one we travel into when we sleep and also when we have passed away. Death as something empty or hollow does not exist. When a person dies his teachings remain in the surviving descendants and through the help of *koka* or *ambil* it is possible to get into contact with them. The deceased may appear and predict present events.

The third world is similar to the second world. It is the world we live in. But the second world is calmer and brighter. We find no worries or sorrows. It is the world the *curandero* travels to be inspired to do certain treatments. He gains therapeutical knowledge in this world.
The second world, the world of the dead, represents peace for the body, the third world means reason. Between the second and the third world an aisle can be found where dark and evil assembles. Sorcerers of the Indian folks visit this place and act from there. This distinguishes the sorcerer from the *curandero*, who only works with the "bright" side. The mythology names *Araracura* as the focus of the world and the *Huitotos* as the humans of the center. This city is the origin of the world in which two persons were found: the white and the dark-skinned. The white emigrated to the north and started the white race; the Indian race originates from the dark-skinned person.
The creator gave him the tabacco. The Indians that emigrated to the north had the gift to smoke the tabacco and use the upgoing smoke for their science of astronomy and calendars. The Indians from *Araracura* were given the responsibility to guard the country.

The *Curandero*
During his education the *curandero* is tought that good and bad do not exist. There is light and shade, sun and moon. The right side of a human shines, the left is dark. Next to the right ear is "*Jora*" and advises the person what needs to be done. Next

to the left ear is "*Jana*", spirit of the shade, and tries to confuse the human. *Jana* symbolizes death, which is closer to the human beings than life.

The human body's consideration is another part of the education. An essential thing for a persons well-being is the feeling of being in-balance and being in-its middle between extremes. To be in the middle is like standing in the center of a clock: motionless, but at the origin of motion. The middle of a person is his navel, a spot of extreme energy. According to the *curandero*, the 'self' of a person is like a bottle: it glows in its center.

The *curandero* sees the microcosm in his patient. His most important healing tool is the *logos*.

He finds out how the disease started: Was it lightning or rain, a spirit's movement or fire? Then he tries to find a basis of trust with the patient to let the healing process take its way. *"Your disease was initiated by fire, but you turned into fire yourself. Your fire is friendly, your fire guards you. Your fire can balance harming fire."*

There are six senses to be seen in a human, represented as six persons:

- The hearing sense makes us hear.
  (We have to learn the exact hearing, the knowledge of the sounds of the jungle)
- the heart
- the brain
- the eyes, which let us see; "real seeing" lies a lot deeper
- the mouth connected to the eyes and the heart;
- Everything flows through the mouth; what comes back out has to carefully be watched. Word and prayers leave the mouth. Therefore, medicine and plants a special relation to the mouth, the verbal element.
- The sense of smell is the sixth person

There are ritual sayings or prayers that are used, general prayers are not common. So you find prayers to heal a snake bite and to be sucessful at fishing. *Yagé* and *mambe* are taken with a prayer. It is impossible for a *Huitoto* to drink *yagé*, not knowing what prayer, banishment or chanting to use with it.

The *curandero* learns something about the general strengthening of the vividness. Water is an important element. So we find it very healthy to bathe in the river in the morning, before the white butterfly has touched the water three times and the crab has spread its arms. One is supposed to throw oneself into the water so that the body hits the surface hard. One should be careful with air and food.

Before a *curandero* can start with healing treatments he has to go through certain diets. He has to avoid contact with women for a certain period of time. The spirit

Horia at the *curandero's* ear is female. If a woman came too close, her warmth could draw *Horia* away.

Every disease is an expression of misfortune. This fact must be understood by every patient and must inspire him to work on his inner processes. If he fails, the healing process cannot develop. The therapist often meets barriers not only from the patients but built on social rituals. Holistic therapies, like the *Unicista homoeopathy*, request great readiness from both patient and doctor. The medical guidance is essential for the success of the therapy.

Use in modern therapy

One has to bring spirit, body and soul into a unit and discover the cause of the disease. Chronical diseases find their causes often in hidden inner conflicts. These and other processes need to be looked at. It was possible to do group therapies in Columbia, where *mambeo* and *duca* (or *mambe*, the *koka-ambil-* mixture) was used. International law forbids the work with koka plants, therefore we use the most potential *mambe*, even though no case of addiction with Indians is known when *mambe* was used in the traditional sense. Drug addicts have even been cured through *mambe*. But *ambil* opens a wide field of treatment possibilities for a modern therapist.

Small portions are given and kept in the mouth, not swallowed. Then the patient is animated to speak about his worries and fears. *Ambil* does not have a pharmacological effect, but it activates the inner oracle which is most effective and healing. *Ambil* opens the conciousness and is necessary for a new order of social and energetic aspects. The treatment with *ambil* is often assigned with traditional or alternative medical treatments. Since tobbaco is only used once, other methods need to be found. For a successful treatment the direct experience and working on inner processes are important.

Author
Dr med Fabio Alberto Ramirez
Doctor in his own hospital close to Bogota, Columbia.
Connects yagé-shamanism with modern medicine. Student of the well-known shaman Isaysas Mavisoy of the Incas, who initiated him to a ritual leader.
After ethnopharmacological studies in sacral ceremonies of the Huitotos he began to integrate archaic rituals in modern medical therapies eight years ago.
Contact: E-Mail: framirez@cable.net.co

References

Jürgen Falbe, Manfred Regnitz (Hrsg.). 1999. *Römpp Lexikon Chemie,* Bände 1-6, 10. Auflage, Georg Thieme Verlag

http://galeon.hispavista.com/culturasamerica/Huitotos.htm
http://www.sacharuna.com/Shamanism.html
http://www.reichertorga.de/konferenz00/schamanen/schaman.html
http://www.warwick.ac.uk/society/PILAS/1999/ForTEMP
http://www.biopark.org/peru/mapacho.html
http://www.mamacoca.org/feb2002/art_constantino_posibles_impactos_fusarium_fr.html

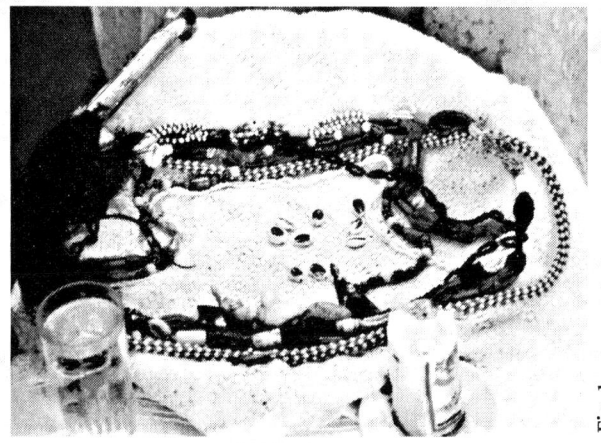

HEILUNG IM CANDOMBLÉ IN BRASILIEN

von Christiane Pantke

Zur therapeutischen Bedeutung von Hexereiauflösungsritualen

Die afrobrasilianische Kultur ist geprägt durch die ehemaligen Sklavereibedingungen. Viele Afrikaner wurden als Sklaven nach Brasilien verschifft, auf den Zuckerrohrplantagen im Hinterland von Salvador als Arbeitskräfte eingesetzt und zum Katholizismus zwangsbekehrt. Sie konnten jedoch viele Elemente ihrer ehemaligen Kulturen im Verborgenen weiter ausüben. Ein wichtiger Bestandteil stellt hierbei die Religion dar, die lokal unterschiedliche Namen erhielt.

In Bahia ist ihr Name *candomblé*. Afrikanische Weltanschauungen, Kosmologien und Heilungstraditionen konnten bis heute fortbestehen. Der *candomblé* ist eng mit der Religion der *Yoruba* und anderer afrikanischer Ethnien verwoben. Mitglieder vieler verschiedener afrikanischer Nationen haben Brasilien im Laufe der Jahrhunderte als Sklaven erreicht.

Es haben sich verschiedene religiöse Gruppen gebildet, deren Namen sich an den jeweiligen Nationen, *(nações)* orientierten. Am verbreitetsten in Bahia ist die Ethnie *Nagô*, bestehend aus Mitgliedern der *Yoruba*. Die anderen *nações* wie *Ketu* und *Angola* haben unterschiedliche Ausprägungen des *candomblé* gebildet. Andere *nações* nennen sich nach den *Yoruba*-Reichen *Ketu* und *Ijexá*. Zudem existieren die *nações Jeje*- das sind die afrikanischen *Ewe* und die *nações Kongo*,

Abb. 1: *jogo-de-buzius* (Wahrsageorakel). Nachdem die *mãe-de-santo* konkrete Fragen gestellt hat, übermittelt das Orakel die Antworten der *orixás* und ihre Anweisungen bezüglich Opfergaben und Heilungsritualen.

Kongo-Angola und *Angola* (Vgl. Pinto 1991:161; Pantke 1997:54). Demzufolge sind auch die Heilungsansätze der verschiedenen *candomblé*-Traditionen unterschiedlich. Hinzu kommen z.T. auch Elemente traditioneller Volksmedizin, indianische und katholische Volkspraktiken (vgl. Minz 1992).
Die gesellschaftlichen und persönlichen Probleme, die aus der Unterdrückung durch die Kolonisatoren resultierten, konnten auch nach Aufhebung der Sklaverei (1888) und bis heute nicht gänzlich überwunden werden. Zwischen Afrobrasilianern und Weißen gibt es bis heute ein starkes soziales Gefälle. Brasilien ist von Rassenvorurteilen geprägt. Die dunkelhäutige Bevölkerung, oftmals mit geringer Schulbildung und wirtschaftlich schlecht gestellt, kann ihr Selbstbewusstsein zum Teil im *candomblé* stärken (Vgl. Bacelar 1989 &1995).
Im Rahmen ihrer Subkulturen nehmen die Priesterin/ der Priester *(mãe-desanto/pai-de-santo)* eine sozial hohe gesellschaftliche Stellung ein. Außerhalb jedoch stoßen sie auf Widerstand. Der *candomblé* wurde in Bahia bis in die siebziger Jahre des letzten Jahrhunderts polizeilich verfolgt. Heute interessieren sich Intellektuelle für den *candomblé*. Die Kultstätten *(terreiros)*, die Kontakte mit Forschern und Intellektuellen und Touristen haben, konnten ihren Status innerhalb der Gesellschaft und ihr Äußeres aufwerten (Pantke 1997). Dies trifft jedoch auf die Mehrzahl der *terreiros*, in der Peripherie Salvadors nicht zu.
Dementsprechend ist die Position der afrobrasilianischen Heiler zu deuten: Er wirkt meist im Verborgenen, in armen Stadtteilen und stellt hier für viele Afrobrasilianer eine Alternative zur europäischen Schulmedizin und anderen Heilmethoden dar.

Traditionelle Bedeutung von Gesundheit, Krankheit und Heilung

Zur Diagnose der Krankheitsursache wird ein Orakel, das *jogo-de-búzios* befragt (Braga 1988). Das Orakel entscheidet hierbei, ob es sich um eine materielle oder eine "spirituelle" Krankheit handelt. Die materielle, d. h. organische Krankheit wird durch Medizin, Heilkräuter oder schulmedizinische Heilmethoden geheilt. Hier sind Verursacher für Krankheiten, Bakterien oder Viren, die durch Ansteckung übertragen werden. Erbkrankheiten gehören auch zu diesem Bereich.

1. Krankheit kann durch *orixás*, die Gottheiten des *candomblé*, verursacht werden, wenn die Person die Pflege ihrer *orixás* vernachlässigt hat oder Priesterin werden soll und diesem Ruf nicht Folge leisten will.

2. Krankheit kann durch Hexerei entstehen. Aus Neid, Eifersucht, Missgunst und Begierde sucht eine Person eine Priesterin auf, die für sie ein Hexereiritual durchführt. Diese *trabalhos* (Arbeiten) werden auch als *quimbanda* (Schadenszauber) oder *macumba* (Hexerei) bezeichnet.

3. Ahnen und Geister, die ihr Leben nicht vollendeten, in dem Sinne, dass sie mit Hass, Neid, niedrigen Begierden oder besitzergreifender Liebe die Welt verlassen mussten, können Krankheiten bringen (Braga 1988).

Bei allen drei Krankheitsursachen werden auch Unwohlsein, soziales Unglück, psychisches Leid, psychosomatische Krankheiten, Nervosität, Ängste,

Schwächezustände und sozialer Misserfolg, wie Arbeitslosigkeit und Armut miteinbezogen. Der Bereich der unerfüllten Wünsche und Bedürfnisse gehört auch hierzu. Die Therapie der Krankheiten und Symptome wird durch den jeweiligen *orixá* im Orakel, in dem schon die Diagnose gestellt wurde, angeordnet.

Die hauptsächlichen therapeutischen Tätigkeiten einer *mãe-de-santo* sind: Orakelbefragungen, Heilungsrituale mit Opfergaben *(ebós)* und Heilkräutern, Reinigungsrituale, Feste zu Ehren der *orixás*, der *candomblé*-Gottheiten und soziale Events, deren therapeutische Funktionen als sozial integrierende Momente gedeutet werden können.

Heilrituale und Therapien mit Ursache

> "*Gesundheit, als Wohlbefinden des Einzelnen, und Krankheit in der Moderne muss notwendigerweise über das klassische Krankheitsbild der "sogenannten Schulmedizin" im medizinischen, psychologischen und psychoanalytischen Sinn hinausführen.*"
> (GREIFELD 1995:21, vgl. auch KELLER 1995 und DIALLO 1995).

Dies wird durch die folgende Beschreibung einer Heilung allergischer Hautausschläge, die durch einen verärgerten Ahnengeist ausgelöst wurden, erläutert. Die Ritualbeschreibung verdeutlicht den Ablauf der Rituale, die Grundelemente, und deren vielschichtige Bedeutung.
Ein kleines Mädchen (eineinhalb Jahre alt) leidet schon mehrere Monate unter Hautausschlägen, vor allem am Hals und im Nackenbereich. Andere Stellen des Körpers sind ebenfalls sporadisch betroffen. Nun hat sie Windpocken bekommen und die Ausschläge wurden dabei schlimmer und entzündeten sich. Der Hautarzt verschrieb Antibiotika, aber die Mutter ist weiterhin beunruhigt. Der Arzt weiß nicht, ob es eine Allergie gegen Hitze, Sonne oder Lebensmittel ist und er schlägt vor, dies später auszutesten. Die Mutter entschließt sich daraufhin zur Konsultation einer ihr empfohlenen *mãe-de-santo*. Diese lernte in der *candomblé-nagô*-Tradition und war zuvor ca. zwanzig Jahre beim Kardezismus aktives Mitglied, bis ihr dort *Oxum* erschien und ihr mitteilte, sie solle *mãe-de-santo* werden und ein eigenes *candomblé-terreiro* aufmachen. Sie erzählte mir, dass sie von den *orixás* die Erlaubnis habe, auch Elemente des Kardezismus wie "*mesa branca*" (weißer Tisch) etc. zu verwenden. Die *mãe-de-santo* befragt das Orakel und erfährt, dass ein Ahnengeist verärgert ist und dies nicht nur das Mädchen, sondern auch ihren Bruder sowie die Mutter betrifft. Erstaunlich hierbei ist, dass nicht der *orixá Omulu*, dem die Hauterkrankungen zugeordnet werden, Verursacher ist und ein *ebó* erhält. Der Ahnengeist, der Verursacher ist, soll jedoch Kind von *Omulu* sein, so die *mãe-de-santo*. Die "Wege seien verschlossen", gutes Gelingen kann für alle drei nicht stattfinden. Es muss eine "Arbeit" *(trabalho)* für einen *egun*, einen Totengeist, getätigt werden. Die *mãe-de-santo* beschließt, dass ein Versöhnungsritual mit dem Ahnengeist stattfinden muss. Er oder sie, es kann sich auch um eine Ahnin handeln, will gespeist werden. Die drei betroffenen Personen sollen von den negativen und bösen Mächten des Geistes befreit werden. Bei diesem Reinigungsritual (port.: *limpeza do corpo*) werden sie auch vor weiterer Hexerei geschützt. Zudem sollen Feinde aus dem Bereich der Familie, Nachbarn oder Freundeskreis gebannt werden. Das Orakel erteilt der *mãe-de-santo* die Anweisung was an Utensilien, wie Essensgaben und Kräutern benötigt wird.

Speisen und Kräuter werden, wie auch Farben und Tiere u.a. den jeweiligen *orixás* nach einem Analogieprinzip zugeordnet, z.B. feine Pflanzen für weibliche *orixás*, fleischige, großblättrige für männliche *orixás*. Die Zuordnungen können lokal und je nach Beeinflussung des jeweiligen *terreiros* Unterschiede aufweisen. (Vgl. MINZ 1992:71, PORTUGAL 1987 mit Pflanzen und Rezepten, LÜHNING 1999: (301-331) mit dem Vergleich bahianischer und afrikanischer Pflanzenkunde und ORDEP (1999:289-302) zu Mythen als kosmologischem Ursprung von Heilungsritualen des *candomblés* und COSTA DA LIMA (1999:319-326) zur Ernährung und Diät im *candomblé*. Vgl. auch einige Heilungsrituale bei HOHENSTEIN 1991)

• Ein Pärchen kleiner Küken;

• ein Kilo weiße Bohnen, weißer Mais, schwarze Bohnen, *fradinho* Bohnen, Hühnermais, *tapioca:* weißes Yuccamehl; *carimã:* eine Maniokmasse, Juccawurzel, *iahme:* aus der Maniokfamilie;, Mehl, Reis, Gemüse: *chuchu:* gurkenähnliches Gemüse, das gekocht werden muss; Karotten, *repolho:* Kohl; Gurke, *acaçá:* in Bananenblätter gehüllter und darin gekochter weißer Mais (Gabe für *Oxalá*).

• Für das Ritual wird zudem benötigt: zwei *algidaes:* Tongefäße; Baumwolle; je ein Meter weißes, schwarzes und rotes Tuch, Kerzen, Räucherwerk *(defumador)* und folgende Kräuter:
    nativo (Yoruba: Piperegun, (Vgl. PORTUGAL 1987:19)*),*
    aroera (Aroeira de Ogum) (lat.: schinus molle l.), *Xoroquê/Exú.* Es findet
        Verwendung bei vielen Hexereiauflösungsritualen, bei denen die
        orixás Ogum und *Exú* beteiligt sind. Es hat sich bewährt bei
        Hautgeschwüren und Entzündungen. Vgl.: FARELLI (1999:23) und
        MINZ (1992:83).)
    und *espada de Ogum* (Sansevieria Ceynaica: *Oguns* Schwert), diese Pflanze
        wird auch häufig gegen den bösen Blick (*mal olhada*) verwendet;
        Vgl.:MINZ (1992:59). (*Yoruba: Junça,* für den *orixá Ossaim.* Vgl.
        PORTUGAL, 1987:19)

• Für die Reinigungsbäder sollen für die ersten drei Tage
    vassurinha (*Vassourinha de Nossa Senhora* (lat.: Scoparia dulcis L.) soll
        mit *Omolu* im Zusammenhang stehen. Vgl. MINZ (1992:83).
    folha da costa (Pflanze der Küste: (lat.: calanchoe brasiliensis camb.);
        gehört zum *orixá Oxum* und wirkt entzündungshemmend. Vgl.
        MINZ (1992:72). (*Yoruba: Odum-dum* für die *orixás: Oxalá,*
        Yemanjá, Xangô, Ossaim, Oxossi und *Exú*; Vgl: PORTUGAL
        1987:19.))
    und *folha Manjerição* (Lat.: Ocimum basilicum L. (MINZ 1992:82.))

benutzt werden. Für die darauffolgenden drei Tagen sollen die drei Kräuter
    tomba todo (auch *pinhão-roxo* genannt (lat.: Jatrofa Multifida-Lineu), für
        Ogum und *Exú*. Kräftige Pflanze für Reinigungsbäder; Vgl:.
        PORTUGAL 1987:120)
    folha de araçá (auch folha *araçá-de-coroa* genannt (lat.: Psidium
        Variabilis-Bergius), für *Oxóssi* und *Oxalá* für Reinigungsbäder.
        Vgl:.PORTUGAL 1987:39)
    und *folha (espada) de Manga* (Auch *folha de mangueira* genannt (lat.:

Manjifera Indica- Lineu). *Ogum* und *Exú* zugeordnet; für Reinigungsbäder; *Yoruba: mongoro*, vgl.: PORTUGAL 1987:102) zerrieben und in Wasser eingelegt werden.

Die Eltern sollen auf einen Zettel die Namen der Ahnen, die sie kennen, sowie die Namen von lebenden nicht wohlgesonnenen Menschen notieren. MINZ (1992:57) beschreibt eine "Arbeit" zur Verhexung von Personen, bei der Namen auf Zettel notiert und danach verbrannt werden. Dieser Zettel wird in den Hinterhof, wo das Ritual stattfinden wird, gelegt. Es dürfen keine Fotos und keine Filmaufnahmen getätigt werden, da die Wirksamkeit des Rituals darunter leiden würde.

Das Ritual findet in Salvador, im Wohnhaus bzw. Hinterhof des Wohnhauses, der *mãe-de-santo* statt. Ihr *terreiro* ist im Hinterland, zwei Stunden Reisezeit entfernt. Hier behandelt sie normalerweise Personen, die Zeit und Geld für die Reise haben. Einfachere Behandlungen führt sie in Salvador durch.

Die *filha-de-santo*, die bei der *mãe-de-santo* ihre Initiationszeit verbringt und alle Rituale erlernt, hat das Essen für die Ahnengeister vorbereitet. In der Küche stehen je drei Teller mit jeder der gekochten Speisen bereit. Alle Speisen sind separat angerichtet, nur die Gemüsesorten wurden gemischt. In einem anderen Raum befinden sich die lebenden Küken. Im Hinterhof in einer Ecke liegen die Kräuter. Hier wird als erstes das kleine Mädchen mit den Hautausschlägen von der *mãe-de-santo* mit jeder dieser Speisen nacheinander abgerieben. Dies geschieht in der Reihenfolge der oben genannten Auflistung der benötigten Artikel. Die Reihenfolge ist: Kopf, Vorder- und Hinterseite des Körpers, Arme und danach die Beine. Dabei murmelt sie Gebete, zum Teil auf *Yoruba*, zum Teil auf Portugiesisch. Sie fordert den Ahnengeist auf, das Mädchen in Ruhe zu lassen.

Als nächstes wird sie mit einem der Küken abgerieben, dem danach der Hals umgedreht wird. Feuerpulver wird entzündet und es knallt, um den Geist zu erschrecken. Danach wird eine Kerze vor dem Kind durchgebrochen. Weiße, schwarze und rote Tuchfetzen, die mit dem Körper in Berührung kamen, sollen die negativen Kräfte binden. Sie werden von der *mãe-de-santo* zusammengeknotet. Zum Schluss wird der Körper mit den Heilkräutern abgewedelt.

Danach wird das kleine Mädchen entfernt, es soll nicht mehr mit den Speisen und Gegenständen in Berührung kommen, mit denen sie abgestrichen wurde. Als nächster wird der Bruder und danach die Mutter der Beiden in gleicher Weise behandelt. Der Vater der Kinder, der unerwartet mitgekommen ist, und mit dem die *mãe-de-santo* nicht gerechnet hatte, wird ebenfalls behandelt. Sie entscheidet dies spontan, indem sie die Teller mit den Speisen begutachtet und bemerkt, dass für die Behandlung aller Anwesenden genug vorhanden sei.

Die Kinder und die Mutter erscheinen mit einer Tüte mit frischen Kleidern. Nach dem Ritual nehmen sie ein erstes Reinigungsbad und ziehen daraufhin die neuen Kleider an. Die Kleider, welche sie vorher am Leib trugen, werden in eine Tüte gepackt und sollen von einer anderen Person gewaschen werden. Die Mutter bekommt den Auftrag, während der Zeit der Reinigungsbäder während einer Woche sexuell enthaltsam zu sein, dies soll sie auch dem Vater der Kinder mitteilen. Der Vater musste die getragenen Kleider wieder verwenden, da er keine anderen dabei hatte. Die *mãe-de-santo* bestätigte ihm, dass das nicht schlimm sei, da sie damit rechnet, dass der die Krankheit verursachende Ahnengeist aus der Verwandtschaftslinie der Frau stamme. Zu dieser Überzeugung gelangt sie, da sie keine gegenteilige Information hierzu hatte und zudem die Mutter das Ritual in Auftrag gegeben hatte.

Die *filha-de-santo* fegt zum Abschluss des Rituals die Speisen und Kräuter zusammen. Eine nicht genannte Person wird sie entfernen, irgendwohin weit weg bringen, wo wenn möglich, niemand damit in Berührung kommt. Dieser Teil des Rituals wird von der *mãe-de-santo* als der Schwierigste beschrieben, da die Reste jetzt mit negativen Kräften durchtränkt sind. Die Person, welche die Speisen wegbringt, schwebt in der Gefahr, dass die Kräfte auf sie übertragen werden. Dies gilt für alle Personen, die mit dem Essen in Berührung kommen. Als Orte werden hierfür, wenn die Opfer *Exú* gelten, oftmals Wegkreuzungen ausgewählt.
Exú, dem Wegkreuzungen zugeordnet sind, kann hier seine Speisen empfangen. Friedhofseingänge eignen sich bei *ebós* für *eguns*, damit sie wieder an die für sie bestimmten Orte zurückkehren. In dem Ritual vorangehenden *jogo-de-búzios* hatte die *mãe-de-santo* festlegen lassen, was das Wegbringen der Reste kosten wird. Dieser Teil der Behandlung war der Kosten aufwendigste (136 *reais*, zur damaligen Zeit ca. 76 EURO). Hierdurch sind "die Wege der Personen wieder geöffnet", was eine gängige Ausdrucksweise dafür ist, dass gutes Gelingen für die Zukunft und die Wege, die man zu gehen hat, vorbereitet und gewährleistet ist (Port.: *abrir os caminos*; sprachlicher Ausdruck aus dem *candomblé* in Bahia.). Die Mutter der Kinder ist beruhigt. Der übelbringende Ahnengeist wurde gefunden und das Unheil aus dem Weg geschafft in Form seiner Besänftigung und Beschwichtigung. Das Ritual beabsichtigt nicht, das Böse, hier in Form eines krankheitsbringendem Geist zu vernichten. Er wird integriert, geehrt und berücksichtigt mit Speisen, die er liebt. Hierbei wird ihm der Ort gezeigt, der ihm zugeordnet ist. Er wird zurück nach Hause geführt. Erstaunlicherweise beschränkte sich das Ritual nicht darauf, den *egun* zu beschwichtigen, sondern die *mãe-de-santo* öffnete Raum für Hexereiverdächtigungen von Lebenden. Die Personen sollten hier vor lebenden Feinden beschützt werden, die *mãe-de-santo* wollte aber keine *trabalho* gegen diese verrichten. Bei vielen der bekannten Behandlungen sind dies zwei getrennte Bereiche: *ebós* für Ahnengeister und *orixás* und *trabalhos* gegen Feinde. Vgl. z.B. MINZ 1992. Nicht das erkrankte Kind stand im Mittelpunkt des Geschehens, sondern die Familienmitglieder wurden in das Heilgeschehen integriert. Alle wurden gleichrangig mitbehandelt. Der Vater, mit dessen Erscheinen die *mãe-de-santo* nicht gerechnet hatte, wurde gleichfalls sofort integriert, mitbehandelt und gereinigt. Vater und Mutter wurden aufgefordert, die Namen aller mutmaßlichen Feinde der Familie zu notieren und das Ritual versprach, außer den Ahnengeist zu beschwichtigen, gleichzeitig Schutz vor allen mutmaßlichen Feinden der Familie zu bringen. Die *mãe-de-santo* zählte auf, wer auf dem Papier notiert werden darf, wer in Frage kommt, Feind zu sein, wie z.B. Familienmitglieder. Durch das Papier konnte eine Anonymität aufrecht erhalten werden, die es der Familie erlaubte, frei zu assoziieren und Personen zu verdächtigen, die sie nicht verdächtigen wollen, da Abhängigkeiten, Verbindlichkeiten oder Versprechungen bestehen. Oder mit anderen Worten: Die Personen dürfen im realen Leben nicht verdächtigt werden, es darf ihnen gegenüber kein Verdacht oder Vorwurf ausgesprochen werden, um keine neuen Probleme zu kreieren, die dann einer neuen Bewältigung bedürfen. Die Ambivalenz der Gefühle zu Personen, welche die Familie feststellt, sowie die Ambivalenz der Gefühle von Personen, welche die Familie empfindet, muss oftmals in der Gesellschaft auf Grund von sozialen Normen und/oder nicht gewollter Konsequenzen verschwiegen werden.
Das Papier, das zu einem entfernten Ort getragen wird, ist somit willkommenes Medium zur Bewahrung der Intimsphäre und Diskretion. Es muss keiner

Verdächtigung Stimme gegeben werden, es darf leiser Unwillen gegen leise und/oder laute Unfriedenstifter geäußert werden. Soziale Konflikte, die nicht ausgetragen werden, schwächen die Personen. Krankheit wird oftmals als Unterlegenheit und persönlicher Schwächezustand gedeutet. Man kann hier eine Parallele zur gesellschaftlichen Situation ziehen: Soziale Marginalisierung führt selten zu gesellschaftlichem Protest und wird eher an Personen der direkten Umgebung abreagiert, z.b. durch *trabalhos* im *candomblé* (Vgl. POLLAK-ELTZ: 1982). Sollte jedoch, wider Erwarten, ein Ahnengeist aus der männlichen Linie der Verursacher der Krankheit sein, würde dieser ebenfalls mitbehandelt werden, da der Vater auch seine Ahnen, von denen er Kenntnis hat oder das Wissen, dass sie ihm oder seinen Eltern zu Lebzeiten übel gesonnen waren, auf das Papier notiert hatte. Verdeckte Aggressionen konnten projiziert und abreagiert werden.

Die Stimmung während und nach dem Ritual war fröhlich und die Gemeinschaft der Familie wurde währenddessen bestätigt. Ihre Probleme wurden ernst genommen, das Gewicht nicht auf die "ungesunde" Person, das Mädchen, gelegt, es wurde kein "Sündenbock" geschaffen. Alle beteiligten Personen wurden gleichermaßen am guten Gelingen beteiligt, z.B. durch gemeinsames Aufpassen, dass die Kinder nicht mit den Essensgaben, mit denen sie abgerieben wurden, spielen oder sie gar selbst verspeisen. Zum Prozess der Gesundung einer Person gehört die Akzeptanz der jeweiligen sozialen Gruppe oder Subkultur. Wie beschrieben wird die Familie, in anderen Fällen die soziale Gruppe mit angesprochen und der Kranke, bzw. "Ungesunde" wieder integriert. Die Familie, bzw. Gemeinschaft wird gleichberechtigt mitbehandelt, nimmt aktiv teil an Leid und Heilung der Einzelperson. Eine Bestätigung ihrer selbst, sowie bestehender Strukturen wird vollzogen (Vgl. LEWIS 1971, der Teile afrikanischer "Besessenheitsrituale" in ähnlicher Weise interpretierte.). Die Krankheit bzw. das Leid wird nicht individuell auf die eine durch Krankheit betroffene Person bezogen, sondern das Leid bzw. Unheil wird als Bestandteil der gesamten sozialen Gruppe interpretiert. Zum kosmischen Einklang gehört, dass die Familie bzw. Gruppe im Einvernehmen mit der leidenden Person gemeinschaftlich während des Rituals agiert.

Das kosmische Gleichgewicht, das Einverständnis der Geistwesen mit der sozialen Gruppe wird zurückgewonnen und bestätigt (Vgl. in diesem Zusammenhang z.B. LEVI-STRAUSS (1967:204-255), der anhand des Beispiels eines schamanistischen Heilungsrituals bei den *Cuña*-Indianern in Panama die therapeutische Funktion des Rituals darstellt. Nicht nur das Individuum, das Hilfe benötigt, sondern ebenfalls die ganze Gemeinschaft erlebt hier durch den Prozess des Rituals eine psychologisch heilsame Wirkung. Der männliche oder weibliche Ahnengeist wird zur Familie, sozialen Gruppe oder jeweiligen Subkultur zugehörig gezählt. Er wird in erster Linie vorrangig "behandelt", d.h. in die Kommunikation miteinbezogen und mit Speisung durch seine Lieblingsmahlzeit verwöhnt oder beschwichtigt, je nach Betrachtungsweise und dem Gefühl der Bedrohung der jeweiligen in Mitleidenschaft gezogenen Personen. Die Behandlung beinhaltet seine Anerkennung, Respektierung und Rehabilitation. Nach der Kanalisation der Ängste und der Projektion von Konflikten und Aggressionen auf ihn, erfolgt die Wiederherstellung der kosmischen Harmonie. Er hat die gleiche Existenz- berechtigung wie die real lebenden Personen und sein Platz wird neu definiert. Gesundheit, und dies bezieht sich auf alle Ebenen physischen, psychischen, geistigen und sozialen Wohlbefindens besteht, wenn Kosmos und Menschen im Einklang sind.

Autorin
DR. PHIL. CHRISTIANE PANTKE
Ethnologin mit Nebenfächern Altamerikanistik und Religionswissenschaft am Institut für Religionswissenschaft an der Freien Universität Berlin. Feldforschungen zum Thema "Afro-Brasilianische Kultur, Religionen (*candomblé*) und Pfingstkirchen *(igrejas pentecostais)*", Brasilien. Studie zur Religionsentwicklung spiritistischer Religionen, Thema:. "Kardezismus" in Brasilien. Projekte am Haus der Kulturen der Welt, Berlin Wissenschaftliche Mitarbeiterin beim DFG-Projekt: "Die bahianische Gesellschaft im Spannungsfeld von Trance und Puritanismus. Familie und Ersatzfamilie in Religionsgemeinschaften in Bahia, Brasilien", mit Lehrveranstaltungen und Vorträgen zum Thema "Religionen in Brasilien". Kontakt: E-Mail: jane.pantke@t-online.de

Literatur

BACELAR, J. 1989. *Etnicidade. Ser Negro em Salvador. Ianamá.* Salvador.
BACELAR, J. 1995. Modernização e a Cultura dos Negros em Salvador. In: *Simpósio International: Culturas Marginalizadas e Processos de Modernização na América Latina,* S.2-17. Hg.: Centro de Estudos Afro-Orientais. Salvador.
BRAGA, J. 1988. *O Jogo de Búzios. Um estudo da advinhação no Candomblé.* São Paulo.
DIALLO, T. 1995. Vorwort. In: *Ritual und Heilung. Eine Einführung in die Ethnomedizin.* Hrg.: B. Pfleiderer, K. Greifeld; W. Bichmannn. Berlin.
GREIFELD, K. 1995. Einführung in die Medizinethnologie, S.11-33. In: *Ritual und Heilung. Eine Einführung in die Ethnomedizin.* Hrg.: B. Pfleiderer, K. Greifeld, W. Bichmann. Berlin.
HOHENSTEIN, de E. 1991. *Das Reich der Magischen Mütter. Eine Untersuchung über die Frauen in den afro-brasilianischen Besessenheitskulten candomblé.* Frankfurt.
KELLER, F.B. 1995. *Krank warum? Einführung und These.* S.:10-24. Ostfildern.
LEVI-STRAUSS, C. 1967. *Strukturale Anthropologie.* Frankfurt. Original: Paris.
LEWIS, I. M. 1989. *Ecstatic Religion. A study of shamanism and spirit possession.* London/ New York.
LIMA DA COSTA, V. 1999. As Dietas Africanas no Sistema Alimentar Brasileiro. In: *Faces da Tradição Afro-Brasileira. Religiosidade, Sincretismo, Anti-Sincretismo, Reafricanização, Prácticas Terapeuticas, Etnobotânicas e Comida,* S.319-326. Hrg.: Carlos Caroso e Jeferson Bacelar. Rio de Janeiro /Salvador-BA.
LÜHNING, A. 1999. Ewé. As Plantas Brasileiras e seus Parentes Africanos. In: *Faces da Tradição Afro-Brasileira. Religiosidade, Sincretismo, Anti-Sincretismo, Reafricanização, Prácticas Terapeuticas, Etnobotânicas e Comida,* S.303-31. Hrg.: Carlos Caroso e Jeferson Bacelar. Rio de Janeiro /Salvador-BA.
MINZ, L. 1992. *Krankheit als Niederlage und die Rückkehr zur Stärke. Candomblé als Heilunsprozeß.* Bonn.
PANTKE, C. 1998. *Favelas, Festas und Candomblé. Zum interkulturellen Austausch zwischen Afro-Brasilianern und Touristen im Rahmen kultischer und profaner Festveranstaltungen in Salvador da Bahia.* Ketsch bei Mannheim.
PINTO, T. DE OLIVEIRA 1991. *Capoeira, Samba, Candomblé. Afro-brasiliansiche Musik im Recôncavö, Bahia.* Berlin.
POLLAK-ELTZ, A. 1982. *Folk-Medicine in Venezuela.* Wien.
PORTUGAL, F. 1987. *Rezas. Folhas- Chás e Rituais dos Orixás. Folhas, Sementes, Frutas e Raízes de Uso Litúrgico na Umbanda e no Candomblé. Com uso práctico na Medicina popular.* Rio de Janeiro.
SERRA, O. 1999. Etnobotânica do candomblé Nagô da Bahia: Cosmologia e Estrutura Básica do Arranjo Taxonômico. O Modelo da Liturgia- in: *Faces da Tradição Afro-Brasileira. Religiosidade, Sincretismo, Anti-Sincretismo, Reafricanização, Prácticas Terapeuticas, Etnobotânicas e Comida,* S. 289-302. Hrg.: Carlos Caroso e Jeferson Bacelar. Rio de Janeiro /Salvador-BA.

HEALING IN CANDOMBLÉ IN BAHIA IN BRAZIL*

by Christiane Pantke

The therapeutic importance of witchcraft-eliminating rituals

The Afro-Brazilian culture is characterized by past slavery conditions. Many Africans were shipped as slaves to Brazil, used as workers on the sugar cane plantations of the Salvadorian hinterland, and compulsorily converted to Catholicism.

Despite this, they were able to practice many elements of their past culture in seclusion. One important factor in this was a religion that was given locally differing names. In Bahia it is named *candomblé*. African world views, cosmologies, and healing traditions were able to survive until today. The *candomblé* is closely interwoven with the religion of the *Yoruba* and other African ethnic groups. Over the centuries members of many different African nations reached Brazil as slaves.

As a result, a variety of religious groups came into being whose names frequently related to the respective nations (*nações*). The most wide-spread ethnic group in Bahia is the *Nagô* consisting of members of the *Yoruba*. The other *nações*, such as *Ketu* and *Angola* have formed different versions of *candomblé* [1]. Other *nacoes* name themselves after the *Yoruba* kingdoms *Ketu* and *Ijexá*. Moreover there exist the *nacoes Jeje*. Therefore the healing approaches of the various *candomblé* traditions

---

Fig. 1: *jogo-de-buzius* (oracle). *mãe-de-santo* is questioning, then the oracle gives the answer of *orixás* and instructions for offerings and healing rituals.

* Translated by Gert Venghaus

are different. Additionally we find traditional folk medicine as well as Indian and Catholic practices [2].

Despite the abolition of slavery (1888), the societal and individual problems resulting from oppression by colonial powers have still not been overcome. There remains a huge social imbalance between Afro-Brazilians and Whites. Brazil is marked by racial discrimination. The dark-skinned population, often with poor school education and low economical status, can strengthen its self-confidence partly through the *candomblé* [3]. In their sub- culture the priestesses/priests (*mãe-de-santo/pai-de-santo*) hold a socially high position, outside they experience resistance.

The *candomblé* in Bahia was prosecuted up until the seventies of the past century. Today intellectuals get interested in the *candomblé*. Those places of worship (*terreiros*) with contacts to scientists, intellectuals and tourists are able to increase their status within society as well as their external image. However, this does not apply to the majority of *terreiros* in the periphery of Salvador.

The image of the Afro-Brazilian healer can be so described: The healer acts mostly in secret, in poor suburbs, and often represents the only alternative to European school medicine and other curative methods for many Afro- brazilians.

Traditional meaning of health, illness and healing

To diagnose illnesses, an oracle - the *jogo-de-búzios* - is consulted [5]. The oracle determines whether the illness is of a material or 'spiritual' nature. The material, i.e. organic illness will be treated with medicines, herbs or orthodox medical methods. These illnesses are caused by bacterial or viral infections. Hereditary diseases also fall into this category.

> 1 A spiritual illness can be caused by *orixás*, the divinities of the *candomblé*, either if a person has neglected the care of their *orixás* or if the person has been called to become a priestess but has refused to follow this calling.

> 2 Spiritual Illnesses can be caused by witchcraft. Driven by envy, jealousy, resentment, or greed, a person will consult a priestess who will perform a witchcraft ritual This work (*trabalhos*) is also called *quimbanda* or macumba (black magic). 6

> 3 They can also be caused by ancestors or spirits who have not completed their lives in the sense of leaving this world still filled with hate, envy, poor desires or possessive love. [7]

All three categories usually encompass general malaise, social misfortune, emotional pain, psychosomatic illnesses, nervousness, anxiety, fatigue and social unsuccessfulness, such as unemployment and poverty.

This also includes unfulfilled desires and needs. The therapy for the illness or symptom is prescribed by the *orixá* of the same oracle that was consulted for a diagnosis.

The main therapeutic interventions of a *mãe-de-santo* are: consultation of the oracle, healing rituals with sacrifices (*ebós*) and herbs, cleansing rituals, ceremonies in honour of the *orixás* - the *candomblé* divinities - and social events whose therapeutic function could be interpreted as socially integrating factors.

Healing rituals and therapies with causes

'Health as wellness of the individual, and illness in the modern age must necessarily exceed the classical symptoms of the 'so-called orthodox medicine' in both, the medical, psychological as well as psychoanalytical sense.'
(GREIFELD 1995:21, KELLER 1995, DIALLO 1995) [8]

This will be illustrated in the following description of healing an allergic rash caused by an angry ancestral spirit [9]. The description of the ritual shows the process of the rituals, the basic elements, and their multi-layered meanings.

For several months, a small girl (one and a half years old) suffers from a rash, mainly on the throat and neck. Sporadically other parts of the body are also affected. Then she had caught chickenpocks, the rash intensified and became infected. The family´s physician prescribed antibiotics. However, the mother remained concerned. The physician was not completely certain whether the allergy was caused by heat, sunlight or food, and suggested to test this at a later stage.

Following this, the mother decided to consult a recommended *mãe-de-santo* [10] who consulted the oracle and learned that an ancestral spirit was angered and that this not only affected the girl but also her brother and the mother. [11] All 'paths are closed', thus preventing a good outcome for all three. Some 'work' (*trabalho*) for an *egun* - a death spirit - must be done. The *mãe-de-santo* decides that an appeasement ritual with the ancestral spirit is needed. He or she (it can also be a female spirit) wants to be fed. Aim of the ritual is to free the three affected persons from the negative and evil powers of the spirit. This cleansing ritual (port.: *limpeza do corpo*) will also protect them from future witchcraft. Further, enemies shall be banned from the immediate area of the family, neighbours and circle of friends.

The oracle instructs the mãe-de-santo in the use of utensils, food offerings and herbs [12]:

- a pair of small baby chicks;

- one kilo of white beans, white maize, black beans, fradinho beans, chicken maize, tapioca: white Yucca flour; carimã: a cassava paste, Jucca root, iahme: of the cassava family; flour, rice, vegetables: chuchu: cucumber-like vegetable that must be boiled; carrots, repolho: cabbage; cucumber, acaçá: white maize wrapped and boiled in banana leaves (offering for *Oxalá*).

- The following additional items are required for the ritual: two algidaes: clay pots; cotton; one meter each of white, black and red cloth, candles, incense (fumador) and the following herbs: nativo13, aroera14, and espada de Ogum [15].

- For cleansing baths, vassurinha[16], *folha da costa*[17], and *folha Manjerição*[18] should be used during the first three days. For the following three days, the three herbs *tomba todo*[19], *folha de araça*[20] and *folha (espada) de Manga*[21] should be ground and immersed in water.

The parents write on a piece of paper the names of known ancestors as well as names of ill-meaning living persons [22]. This paper is then placed in the backyard where the ritual takes place. It is not allowed to take photographs or record films since the effectiveness of the ritual would be adversely affected by this.
The ritual takes place in Salvador, in the house or backyard of the *mãe-de-santo*. Her *terreiro* is located further in the hinterland, approximately two hours travel. Here, she normally treats individuals who have the time and money for the journey. Simple treatments are done in Salvador.

The *filha-de-santo*, who undergoes her initiation period with the *mãe-de-santo* and learns all rituals, has prepared the food for the ancestral spirits. All dishes are prepared separately, only the vegetables were mixed together. The living chicks are in a separate room.

The necessary herbs are placed in a corner of the backyard. It is here where the little girl suffering the rash is given a rub down with each of the dishes by the *mãe-de-santo*[23.] The sequence is: head, front and back of the body, arms, followed by the legs. In the process she mumbles prayers, partly in *Yoruba*, partly in Portuguese. She invites the ancestral spirit to leave the girl alone.

As a next step, the girl is rubbed down with one of the chicks which, afterwards, is then strangulated. Gunpowder is lit and explodes to frighten the spirit. After that, a candle is broken in halves in front of the child. White, black and red pieces of cloth that were in touch with the body are supposed to trap the negative forces. They are tied into a knot by the *mãe-de-santo*. Finally, the body is wafted with the healing herbs.

The little girl is taken away after this procedure since she is not supposed to have any further contact with the items or food dishes. Next her brother and then her mother are treated in the same way. The father of the children who had arrived unexpectedly is also treated by the *mãe-de-santo*. She decides this spontaneously after examining the plates with the food, noting that sufficient food is available for treatment of the entire family.

First the children and the mother appear with a bag of clean clothes. After the ritual, they take a cleansing bath and dress in the new clothes. The discarded clothes are packed into a bag and must be washed by a third person. The mother is asked to abstain from sexual activity during the week-long period of cleansing baths and to inform her husband accordingly.
The father has to wear the same clothes again since he did not bring a change of clothes. The *mãe-de-santo* assures him that this does not matter since the illness causing ancestral spirit comes from the ancestral lineage of the wife. She concludes this in the absence of any information to the contrary and because the mother had requested the ritual.
At the end of the ritual the *filha-de-santo* brushes the food and herbs together. An

unnamed person will remove them later and carry them somewhere far away where no-one can come in contact with them. This part of the ritual is regarded by the *mãe-de-santo* as the most difficult since all remnants are now saturated with negative energies. The person who takes away the food is in danger of contracting these negative energies. If offerings are made for *Exú* (to whom cross-roads are assigned), cross-roads are best suited for the disposal and for him to receive the offerings. Entrances to cemeteries are better suited for *ebós* for *erguns* so that they can return to their destined places. The cost for this is the disposal of the ritual's remnants, and was the most costly part (136 reais, at the time approximately 76 EURO).

Through this ritual, the 'paths of the persons involved have been reopened' - a common phrase for the preparation and assurance of good luck in future undertakings. [24] The mother of the children is pleased. The ominous ancestral spirit was identified and the pending disaster removed through soothing and appeasement. The ritual is not intended to destroy evil, for instance in the form of an illness causing spirit. Rather the spirit is being integrated, honoured and offered favourite food. In this process, the spirit is shown the location that is allocated to him and guided back home.

Surprisingly, the ritual was not limited to pacifying the *egun*, but the *mãe-de-santo* also opened an opportunity to address suspicions of witchcraft amongst the living.[25]
The sick child was not sole focus of the ritual but family members were integrated into the treatment. All were treated equally. The father whose appearance was not planned by the *mãe-de-santo* was also immediately integrated, treated and cleansed. Father and mother were asked to note down the names of all potential enemies of the family and, besides pacifying the ancestral spirit, the ritual also promised to offer protection against the supposed enemies of the family. The *mãe-de-santo* determined who was allowed to be noted down on paper, who should be considered to be an enemy (for instance family members). Through this paper it was possible to maintain anonymity which allowed the family to associate freely and suspect individuals whom they normally would not be able to suspect openly due to dependencies, obligations or promises.

In other words: In real life, suspicion must not be cast on these individuals nor must they be accused in any way since this will create new problems that need to be overcome. In society, and based on social norms and/or unwanted consequences, the ambivalence of emotions felt by the family towards and from other people, often needs to be concealed. The piece of paper that is carried to a remote location is a welcome medium for the maintenance of discretion and privacy. Suspicions need not to be voiced, but quiet indignation against quiet and /or loud troublemakers can be expressed. [26] Should, against all odds, an illness be caused by an ancestral spirit of the male lineage, this spirit would also be included in the treatment since the father has also noted down on paper his own ancestors whose ill will towards himself or his family is known. Through this process, covered aggressions can be projected and dealt with.
The atmosphere during and after the ritual was merry and the unity of the family was reaffirmed. Their problems were taken seriously. Emphasis was not only placed on the 'ill' person (the girl), and it was avoided to create a scapegoat. All

persons were equally involved in the good outcome, for instance by watching the children and preventing them from playing with or eating the food that had been used for the rub-downs.

Part of a person's healing process is the acceptance by the respective social group or sub-culture. As described, the entire family, or, in other cases a social group, are included in the treatment process and the patient or 'un-healthy' person is being integrated. The family or community is treated equally and participates actively in the sorrow and healing of the individual. They themselves as well as existing structures, are reaffirmed. [27] The illness or pain is not related individually to the person suffering from an illness, but regarded as integral part of an entire social group. As part of the cosmic union, the family or group act with the consent of the suffering person and in unity during the ritual. The cosmic balance and the consent of the spirits to the social group are regained and confirmed. [28]

A male or female ancestral spirit is added to the family, social group or respective sub-culture. It is treated with priority, i.e. is being involved in communication and pacified through offerings of its favourite foods depending on the different ways of looking at and experiencing the threat towards the affected persons. The treatment incorporates the spirits recognition, respect and rehabilitation. [29] He has the same right of existence as the people in real life, and his place is being newly defined. Health in the total sense, i.e. physical, psychological, mental and social well-being, exists when cosmos and people are in union.

Author

DR. PHIL. CHRISTIANE PANTKE

Ethnologist with minor subjects *Old Americanism and Religion Science* at the Institute for Religion Science at the University of Berlin. Field studies about "afro- brasilian culture, religion (candomblé) and pentecostal congregations (igrejas pentecostais)", Brazil. Inquiry about religion development of spiritual religions, subject: "Cardezism in Brazil". Projects in the house of cultures of the world in Berlin. Scientific collaborator in DFG projects: "the baihanian society in tenseness of trance and puritanism, family and substitute family in the religion society in Bahia, Brazil". Lectures and lessons about "religion in Brazil".

Contact: E-Mail: jane.pantke@t-online.de

Footnotes

1 Other *nações* are named after the Yoruba-realms of *Ketu* and *Ijexá*. In addition, there are the *nações* Jeje, i.e. the African *Ewe* und die *nações* Kongo, Kongo-Angola, und Angola (cf PINTO 1991:161; PANTKE 1997:54).
2 cf: MINZ, L. 1992.
3 cf: BACELAR, J. 1989 & 1995
4 cf: PANTKE 1997.
5 For details: BRAGA 1988.
6 These *trabalhos* (work) are often referred to as *quimbanda* (harming magic) or *macumba* (witchcraft)
7 cf: BRAGA 1988.
8 For details, please see: KELLER 1995 and DIALLO 1995.

9 This example (1999) is part of my field research within the framework of the DFG-project: The Bahian society in conflict between ecstasy and Puritanism.
10 She was trained in the *candomblé-nagô*-tradition and was, some twenty years ago, actively practicing spiritism until Oxum appeared to her and instructed her to become a *mãe-de-santo* and establish her own *candomblé-terreiro*. Sie told me that she was given permission by the *orixás* to utilise also elements of spiritism such as the 'mesa branca' (white table).
11 It is noteworthy that it is not the *orixá Omulu* who causes the illness although he was identified as being responsible for the rash and who was given an *ebó*. However, according to the *mãe-de-santo*, the ancestral spiriti who causes the illness is a child of Omulu.
12 Like colours and animals, food and herbs are assigned to respecive *orixás* according to specific analogies. For instance, delicate plants to female *orixás*, fleshy, leafy plants to male *orixás*. This assignment, however, can be different depending on location and the influence of the respective terreiros. (cf:: MINZ 1992:71). Also cf: Portugal 1987 regarding plants and recipes, LÜHNING 1999: (301-331) regarding the comparison of Bahian and African botany, and ORDEP (1999:289-302) regarding myths as cosmological origin of healing rituals of the *candomblés*, and COSTA DA LIMA (1999: 319-326) regarding nutrition and diet in *candomblés*. Also cf: some healing rituals by HOHENSTEIN 1991.
13 *Yoruba*: Piperegun, (cf: Portugal 1987:19)
14 *Aroeira de Ogum* (lat.: schinus molle l.), *Xoroqué/Exú*. It finds application in many witchcraft eliminating rituals in which the *orixás Ogum* and *Exú* are involved. It is beneficial in eczema and inflammatory diseases. cf: FARELLI (1999:23) and MINZ (1992:83)
15 (*Sanseviera Ceynaica*: Oguns Sword), this plant is frequently used against evil eye (*mal olhada*); cf: MINZ (1992:59). (*Yoruba: Junça*, for the *orixá Osaaim*. cf: Portugal, 1987:19)
16 *Vassourinha de Nossa Senhora* (lat.: Scoparia dulcis L.); is supposed to be linked with *Omulu*. cf: MINZ (1992:83
17 Plant of the coast: (lat.: calanchoe brasiliensis camb.); supposedly belongs to *orixá Oxum* and has anti-inflammatory properties. cf: *Minz* (1992:72). (*Yoruba: Odum-dum* for the *orixás: Oxalá, Yemanjá, Xangô, Ossaim, Oxossi and Exú*. cf: Portugal, 1987:19.)
18 Lat.: Ocimum basilicum L. (MINZ 1992:82)
19 also *pinhão-roxo* (lat.: Jatrofa Multifida-Lineu), for *Ogum* and *Exú*. Strong plant suitable for cleansing baths., cf: PORTUGAL 1987:120.
20 also *folha araçá-de-coroa* (lat.: Psidium Variabilis-Bergius), for *Oxóssi* und *Oxalá* for cleansing baths. cf: PORTUGAL 1987:39
21 also *folha de mangueira* (lat.: Manjifera Indica-Lieu), linked to *Ogum* and *Exú* , for cleansing baths; *Yoruba: mongoro*, cf. PORTUGAL 1987:102
22 MINZ (1992:57) describes a ‚session' to bewitch a person. During this procedure, names were written on pieces of paper that were later burned.
23 This is done in the same order as described earlier.
24 Port.: *abrir os caminos;* linguistic term from the *candomblé* in Bahia.
25 Here, the persons are meant to be protected from living enemies. However, the *mãe-de-santo* did not want to carry out a *trabalho* against them. In many of the known treatments, these are two separate areas: ebós for ancestral spirits and *orixás* and *trabalhos* against enemies. cf: for instance MINZ 1992.
26 Unresolved social conflicts weaken individuals. Illness is often interpreted as inferiority and personal weakness. A parallel can be drawn to situations in society: Social marginalisation rarely leads to social protest but ia usually directed towards persons within the immediate vicinity, for instance through *trabalhos* in the *candomblé* (cf: POLLAK-ELTZ: 1982)
27 cf: LEWIS 1971, who interpred parts of African 'obsession rituals' in a similar manner.

28 cf in this context: Levi-Strauss (1967:204-255), who described the therapeutic function of the ritual by analysing the shamanistic healing rituals of the *Cuña*-Indians of Panama. Not only the individual who requires help but also the entire community experiences the psychologically healing effect through the process of the ritual.
29 After first channelling the fears, and following the projection of conflicts and aggressions onto him, the cosmic harmony is being restored.

References
Bacelar, J. 1989. *Etnicidade. Ser Negro em Salvador. Ianamá.* Salvador.
Bacelar, J. 1995. Modernização e a Cultura dos Negros em Salvador. In: *Simpósio International: Culturas Marginalizadas e Processos de Modernização na América Latina,* S.2-17. Hg.: Centro de Estudos Afro-Orientais. Salvador.
Braga, J. 1988. *O Jogo de Búzios. Um estudo da advinhação no Candomblé.* São Paulo.
Diallo, T. 1995. Vorwort. In: *Ritual und Heilung. Eine Einführung in die Ethnomedizin.* Hrg.: B. Pfleiderer, K. Greifeld; W. Bichmannn. Berlin.
Greifeld, K. 1995. Einführung in die Medizinethnologie, S.11-33. In: *Ritual und Heilung. Eine Einführung in die Ethnomedizin.* Hrg.: B. Pfleiderer, K. Greifeld, W. Bichmann. Berlin.
Hohenstein, de E. 1991. *Das Reich der Magischen Mütter. Eine Untersuchung über die Frauen in den afro-brasilianischen Besessenheitskulten candomblé.* Frankfurt.
Keller, F.B. 1995. *Krank warum? Einführung und These.* S.:10-24. Ostfildern.
Levi-Strauss, C. 1967. *Strukturale Anthropologie.* Frankfurt. Original: Paris.
Lewis, I. M. 1989. *Ecstatic Religion. A study of shamanism and spirit possession.* London/ New York.
Lima da Costa, V. 1999. As Dietas Africanas no Sistema Alimentar Brasileiro. In: *Faces da Tradição Afro-Brasileira. Religiosidade, Sincretismo, Anti-Sincretismo, Reafricanização, Prácticas Terapeuticas, Etnobotânicas e Comida,* S.319-326. Hrg.: Carlos Caroso e Jeferson Bacelar. Rio de Janeiro /Salvador-BA.
Lühning, A. 1999. Ewé. As Plantas Brasileiras e seus Parentes Africanos. In: *Faces da Tradição Afro-Brasileira. Religiosidade, Sincretismo, Anti-Sincretismo, Reafricanização, Prácticas Terapeuticas, Etnobotânicas e Comida,* S.303-31. Hrg.: Carlos Caroso e Jeferson Bacelar. Rio de Janeiro /Salvador-BA.
Minz, L. 1992. *Krankheit als Niederlage und die Rückkehr zur Stärke. Candomblé als Heilunsprozeß.* Bonn.
Pantke, C. 1998. *Favelas, Festas und Candomblé. Zum interkulturellen Austausch zwischen Afro-Brasilianern und Touristen im Rahmen kultischer und profaner Festveranstaltungen in Salvador da Bahia.* Ketsch bei Mannheim.
Pinto, T. de Oliveira 1991. *Capoeira, Samba, Candomblé. Afro-brasiliansiche Musik im Recôncavö, Bahia.* Berlin.
Pollak-Eltz, A. 1982. *Folk-Medicine in Venezuela.* Wien.
Portugal, F. 1987. *Rezas. Folhas- Chás e Rituais dos Orixás. Folhas, Sementes, Frutas e Raízes de Uso Litúrgico na Umbanda e no Candomblé. Com uso práctico na Medicina popular.* Rio de Janeiro.
Serra, O. 1999. Etnobotânica do candomblé Nagô da Bahia: Cosmologia e Estrutura Básica do Arranjo Taxonômico. O Modelo da Liturgia- in: *Faces da Tradição Afro-Brasileira. Religiosidade, Sincretismo, Anti-Sincretismo, Reafricanização, Prácticas Terapeuticas, Etnobotânicas e Comida,* S. 289-302. Hrg.: Carlos Caroso e Jeferson Bacelar. Rio de Janeiro /Salvador-BA.

O LE FOFO – DIE HEILER VON SAMOA

von Christian Lehner

Traditionelle Glaubensvorstellungen der Samoaner
Die medizinischen Glaubensvorstellungen und Praktiken der Samoaner bezeichnen die Einheimischen als ihre eingeborene Medizin.
Mein Interesse an den medizinischen Glaubensvorstellungen und Praktiken der Samoaner entwickelte sich unter dem Eindruck verschiedener Erlebnisse während mehrerer Aufenthalte auf den Inseln Upolu und Savai'i. Diese Inseln stellen die Hauptlandmasse der westsamoanischen Inseln dar, und dort lebt die Mehrzahl der samoanischen Eingeborenen.
Die üppig-grünen Inseln von West-Samoa liegen 1026 Kilometer westlich von Tahiti mitten im Herzen von Polynesien auf halbem Weg zwischen dem Äquator und dem Wendekreis des Steinbockes. Samoa ist der Sage nach die Heimat der Polynesier - HAWAIKI - von der aus Ostpolynesien (die Marquesas und die Gesellschaftsinsel) und viele andere Teile der Südsee besiedelt wurden.
Tausende von Jahren blieb diese Inselgruppe vor fremden Einflüssen verschont. Prähistorische Bauten, wie zum Beispiel die PULEMELEI Steinpyramide auf der Insel Savai'i, werden von Experten auf ein Entstehungsjahr um 1000 vor Christus datiert. Dort entwickelte sich eine eigenständige kulturelle und soziale Struktur, in die seit Jahrtausenden die eingeborene Medizin eingebunden war und auch heute noch ist.
Auch das Auftreten des ersten europäischen Missionars Reverend John Williams von der Londoner Missionsgesellschaft im Jahre 1830, der im übrigen im gesamten

pazifischen Raum sehr erfolgreich Christianisierungen durchführte, war nicht geeignet die alten Traditionen und Gebräuche der Samoaner wesentlich verändern zu können. Der tägliche Umgang und der enge Kontakt mit den verschiedenen Pflanzen und Pflanzenarten, von denen viele Spezies in keinem anderen Teil der Welt gefunden werden können, lehrte die Samoaner Nutzen aus den verschiedenen Pflanzen und Pflanzenteilen zu ziehen und deren Heilkräfte für sich zu verwenden.

Gesundheit, Krankheit und Kultur

Die Zusammenhänge zwischen Gesundheit, Krankheit, Kultur und sozialer Organisation werden jenen, die daran gewöhnt sind, über sie als getrennte Sphären der menschlichen Aktivitäten zu denken, nicht immer auf den ersten Blick ersichtlich. Unter den Angelegenheiten, die von der Kultur definiert und erklärt werden, befinden sich auch Gesundheit und Krankheit. Die verschiedenen Vorstellungen über das Kranksein, die sich in den menschlichen Gesellschaften nachweisen lassen, finden ihr Spiegelbild in den unterschiedlichen Antworten der einzelnen Sozietäten auf die Krankheit.

Die Kultur setzt sich aus einer Reihe von Glaubensvorstellungen, Ideen und Wertvorstellungen zusammen, die in menschliche Aktivitäten transponiert werden müssen und wird am besten im Zusammenhang mit der sozialen Organisation gesehen und verstanden werden. Die Kultur stellt die Prinzipien dar, die als Muster des häufigsten sozialen Verhaltens dienen. Demzufolge können Krankheiten und die Antworten auf die Krankheiten am besten in ihrem kulturellen und sozialen Zusammenhang studiert werden. Die Art in der eine bestimmte Gruppe von Menschen über die Entstehung der Krankheiten und die Antworten darauf denkt, wird am ehesten in den gruppeneigenen Begriffen verstanden.

Die drei Welten

Die Kultur der Samoaner setzt voraus, dass der Mensch innerhalb von drei "Welten" lebt: einer natürlichen Welt, einer sozialen Welt und einer spirituellen Welt. Der Zustand des Menschen wird zu jeder Zeit durch die Beziehungen zwischen dem Individuum und der natürlichen, der sozialen und der spirituellen Weltordnung beeinflusst. Der ersehnte Zustand, den es anzustreben gilt, ist jener in dem die Beziehungen zwischen dem Menschen und jeder einzelnen dieser Welten stabil und ohne Spannung ist. Wenn ein solches Äquilibrium besteht, ist ein Gefühl des Wohlbefindens zu erwarten. Wenn der Einzelne diesbezüglich betroffen ist, wird dieser Zustand SOIFUA MALOLOINA genannt und wenn er ein Kollektiv betrifft, wird er MAOPOOPO bezeichnet.

Diese Befindlichkeit ist jedoch kaum ein perfektes Äquilibrium. Einige verbleibende Spannungen erscheinen unausweichlich, wobei die Kultur akzeptable Grenzen definiert und die soziale Organisation dazu dient Konflikte die meiste Zeit innerhalb gewisser Grenzen zu halten. Ernste Störungen dieses Gleichgewichtes sind jedoch auch in der samoanischen Gesellschaft unausweichlich, wie folgendes samoanische Sprichwort festhält: TUAOI AFA MA MANINOA – "*Der Sturm und die Ruhe sind Nachbarn*" -. Die Tatsache, dass ernste periodische Störungen dieses Gleichgewichtes unausweichlich sind, macht sie aber auch nicht erstrebenswert. Historisch gesehen hingen viele ökonomische und soziale Aktivitäten, die zum Überleben sowohl des Einzelnen als auch der Gruppe notwendig waren, von der Zusammenarbeit und Kooperation, ab und ungelöste Spannungen wurden bei den Samoanern in allen Zeiten für problematisch gehalten, da sie die Basis des gemeinsamen Überlebens bedrohten. Bis zu einem gewissen Grad gilt dies auch heute noch, wobei eine geteilte, uneinige Gruppe eine verletzbare Gruppe darstellt. Die Fähigkeit politischen und sozialen Boden festzuhalten und das Ansehen, das von diesem abgeleitet werden kann, ist stets von der Einheit der Gruppe abhängig gewesen. Interne Spannungen und Konflikte, die eine Gruppe als verletzlich zurückließen, waren eine ständige Quelle der Betroffenheit und es wurden unaufhörlich Bemühungen unternommen Spannungen zu vermeiden um die Einheit der Gruppe oder zumindest deren Anschein zu erhalten.

Die Instandhaltung eines Zustandes, der am ehesten als unvollkommenes komplexes Fließgleichgewicht bezeichnet wird, erscheint durch die frühe und vorzeitige Entdeckung und Behandlung jeglicher Spannungen gesichert. Das

Konfliktmanagement und die Auflösung derselben waren immer ein zentrales Anliegen der samoanischen Gesellschaft. Die Häuptlinge - MATAI -, die Priester - FAIFE'AU -, die Heiler - FOFO - und andere Samoaner sind alle auf unterschiedlichen Wegen in diesen Prozess innerhalb des Zusammenhanges eines Dorfes eingebunden. Wer in die Konfliktlösung eingebunden wird und die äußere Form, die der Prozess annimmt, hängt von den Trägern des Konfliktes und dem Ursprung und der Natur der Spannungen ab, wobei aber alle Beteiligte in Rollen eingebunden sind, die in der samoanischen Gesellschaft stets für wichtig gehalten werden.

Während Parallelen in der Tätigkeit all jener bestehen, die versuchen die Gründe der Störung zu identifizieren und das Äquilibrium wiederherzustellen, gibt es auch signifikante Unterschiede. Die Gründe der Spannungen und der Konflikte zwischen den einzelnen Dörfern, Familien oder Individuen werden meist relativ einfach erkannt und besitzen üblicherweise die Tendenz aus weltlichen Aktivitäten zu entspringen. Diese Gründe können meist auf ein bestimmtes Ereignis rückgeführt werden, welchem oftmals von unbeteiligten Personen als Augenzeugen beigewohnt wurde, und welches meist alle bekannte Personen einschließt. Die Verantwortlichkeit, diese Ereignisse festzuhalten und Lösungen herbeizuführen, fällt üblicherweise dem MATAI oder dem FAIFE'AU zu, die beide unterschiedliche Rollen verkörpern.

Der Priester

Die wesentliche Rolle der Priester - FAIFE'AU - ist meist eine präventive. In ihrem Unterricht betonen sie die Bedeutung der Werte und des Verhaltens auf welchem die empfindliche soziale Ordnung ruht. Wenn sie auf entstehende Spannungen aufmerksam werden, versuchen sie diese mit subtiler und manchmal weniger subtiler Führerschaft jenen gegenüber zu entschärfen, die darin direkt involviert sind und jenen die möglicherweise miteinbezogen werden könnten. Die Tatsache, dass sie selbst nicht direkt in diesen Konflikt und die politischen Interessen, die ihn umgeben, verwickelt sind, erlaubt den Pastoren meist Standpunkte einzunehmen, die von keinem anderen eingenommen werden könnten ohne den Konflikt eskalieren zu lassen.

Einige Konflikte entstehen jedoch trotz dieser Präventionen, wobei die Priester sehr oft auch als Vermittler eingebunden werden. Sie spielen dabei oft eine wichtige Rolle, weil es ihnen möglich ist für den Frieden, die Vergebung und die Wiederversöhnung in Situationen zu argumentieren, in denen sich die Streitparteien, die vom Konflikt betroffen sind, bedingt durch ihre eigenen Ehrvorstellungen verpflichtet fühlen den Streit fortzusetzen bis die eine oder andere Seite die Oberhand gewinnt. Auch können die Priester eingeladen werden eine bestimmte Rolle beim Wiederversöhnungsfest - FA'ALELEIGA - zu übernehmen, das üblicherweise dem offenem Konflikt folgt. In dieser Rolle wird der Priester versuchen die einzelnen Fraktionen zu überzeugen, dass Vergebung und Wiederversöhnung die einzige akzeptable Vorgangsweise darstellt.

Die MATAI können einzeln oder im Kollektiv die Spannungen in einer Gruppe, der sie als Führer voranstehen, begrenzen und festhalten. Ihr Ansehen und ihre effektive Macht ruht auf ihrer Fähigkeit Ressourcen zu mobilisieren, was offensichtlich nur so lange möglich ist, solange es ihnen gelingt die Einheit der Gruppe zu erhalten. Demzufolge versucht ein MATAI Spannungen, die sich innerhalb verschiedener Sektionen der Familie entwickeln, festzuhalten und einer

Lösung zuzuführen, um im Falle einer Krise vorbereitet zu sein, wenn die Einheit der Familie gefordert wird. Auf ähnliche Weise werden auch die einzelnen Köpfe einer Familie versuchen, innerhalb ihrer verschiedenen Teile die Spannungen festzuhalten und einer Auflösung zuzuführen, um es im Krisenfalle der Familie zu ermöglichen die Ressourcen der gesamten Familie zu mobilisieren. Aber Konflikte können auch in gut geführten Familien entstehen und die einzelnen Dörfer und deren MATAIs werden wiederkehrend gefordert diese Situationen zu entschärfen. Sie identifizieren die Unruhestifter und die Beleidigungen und setzen mit der Autorität, die in sie als Führer ihrer umfangreichen Familien oder als Versammlung der MATAIs - FONO A MATAI - gesetzt wurde, sozial vorgeschriebene "Lösungen" fest und überwachen deren Durchführung auch.

Sowohl MATAI als auch FAIFE'AU unterstützen ebenso jene Menschen, die damit befasst sind verschleppte und ernstere Zerreißungen des sozialen Gefüges zu verhindern, welche entstehen können, wenn eine größere Gruppen von Menschen in einen Konflikt verwickelt wird. Die Gründe und die Konsequenzen der sozialen Spannungen, welche die MATAI und die FAIFE'AU identifizieren und behandeln, und ihre Rolle in diesem Prozess sind verhältnismäßig offensichtlich.

Die Heiler

Aber auch die Heiler spielen eine wesentliche Rolle in diesem Prozess. Ihre Funktion ist jedoch weit komplexer und weniger offensichtlich. Sie ist komplexer, da die Menschen zu jeder Zeit gegenüber physischen, sozialen und spirituellen

Mächten verletzbar sind, die alle ihr persönliches Äquilibrium stören und Krankheiten verursachen können und weniger offensichtlich, da die sozialen Konsequenzen der Krankheit durchaus weniger augenscheinlich sein können, wie zum Beispiel im Falle einer Dorffehde. Da die Krankheit eine Störung in den Beziehungen des Einzelnen und einer der Welten innerhalb derer dieser lebt wiederspiegelt, muss ein Heiler mit einer Reihe von physischen, spirituellen und sozialen Ursachen und Gründen umgehen und muss sich immer der Möglichkeit gegenwärtig sein, dass die Krankheit und ihr sozialer Zusammenhang miteinander verbunden sind.

Die Aufgabe des Heilers ist es den wahrscheinlichsten Ursprung jeglicher vorgegebener Folge von Symptomen und ihre Bedeutung festzusetzen und eine Antwort vorzuschlagen, welche die Spannungen lösen kann. Das diagnostische Modell, das in einem späteren Kapitel ausführlicher beschrieben wird, ist äußerst komplex, da es mit drei Ebenen der Realität umgehen muss und ebenso die Möglichkeit besteht, dass vorgegebene Symptome mit mehr als einer Ebene verbunden sind. Dieser Prozess wird auch noch durch die Tatsache erschwert, dass das Opfer diese Verbindungen nicht verstehen kann und nur eine beschränkte und passive Rolle in der Diagnosefindung spielen kann.

In vielen Fällen kommen die Heiler zum Schluss, dass eine Krankheit organische Ursachen hat: die Symptome werden von organischen Störungen verursacht, die im allgemeinen mit der natürlichen Welt in Verbindung stehen. Der Heiler empfiehlt eine Form der Therapie und manchmal eine Änderung des Lebensstiles bei der Ernährung, der persönlichen Hygiene, der Organisation von körperlicher Tätigkeit und so weiter.

Die Erkennung der richtigen Verbindungen und die Kombination von Therapie und Lebensstiländerung werden ausschließlich für notwendig erachtet um die Balance und demnach auch die Gesundheit wiederherzustellen. Organische Krankheiten besitzen aber auch soziale und ökonomische Konsequenzen, die sich mit dem sozialen Status des Opfers und der Natur und der Dauer der Krankheit ändern.

Das Opfer

Die Rolle eines Krankheitsopfers in der familieninternen Arbeitsaufteilung bestimmt die unmittelbaren wirtschaftlichen Konsequenzen seiner oder ihrer Krankheit. Die Rolle eines Opfers in der Familie und den Angelegenheiten des Dorfes bestimmen die sozialen und politischen Konsequenzen der Krankheit. Je zentraler die Rolle des Opfers auf diesen Gebieten ist, um so ernster sind die Konsequenzen durch die Krankheit.

Das erfolgreiche Einschreiten eines Heilers begrenzt somit die aktuellen und potentiellen Kosten der Krankheit. Das erfolgreiche Zurückhalten einer organischen Infektionskrankheit, welche unter Umständen erhebliche soziale und ökonomische Auswirkungen besitzt, kann für die Familie und das Dorf des Opfers von größter Bedeutung sein. Die Folgen und die Kosten von organischen Krankheiten werden relativ einfach verstanden und abgeschätzt.

Es besteht auch eine weitere Reihe von Symptomen, die vermuten lassen, dass die Beziehungen eines Individuums zum sozialen Weltreich gestört sind. Da jedoch bereits durch die Definition bedingt diese auch andere Menschen und Gruppen einschließen, besitzen diese Symptome eine noch größere Bedeutung. Wenn die Quellen der Spannungen innerhalb dieser Beziehungen nicht erkannt und

eliminiert werden, können sie für den Einzelnen und die Gruppe bedrohlich werden.
Der Heiler ist mit der Aufgabe betraut die Lokalisierung der Beziehung oder der Beziehungen, die belastet werden, durchzuführen, die Ursprünge der Spannungen zu identifizieren, diese der Aufmerksamkeit der anderen, die darin verwickelt sind, zuzuführen und möglicherweise eine gewisse Rolle in der Vermittlung zwischen ihnen zu bekleiden.
Die soziale Bedeutung einer frühzeitigen Diagnose und Behandlung dieses Typs einer Erkrankung liegt in der Tatsache, dass sie verhindern kann, dass einfache Konflikte in weitaus zerstörerische Prozesse eskalieren, die eine größere Zahl von Menschen betreffen und die Ursprünge für Sekundärkonflikte bilden können. Der folgende Fall soll versuchen, die Abfolge der Ereignisse zu illustrieren, die in solchen Beziehungen entstehen kann, wenn eine frühzeitige Intervention ausbleibt.

Fallbeispiel

Die Ereignisse
Eine junge Frau erkrankte auf dem Heimweg nachdem sie in der Pflanzung gearbeitet hatte, indem sie angab fremde Stimmen zu hören und fallweise in unverständlichen Worten und Tonlagen sprach. Ihre Familie war um ihren Zustand besorgt und brachte sie zu einem FOFO um sie behandeln zu lassen. Der Heiler kam zu dem Schluss, dass die Frau auf ihrer Rückkehr aus der Pflanzung von einem bösem Geist - FASIA - befallen wurde. Der Heiler beschwor den Geist, der sich als der Geist des verstorbenen Großvaters der jungen Frau zu erkennen gab, seine Gründe zu entdecken weshalb er das Mädchen befallen habe. Dieser erklärte daraufhin seinen Ärger:
In den alten Zeiten wurden die Menschen unmittelbar hinter dem Dorf in flachen Erdgräbern bestattet, welche von Steinsäulen markiert wurden. Die jüngeren Gräber wurden näher zum Dorf angelegt und mit fein ausgearbeiteten Zementtafeln mit eigener Überdachungen und in einigen Fällen sogar mit importierten Grabsteinen gekennzeichnet.
Die Klage des Geistes bestand darin, dass die Nachkommen der Verstorbenen, die im alten Friedhof begraben wurden, diese vergessen hätten und dass dies ohne Zweifel aus den mit Gras und Unkraut überwachsenen Gräber und der allgemeinen Ablehnung des alten Friedhofes ersichtlich sei. Unter der Annahme, dass der Geist und jene, die mit ihm begraben wurden, das Dorf errichtet hatten und dadurch das Ansehen gewonnen hatten, dass sie stark und einig seien, wäre dies ein bedauernswerter Zustand. Zur gleichen Zeit machten die noch Lebenden erheblich mehr Aufsehen über die Gräber der Menschen, die im oder in der Nähe des Dorfes in den neuen Gräbern bestattet wurden, welche zu keiner Zeit um die Ehre des Dorfes kämpfen mussten.
Während der Geist den Respekt für die Toten verstand und hoch achtete, wurde er durch die Tatsache verärgert, dass einige Leute aus dem Dorf sangen und frivole, manchmal sogar obszöne Reden führten, wenn sie Abkürzungen durch den alten Friedhof nahmen. Die Kinder verwendeten die Steine von den Gräbern um damit nach Flughunden zu jagen und die Erwachsenen hatten die Steine von den Gräbern entfernt um damit die Fundamente ihrer Häuser zu bauen, nur weil sie zu faul waren diese aus dem Meer oder dem Hinterland zu sammeln.

Die Konsequenzen
Als der Inhalt dieser Beschwerde im Dorf bekannt wurde, traf sich sofort die Ratsversammlung der Häuptlinge - FONO A MATAI - um dieses Thema zu diskutieren. Die involvierten Familien beschlossen die Gebeine der Verstorbenen wieder auszugraben und sie in den neu errichteten und neu geschmückten Familiengräbern, die näher zum Dorf gelegen waren in einer Zeremonie zu überführen, die unter dem Namen LIUTOFAGA in Samoa bekannt ist. Die Ratsversammlung organisierte eine vielbesuchte Zeremonie, bei der die Knochen aus dem alten Friedhof enterdigt, gereinigt, geölt und in TAPA Stoffe gewickelt wurden und anschließend zu ihren neuen Ruheplätzen gebracht wurden. Das Ereignis, eine interessante Kombination aus christlichen und vorchristlichen Riten, erinnerte die Lebenden an jene, die das Dorf gegründet hatten. Dieses Ereignis wird bis heute für ein wesentliches Geschehen in der gegenwärtigen Geschichte des Dorfes gehalten.
Es erscheint einfach über die psychologischen Dimensionen dieses Falles zu

spekulieren. Es ist durchaus möglich, dass die Enkeltochter eine enge Beziehung zu ihrem Großvater besaß, da er sie aufgezogen hatte und dass sie enorm stolz auf ihn war und sehr verärgert über die Tatsache war, dass die Menschen seinen Ruheplatz ohne nötigen Respekt behandelt hatten. Es wäre allerdings zu einfach anzunehmen, dass sie diese Tatsache dazu verleitet hätte eine sogenannte Geisterkrankheit - MA'I AITU - vorzutäuschen um die Aufmerksamkeit darauf in der ihr einzig möglichen Art und Weise zu lenken.

Weit interessanter und zumindest ebenso bedeutend erscheinen die weitreichenden sozialen Konsequenzen der Tätigkeit des Heilers. Die Fähigkeit des Heilers, die Hintergründe der Krankheit zu erkennen und die Möglichkeit im Lauf der Behandlung die Aufmerksamkeit auf eine Quelle von Spannungen zwischen dem Einzelnen und der übernatürlichen Welt zu lenken, waren in der Folge für alle Dinge wesentlich, die sich danach entwickelten.

Im Aufzeigen der zukünftigen Möglichkeit des Befallenswerdens, dadurch dass andere übelwollende Geister im abgelehnten Friedhof ihr Missfallen ausdrückten, zieht der Heiler das allgemeine Interesse der weiter reichenden Bedeutung dieser Quelle von potentiellen Schwierigkeiten darauf und erlaubt es dem Dorf zu überlegen und einem Thema gegenüber zu handeln, das offensichtlich seiner Aufmerksamkeit entgangen ist.

Als die Dorfversammlung die Notwendigkeit des gemeinsamen Handelns erkannte, wurde die Bedeutung des Ideals der kollektiven Solidarität wieder gestärkt. Als die Bewohner des Dorfes die Ausgrabungen und Wiederbestattungen gemeinsam durchführten, wurde dem kulturellen Ideal eine soziale Form gegeben und diese wiederbehauptet. Schlussendlich wurde es, indem die Wirkung der übernatürlichen Kräfte in der Krankheit erkannt und es dem Dorf dadurch ermöglicht wurde seine darüber hinausgehende Bedeutung zu überdenken und danach zu handeln, dem Heiler möglich sowohl die Bedeutung der Wirkung der übernatürlichen Kräfte als auch der Notwendigkeit jener wiederzuerstärken, die sie zu erkennen vermögen.

Demzufolge muss, obwohl die primäre Rolle des Heilers darin gelegen sein mag bestimmte Krankheiten bei den Individuen, die sie umgeben, zu erkennen und zu behandeln, dies in einem weiteren Zusammenhang gesehen werden. Diese Aktivität stellt einen Versuch dar das Gleichgewicht in und zwischen den natürlichen, den sozialen und den übernatürlichen Elementen des Lebens der Individuen wiederherzustellen. Bei diesem Prozess kann der Heiler Umstände erkennen, die für das Kollektiv, dem der Einzelne angehört, wesentliche Bedeutung haben.

Indem er die Aufmerksamkeit auf sie lenkt kann der Heiler frühzeitige Interventionen erlauben und Umstände verhindern, die sich in zerreißende Konflikte entwickeln können und welche in weiterer Folge eine große Zahl von Menschen einbeziehen und potentiell ernste soziale, ökonomische und politische Konsequenzen nach sich ziehen können.

Schlussfolgerung

Die Vorstellung der Samoaner vom Wohlbefinden und die Rolle, welche die Heiler bei seiner Erhaltung spielen, macht ihre soziale Signifikanz zumindest ebenso interessant wie ihre medizinische.

In der westlich orientierten Medizin wäre dieses Mädchen vermutlich mit der Diagnose halluzinatorische Psychose in stationäre Behandlung gekommen und mit Hilfe von dämpfenden Neuroleptika behandelt worden um die Halluzinationen zum Verschwinden zu bringen. Damit wären sowohl dem Mädchen als auch der sie umgebenden Sozietät die Möglichkeit genommen worden die bestehende Hintergrundproblematik einschließlich der verursachenden Faktoren aufzuarbeiten.

Dem samaonischen Mädchen ist bis zum heutigen Tage ein Krankenhausaufenthalt erspart geblieben und die sporadisch auftretenden Halluzinationen kamen zum völligen Erliegen nachdem die Ratsversammlungen einberufen wurde und die Erscheinungen öffentlich zum Thema gemacht wurden.

Autor
ORR Dr. Christian Lehner
Studium der Medizin, Ethnologie und Psychologie an der Universität Wien, im ärztlichen Beruf tätig.
Ethnomedizinische Studien in Indonesien, China, Thailand und Ozeanien. Seit sechs Jahren regelmäßige Forschungsreisen nach West-Samoa, um die Sprache und die Medizin der Eingeborenen zu studieren. Seit 1996 Vorstand des Institutes für Ethnomedizin der Sir Karl Pooper Society.
Kontakt: E-Mail: Christian.Lehner@bgld.gv.at

Literatur
PARNHAM, B. E. V., 1972. Plants Of Samoa. *DSIR Information Series* no. 85. Wellington DSIR.
MacCUDDIN, Charles R., 1974. *Samoan Medical Plants and Their Usage. Office of Comprehensive Health Planning* , Dept. of Medical Service, Pagopago, Govt. of America Samoa.
MOYLE, Richard M., 1974. "Samoan Medicinal Incantations", *Journal of the Polynesian Society,* 83, pp.155 - 179.
MOYLE, Richard M., 1974. "Samoan Medicinal Incantations", *Journal of the Polynesian Society,* 83, pp.155 - 179.
TURNER, George, 1861. *Nineteen Years In Polynesia: Missionary Life, Travels And Researches In The Islands of The Pacific.* London, Snow.
KINLOCH, P.J. 1985. *Talking Health, But Doing Sickness: Studies in Samoan Health.* Wellington, Viktoria Univ. Press.
HEATH, Timothy, 1973. *The Diagnosis and Treatment of Disease in a Rural Village in Western Samoa.* MA Thesis, Univ. of Auckland.
KINLOCH, P. J. 1985. *Midwives and Midwifery in Western Samoa.* C. D. F. Parsons ed.
TE RANGI HIROA, 1930. Samoan Material Culture. Honolulu, Bernice P. Bishop *Museum Bulletin* no. 75
WILLIAMS, John, 1838. *A Narrative of Missionary Enterprises in the South Sea Islands.* London Snow. Seite 354
CHURCHWARD, William B.; 1971. My Consulate in Samoa. Erstmals publiziert 1887, Folkstone, Dawsons.
DILLON, Peter, 1829. *Narrativ and Successful Result of a Voyage in the South Seas to ascertain the Fate of La Perouse's Expedition.* London, Hurst, Chance & Co.

O LE FOFO – THE HEALERS OF SAMOA*

by Christian Lehner

Traditional belief systems in Samoa

This lecture is an attempt to describe the medicinal ideas and practices that are called native medicine among Samoans and which they consider as their indigenous therapeutic medicine. My interest in the medicinal beliefs and practices of Samoa developed from the impression of several different experiences and circumstances during stays on the islands Upolu and Savai´i, where the majority of the indigenous people of Samoa live and that also is the main landmass of the Western Samoan Islands.

The lush green islands of Western Samoa are located 1026 kilometers west of Tahiti in the heart of Polynesia, halfway between the equator and the tropic of capricorn. Samoa is said to be the original home of Polynesians HAWAIKI from where Eastern Polynesia (Marquesas and Society Islands) and many other parts of the South Pacific were populated.

During thousands of years these islands, with their prehistoric architecture, like the stone pyramid PULEMELEI on the island of Savai´i, that was estimated by experts on a date of origin around 1000 b.c., escaped any foreign influences and developed an independent cultural and social structure, where native medicine was integrated and still is today. Even the appearance of the first european missionary Reverend John Williams from London Missionary Society in 1830, who

---

* Translated by Christian Abele

in the entire pacific area very successfully implemented conversions to Christianity, was not able to considerably change the old traditions and customs of Samoa. The daily use and close contact to various plants and plant species - whereas many species in no other part of the world can be found - taught the people of Samoa, because of a lack of western medicine, to benefit from several plants and to use their healing powers.

Health, illness and culture

The connections between health, illness, culture and social organization will not be noticed immediately by those used to think of them as separate spheres in human activities. Health and illness are part of the topics, that are defined and explained by culture.

The various beliefs of illness, which can be proved in human societies, are reflected by various different answers of the societies on what illness is. Culture consists of beliefs, ideas and values that need to be transposed into human activities, and is displayed and understood best in connection to social organization. Culture represents the principles, which are patterns of the most common social behavior. Therefore, diseases and the answers to illnesses are studied best in their cultural and social context.

The way of how a specific group of people thinks about the origin of illness and the answers to it are understood most likely in its own terms.

The three worlds

The Samoan culture presupposes that a person lives in three "worlds": a natural world, a social world and a spiritual world. The condition of the people is influenced at all time by the relations of the individual with the natural, the social and the spiritual worldorders. The longed-for condition, that is meant to strive for, is where the relations between the person and every single one of these worlds is stable and without tension.

If such an equilibrium exists, a feeling of well-being can be expected. If a single individual is affected regarding this, its condition is called SOIFUA MALOLOINA and if it affects a collective, it is called MAOPOOPO.

However, this condition is hardly a perfect equilibrium. A few remaining tensions seem to be inevitable, culture though defines acceptable boundaries and social organization is of help to limit conflicts most of the time. Serious interference of this balance, however, is also in the Samoan society inevitable, as the following saying states: TUAOI AFA MA MANINOA "Storm and silence are neighbours."

The fact that serious periodical disorders of this balance are inevitable does not make them desirable. Historically, many economic and social activities that were essential to the survival of the individual, as well as the collective, depended upon cooperation.

Unresolved tensions were considered by Samoans at all times as problematic, since they threaten the foundation of common survival. To a ceratin extent this is still valid today, where a divided and disagreeing group is a vulnerable group. The ability to keep a firm political and social ground and the reputation resulting from it, has always been dependent on the unity of the group.

Internal tensions and conflicts, that left a group vulnerable were a permanent source of consternation, and incessant endeavors were undertaken to avoid tensions to keep the unity of the group or at least its reputation. The maintenance of the condition described most likely as an incomplete and complex balanced flow, seems to be secured by an early detection and treatment of any tensions. Conflict management and dissolving of the same has always been a central concern of Samoan society.

The priests
MATAI -, priests FAIFE´AU -, healers FOFO and other Samoans are all in different ways part of this process within the connections of a village. Who is part of the conflict solution and the outer performance of the process depends on the participants of the conflict, its origin and the nature of tensions, but all parts are taking roles considered as important in Samoan society.
While there are similarities of the actions taken by those trying to identify the origin of the interference and to restore the equilibrium, there are also significant differences. The cause of tensions and conflicts between villages, families and

individuals are most of the time relatively easy recognized and usually they have the tendency to originate in worldy activities. These causes can mostly be traced back to a certain incident, which has often been witnessed by uninvolved persons and that most of the time includes all persons known. MATAI or FAIFE´AU, both embodying different roles, have the responsibility to hold on to these incidences and to lead to solutions. The essential role of priests FAIFE´AU is most of the time preventive. In their teachings they emphasize on the meaning of values and behavior on which the sensitive social order is based. If noticing arising tensions, they try to neutralize them in a subtile and sometimes in a less subtile way of leading the directly involved and those possibly able to be included.

The fact of not being involved in these conflicts and its surrounding political interests permits the priests to take a point of view that no one else could take without escalating the conflict. Still some conflicts arise despite these preventions, where priests then very often take part as mediators. They often play an important role, since it is possible for them to stand up for peace, forgiveness and reconciliation in situations, where the affected parties of the conflict, due to their ideas of pride and reputation, are obliged to take on the conflict until one or the other takes the winning side. Priests can also be invited to take certain roles at the celebration of reconciliation FA ALELEIGA, usually following the public conflict. In this role, the priest will try to persuade the seperate parties that forgiveness and reconciliation is the only acceptable action to proceed. MATAI can individually or collectively limit tensions in the group they are leading.

Their respect and effective power is based upon their ability to mobilize resources and obviously it is only possible to them as long as they succeed in maintaining the unity of the group. Accordingly a MATAI tries to stop and will lead to the solution of tensions that arise in the different parts of families, in order to be prepared in case of a crisis, where the unity of the family is challenged. In a similar way the individuals of a family will try their parts to hold in and stop the tensions, leading to a solution, so that in case of a crisis the family is able to mobilize the resources of the whole family.

Still conflicts can arise in carefully lead families and the single villages with their MATAIs are recurringly challenged to ease these situations. They identify troublemakers and offences, and with their authority, given to them by their extensive families and in gatherings of the MATAIs FONO A MATAI, they lay down socially stipulated solutions and also supervise their realization. MATAI, as well as FAIFE´AU, also support those people, concerned with preventing any carried on and serious seperations of the social fabric that can arise, if a larger group of people is involved in a conflict. The cause and the consequences of social tensions that MATAI and FAIFE´AU identify and deal with and their role in this process are reasonably obvious.

Healers

But also healers take an essential role in this process. Though their function is a lot more complex and less obvious. It is more complex, since people are at any time vulnerable to physical, social and spiritual powers, that all interfere with their personal equlibrium and are able to cause illness, and less obvious, since the social consequences of an illness can be quite less apparent, like in the case of a village feud. Since the illness reflects an interference of the relations of the individual and one of the worlds that the person lives within, a healer has to deal with various physical, spiritual and social causes and reasons. He must be aware of the fact that the illness and its social context are connected. The healer´s work is to identify the most likely cause of a series of symptoms with their meanings and to propose an answer that can resolve the tensions. The diagnostic model that will be discussed more detailed in a later chapter is extremely complex as it deals with three levels of reality, since there is a possibility that the given symptoms are connected to more than one level.

This process becomes even more difficult, because the victim cannot understand these connections and can only play a limited and passive part in the diagnosis. In many cases healers come to the conclusion that the illness is of organic cause: symptoms are caused by organic disorder that usually are connected to the natural world.

The healer recommends a way of therapy and sometimes a change in lifestyle or nutrition, personal hygiene, the arrangement of physical work and so on. Identification of the right connections and combination of therapy and change in lifestyle are solely seen necessary to restore the balance and therefore health. Organic illnesses also have social and economic consequences, varying with the social status of the victim and the nature and duration of sickness.

The victim

The part a victim of an illness plays inside the family and their division of work determines the direct economic consequences of his or her illness. The part a victim plays in family and village affairs determines the social and political consequences of the illness. The more central the victim's part in these areas is, the more serious are the consequences of the illness. Successful intervention of a healer therefore limits the actual and potential costs of the illness.

The successful restraint of an organic infectious disease, that under circumstances will result in considerable social and economic consequences, can be of great importance to the family and village of the victim. The consequences and costs of organic diseases are fairly easy understood and foreseen.

There are also a lot of symptons presuming that the relations of the individual with the social world is disturbed. Since they also include, due to the definition, other people and groups, these symptoms are of even greater importance. If the roots of tensions within these relations are not identified and eliminated, they might become dangerous to both individual and group.

The healer's work is to localize the relation or relations that are pressured, to identify the cause of tensions, to let others involved become aware of these and perhaps take a certain role of mediation between them. Social implications of early diagnosis and treatment of this type of illness, are based upon the fact, that it can prevent simple conflicts from escalating into far more destructive processes, which might affect a greater number of people and could be the cause for secondary conflicts. Following case will try to illustrate the sequence of events that might arise in such relations, if an early intervention doesn't take place.

Case study

The Events
A young woman became sick after working in the fields, she stated that she heard strange voices that partly spoke in incomprehensible words and tones. Her family was worried about her condition and brought her to a FOFO for treatment. The healer came to the conclusion that the woman on her return from the fields had been attacked by a bad spirit FASIA. The healer conjured the spirit, who disclosed his identity as the passed away grandfather of the young woman, to reveal his reasons for attacking the girl.

He then explained his anger: In former times people were burried right behind the village in flat earthgraves marked by stonecolumns. More recent graves were built closer to the village with gracefully designed plaques, their own rooftops and in some cases even with imported gravestones.

The spirit's complaint consisted of the descendants oblivion of the dead that were burried at the old graveyard, the weed overgrown graves evidentely leaving no doubt about the general dislike of the old graveyard. On the assumption that the spirit and those burried with him founded the village and therefore held the respect of being strong and united, this was an unfortunate condition.

At the same time the living caused a stir about the people's graves in or close to the village being burried in the new graves, even though they at no time had to fight for the honor of the village.

While the spirit understood the respect for the dead and highly respected it, he was upset by the fact that some people of the village sang and talked frivolously, sometimes even obscenely, when taking shortcuts through the old graveyard. Children used rocks of graves to hunt after bats and adults had taken away rocks to built the foundations of their houses, only because they were too lazy to collect these out of the ocean or the backcountry.

The consequences
As the contents of this complaint became known in the village, the council of chiefs FONO A MATAI gathered right away to disuss the matter. The involved families decided to dig out the skeletons of the dead and take them in a ceremony to the recently built and decorated familygraves that are closer to the village and known in Samoa as LIUTOFAGA.

The council of chiefs organized a very well attended ceremony, where the bones from the old graveyard were digged out, cleaned, oiled and wrapped in TAPA cloth and afterwards brought to their new resting places. The event, an interesting combination of christian and pre-christian rites, made the living remember those who founded the village.

This event is considered to be an essential happening in the present history of the village up to this day. It seems easy to speculate on the psychological dimensions of this case. It is quite possible that the granddaughter had a close relationship to her grandfather, since he raised her, and that she honored him tremendously and was very upset about the fact that people treated his place of rest without the needed respect. It would be oversimplified, though, to view this fact as the motivation that had tempted her to pretend a so-called spirit-illness MA'I AITU in order to focus the attention on this matter in her only possible way. A lot more interesting and just as plausible explanation is the far-reaching social consequences of the healer's work.

The ability of the healer to realize the background of the illness and the chance to draw the attention on a root of tensions of the individual and the supernatural world during treatment were essential to all things evolving after. In showing future chances of being attacked by other harmful spirits of the disliked graveyard expressing their disapproval, the healer draws public interest on the far reaching cause for potential trouble and offers the village a chance to reconsider and to take action in a matter, that apparently escaped their attention.

As the village gathering realized the necessity to act in a concerted effort, the meaning of the ideal of collective solidarity was strengthened. While the village people carried out the digging and reburial together, the cultural ideal was given a social form and reclaimed. Finally, by realizing the effect of the supernatural powers in the illness and the given chance for the village to reconsider and then to act upon, it was made possible to the healer to emphasize on the meaning of supernatural powers as well as the necessity to strengthen those able to perceive them.

Accordingly this must, though the primary role of the healer lies in identifying specific illnesses of individuals and to treat those affected, be seen in a wider context. This action is an attempt to balance within and between the natural, social and supernatural elements of the life of the individuals. In this process the healer can realize conditions, that are of essential meaning to the collective the individual is part of. In drawing attention on them, a healer is able to intervene in advance and prevent situations, that could build up into tearing conflicts, which subsequently might involve a greater amount of people and result in potentially serious social, economic and political consequences.

Conclusion

The Samoans idea of well-being and the part healers play in its maintenance makes their social significance at least as interesting as their medicine. In western oriented medicine the girl presumably would have been diagnosed with hallucinatory psychosis and treated in an in-patient hospital with the help of supressing neuroleptics to get rid of the hallucinations. As a result, the girl as well as her surrounding society would have been taken the chance to work through the existing problems in the background including the causes.

The Samoan girl had not to be treated in a hospital to this day and the sporadically occuring hallucinations came to a complete standstill after the council was held and the apparition phenomena were brought to public attention.

Author

ORR DR. CHRISTIAN LEHNER
studies of medicine, ethnology and psychology at the university of Vienna, works in his medical profession.
Ethnomedical studies in Indonesia, China, Thailand and Oceania. Regular field studies in West- Samoa to learn the language and the medicine of the natives since six years. Since 1996 director of the Institute of Ethnomedicine of the Sir Karl Pooper Society.
Contact: E-Mail: Christian.Lehner@bgld.gv.at

References

PARNHAM, B. E. V., 1972. Plants Of Samoa. *DSIR Information Series* no. 85. Wellington DSIR.
MacCUDDIN, CHARLES R., 1974. *Samoan Medical Plants and Their Usage. Office of Comprehensive Health Planning* , Dept. of Medical Service, Pagopago, Govt. of America Samoa.
MOYLE, RICHARD M., 1974. "Samoan Medicinal Incantations", *Journal of the Polynesian Society,* 83, pp.155 - 179.
MOYLE, RICHARD M., 1974. "Samoan Medicinal Incantations", *Journal of the Polynesian Society,* 83, pp.155 - 179.
TURNER, GEORGE, 1861. *Nineteen Years In Polynesia: Missionary Life, Travels And Researches In The Islands of The Pacific.* London, Snow.
KINLOCH, P.J. 1985. *Talking Health, But Doing Sickness: Studies in Samoan Health.* Wellington, Viktoria Univ. Press.
HEATH, TIMOTHY, 1973. *The Diagnosis and Treatment of Disease in a Rural Village in Western Samoa.* MA Thesis, Univ. of Auckland.
KINLOCH, P. J. 1985. Midwives and Midwifery in Western Samoa. C. D. F. Parsons ed.
TE RANGI HIROA, 1930. Samoan Material Culture. Honolulu, BERNICE P. BISHOP *Museum Bulletin* no. 75
WILLIAMS, JOHN, 1838. *A Narrative of Missionary Enterprises in the South Sea Islands.* London Snow. Seite 354
CHURCHWARD, William B.; 1971. My Consulate in Samoa. Erstmals publiziert 1887, Folkstone, Dawsons.
DILLON, PETER, 1829. *Narrativ and Successful Result of a Voyage in the South Seas to ascertain the Fate of La Perouse's Expedition.* London, Hurst, Chance & Co.

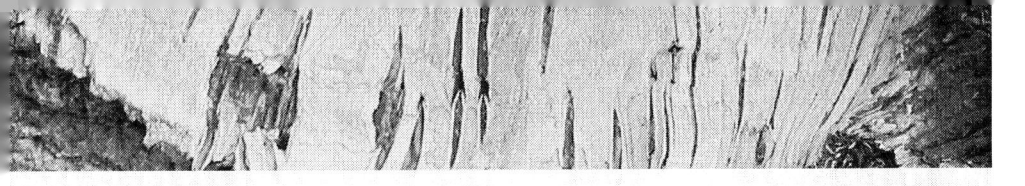

HERAUSGEBER
EDITORS

CHRISTINE E. GOTTSCHALK-BATSCHKUS
Ärztin, Vorstands- und Gründungsmitglied von ETHNOMED - Institut für Ethnomedizin e.V.. Mutter von vier Kindern, Organisatorin internationaler ethnomedizinischer Kongresse und Seminare; Herausgeberin und Autorin zahlreicher Bücher und Buchreihen wie "Gebären- ethnomedizinische Perspektiven und neue Wege", "Frauen und Gesundheit", "Ethnomedizinische Perspektiven zur Frühen Kindheit", "Ethnotherapien - Therapeutische Konzepte im Kulturvergleich", "Ethnomedizin - Schätze der Gesundheit", "Ins Leben tragen", "Wanderer zwischen den Welten - Schamanismus im neuen Jahrtausend".
Physician, Member of the board of ETHNOMED - Institute for Ethnomedicine. Mother of four children; organisor of International ethnomedical congresses, editor and author of books like "Giving Birth - Ethnomedical Perspectives", "Women and Health", "Ethnomedical Perspectives on Early Childhood", "Ethnotherapies - Therapeutical Concepts in Transcultural Comparison".
Contact: E-Mail: ethnomedizin@web.de

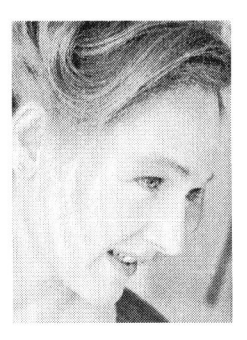

JOY C. GREEN
vier Jahre Arbeit im Rettungsdienst und in der Unfallambulanz verschiedener Münchner Kliniken. Studium der Biologie und Chemie an der Universität Bayreuth Lehrtätigkeit in München, Bayreuth & dem State Junior College Enterprise, Alabama, USA. Ausbildung als Heilpraktikerin und Shiatsu- Praktikerin. Gründungs- und Vorstandmitglied von ETHNOMED und dem Institut GREEN VOICES - Stimme, Musik und Gesundheit. Aktuelles Projekt: Körperliche und geistige Gesundung und Gesunderhaltung durch Musik- und Gesangstherapie. Mutter von drei Kindern.
Worked in the emergency car and ambulance room of several hospitals for four years; study of biology and chemistry at the University of Bayreuth. Teaching profession in Munich, Bayreuth and at the State Junior College Enterprise, Alabama, USA. Education as a naturopath and shiatsu therapist. Member of the board of ETHNOMED- Institute for Ethomedicine and GREEN VOICES Institute for Voice, Music and Health. Current project: Physical and mental recovery and health through music and vocal therapy. Mother of three children.
Contact: E-Mail: JoyCGreen@compuserve.com

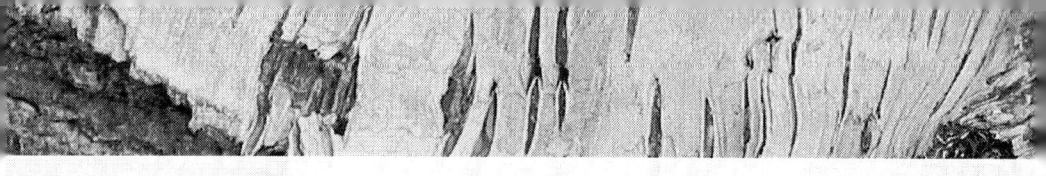

AUTOREN-REGISTER
CONTRIBUTORS

	Seite/Page
Aldridge, David	53 / 65
Assion, Hans- Jörg	269 / 281
Buccalo, Sharyn	407 / 413
Dattenberg- Holper, Traute	347 / 355
Erdtsieck, Jessica	119 / 133
Greenberg, Ofra	221 / 229
Iroegbu, Patrick	145 / 157
Kalweit, Holger	37 / 45
Khan, Mahmoud Tareq H.	373 / 381
Kosack, Godula	169 / 183
Krippner, Stanley	21 / 29
Krippner, Stanley	431 / 437
Lehner, Christian	491 / 501
Lussi, Kurt	77 / 87
Müller-Ebeling, Claudia	13 / 17
Neumann Fridmann, Eva J.	291 / 301
Ojewole, John A. O.	197 / 209
Pantke, Christiane	475 / 483
Pieroni, Andrea	97 / 109
Quave, Cassandra Leah	97 / 109
Ramirez, Fabio Alberto	463 / 469
Rätsch, Christian	443 / 453
Reimers, Andreas	387 / 397
Roy, Babul	361 / 367
Schenk, Amélie	311 / 317
Schmidt, Bettina E.	419 / 425
Singh, Ranjay K.	337 / 341
Tietze, Dierk	323 / 331
Tucek, Gerhard Kadir	237 / 253

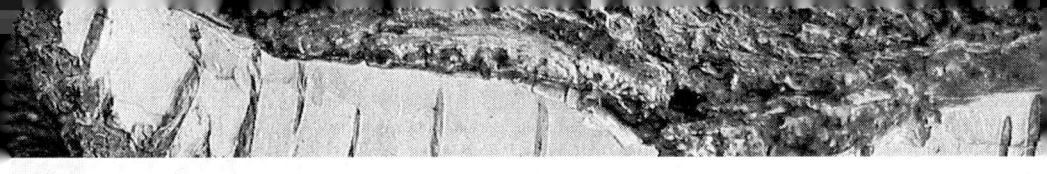

BILDNACHWEIS
PICTURE CREDITS

0-10	Batschkus, M.M.	249-261	Batschkus, M.M.	397-399	Reimers, A.
13/17	Rätsch, C.	263	Tucek, G.K.	403	Reimers, A.
21	Batschkus, M.M.	265-266	Batschkus, M.M.	405	Gottschalk-Batschkus, C.
28	Krippner, S.	275-287	Assion, H.-J.	407	Batschkus, M.M.
29	Batschkus, M.M.	291-307	Neumann Fridman, E.J.	407-412	Buccalo, S.
35	Krippner, S.	311-322	Schenk, A.	413	Batschkus, M.M.
37	Batschkus, M.M.	323	Tietze, D.	413-418	Buccalo, S.
37-43	Kalweit, H.	327	Batschkus, M.M.	419	Batschkus, M.M.
45	Batschkus, M.M.	331	Tietze, D.	421-424	Schmidt, B.
45-51	Kalweit, H.	335/337	Batschkus, M.M.	425	Batschkus, M.M.
53/61		337-340	Singh, R.K.	427-430	Schmidt, B.
65/72	Batschkus, M.M.	341	Batschkus, M.M.	431-442	Krippner, S.
77-95	Lussi, K.	341-346	Singh, R.K.	443/445	Rätsch, C.
97	Batschkus, M.M.	347	Batschkus, M.M.	452	Gottschalk-Batschkus, C.
97-108	Quave, C./Pieroni, A.	353	Dattenberg-Holper, T.	453/455	Rätsch, C.
109	Batschkus, M.M.	355	Batschkus, M.M.	462	Gottschalk-Batschkus, C.
109-118	Quave, C./Pieroni, A.	360	Dattenberg-Holper, T.	463	Batschkus, M.M.
119-144	Erdtsieck, J.	361	Batschkus, M.M.	468	Gottschalk-Batschkus, C.
145	Batschkus, M.M.	365	Roy, B.	469	Batschkus, M.M.
149-155	Iroegbu, P.	367	Batschkus, M.M.	473	Gottschalk-Batschkus, C.
157	Batschkus, M.M.	371	Roy, B.	475	Batschkus, M.M.
161-166	Iroegbu, P.	373	Batschkus, M.M.	475/482	Pantke, C.
169	Kosack, G.	379	Khan, M.T.H.	483	Batschkus, M.M.
170-195	Kosack, G.	381	Batschkus, M.M.	483/488	Pantke, C.
197	Batschkus, M.M.	386	Khan, M.T.H.	491-509	Lehner, C.
197-208	Ojewole, J.O.A.	387	Reimers, A.	511-554	Batschkus, M.M.
209	Batschkus, M.M.	389-393	Reimers, A.		
209-219	Ojewole, J.O.A.	395	Gottschalk-Batschkus, C.		
221-245	Batschkus, M.M.				
247	Tucek, G.K.				

SCHLAGWORTREGISTER

Aargau, Kanton 81
abendländische
  Besessenheit 347
Aberglaube 272
Aberglaube, Italien 99
Abgeschiedenheit, Vodou- 422
Abholzung, Mexiko 445
Abrus precatorius 202
Abtreibungszwecke 337
Abwehr böser Einflüsse 271
Abwehrmechanismen 150
Acaçá, Brasilien 478
Acacia karroo 202
Acanthaceae, Fam. 375
Acanthus ilicifolius Linn. 375
Achyranthus aspera Linn. 377
Ackerbau auf
  Bergabhängen, Indien 361
Ackerbegrenzung, Indien 338
Acorus calamus Linn. 377
Adler, Türkei 272
Adler, Indien 363
Adstringenz, Amish 409
Aegle marmelos 377
Affektzustand 242
Affenfleisch 451
Affenfleisch, Lakandonen 444
Affengott 351, 391
Affenkopf 151
Afrika
---, Heilerrolle 120
---ner, Kultur 475
---nische Götter 419
---nische Religionen 419
---nisches religiöses Leben 119
Afrobrasilianer, Brasilien 476
afrobrasilianische Kultur 475
Aggression 126, 147
Aggressionen, Brasilien 481
Agnideva (nepali) 395
Agwu 146
Ahnen
---, Brasilien 476
---, Geister der 197
---, Kamerun 169
---, Kolumbien 464
---, Wohlwollen der 122
---, Zorn der 146
---geist, Brasilien 477
---geister 314
---opfer 170
---tradition 155
AIDS-Patienten 59
Ainu 292
Aiutare, Italien 100
Ajna Cakra 326

Akasha 388
Akbar 324
Äkinchob, Lakandonen 447
Akupressur 174, 179
Akupunkturpunkte 298
Akutsituationen 391
Äkyantho, Lakandonen 448
Alap 324
Alb, Schweiz 79
albanische Sprache,
  toskisch- 98
albanische Kultur,
  arbëresch- 98
Albtraum, Schweiz 79
Aldridge, David 53
Algidaes, Brasilien 478
Alkaloid Harmin 464
Alkoholismus 54
Alkoholmissbrauch 54
Allergie, Brasilien 477
allergische Hautausschläge,
  Brasilien 477
Allium cepa Lam. 377
Allium sativum Lam. 377
Allmacht 390
Alltagsbewusstsein 246, 395
Alocacia indica 377
Aloe indica 377
Aloe vera 374, 377
Alpen 78
Alpina nigra 377
Alpinia malaccensis Rose 377
Altar, Nepal 389
alternative Behandlungs-
  methoden, Israel 221
Amalgam 375
Amaquira 198
Amaranthus gangeticus
  Linn. 377
Amaranthus spinosis
  Linn. 377
Amaranthus viridis 377
Amazonas 463
Ambil, Huitotos 464
Amerbel 339
Amerika, Vodou 419
Amish, Heilverfahren 407
Ammbaa 294
Amnesie nach Trance 351
Amöbenruhr,
  Lakandonen 448
Amputation 408
Amulett 271, 149, 175, 225, 273
Amulette, Kallawaya 434
Amuletten, Tansania 120
Anacardiaceae 200
Anahata Cakra 326
Analogieprinzip, Brasilien 478
Ananas comosus Merr. 377

Andachtsbildchen,
  Schweiz 82
Anden, Peru 463
Andengebiet,
  Heilungssystem 431
Anforderungsprofile 244
Angola, Brasilien 476
Angst 146
Angstanfälle 351
Ängste 58, 391
Ängste, Brasilien 476
Ängste, Lakandonen 446
angstlösend 326
Angstneurose 350
Angststörung 244, 272
animistische Kräfte 269
Annona reticulata Linn. 377
Anrufungen 314
Ansteckung 169
Ansteckung, magische 99
Anteilnahme 392
Anteilname, Lakandonen 444
Antennen 314
Anthocephalas chinensis
  Lamk. 377
Anthropologie als
  Wissenschaft 444
anthropologische
  Untersuchung, Italien 97
anthropomorpher
  Glauben 148
antibakterielles Mittel 408
Antibiotika 55
antiepileptische Pflanzen 199
Antonius, hl., Schweiz 79
Anwendungsbereiche,
  klinische 244
Anxiolyse 248
Apallisches Syndrom 244
Aphrodisiacum 451
Apocynaceae 200
Apollonia, St. 81
Appetitlosigkeit, Susto 436
Apulien, Italien 98
Apuria-Nation 27
arabischer Arzt 270
Arakani, Bangladesh 373
Araracura, Huitotos 465
Araracura, Kolumbien 464, 466
Arbeiterfamilien 277
Arbeitsaktivitäten 407
Arbeitslosigkeit, Brasilien 477
Arbeitsunfähigkeit,
  Andenraum 431
arbëresch-albanische Kultur,
  Italien 98
arbëresche Gemeinden,
  Italien 97

514 Aargau — arbëresche Schlagwortregister

archetypische Kräfte	388	
Arctium	410	
Argentinien, Kallawaya	431	
Aristolochia indica Linn.	377	
Armulett, Knochen als, Indien	364	
Armut, Brasilien	477	
Aroeira de Ogum, Brasilien	478	
Aroera, Brasilien	478	
Ars medica	242	
Arthritis	339	
Arthritis, Indien	364	
Artocarpus heteophyllus	377	
Artocarpus lakoocha Roxb.	377	
Arzan Shivilig	299	
Arzneimittelkunde, westliche	100	
Ärzte, Islamische	239	
Ärztekrankheit	277	
Asien, Schamaninnen in Zentral	291	
Assam	362	
Assam, Indien	361	
Assion, Hans-Jörg	269	
Assoziationsarbeit, Musik	248	
assoziative Regression	246	
Astanaga (nepali)	395	
Asteraceae	200	
Asterocantha longifolia Ness.	377	
Astrologische Kräfte	349	
Astronomie, Kolumbien	466	
Atatürk	269	
Atem	323, 391	
Atemwegsprobleme	432	
Ätiologie, Krankheits-, Lakandonen	446	
Atmen, verstärktes	347	
Atmung, Diagnose	432	
Aufmerksamkeit	244	
Aufschließen	150	
Auge, Stofffetzen im	176	
Augen, blaue	271	
---, Diagnose	432	
---, Huitotos	466	
---amulett	274	
---brauen	326	
---diagnostiker	408	
---krankheit	176	
---zauber	270	
Aura	298	
Aussaugen durch den Heiler	172	
Ausscheidungen, Diagnose	432	
außergewöhnliche Bewusstseinszustände	347	
Aussprache	326	
Ausspucken	271	
Austreibung, Indien, Geister-	347	
Authoritätssymbolen	154	
autistische Personen	248	

autoerotische Handlungen	272	
Autorität	352	
Autosuggestion	347	
Auto-Suggestion	54	
Ave Maria, Italien	103	
axis mundi	389	
Aymara, Kallawaya	431	
Ayoco, Kolumbien	464	
Ayurveda	349	
Ayurveda-Heilern	349	
ayurvedische Heilmittel	373	
Azadirachta indica	377	

Baatar, Region 337

Baba Gopal	324	
Baba Imam Khan	324	
Bad, öffentliches	272	
Bahia, Kultur	475	
Baikalsee	296	
Bai-Khaakh Region	299	
Baiuu	375	
Bakseschamanen	239	
Bakterientötend	410	
Bakterienwachstum	409	
Balance	432	
Balance, Samoa	496	
balche, Lakandonen	451	
Balkan-Gruppe, Paleo-	98	
Bananenblätter, Brasilien	478	
Bandarban, Bangladesh	373	
Bangladesh, Therapeutisches System	373	
Banisteriopsis caapi	464	
Bantu, Tansania	121	
Barbier	270	
Barhim-baba	296	
Barile, Italien	97, 101	
Basilicata-Region, Süditalien	97	
Basilikata, Italien	97	
Basiliskenblick	270	
Bauch	326	
---nabel	326	
---raum	178	
---schmerzen	100, 103, 176	
---schmerzen, Schwangerschaft	179	
Bauern, Bangladesh	379	
Bauernkaste	349	
Bäume, Bedeutung der	148, 314	
Baumhuhn	450	
Baumreihen	314	
Baumwolle, Brasilien	478	
Baumwollfaden	451	
Bauthinia malabarica Roxb.	377	
Beatmungsgeräte	55	
Becken	326	
Bedrängnis	147	
Beerdigungsstätte, Tansania	122	
Befindlichkeit	57	

Befindlichkeit, Störung der	350	
Befreiung des Patienten	152	
Befreiung	151	
Begierde, Brasilien	476	
Begierden, niedrige, Brasilien	476	
Begräbnis von Säuglingen	434	
Behandlung durch		
--- magische Kräfte	374	
--- übernatürliche Kräfte	374	
--- von Geisteskrankheiten	238	
--- von Grenzen, Italien	104	
Behandlung, Beziehungsmedizinische	239	
---, Biomedizinische	239	
---, erfolglose	56	
---, ganzheitliche	57	
---, symbolische	147	
---smethoden, alternative, Israel	221	
Beinwell	409	
Beinwil, St. Burkard von, Schweiz	80	
Beischlafen, Maßhalten beim	273	
bekreuzigen, Italien	103	
Beleidigung	126	
Benedictionale Constantinese, Schweiz	83	
Benincasa hispida	377	
Berge, Herren der	292	
Berufung, Nepal	388	
Berührung	295	
Berührungsreliquie, Schweiz	79	
Berührungstherapie	296	
Beschneidung	154	
Beschwerdeerleichterungen	409	
Beschwörung, Huitotos	467	
Beschwörungen	198	
Besen	391	
Besessenheit	154	
---, Indien	347	
---, Schweiz	79, 84	
---, Tansania	120	
---, Vodou	419	
---tsrituale, Brasilien	481	
----Zustand	351	
Besorgnis, Susto	436	
Bestatter	174	
Bestrafung	222	
Beten	54	
Betreuende	58	
Betreuung, soziale, Lakandonen	444	
Bevölkerungsdichte	379	
Bevölkerungswachstum, Kampf gegen	448	
Bewältigungsstrategie	54	
Bewegung, Ursprung der	466	
Bewegungsabläufe, harmonische	239	
Bewegungsabläufe, ritualisiierte	391	

Bewegungsaffekt	246	
Bewegungsfähigkeit	245	
Bewegungsmuster, universelle	243	
Bewegungstherapie	242	
Bewegungsübungen	246	
Bewusstsein	152, 198	
---, Alltags-	246	
---, Huitotos	467	
---, Lakandonen	446	
---, Shiva-	326	
Bewusstseinspotentiale	326	
---therapie	242	
---verlust, Tansania	123	
---zustand	56	
---zustand, veränderte	130, 243, 292, 338	
---zustände, außergewöhnliche	347	
Bezahlung	409	
Beziehung, Eltern-Kind-, Vodou	420	
Beziehung, transzendente	243	
Beziehungen, harmonische, Anden	432	
Beziehungen, zerstörte	147	
Beziehungsebene	246	
---konflikte	271	
---medizinische Behandlung	239	
---modell, therapeutische	243	
---muster, gestörte	392	
---problem, Tansania	124	
Bezugsaufnahme	248	
Bhakti-Tradition	327	
Bharatpur bei Dheli	351	
Bhraj, Volkssprache	324	
Bhuta-Geist	351	
Bhutavidya	349	
Bienenkundler	408	
Bienenwachs	409	
Bier, selbstgebrautes, Tansania	122	
Bieropfer	170	
Bignoniaceae	200	
Bildstöcke, Schweiz	78	
Bildungsniveau, Israel	222	
Bindfäden	149	
Bindung zu sich selbst	388	
--- zum Universum	388	
--- zur Gemeinschaft	388	
Binnenmigrantinnen, Türkei	277	
Biomedizinische Behandlung	239	
Birke	299	
Birkenwald	314	
Bisswunde, Zecke	450	
Bittgebete, Schweiz	80	
Blähungen, Susto	436	
Blaseninfektion	226	
Blasetechnik	391	
Blätter, herzförmige	407	
Blätter, Talik	376	
Blei	375
Bleigießen	274
Blick, Böser	270
Blick, böser, Brasilien	478
Blick, Böser, Italien	99
Blicks, Abschirmen des	271
Blinddarmgegend	179
Blitz, Huitotos	466
Blockade	327
blockierte Energien	388
Blumea alata	200
Blut	151
---, Rhinozeros	375
---, Schweiz	80
Blutdruck, Diagnose	432
Blutdruck, niedriger	226
Blütenköpfe, rotviolette	407
Bluthochdruck	379
blutige Darmerkrankungen	451
blutiger Durchfall, Lakandonen	449
Blutproben	22
Blutungen, Schwangerschaft	179
Bogota, Kolumbien	469
Bohnen, Brasilien	478
Bohnen, schwarze, Brasilien	478
Bohnen, weiße, Brasilien	478
Bonavasi (nepali)	395
bonjhankri	388
Boomerang Gesetz	436
Boo-zaarins	294
Bordunstrument	325
Boscia albitrunca	201
böse Einflüsse, Abwehr	271
böse Geister	197
böse Geister, Israel	222
Böser Blick	172, 222, 270
---, Brasilien	478
---, Italien	99
böser Geist	227
böser Geist, Samoa	498
Bosheit	172
Bossiedoktor	198
Brahmanen	324
Bramssica napus	377
Brandrodungsfelder, Mexiko	444
Brandwunde	411
Brasilia, Universität in	21
Brasilien, candomblé	475
Brautbett, Amulett	274
Breitwegerich	411
Brij Chand	324
Brooklyn, New York	422
Brotfrucht	149
Broussonetia paperifera Linn.	377
Brüche, Indien	363
Brücke	276
Brunnen, heiliger, Schweiz	81
Brust	150, 326
Brustbeerbaumrinde	177
Brustentzündung, Italien	100
Brusthaarkrankheit, Italien	103
Brustkorb	172
Brustwarze, Indien	364
Bryatia	296
Buccalo, Sharyn	407
Buddha Maitrea	295
Buddhismus	294
Buddhismus	387
Buddhist	291
buddhistische Gottheiten	296
buddhistische Mantras	294
buddhistische Tankas	296
Bumeraja (nepali)	395
Bumerani (nepali)	395
Burjaten	312
burjat-mongolischer Schamane	311
Burkard von Beinwil, St.	80, 81
Burn-Out-Syndrom	244
Buryat	296
Bußtage, Tansania	120
Bußwallfahrten, Schweiz	80
Butterverbot	296
Büyü	271
büyüyü cözmek	271
Byrds Studie	54

Caesalpina crista 338

Cajanus indicus	377
Cakra	326
Calabrien, Italien	98
Calamus viminalis	377
calanchoe brasiliensis camb., Brasilien	478
Calotropis gigantia	377
Calotropis procera	377
Camp der pajes	21
Campanien, Italien	98
Canabis sativa	377
Candomblé, Brasilien	475
Capparaceae	201
Capparis tomentosa	201
Capsicum annum	377
Caquetá, Kolumbien	463
Carica papaya Linn.	377
carimã, Brasilien	478
Cassia alata	377
Cassia siamca Linn.	377
Cassytha filiformis L.	339
Catunaregam spinosa	203
Cau-Tala	325
Cedrus deodar	375
Celastraceae	201
Centella asiatica Linn.	377
Centipeda minimal Linn.	377
Chakma Talik	374
Chakma Talika Cikitsa, Bangladesh	373
Chakma, Bangladesh	373
Chandrama (nepali)	395
Chhatisgarh	337
Chhoti Dudhi	338

Chiapas, Mexiko	443	
Chicrassia tabularis Jubs.	377	
Chile, Kallawaya	431	
Chinin-Mixtur	434	
chinta	389	
chirurgische Eingriffe	174	
Chittagong Hill Tract, Bangladesh	373	
Cholera, Lakandonen	448	
Christen, Italien	98	
Christentum	419	
---, Afrika	122	
---, Schweiz	78	
Christianisierung, Indien	362	
Christianisierung, Samoa	492	
christliches Kreuz, Anden	435	
Chronische Beschwerden	56	
--- Erkrankungen	226	
--- Erkrankungen, Huitotos	467	
Chuchu, Brasilien	478	
Chuckchee	292	
Cin carpmasi	272	
cinler basima üsüstü	272	
Cinler	271	
Citrus maxima Linn.	377	
Citrus medica Linn.	377	
Clausena anisata	203	
Cleodendrum viscosum	377	
Clerodendrum glabrum	204	
Coca-Blatt	432	
Coca-Blätter, Werfen von	431	
Coccinia cordifolia	377	
Coccinia medica	377	
Colocasia esculentus Linn.	377	
Commelina africana	201	
Commelinaceae	201	
Conyza scabrida	200	
Corchorus capsularis Linn.	377	
Coriandrum sativum Linn.	377	
Cotyledon orbiculata	201	
Crassula alba	201	
Crassulaceae	201	
Crassulaceae	201	
Croton gratissimus	202	
Cucumis hirsutus	201	
Cucumis sativa Linn.	377	
Cucurbitaceae	201	
Curandero	465	
---, Kallawaya	431	
---, Kolumbien	463	
Curcuma amada Roxb.	377	
Curcuma caesia Roxb.	377	
Curcuma domestica	377	
Curcuma longa Linn.	377	
Cuscuta reflexa Roxb.	377	
Dagar-Schule	324	
Damm	326	
Dämonen	274, 391	
---, Indien	348	
---, Italien	78	

---, Türkei	272	
Dampf, Wesen aus	272	
Dampfbox, Kallawaya	434	
Dankzeremonie, Lakandonen	451	
Darbhanga, Schule von	324	
Darmerkrankungen, blutige	452	
Dattenberg-Holper, Traute	347	
Datura fastuosa Linn. var. D. alba	377	
Datura metel Linn.	377	
Datura stramonium	204	
Defumador, Brasilien	478	
Dehasia kurzi King	377	
Dekonditionierung	243	
Demenz	146	
Denkmuster	243	
Depression	126, 146, 222, 226, 244, 390, 391	
---, Susto	436	
---, wahnhafte	272	
Depressionssymptomatik, reaktive	249	
depressive Episoden	276	
Derwisch	270	
Derwische, drehende	238	
Dhamar	325	
dhami	387	
Dhariti	388	
Dhrupad	323	
Dhruva	323	
Diagnose, Kallawaya	431	
Diagnosefindung, Samoa	496	
Diagnosesitzung, Afrika	124	
Diagnosestellung, Nepal	389	
diagnostische Trance	389	
Diarrhoe	451	
Diäten, Huitotos	467	
Diätetik	242	
Diätetische Maßnahmen	272	
Diazepam	205	
Dibia, Nigeria	146	
Diebstahl des Wissens	24	
Diesseits	314	
Dillenia indica Linn.	377	
Diospyros peregrina Linn.	377	
Dipterocarpaceae	373	
Dipterocarpus alatus	377	
Dipterocarpus gracilis	377	
Dipterocarpus turbinatus	377	
Disharmonie	126	
Disharmonie, Diagnose	432	
Diskretion, Brasilien	480	
Diskriminierung	27	
Dissoziation	347	
Divination	149	
Divination, Lakandonen	448	
Divination, Vodou	419	
Djinnen	271	
Don, Flüsse	295	
Donnerkeil Gottes	391	
Doppelkonustrommel	325	

Dorffehde, Samoa	496	
Dorfgemeinschaft, Lakandonen	449	
Drachen	294	
Drachen, Schweiz	77	
Dreiecksform, Amulett	274	
Dreieinigkeit	103	
Drogenabhängigkeit	54, 467	
Dschalaleddin Rumi	238	
Du - Bezug, Ich -	243	
Duca, Huitotos	465	
Duca, Kolumbien	464	
Düdger Waantschig	311	
dulcis-Halm	179	
Dunkeltherapie	40	
Durchfall bei Kindern	338	
Durchfall, blutiger, Lakandonen	449	
Dürreperiode	324	
Dyonisios, St., Schweiz	81	
Ebenaceae	201	
Ebós, Brasilien	477, 480	
Ebru	241	
Ecce crucem, Schweiz	79	
Echse	375	
Edelpflanzen	198	
Edelsteinzentrum	326	
Egun, Brasilien	477, 480	
Ehebrecherisch	351	
Ehefrauen, Konformität	352	
Ehemann, Zuordnung zum	349	
Eibischwurzel	409	
Eichenrinde, Weiße	409	
Eier	150, 314	
Eiern, Ritual mit	225	
Eifersucht, Brasilien	476	
Einbildungen, phantastische	350	
Einflußwille	243	
Eingangsanrufungen	312	
Einlauf	412	
Einnistung eines Eis	337	
Einsamkeit	40	
Einweihung in die Natur	37	
Eisen, Mineralstoffe	464	
ekstatische Raserei	352	
Elaeocarpus rugosus Roxb.	377	
Elefant, Zähne von	375	
Elementsymbolik	248	
Elfenbein-Tambura	324	
Elixiere, Anden	433	
Eltern, Zurückweisungen der	272	
Eltern-Kind-Beziehung, Vodou	420	
Emblica officinalis Gaertn.	377	
emotionale Gesundheit	146	
Emotionale Offenheit	248	
emotionale Wärme	392	
Emotionen, aufgestaute	394	
Emotionslage der Vergangenheit	246	
Endorphine, Beta-	243	

Energie, kosmologische	151	
---, weibliche	326	
---, blockierte	388	
---, schlechte	296	
Energiewesen	314	
Englerophytum magalismontanum	204	
Enokaye-Clan, Kolumbien	465	
Entgiftungsmittel	410	
Enthaltsamkeiten	434	
Entsagung	38	
Entspannung	244, 325	
Entspannung, Tansania	129	
Entspannungsmethoden	54	
Enttäuschung	152	
Entwicklungspolitik, Indien	362	
Entzündungen, Brasilien	478	
Entzündungen, penile, Italien	100	
entzündungshemmend, Brasilien	478	
Epidemie	379	
Epidemiologe	379	
epidemische Krankheiten, Lakandonen	448	
Epilepsie	146, 197	
Epilepsie, Behandlung von	151	
Epilepsie, Schweiz	81	
Erasmus, St. , Schweiz	81	
Erbrechen	375	
Erde, Mutter -	434	
Erde, Schweiz	80	
Erde, Verbindung	314	
Erdgräber, Samoa	498	
Erdtsieck, Jessica	119	
Erholung	54	
Erholungspotential	57	
Erickson	243	
Erkältungen	271	
Erkältungen, Lakandonen	448	
Erkenntnisprozess	238	
Erkenntnistheorie, Evolutionäre	243	
Erklärungsmuster, vertraute	279	
Erkrankten, Seele des	450	
Erkrankung, psychischer	269	
Erkrankungen, Chronische	226	
Erkrankungen, Schizophrene	272	
erlebnisorientierte Therapieformen	394	
Ernährung	272, 408	
---, ausgeglichene, Kallawaya	434	
---, maßvolle	239	
---, Samoa	496	
Erregungsleitung, Nervensystem	465	
Erschöpfungssyndrom	244	
Erschrecken	276	
Erwachsenendiabetes	379	
Erythrina variegata Linn.	377	
Erythroxilon coca	464	
Eskimo	292	
espada de Ogum, Brasilien	478	
Essen, Maßhalten beim	273	
ethische Reflexion	243	
Ethnoantomie, Lakandonen	446	
Ethnobotaniker	379	
Ethnoepidemiologie	378	
Ethnographie als Wissenschaft	444	
ethnologische Erkenntnisse, Italien	97	
Ethnomusiktherapie, Institut für	250	
Ethnoökologie	378	
ethnopharmakologische Untersuchung, Italien	97	
Ethnopsychiatrie, Nigeria	145	
Ethnotrance	243	
Ethoslehre	242	
Euclea divinorum	201	
Euphorbia thymifolia	338	
Euphorbiaceae	202, 373	
europäische Volksmedizin, Italien	97	
europäischen Krankheiten	452	
Evolutionäre Erkenntnistheorie	243	
Ewigkeit	148	
Exorzismen, Schweiz	80	
Exorzismus	154, 198	
Exorzisten, Indien	349	
Exorzistenbüchlein, Schweiz	84	
Exstase	347	
Extraktion	390	
Exú, Brasilien	478, 480	
FA'ALEIGA, Samoa	494	
Fabaceae	202	
Fächerpalmenblättern	451	
Fackeln	324	
Faden, geweihter	276	
Faden, goldener	314	
Fäden, schwarze	298	
FAIFE'AU, Samoa	494	
Familie, Gesundheit der	352	
Familie, lamaische	494	
Familien, Miteinbeziehung der	432	
Familienmitglieder, Brasilien	480	
Familienmitglieder, Mongolei	292	
Familienmitglieder, Tansania	128	
Familiennetzwerk	408	
Familienspannungen, Samoa	495	
Familienstreit, Tansania	124	
Familienstruktur, Huitotos	464	
Familientherapie	352	
Farbe, blaue	271	
Farben	152	
Farben, Werte der	154	
Farbgestaltung, harmonische	239	
FASIA, Samoa	498	
Fasten	388	
Faulheit, Susto	436	
Feder	178	
Federn	151	
Feind, metaphysischer	350	
Feinde	149	
Feinde, Brasilien	480	
Feindliches, Schutz	314	
Feindschaft	271	
Felsen	323	
Fesseln	149, 153	
Fesselritual	148	
Festschmaus	451	
Fetischzauberer	15	
Fettleibigkeit	379	
Feuer, Huitotos	466	
Feuer, Schweiz	80	
Feuer, Wesen aus	272	
Feuerflamme	272	
Feuerkrankheit, sankt Antonius	101	
Feuerkrankheit, tote, Italien	101	
Feueropfer	42	
Feuerpulver, Brasilien	479	
Feuer-Raga	324	
Feuerstein	375	
Ficus racemosa Linn.	377	
Fieber, Susto	436	
Fiebererkrankung, Lakandonen	449	
Fipa, Tansania	121	
Flammen	299	
Fleischverbot	296	
Fleurya interrupta	377	
fliegendes Pferd	299	
Flöte der Unendlichkeit	327	
Flöte	323	
Fluch	296	
Fluch, Italien	105	
Fluch, Vodou	421	
Flüche	272	
Flüsse, Herren der	292	
FOFO, Samoa	494	
folha araçá-de-coroa, Brasilien	478	
folha da costa, Brasilien	478	
folha de araçá, Brasilien	478	
Folha de Manga, Brasilien	478	
folha de mangueira, Brasilien	478	
folha Manjerição, Brasilien	478	
Formeln, Brasilien	292	
Fötus eines Lamas	434	
fradinho , Brasilien	478	
Frakturen	408	
Frau, Sexualität der	349	
Frau, weise	270	
Frauen, gebärfähige	451	

Frauen		
---, indische		349
---, Kompensation für die		352
---, Kontakt mit, Huitotos		467
---, menstruationsfähige		451
---, Missbrauch der		23
Fremdkörper im Leib		176
Fremdkörper		172
Frieden	154,	239
Friedens, Gefühl des		55
Friedensarbeit		244
Friedhof, Samoa		498
Friedhöfe		272
Friedhofseingänge, Brasilien		480
Frieundshaft (Amish)		408
Fruchtbarkeit	171,	274
Früchte, rituelle		273
Frustration		152
Fuchs, Indien		364
Führungskräfte		154
Fundacao National de India		21
fuoco di sant antonio, Italien		101
Fürbitte, Schweiz		80
Furcht		350
Fürsprechende Gebete		55
Fürsprecher		55
Fuß		323

G

Gähnen, Italien		103
Galen		242
Gallenblase		375
Gallensalze		375
Ganzheit		238
Garaine		338
Gardenia ternifolia		203
gastroenterologischer Bereich		244
Gataine		338
Gebären, Maloca		464
Gebärenden, Patronin der, Schweiz		81
gebärfähige Frauen		451
Gebet		53
Gebet, Afrika	122,	175
Gebet, Tee mit		273
Gebetbücher, Schweiz		80
Gebete, Huitotos		467
---, katholische, Italien		103
---, meditative		273
---, Schweiz		80
---, Tansania		127
Gebetskranz		296
Gebetsmatte		296
Gebetstechniken		54
Gebirge der Assam, Indien		362
Geborgenheit		154
Geburt, Nigeria		148
Geburtshelfer, traditionelle		199
Geburtshelferinnen		174
Gecekondu		277

Gedankentätigkeit		326
Gedicht, vertontes		325
Gefühle, Ausdruck der		323
Gefühle, exaltierte		350
Gefühle, Lakandonen		447
Gegenmagie		271
Gegensätze, Überwindung der		152
Gegenwart, Mongolei		312
Geheimhaltung magischer Handlungen, Italien		106
Gehirn		151
Gehirn, Huitotos		466
Gehörsinn, Huitotos		466
Geist der Krankheit, Italien		103
--- der Vorväter, Tansania		122
---, böser		227
---, böser, Samoa		498
---, tobender		351
---, verstorbener		126
Geister der Ahnen		197
---, böse		197
---, böse, Israel		222
---, Brasilien		476
---, heilende, Tansania		123
---, Indien		348
---, Kamerun		169
---, kopflose, Schweiz		78
---, Lebensraum der		152
---, Nepal		389
---, Nigeria		145
---, Schweiz		77
---, Tansania		120
---, Türkei	271,	272
---, vier, Lakandonen		446
----Austreibung, Indien		347
----Besessenheit, Indien		347
---kanu		42
---kraft		150
---leitung		314
--- der Verstorbenen		314
Geistern, Nachrichten von		421
Geistertanz		42
Geisterwanderung, Huitotos		466
Geisterwelt, Nigeria		148
Geistes, Verlust des		432
Geisteskraft	126,	126
Geisteskrankheiten, Behandlung von		238
Geisteskrankheiten, Nigerien		145
Geistheiler		198
Geisthelfern		294
geistige Abwesenheit		126
--- Gesundheit		146
--- Prinzipien		242
--- Welt, Mongolei		292
Geistwelt, Mongolei		292
Geistwesen, Mongolei	299,	313
Geistwesen, Zentral Asien		291
Gelbfieberepidemie		169
Gelbsucht		338

Gelbsucht, Lakandonen		448
Gelbsuchtheiler	270,	277
Geld, Opfer-		351
Geldgaben		276
Gelenkbeschwerden, Indien		364
Gemeinschaft, Bindung zur		388
Gemeinschaft, Brasilien		481
Gemeinschaft, Harmonie in der		436
Gemütsleben		242
Genesung		239
Genesungsprozess		248
Genesungsprozess, Nigeria		147
geriatrische Probleme		244
Gerichtsverfahren, Ritual als		350
Geruch		242
Geruchssinn, Huitotos		466
Gesang Nord-Indiens, klassischer		323
Gesang		239
Gesang-Sessions		126
Geschlechter		242
Geschlechtsverkehr		272
Geschmack		242
Geschwüre	407, 408,	434
Gesellschaft, Nigeria		146
Gesellschaft, pluralistische		221
gesellschaftliche Ordnung, Indien		349
gesellschaftlichen Realitäten, Indien		348
Gesetze		24
Gespräch, therapeutisches		241
Gespräche		155
Gespräche, Kranken-, Lakandonen		448
Gesprächstherapie, Klientenzentrierte		394
Gestalten, künstlerisches		241
Gestalttherapie		394
Gesten		327
gestörte Beziehungsmuster		392
Gesundheit der Familie		352
Gesundheit, emotionale & geistige		146
Gesundheitsbehörden, israelische		222
Gesundheitssystem, Israel		222
gewaltsamer Tod		348
Gewehrkugeln		375
Gewichtsverlust		126
Ghanghchi		337
Gibbon, Indien		364
Gichtzettel		274
Gift, tödliches		375
giftige Tiere, Lakandonen		447
giftiger Blick		270
Giftpfeil, Lakandonen		448
Giftstoffe, Ausleitung der		412
Ginestra, Italien		97

Glauben, anthropomorpher	148
Glaubensheilung	56
Glaubenssystem	227
---, Mongolei	292
---, schamanisches	292
---, sozio-religiöses, Italien	98
Glaubensüberzeugungen	348
Glaubensvorstellungen, Samoa	491
Gleichgewicht, kosmisches, Brasilien	481
Gleichgewichtes, Störungen des, Samoa	492
Gliederschmerzen	391
Glocken	298
Gloria al Padre, Italien	103
Glückstalismanen	150
Glycerine, Pflanzliche	409
Glycosmis pentaphylla Retz.	377
Glycyrrhiza globera	337
Gnadenbilder, Schweiz	81
Gold	375
goldener Faden	314
Goldhase	450
Gond in Jalpur, Volksstamm	337
Göschenen, Teufelsstein von, Schweiz	78
Gott der Nichtindianer, Lakandonen	448
Gott der Weißen, Lakandonen	448
Gott	243
Gott, Afrika	122
Gott, Tansania	127
Götter, afrikanische	419
---, Indien	348
---, Lakandonen	444
---, Pferde der	299
---bote, Lakandonen	447
---haus, Lakandonen	448
---schalen	450
---welt	388
Gottes	
--- Wille	269, 271, 408
---, Donnerkeil	391
---bild	351
---suche	238
---wort, außerkor'anisches	237
Gotthardtunnel, Schweiz	78
Gottheit	227
---, höchste, Nepal	390
---, Nigeria	148
---en, Brasilien	476
---en, buddhistische	296
---en, Mongolei	292
Göttin des verdrängten Waldes	391
göttliche	
--- Dreiheit	391
--- Einheit	238
--- Geister, Tansania	123
---, das	323
---n, Suche nach dem	60
---r Shiva	326
---s Gebot	272
Grab, heiliges	276
Grab, Tansania	125
Gräber	148
Grabstätten von Heiligen	226
Grabsteinen, Samoa	498
Greenberg, Ofra	221
Grenzen, Behandlung von, Italien	104
Grippe, Lakandonen	448
Grippeepidemien	452
Großhirnrinde, Schädigung der	244
Gruppenbehandlungen, Huitotos	467
Gruppentherapie	54, 126
Gujarat	352
Gurke, Brasilien	478
Gurung	387
Güvenç, Oruç	240
Gwalior	323
Haare ziehen	350
Haare	151, 273
Haaren, helle	271
Haaren, Verschnüren von	276
hach winik, Lakandonen	444
Hachäkyum, Lakandonen	446, 448
Hadith Qudsi	237
Hähnchenschnabel	176
haitianische Migranten	420
haitianische Religion Vodou	419
hakim arabi	270
Halluzinationen, Huitotos	464
Halluzinationen, Samoa	499
halluzinatorische Psychose, Samoa	499
Halluzinogene	388
Halsleiden, Schweiz	81
Halsschmerzen, Italien	103
Hammam	272
Handamulett	274
Handauflegen	56, 174
Händezittern	226
Händlerkaste	349
Handpostille, katholische, Schweiz	82
Hanuman	351, 391
Haridas, Swami	324
Harmin, Alkaloid	464
Harmonie	154, 390
--- in der Gemeinschaft	436
---, kosmische, Brasilien	481
---, Störung der, Anden	432
harmonische	
--- Beziehungen, Anden	432
--- Farbgestaltung	239
--- Klänge	239
Harmonisierung	242
Harn, Schweiz	80
harntreibende Mittel	55
Hartgummistift	295
Harz	451
Hass	21, 476
Häuptling, Samoa	494
Hausbesuch, Kallawaya	434
Haustiere, Lakandonen	445
Hautausschlag, Italien	102
Hautausschläge, Brasilien	477
Hautbeulen	451
Hautentzündungen, Italien	100
Hautgeschwüren, Brasilien	478
HAWAIKI, Samoa	491
Hazardana	338
Hebamme, traditionelle	270
Hebammen, Andenraum	431
Hegatangpui, Indien	363
heidnische Riten, Schweiz	78
Heidnische Zeremonie, Italien	105
Heilbehandlung, Nepal, Schamanische	387
Heilen in Afrika	120
Heilen, traditionelles, Italien	98
heilende Geister, Tansania	123
Heiler	
---, Afrika	15
---, Balinesen	15
---, Brasilien	15
---, Haiti	15
---, irakischer	224
---, Italien	97
---, Karibik	15
---, Nigerien	145
---, Nordamerika	15
---, Samoa	491, 494
---, türkischer	275
---, Vielfalt der	13
Heilerfolge, fantastische	60
Heilerin	
--- in Tansania	119
--- sheik's wife	225
---, PEPO, Tansania	119
---nen, Mongolei	291, 293
Heilerrolle der Geistheiler, Afrika	120
Heilerrolle der Schamanen, Afrika	120
Heilgesänge	391
Heilgesänge, Kallawaya	434
heilige Geisteskraft	126
--- Laute	323
--- Pflanzen, Huitotos	464
--- Pflanzen, Huitotos	464
--- Quelle	299
Heilige	
---, Italien	103
---n, Grabstätten von	226
---nverehrung, volkstümliche	419
heiliger Brunnen, Schweiz	81

heiliger Geist, Italien 103
heiliges Grab 276
Heilinstanzen der türkischen
   Volksmedizin 269
Heilkräfte, Samoa 492
Heilkräuter 375
---, Bangladesh 374
---kundige 431
---, Brasilien 476
---n, Sammeln von 106
Heilmittel, ayurvedische 373
Heilmittel, kirchliche,
   Schweiz 80
Heilmittel, krampflösende 197
Heilpädagogik 244
Heilpflanzen
--- Wurzeln 174
---, Huitotos 464
---, Lakandonen 451
Heilpraktiken, Türkei 270
Heilriten, Zulus 198
Heilrituale, Magisch,
   Religiöse Schweiz 77
Heilsitzungen,
   musikalische 126
Heiltempel, Indien 350, 351
Heiltradition, Huitotos in
   Kolumbien 463
Heilung
---, candomblé 475
---, Huitotos 466
---, Italien 102
---, Tansania 127
---, Magische, Italien 97
---, spirituelle 53
---skonzepte 169
---smodelle, Nigeria 147
---sphänomene, spiritueller 56
---sprozess 55
---sritual, Indien 350
---srituale, Brasilien 475, 477
---sschrein, LaPaz 435
---ssprüche, Huitotos 467
---ssymbolik 152
---ssystem, Kallawaya 431
---sverständnis, Nigeria 145
Heilverfahren, Indien 361
Heilverfahren, traditionelle,
   Indien 361
Heilzeremonien 198
Heilzeremonien,
   musikalische 237
Heinei, Indien 364
Heirat, Nigeria 148
Helfer, Italien 100
Helminthiasis, Italien 101
Helung, Indien 363
Helungmau, Indien 363
Hemeube, Indien 363
Henna 224
Henne 178
Hepatitis, Italien 100
Hepobei, Indien 364

Heradi, Indien 364
Heraka-Bewegung, Indien 362
Herbalarios, Kallawaya 431
Herbalismus 148
Herbalist 198, 270
Herbalist 408
Herbarium in Durban,
   Südafrika 199
Herz, Huitotos 466
Herzerkrankungen 379
Herzhöhe 326
Herzklopfen 126
Herz-Lungen-Stillstand 55
Herzoperation 54
Hethei, Indien 364
Heth-Rangma 375
Hexen 169, 175, 197, 389
---, Anrufung der 198
---, Tansania 120
Hexerei 154
---, Brasilien 476
---, Indien 364
---, Lakandonen 446, 447
---, Tansania 122
---auflösungsrituale,
   Brasilien 478
hexerische Angriffe 171
hexerische Energien 145
Hexerkraft 171
Hibiscus esculentus Linn. 377
Hierarchie, kosmische 348
Hilflosigkeit 348
Hilfsgeister, Nepal 388
Hilfsmittel, medizinische 407
Himalayische Zeder 375
Himmel, Anrufung der vier 42
Himmels
---briefe 274
---geist, weiblicher 179
---geister 294
---richtungen 314
---schmied, Söhne des 313
Himmlische, der 311
Hinduismus 348
Hinduismus, Indien 362
Hingkuipau, Indien 364
Hirnstamm, Schädigung 244
Hirsch 450
Hirsebier 379
Hirte, Bangladesh 379
HIV-Patienten 59
Hoca 270
Hoca-Krankheiten 277
Höhlen 272
Hokkaido Insel,
   japanische 292
holistische Körperkonzept 423
Holunderbeeren, Italien 103
Holz, Talik 376
Holzasche 375
Homöopathie 407
Homöostase 241
Hordeum vulgare Linn. 377

Hören 240
Horia, Huitotos 467
Horn, Rhinozeros 375
Horn-Tambura 324
Hotgoid 294
Hövsgöl Gegend 294
Hövsgöl 294
Hufschmied 408
Hüfte 150
Huhn 375
Hühnermais, Brasilien 478
Hühneropfer 170
Huitotos, Kolumbien 463
Humoralmedizin 242
Hund 450
Hunde, schwarze, Schweiz 78
Hundekopf 151
Hunger 348
Husten des Heilers, Italien 103
Hydnocarpus kurzii 377
Hygiene, Samoa 496
Hyperventilation 347, 388
Hypnose 347
Hysterie 350

Iahme, Brasilien 478
Ibni Sina 242
Ich - Du - Bezug 243
Identitätswechsel,
   traumatischer 349
Igbo Heiler, Nigeria 145
Ilex godajam 377
Illyrien, Italien 98
Imagination 241, 394
Imagination, Huitotos 465
Imaginationsarbeit, Musik 248
Imker 408
Immunsystem 248
Improvisation 323
Improvisationsmusik 248
Indianer, Nationale Stiftung
   für 21
Indianer-DANN 22
Indien, Nord- 323
Indien, Pflanzenmedizin
   Zentral- 337
Indien, Volksmedizin 361
indigenen Wissens,
   Prinzipien des 22
indigener Menschen,
   Internationale Charta 26
Indigenes Heilen, Italien 98
indische Kultur 348
Indradeva (nepali) 395
Infektionskrankheiten 379
Infektionsherde, lokale 434
Ingwer 451
Inhalieren von Rauch 273
Initianden, Vodou- 422
Initiation
---, Lakandonen 447
---, Tansania 123

Schlagwortregister   heiliger — Initiation   521

Initiationen	154	
Initiationszeit, Brasilien	479	
Initiationszeremonie, Lakandonen	451	
Inka Imperium	431	
Inka-Kulturen, Prä-	431	
Inkorporieren krafttragender Substanzen	273	
innere Konflikte, Huitotos	467	
innere Stimme	388	
innere Sammlung	391	
Instrumente	323	
Integration, Altorientalische Musiktherapie	243	
integrativen Sinnesakten	239	
interkulturelles Verständnis	244	
Internationale Charta indigener Menschen	26	
Intervention, psychoanalytische	394	
Intimsphäre, Brasilien	480	
Intuition des Therapeutenteams	246	
Intuitive	199	
Ipomoea reptans Linn.	377	
irakischer Heiler	224	
Iridologist	408	
Iris, Diagnose	432	
Iroegbu, Patrick	145	
Islam	324	
Islamische Ärzte	239	
--- Lehre, orthodoxe	269	
--- Medizin	237	
--- Mystiker	238	
--- Volksmedizin	221	
Isolationssymptomatik	249	
Israel, Volksmedizin	221	
Italien, Magische Heilung	97	
italienischer Dialekt, süd-	101	
Ivitimbango, Tansania	122	
Iwa, Tansania	122	
Ixwele	198	
Izangoma	15, 197, 198	
Izinyanga	15, 198	

J

Jagdbedingungen	292	
Jagdglück	292	
Jagdmagie	293	
Jagdopfer	299	
Jäger	292	
Jalpur	337	
Jana, Huitotos	466	
Jangeli	391	
japanische Hokkaido Insel	292	
Jatrofa Multifida-Lineu, Brasilien	478	
Jatropha curcas	202	
Javae-Nation	27	
jemenitischen Rabbi	223	
Jenseits	314	
Jenseits, Schweiz	78	
Jesus Christus, Italien	103	
Jesus Christus, Tansania	127	
Jhalla	325	
Jhankri	387	
Jharphuk, Nepal	387, 390	
Jhum-Anbau, Bangladesh	373	
Jod, Tempo	325	
jogo-de-búzios, Brasilien	475, 476, 480	
Jokhana	389	
Joria, Huitotos	466	
Juccawurzel, Brasilien	478	
Juden, Israel	221	
jüdisch-christlicher Gott	54	
Junça, Brasilien	478	

K

Kaffesatzeinlauf	412	
Kah, Lakandonen	448	
Kaingang-Nation	27	
Kalebasse	177	
Kalebassenkürbis	324	
Kalebassenstückchen	178	
Kalendariographie, Kolumbien	466	
Kalium	464	
Kallawaya Heilungssystem	431	
Kalmykia	294	
kalmykische Heilerinnen	295	
Kalmyks	292	
Kalweit, Holger	39	
Kalziumbedarfs, Huitotos	464	
Kampfmittel gegen Geister	350	
Kanada, Amish	407	
Kanton Luzern	77	
Kapellen, Schweiz	78	
Kapzinerinnen, Salzburg	82	
Karaja-Nation	27	
Karatiana-Nation	27	
Karbi Anglong, Indien	362	
Kardezismus, Brasilien	477	
kardiologischer Bereich	244	
Karitiana-Volk	22	
Karma	348	
Karmische Kräfte	349	
Karotten, Brasilien	478	
Kastenlosen	349	
Kastensystem	348	
Katalysator, Vodou-	423	
Katharina, St. , Schweiz	81	
kathartisches Erleben	394	
katholische Gebete, Italien	103	
katholische Handpostille, Schweiz	82	
katholische Kirche, Schweiz	80	
katholischer Zeremonie, Italien	105	
Katholizismus, Italien	98	
Katholizismus, Zwangsbekehrung	475	
Kaugummibaumes, Rindenextrakt des	451	
Kaukasus	294	
k'ax, Lakandonen	444	
Kehle	326	
Kehlkopf	326	
Keim, J.	407	
Kepe, Indien	364	
Keram, Indien	365	
Kerze	154	
Kerze, Brasilien	478, 479	
Kerze, Flamme der	238	
Keuschheit, Indien	349	
Khagrachari, Bangladesh	373	
khali	325	
Khan, Mahmud Tareq Hassan	373	
Kharisiri, Anden	432	
Khori Familie	296	
Kigelia africana	200	
Kinder, ungeborene	451	
Kinderkrankheiten	271	
Kinderkrankheiten, Lakandonen	448	
kinetische Trance	243	
Kinhiha, Tansania	122	
Kirchenbesuch, kein, Italien	103	
kirchliche Heilmittel, Schweiz	80	
kirchliche Rituale, Schweiz	80	
Kirklama	273	
Kiswahili	120	
Klang	323	
Klangstrukturen	242	
Klassifizierungen von Krankheiten, volkstümlichen	100	
Klassifizierungen, Krankheiten, Italien	100	
Klauen, Rhinozeros	375	
Kleider, frische, Brasilien	479	
Klette	407, 410	
Klettenblätter	412	
Klientenzentrierte Gesprächstherapie	394	
klinische Anwendungsbereiche	244	
Kloster Muri, Schweiz	81	
Knie, in die, zwingen	350	
Knochen als Armulett, Indien	364	
Knochen	273	
---, Samoa	498	
---brüche	174	
---brüche, Indien	364	
---brüche, Lakandonen	447	
---heiler	270, 277	
---heiler, Italien	101	
Knoten, magische	271	
Kobolde, Schweiz	77	
kognitive Ebene, Therapie	248	
Kohl, Brasilien	478	
Koka, Kolumbien	464	
Koka-Blatt	464	
Kokain	464	
Kokastrauch	464	
Kokosnüsse, Opfer-	351	

kollektives Unbewusstes	392	
Kolonialismus		444
Kolumbien, Heiltradition, Huitotos in		463
Kompensation für die Frauen		352
Kompensationstheorie		352
Konditionierung		243
Konflikte, innere, Huitotos		467
---, Samoa		493
---, unbewusste		348
---lösung, Samoa		494
---orientiert, nicht		241
Konformität als Ehefrauen		352
Kongo-Angola, Brasilien		476
Konkurrenz		172
Konservierungsmittel		409
Konsultationsraum, Vodou		422
Kontrollzentrum		326
Konzentration	244, 326, 391
Konzentrationsstörungen		271
Konzepte, philosophische		241
---, psychologische		241
---, religiöse		241
---, spirituelle		241
Kooperation der Patienten		433
Koordinationszentrum		326
Kopf für Kopf		151
Kopf		326
Kopfschmerzen	271, 351, 391, 409
---, Indien		363
---, Italien	100, 103
---, Schweiz		81
Koran		270
koranhaltiger Rauch		273
Koranpapier		273
Körper		
---- - Geist - Seele-Konzept	13, 16
---- - Seele - Verständnis		242
---konzept, holistisches		423
---liche Disposition		239
---lose Wesenheit		314
---säfte		242
---säfte, drei		349
---sensibilisierung		248
---rsensibilisierungs- übungen		246
---sprachlicher Ausdruck		246
---zonen, geschädigte, Reintegration		248
---- -zonenspezifische Tonarten		246
Koryak		292
Kosack, Godula		169
kosmische Hierarchie		348
--- Kräfte, Nepal	388, 392
--- Methoden		298
--- Ordnung	237, 394
---s Gleichgewicht, Brasilien		481
Kosmologie, Mongolei		292
Kosmologie, Nepal		388
kosmologische Energie		151
kosmologischen Verknüpfung		152
Kosmos, Einklangs mit dem		169
Kosmos, Zentrum des		154
Krabbe		170
Krabben, Indien		363
Krabbenorakel		178
Kräfte, archetypische		388
---, Astrologische		349
---, Karmische		349
---, kosmische, Nepal		388
---, negative		389
---, seelische, Nepal		388
---, transzendente	170, 348
---, übermenschliche		349
Kraftfelder		155
Kraftobjekte	149, 151
Krampf		197
Krämpfe		126
krampflösende Heilmittel		197
Krankenamulett		274
Krankenkassen, Israel		222
Krankensegen, Schweiz		80
Krankheit des Regenbogens, Italien		99
---, Geist der, Italien		103
---, Heiler, Tansania		120
---, Nigeria		148
---, Regenbogen-, Italien		101
---, schwere		271
---, Sinn der, Tansania		119
---, Umlenkung der		149
---, Ursache		169
Krankheiten, chronische		434
---, Entstehen der, Schweiz		78
---, epidemische, Lakandonen		448
---, innere		174
---, Lakandonen		446
---, mentale		222
---, neurologische		271
---, psychische	271, 272
---, psychische, Kallawaya		432
---, psychosomatische, Brasilien		476
---, volkstümliche Klassifizierungen von, Italien		100
---serzeugende Einflüsse		391
---sheilige, Schweiz		80
---sursache	227, 389, 476
Kräuter		407
---, Brasilien		478
---arzt		197
---heiler		270
---heiler, Kallawaya		431
---kundige, Tansania		120
---kundige	198, 199, 408
---laden, Anden		433
---mixturen		198
---mixturen, Bäder in		198
---zubereitungen, Kallawaya		434
Krebspatienten	57, 411
Kreise		154
Kreislauf, Lebens-		313
Kreuz, Doppelbalkiges, Schweiz		77
Kreuze, Italien		103
Kreuze, Schweiz		78
Kreuzung, Symbolismus der, Italien		104
Kreuzzeichen, Schweiz		84
Kriegerkaste		349
Krippner, Stanley	21, 28, 431
Krise		408
Krise, Heiler-, Tansania		120
Krisen, Lebens-		244
Krokodil		375
Krschna Verehrung		323
Krschna		323
Kruiedoktor		198
Kruzifix, Schweiz		85
Ksalinaga (nepali)		395
Kuganga, Tansania		120
Küken, Brasilien		478
Kultstätten		40
Kultstätten, Brasilien		476
Kultur, indische		348
Kulturanthropologie als Wissenschaft		443
Kumys		311
Kundalini Yoga	130, 326
Kundalini-Energie		326
Kunstform, befreiende		352
künstlerisches Gestalten		241
Kunsttherapie		239
Kunyah, Lakandonen		449
Kupepea, Tansania		120
Kürbiskerne, Lakandonen		447
Kurumkan		296
Kushagras		391
Kyzyl		299

Lageneria sicearia 377

Lagerstroernia speciosa Linn.		377
Lähmung		222
Lakandonen, Ethnomedizin der		443
Lama Lehrer		294
--- Vorfahren		294
---ische Familie		294
---s, Fötus eines		434
---skeletts, Anden		433
Lamiaceae		202
Landwirt		408
Langenmatt, Schweiz		81
Langhalslaute		324
Langsame Loris, Indien		364
Lannea coromondelica		377
Lannea discolor		200
LaPaz, Kallawaya		435

Lärche	314	
Lathyrus sativus Linn.	377	
Lauraceae	373	
Läuse, Lakandonen	448	
Lebens		
---baum	451	
---energie	394	
---erfahrung	57	
---faden	314	
---führung, Regeln	273	
---geist	272	
---krisen	244	
---linien, Durchtrennen der	390	
---qualitätsstabilisierung	248	
---sinnfindung	244	
---stil, Samoa	496	
Leberprobleme	432	
Lederpeitsche	451	
Legenden, Mongolei	312	
Leguminosae	373	
Lehmboden	422	
Lehner, Christian	491	
Lehre, Schamanen-, Nepal	388	
Lehrer, Lama	294	
Lehrgeschichten	241, 248	
Leibschmerzen	179	
Leibschmerzen, Schweiz	81	
Leichenasche	375	
Leichenteile, Schweiz	80	
Leichenverbrennung	375	
Leid, Brasilien	481	
Leiden	58	
Leidenschaft	146	
Leistungsanspruch	246	
Leonotis leonurus	202	
Lernen am Modell	394	
Lianensäfte	451	
Licuala pellata Roxb.	377	
Liebe	327	
Liebe, besitzergreifender, Brasilien	476	
Liebe, schöpferische	238	
Liliaceae, Fam.	375	
Lippia javanica	204	
Loas, Vodou	419	
Lobelia	409	
Loganiaceae	202	
Logos, Huitotos	466	
Londoner Missionsgesellschaft, Samoa	491	
Loretokind von Salzburg	80, 81	
Loslassen	150	
Lot, Befehl an, Italien	104	
Lucania-Region, Süditalien	97	
Luft	391	
Lungenentzündung	55	
Lunnea grandis	377	
Lussi, Kurt	77	
Luzern, Kanton, Schweiz	77, 81	

Macht 348

Machtmissbrauch	23	
Machtsymbole	154	
Macumba, Brasilien	476	
Macuxi	25	
Mädchen, pubertierendes	451	
madzaf nkhè	180	
mãe-de-santo, Brasilien	475, 476	
Mafa, Kamerun	169	
Magen		
---beschwerden	129, 363	
--- -Darm-Beschwerden	391	
---krämpfe	298	
---probleme	432	
---schmerzen	81, 409	
---verstimmung	451	
Magico veränderte Bewusstseinszustände	243	
Magie	15	
--- der Zahl, Italien	104	
---, negative	271	
---, positive	271	
---, schwarze	126, 271	
---, schwarze, Tansania	120	
---, schwarze, Vodou	420	
---, weiße	271	
magische		
--- Ansteckung, Italien	99	
--- Erklärungen	269	
--- Handlungen, Schweiz	80	
--- Heilrituale, Schweiz	77	
--- Heilung, Italien	97	
--- Knoten	271	
--- Kräfte	374	
--- Quadrate	274	
--- Texte	271	
--- Übertragung, Italien	102	
--- Vergiftung, Italien	104	
---s Weltbild	361	
---s Heilen, Italien	99	
---s Ritual, Türkei	276	
Magnesium	464	
Magnolienblüten, Lakandonen	451	
Mahadev	390	
Mais		
---, weißer, Brasilien	478	
---fladen, , Lakandonen	444	
---körner als Zähne, Lakandonen	446	
---speisen	451	
Makamen	242	
mal d arco, Italien	99, 101	
--- di denti, Italien	104	
--- di gola, Italien	103	
--- di pancia, Italien	103	
--- olhada, Brasilien	478	
Malaria	338, 434, 448	
Mallotus albus	377	
Maloca, Kolumbien	463	
Malocchio, Italien	99, 101	
Mambeodero, Maloca	464	
Mambwe, Tansania	122	
Mangan	464	

Mangfera indica Linn.	377	
Mangifera sp, Indien	365	
Manien	272	
Manifest, schamanisches	21	
Maniok, Brasilien	478	
Manipura Cakra	326	
manische Episoden	276	
manische Syndrome	146	
Manjifera Indica- Lineu, Brasilien	479	
Manjour, Indien	361	
Mänsebäk, Lakandonen	448	
Mantras	323	
Mantras, buddhistische	294	
Mantren	388, 390	
MAOPOOPO, Samoa	492	
Marginalisierung, Soziale, Brasilien	481	
Maria, Schweiz	82	
Marma, Bangladesh	373	
Marquesas, Samoa	491	
Marrons, Vodou	419	
Maschito, Italien	97	
Mashallah	271	
Massage, Italien	100, 294	
Massagetechniken	174, 388	
MATAI, Samoa	494	
Mathura	323	
Mäuse, Test-	205	
ma'uts, Lakandonen	446	
Maxacali-Nation	27	
Maya, Mexiko	444	
Maytenus senegalensis (Lam.)	201	
maytenus senegalensis	174, 178	
Mbachi, Indien	365	
Mbeya Region, Tansania	122	
Mchawi, Tansania	120	
Medikamentenabhängigkeit	54	
Meditationsgebet	273, 296	
Medizin		
--- -Topf	151, 153	
--- Zentralasiens	240	
---, Einführung der modernen, Indien	362	
---, islamische	237	
---, prophetische	240	
---, westliche, Israel	222	
---, wissenschaftliche	240	
----Gottheit	146	
---händler	46	
---ische Pflanzen	199	
---mann, Kolumbien	463	
---männer, Kallawaya	431	
---männer, Nordamerika	15	
---männer, Tansania	120	
---pflanze	198, 199	
---pflanzen, Südafrikanische	197	
Meerschweinchen,Diagnose	432	
Meerwasser	276	
Mehlpackungen	294	
Meidling, Rehabilitationszentrum	244	

Meisterhelfer, Italien	101	Indien	362	Huitotos	464
Melancholikern, Therapie		Mongun-Taiga	299	Nações, Religionen	475
von	240	Moralbewusstsein	155	nada-brahma	323
Melia azedarach	203	Mord	348	Nada-Yoga	323
Meliaceae	203	Mord, Italien	102	Nadeltherapie	296
Melodie	323, 242	Mord, Tansania	124	Naga Stamm,	
Melodieinstrumente	323	Morinda anguistifolia		mongolischer	362
Meningitis	169	Roxb.	377	Nagaland, Indien	361
Mennoniten	407	Moringa oleifera	377	Nagaraja (nepali)	395
Mensäbäk, Lakandonen	448	Moschee, Besuch	276	Nagarani (nepali)	395
Menschen		Motivationssteigerung	244	Nagphani	337
---, Erzeugung des ersten	311	Müdigkeit	271	Naha in Südmexiko	444
---fleisch	172	Muladhara Cakra	326	Naha See, Mexiko	444
---welt	388	Müllhaufen	272	Nahrungsmittelergän-	
Menstruation	224	Mumps, Italien	100	zungen	408
---, weibliche	349	Mund, Huitotos	466	Namensgebung	154
---sblut	172	Mundfäule	451	Narasing (nepali)	395
---sblutungen	178	Murang, Bangladesh	373	Nardostachys jatamansi	
---sfähige Frauen	451	Muri, Kloster	81	Dc.	377
mentale Beschwerden,		Musa ornata Roxb.	377	Nasenbluten, Italien	100
Tansania	120	Musa paradisiacal Linn.		Nationale Stiftung für	
mentale Krankheiten	222	sub sp. sylvestris	377	Indianer	21
mentale Probleme	126	Musa sapientum Linn.	377	Nativo, Brasilien	478
mentales Leiden	145	muscas	271, 273	Natur, beseelte, Schweiz	78
Mesa	434	Muscheln	150	---, Indien	323
Mesa, Zeremonial-,		Musik	347	---, Kräfte der, Mongolei	292
Andengebiet	432	---, Bedeutung von	237	---aufenthalte	40
Messapic, Italien	98	---, Indien	323	---feste	41
Mesua ferrea Linn.	377	---, indische klassische	323	---geist	126
metaphorische Dimension	388	musikalische		---gesetze	243
metaphysischer Feind	350	--- Heilsitzungen	126	---gesetzmäßigkeiten	237
Mevlevi Orden	238	--- Heilzeremonien	237	---heilmedizin, Israel	222
mexikanischen Regenwald,		--- Komposition	323	---kenntnisse	37
Lakandonen	443	Musik-		natürliche Welt, Samoa	492
Mganga, Afrika	120	---erleben, Rezeptives	246	Natur	
Migräne, Italien	100	---hören, tonarten-		---phänomene	243
Migranten, haitianische	420	spezifisches	241	---schau	40
migrationsspezifische Fragen,		---stück-Sequenz-Plänen	242	---schützer	379
Türkei	276	---therapeuten, Aus-		---therapie	37
Mikrokosmos, Huitotos	466	bildung	243	---verehrung	41
Mikrokosmos, Kallawaya	431	---therapie	239	Nazar	270
Mikrotonale Tonskalen	242	---therapie, Alt-		negative Kräfte	389
Milch	299	orientalische	237	Neid	172, 348
Mildtätigkeit	239	---therapien, westliche	242	Neid, Brasilien	476
Mimosa pudica	202	Musizieren	241	Neider	270
Mineralien	409	Muskelleiden, Italien	101	neoschamanischen Suche	292
Mineralsalze	375	Muskelschmerzen	409	Neo-Schamanismus	299
Mineralstein	375	muslimische Gelehrte	272	Nepal, Schamanische	
Mineralstoffe	464	muslimischer Scheich	225	Heilbehandlung	387
Missernten	271	Mustafa Kemal Pascha	269	Nerven, gekreuzte, Italien	102
Missgunst	172	Mutter Erde, Respekt für	23	nervenärztliche Behand-	
Missgunst, Brasilien	476	Mutterbaum	314	lung	276
Missionsgesellschaft, Londoner,		Mutterleib	451	Nervensystem, zentrales	197
Samoa	491	Muzimu, Tansania	122	nervi accavallati, Italien	102
Mogh, Bangladesh	373	Mykhorshibirski Region	298	Nervosität	272
Mohammed, Prophet	271	Mysterienfeier	42	Nervosität, Brasilien	476
Momordia charantia	377	Mystiker, Islamische	238	Nesselraupen,	
Momordia muricata	377	mystische Dimension	237	Lakandonen	447
Mondamulett	274			Nestbaum	314
Monduntergang	276	**N**abel, Mittelpunkt	466	Neumann Fridman,	
Mongolei	291	Nachtfalter	238	Eva Jane	291
Mongolei, Schamane der	311	Nachtschattengewächse,		Neuroleptika, Samoa	499
mongolischer Naga Stamm,				neurologische Krankheiten	271

Schlagwortregister   Meisterhelfer — neurologische   525

neurologische Rehabilitation 244
neuropsychologische Sinnessystem 243
Neurotransmitter, Huitotos 465
New York City, Vodou 419
Ngwozla 174
Nichtraum 315
Nichtwissen 315
Nichtzeit 315
Nicotiana tabacum 464
Nicotiana tobactim Linn. 377
Nierenleiden 294
Nigerien, Südost 145
Nimbus, Schweiz 80
nomadische Völker 292
nome della croce, Italien 103
Norden 314
Nordkamerun 169
Nordkap 198
North Cachar Hill 362
Nosologie, , Krankheits-, Lakandonen 446
Nothelfer, Schweiz 80
Nottingham Health Profile 57
Nqaka 198
Nsawalteva 179
Nswaltewa 178
Nuxia floribunda Benth. 202
Nyakyusa, Tansania 122
Nyamwanga, Tansania 121
Nyiha, Tansania 121
Nymphaea nouchali 377

O

OLE Fofo, Samoa 491
Oberwelt 389
Objekte, rituelle, Italien 100
Obszönitäten 351
Ocakli 270
Ocimum basilicum L., Brasilien 478
Ocimum basilicum Linn. 377
Ocimum gratissimum Linn. 377
Odum-dum, Brasilien 478
Offenbarung, Tansania 119
Oguns Schwert, Brasilien 478
Ohnmacht 226
Ohrengeräusche, Susto 436
Oirat Mongolen 295
Ojewole, John A. O. 197
Ojihas 375
Ökologe 379
ökologische Begebenheiten 147
ökonomische Faktoren, Indien 362
Ökopiraterie 21
Ökosystem 378
Olivenöl 224, 409
OM (nepali) 395
Om, Urlaut 323
Omolu, Brasilien 477, 478

Ongons 294
Onkologiestationen 58
onkologischer Bereich 244
Opfer 38, 390
---, Bier- 170
---, Hühner- 170
---, Mongolei 299
---, Samoa 496
---, Tansania 122, 125
---, Ziegen- 170
---gaben, Brasilien 475, 477
---gaben, Tansania 122
---gaben, Vodou 419
---handlungen 175
---speisen 351
---speisen, Lakandonen 448
---ung 149
---zeremonien 198
Opuntia vulgaris mill 337
Opuntie, Indien 337
Orakel 169, 175
---, Afrika 15
---, Brasilien 475
---, inneres, Huitotos 467
---, Vodou 419
----Ritual 273
Orakelsprecher 169, 175, 178
Orden, Mevlevi 238
Ordnung 390
Ordnung, gesellschaftliche, Indien 349
organische Krankheit, Brasilien 476
orixá Ossaim, Brasilien 478
orixá Oxum, Brasilien 478
Orixás, Brasilien 475, 476, 478
Ornamentik 241
Oroxylum indicum Linn. 377
Orpheus 323
orthodoxe islamische Lehre 269
orthopädische Leiden, Italien 101
Ortswechsel 174
Oryza sativa Linn. 377
Osmanenreich 238
Ossaim, Brasilien 478
Ostafrika 120
Osten 314
Ost-Jalpur, Zentralindien 338
Otter, Indien 365
Oxalá, Brasilien 478
Oxossi , Brasilien 478
Oxygonum dregeanum 203
Ozeans, Grund des 311

P

Pachamama, Kallawaya 434
Pada 323
Padre Nostro, Italien 103
Padua 79
pai-de-santo, Brasilien 476
Pajes 21
Paleo-Balkan-Gruppe,

Italien 98
Palmenblatt 451
Palmöl 178
Panama-Kanal 434
Pandanus lectonis 377
Pankreassekrete 375
Pantke, Christiane 475
Papageienfleisch, Lakandonen 444
Paradies 348
Paradieses, Pforten des 238
Paralyse 126
Parana 22
Paraphernalien 388
Parasiten, äußere 451
Parasiten, Lakandonen 448
Parasitenerkrankungen 378
partidas, Andenraum 431
Partners, Treue des 275
Partnersuche, vergebliche 222
Parvat (nepali) 395
Passary-Shops 374
Patala 388
Pataxo-Nation 21, 27
Patentrechte 24
Patienten türkischer Herkunft 269
Patienten, Befreiung des 152
Patienten, Kooperation der 433
Patronin der Gebärenden, Schweiz 81
Pech 126
pelo alla menna, Italien 103
Penicillin 452
penizilinähnliche Substanz 434
Pentylenetetrazol 205
pepo Erwachung, Tansania 128
--- Heilerin, Tansania 119
--- nzuri 126
--- -Krankheit, Tansania 120
Persönlichkeits-Anteile, abgespaltene 348
Persönlichkeitsentwicklung 244
Perspektivenwandel 248
Peru, Kallawaya 431
Pest, Schweiz 81
Pfauenfedern 375
Pfeffer 338
Pferd 450
Pferd, fliegendes 299
Pferde der Götter 299
Pferdekopf 294
Pflanzen
---, Indien, einheimische 361
---, Kallawaya 431
---, Samoa 492
---extrakte 199, 205
---extrakte, Israel 225
---kenntnis, Bangladesh 374
---medizin, Zentral-Indien 337
---präparate 388
---therapie, Wurzel- 147

Pflanzliche Glycerine	409	Psidium, Brasilien	478	Raga, Feuer-	324
Pflegende	58	Psychiater, Nigeria	147	Raga, Regen-	324
Phakavaj	325	Psychiatrie, Türkei	269	Raja Man Singh Tomar	323
Phallus	42	psychiatrische Krankheits-		Rajastan	324
Phantasien	347	bilder	244	Rakhain, Bangladesh	373
phantastische Einbildungen	350	psychische		Rama	391
philosophische Konzepte	241	--- Krankheiten 269, 271, 272		Ramirez, Fabio Alberto	463
Phook	391	--- Krankheiten, Kallawaya	432	Rangamati, Bangladesh	373
Phukne-Behandlung	391	--- Stimulation, basale	245	ranjayati iti ragaha	324
Phurba	391	--- Stressfaktoren	149	Rasierklinge	151
Phytolacca dodecandra	203	--- Störungen, Türkei	276	Rassenidentitäten	27
Phytolaccaceae	203	---s Leid, Brasilien	476	Rassenvorurteile, Brasilien	476
Phytotherapie, Italien	106	psycho		Rätsch, Christian	443
Phytotherapie, Vodou	420	----aktive Substanzen,		Ratsversammlung, Samoa	498
Picrotoxin	205	Huitotos	464	Rauch	451
Pieroni, Andrea	97	---analytiker, indische	352	Rauch, Inhalieren von	273
Pilatus, Schweiz	77	---oanalytische Intervention	394	Rauch, koranhaltiger	273
Pilgerfahrten	40, 350	---drama	394	Räucherstäbchen	391
Pilztötend	410	---hygiene	244	Räucherwerk, Brasilien	478
pinhão-roxo genannt,		---logie	394	Raupen, Lakandonen	447
Brasilien	478	---logische Ästhetik	239	Raupenkrankheit,	
Piper bettle Linn.	377	---logische Konzepte	241	Lakandonen	449
Piper chaba Linn.	377	---neuroimmunologie 248, 394		Rauschzustand, Huitotos	464
Piperegun, Brasilien	478	Psychose	350	Rauvolfia caffra	200
Plantago ovata Forst.	377	Psychose, halluzinatorische,		Rawalfia serpentina	378
Plantain	411	Samoa	499	Realität, transzendente	243
Platon	242	Psychosomatik	241	Realitätsebenen	389
Plazeboeffekts, Italien	99	psychosomatische		Redekunst, Tansania	125
Pocken	180	--- Beschwerden, Tansania	120	Reflexion, ethische	243
Poesie	239, 241, 248	--- Krankheiten, Brasilien	476	Reflexologist	408
Polson, Montana	27	--- Störungen	244	Reflexzonenkundige	408
Polygonaceae	203	psychotherapeutische Heilung,		Reframings	390
Polygonatrum cirrhifolium		Italien	99	Regen, Huitotos	466
Royle	377	psychotherapeutische		Regenbogenkrankheit,	
Polygonatrum oppositi		Technik	347	Italien	101
folium	377	Psychotherapie	298, 392	Regenguss	324
Polygonum hydropiper	378	Psychotherapie, Italien	106	Regen-Raga	324
Polynesien	491	Psychotherapie, Zentral		Regression, assoziative	246
Porto Velho	22	Asien	291	Reh	447, 450
poteau-mitan, Vodou	422	Pterocarpus santalinus	375	Rehabilitation	
Praktiken, volksmedizinische,		pubertierendes Mädchen	451	---, Brasilien	481
Italien	97	PULEMELEI, Samoa	491	---, neurologische	244
Prana	327	Pulsdiagnose	294, 432	---sphilosophie, moderne	245
Preisgabe	38	Pulsfühlen	390	---szentrum Meidling	244
Priester, Brasilien	476	Pulver, schwarzes	151	Rehlederhaut	294
---, Nigeria	146	Pulvermacher, Lakandonen	448	Reifungsprozess, Krankheit	
---, Samoa	494	Punica granatum Linn.	378	als	238
---, Tempel-	351	Pupillenweite, Diagnose	432	Reimers, Andreas	387
---, Vodou-	419, 420	Python	375	Reinheitsvorstellungen	348
---kaste	349	Pythongalle	375	Reinheitszentrum	326
Prinzipien indigenen				Reinigungs-	
Wissens	21	**Q**uadrate, magische	274	---bäder, Brasilien	478
Privatexorzismus, Schweiz	84			---prozess, Italien	103
Prophet Mohammed	271	Quave, Cassandra	97	---prozess, Tansania	128
Propheten	199	Quecha, Kallawaya	431	---rituale	314
prophetische Medizin	240	Quecksilber	375	---rituale, Brasilien	477
Prophezeiung	146	Quecksilbersulphid, rotes	375	Reis, Opfer-	351
Prophezeiungen, Tansania	127	Quelle, heilige	299	Reisfelder	391
protestantische Sekten,		Quimbanda, Brasilien	476	Reiskörner	390
Mexiko	444			Reizdeprivation	388
Prozess, therapeutischer	239	**R**abbi, jemenitischen	223	Reizintensivierung	388
Prüfung, Krankheit als	238			Religionen, afrikanische	419
Psidium guyava Linn.	378	Raffia-Schnur	149	Religionsausübung	54

religiös veränderte Bewusstseinszustände		243
religiöse Bindungen		54
--- Gebräuche, Afrika		122
--- Heilrituale, Schweiz		77
--- Konzepte		241
--- Verse		224
--- Zugehörigkeit		54
--- Leben, afrikanisches		119
--- Musik		323
--- Aktivitäten, Unterdrückung		291
--- Glauben, Italien		99
--- Hintergrund		223
Religiosität		54
religiös-rituelle Reinigung		273
Reliquienkult, Schweiz		80
Remissionsphase		248
Repolho, Brasilien		478
Repression		294
Repressionen, soziale, Indien		349
Reptilien, Lakandonen		447
Resonanzbereich		326
Resonanzräume		326
Respekt für die große Mutter Erde		23
retikuläre aktivierende System, aufsteigendes		244
Rezeptives Musikerleben		246
Rheumatismus		223, 375
Rhinozeros		375
Rhoicissus tridentata		204
Rhythmus		242, 323
Ricinus communis Linn.		378
Riechen an Körnern		276
Rinde		339
Rinde, Talik		376
Ripacandida, Italien		100
Ripacandida, Italien		97
Riten		
---, Afrika		120
---, heidnische, Schweiz		78
Ritual		
--- mit Eiern		225
---, Magisches, Türkei		276
---, Orakel-		273
---e, Grundlage der		312
---e, kirchliche, Schweiz		80
---e, Mongolei		292
---e, Nigeria		148
---kundige		432
---objkte, Nigeria		152
---objekte		391
---verlauf		394
rituelle Objekte, Italien		100
rituelle Waschungen		272
ritueller Schlüssel		153
Riyazed		242
Roggliswil, Schweiz		77
römisch-katholische Kirche, Schweiz		81
Rondonia		22
Roraima		26
Rosaceae		203
roter Stoff		351
rotes Tuch, Brasilien		478
Roy, Babul		361
Rubiaceae		203, 373
Rubus pinnatus		203
Rückert, Friedrich		238
Rückfälle		148
Rückgrad, Schmerzen		409
Ruhelosigkeit		126, 271
Ruhezeiten		273
Rununculus seleratus Linn.		378
Russland		291
Rutaceae		203
Saccharurn officinarum Linn.		378
Säfte, Ungleichgewicht der		349
Sahasrara Cakra		326
Salbenform		410
Salbung		299
Salvador, Kultur		475
Salz		338
Salz, alkalisches		464
Salz, Einstreuen von		273
Salz, rituelles, Italien		104
Salzburg, Loretokind von, Schweiz		81
Samalia insignis		378
Samaveda		325
Sambucus nigra, Italien		103
Sammler		292
Samoa, Heiler		491
Samskrit		324
Samskrt		323
samvadi		324
San Biagio, Italien		103
San Francisco General Hospital		54
Sanador, Kolumbien		463
Sandelholz		375
Sangoma		197, 198
Sanseviera Ceynaica, Brasilien		478
Santalum album Linn.		378
Sapotaceae		204
Saraca indica Linn.		378
Saugen, Heilbehandlung		177
Säugling		274
Säuglingen, Begräbnis von		434
Savai'i, Samoa		491
Schachtelhalmtee		451
Schädel- Hirn -Trauma		244
Schaden		
--- bereiten		271
---bringer		150
---szauber		222
---szauber, Brasilien		476
---szauber, Italien		105
Schaf		296
Schaf, Wildes, Indien		363
Schaffung der Welt		314
Schakal, Indien		364
Schamanen		
---, Afrika		120
---, Amazonasgebiet		14
---, burjat-mongolischer		311
---, Definition		14
---, Korea		14
---, Mongolei		14, 311
---, Nepal		14
---, Prüfung der		313
---, Verpflichtung des		388
---, Werdegang der, Nepal		388
---, Yagé-		463
---, Vielfalt der		13
---, zentralasiatische		237
---geister		314
---kleid, Mongolei		294
---kostüm, Nepal		388
---lehre, Nepal		388
---spiegel		298
---tum		37
---versammlung		21
Schamaninnen in Zentral Asien		291
Schamanische Familientradition, Nepal		388
Schamanische Heilbehandlung, Nepal		387
schamanische Wahrsager, Afrika		120
schamanisches Manifest		21
schamanisches Universum		14
Schatten, Tansania		125
Schattens, Wesen des		466
Scheich, muslimischer		225
Scheide, Maloca		464
Scheitel		326
Schenk, Amélie		311
Schicksal		146
Schicksal, Akzeptanz		248
Schicksal, Vodou		419
Schicksalsschlägen		390
Schildkröte		375
Schildkröte, Indien		363
Schildkrötengalle		375
Schimmelbildung		409
schinus molle l., Brasilien		478
Schizophrene Erkrankungen		272
Schizophrenie		296
Schlaf		243
---en, Maßhalten beim		273
---entzug		388
---losigkeit		226
---losigkeit, Kallawaya		434
Schlangen		272, 294, 311
---, Lakandonen		447
---biss, Huitotos		467
---biss, Lakandonen		446
---kräfte		388, 389
---weib		311
schlechte Einflüsse		298
schlechte Energien		296
schlechtes Wasser		273

schleimbildend	410	
Schlösser, Ritual-	149	
Schlossöffnung	150	
Schlüssel, ritueller	149, 153	
Schmerz		
---bewältigung	58	
---zen	226, 409	
---en, stechende	178	
---erleichterung	412	
---frei	339	
---lindernd	326	
---stillung	410	
---symptomatik, akute	244	
Schmidt, Bettina E.	419	
Schmiede	174	
schmutzige Abwässer	351	
schmutzige Gewässer	272	
Schmutzwasser	272	
Schnittwunden, Lakandonen	447	
Schnittwunden, Talik	376	
Schnüre	149	
Schockzustände	432	
Schöpfergottheiten, Lakandonen	447	
schöpferische Liebe	238	
Schöpfung, Grundlage der	323	
Schöpfungsdynamik	391	
Schrecken, Krankheit	432	
Schrecken, Lakandonen	446	
Schulbildung, geringe, Brasilien	476	
Schuldzuweisung, Vodou	420	
Schulmedizin, ablehnende Haltung	226	
Schulmedizin, Israel	222	
Schütteln des Körpers, Tansania	128	
Schütteln	350	
Schutzamulett, Schweiz	79	
schützende Geisteskraft	126	
Schutzimpfungen	452	
Schutzmaßnahmen	175	
Schutzpflanzen	175	
Schwäche	126, 150	
Schwächezustände, Brasilien	477	
Schwangere	274	
Schwangerenbehandlung	175	
Schwangerschaft	179	
---, Bauchschmerzen	179	
---, Blutungen	179	
schwarze		
--- Bohnen, Lakandonen	444	
--- Fäden	298	
--- Kleidung	154	
--- Mächte	296	
--- Magie, Vodou	420	
--- Tara	296	
---r Himmlischer	311	
---r Stein	224	
---s Tuch, Brasilien	478	
Schwein	375	
Schwein, Zähne von	375	
Schweiß	80, 172	
Schweiz, Heilrituale	77	
Schwerstversehrte	248	
Schwindel	271	
Schwindel, Indien	363	
Scoparia dulcis L., Brasilien	478	
scoparia dulcis	178, 179	
Seasamum indicum D.C.	378	
Seele - Verständnis, Körper	242	
--- des Erkrankten	450	
---, Abbild der	239	
---, Ausdruck der	323	
---, Lakandonen	446	
---anteil	390	
---körper, Lakandonen	447	
---reisen	451	
---rückholung	390	
---verlust	390	
seelische Kräfte, Nepal	388	
seelische Verletzungen	352	
seelischer Ausgleich	242	
Seen, Herren der	292	
Segen	390	
Segensgebet, Schweiz	80, 83	
Segenskreuz, Schweiz	83	
Sehen, Huitotos	466	
Seile	149	
Seins-Dimensionen	238, 243	
Seinsöffnung	38	
Sekten, absolutistische, Mexiko	444	
Selbstbewusstsein, Brasilien	476	
Selbsterkenntnis	240	
Selbstheilung des Heilers, Italien	103	
Selbstheilung	55	
Selbstheilungskräfte	130, 394	
Selbstmord	348	
Selbstmord, Tansania	125	
Selbstversorgung, Indien	362	
Seldschukenreich	238	
Sensibilisierungsübungen, Körper-	246	
Sequenz-Plänen, Musikstück-	242	
Sesanaga (nepali)	395	
Setinaga (nepali)	395	
Seuchen, pestartige, Schweiz	81	
Seuchenübertragung	379	
Sexualität der Frau	349	
Sexualität	59, 348	
sexuelle Begierde	348	
sexuelle Verfehlungen	348	
shakti	391	
sheik's wife, Heilerin	225	
Shiva (nepali)	395	
Shiva	326, 388	
Sibirien	292	
Sibiriens, Nordosten	292	
Sida cordata	378	
Sida orientalis Cav.	378	
Sida rhombitolia Linn.	378	
Siechtum	170	
Silber	375	
Simaraja (nepali)	395	
Simarani (nepali)	395	
Singen, Schamanen-	388	
Singh, Ranjay K.	337	
Sinne, Rückzug der	326	
Sinnesakten, integrative	239	
Sinnesgenüsse	239	
Sinnessystem, neuropsychologischen	243	
Sinnesverfeinerung	240	
Sinnspruch	325	
Sizilien	98	
Sklavenfänger, Vodou	420	
Sklaverei, Vodou	419	
Sklavereibedingungen	475	
Skorpion	272	
Sodbrennen, Tansania	126	
Sohn, Zuordnung zum	349	
SOIFUA MALOLOINA, Samoa	492	
Solanaceae	204	
Solanaceae, Fam.	375	
Solarium melongena Linn.	378	
Sonne, Vater -	434	
Sonnenaufgang	325	
Sorgen, Lakandonen	446	
Sotho	198	
Sowjetunion	291, 292	
soziale		
--- Betreuung, Lakandonen	444	
--- Ebene, Therapie	249	
--- Marginalisierung, Brasilien	481	
--- Ordnung	146	
--- Repressionen, Indien	349	
--- Welt, Samoa	492	
--- Wiedereingliederung	249	
--- Zuwendung	392	
--- Gefüge	146	
--- Kosmos	178	
--- Misserfolg, Brasilien	477	
--- Unglück, Brasilien	476	
Spanisch, Kallawaya	431	
Spannungen, Samoa	493	
Spasmen, Reduktion der	244	
Speichel, Schweiz	80	
Speisen, Ritual-, Brasilien	480	
Spielerisches Erforschen	248	
Spindel aus Holz	451	
Spinnen, Tote	375	
Spinneraffen	447	
Spirituelle		
--- Entwicklung, Huitotos	465	
--- Heiler	199	
--- Heiler, Andenraum	431	
--- Heilung	53	
--- Konzepte	241	
--- Krankheit, Brasilien	476	
--- Welt, Samoa	492	
--- Kräften, Tansania	119	
--- Wachstum	130	

Spitäler	239
Spondias magnifera	378
Spondias pinnata	378
Sprache, gefährdete, Italien	98
Sprache, schwere, Italien	81
Sprechstimme	326
Springbrunnen	248
Spritzenfau	270
St. Blasius, Schweiz	81
St. Burkard von Beinwil	80
St. Margaretha, Schweiz	81
St. Sebastian, Schweiz	81
Stadt des Friedens	21
Stammenhaus/Stammhäusel, Schweiz	82
Stammes	
---ältester	291
---kulturen	37
---schamanen, Mongolei	292
---strukturen, Mongolei	292
---traditionen	23
Stammrinde	198
Stärke	150
Staudamm, Mexiko	445
Stauungsinsuffizienz, Abnahme an	55
Stein, schwarzer	224
Steinbockes, Wendekreis des	491
Steine	150, 170, 274
Steine, kraftgeladene	175
Steinorakel	170
Steinsalz	375
Steinsäulen, Samoa	498
Steißbein	326
Stendnera virosa Prain	378
Sterbebett	296
Sterbende, Betreuung	58
Stieren, Urin von	375
Stiftung für Indianer, Nationale	21
Stille	239
Stillen, Indien	364
Stimme	323
---, innere	388
---, Sprechen mit fremder	350
---nhören, Samoa	498
Stimmvolumen	326
Stimulation, basale psychische	245
Stoff, roter	351
Stofffetzen im Auge	176
Stoffstreifen	294
Storchenschnabelgewächse	464
Störung der Befindlichkeit	350
--- der Harmonie, Anden	432
--- des Gleichgewichtes, Samoa	492
---, psychosomatische	244
Strahlentherapien	411
Streichhölzer	298

Streitparteien, Samoa	494
Stressfaktoren, psychische	149
Stresssyndrom	244
Stricke	149
Strychnos nuxvomica	378
Stutenmilch	311
Substanz, krampflösende	197
Suchterkrankungen, Huitotos	467
Südafrikanische Medizinpflanzen	197
Süden	314
Südmexiko, Naha in	444
Sufi	237, 270
Suggestibilität	243
Suggestibilität, starke	350
Suggestion	54
Sühnetaten	421
Suizid, Kallawaya	434
Sukkulentenarten	174
Sumkuma, Tansania	122
Sünden, Vergebung der	198
Sündenbock, Brasilien	481
Suren, Koran	273
Suryadeva (nepali)	395
Süßigkeiten	351
Susto, Anden	432
Svadisthana Cakra	326
Swami Haridas	324
symbolische Behandlung	147
--- Dimension	388
--- Erlösung	147
--- Weltbild	361
---sprache	40
Syndrom, Apallisches	244
Syphilis, Lakandonen	448
Tabak	451
Tabak, Kolumbien	464
Tabaksirup	464
Tabernae montana divericata Linn.	378
Tabu, Essen	348
---, gebrochenes, Tansania	122
---, Mongolei	292
---s, Verletzung eines	126
---bruch	270, 421
Tageszeiten	242
Tahiti	491
Tala	324, 325
Talik	374
Talismanen, Tansania	120
Tamang, Nepal	387, 389
Tamarindus indica Linn.	378
Tambillo-Krankenhaus, LaPaz	436
Tambura	324
Tamil Nadu	352
Tangayika Nyasa Korridor Gegend, Tansania	122
Tankas, buddhistische	296

Tansania	119
Tansania, Heilerin in	119
Tansen	323
tantro-mantro-jhar-funk-tabij-kabach-bali-utsharga	374
Tanz	238, 241, 347
Tänze, Kallawaya	434
Tanztherapie	239
Tapioca, Brasilien	478
Tapir	450
Tara, Grüne	295
Tara, Schwarze	296
Tara, Weisse	295
Tataente, Kallawaya	434
Taube	450
Tauschpraktiken	151
Tecomaria capensis	200
Tee mit Gebet	273
Teeli	299
Telepathie, Huitotos	464
Telepathin	464
Tempel, Vodou-	420
Tempelgemeinschaft	352
Tengri	296
Tengris	298
Terminalia belerica Retz.	378
Terminalia chebula Retz.	378
Terreiros, Brasilien	476
Tetramycin	434
Teufel	347
Teufel, Schweiz	78
Teufelsstein von Göschenen, Schweiz	78
Teüffel, Schweiz	84
Texte, magische	271
Than	389
Theater-Aufführung, Ritual als	350
therapeutische	
--- Berührung	55
---r Prozess	239
---r Wille	148
---s Beziehungsmodell	243
---s Gespräch	241
---s System, Bangladesh	373
Therapie	
--- von Melancholikern	240
---, Bewegungs-	242
---, Bewusstseins	242
---, Vodou	421
---, Zaubersprüche als	443
---formen, erlebnisorientierte	394
---prozess	394
Thrakien, Italien	98
Tiahuanaco Kultur	431
Tibetanischer Buddhismus	294
Tiefenentspannung	325
Tier	
---, energiereiches, Indien	364
---, nachtaktives, Indien	364
---, schlaues, Indien	364
---, getötetes	292

Tier		
---e, Herren der		292
---geist, Lakandonen	446,	447
---ische Materialien		205
---ische Sekrete		374
---kreiszeichen		242
---produkte, Heilung durch, Italien		100
Tietze, Dierk		323
Tiger, Indien		364
Tiger, Zähne von		375
Timaios		242
Tintriloka		388
Titelverleihung		154
Titiskoti (nepali)		395
Tod	146, 271,	299
--- von Kindern		348
---, gewaltsamer		348
---, Huitotos		465
---, Mongolei		313
---, Nigeria		148
---, plötzlicher	125,	126
---, vorzeitiger		348
Todesfälle		169
tödliches Gift		375
tomba todo, Brasilien		478
Ton/ Erde, Lakandonen		446
Tonarten, körperzonenspezifische		246
tonartenspezifisches Musikhören		241
Tongefässe, Brasilien		478
Tonikum		451
Tonskalen, Mikrotonale		242
Töpferinnen		174
toskisch-albanische Sprache, Italien		98
tote Feuerkrankheit, Italien		101
tote Spinnen		375
töten		292
Toten		
---, Heer der, Schweiz		77
---fluss		42
---geist, Brasilien		477
---geister, Vodou-		422
---welt, Huitotos		465
---zähne, Schweiz		80
Trabalhos, Brasilien		476
traditionelle		
--- Gebräuche, Afrika		122
--- Heilverfahren, Amish		407
--- Heilverfahren, Indien		361
---s Heilen, Italien		98
---s Wissen		24
Tragia involucrata Linn.		378
Trance		315
---, Amnesie nach		351
---, Definition		14
---, diagnostische		389
---, kinetische		243
---, Schamanen-		388
---, Vodou-		424
----basierte Heilung, Italien		99

---reisen		389
---rituale, Nepal		387
---zustand	299,	390
---, Israel		347
---, Tansania	121,	124
Transkulturelle Fragen, Türkei		276
transzendente Beziehung		243
--- Kräfte	170,	348
--- Realität		243
--- Sphären, Kolumbien		464
--- Welt		238
Traum, Huitotos		465
Traum, Lakandonen		446
Trauma, Schädel- Hirn -		244
Traumata		432
traumatischer Identitätswechsel		349
Traumdeutung, Lakandonen		448
Träume, Tansania		127
Träumer		199
traurige Stimmung		276
Treue des Partners		275
Treue, Indien		349
Tribulus terrestris Linn.		378
Tricosanthes tricuspidata		378
Tridoshas		349
Trimphetta-Seil		149
Trommel		
---, Schamanen-		294
---n, Schamanen-		388
---n, Vodou		422
---rhythmen		390
Tropenmedizin, Lakandonen		444
Tsaagantan Khori Stamm		298
Tschanar		313
Tucek, Gerhard		237
Tuch, rotes, Brasilien		478
Tuch, Schwarzes, Brasilien		478
Tuch, Weißes, Brasilien		478
Tumor		411
Türken, Vater der		269
Türkische Migranten		278
türkische Volksmedizin		269
türkischer Herkunft, Patienten		269
Türstzug, Schweiz		78
Tusta, Lakandonen		445
Tütsüleme		273
Tuva		294
Tuxtla Gutiérrez, Chiapas		445

U

....S.A., Amish		407
Übelkeit		271
Übelkeit, Italien		106
Übelkeit, Susto		436
Überforderung		272
Übergangssituation		152
übermenschliche Kräft		349e
übernatürliche Kräfte		374

Übertragung, magische, Italien		102
Uchawi, Tansania		120
Udagan		294
UDSSR		291
Ulan-Ude		298
Umgangssprache, Schweiz		78
Umwelt, Einflüsse der		269
Umweltimpulse		246
Unabhängigkeit, Afrika		122
Unberührbare		349
unbewusste Konflikte		348
Unbewusstes, Huitotos		465
Unbewusstes, kollektives		392
Unehre, Indien		349
Unendlichkeit, Flöte der		327
Unfälle		271
Unfalltod		348
Unfalltod, Tansania		125
Unfriedenstifter, Brasilien		481
Unfruchtbarkeit		179
Ungewissheit, Bewältigung der		58
Ungleichgewicht der Säfte		349
Unglück	146, 169,	170
---, Huitotos		467
---, Indien		349
---, soziales, Brasilien		476
Unglücksbringer		150
Unheil, Brasilien		481
Unicista-Homöopathie		467
Universelle Bewegungsmuster		243
Universität in Brasilia		21
Universum		326
Universum, Bindung zum		388
Universum, schamanisches		14
Unkraut	338,	410
Unterbewusstsein, Tansania		125
Unterdrückungs-Theorie		352
Unterleib, Schmerzen	81,	100
Unterwelt		389
Unterwelt, Lakandonen		447
Unwetter		170
Upolu, Samoa		491
Urin		172
--- von Stieren		375
---, Diagnose		432
---, Italien		104
Urklangs		326
Urkulturen		42
Urlaut Ohm		323
Ursprung		312
Ursprung der Bewegung		466
Ursprung der Welt, Kolumbien		465
ursun dökme		274
Urteilsfähigkeit		60
Urzeit	311,	314
Usumacinta, Mexiko		445

V

Vadi	324
Vaids	349
Variabilis-Bergius, Brasilien	478
Vassourinha de Nossa Senhor, Brasilien	478a
Vassurinha, Brasilien	478
Vater Unser, Italien	103
Vater, Zuordnung zum	349
Vaterbaum	314
Vayudeva (nepali)	395
vedische Rezitationen	323
Veit, St., Schweiz	81
Venosa, Italien	97
Venushügel	326
Verarbeitungsmechanismen	248
Verbenaceae	204
Verbrennen von Dingen	273
Verbrennen, Zettelchen	226
Verbrennungen	410
Verdauungssäfte	375
Verdauungsstörungen	298
Verfehlungen, Schweiz	80
Verfluchen, Italien	105
Vergangenheit, Mongolei	312
Vergiftung, magische, Italien	104
Vergiftung, rituelle, Italien	102
Verhalten	
---, unsittliches	348
---skrisen	150
---smuster	243
---smuster, auffällige	388
---sregeln	394
---sstörungen	146
---stherapie	238
---sweisen, lächerliche	146
---sweisen, unreine	270
Verhexung, Brasilien	479
Verhör	351
Verletzung	174
--- durch eine Gräte, Indien	365
---, Lakandonen	446, 447
---en, seelische	352
---en, Talik	376
Vermittler, Samoa	494
Vernonia neocorymbosa	200
Verpflichtung des Schamanen	388
Verrenkung, Indien	363
Verrücktwerden	272
Versmaß	323
Versöhnungsritual, Brasilien	477
Verspannungen	409
Verständnis, interkulturelles	244
Verstopfung	129
Verstorbene	348
---, Huitotos	465
---, Samoa	498
---, Geistern der	314
---, Tansania	125
---, Zeremonien für die	170
Vertrauensbasis, Huitotos	466
verwandtschaftliche Verhältnisse	147
Verwirrung	126
Verwirrung, Tansania	122
Verzicht	421
Vestibularapparat	243
Vibrationen, Tansania	124
Vision, Nigeria	148
visionäres Sehen, Tansania	119
Visionen	388
---, Afrika	121
---, Tuva	299
Visionssuchen	40
Visuddha Cakra	326
Vitaceae	204
Vitalkraft eines Menschen	172
Vitamin E	409
Vitamine A, C	464
Vitamine	408
Vodou / Voodoo	15 / 419
Vogel Garuda	391
Vögel	323
Volksglaube, Schweiz	82
Volksglaube, Türkei	269
Volksheiler, Nigeria	147
Volksheiler, türkischer	275
Volksmedizin	
---, europäische	97
---, Indien	361
---, Islamische	221
---, Israel	221
---, zeme nagas	361
---, Zulu-	197
---ische Praktiken, Italien	97
Volkssprache Bhraj	324
Volkstümliches Heilen, Italien	98
Vorfahren, Lama	294
Vorfahren, Mongolei	299
Vorfahrenanrufung, Huitotos	465
Vorzeichendeutung, Lakandonen	448
Vrindavan	323, 324
Vulturgebiet, Italien	97
Vulva	42, 178
VWB	243

W

Wachbewusstsein	243
Wachbewusstsein, verändertes	243
Wachheitsgrad	244
Wachheitszentrum	244
Wacholderzweig	298
Wachstum, Nigeria	148
Waganga wa pepo, Afrika	120
Waganga, Afrika	120
Wahn	350
wahnhafte Depressionen	272
Wahrheit	327
Wahrnehmungsveränderungen, Huitotos	464
Wahrsageorakel, Brasilien	475
Wahrsager	350
---, schamanische, Afrika	120
---, Tansania	120, 122
---sitzungen, Tansania	124
Wälder, Rodung der, Indien	362
Waldes, Abholzung des, Mexiko	445
Waldes, Göttin des verdrängten	391
Waldgebiet, Assam	362
Wallfahrten, Schweiz	80
Wallfahrtsstätten	270, 277
Wanda, Tansania	121
Wanzen, Lakandonen	448
Waschungen, rituelle	272
Wasser	298
---, Bedeutung	272
---, Herren der	292
---, Huitotos	467
---, schlechtes	273
---, Schweiz	80
---klänge	248
---pfützen	272
---plätschern	239
---schalen	248
---strömung	243
Wegerichblätter	410
Wegkreuzungen, Brasilien	480
weibliche Energie	326
--- Himmelsgeist	179
--- Menstruation	349
--- Topf	179
Weihrauch	154, 450
Weihwasser, Schweiz	85
Wein	375
Weissagen	293
weiße Mächte	296
Weißes Tuch, Brasilien	478
Weizenkeimöl	409
Weizenmehl	337
Welt	
---, Schaffung der	314
---, transzendente	238
---, Ursprung der, Kolumbien	465
---all	323
---bild, symbolisches u. magisches	361
---en, drei, Samoa	492
---enberg	311
---erkenntnis	240
---ordnung, Nigeria	145
---ordnung, Samoa	492
Werfen von Coca-Blättern	431
Wermut	409
Wertesystems	54
Wesen aus Dampf oder Feuer	272
Wesenhaftes	243
Wesenheit, körperlose	314
Wesensschau	41

Wespen, Lakandonen	447	Wut	348	Zeme, Indien	362
Westkap	198	Wutausbrüche	351	Zementtafeln, Samoa	498
westliche Arzneimittelkunde, Italien	100	**X**angô, Brasilien	478	zentralasiatische Schamanen	237
westliche Medizin, Israel	222			Zentralasien	242
Whisky	375	Xeromphis spinosa	378	Zentralasiens, Medizin	240
Wiedergeburten	348	Xhinestra, Italien	97	Zentralschweiz	77
Wiederversöhnungsfest, Samoa	494	Xhosa	198	Zeremonial-Mesa, Andengebiet	432
		Xoroquê/Exú., Brasilien	478		
Wildnis, Mongolei, Sibirien	293	**Y**agé-Schamismus	463	Zeremonie	
				---, heidnische, Italien	105
Wildnis, Zwiegesprächs in der	40	Yamuna	324	---, katholische, Italien	105
Wildschwein	447, 450	Yarumo-Palme	464	--- für die Verstorbenen	170
Wille, Einfluss-	243	Yatiris, Andenraum	431	---, Vodou-	423
Willenskraft, Tansania	129	Yemanjá, Brasilien	478	Zerstörung der Wälder, Flüsse und Tiere	24
Wind	272	yerbateros, Kallaway	431	Zettelchen, Verbrennen	226
---, starker	432	Yoga, Kundalini-	130, 326	Ziegenopfer	170
---, Tansania	120	Yoruba, Brasilien	475, 478	Zingiber casumumum	378
---e, Lakandonen	447	Yuccamehl, weißes, Brasilien	478	Zingiber officinalis	378
---inkontinez, Italien	101			Zingiber purpureum	378
---strömung	243	**Z**aarin	294	Zink	464
Wirbelsäulen-Achse	326			Zinngießen	274
Wirklichkeitsebenen	392	Zahl, Magie der, Italien	104	Zinziber rubens Roxb.	378
Wirklichkeitsveränderung, Lakandonen	449	Zähne	375	Zittern	350, 390
		Zähne, Rhinozeros	375	Zittern, Pepo-, Tansania	124
Wissender, Lakandonen	449	Zähne, Toten-, Schweiz	80	Zittern, Susto	436
wissenschaftliche Medizin	240	Zahnschmerzen, Italien	100, 104	Zivilisation	23
Withania somnifera Dunal	375	Zahnschmerzen, Schweiz	81	Zivilisierung, Indien	362
Withania somnifera	204	Zauberärzte, Tansania	120	Zizyphus jujuba	378
Wochentage	242	Zauberblick	270	Zizyphus sativa	378
Wodka	298	Zauberei	298	ZNS	197
Wohlbefinden	55, 244	---, Anden	432	Zoologe	379
Wohlbefinden, Tansania	126	---, Indien	364	Zoonosen	378
Wohlgerüche	239	---, Schweiz	80	Zucker, geweihter	276
Wolga, Flüsse	295	---, Tansania	124	Zuckung	197
Wortzauber, Schweiz	80	Zauberer	197, 271	Zug, Kanton	81
Wunde, Behandlung	407	---, Anrufung der	198	Zukunft, Vorhersehen der	293
Wunderblick	270	---, Huitotos	465	Zukunftsvoraussage	275
Wunderzeichen, Schweiz	82	---, Tansania	120	Zulumedizin	199
Wundheilung	169	Zaubergeräte, Tansania	127	Zulu-Volksmedizin	197
Wünsche, unsittliche	352	Zaubersprüche	198, 325	Zunge, Diagnose	432
Wünsche, unterdrückte	348	--- als Therapie	443	Zunge, Herausstrecken der	271
Würmer, intstinale, Lakandonen	448	---, Lakandonen	446, 448	Zusammenarbeit, Samoa	493
		---, Tansania	120	Zwangsstörung	244
Wurzel		Zecken, Lakandonen	447	Zwangsumsiedelung	292
--- einer Zinginber, Indien	364	Zeckenart, rote, Lakandonen	449	Zweiheit	314
---, Talik	376			Zwei-Hügel-Distrikt, Indien	362
---cakra	326	Zeder, Himalayische	375	Zyklus des Lebens	23
----Pflanzentherapie	147	Zeitgefühl, verändertes	276	Zyste	179
---stücke	174	Zellproduktion	409	Aargau, Canton, Switzerland	90
---suche, Tansania	127	zeme nagas, Indien	361	Tabacco plant, Huitotos	470
---zentrum	326				

INDEX

Aargau, Canton,
  Switzerland 90
Abandonment 48
abdominal cavity,
  Cameroon 191
abdominal pain 112
abortion 341
abrus precatorius 214
abuses, women 31
acaçá, Brazil 485
acacia karroo 214
Acanthaceae, Fam. 382
Acanthus ilicifolius Linn. 382
acceptance of one's fate 264
accident, death of 356
Achyranthus aspera Linn. 384
Acorus calamus Linn. 384
action, unlocking, Nigeria 161
active AM 258
active movement 257
Acupuncture, Mongolia 308
addiction 473
Aegle marmelos 384
aesthetic
--- experiences 255
--- expression 256
--- impressions 256
--- senses 255
African gods 425
African Medicinal Plants,
  South 209
African slaves 425
African traditional healer 210
Afro-Brazilian culture, Brazil 483
Afro-Brazilian healer, Brazil 484
afterbirth, Nigeria 159
aggression, Africa 139, 158, 487
agitates, rhythm 256
Agnideva (nepali) 404
AIDS 70
Ainu groups 302
Air, treatment with 401
Ajna Chakra 334
akasha (nepali) 399
Akbar, great- mogul 331
Akinchob, Lakandon 457
akupressure, Cameroon 188
Akyantho, Lakandon 458
Al Farabi 255
Alap 332
Alb, Switzerland 88
Albanian culture, Italy 110
Albanian languages, Italy 110
alcaline salt, Huitotos 470
alcaloid harmin, Huitotos 470
alcohol abuse 66
alcoholism 66
ALELEIGA, Samoa 504

alien elements, Cameroon 190
allergic rash, Brazil 485
allergy, Brazil 485
Allium cepa Lam. 384
Allium sativum Lam. 384
allopathic concept 258
Alocacia indica 384
Aloe indica 384
Aloe vera 382, 384, 415
Alpina nigra 384
Alpinia malaccensis Rose 384
Alps, Low, Switzerland 87
altar, Mongolia 304
altar, Nepal 399
altered state of consciousness
  259, 302, 309, 397
alternative medicine 229
AM, clinical application of 256
AM, Integration of 259
AM, Traditional Oriental Music
  Therapy 253
amalgum 382
Amaquira, Africa 210
Amaranthus gangeticus 384
Amaranthus spinosis Linn. 384
Amaranthus viridis 384
Amazonas 469
ambil, Huitotos 470
Amerbel bark 346
Amish Culture, Traditional
  Healing 413
amoebic dysentery,
  Lakandon 458
amputation 414
amulets 283, 285
---, Africa 134
---, Cameroon 188
---, Kallawaya 440
---, guarding, Switzerland 89
--- of bone 370
Anacardiaceae 212
Anahata Chakra 334
analgesic, Israeli 231
analogy 370
Ananas comosus Merr. 384
anarchical community,
  Mexico 453
ancestor 30, 417
--- - offerings, Cameroon 184
---, Africa 136
---, Amish 413
---, angry, Cameroon 183
---, Brazil 484, 486
---, Burjat 306
---, Cameroon 183, 184
---, connection with,
  Nigeria 166
---, goodwill of the, Africa 209
---, Huitotos 470

---, Huitotos 471
---, lama, Mongolia 303
---, Mongolia 319
---, shaman, Mongolia 301
---, Switzerland 88
ancestral
--- knowledge, Nigeria 159
--- spirits, Africa 135, 209
--- spirits, Brazil 486
--- spirits, Mongolia 309
ancient wisdom 46
Andes, Kallawaya Healing
  System 437
anger 356, 359
Angola, Brazil 483
animal
--- bodies, secrets 382
--- capture, Mongolia 302
----derived products 382
--- diseases 385
---, domestic, Mongolia 304
---, injured 414
--- Material, Africa 211
--- products, Italy 111
--- spirits, Lakandon 457
---, dead, Mongolia 302
---, Masters of the, Mongolia 302
animistic forces 281
Annona reticulata Linn. 384
antennae 369
antennas, Mongolia 320
Anthocephalas chinensis
  Lamk. 384
anthropological research,
  Italy 109
anthropomorphic belief,
  Nigeria 159
antibacterial 414
antibiotics, Brazil 485
anticonvulsant drugs,
  Africa 209, 211
antiepileptic drugs, Africa 217
antiseptic 415
antisocial emotions fight 359
antivomiting agent 383
Antonio´s fire illness, St.,
  Italy 112
Antonius, wholy, Switzerland 89
anxiety 260, 357
---, Brazil 484
---, Lakandon 456
---, situational 69
---, susto 441
Anxiolysis 264
Apallic Syndrom 260
ape-god 358
aphrodisiac, Lakandon 461
Apocynaceae 212, 217
Apollonia, St., Switzerland 90

534   Aargau — Apollonia   Index

appetite, loss of,	441
Apulia, Italy	110
Apurian Nation	34
Arab 'sheik's wife, healer	232
Arabic cultural history	255
Arabic physician	282
Arakani, Bangladesh	381
Araracura, Huitotos	470, 471
Arbëresh communities, Italy	109
arbor vitae, Lakandon	461
archaic nature-knowledge	46
archetypes	50
archetypical energies	399
architecture, harmonious	255
Argentina, Kallaway	437
argueing	358
Aristolochia indica Linn.	384
aromatic scents	255
Ars medica	258
art therapy	255
art, liberating form of	359
arthritis	346
articulation	334
artish, Mongolia	308
artistic expression	257
artistically integrated therapies	255
Artocarpus heteophyllus	384
Artocarpus lakoocha Roxb.	384
arts, oriental healing	258
Arzan Shivilig, Mongolia	308
ashes of the dead, Nigeria	159
ashes	382, 401
Asia, Central	258
Asia, Women Shaman Healers, Inner	301
Assam, India	367
Assion, Hans-Jörg	281
Astanaga (nepali)	404
Asteraceae	212, 217
Asterocantha longifolia Ness	384
astringent	415
astrological origin	357
astronomy, Huitotos	471
Atatürk	281
atmosphere, Mongolia	320
attacks from outside, Cameroon	183
attention span, increased	260
attention, public, Samoa	508
aura, personal, Mongolia	306
Austria, AM	260
authority, Samoa	504
autistic person	264
autoerotic actions	283
auto-suggestion	66
Ave Maria, Italy	114
avoidance, Nigeria	164
awakening, pepo, Africa	133
awareness	260
awareness, intercultural	260
axis mundi	399

axis of the world	399
Aymara	437
Ayoco, Huitotos	470
ayurveda	357
ayurvedic doctors	357
Ayurvedic sources	382
ayurvedic teaching	357
Azadirachta indica	384
Baba Gopal Das	332
Baba Imam Khan Dagar	332
baby's spirit, Kallaway	438
bacterial growth	415
bacterial infections, Brazil	484
bad influence, Mongolia	308
bad spirit, Samoa	506
Bahia, Brazil	483
Baikal, Buryatia	306
Bai-Khaakh region	308
Baiuu	383
Bakse shamans, Central Asian	255
balance	397
--- of power	356
--- of the cosmos, Cameroon	186
---, Africa	134
---, cosmic, Brazil	488
---, Huitotos	472
---, physical & emotional	256
---, Samoa	502
---, state of, Africa	139
balancing polar opposites	258
Balche, Lakandon	461
Balche´-Trank, Lakandon	455
Balkan group, Paleo, Italy -	110
banana leaves, Brazil	485
bananas, fungus of	440
Bangladesh	381
Banisteriopsis caapi, Huitotos	470
Bantu, Africa	135
Barber	282
Barhim-baba, Mongolia	306
Barile, Italy	109
Barriers, Huitotos	473
base stimulation	260
Basilicata region, Italy	109
Bastar district	341
Bath, cleansing, Brazil	486
Bathes, public	283
baths, Vodou	426
Bauthinia malabarica Roxb.	384
beans, black	455
beans, black, Brazil	485
beans, fradinho, Brazil	485
beans, white, Brazil	485
beat, empty	333
bee man	414
beer, Cameroon	184
beer, home brewed, Africa	136
Beeswax	415

behaving patterns	402
behavior
---, congruent	402
---, every day	400
---, social, Samoa	502
---, foreign	454
---, Lakandon	459
---ral disorders, Nigeria	158
---al therapy	254
Beinwil, St. Burkard von	90
belief
--- in a nature, Switzerland	88
--- in spirits	355
--- system	69
--- system, religious, Italy	110
--- systems, Israel	230, 234
--- Systems, Samoa, Traditional	501
---, anthropomorphic, Nigeria	159
---s, Nigeria	157
bells, shaman, Mongolia	306
Belly pain, pregnancy, Cameroon	193
Benedictionale Constantiense, Switzerland	93
Benincasa hispida	384
beta-endorphins	259
bewitchment, Nigeria	166
Bharatpur, north of Delhi	358
Bhraj	331
bhuta	358
bhutavidya	357
Bignoniaceae	212, 217
Bildstöcke, Switzerland	88
bile salt	382
bile secretions	382
bio-diversity, South Africa	210
biogenetic resources, regional	367
biomedicine, Western	229
birch tree, Mongolia	308
birch wood, Mongolia	320
Birds	331
birth attendants, traditional, Africa	210
birth rituals, Mongolia	318
birth, Nigeria	159
Bishop of Würzburg	90
black
--- cloth, Brazil	486
--- creatures	317
--- divine, Mongolia	317
--- kettle, Mongolia	308
--- magic	283
--- magic, Vodou	426
--- pepper	343
--- powder, Nigeria	162
--- smith, sons of divine	319
--- Tara	305
--- threads, Mongolia	306
---, Nigeria	165
---smithing	414

bladder infection, Israeli	233	
Blasius, St.	90	
bleeding, menstrual, Cameroon	191	
Bleedings, pregnancy, Cameroon	193	
bleeds, nose, Italy	112	
blessing		
--- prayer, Switzerland	90, 92	
---, praying for	400	
---, Mongolia	306	
blockage	334	
blocked energies	399	
blood		
--- contact, Nigeria	162	
--- pressure, low, Israeli	233	
--- pressure, patients', Andes	437	
--- samples	30	
---, Africa	138	
---, Lakandon	456, 457	
---, menstrual, Nigeria	165	
---, Nigeria	162, 165	
---, rhinoceroses	383	
---, Switzerland	90	
---y cockerel bill, Cameroon	189	
---y diarrhoea, Lakandon	459	
blow, heavy	400	
blowing technique	401	
Blowing, way of	256	
Blumea alata	212	
bodies, deceased	356	
bodies, foreign, Cameroon	188	
bodily humours	258	
bodily illnesses, Nigeria	157	
body		
--- aches	401	
--- as microcosm	437	
--- in the body, Cameroon	190	
--- oriented medicine	17	
--- relation, mind-, Nigeria	159	
--- sensibilisation, sensory	262	
--- setting, Nigeria	164	
--- -spirit-soul unity	17	
---, trembling of the	400	
-- -concept, holistic, Vodou	429	
---fluids, three	357	
---- -language	262	
---parts, Switzerland	90	
Bogota, Columbia	473	
Bolivian Society of Traditional Medicine	440	
Bonavasi (nepali)	404	
bonding, emotional	334, 399	
bone displacement	369	
bone		
--- -fracture	370	
---healer	113, 282	
----joint-pain	370	
---s, Samoa	507	
boomerang law, Kallaway	442	
boo-zaarins, Mongolia	303	
Boscia albitrunca	213	

Bossiedokter, Africa	210	
boundaries treatments of, Italy	115	
Brahma	331	
brahmin language	331	
Brahmins	332	
brain, Huitotos	472	
brain, patient's, Nigeria	162	
brainstem	260	
Bramssica napus	384	
Brazil	29	
---, Healing	483	
---, shamans from	29	
---ian government	31	
---ian Indians	30	
bread, corn	455	
breadfruit, Nigeria	160	
breast cancer outpatients	65	
breast, female	370	
breast-hair illness, Italy	114	
Breath	331, 401	
breath, patients', Andes	437	
breathing	334	
breathing, heavy	355	
bride	356	
bridge, crossing a certain	286	
Broadleaf plantain	417	
Broom, kushagras	401	
Broussonetia paperifera Linn.	384	
Buccalo, Sharyn	413	
Buddha Maitrea	304	
Buddhism	398	
Buddhist mantras	304	
Buddhist tankas, Mongolia	305	
Buddhists	301	
Bugs, Lakandon	458	
Bumeraja (nepali)	404	
Bumerani (nepali)	404	
burdock leave	417	
Burdock	413, 415	
burial of infants, Kallaway	439	
Burjat-Mongolia	317	
Burkard von Beinwil, St., Switzerland	90	
burn out	260	
burn	417	
burning, Mongolia	320	
Burns	413	
Buryat shaman-healer, Mongolia	306	
butter, Mongolia	308	
Büyü (turkish)	286	
Büyü	283	
Byrd's study	66	
Cabbage, Brazil	485	
Cachar Hills district, India, North	367	
Caesalpinia crista	343	
Cajanus indicus	384	
calabash, Cameroon	190	

Calabria, Italy	110	
Calamus viminalis	384	
Calcium, Huitotos	470	
calebass- pumpkin	332	
Calendars, Huitotos	471	
calms, rhythm	256	
Calotropis gigantia	384	
Calotropis procera	384	
Cameroon, Northern	183	
Campania, Italy	110	
Canabis sativa	384	
Canada, Amish	413	
cancer	30	
cancer outpatients, breast	65	
cancer patient	69	
candle's flame	254	
candles, Nigeria	165	
Candomblé	19, 425, 483	
Capparaceae	213, 217	
Capparis tomentosa	213	
Capsicum annum	384	
Capuchin convent in Salzburg, Switzerland	91	
Caquetá, Columbia	469	
Caquetá, Huitotos	470	
cardiac surgery	66	
cardiological sector	260	
cardio-pulmonary arres	67	
care group, Nigeria	158	
Caregivers	69	
caregivers, Nigeria	159	
Carica papaya Linn.	384	
carimã, Brazil	485	
carrots, Brazil	485	
cassava family, Brazil	485	
cassava paste, Brazil	485	
Cassia alata	384	
Cassia siamca Linn.	384	
Cassytha filiformis L.	346	
caste		
---, merchants	356	
---, farmer	356	
---, priest	356	
---, warrior	356	
---, system of	356	
Caterpillars, Lakandon	457	
caterpillars, Lakandon	457	
catholic		
--- church, Switzerland	90	
--- cross, Italy	114	
--- prayers, Italy	114	
---ism, Brazil	483	
---ism	109, 425	
Catunaregam spinosa	215	
causes of illness, Israeli	234	
Cau-tala	333	
Caves	283	
Cedrus deodar	382, 384	
Celastraceae	213	
celebrate the origin, Mongolia	318	
celebrations, nature	49	
cell repositories	30	

Celtic myths	46
cemeteries	283
cemeteries, Brazil	487
Centella asiatica Linn.	384
Centipeda minimal Linn.	384
Central Asia	253, 258
Central Asian Bakse shamans	255
centre of the cosmos, Nigeria	165
cerebral cortex	260
cerebral trauma	260
ceremonies	
---, musical healing	255
---, musical shamanic healing	253
---, Vodou	425
---, nature	49
Chakma Talika Cikitsa, Bangladesh	381, 382
chakma Tribe, Bangladesh	381
chakras	334
Chandrama (nepali)	404
channel healing energies	68
Chapels, Switzerland	87
character, development of	254
charms, Africa	134
Chemoshock, Africa	211
chest	334
chest, Nigeria	161
Chhatisgarh, India	341
Chhoti Dudhi	345
Chiapas, Mexico	454, 455
chicken	455
chicken- offering, Cameroon	184
chickenpocks, Brazil	485
chicks, baby, Brazil	485
Chicrassia tabularis Jubs.	384
child, divine, Switzerland	92
children of God, Mongolia	320
Children	
---, Dysentery	345
---, education of the, Huitotos	470
---, mistreats their	31
---, unborn, Lakandon	461
---´s diseases, Lakandon	458
---s injuries	401
Chile, Kallawaya	437
Chinta (nepali)	400, 401
Chittagong Hill Tract, Bangladesh	381
choice of treatment	229
cholera, Lakandon	458
Christian	
--- faith, Nigeria	158
--- life	66
--- rites, pre-, Samoa	507
---ity, Africa	135
---ity, Samoa	502
---ity, Switzerland	88
chronic	
--- complaints	68
--- illnesses	440
--- illnesses, Israel	234
---al diseases, Huitotos	473
chuchu, Brazil	485
Chuckchee	302
church, catholic, Switzerland	90
church, not entering the, Italy	114
cigli alla testa, Italy	112
Cinler	283
circle of reinkarnations	356
circles, Nigeria	165
circumcision, Nigeria	165
Citrus maxima Linn.	384
Citrus medica Linn.	384
City of Peace	29
civilization	31
clan elders, Mongolia	301
clan structure, loss of, Mongolia	302
classical music therapy	255
Clausena anisata	215
clay bowl, Cameroon	184, 192
clay, Vodou temple	428
cleaning rite	357
Cleodendrum viscosum	384
Clerodendrum glabrum	216
client concentrated	404
climate, tropical monsoon	381
clinical application of AM	256, 260
cloth	
---, beautiful red	359
---, strips of, Mongolia	304
---, white, black and red, Brazil	486
---s, clean, Brazil	486
---s, shaman, Mongolia	303
CNS	209
coca leaves	437
coca mixture	440
cocain, Huitotos	470
Coccinia cordifolia	384
Coccinia medica	384
coccyx	334
Coconuts	358
coffee enemas	417
cognitive anthropology	453
cognitive reflection	264
cognitive work, AM	264
Coke, Huitotos	470
cold	30, 283
coldness, Mongolia	306
colds, Lakandon	458
colitis, Lakandon	461
Colocasia esculentus Linn.	384
colonial powers, Brazil	484
colonization, Huitotos	469
colour designs	255
colours, Nigeria	164
Commelina africana	213
Commelinaceae	213, 217
communication theories, interpersonal	259
community members, Kallawaya	438
community, Brazil	488
community, health, Nigeria	157
compensation, theory of	359
complaints, mental, Africa	134
complaints, psychosomatic, Africa	134
composition, musical	331
concentration disturbances	283
concentration	334, 401
concept	
--- of healing, Cameroon	186
--- of illness, Cameroon	183
--- of illness, turkish	281
--- of sorcery, Cameroon	185
---, allopathic	258
concoctions, Africa	210
conditioning, mental	259
confidence, Kallawaya	438
confidence, self-	404
conflict	
--- orientated treatment, non-	256
---s, inner, Huitotos	473
---s, Samoa	502
---s, unconscious	356
conformity as wives	359
confusion, Africa	139
connection to transcendency	355
consciousness	253
--- for the whole	318
--- potentials	334
--- therapy	258
---, altered state of	302, 309, 397
---, changed	402
---, Huitotos	473
---, Lakandon	456, 457
---, state of, Switzerland	90
contagion, magical, Italy	111
contagion, magico-religious, Italy	113
continuity, genealogical, Nigeria	160
contradictions	359
contradictions, Nigeria	158, 164
control	334
convent in Salzburg, Capuchin, Switzerland	91
conversation therapy	404
convulsion, Africa	139, 209
convulsive disorders, Africa	209
Conyza scabrida	212
Coordination	334
coping factor	66
coping mechanism	66
Corchorns capsularis Linn.	384
cord, trimphetta, Nigeria	160
Coriandrum sativum Linn.	384
corn bread	455

corn, fungus of	440
corpeless spirits, Mongolia	320
cortical disorder, Africa	209
cosmic		
--- disorder	357
--- hierarchy	356
--- methods	308
--- order, universal	253
--- powers	397
--- principles, universal	255, 258
--- union, Brazil	488
cosmical		
--- energies	398
--- order	400, 402
--- powers	400, 402
cosmological energy, Nigeria	162
cosmological interweaving, Nigeria	164
cosmologies, African, Brazil	483
cosmology, Nepal	399
cosmos		
---, balance of the, Cameroon	186
---, centre of the, Nigeria	165
---, disorder in the, Cameroon	183
---, harmony with the	183
---, Huitotos	469
cottage industry	414
cotton thread, Lakandon	461
Cotyledon orbiculata	213
coughing, Italy	114
council of chiefs, Samoa	507
counselling, Nigeria	157
countries, developing	341
court procedure	357
crab	369
Crab, Cameroon	184
crab-oracle, Cameroon	192
cranial -cerebral damage	260
cranial trauma	260
Crassula alba	213
Crassulaceae	213, 217
creation, love of	254
creation, multiplicity of	254
creative self-expression	255
Creator, Huitotos	471
creatures, black, Mongolia	317
crisis	414
---, Africa	136
---, healer, Africa	134
---, Nigeria	157, 160, 164
---, Samoa	504
crop, good, Africa	136
crosses, Switzerland	87
crossroads, treatments of, Italy	115
Croton gratissimus	214
Crucifix, Switzerland	88, 94
cucumber, Brazil	485
cucumber-like vegetable, Brazil	485

Cucumis hirsutus	213
Cucumis sativa Linn.	384
Cucurbitaceae	213
cultivation, shifting	367
cultivation, slash-and-burn	455
cultural anthropology	453
cultural system, Nigeria	158
cultural work, socio-psycho-, Nigeria	158
culture organization, Samoa	502
culture, Lakandons	453
curandero, Andes	437
curandero, Huitotos	469
curative practices, India	367
Curcuma amada Roxb.	384
Curcuma caesla Roxb.	384
Curcuma domestica	384
Curcuma longa Linn.	384
curses, Italy	116
Cuscuta reflexa Roxb.	384
customs, Africa	135
cut of the life line	400
cuts on the head, Nigeria	162
cyste, Cameroon	192
Daily reality	398
dance	355
dance therapy	255
dance, AM	257
dances, Kallawaya	440
danger, Nigeria	165
Darbhanga, school of	332
darkness therapy	46
Dattenberg-Holper, Traute	355
Datura fastuosa Linn. var. D. alba	384
Datura metel Linn.	384
Datura stramonium	216
dead		
--- animal, Mongolia	302
--- bodies	383
--- fire illness, Italy	112
---, ashes of the, Nigeria	159
---, respect for the, Samoa	506
---, teeth of, Switzerland	90
deadly poisons	383
death	283, 356
--- of infants, Kallawaya	439
--- rituals, Mongolia	318
--- spirit, Brazil	485
---, accidental, Africa	138
---, Africa	138
---, Cameroon	186
---, Huitotos	471
---, Lakandon	457
---, Mongolia	309
---, natural, Africa	139
---, Nigeria	159
---, sudden, Africa	139
----bed, Mongolia	306
decoctions, Africa	210
de-conditioning	259

deeds in prior lives	356
deer, Lakandon	460
deficiencies, physiological & emotional	258
Dehasia kurzi King	384
delights, rhythm	256
delusion	357
demons	356, 401
---, Switzerland	88
dependencies, Brazil	487
depression	70, 260, 400, 401
---, Africa	139
---, Israeli	230
---, Israeli	233
---, reactive	265
---, susto	441
---, treating	256
depressive episodes	286
deprivation	440
dermatitis, Italy	112 114
Dervish	282
desease, transcendential cause of	399
desires, poor, Brazil	484
destination, original, Mongolia	318
destruction of forests, rivers, animals	31
developing countries	341
development, personality	260
Devil Stone, Switzerland	87
devil	355
devine	331
Dhagar school	332
Dhamar	333
dhami (nepali)	397
dhariti (nepali)	399
dherwishes, whirling	254
Dhrupad	331
Dhruva	331
diagnosing	284
diagnosis		
---, Brazil	484
---, Nepal	400
---, pulse	400
---, Vodou	426
diagnostic model, Samoa	505
diagnostic session, Africa	136
diarrhoea, bloody, Lakandon	459, 461
diazepam	211, 217
Dibia, Nigeria	157
diet	414
---, moderate	255
---ary measures	284
---etic rules	258
---etics	258
Dillenia indica Linn.	384
dimension, methaphoric-symbolistic	399
dimension		
---, physio-psychological	258
---, spiritual-mental	256

dimensions
--- of being 259
---, emotional 254
---, physical 254
---, spiritual 254
Diospyros peregrina Linn. 384
Dipterocarpaceae 381
Dipterocarpus alatus 385
Dipterocarpus gracilis 385
Dipterocarpus turbinatus 385
directions, Mongolia 320
dirty sewage 359
discernment 71
discretion, Brazil 487
discrimination, Brazil 484
disease
---, infectious, Samoa 506
---, mental 281
---, internal, Cameroon 188
---s, magical 382
---s, plague, Switzerland 90
disharmony, Africa 139
disharmony, Kallawaya 438
disorder 397
--- in the cosmos,
  Cameroon 183
---, cosmic 357
---s, convulsive, Africa 209
dissatisfaction, Nigeria 164
distress factors, Nigeria 159
disturbance, Nigeria 158, 162
disturbing facts, Nigeria 160
diuretic medication 67
divination
--- interpretation, Lakandon 458
--- methods, Lakandon 458
--- sessions, Africa 136
---, Nigeria 157, 160
divinator, Cameroon 183
divine 253
--- black smith, sons of the 319
--- child 92
--- paradise 356
--- skill, Mongolia 319
--- unity 254
---, black, Mongolia 317
---, Mongolia 317
diviner, Africa 134, 136, 210
diviners, shaman 133
divinities, Brazil 484, 485
divinity, Israeli 234
Djinns 283
DNA, Indians' 30
Doctors, Islamic 255, 258
dog, head of, Nigeria 162
dog, Lakandon 460
dogs, black, Switzerland 88
donations 414
dragons, Mongolia 304
draining, Cameroon 186
dream, Huitotos 471
dream, interpretation,
  Africa 140

dreamers, Africa 210
dreams, Interpretations of,
  Lakandon 458
drought 332
drug addicts 473
drum rythms 400
drum, konus- 333
drum, Mongolia 303
drum, shaman, Mongolia 304
drumming, way of 256
Dschalaleddin Rumi 254
duality mother and father 320
Duca, Huitotos 470
Düdger Waantschig 317
dying 69
dynamical process in
  shamanism 399
Dyonisios, St., Switzerland 90
dysentery, amoebic,
  Lakandon 458
dysentery, children 345

Eagle 283, 369
earth
---, Mongolia 320
---, Nigeria 164
---, spirits of, Cameroon 183
---, Switzerland 90
---graves, Samoa 506
East Africa 134
East, Mongolia 320
Ebenaceae 213
ebós, Brazil 485
Ebós, Brazil 487
Ebru 257
eccentric feelings 357
economic consequences,
  Samoa 505
economic hardship 230
economical status, bad,
  Brazil 484
economy, market 368
ecopiratism 29
ecosystem, Bangladesh 381
ecstatic furiousness 359
ecstatic religion 355
education of the children,
  Huitotos 470
effects, trans-cultural 256
eggs, Mongolia 320
eggs, Nigeria 161
eggs, ritual, Israeli 233
ego- strength 402
ego, limited 253
Elaeocarpus rugosus Roxb. 385
elderberry tree, Italy 115
elderly, abandons the 31
elemental symbolism 264
elements, use of, Nigeria 166
elements, work with 257
Elephant, teeth of 383
elevation of the head 400

elixiers, bottled, LaPaz 439
Emblica officinalis Gaertn. 385
embryo formation 342
embryo, undesired 341
emotion, expression of 331
emotional
--- balance 256, 258
--- bonding 399
--- deficiencies 258
--- dimensions 254
--- healing 255
--- health 259
--- pain, Brazil 484
--- problems 308
--- processes, inner 255
--- resources, strengthening 261
--- warmth 402
emotions fight, antisocial 359
enema 417
enemies, Brazil 485
enemies, protection,
  Mongolia 319
energies
---, blocked 399
---, central archetypical 399
---, cosmical 398
---, psychical 398
---, snake 399
---, transfer of 404
energy
--- spirits, Mongolia 320
--- stones, Cameroon 188
---, bad 306
---, cosmological, Nigeria 162
Englerophytum
  magalismontanum 216
enjoyment 260
Enokaye, Huitotos 471
environment, social,
  Nigeria 159
environmental impulses 262
envy 356, 484
epidemics, Lakandon 458
epidemiology, Bangladesh 385
epilepsy, Africa 209
epilepsy, Switzerland 90
epileptic fits, Nigeria 162
epistemology, evolutionary 259
equilibrium, dynamic,
  Kallawaya 442
equilibrium, Samoa 502
Erasmus, St., Switzerland 90
Erdtsieck, Jessica 133
Erguns, Brazil 487
Erickson 259
Erythrina variegata Linn. 385
Erythroxilon coca, Huitotos 470
Eskimo 302
esoteric forces, Nigeria 159
eternity, Nigeria 159
eternity, way to,
  Switzerland 88
ethnic belief, Turkey 281

ethno		
--- -anatomy		456
---biology		386
---ecology		385
---epidemiology		385
---grapher, view point		454
---graphers realities		454
ethnographic interview		454
---graphy		453
----Medicine, Lacandon Indians		453
----medicine, system		454
---musiktherapie, Institute for		266
---pharmacological research, Italy		109
--- -trance		259
ethos, philosophy of		258
Euclea divinorum		213
Euphorbia thymifolia		345
Euphorbiaceae	214, 217, 381	
European		
--- family, Indo-, Italy		110
--- folk-medicine, Italy		116
--- healing system		17
event- oriented therapy		404
evil		
--- acts, Italy		116
--- eye	230, 281	
--- eye, Cameroon		186
--- eye, Italy		111
--- spirits		
---, Africa		209
---, Israeli		230
---, Nigeria		159
evolutionary epistemology		259
exhaustion		260
existence, human		253
existence, superhuman		47
existentialist quests		260
exorcism		
---, Africa		209
---, India		355
---, Nigeria		165
---, Private, Switzerland		93
---, Switzerland	90, 93	
experiences, joyful		261
expression		331
Exú, Brazil		487
eye		
---- brows		334
---, cloth in the, Cameroon		189
---, evil		230
---s, Huitotos		472
---s, patients', Andes		437

Fabaceae 214

Fabaceae	214, 217	
FAIFE´AU, Samoa		503
failure, Africa		136
fainting, Israeli		233
faith, Christian, Nigeria		158

faith-healing		68
family		
--- life, Africa		134
--- members		265
--- members, loss of, Mongolia		302
--- therapy		359
--- tradition, shamanism		398
---, Brazil		487
---, equlibrium, Samoa		503
---, Kallawaya		438
---, ritual with		402
---, role of, Samoa		504
---, graves, Samoa		507
----life, difficult		426
----substitute, Vodou		428
farmer caste		356
farmer, Amish		413
FASIA, Samoa		506
fate, acceptance of one's		264
fate, human		425
Father Sun, Kallawaya		440
father tree, Mongolia		320
fatigue , Brazil		484
fattura		116
fauna, Bangladesh		381
fears	334, 401	
feather, Cameroon		191
feather, peacocks´s		383
feathers, Nigeria		162
feces, patients', Andes		437
feelings, eccentric		357
female breast		370
female energy		334
female sky-spirit, Cameroon		193
ferment		317
ferrum, Huitotos		470
fertility, Cameroon		192
feticide		341
fetish sorcerer		19
fever antibiotics		67
fever, susto		441
fiber, Cameroon		186
Ficus racemosa Linn.		385
field, Tschanar		320
filha-de-santo, Brazil		486
Fipa, Africa		135
fire	254, 283	
--- illness, dead, Italy		112
---, Huitotos		472
---, inner		332
---, Sacrifice of		50
---, Switzerland		90
----raga		332
----stone		383
first human being, Mongolia		317
flame		283
flame, candle's		254
flame, Mongolia		308
fleece vest, Mongolia		309
Fleurya interrupta		385
flora, Bangladesh		381

flour poultices, Mongolia		304
flour, Brazil		485
flute, sound of		331
flying horse, Mongolia		308
FOFO, Samoa		503
folha da costa, Brazil		486
folha Manjerição, Brazil		486
folk		
--- healers, nigeria		159
--- healing, LaPaz		439
--- Medicine, India		367
--- Medicine, Isreal		229
--- Medicine, Zulu		209
----medical practices, Italy		109
food restrictions, Africa		143
food supplies, Mongolia		302
food, needs for		356
foot		331
force		
---, death of		356
---, mediating		258
---s, field of, Nigeria		165
---s, organisation of, Nigeria		158
---s, taunting, Nigeria		162
---s, transcendental, Cameroon		184
forefather, Africa		136
foreign		
--- behaviour		454
--- bodies, Cameroon	188, 190	
--- elements, Cameroon		186
--- entitie		355
forest		283
--- animals, Mistress of		50
---, displaced		401
---, India		367
---, Mexico		454
forgiveness , Samoa		504
fortune for hunting, Mongolia		302
fortune teller		358
Foundation for the Indians, National		29
fountain		264
fox		369
fracture		369
fractures		414
fractures, Cameroon		188
framework, ritual, Nigeria		160
friends, ritual with		402
Frieundshaft, Amish		414
frightens, rhythm		256
frivolous, talking, Samoa		506
fumigation		400
Fundacao Nacional de India		29
fungus of corn or bananas		440
fuoco di Sant´ Antonio, Italy		112
fuoco morto, Italy		112
furiousness, ecstatic		359

G

Galen 258
galenicals, Africa 210
gall bladder 382
gallbladder, Lakandon 456
garbage heaps 283
Gardenia ternifolia 215
gas, passing, susto 441
gastric disorders 382
gastritis, Lakandon 461
gastro-enteriological sector 260
gathering, village, Samoa 508
Gatine 343
gem center 334
generations, Mongolia 320
genies, Nigeria 159
geriatric problems 260
Germany, AM 260
Ghonghchi 342
Ghost Canoe 50
Ghost Dance 50
Ghost, Holy, Switzerland 92
Gibbon 370
Ginestra, Italy 109
ginger , Lakandon 461
glass of water 284
Gloria al Padre, Italy 114
Glycerine, Vegetable 415
Glycosmis pentaphylla Retz. 385
Glycyrrhiza globera 342
goat-offering, Cameroon 184
God 133, 254, 332
--- of the Whites, Lakandon 458
---, children of, Mongolia 320
---, concept of 69
---, dialogue with, Samoa 91
---, monkey 401
---, quest for 254
---, relationship 259
---, tying of, Nigeria 161
---'s will 414
Goddess, Naked 50
gods 356, 399,
--- will 281
---, african 425
---, invocation of the 358
---, obsession by 355
---, steps to the 400
---, Switzerland 88
--- -house, Lakandon 455
gold rabbit, Lakandon 460
gold 382
golden thread, Mongolia 320
gond, India 342
Göschenen, Switzerland 87
Gotthard-Tunnel, Switzerland 87
government, Brazilian 31
gratitudes for the spirits 400
grave

---, Africa 139
---, holy 286
---s of holy men, Israeli 234
---s, Nigeria 159
---yard, Samoa 506
Green Tara, Mongolia 304
Greenberg, Ofra 229
grief, Lakandon 457
grimaces with pain 358
group therapy, Africa 139
growth, Nigeria 159
guarding amulett, Switzerland 89
Guaritore, Italy 112
guided visualization 257
guilt, Vodou 426
guinea pig diagnosis, Kallawaya 438
Gujarat 359
gulags, Mongolia 302
gunpowder, Brazil 486
Gurung folks 398
Güvenç, Oruç 266
Gwalior 331

H

Hach k´ay, Lakandon 455
hach winik, Lacandon 454
Hachakyum, Lakandon 456, 457
Hadith Qudsi, central 253
Hafiz 253
hair 286
Haiti, migrants from 426
Haiti, religion of 425
hakim arabi 282
hallucinations, Huitotos 470
hallucinations, Samoa 508
hallucinatory psychosis, Samoa 508
halo, Switzerland 90
Hammam 283
Handpostille, Switzerland 91
Hanuman 358, 401
harmin, alcaloid, Huitotos 470
harmonic sounds 255
harmonious architecture 255
harmonious interior designs 255
harmonious relationships, Kallawaya 438
harmonisation 258
harmonise the contradictions, Nigeria 164
harmony with the cosmos 183
harmony, Nigeria 165
Hasse 29
hate, Brazil 484
HAWAIKI 501
Hazardana 344
head 334
--- pain 414
---, bare, Nigeria 162
---, cakra 334
---, cuts on the, Nigeria 162

---, elevation of the 400
headache 283, 369, 401
---, Italy 112
---, severe 358
---, Switzerland 90
Healer 282
--- in Tanzania, traditional 133
--- of Iraqi 232
---, African traditional 210
---, Afro-Brazilian, Brazil 484
---, Arab 'sheik's wife 232
---, definition 17
---, Pepo- 133
---, Yellow Jaundice 282
---s, bone-, Italy 113
---s, Inner Asia, Women Shaman 301
---s, Italy 112
---s, Samoa 501, 503
---s, spiritual Zulu 210
---s, spiritual, Andes 437
---s, traditional, Bangladesh 382
healing
---, alternative 17
--- arts, oriental 258
--- ceremonies, Cameroon 189
--- ceremonies, Lakandon 460
--- ceremonies, musical shamanic 253, 255
--- experts, overview 19
--- insanity, Nigeria 157
--- mechanisms, self, Kallawaya 438
--- plants, Cameroon 188
--- potency 258
--- powers 284
--- powers, Samoa 502
--- process 397, 113
--- research 66
--- rites, magical or spiritual, Italy 109
--- ritual, Lakandon 455
--- ritual, shamanistic, Nepal 397, 398
--- sanitation process, post-,Italy 114
--- sessions, Africa 139
--- shrine, LaPaz 441
--- System, Kallawaya 437
--- tradition, Huitotos 469
---, Bahia 483
---, candomblé 483
---, Concept of, Cameroon 186
---, Conception of, Nigeria 158
---, emotional 255
---, faith 68
---, Magical, Italy 109
---, Northern India 331
---, perception of, Italy 112
---, physical 255
---, spiritual 65
---, trance-based, or psycho-therapeutic, Italy 111

Index   Galen — healing   541

health
--- authorities, Israeli 230
--- beliefs, Amish 414
--- care practice, traditional,
    Africa 134
--- systems, Isreal 229
---, beliefs, Israeli 231
---, emotional 259
---, Nigeria 159
---y community, Nigeria 157
hearing noises in the ears,
    susto 441
hearing 256
hearing sense, Huitotos 472
heart
--- failure, congestive 67
--- level 334
---, Huitotos 472
---, Lakandon 456
---burn, Africa 139
----palpitation, Africa 139
heavens, Four 50
Hegatangpui 369
helminthiasis, Italy 112
helpers, Italy 112
helplessness 356
Helung 369
helungmau 369
Hemeube 369
Henei 369
henna, Israeli 232
hepatitis, Italy 112
Hepobei 370
Heradi 370
Herbaceous 345
herbal
--- concoction, Africa 210
--- doctor, Africa 209
--- drugs, Africa 209
--- medicine, Africa 142
--- products, Bangladesh 383
--- supply shop, LaPaz 439
--- therapy, Nigeria 158
Herbalarios, Andes 437
herbalism, Nigeria 159
herbalist 282, 414
herbalist, Africa 210
herbalists, Africa 134
herbals 382
herbs 413
--- mixtures, Nigeria 162
---, Brazil 484
---, Himalaya 401
---, therapy with 398
---, use of, Nigeria 158
Hethei 370
Heth-rangma 383
hex, Nigeria 159
Hibiscus esculentus Linn. 385
Hinduism 355
Hingkuipau 370
Hispanic era, pre- 454
HIV-infected patients 70

Hoca disease 282, 286
Hokkaido Island in Japan 302
holistic body-concept,
    Vodou 429
holy
--- entity, Italy 115
--- fountain, Switzerland 91
--- ghost, Switzerland 92
--- men, graves of 234
--- Michael, Switzerland 94
--- plants, Huitotos 470
--- Spirit, Italy 115
--- Trinity, Switzerland 92
--- water, Switzerland 95
Homeopathy 413
homeostasis 256
honey beer, Lakandon 455
Honey 414
Hope, sources of 69
Hordeum vulgare Linn. 385
Horia, Huitotos 473
horn 332
horns, rhinoceroses 383
horse
--- head, Mongolia 304
---, flying, Mongolia 308
---, Lakandon 460
----tail , Lakandon 461
hot water, Cameroon 190
Hotgoid tribe, Mongolia 303
houses, abandoned 283
houses, spirits of,
    Cameroon 183
Hövsgöl province, Mongolia 303
Huitotos, Columbia 469
human
--- being, first, Mongolia 317
--- existence 253
--- flesh, Cameroon 185
humanity 31
humoural medicine 258
hunting
--- magic, Mongolia 302
--- offerings, Mongolia 308
--- rites, Mongolia 309
---, fortune for, Mongolia 302
---, Mongolia 301
husband, Nigeria 157
Hydnocarpus kurzii 385
Hygiene 341
hygiene, personal, Samoa 505
hysteria 357

I ahme, Brazil 485
Ibn Sina 258
Ibn-Hindu 256
Identification, Samoa 505
identity, traumatic change of
356
Igbo Medicine 157
Ijexá, Brazil 483
Ilex godajam 385

illness
--- of the rainbow, Italy 111
---, breast-hair, Italy 114
---, cause, Africa of 134
---, causes of, Israeli 234
---, dead fire, Italy 112
---, material, Brazil 484
---, mental, Africa 139
---, mental, Israeli 230
---, Nigeria 157
---, Nigeria 159
---, organic, Brazil 484
---, pepo-, Africa 134
---, rainbow, Italy 112
---, severe 283
---, spirit 133
---, spirit-, Samoa 508
---, spiritual, Brazil 484
---, St. Antonio´s fire, Italy 112
---, transfer of, Italy 111
---, turkish, concept of 281
---, wind-, Italy 112
---, bodily, Nigeria 157
---, chronic 440
---, chronic, Israeli 234
---, origin of 88
---, patron of, Switzerland 90
Illyrian, Italy 110
image of the soul 255
imagery, Mongolia 309
images, mercy, Switzerland 91
imagination, Huitotos 471
imagination, phantastic 357
immaculate Virgin,
    Switzerland 92
immoral behaviour 356
immune system 264
impulses, environmental 262
impurity 357
Inca cultures, pre-
incarnations, Africa 209
incense, Lakandon 455, 461
incisions, seven, Nigeria 162
independence, Tanzania 135
independent visualization 257
India, Central 341
India, Exorcism 355
India, Northern 331
Indian obsession 355
Indians' DNA 30
Indians, National Foundation
    for the 29
indigenous
--- healers in Africa 134
--- Knowledge, Principles of 29
--- peoples, Bangladesh 381
individuals, equlibrium,
    Samoa 503
individuation process 259
Indo-European family, Italy 110
Indradeva (nepali) 404
infants, death and burial of,
    Kallawaya 439

infection		
---, Cameroon		183
---, bacterial, Brazil		484
---, local		440
---, viral, Brazil		484
--- disease, Samoa		506
Infertility, Cameroon		192
infirmity, Cameroon		184
inflammation of the pelvis, Israeli		232
inflammation, penile, Italy		112
influenza, Lakandon		458
infusions, Africa		210
inherent quintessential nature		254
initiation		
--- into nature		45
--- of the shaman, Mongolia		319
---, ritual, Nigeria		157
---, Africa		136
---, Brazil		486
---, Vodou		428
---s, social, Nigeria		165
injuries, Cameroon		188
injury, physical		230
inner		
--- changes		259
--- conflicts, Huitotos		473
--- experience		397
--- fire		332
--- oracle, Huitotos		473
--- voice		398
--- World, Mongolia		301
insanity, Healing, Nigeria		157
insomnia, Israeli		233
insomnia, Kallawaya		440
Institute for Ethnomusiktherapie		266
Integration of AM		259
interactive music making		257
intercessors, Mongolia		302
intercultural awareness		260
interest, intense		402
interior designs, harmonious		255
internal diseases, Cameroon		188
interpersonal communication theories		259
interview, ethnographic		454
intestinal disorders		382
intestinal worms, Lakandon		458
intestiny problems		401
intoxicating drink		317
intoxicating drink, Lakandon		455
intoxication, Huitotos		470
intuitives, Africa		210
invisible world, Lakandon		458
invocation of the gods		358
Ipomoea reptans Linn.		385
Iraqi, healer of		232
iridologist		414
iris diagnosis, Kallawaya		438
Iroegbu, Patrick		
Islam		332
--- countries		229
--- culture		285
--- doctors		255
Islamic		
--- medicine		253
--- mystics		254
--- orthodoxy		255
Island of Now		50
Israeli health authorities		230
Italy, Folk-medical practices, Italy		109
Italy, Southern		109
ivory		332
Iwa, Africa		135
Ixwele, Africa		19, 210
izangoma, Africa		19, 209, 210
Jabalpur, India		342
Jackle		370
Jahr (nepali)		401
Jana, Huitotos		472
Jangeli (nepali)		401
Japan, Hokkaido Island in		302
Jatropha curcas		214
jaundice		344
Javae Nation		34
jealous individuals, Israeli		230
Jeje, Brazil		483
Jesus Christ, Italy		115
Jewish experts, Israeli		234
Jews, Oriental, Israel		229
Jhalla		332
jhankri (nepali)		397
Jharphook (nepali)		401
Jharphuk, Nepal		397
Jod		332
jogo-de-búzios, Brazil		483, 484
joints, stiffness of		346
joyful experiences		261
Jora, Huitotos		471
Jucca root, Brazil		485
Judeo-Christian God		66
Jungle, Columbia		469
juniper branch, Mongolia		308
K´ax, Lacandon		454
Kah, Lakandon		457
Kaingang Nation		34
Kallawaya Healing System, Andes		437
Kalmykia, Mongolia		304
Kalmyks, Mongolia		302
Kalweit, Holger		45
Karaja Nation		34
Karatiana Nation		34
Karitiana tribe		29
karmic origin		357
Katharina, St., Switzerland		90
Keim, J.		413
Kepe		370
Keram		370
kettle, black, Mongolia		308
Ketu, Brazil		483
key, ritual, Nigeria		160
khali		333
Khan, Mahmud Tareq Hassa		381
kharisiri, Kallawaya		438
Khori kinship, Mongolia		306
kidney diagnosis, Kallawaya		438
kidney malfunctions		304
kids, death of		356
Kigelia africana		212
kinetic trance		259
kinship, symbols of, Nigeria		160
Kinyiha, Africa		136
Kirklama		285
Kiswahili, Africa		134
knots, magic		283
knowledge		
---, indigenous		31
---, leaf of, Huitotos		470
---, local, Bangladesh		381
---, therapeutical, Huitotos		471
Koka, Huitotos		470
konus-drum		333
Kootenai Tribe		34
Koran		283
Koranic spiritual maxim, non-		253
Koran-paper		284
Koryak		302
Kosack, Godula		183
Kraho Nation		34
Krippner, Stanley		29, 437
Krshna		331
Kruiedokter, Africa		210
kruierate, Africa		210
Ksalinaga (nepali)		404
Kuganga, Africa		134
Kumys		317
Kundalini yoga		143, 334
kunyah, Lakandon		455, 459
kursun dökme		285
Kurumkan region, Mongolia		306
Kushagras, Broom		401
Kyzyl, Tuva		308
Lageneria siceraria		385
Lagerstroernia speciosa Linn.		385
lake, Masters of the, Mongolia		302
lama ancestor, Mongolia		303
lama teachers		304
Lama, Mongolia		303
Lamiaceae		214, 217
Langenmatt, Switzerland		91
language		
--- group, tibetanian		398

language	Lucania region, Italy	109
---, endangered, Italy	110	luck, bad, Africa	139
---, hard, Switzerland	90	lumbal region, Cameroon	192
---s, Albanian, Italy	110	Lunnea grandis	385
Lannea coromondelica	385	Lussi, Kurt, Switzerland	87
Lannea discolor	212	Luzern, Canton,
larch, Mongolia	320	Switzerland	87, 90
Lathyrus sativus Linn.	385
Lauraceae	381	**M**ababu, Africa	136
law		
---, boomerang, Kallawaya	442	Macuxi	33
--- of nature	253	madzaf nswaltewa, Cameroon 191
---, patent	31
---, universal	254	mãe-de-santo, Brazil	483
laziness, susto	441	Mafa, Northern Cameroon	183
Lead	285, 382	magic
leaf of knowledge, Huitotos	470	--- forces	281
learning by the model	404	--- healing rituals,
Leguminosae	381	Switzerland	87
Lehner, Christian	501	--- knots	283
Leonotis leonurus	214	--- objects, Switzerland	90
Lesser burdock	415	--- of threes, Italy	115
liana, Lakandon	461	--- products	382
liberate a patient, Nigeria	164	--- remedies, Switzerland	90
liberating form of art	359	magic spell	332
liberation of pepo, Africa	143	---, Lakandon	455
Lice, Lakandon	458	---, Lakandon	459
Licuala pellata Roxb.	385	---, Switzerland	90
life		---, Therapy, Lacandon	453
--- crises	260	magic texts	283
--- line, cut of the	400	magic, Cameroon	186
---, harming, Nigeria	165	Magic, Black	283
---, symbols of, Nigeria	159	---, Africa	134
--- -giver, Nigeria	157	---, Africa	139
---style, Samoa	505	---, Vodou	426
--- -world, Nigeria	159	magic
light-disc, Switzerland	90	---, Cameroon	188
Liliacea, Fam.	382	---, hunting, Mongolia	302
limited ego	253	---, White	283
Lippia javanica	216	magical
LIUTOFAGA, Samoa	507	--- contagion, Italy	111
liver, Kallawaya	438	--- diseases	382
living, principles of	254	--- healing rites, Italy	109
lizard swallows	383	--- healing, Italy	109
Llama fetuses	440	--- interpretation, India	367
llama skeletons, LaPaz	439	---ly contagious, Italy	114
Loas, Vodou	425	magico-religious transfer,
Lobelia	415	Italy	113
local popular pharmaco-		magnesium, Huitotos	470
poeias, Italy	109	magnolia flowers, Lakandon	461
locking action, Nigeria	161	maize, chicken, Brazil	485
locks, Nigeria	160	maize, white, Brazil	485
Loganiaceae	214	Makamen	258
logging, forests	455	mal
logos, Huitotos	472	--- d`arco, Italy	111, 112
Lonchocarpus violaceaus,		--- di gola, Italy	112
Lakandon	455	--- di pancia, Italy	114
London Missionary		--- di testa, Italy	115
Society	501	--- viento, Italy	112
loss of one's spirit,		malaise, general, Brazil	484
Kallawaya	438	Malaria	343, 440
love of creation	254	malaria, Lakandon	458
love, possessive, Brazil	484	male cults	357

malevolence, Italy	115
malice, Cameroon	185
Mallotus albus	385
Maloca, Huitotos	469
malocchio, Italy	111, 112
Mambeodero, Huitotos	470
mambo priest	429
Mambwe, Africa	135
man, sitting, Huitotos	470
man, wise, Huitotos	470
mangan, Huitotos	470
Mangifera indica Linn.	385
Mangifera sp.	370
manic episodes	286
Manipur, India	367
Manipura Chakra	334
Mantra	332
mantras, Buddhist	304
MAOPOOPO, Samoa	502
Margaretha, St.,
Switzerland	90
Maria, Switzerland	92
Marma, Bangladesh	381
Marquesas, Samoa	501
marriage partner, Israeli	230
Marriage	283, 285
marriage, force into	359
marriage, Nigeria	159
Marrons	425
Marshallah	283
Marshmallow root	415
Maschito, Italy	109
Massage	414
---, Cameroon	188
---, Italy	111
---, Mongolia	304
massaging techniques	398
mastitis, Italy	112
MATAI, Samoa	503
Matches, Mongolia	306
material illness, Brazil	484
Mathura	331
Maxacali Nation	34
Mayans	454
Maytenus senegalensis	213
maytenus senegalensis,
Cameroon	191
Mbachi	370
mchawi, Africa	134
meat, monkeys	455
meat, parrot	455
meat, sacred, Mongolia	308
mediating force	258
mediation, Nigeria	160
medical anthropological
research, Italy	109
medical plants, Lakandon	461
medical system, foreign	454
medicinal plants, South
African	209
medicinal plants, Vodou	426
medicine
--- man, Nigeria	157

medicine	midwives, Andes	437
--- men, Africa	134	migraine, Italy	112
--- men, North America	19	migraines, Italy	112
--- pot, Nigeria	162	migrants from Haiti	426
---, alternative	17, 229	milk	317
---, Folk, Isreal	229	milk, Mongolia	308
---, humoural	258	Mimosa pudica	214
---, Islamic	253	mind-body relation,
---, prophetic	255	Nigeria	159
---, tied, Nigeria	160	mineral salts	382
---, Zulu Folk	209	minerals	415
meditation	48, 69	miracles, signs of	91
Meditation, Switzerland	91	mirror , shaman, Mongolia	306
medium	19	mirror image, Lakandon	456
Melia azedarach	215	mischievous, Nigeria	159
Meliaceae	215, 217	misfortune	357
melody	331	---, Africa	134
melody, type of	256	---, Cameroon	183
meningitis, Cameroon	183	---, Huitotos	473
Mensabak, Lakandon	457	---, social, Israel	230
menstrual		Missionary Society,
--- bleeding, Cameroon	191	London	501
--- blood, Cameroon	186	mistreats their children	31
--- blood, Nigeria	165	modern societies	45
--- women, Lakandon	461	modern Western society	229
menstruation	356	Mogh, Bangladesh	381
Menstruation, Israel	231	Mohammed, prophet	283
mental		Momordia charantia	385
--- processes, inner	255	Momordia muricata	385
--- complaints, Africa	134	money	358
--- conditioning	259	Mongolia	301
--- dimension	256	Mongolia, shaman of	317
--- disease	281	Mongoloid Naga tribe	367
--- disorders	383	Mongols, Oirat	304
--- disturbance, Nigeria	158	monkey god	401
--- illness, Africa	139	monkey, head of, Nigeria	162
--- illness, Israel	230	monkeys meat of	455
--- resources, strengthening	261	mons pubis	334
merchants caste	356	moral conduct	356
mercuric sulphide, red	382	Morinda anguistifolia Roxb.	385
mercury	382	Moringa oleifera	385
mercy images	91	Moslem wise men, Israeli	234
mesa, ceremonial	437	Mosque	286
Messapic, Italy	110	Mother
Mesua ferrea Linn.	385	--- Earth	31
metal working, Mongolia	319	--- Earth, Kallawaya	440
metaphysical causes of		--- tree, Mongolia	320
desease	399	---s' womb, Huitotos	470
methaphoric- symbolic		motion, origin of, Huitotos	472
dimension	399	motivation	262
metrazol	217	mountain of the world,
Metrazol, Africa	211	Mongolia	317
Metrum	331	mountain, Masters of the,
Mevlevi Order	254	Mongolia	302
Mexican rain forest	453	mouth, Huitotos	472
Mganga, Africa	134	movement
Mice, test, Africa	211	--- -therapy	258
Michael, Holy	94	---, active	257
microcosm, body as	437	---, universal patterns of	258
microcosm, Huitotos	472	---, ritualised	258
middle world	399	---, therapeutic	258
Midwife, Traditional	282	Muladhara Chakra	334
midwives, Cameroon	188	Mulhati	342

multiplicity of creation	254
mumps, Italy	112
Murang, Bangladesh	381
murder, Africa	138
murder, death of	356
murdered person, Italy	114
Muri, monastery,
Switzerland	91
Musa ornata Roxb.	385
Musa paradisiacal Linn.
sub sp. sylvestris	385
Musa sapientum Linn.	385
muscle soreness	415
muscular ailments, Italy	113
music	253, 254, 355
--- making, interactive	257
--- therapy	68
--- therapy, classical	255
--- therapy, Oriental schools
of	258
--- Therapy, Traditional
Oriental	253
---, India	331
musical
--- composition	331
--- experiences, Receptive	262
--- healing ceremonies	255
--- sessions, Africa	139
--- shamanic healing
ceremonies	253
--- sound	256
Mustafa Kemal Pascha	281
Muwene, Africa	135
muzimu, Africa	136
Mykhorshibirski region,
Mongolia	308
Myrtaceae	217
mystical depth,
Switzerland	91
mystical Dimension,
Music Therapy	253
mystics, Islamic	254
myths, Nepal	397
myths, Teutonic & Celtic	46
mzimu, Africa	139

Nações, Brazil 483

nada brahma	331
Naga tribes, India	367
Nagaland, India	367
Nagaraja (nepali)	404
Nagarani (nepali)	404
Nagô, Brazil	483
Nagphani	341
Naha´, Lakandons	453
nails, rhinoceroses	383
naming, Nigeria	165
Narasing (nepali)	404
Nardostachys jatamansi Dc.	385
native medicine dealer,
Nigeria	157
natural forces, Mongolia	309

natural world, Samoa	502
nature	
--- celebrations	49
--- ceremony	49
--- reverence	49
--- spirit, Africa	139
--- therapy	45
---, belief in a, Switzerland	88
---, India	331
---, inherent quintessential	254
nature, laws of	253
nausea	283
nausea, susto	441
navel	334
Nazar	282
needle therapy, Mongolia	305
needs, Brazil	484
neighbours, ritual with	402
neo-shamanic quest	301
neo-shamanism, Mongolia	308
Nepal, shamanistic healing ritual	397
Nepali	398
nerves, crossed, Italy	113
nervi accavallati, Italy	113
nervous system, central	209
nervous system, human, Huitotos	470
nervousness, Brazil	484
nest tree, Mongolia	320
Network, extended family	414
Neumann Fridman, Eva Jane	301
neuroleptics, Samoa	508
neurological rehabilitation centre	260
Neurological Rehabilitation Centre, Meidling	260
neuropsychological sensory system	259
neurosis	357
New York City, Vodou	425
ngwozla, Cameroon	186
nicotiana tabacum, Huitotos	470
Nicotiana tobactim Linn.	385
Nigeria, southeastern	157
Nightmares, Switzerland	88
Nimbus, Switzerland	90
nipple	370
nocturnal creature	370
nomadic clan, Mongolia	302
nome della croce, Italy	114
non- space, Mongolia	320
non- time, Mongolia	320
non-conflict orientated treatment	256
normality, Nigeria	159, 164
north, Mongolia	320
nose bleeds, Italy	112
not- knowing, Mongolia	320
Nottingham Health Profile	68
nourishment for the soul	255
nourishment	414
novice healers, Africa	143
Nqaka, Africa	210
Nsawalteva, Cameroon	192
nswaltewa, Cameroon	191
nutrition, Samoa	505
nutritional consultant	417
Nuxia floribunda Benth.	214
Nyakyusa, Africa	135
Nyamwanga, Africa	135
Nyiha ethnic group, Africa	135
Nymphaea nouchali	385
O LE FOFO, Samoa	501
obligations, Brazil	487
obscene, talking, Samoa	506
obscenities	359
obsession by gods	355
obsession	260
obsession, Indian	355
obsession, Spirit	355
obsession, Switzerland	89, 93
obstruction, Africa	142
Ocakli	282
Occident, Romanised	256
Ocimum basilicum Linn.	385
Ocimum gratissimum Linn.	385
odorous waters, Vodou	426
offering	401
---, Mongolia	308
---, Nigeria	160
---s, Brazil	483
---s, Cameroon	184
---s, sacrificial, Cameroon	188
oil, olive	415
oil, olive, Israel	232
oil, wheat germ	415
Oirat Mongols	304
Ojewole, John A. O.	209
Ojhhas	383
OM (nepali)	404
omen interpretation, Lakandon	458
oncologic sector	260
ongons, Mongolia	304
opening of a key, Nigeria	161
opposites, balancing polar	258
oppression, Africa	142
Opuntia vulgaris mill	341
oracle	
- speaker, Cameroon	192
---, Brazil	483
---, Cameroon	188
---, inner, Huitotos	473
--- -ritual	19, 284
--- -speaker, Cameroon	183
oral formulas, Italy	111
oral-formulas, Italy	112
order	
---, cosmical	400
---, Mevlevi	254
---, social, Samoa	504
---, world, Samoa	502
ordering principle, higher	254
organic illness, Brazil	484
oriental healing arts	258
Oriental Music Therapy, traditional	253
origin of sound	334
origin, celebrate the, Mongolia	318
orixás, Brazil	483, 484
ornamentic	257
Oroxylum indicum Linn.	385
Orpheus	331
Orthodoxy, Islamic	255
orthopedic ailments, Italy	113
Oruç Güvenç	256
Oryza sativa Linn.	385
Otherworld, Switzerland	87
otter	370
Ottoman Empire	254
outcastes	356
overtones	332
Oxygonum dregeanum	215
P achamama, Kallawaya	440
Pacific, South	501
pacifying	358
Pada	331
Padre Nostr, Italy	114
Padua, Switzerland	89
pai-de-santo, Brazil	484
pain	69, 254, 334, 415
--- relief	417
--- symptomatology	260
---, bodily, Switzerland	90
---, grimaces with	358
---, severe, Israel	233
---, stinging, Cameroon	186
Pajes	29
Paleness, unnatural	358
Paleo-Balkan group, Italy	110
palliative interventions	69
palm leaf, Lakandon	458
palmoil, Cameroon	191
pancreatic juice	382
Pandanus lectonis	385
Pantke, Christiane	483
paper, Slips of	284
parables	257, 264
paradise, divine	356
paradise, gates of	254
paralysis	230
paralysis, Africa	139
Parana	30
parasites, external, Lakandon	461
parasites, Lakandon	458
parasitic diseases, human	385
parent-child-relationships	426
parents, rejection of the	283
parrot, meat of	455

partidas, Andes	437	
partnership-oriented community, Mexico	453	
Parvat (nepali)	404	
passaries	382	
passion	254	
past, Mongolia	318	
patala (nepali)	399	
Pataxo Nation	29, 34	
patent laws	31	
patients´		
--- willingness, Italy	111	
---' blood pressure, Andes	437	
--- brain, Nigeria	162	
--- of Turkish Origin	281	
---' pulse, Andes	437	
--- soul	400	
---, psychiatric	254	
---' conscious, Africa	138	
patrilineal ancestors, Africa	136	
patron of illnesses, Switzerland	90	
patron of the pregnant, Switzerland	90	
peace	31	
--- work	260	
---, Nigeria	165	
---, Samoa	504	
---fulness, sanctuaries of	255	
peacocks´s feather	383	
pelo alla menna, Italy	114	
pelvis	334	
pelvis, inflammation of the, Israel	232	
penicillin, similar	440	
Pentylenetetrazol, Africa	211	
peoples, moving of, Mongolia	302	
Pepo Healer	133	
pepo illness, Africa	139	
pepo-illness, Africa	134	
perception of healing, Italy	112	
performance, theater	357	
Persian poets	253	
personal call, Nepal	398	
personality	254	
--- development	260	
--- portions, schismatic	356	
Peru	469	
Peru, Kallawaya	437	
Phakavaj	333	
pharmacological screening, plant, Africa	211	
pharynx level	334	
phenobarbitone	217	
philosophical concepts	257	
philosophy of ethos	258	
Phook (nepali)	401	
Phrasing	333	
phukne treatment	401	
Phurba (nepali)	401	
physical		
--- balance	256	
--- balance	258	
--- complaints, Africa	137	
--- dimensions	254	
--- healing	255	
--- injury	230	
--- movements	255	
--- therapy	262	
physiological deficiencies	258	
physio-psychological dimension	258	
physiotherapeutic rehabilitation	258	
Phytolacca dodecandra	215	
Phytolaccaceae	215	
phytotherapy, Vodou	426	
picrotoxin	217	
Picrotoxin, Africa	211	
Pieroni, Andrea, Italy	109	
pigeon, Lakandon	460	
Pilatus, Switzerland	87	
pilgrimage	48, 282, 358	
pilgrimages, Switzerland	90	
Piper bettle Linn.	385	
Piper chaba Linn.	385	
Piper longum Linn.	382	
Piperaceae, Fam.	382	
placebo effect, Italy	110	
placebo response	67	
plant extracts, Africa	217	
plant material, Africa	210	
Plantago ovata Forst.	385	
plantain leaves	417	
plants		
---, healing, Cameroon	188	
---, Holy, Huitotos	470	
---, medical, Lakandon	461	
---, medicinal, Vodou	426	
---, Samoa	502	
---, sanctified, Italy	115	
---, South African Medicinal	209	
---, use of native, Italy	110	
Plato	258	
pleasurable sensory exploration	261	
pneumonia	67	
poem	333	
poetry	264, 255, 257	
poets, Persian	253	
poisonous animals, Lakandon	457	
poisons, deadly	383	
political repression, Mongolia	301	
Polson, Montana	34	
Polygonaceae	215, 217	
Polygonatrum cirrhifolium Royle	385	
Polygonatrum oppositifolium	385	
Polygonum hydropiper	385	
Polynesia	501	
pom, Lakandon	455	
poor desires, Brazil	484	
poor economic situations	341	
Porto Velho	30	
Portuguese, Brazil	486	
posessed, phantasies of being	355	
Position	334	
possessed by spirits, Africa	134	
possession of a human	355	
Possession, Switzerland	88	
possessions, Vodou	427	
possessive forces, Nigeria	165	
possessive love, Brazil	484	
pot gutters, Cameroon	186	
potassum, Huitotos	470	
poteau-mitan, Vodou	428	
potency, healing	258	
poverty, Brazil	484	
powder		
---, Africa	210	
---, Lakandon	457	
---, ritual, Nigeria	162	
--- of symbols, Nigeria	159	
---, needs for	356	
powerlessness	359	
powers		
---, cosmic	397	
---, cosmical	400	
---, healing	284	
---, shamanistic	398	
---, spiritual, Andes	437	
---, supernatural , Vodou	429	
---, super-natural	382	
---, supernatural, Africa	209	
---, supernatural, Israel	234	
---, transcendental	356	
---, world of spiritual	398	
practitioners, Igbo Medicine	157	
practitioners, Nigeria	157	
Prana	331, 334	
prayer	65, 284	
---, Africa	136	
---, Blessing, Switzerland	92	
---, Kallawaya	438	
---, tea with	284	
---s, Cameroon	188	
---s, Italy	112	
---s, Mongolia	304	
---s, Mongolia	306	
---s, Switzerland	90	
praying for blessing	400	
pregnancy	285, 341	
pregnancy, Belly pain, Cameroon	193	
pregnancy, Cameroon	193	
pregnant, Cameroon	190	
pregnant, patron of the, Switzerland	90	
prestige, social	356	
priest		
--- caste	356	
---, Nigeria	157	

priest
---ess, Brazil 484
---ess, Vodou 427
---s, Samoa 503
---s, Vodou 426
primeval times, Mongolia 317
principles of Indigenous
   Knowledge 29
principles of living 254
principles, universal
   cosmic 255
principles, universal
   cosmic 258
privacy, Brazil 487
private altar, Vodou 428
process
---, individuation 259
---, therapeutic 255
---, therapeutic, AM 256
----centred method, AM 262
promises, Brazil 487
property, loss of, Israeli 230
prophet Mohammed 283
prophetic medicine 255
prophets, Africa 210
protection, Mongolia 302
Psalms, Switzerland 94
Psidium guyava Linn. 385
psychiatric
--- complexes 260
--- patients 254, 287
--- stress factors, Nigeria 160
--- treatment 286
psychiatrists, Nigeria 158
psychiatry, Turkey 281
psychical areas 334
psychical centers 334
psychical energies 398
psycho drama 404
psycho-active substances,
   Huitotos 470
psycho-cultural work, socio-,
   Nigeria 158
psycho-hygiene 260
psychological concepts 257
psychological dimension,
   physio- 258
psychological disorders 383
psychological symptoms,
   Israeli 230
psycho-neuro-immunological
   mechanisms 402
Psychoneuroimmunology 264
psychosis 357
psychosis, hallucinatory,
   Samoa 508
psychosomatic
--- complaints, Africa 134
--- disturbances 260
--- illnesses, Brazil 484
--- model 256
psychotherapeutic
--- healing, Italy 111

--- principles 301
--- techniques 355
--- treatment, Africa 139
psychotherapy 308
Pterocarpus santalinus 382
puberty, Lakandon 457
public attention, Samoa 508
pulling motions, Mongolia 306
pulse
--- diagnosis 400
--- diagnosis, Mongolia 304
---, patients', Andes 437
pumpkin seeds, Lakandon 457
Punica granatum Linn. 385
punishment, Israeli 230
pupil diagnosis, Kallawaya 438
Purification 48
purity 334, 356
python, Large 382

Quality check, shamans,
   Mongolia 319
Quave, Cassandra, Italy 109
Quechua 437
Quelli che possono aiutare,
   Italy 112
quest for God 254
quimbanda, Brazil 484
quinine mixture 440
quintessential nature,
   inherent 254

Rabbi of Yemenite origin 231
radiation treatment 417
raga, fire- 332
rain forest, Mexico 453
rainbow illness, Italy 112
rainbow, illness of the,
   Italy 111
rain-raga 332
Raja Man Singh 331
Rakhain, Bangladesh 381
Rama, god 401
Ramirez, Fabio Alberto 469
ranjayati iti ragaha 332
rash, Brazil 485
Rätsch, Christian 453
Rauvolfia caffra 212
Rawalfia serpentina 385
rayers, Lakandon 455
razor blade, Nigeria 162
realities, ethnographers 454
realities, social 356
reality, everyday 262
realms, transcendental 254
reawakening 262
rebalancing 399
rebalancing, Nigeria 158
recalcitrance 68
receptive AM 257
receptive musical

experiences 262
reconciliation, Samoa 504
recovery, Nigeria 165
recovery, Vodou patient 427
red cloth, beautiful 359
red cloth, Brazil 486
red, Nigeria 165
re-empowerment, Nigeria 158
reflexologist 414
regain of the soul 400
regional biogenetic
   resources 367
Rehabilitation Centre, Meidling,
   Neurological 260
rehabilitation, Brazil 488
rehabilitation, neurological 260
rehabilitation, physio-
   therapeutic 258
Reimers, Andreas 397
reincarnation, Nigeria 159
reinforcement 258
reinkarnations, circle of 356
relationship, trusting 262
relationships, parent-child- 426
relaxation 69, 333
relaxes, rhythm 256
religion, ecstatic 355
religion, Switzerland 88
religiosity 66
religious
--- activity, suppression of 301
--- affiliation 65
--- belief system, Italy 110
--- concepts 257
--- customs, Africa 135
--- healing rituals,
   Switzerland 87
--- life, Africa 133
--- phenomenon of
   obsession 355
--- practitioners, killing of,
   Mongolia 302
--- transfer, Italy 113
religon of haiti 425
remission phases 262
renal patients 66
renunciation 48
repolho, Brazil 485
repression of male shamans,
   Mongolia 303
repression, Political 301
reptiles, Lakandon 457
resonance center 334
resource-poor people 341
resources, regional
   biogenetic 367
respect for the dead, Samoa 506
respiratory problems,
   Kallawaya 438
restlessness 283
restlessness, Africa 139
restrictions, food, Africa 143
reticular activating system 260

retreat of senses	334	
Reuss, Switzerland	87	
reverence, Nature	49	
reverence, Switzerland	91	
revival of shamanic healing, Mongolia	309	
revival, Mongolia	301	
rheumatism	383	
rheumatism, Israeli	231	
Rhoicissus tridentata	216	
rhythm	331	
rhythm, AM	258	
rhythm, type of	256	
ribbons, Mongolia	308	
rice counting	400	
Rice	358, 401	
rice, Brazil	485	
Ricinus communis Linn.	385	
ridiculing	358	
righteousness	259	
Ripacandida, Italy	109	
Ripacandida, Italy	112	
rite, cleaning	357	
rites, pre-christian, Samoa	507	
ritual		
--- healing procedures, Italy	109	
--- key, Nigeria	160	
--- meeting, Huitotos	469	
--- powder, Nigeria	162	
--- washings	283	
---, eggs, Israeli	233	
---, initiation, Nigeria	157	
---, tying, Nigeria	160	
---ised movements	258	
---ly salt, Italy	115	
---s, birth, Mongolia	318	
---s, death, Mongolia	318	
---s, social, Huitotos	473	
---s, Structure of the	400	
---s, witchcraft eliminating Brazil	483	
River of Death	50	
river, Masters of the, Mongolia	302	
Riyazed	255, 258	
robes of the shaman	397	
Rocks	331	
rocks, spirits of, Cameroon	183	
rock-salt	382	
Roggliswil, Switzerland	87	
roman-catholic church, Switzerland	91	
Romanised Occident	256	
Rondonia	30	
root chakra	334	
root maytenus senegalensis, Cameroon	189	
root maytenus senegalensis, Cameroon	191	
root therapy, Nigeria	158	
roots mixtures, Nigeria	162	
roots, Africa	140	
Roots, use of, Nigeria	158	
rope, Nigeria	160	
Roraima	33	
Rosaceae	215, 217	
Roy, Babul	367	
rubber-tree, Lakandon	461	
Rubiaceae	215, 217, 381	
Rubus pinnatus	215	
Rueckert, Friedrich	254	
rules, dietetic	258	
Rununculus seleratus Linn.	385	
Russia	301	
Rutaceae	215, 217	

Sabal palmetto leaves, Lakandon 461
Saccharurn officinarum Linn. 385
sacred
--- animal, Kallawaya 440
--- meat, Mongolia 308
--- spring, Mongolia 308
sacrifice 48
---, Africa 136
---, Africa 139
---, Nigeria 160
---s, Africa 209
sacrificial gifts 425
sacrificial offering, Cameroon 185, 188
sadness 256
Sahasrara Cakra 334
Saints, Switzerland 90
Salish Tribe 34
saliva, Switzerland 90
salt 343
salt, alcaline, Huitotos 470
salt, ritually , Italy 115
Salvador, Brazil 484
Salzburg, Capuchin convent in, Switzerland 91
Samalia insignis 385
Sambucus nigra, Italy 115
Samoan Islands 501
Samscrt 331
samvadi 332
San Biagio, Italy 115
Sanador, Huitotos 469
sanctification of objects, Italy 116
sanctified plants, Italy 115
sanctuaries of peacefulness 255
Sanctuaries 48
sandal, red 382
sandal-wood, red 384
sangoma, Africa 209
Santalum album Linn. 385
Sapotaceae 216, 217
Saraca indica Linn. 385
Savages, lazy 31
Savai´i, Samoa 501
savuco, Italy 115
scales, micro-tonally 258

scarring	415
Schenk, Amélie	317
schismatic personality portions	356
Schizophrenia	306
Schmidt, Bettina E.	425
school education, poor, Brazil	484
school of Darbhanga	332
School, Dagar	332
science	31
sciences, profane	254
scientific treatment	255
scientist´s approach	454
scoparia dulcis, Cameroon	191
scorpion	283
Seasamum indicum D.C.	385
sedates, rhythm	256
seek for goddess	357
self- understanding	256
self-expression, creative	255
self-healing	67
Seljuk Turks	254
senses, aesthetic	255
senses, retreat of	334
sensory	
--- body sensibilisation	262
--- experiences	255
--- openness	254
--- system, neuropsychological	259
--- awareness	256
Sesanaga (nepali)	404
Setinaga (nepali)	404
settlement, Nigeria	165
seven tunnels	400
sexual	
--- desire	356
--- intercourse	283
--- misconduct	356
--- relations	357
sexuality of women	356
sexuality, needs for	356
shade, spirit of the, Huitotos	472
shadow, Africa	139
shaking	357
shaking, susto	441
shakti (nepali)	401
shaman	
--- ancestors, Mongolia	301
--- clothes, Mongolia	303
--- diviners	133
--- Healers, Inner Asia, Women	301
--- of Mongolia	317
--- travel	400
---, Initiation of the, Mongolia	319
---, robes of the	397
----healer, Buryat, Mongolia	306
shamanic healing ceremonies, musical	253

Shamanic Manifesto	29
Shamanism	45
---, Amazonas	18
---, definition	18
---, inner essence of	45
---, Korean	18
---, Ladakh	18
---, Mongolia	18, 301, 317
---, Nepal	18, 397
---, Siberia	18
---, yagé	469
shamanistic	
--- healing ritual, Nepal	397
--- knowledge, Mexico	453
--- powers	398
shamans from Brazil	29
shamans, Africa	133
shamans, Central Asian Bakse	255
shavegrass, Lakandon	461
sheep, Mongolia	308
sheep, Wild	369
Sheik	282
shells, cowrie, Nigeria	161
Shiva (nepali)	334, 399, 404
shivering	357
shivering, Africa	137
shocks, Kallawaya	438
shrine, Healing, LaPaz	441
shrines, Africa	136
Siberia	302
Sicily	110
sick funds, Israel	230
sickness	254
sickness, beliefs, Israeli	231
Sida cordata	385
Sida orientalis Cav.	385
Sida rhombitolia Linn.	385
silk, Mongolia	309
Silver	382
Simaraja (nepali)	404
Simarani (nepali)	404
Singh, Ranjay K.	341
singing	255
singing of mantras	400
singing, rhythmic, Africa	139
sins, forgiveness of, Africa	209
sitting man, Huitotos	470
situational problems	308
skeletons, Samoa	507
skin affections, Lakandon	461
skin rash, Italy	113
skin, ulcerated	440
skull of monkey, Nigeria	162
sky spirit, Mongolia	304
sky	317
sky, spirits of	183
sky-spirit, female, Cameroon	193
slash-and-burn cultivation	455
slavery	425
slaves, Brazil	483
sleep, Huitotos	471
sleeplessness	256
Slow Loris	370
smallpox, Cameroon	194
smell, AM	258
smell, Huitotos	472
smith, sons of the divine black	319
smiths, Cameroon	186
smoke	284
snake	283
--- bite	383
--- bite, Lakandon	456
--- energies	399
--- woman, Mongolia	317
---, Lakandon	458
---, Mongolia	317
---s, Lakandon	457
---s, Mongolia	304
social	
--- bonds, Nigeria	159
--- competence	404
--- cosmos, Cameroon	192
--- environment, Nigeria	159
--- group, Brazil	488
--- group, Nigeria	159
--- imbalance, Brazil	484
--- initiations, Nigeria	165
--- interaction, Lakandon	460
--- methods	66
--- misfortune, Brazil	484
--- misfortune, Israel	230
--- organization, Samoa	502
--- prestige	356
--- realities	356
--- reintegration	265
--- rituals, Huitotos	473
--- structure	501
--- structure, Huitotos	469
--- surroundings, Cameroon	188
--- unsuccessfulness, Brazil	484
--- world, Samoa	502
socialist period, Mongolia	304
society, modern Western	229
society, pluralistic, Israel	229
society, renewal of the, Nigeria	158
socio-cultural transition, Italy	112
socio-psycho-cultural work, Nigeria	158
SOIFUA MALOLOINA, Samoa	502
soil, fermented	440
Solanaceae	216, 217
Solanaceae, Fam.	382
Solarium melongena Linn.	385
solidarity, Samoa	508
solonaceae, Huitotos	470
songs, Nepal	397
sons of the divine black smith	319
sorcerer	283
sorcerer, Africa	134
sorcerers, Huitotos	471
sorcerous attacks, Nigeria	166
sorcery	369
---, Cameroon	184
---, Kallawaya	438
---, Nigeria	165
sore throat, Italy	112
sores	413
sorrow, Lakandon	457
sorrows, Lakandon	456
Sotho, Africa	210
soul	331
---, image of the	255
---, Lakandon	456, 457
---, lost	401
---, Mongolia	306
---, nourishment for the	255
---, patients	400
---s, army of, Switzerland	88
---s, Nigeria	159
sound of flute	331
sound, AM	258
sound, musical	256
sounds, harmonic	255
sounds, Nigeria	159
south, Mongolia	320
Soviet Period	301, 303
space, creator, Mongolia	321
Spanish conquest, Andes	437
speech, AM	258
spells, magic, Switzerland	90
spiders, dead	383
spine pain	414
spine	334
spirit	
--- healers	133
--- helpers, Mongolia	304
--- illness	133
--- obsession	355
--- of the shade, Huitotos	472
--- world, Inner Asia	302
---, 'alien', Africa	139
---, bad, Samoa	506
---, death, Brazil	485
---, female sky-, Cameroon	193
---, impure	357
---, loss of one's, Kallawaya	438
---, sky, Mongolia	304
----illness, Samoa	508
----journey, Mongolia	309
Spirito Santo, Italy	115
spirits	356
--- without heads, Switzerland	88
---, ancestral, Africa	135
---, ancestral, Africa	209
---, animal, Lakandon	457
---, appearance of, Nigeria	165
---, belief in	355
spirits	
---, Brazil	484

spirits	
---, Cameroon	183
---, corpeless, Mongolia	320
---, energy, Mongolia	320
---, evil, Africa	209
---, evil, Israeli	230
---, evil, Switzerland	88
---, instruction of the, Africa	134
---, Nepal	399
---, Turkey	281
---, tying of, Nigeria	161
---, Vodou	427
spiritual	
--- belief models, Italy	110
--- bonding, Mongolia	320
--- concepts	257
--- dimension	254, 256
--- forces	400
--- Healers in England, National Federation of	67
--- healers, Andes	437
--- healers, Zulu	210
--- healing rites, Italy	109
--- healing	65, 67
--- illness, Brazil	484
--- intrusion, Africa	134
--- maxim, non-Koranic	253
--- powers, Andes	437
--- products	382
--- restrictions, Italy	114
--- techniques of prayer	66
--- world, Samoa	502
spitting	283
splendor	334
Spondias magnifera	385
Spondias pinnata	385
spring, sacred, Mongolia	308
St. Sebastian	
Stability, Nigeria	164
stag, Lakandon	460
Stammenhaus, Switzerland	91
Stammhäusel, Switzerland	91
stand	334
states of trance	355
steam box	440
steam	283
Stendnera virosa Prain	385
Steppe, Mongolia	303
stiffness of joints	346
stimulation, base	260
stock roots, Cameroon	188
stomach	334
--- ache, Cameroon	192
--- complaint	369
--- cramps	306
--- diagnosis, Kallawaya	438
--- pain	414
---, Kallawaya	438
stomachache, Italy	114
stomachaches, Italy	112
stomatitis, Lakandon	461

stone, Nigeria	161
stone-circles	45
stonecolumns, Samoa	506
stone-oracle, Cameroon	184
stones, energy, Cameroon	188
strength	
--- of the body	255
---, Nigeria	158, 164
---, vital, Cameroon	185
strengthen words, Huitotos	471
strengthening emotional resources	261
strengthening mental resources	261
stress	308, 260
--- factors, psychiatric, Nigeria	160
--- of cardiac surgery	66
String, blessed	286
string, raffia, Nigeria	160
strong suggestibility	357
Strychnos nuxvomica	385
studies with a teacher, shamanism	398
suffering	69, 254
Sufi	253, 282
sugar, blessed	286
suggestibility	259
suggestion	66
suicide, Africa	138
suicide, death of	356
sukkulents, Cameroon	188
Sukuma, Africa	135
sunrise	333
supernatural	
--- causes	281
--- powers, Israeli	234
--- powers, Vodou	429
--- world, Samoa	508
suppression, shamanism	301
suppression, theory of	359
supressed wishes	356
sures of the Koran	285
surgical operations, Cameroon	188
Surui	32
survival, common, Samoa	502
Suryadeva (nepali)	404
Suspicion, Brazil	487
Susto, Kallawaya	438
Svadisthana Chakra	334
Swahili, Africa	136
Swami Haridas	332
sweat, Cameroon	186
sweat, Switzerland	90
sweets	359
swindles	283
swine, teeth of	383
Switzerland, healing rituals	87
Syllabels	332
symbolic	
--- interpretation, India	367
--- objects, incorporation of,	

Italy	111
--- Release, Nigeria	158
--- treatment, Nigeria	158
Symbolism, Elemental	264
symbols of kinship, Nigeria	160
symbols of life, Nigeria	159
symbols, power of, Nigeria	159
synovial fluid	346
syphilis, Lakandon	458
syringe woman	282
syrup, Huitotos	470
system of beliefs	66
system of castes	356

T´ani k´uh, Lakandon 455

Tabacco plant, Huitotos	470
Tabernae montana divericata Linn.	385
taboo	
---, broken, Africa	136
---, sharing	356
---, violation of a, Africa	139
---s, Mongolia	302
Tahiti	501
Tala	332
Talik	382
talking frivolous, Samoa	506
talking obscene, Samoa	506
Tamang folks	398
Tamarindus indica Linn.	385
Tambura	332
Tamil Nadu	359
Tanganyika Nyasa Corridor area	135
Tankas, Buddhist, Mongolia	305
Tansen	331
tantric traditions	397
tantro-mantro-jhar-funk-tabij-kabach-bali-utsharga	382
Tanzania	133
Tanzania, traditional healer in	133
tapioca, Brazil	485
tapir, Lakandon	460
Tara, Black	305
Tara, Green, Mongolia	304
Tara, White	304
tara'iq'	256
taste, AM	258
Tataente, Kallawaya	440
tea with prayer	284
teachers, lama, Mongolia	304
teachers, shaman, Mongolia	304
teaching, ayurvedic	357
teas, Vodou	426
techniques, transforming, Nigeria	160
Tecomaria capensis	212
Teeli, Tuva	308
teeth	
--- of elephant	383
--- of swine	383

Index   spirits — teeth   551

Entry	Page
teeth	
--- of the dead, Switzerland	90
--- of tiger	383
--- troubles	283
---, rhinoceroses	383
telepathic contact, Huitotos	470
telepathin, Huitotos	470
temperance movement	66
tempest, Cameroon	184
temple dancers	19
temple, Vodou	426
Tengri, Mongolia	306
tensions, Samoa	502
tentacles	369
Terena Nation	34
Terminalia belerica Retz.	385
Terminalia chebula Retz.	385
terreiros, Brazil	484
territory, loss of, Mongolia	302
tetramycin, similar	440
Teufelsstein, Switzerland	87
Teutonic myths	46
texts, magic	283
than (nepali)	399
theater performance	357
therapeutic	
aspects, Vodou	425
--- movements	258
--- process	255
--- process, AM	256
--- System, Bangladesh	381
--- touch	67
--- knowledge, Huitotos	471
therapies, artistically integrated	255
therapy	
--- methods, Lakandon	459
--- process	404
---, art	255
---, behavioural	254
---, classical music	255
---, complementary	65
---, consciousness	258
---, conversation	404
---, dance	255
---, darkness	46
---, event- oriented	404
---, family	359
---, movement	258
---, needle, Mongolia	305
---, Physical	262
---, root-herbal, Nigeria	158
---, touch, Mongolia	305
---, Traditional Oriental Music	253
thinking	334
thinking, Lakandon	457
thorax, Cameroon	186
thousandfold center	334
Thracian, Italy	110
threatening	358
threes, magic of, Italy	115
throat	334
---, problems with, Switzerland	90
---, sore, Italy	112
---s, Africa	136
thunder of the sky	383
Tiahuanaco cultures, Andes	437
Tibetan Buddhism	304
tibetanian language group	398
tics, Lakandon	457
Tietze, Dierk	331
Tiger	370
Tiger, teeth of	383
tinctures, Africa	210
tinctures, Vodou	426
tin-pouring	285
tintriloka (nepali)	399
tiredness	283
Titiskoti (nepali)	404
tobaccho, Lakandon	461
Tobacco, Huitotos	470
tomba todo, Brazil	486
Tonality, ninth	258
tones, Single	333
tongue, color of the, Kallawaya	438
tongue, patients', Andes	437
toothache, Italy	112
toothaches, Switzerland	90
torches	332
tortoise	369
tortoise shell, Lakandon	461
touch therapy, Mongolia	305
touch, AM	257
traditional	
--- belief systems, Samoa	501
--- concept of illness, turkish	281
--- customs, Africa	135
--- healer in Tanzania	133
--- healing, Amish Culture	413
--- medicine, Bolivian	440
--- medicine, Turkey	282
--- midwife	282
--- Oriental Music Therapy	253
--- practices, Italy	109
--- singing, Northern India	331
Tragia involucrata Linn.	385
trance	259
--- state, Africa	135
--- state, semi-, Africa	137
--- status	400
--- vision	400
---, Mongolia	320
---, Nepal	397
---, states of	355
-- -based healing	111
-- -rituals, Nepal	398
-- -state	400
tranquillity, sanctuaries of	255
transcendency, connection to	355
transcendental forces, Cameroon	184
transcendental	
--- powers	356
--- realms	254
--- world	183
--- causes of desease	399
trans-cultural effects	256
transfer of energies	404
transformation, Nigeria	161
transforming techniques, Nigeria	160
transitional situation, Nigeria	164
trauma, cranial/ cerebral	260
traumas, Kallawaya	438
traumatic change of identity	356
traveller to destination, Mongolia	318
treating depression	256
treatment	
-- methods, AM	257
---, choice of	229
---, non-conflict orientated	256
---, psychiatric	286
---, scientific	255
---, symbolic, Nigeria	158
---s ceremonies, Cameroon	189
---s of boundaries, Italy	115
---s of crossroads, Italy	115
---s of directions, Italy	115
tree	
---, birch, Mongolia	308
---, father, Mongolia	320
---, mother, Mongolia	320
---, nest, Mongolia	320
---s, meaning of the, Mongolia	320
---s, Nigeria	159
---s, spirits of, Cameroon	183
trembling hands, Israeli	233
trembling of the body	400
triangle form	285
tribal cultures	45
tribal knowledge	29
tribal people, India	341
tribal women's, Bangladesh	381
Tribulus terrestris Linn.	385
Tricosanthes tricuspidata	385
tridoshas	357
Trinity, holy	92
tropical monsoon climate	381
troublemakers, Brazil	487
troublemakers, Samoa	504
Tsaagantan Khori clan, Mongolia	308
Tschanar, Mongolia	319
tubers, Cameroon	188
Tucek, Gerhard	253
tumor	417
tunnels, seven	400
Turkey, AM	260
Turkey, Ethnic Belief	281

turkey, Lakandon	460	
turkeys	455	
turkish ethnomedicine	281	
Turkish-Islamic cultural history	255	
Turks, Father of the	281	
Turks, Seljuk	254	
Türstzug, Switzerland	88	
turtles	383	
turtles' bile	382	
tütsüleme	284	
Tuva	303	
Tuxtla Gutiérrez, Chiapas	455	
twine, Nigeria	160	
tying of man, Nigeria	161	
tying thread, Nigeria	160	

Udagan, Mongolia 304

Ulan-Ude, Mongolia	308	
ulcerated skin	440	
ulcers	413, 414	
umbilical cord, Nigeria	159	
unconciousness, Huitotos	471	
unconscious conflicts	356	
understanding, self- and world	256	
underworld	399	
underworld, Lakandon	457	
unemployment, Brazil	484	
UNESCO Redbook of the Endangered Languages, Italy	110	
unfulfilled desires, Brazil	484	
Unicista homoeopathy	473	
unio mystica	254	
union, cosmic, Brazil	488	
United States, Amish	413	
unity, divine	254	
universal		
--- cosmic order	253	
--- cosmic principles	255, 258	
universal laws	254	
--- patterns of movement	258	
universe	331, 334	
untouchables	356	
Upolu, Samoa	501	
upper world	399	
upper World, Mongolia	301	
urinating	283	
urine		
--- of bull	383	
---, Cameroon	186	
---, ceremonially collected, Italy	115	
---, patients', Andes	437	
---, Switzerland	90	
USSR	301	
Ustad Ziya Fariduddin Dagar	331	
Usumacinta, Guatemala	455	

Vadi 332

vagina, Huitotos	470	
vaids	357	
Vayudeva (nepali)	404	
vegetable glycerine	415	
vegetables, Brazil	485	
veins, Huitotos	470	
Veit, St. , Switzerland	90	
Veloso	30	
Venosa, Italy	109	
ventilator support	67	
Verbenaceae	216, 217	
vermi	112	
Vernonia neocorymbosa	212	
vestibular apparatus	259	
vibrates untouched	334	
vibrations	333	
victim		
---, Cameroon	186	
---, Samoa	505	
---, Vodou	429	
---s body, Cameroon	186	
view point, ethnographer	454	
villages, equlibrium, Samoa	503	
violence, Nigeria	164	
vipembe, Africa	141	
viral infections, Brazil	484	
Virgin, immaculate	92	
Vision Quest	48	
vision		
---, Nigeria	159	
---, trance	400	
---ary sights, Africa	134	
---ary sights, Africa	135	
---s	398	
---ns, strange, Mongolia	308	
visualisation	69, 257	
Visuddha Chakra	334	
Vitaceae	216, 217	
Vitamin E	415	
vitamins A and C, Huitotos	470	
Vitamins	414, 415	
Vodka, Mongolia	306	
Vodou / Voodoo	19, 425	
voice	331	
--- of the spirit	359	
---s' volume	334	
---s, hear strange, Samoa	506	
vowel	334	
Vrindava	331	
Vrindavan	332	
Vulture area, Italy	109	
vulva	50	
vulva, Cameroon	191	

Waganga wa pepo, Africa 134

waist, Nigeria	161	
Wanda, Africa	135	
warmth	306	
warnings, Africa	140	
warrior caste	356	
washings, ritual	283	
wasps, Lakandon	457	
wastewater	283	
water	284	
--- puddles	283	
---, Brazil	486	
---, cutting, Mongolia	306	
---, glass of	284	
---, holy	95	
---, hot, Cameroon	190	
---, running	255	
---, spirits of, Cameroon	183	
---, Switzerland	90	
---s, dirty	283	
---s, masters of, Mongolia	302	
---sound	264	
ways, spirits of, Cameroon	183	
weakened areas	401	
weakness, Africa	139	
weakness, Nigeria	158, 160	
weight loss, Africa	139	
well-being	67	
---, Africa	139	
---, Huitotos	472	
---, Nigeria	164	
---, Samoa	508	
west, Mongolia	320	
western music therapy	257	
Western school medicine	17	
Wheat germ oil	415	
whisky	383	
white		
--- cloth, Brazil	486	
--- magic	283	
--- maize, Brazil	485	
--- oak bark	415	
--- Tara	304	
---, Nigeria	165	
wholeness	254	
wholy Antonius, Switzerland	89	
widow	356	
wild		
--- animal, Mongolia	308	
--- deerskin, Mongolia	304	
--- pig, Lakandon	460	
wilderness	398	
wilderness, soul of the	45	
will, Nigeria	159	
willpower, Africa	142	
wind	283	
---, Kallawaya	438	
--- -illness, Italy	112	
---s, cold or strong, Italy	114	
---s, Lakandon	457	
wines	383	
wise man, Huitotos	470	
wise woman	282	
wishes, indomitabale	356	
wishes, supressed	356	

witch doctors, Africa 134
witchcraft 369
--- eliminating rituals, Brazil 483
---, Africa 136, 141
---, Brazil 484, 487
---, Cameroon 185
---, Lakandon 456
---, Mongolia 306
---, Nigeria 165
witches 399
--- house, Cameroon 189
---, Africa 134, 209
---, Cameroon 184
Withania somnifera Dunal 382
Withania somnifera 216
withdrawal, Africa 139
wives, conformity as 359
wizards, Africa 209
women
--- healers, Inner Asia 303
---, abuses 31
---, menstrual, Lakandon 461
---, sexuality of 356
---, tribal 341
wood, birch, Mongolia 320
woods, Nigeria 159
words, strengthen, Huitotos 471
work, physical, Samoa 505
world
---, axis of the 399
--- of spiritual powers 398

--- order, Nigeria 158
--- structure 399
--- understanding 256
---, inner, Mongolia 301
---, middle of the 399
---, mountain , Mongolia 317
---, supernatural, Samoa 508
---, under 399
---, upper 399
---, upper, Mongolia 301
---s, three, Samoa 502
worms, intestinal, Lakandon 458
Wormwood 415
worship, Brazil 484
worship, places of 51
worship, Switzerland 91
wounds 414
Würzburg, bishop of, Switzerland 90

Xavante Nation 34
Xerente Nation 34
Xeromphis spinosa 385
Xhinestra, Italy 109
Xhosa, Africa 210

Yagé shamanism 469
Yanuma 332
yaruma palm, Huitotos 470

yatir 282
yatiris, Andes 437
yatoch k´uh, Lakandon 455
yawning 114
yellow fever epidemic 183
yellow fever, Lakandon 458
Yellow Jaundice Healer 282
Yemenite origin, rabbi of 231
Yerbateros, Andes 437
yoch k´uh, Lakandon 455
yoga 397
yoga, kundalini 334
yoga, Kundalini, Africa 143
Yoruba, Brazil 483, 486
Yucca flour, white, Brazil 485
Yurt, Mongolia 303

Zaarin, Mongolia 304
zeme nagas, India 367
zinc, Huitotos 470
zinger 370
Zingiber casumumum 385
Zingiber officinalis 385
Zingiber purpureum 385
Zinginber sp., Rhizome of a 370
Zinziber rubens Roxb. 385
Zizyphus jujuba 385
Zizyphus sativa 385
zoonoses 385
Zug, Canton, Switzerland 90
Zulu Folk Medicine 209